T0364129

The Financing of
Catastrophe Risk

A National Bureau
of Economic Research
Project Report

The Financing of Catastrophe Risk

Edited by Kenneth A. Froot

The University of Chicago Press

Chicago and London

KENNETH A. FROOT is the Industrial Bank of Japan Professor of Finance and director of research at the Harvard Business School and a research associate of the National Bureau of Economic Research.

The University of Chicago Press, Chicago 60637
The University of Chicago Press, Ltd., London
© 1999 by the National Bureau of Economic Research
All rights reserved. Published 1999

08 07 06 05 04 03 02 01 00 99   1 2 3 4 5
ISBN: 0-226-26623-0 (cloth)

Library of Congress Cataloging-in-Publication Data

The financing of catastrophe risk / edited by Kenneth A. Froot.
        p.   cm.—(A National Bureau of Economic Research project report)
    A collection of papers written for this volume and for the conference, "The Financing of Property Casualty Risks," organized by the editor under the auspices of the National Bureau of Economic Research and its Insurance Program.
    Includes bibliographical references and index.
    ISBN 0-226-26623-0 (alk. paper)
    1. Insurance, Disaster—United States.   I. Froot, Kenneth.
II. Series.
HG9979.3.F56   1999
368.12'201'0973—dc21   98-31580
                                                                    CIP

Relation of the Directors to the
Work and Publications of the
National Bureau of Economic Research

1. The object of the National Bureau of Economic Research is to ascertain and to present to the public important economic facts and their interpretation in a scientific and impartial manner. The Board of Directors is charged with the responsibility of ensuring that the work of the National Bureau is carried on in strict conformity with this object.

2. The President of the National Bureau shall submit to the Board of Directors, or to its Executive Committee, for their formal adoption all specific proposals for research to be instituted.

3. No research report shall be published by the National Bureau until the President has sent each member of the Board a notice that a manuscript is recommended for publication and that in the President's opinion it is suitable for publication in accordance with the principles of the National Bureau. Such notification will include an abstract or summary of the manuscript's content and a response form for use by those Directors who desire a copy of the manuscript for review. Each manuscript shall contain a summary drawing attention to the nature and treatment of the problem studied, the character of the data and their utilization in the report, and the main conclusions reached.

4. For each manuscript so submitted, a special committee of the Directors (including Directors Emeriti) shall be appointed by majority agreement of the President and Vice Presidents (or by the Executive Committee in case of inability to decide on the part of the President and Vice Presidents), consisting of three Directors selected as nearly as may be one from each general division of the Board. The names of the special manuscript committee shall be stated to each Director when notice of the proposed publication is submitted to him. It shall be the duty of each member of the special manuscript committee to read the manuscript. If each member of the manuscript committee signifies his approval within thirty days of the transmittal of the manuscript, the report may be published. If at the end of that period any member of the manuscript committee withholds his approval, the President shall then notify each member of the Board, requesting approval or disapproval of publication, and thirty days additional shall be granted for this purpose. The manuscript shall then not be published unless at least a majority of the entire Board who shall have voted on the proposal within the time fixed for the receipt of votes shall have approved.

5. No manuscript may be published, though approved by each member of the special manuscript committee, until forty-five days have elapsed from the transmittal of the report in manuscript form. The interval is allowed for the receipt of any memorandum of dissent or reservation, together with a brief statement of his reasons, that any member may wish to express; and such memorandum of dissent or reservation shall be published with the manuscript if he so desires. Publication does not, however, imply that each member of the Board has read the manuscript, or that either members of the Board in general or the special committee have passed on its validity in every detail.

6. Publications of the National Bureau issued for informational purposes concerning the work of the Bureau and its staff, or issued to inform the public of activities of Bureau staff, and volumes issued as a result of various conferences involving the National Bureau shall contain a specific disclaimer noting that such publication has not passed through the normal review procedures required in this resolution. The Executive Committee of the Board is charged with review of all such publications from time to time to ensure that they do not take on the character of formal research reports of the National Bureau, requiring formal Board approval.

7. Unless otherwise determined by the Board or exempted by the terms of paragraph 6, a copy of this resolution shall be printed in each National Bureau publication.

(Resolution adopted October 25, 1926, as revised through September 30, 1974)

Contents

Acknowledgments

The subject of this book—the financing of catastrophe risk—is one of the most rapidly changing in all of insurance and finance. In just a few short years, we have gone from theorizing about possible capital market activities to watching new and innovative transactions occur in both capital markets and traditional insurance and reinsurance markets. Individualized securities, innovative insurance contracts, standardized exchange-traded securities based on indexes, over-the-counter derivatives have all come into being. And these transactions themselves are only the tip of the iceberg; beneath the surface are massive early changes in the relationship between the insurance and financial markets and the companies that operate in them. Insurance and reinsurance activities are becoming explicitly intermingled with investment and commercial banking. The greater fungibility of capital—belonging to banks, the insurer sector, and investors—means more opportunities to deploy savings and better ways to share risk. There is a decade of powerful change in the offing as new and changed companies develop responses to this greater array of opportunity.

This book is one attempt to bring these issues forward. As with any undertaking, it required many minds plus lots of energy and hard work. First and foremost, the book and its editor are deeply indebted to all the authors for their careful and interesting papers as well as their diplomacy and responsiveness in accommodating others' suggestions. The discussants, too, contributed important ideas, both in shaping the authors' comments and in their own statements. These individuals plus the attendees of the conference in November 1996 in West Palm Beach, Florida, made it one of the most stimulating I have attended.

On behalf of the National Bureau of Economic Research, Marty Feldstein and I are grateful to the Insurance Information Institute, J. P. Morgan, and J&H Marsh & McLennan for their important financial support. Gordon Stewart of the Insurance Information Institute was particularly helpful throughout the organization of the conference, and helped to edit the panelists' comments included in the book. I also wish to thank David Tralli, of the Targeted Commercialization Office of NASA's Jet Propulsion Laboratory, for his and NASA's help in providing an image for the book jacket. Finally, thanks go to Marty Feldstein for his encouragement and to Kirsten Foss Davis and the NBER's conference department for their renowned organizing savvy and efficiency.

Ken Froot

Introduction

Kenneth A. Froot

In recent years, the magnitude of catastrophic property-casualty disaster risks has become a major topic of debate. The insurance industry now regularly discusses potential U.S. earthquake or hurricane losses of $50–$100 billion, a magnitude of loss that was unthinkable ten years ago. The disasters of Hurricane Andrew and the Northridge Earthquake alone totaled over $45 billion in 1997 dollars, with the insured component running to almost $30 billion. This compares with cumulative insured losses from natural catastrophes in the decade prior to those events (roughly 1980–92) of only about $25 billion (according to data from Property Claims Services).

These enormous increases in potential losses are likely to be permanent and even to increase over time. During the period 1970–90, the population of the Southeast Atlantic coastal counties increased by nearly 75 percent, a rate almost four times that of the nation as a whole. Annual growth rates in population per square mile in California and Florida have been two or three times the national average for the last three decades (Lewis and Murdock, chap. 2 in this volume). Indeed, analysis by Guy Carpenter and Co. suggests that, because of

Kenneth A. Froot is the Industrial Bank of Japan Professor of Finance and director of research at the Harvard Business School and a research associate of the National Bureau of Economic Research.

This introduction expounds on the collection of papers written for this volume and the conference, "The Financing of Property Casualty Risks," organized by the author under the auspices of the National Bureau of Economic Research and its Insurance Program.

The author is deeply indebted to many individuals for their comments and help, particularly many NBER conference participants, too numerous to mention. He has particularly benefited from conversations with Clem Dwyer, Peter Diamond, Marty Feldstein, David Govrin, Chris McGhee, Roberto Mendoza, Brian Murphy, Paul O'Connell, Steve Ross, Jeremy Stein, Gordon Stewart, and Joe Umansky. He also thanks Howard Kunreuther, David Moss, Frank Pierson, and George Segelken for detailed and extremely helpful comments on this essay. Thanks go as well to the NBER's Insurance Program sponsors, the sponsors of the Global Financial Systems Project at Harvard Business School (HBS), and the Department of Research at HBS for generous research support. Responsibility for any errors or omissions lies solely with the author.

growth in hazard-prone areas since 1950, real-dollar damages of a given-size natural event have been doubling every fourteen years.

With prospective event losses that can easily exceed $50 billion, it would appear that the insurance industry is not ready for a major event. The capitalization of the bearers of catastrophe risk is a major problem. Estimates (from the A. M. Best Co. as of 30 September 1996) of total capital and surplus of U.S. insurers run to about $239 billion. While a large natural disaster would not bankrupt the entire industry, this capital and surplus apply to *all* risks (property-casualty, liability, worker's compensation, etc.), not just catastrophes. A large event could, therefore, place firms' capital under severe stress, potentially jeopardizing the rewards of both policyholders and investors.

Traditionally, the insurance industry has avoided these financial stresses by pooling its exposures for large events. This occurs through reinsurance treaties with separately capitalized reinsurers. Insurers can pass along the risks of low-probability, high-cost events to these reinsurers, who accomplish the pooling. The pass-through is, however, only partial. Very little of the reinsurance in place provides protection against industrywide losses for catastrophic (cat) events greater than $5 billion. That is, for a $50 billion cat event, the overwhelming majority of the last $45 billion of losses (after the first $5 billion) is not covered by reinsurance. In a narrow sense, this is not surprising, given the relatively small capital and surplus of the reinsurance industry ($26.7 billion for U.S. reinsurers, $6.5 billion for Bermudan reinsurers, $7.0 billion for German reinsurers, and $16.8 billion for others) (Guy Carpenter 1997). Thus, at present levels of capital, the worldwide reinsurance industry is not capable of funding large-event risks in the United States, let alone the rest of the world.

The paucity of reinsurance protection at high layers of exposure can be observed directly from reinsurance-buying patterns. To do this, I assembled data on property-casualty contracts brokered by Guy Carpenter. These data cover a large fraction of all catastrophe-reinsurance purchases by U.S. insurers.[1] From them, it is possible to gain a sense of the paucity of reinsurance coverage at high levels of losses. Figure 1 shows the relation in these data between the fraction of pooled insurer exposure covered by reinsurance and the size of industrywide events.[2]

---

1. Catastrophe-reinsurance contracts oblige the writer to pay the cedent insurer for its insurance losses associated with a natural hazard. The contracts are typically in an "excess-of-loss" form. This means that the writer is obliged to pay up to a fixed-limit amount for all losses in excess of a given deductible ("retention"). To see how such contracts work, consider an insurer that purchases a layer of reinsurance covering $100 million in cat losses in excess of $200 million. These terms imply that, if the insurer's losses from a single catastrophic event during the contract year exceed $200 million retention, the layer is triggered. The reinsurer pays the insurer the amount of any losses in excess of $200 million, with the loss capped at a limit of $100 million. By purchasing this contract, the insurer cedes its exposure to single-event catastrophe losses in the $200–$300 million range. In return for assuming this exposure, the reinsurer receives a premium payment. If the insurer wishes to cede a broader band of exposure, it could purchase additional layers—$100 million in excess of $300 million, $100 million in excess of $400 million, and so on.

2. The procedure for attaching individual reinsurance-contract layers to industry losses is described in Froot and O'Connell (chap. 5 in this volume).

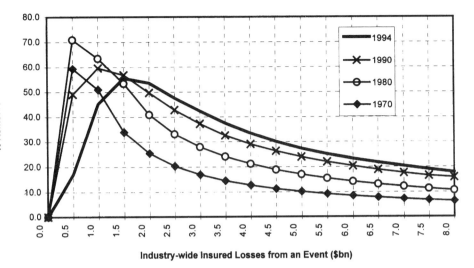

Fig. 1   Percentage of exposure that insurance companies reinsure (by various event sizes)
Note: Event losses are given in 1994 dollars and are adjusted for changes in demographics and GNP.

There are two important points to be made from figure 1. First, reinsurance coverage as a fraction of exposure declines markedly with the size of the event, falling to a level of less than 30 percent for events of only about $5 billion.[3] Clearly, only a small fraction of large-event exposures is covered, and, remarkably, this figure *overstates* that fraction. That is because the only insurers included in the data are those that actually purchase reinsurance.[4] The implication is that insurance companies overwhelmingly retain, rather than share, their large-event risks.

This point must be expanded in one important respect. Many exposures faced by the corporate and household sectors are self-retained and *never even reach insurers in the first place.* Corporations, for example, tend to self-insure, particularly against large losses—even while purchasing insurance against small losses. One study documents that insurance coverage is extremely limited for corporate cat losses of between $10 and $500 million (for a single corporation) and virtually nonexistent for losses above $500 million (Doherty and Smith 1993). This suggests that the vast majority of primitive cat risk in the economy is being retained. The implication is that the problem of inadequate risk sharing—and the failure of the reinsurance sector to help accomplish it—is on a far larger scale than can be directly indicated by figure 1.[5]

3. Indeed, the figure shows that 30 percent is an improvement over the past. In 1970, coverage of similar event sizes was less than 20 percent.
4. For firms that did buy reinsurance and are in the database, I observe the entire reinsurance program.
5. Of course, some types of risk are subject to asymmetrical information or manipulation, and the resulting adverse selection or moral hazard makes sharing them inherently problematic. I dis-

There is a second, more subtle point to be taken from figure 1. It is apparent that, after a large event, like Hurricane Andrew in 1992, retentions (or "deductibles") tend to increase. After an event, the total amount of coverage does not rise (indeed, it appears to fall somewhat). Most of the action is that a typical firm's window of coverage shifts toward higher layers of protection. In other words, coverage for large events apparently increases only at the expense of coverage for small events. I return to this point in the discussion below.

It is striking that so little reinsurance is in place for large-event losses. After all, it is large events whose risks need most to be shared. This paucity of risk sharing is costly for two reasons. First, poor risk sharing means that individuals bear higher portfolio risks. With higher portfolio risk, hurdle rates for new investments are higher, and, therefore, investment spending is lower, than if risk sharing were perfect.

There is a second cost that makes hurdle rates higher and investment lower. This comes from ex post burden sharing. Ex post burden sharing occurs when those who bear risk try to get someone else to pay their losses. This behavior is costly because it creates bad incentives. If someone else will pay, then risk-increasing investments are subsidized, while risk-reducing investments, such as mitigation, are taxed. For example, homeowners overbuild on exposed coastline because of subsidized insurance rates or because they expect to be bailed out by a government program; insurers are tempted to take too much risk relative to their capital, thereby shifting part of the cost of disasters onto other insurers, state agencies, and insurance customers; and some households and companies decline to purchase sufficient insurance, under the assumption that they will receive de facto protection. Bad incentives increase the aggregate level of risk. They also further worsen its distribution, as those with the greatest cat risks have the greatest marginal incentive to take more on.

It is not my goal here to gauge the magnitude of these costs. But both these mechanisms raise costs of capital and reduce economic growth. While the link between lower capital costs and higher growth rates is not well established, it is worth noting that lowering capital costs by enough to spur even a single basis point of additional growth is worth $700 million per year in a $7 trillion economy such as that of the United States.

The discussion below takes as its central premise the argument that the system of redistributing large catastrophe risks has not spread risks into and beyond insurer balance sheets and out evenly across investors. The discussion also takes as given that there are large costs associated with an equilibrium in which risk sharing is inefficient. I then go on to ask whether the current framework for managing cat risk is functioning as well as is possible. What barriers (if any) prevent higher-layer risks from being spread and/or mitigated? Are the capital markets likely to solve the problem?

---

cuss this issue below. For now, however, it is sufficient to note that catastrophe events—so-called acts of God—are basically exogenous to mankind. These risks (as opposed to, say, liability risks) are, therefore, relatively free from asymmetrical information and moral hazard.

These are the issues that motivate this volume and the papers in it. The objective of the volume is to facilitate a better understanding of the issues and to serve as a starting point for serious discussion among practitioners, academics, and policymakers about the basic problems.

In what follows, I enumerate eight different explanations for barriers to better risk sharing. These explanations serve as ways of introducing the ideas of each chapter and set of panelist comments. Naturally, one's view of the solution to the problem of inadequate catastrophic risk sharing depends on the assumed cause. The introduction then turns to solutions that have been suggested, many during the conference itself, with a focus on the role of the capital markets and alternative means of redistributing cat risk.

Explanations for the Paucity of Catastrophe Risk Sharing

Explanation 1: Prices of Catastrophe Reinsurance Are High
because of Insufficient Reinsurance Capital

This explanation relies on the premise that prices are high. Thus, before evaluating the sufficiency of reinsurance capital, we must first examine whether reinsurance prices are high relative to some natural benchmark. A comparison of actual prices with a benchmark that somehow represents fair prices is a useful indicator. For the sake of argument, I assume that fair prices are those that would prevail if the system for redistributing cat risk were perfect and frictionless. In such a system, catastrophe-risk prices would be determined by investors. This makes sense because it is investors who, in one form or another, must ultimately provide catastrophic risk–bearing capacity.

As is generally argued by both practitioners and financial economists, investors require relatively low average returns for bearing risk exposures that provide large diversification benefits. Take, for example, investments that are a small part of total wealth and that are uncorrelated with the returns on other forms of wealth (such as stocks and bonds). Such investments improve the reward-to-risk ratio of investor wealth as long as their average returns exceed the return on risk-free investments like U.S. Treasury bills. This suggests that the (relatively low) short-term U.S. Treasury rate is the threshold required return for a small, uncorrelated investment.

Historical data suggest that catastrophe risk is one such investment since returns from bearing cat risk through reinsurance contracts are uncorrelated with all other major investor asset classes.[6] If this is true, then, with wide risk distribution, the fair catastrophe premium on a reinsurance contract is just the actuarial contract loss. In other words, the contract premium should equal actuarial insurer losses covered by the reinsurance contract. Of course, actuarial

---

6. See Froot et al. (1995), which presents data showing that recent returns from bearing catastrophe risk are uncorrelated with other major financial asset classes, such as U.S. and foreign stocks and bonds as well as currencies.

losses are not known with certainty. One can only estimate actuarial losses. Nevertheless, as long as the estimate of expected loss is unbiased and the uncertainty in actuarial losses is itself uncorrelated with investor wealth, then the premium should on average equal estimated actuarial losses.

To those in the industry, it comes as no surprise that reinsurance premiums are today considerably greater than estimates of actuarially expected losses covered by reinsurance. A good and very visible example is the recent purchase of reinsurance by the California Earthquake Authority (CEA) from National Indemnity, a subsidiary of Berkshire Hathaway. Under the structure of that contract, National Indemnity receives an annual premium that exceeds actuarially expected losses by 530 percent. To see this, note that the average annual premium for the four-year aggregate cover is 10.75 percent of the annual limit, whereas the likelihood that the reinsurance is triggered is 1.7 percent or (10.75/ 1.7) − 1 = 530 percent (according to EQE International, a catastrophe-risk-modeling firm). In other words, Berkshire Hathaway has a 1.7 percent chance per year of losing the $1.05 billion it has put up; in return, it receives $113 million per year in premiums. Indeed, under the contract specifications, Berkshire Hathaway receives four years' worth of premiums in the first two years. Since the $1.05 billion cover aggregates over the four-year period, Berkshire Hathaway is effectively putting up about $600 million in net exposure for a 93.4 percent chance to make about $400 million in premium.[7]

The pricing of this contract is, in today's market, not unusual. Historically, reinsurance-contract premiums have exceeded actuarial contract losses by large amounts. Figure 2 shows a computation of the percentage excess of premiums over expected losses. While a multiple of five appears relatively high by the standards of the early 1980s, prices are on average nearly that high since Hurricane Andrew. In many instances, the prices are greater than those shown in figure 2, which averages across both high and low reinsurance layers. In general, the multiples on low-probability, higher layers (such as the CEA tranche) have been particularly high (see fig. 3), the more so since Hurricane Andrew.

Once reaction to the Berkshire Hathaway example and the numbers shown in figure 2 is healthy skepticism. The computations require one to measure actuarial value, which is not really possible. The actuarial values behind the figure are derived from the historical distribution of catastrophe losses.[8] And this historical distribution is likely to differ from what market participants considered to be relevant at various times. Indeed, a portion of what appears to be a secular increase in prices in figure 2 may actually be attributable to increasingly large losses expected by the market.

---

7. Based on a probability of 1.7 percent per year, the chance of no event over the four years is $(98.3\%)^4 = 93.4\%$. Data in this paragraph are from *IBNR Insurance Weekly* (Dowling and Partners Securities) (vol. 3, no. 46) and from remarks by Richard Sandor.

8. For a description of how these numbers are calculated, see Froot and O'Connell (chap. 5 in this volume).

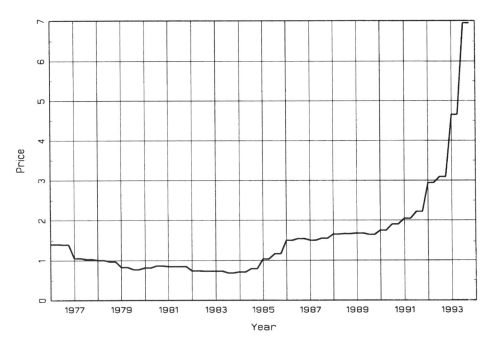

Fig. 2 Industry price per unit of ceded exposure

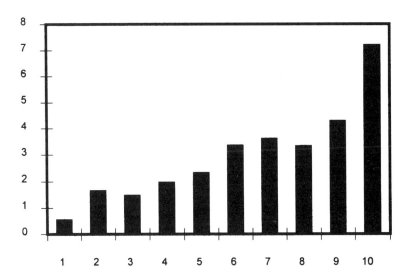

Fig. 3 Relation of price to attachment probability (layer 10 is highest retention)

However, none of this skepticism changes the fact that, while the numbers in the figure seem high by actuarial standards, they are not high by the standards of current market prices for catastrophe risk, at least as shown by the National Indemnity/CEA reinsurance layer. Indeed, Berkshire Hathaway shareholders appear to have rejoiced at having written the reinsurance: on the day the contract was announced, Berkshire's stock market valuation rose by over $400 million, or 1 percent, in excess of the broad stock market change. This suggests that shareholders saw the reinsurance contract (and those that might follow) as providing net present value.

With these arguments about catastrophe-reinsurance prices in mind, it is worth exploring the reasons why prices might indeed be too high. (Below, I also consider explanations that assume that current prices are fair.) The specific explanation considered in this section is that prices are high because catastrophic risk-taking capital is somehow limited. Even if such capital shortages are relatively temporary, they might exist for a number of structural reasons: it may be costly for existing reinsurers to raise additional funds in the capital markets; it may be hard to find investors and names who expect adequate rewards for bearing catastrophic risks; it may also be that it is costly for reinsurers to accumulate large amounts of collateral on their balance sheets.

Shortages of capital are an important rationale for Berkshire Hathaway's strategy in reinsurance. In his 1996 letter to shareholders in Berkshire Hathaway's annual report, Warren Buffett observes, "Our . . . competitive advantage [in writing 'supercat' risks] is that we can provide dollar coverages of a size neither matched nor approached elsewhere in the industry. Insurers looking for huge covers know that a single call to Berkshire will produce a firm and immediate offering." Given that easy access by new and existing reinsurers to additional capital would remove this competitive advantage, it seems clear that Buffet believes in—and profits from—capital shortages.

Indeed, there is a perception that the shortage may become even worse once reinsurer capital is depleted by a large event. Again in Berkshire Hathaway's 1996 annual report, Buffett writes, "After a mega-catastrophe, insurers might well find it difficult to obtain reinsurance even though their need for coverage would then be particularly great. At such a time . . . it will naturally be [Berkshire's] long-standing clients that have first call on it. That business reality has made major insurers and reinsurers throughout the world realize the desirability of doing business with us. Indeed, we are currently getting sizable 'standby' fees from reinsurers that are simply nailing down their ability to get coverage from us should the market tighten." Buffett's entire discussion of "supercat" risks emphasizes the value to Berkshire's shareholders of the company's substantial financial capacity. In a world of no capital shortages, large capital capacity is nothing to write home about.

Are there more concrete facts to suggest that capital shortages are behind high prices? There are some. A second important feature of figure 2 is that prices appear to rise in the aftermath of major catastrophic events and then fall

Table 1   **Event Study of Hurricane Andrew**

	A. Southeast Exposure			B. Hurricane Exposure		
	Mean Exposure	Mean $\Delta\ln(p_{j,t})$	Mean $\Delta\ln(q_{j,t})$	Mean Exposure	Mean $\Delta\ln(p_{j,t})$	Mean $\Delta\ln(q_{j,t})$
5 most-exposed insurers	.707	.415	$-.021$	.918	.583	$-.082$
5 least-exposed insurers	.000	.335	$-.013$	.561	.336	$-.047$

Source: Froot and O'Connell (chap. 5 in this volume).

Note: Comparison of price responses in the year after Hurricane Andrew, for different insurers. Panel A contrasts insurers that have high and low exposure to the Southeast (as measured by market share). Panel B contrasts insurers that have high and low exposure to hurricanes. The table shows the mean exposure and the mean price change of the five most extreme contracts in each case. The mean price change for the insurers with lesser exposure to the Southeast is calculated using all fourteen of the insurers that have zero market share in that region.

afterward. This can be seen most clearly in the period around Hurricane Andrew (1992). Prices rose substantially in 1993 and have consistently fallen since. While the figure does not include 1995 and 1996 price data, preliminary estimates suggest that prices have fallen by approximately 27 percent during that time.[9]

It is perhaps not surprising that the price of reinsurance increases in the aftermath of an event since event losses are likely to raise the demand for insurance and reinsurance. Of course, one reason for an increase in demand is that capital and surplus are depleted and in short supply at the insurer level.[10] In a world of perfect markets, this depletion would, by itself, have no effect on reinsurance demand. Insurance companies would simply enter the capital markets, raising equity and even debt as needed, in order to put their capital back to original levels. Indeed, given the increase in consumer demand for insurance in the aftermath of a catastrophe, one might expect insurance companies to raise considerable amounts of capital. Thus, one might argue that the increase in reinsurance prices is prima facie evidence that there are capital shortages somewhere in the system.

However, the behavior of prices alone cannot be decisive for whether the supply of reinsurance capital is relatively restricted after events. The combination of prices and quantities, on the other hand, is more decisive. Indeed, the cyclic price patterns turn out to be mirrored by synchronized declines in the "quantity" of reinsurance purchased.

Table 1 provides a kind of event study to demonstrate this. The table shows both price and quantity responses in reinsurance purchased during the year following Hurricane Andrew. (Prices and quantity are measured using the same

9. Paragon produces a catastrophe-price index that, since peaking in late 1994 at 2.47 (and beginning on 1 January 1984 at 1.00), shows the following prices: 2.32 on 1 January 1995; 2.16 on 1 July 1995; 2.14 on 1 January 1996; and 2.06 on 1 July 1996.

10. For a study of demand and supply issues in pricing, see Gron (chap. 1 in this volume).

actuarially expected annual reinsurance benefits that lie behind figs. 1 and 2 above.) It is evident that, in the aftermath of large events like Hurricane Andrew, reinsurance purchases fall. (In practice, this occurs primarily through an increase in insurer retentions.) Indeed, the table shows that the quantity purchased fell by more—and prices rose by more—for those insurers that had greater exposure to the southeastern United States and to hurricanes wherever they occur.

The combination of a postevent increase in price and decrease in quantity cannot be explained by an increase in demand. High demand would be associated with high prices *and* high quantities sold, much as if one were to observe transaction prices and quantities of electric generators sold during a blackout. What is going on in the reinsurance market is different: in the aftermath of events, there is *less* provision of reinsurance capacity even though prices are higher. This can be explained only by a temporary shift backward in the supply of capital.

In some sense, it should also not be surprising that the supply of cat-risk-bearing capital is restricted immediately following an event: after all, large-event losses deplete reinsurers' capital and surplus going forward. For at least a time, however, the high prices and low quantities are consistent with a view that additional capital has trouble flowing into the reinsurance sector.[11]

The final point in this section is that there is a kind of irony in capital market shortages and paucity of reinsurance: much primitive cat risk could be reduced through investments in mitigation, investments that are inexpensive in an actuarial sense. However, many of these investments are not made because they require individuals and corporations, who have scarce capital themselves, to raise (or deplete internal) capital. Thus, capital market shortages are in part responsible for the large and growing risk pool needing insurance and reinsurance. Without capital shortages, reinsurance capacity would be greater, but there would also be fewer risks to reinsure in the first place (see Kleindorfer and Kunreuther, chap. 4 in this volume).

Explanation 2: Prices of Catastrophe Reinsurance Are High because Reinsurers Have Market Power

A number of observers have suggested that the evidence presented above on prices and quantities might be explained by market power rather than by a capital shortage per se. Under this explanation, prices rise, and quantities decline, not because reinsurance capital is impossible or costly to obtain, but because reinsurers have no incentive to increase their capital. By putting less money at risk, reinsurers keep prices high. James M. Stone (see chap. 11 in

---

11. It is common in the industry for reinsurers to require "paybacks" for event losses and to do so through higher premiums and retentions. Note that, to the extent that it explains the data, there is nothing in this practice to contradict explanation 1. However, an important question remains as to why this kind of contracting prevails and what it tells us about reinsurance markets. For one potential answer, see explanation 5 below.

this volume) has argued that market power among reinsurers may be one reason that, for catastrophe exposures, reinsurance is a much more attractive business than insurance.

It is, of course, very hard to provide evidence that market power among reinsurers has increased secularly over time or cyclically in the aftermath of events. There is a general view that the reinsurance industry has been consolidating over time. There has been a distinct drop, for example, in the number of Lloyd's syndicates since the 1960s and 1970s. There has also been an increase over time in the capital and market share of large reinsurers. But neither of these facts is necessarily associated with increased market power in setting prices or restricting supply. For example, even when there were many more Lloyd's syndicates, catastrophic risk pricing was not typically determined by individual syndicates.

Furthermore, even if consolidation has occurred in the industry, it need not be associated with greater market power. Consolidation may be a natural result of economies of scale in the reinsurance business. Information intensity is one possible source of scale economies. For example, there may be high fixed costs of developing analytic capabilities and systems (see remarks by Stewart C. Myers, chap. 11 in this volume). Once these systems are in place, optimal reinsurer size grows as the required investment in fixed-cost systems increases. Consolidation may also be an efficient industry response to the costs of obtaining reinsurer capital from outside markets. (Size may help here as well.) If, in the extreme case, outside capital was effectively unavailable, then consolidation would follow from reinsurers' desire to diversify exposures and reduce the probability of ruin.

There may also be a kind of interplay between explanations 1 and 2—the insufficient capital and market power stories. Figure 2 above suggests that prices have both increased secularly and undergone cyclic fluctuations associated with cat events. One would be hard-pressed to explain the secular price increase with the insufficient capital story. For example, entry of capital into the Bermudan reinsurers, beginning in 1993 with Mid-Ocean Ltd., suggests that the barriers to capital entry are not overwhelming, at least not over time periods of more than a few years. The insufficient capital story by itself is therefore likely to be better at explaining cyclic fluctuations in prices. However, to the extent that insufficient capital also drives consolidation, it may contribute to market power, thereby indirectly driving prices up on a secular basis.

Explanation 3: Prices of Catastrophe Reinsurance Are High
because the Corporate Form for Reinsurance Is Inefficient

Under this explanation, the corporate organizational form of reinsurers is costly. Observers of corporate governance often point out that there are costs associated with discretion given to managers to run a business. In principal, managers could act in ways not in the shareholders' interests. It may be difficult for shareholders both to identify this behavior and to discipline it. Even if most managers are benevolent, the prospect that a bad manager might use his agency relation against shareholders reduces stock prices and drives up the cost of capital.

This generic corporate-finance argument of "agency costs" has application in a number of arenas. First, it clearly can be applied to insurers and reinsurers. Many of the details of the reinsurance business and the specific contracts are not transparent to arm's-length capital providers. And, given the occasional big-loss nature of reinsurance, it takes many years to evaluate management efficacy and business profitability. In the reinsurance business, bad managers may have an unusually large incentive to take the money and run.

How costly is it to delegate discretion to managers? In the case of some businesses, it is possible get a partial answer. Closed-end funds are one such business. Closed-end funds invest in publicly traded securities and then sell stakes in their portfolio to shareholders, much like mutual funds do. The difference is that mutual funds are "open-ended"; shareholders can sell their shares back to the fund at a price dictated by the net asset value of the portfolio. Closed-end funds do not automatically buy and sell their shares; a shareholder wishing to sell must find another investor. And, like the price of most traded stocks, the price of the closed-end-fund shares must find its own value in the marketplace in accord with supply and demand.

There is a puzzle associated with closed-end-fund shares: their prices are, on average, considerably below their net asset values. This cannot happen with open-ended-fund shares. Closed-end-share discounts average about 10–20 percent and are pervasive across funds. And it is often argued that agency costs account for these discounts. The story is that closed-end funds must pay an average return in excess of what would be required for holding the underlying net assets. The reason is that shareholders can neither observe managers nor easily discipline managers should they turn out to misbehave. The lack of transparency and control means higher capital costs for running a fund, even for ostensibly good managers.

This agency cost of capital may explain why the costs of reinsurance capital—and, by inference, reinsurance prices—are high. This agency argument is buttressed by two regularities. The first is that managers of reinsurers regard their capital costs as "equity-like"—that is, as requiring a return considerably above U.S. Treasury rates. Writing reinsurance at anywhere near actuarially fair premiums is viewed as being against shareholder interest. Yet, given that catastrophe risks are uncorrelated with those of other financial assets, shareholders' required returns on cat risk should, as argued above, be low. Agency costs may be one factor forcing up required returns. The agency-cost explanation may, therefore, help us understand the view in the industry that, for many risks, there is too much capital and prices are too low. Indeed, some public reinsurers (such as Renaissance Re) are, as of this writing, in the process of repurchasing stock because the returns on writing reinsurance are so low.

There is a second regularity behind the view that the corporate form is inefficient for the provision of reinsurance. This is that, even without agency costs, there is evidence that shareholders expect reinsurer equity returns to be well above U.S. Treasury rates. Evidence for this comes from the behavior of stock prices of public Bermudan reinsurers, such as Mid-Ocean, Renaissance Re, and Partner Re. These firms hold large property-catastrophe liabilities and generally hold assets in the form of short-term notes and bills. Neither their assets nor their liabilities are correlated with the stock market, yet their share prices comove strongly with the stock market. Specifically, a 10 percent increase in the level of the S&P 500 is associated with an increase in the average value of these firms of about 6.5 percent.[12] All I know about the source of this comovement suggests that it does not emanate from the companies themselves.

If the source of the comovement lies outside the companies, there is an inefficiency. Investors who see a stock with higher systematic risk of moving with the market expect the stock to deliver a higher, more equity-like return. As a result, benevolent managers of reinsurers may be maximizing shareholder value by requiring high hurdle rates for writing reinsurance. This suggests that equity-financed reinsurance may be inefficient even if agency costs are completely unimportant. If equity capital requires an equity-like return and reinsurer assets and liabilities contain no broad equity market risks, then equity is an expensive form of capital, pure and simple. And, if reinsurance is financed in an expensive manner, then reinsurance prices will be high.

Offsetting these arguments are several facts. Roberto Mendoza of J. P. Morgan has argued that Bermudan reinsurers, in particular, have a number of advantages that reduce their costs of equity capital. First, Bermuda's low corporate income tax rate means that reinsurers do not suffer by using equity finance as opposed to debt since there are no interest tax deductions available in the first place. Second, Bermudan reinsurer balance sheets provide an opportunity to achieve tax-free compounding on invested assets (remarks by Roberto Mendoza, chap. 11 in this volume). Both these features tend to lower the cost of equity relative to what it would otherwise be.

Third, rather than an agency "cost," reinsurer managerial discretion may provide an agency "benefit." Smart managers may be able to cherry pick the better risk-writing opportunities, thereby raising share prices.[13] This set of features may imply that the typical corporate form of reinsurers, particularly those in Bermuda, is not so inefficient after all. Indeed, Mendoza (see chap. 11 in this volume) argues compellingly that these advantages make the Bermudan corporate form the most efficient reinsurance delivery mechanism.

Explanation 4: Prices of Catastrophe Reinsurance Are High
because Frictional Costs of Reinsurance Are High

This explanation says that prices are high because, as financial instruments, reinsurance contracts are illiquid, have high transactions costs, brokerage, etc.

---

12. Data on unadjusted stock betas from Bloomberg.
13. Of course, the same argument is often made in defense of closed-end-fund managers.

These sources of friction imply that there are important costs in getting capital and reinsurance contracts together in a repository called a *reinsurer.*

There is abundant evidence that illiquid assets trade at significant discounts. For example, letter stock, as opposed to publicly traded stock, typically trades at discounts of 25 percent; on-the-run bonds trade at significantly higher premiums than less liquid off-the-run bonds; and so on.

However, illiquidity of reinsurance contracts is not enough to drive prices up. In order to raise the cost of capital for reinsurers, reinsurers would themselves need to be financed through illiquid placements. It can be argued that this may have been the case for Lloyd's commitments from names; it is unlikely to be true for publicly traded reinsurers in Europe, the United States, and Bermuda.

Other frictions such as brokerage costs and servicing expenses can legitimately raise the cost of procuring reinsurance. However, these costs are not out of line with other financing charges. For example, in the National Indemnity transaction described above, annual brokerage fees were less than 1 percent of premium and 0.1 percent of limit. If the reinsurance had been issued as a capital market instrument, as had been anticipated by some, these costs would have amounted to about 5 percent of the annual premium. Brokerage/underwriting costs for both traditional and new capital market instruments can be expected over time to be competitive with those on other instruments.

Another kind of frictional inefficiency is the means by which reinsurer portfolios are managed. Often today, and in many more cases in the past, reinsurers manage their portfolios by aggregate limits rather than exposures. For example, a reinsurer might decide that it will risk up to $100 million on Florida, but without specifying the *probability* of Florida losses on contracts written or the covariance of Florida losses with potential losses on North Carolina contracts. Removing such portfolio inefficiencies could have a substantial effect on the cost of risk transfer.

However, the main point here is that the high level of prices seems well above anything that can be explained by brokerage and underwriting costs. Even if brokerage and underwriting expenses had come to a high of 10 percent of premium in the National Indemnity deal, complete elimination of these expenses would have driven down the multiple of premium relative to actuarially expected losses by about 0.6 from 5.3 to 4.7. Brokerage and underwriting expenses cannot explain observed price levels.

Finally, it is hard to argue that inefficient reinsurance portfolio practices keep prices high. The financial technology to improve efficiency exists and can be transferred fairly cheaply. Indeed, the fact that these inefficiencies prevail today seems to be evidence for the lack-of-competition view (explanation 2).

Explanation 5: Prices of Catastrophe Reinsurance Are High because
of Moral Hazard and Adverse Selection at the Insurer Level

There is often agreement, implicit or explicit, that reinsurers will charge more in the aftermath of a catastrophe loss. In this sense, property-catastrophe reinsurance is much like "finite" reinsurance. Finite reinsurance does not so much transfer risk from the cedent as it smooths the risk over time. The insurer uses the reinsurance more as a financing vehicle than as an instrument of risk transfer. During an event, the reinsurer makes funds available, expecting to be paid back later. In its purist form, the arrangement is just event-contingent borrowing.[14] Thus, to the extent that catastrophe reinsurance resembles finite reinsurance, it may be transferring even less risk than might appear on a year-by-year basis. Indeed, a prevalent view in the industry is that it is appropriate to have a "payback" to reinsurers after an event loss and that this drives retention levels up.

While this theme is frequently echoed among practitioners, it further begs the question of why there is so little risk transfer in the first place. Two mechanisms that would explain the use of finite-risk-type contracts as well as high prices and low quantities would be moral hazard and adverse selection.

Moral hazard says that an insurer's behavior might change if it were too easily allowed to transfer risk to reinsurers. Once the risks are transferred, insurers have much less stake in prudent underwriting in the first place. Thus, it may be that the most efficient form of reinsurance is to allow very little risk transfer at all: only by forcing cat risk back on insurers (or by charging a very high price to assume risk) can reinsurers get insurers to expend the resources to monitor and mitigate exposures. A reinsurance intermediary who came along willing to charge a low price and take a substantial quantity of risk from an insurer might find that the insurer misbehaves.

Adverse selection is a related problem. It says that insurers know more about their exposures and underwriting than do reinsurers. Those that are most eager to reinsure at any given price probably have private information that their exposures are worse than average. Similarly, those that are least eager to reinsure have private information that their exposures are better than average. The result is that, at any given price, reinsurers will do business with an adversely selected group of (the worst) insurer risks. Clearly, in the presence of adverse selection, the reinsurer needs to charge more to make up for the degree of adverse selection.[15]

This explanation has some interesting implications (see the discussion below). Unlike explanation 4, it does have the ability to explain high levels of prices. However, it is not clear how it fits all the facts. For example, it is hard to see how the cyclic pattern of prices and quantities would emerge. Why, for example, are reinsurers worried that insurers have a greater motive to forgo monitoring after cat events? Why might the information gap between insurers and reinsurers be greater in the aftermath of an event? Is there a pattern whereby insurers who transfer more risk are less profitable? Much needed is

---

14. The contingent credit arranged for the Nationwide by J. P. Morgan has many of these features.

15. In some circumstances, higher prices may actually exacerbate the problem, making it impossible for the market to function. For a discussion of the implications of adverse selection on reinsurance contracts, see Cutler and Zeckhauser (chap. 6 in this volume).

further evidence along these lines that moral hazard and adverse selection are operative in the behavior of prices and quantities. Personally, I am skeptical that these explanations can explain prices and quantities, particularly at higher layers. These layers should be relatively immune to moral hazard and adverse-selection considerations because the retentions (deductible amounts) are so high.[16]

Explanation 6: Regulation Prevents Primary Insurers from Pricing Cat Properly

This explanation observes that a number of major high-catastrophic-risk states use regulatory barriers to keep insurance prices down. In some states, lines of business, and specific geographic areas, insurers must underwrite risk at prices well below those that are actuarially and financially profitable. This is perhaps not a surprising state of affairs when the insurance commissioners are publicly elected officials in twelve states, including California and Florida.

Clearly, this situation cannot lead to a high level of prices in the reinsurance market. However, it can explain why there is so little reinsurance purchased even if prices are actuarially fair. The basic reasoning is that, if insurers are unable to earn a profitable return by underwriting risk, they need to cut costs. One way of cutting costs is to avoid purchasing reinsurance.

The mechanism here is analogous to that of rent control. Rent control is intended to make housing more affordable. It does so by reducing the return that owners receive from making improvements in the housing stock. Owners, therefore, make fewer improvements, and the quality of the housing stock falls. This goes on until equilibrium is reached: eventually, the low rents are matched by a similarly low level of housing quality. The equilibrium rental rate—high or low—is none other than a fair one. The old saw, You get what you pay for, holds even in regulated markets.

In response to price controls, insurers likewise have an incentive to provide a product that is of lower quality and therefore cheaper to produce. They have less incentive to purchase reinsurance, even at fair prices, since much of the benefit of that reinsurance accrues to others (policyholders, state-guarantee funds, other insurers, taxpayers, etc.). The result is that state-guarantee funds must bear considerably greater risks that a large catastrophe will become their responsibility or the responsibility of policyholders and taxpayers. In short, everyone suffers if regulation makes it unprofitable for insurers to provide high-quality insurance contracts.

This explanation also fits the cyclic behavior of quantities. After a big event, insurers may feel that their underwriting prices are particularly low. Thus, even with reinsurance offered at a fair price, they will cut back more on reinsurance purchases. The major weakness of this explanation is that it cannot explain

---

16. For the way in which capital market innovations might help solve these problems (to the extent that they exist), see also the discussion below.

high prices. However, it does explain why insurers may perceive reinsurance prices as high, that is, as being in excess of what they can profitably afford to pay.

Much as with rent control, there is a social policy issue here that will not be dispensed with so easily. What if, for example, the risk of an earthquake occurring along an old fault line in a working-class town suddenly surges? Charging the actuarially justified rate on homeowner's insurance would result in reduced insurance purchases. Housing values would be hit with high homeowner's rates in addition to the hit from the initial earthquake risk. And what of the uninsured? What is the appropriate policy? Should the state or the federal government transfer taxpayer funds to subsidize insurance purchases? Should insurers be forced to bear the cost and spread the burden across all their policyholders by either raising general homeowner's rates or lowering the quality of their product? And, whatever the answer, how does it change if the affected area is not a single town but all of California?

Explanation 7: The Presence of Ex Post Third-Party Financing

Ex post financing of catastrophes occurs when other parties step in to prevent losses from being financed by policyholders. Chief among these entities is, of course, the U.S. government. As is well known, the government has a major role in funding disasters at both the state and the federal levels, through a number of agencies and through both the executive and the legislative branches. During the period 1977–93, the average federal expenditure for disaster assistance was $7.04 billion (in 1993 dollars; see Moss, chap. 8 in this volume). This is far greater than the average annual loss borne by reinsurers on U.S. catastrophe coverage. In some forms of disasters, notably floods, the federal government has effectively eliminated the incentive for the creation of private market insurance contracts. Indeed, before the federal government stepped in to provide disaster relief, private insurers *did* offer flood insurance (see Moss 1996).

The federal government is not the only entity involved in ex post financing of catastrophes. State-guarantee funds and other insurers are often the next line of defense if an insurer is unable to meet its customer obligations. And, if the fund is exhausted, then in many cases solvent insurance companies are to make good on claims against insolvent companies. This creates two types of bad incentives. First, companies have an incentive to shift the burden onto the fund or other insurers before the fund is exhausted. Second, companies who do not act to shift high-layer losses onto the pool are themselves likely to have to pay for others. Well-behaved insurers will wish to avoid doing business in states with guarantee funds and pools. This is another way in which adverse selection can increase the cost of insurance. Overall, the outcome is an incentive for insurers to enter a race to the bottom in customer credit quality (see Bohn and Hall, chap. 9 in this volume). This strengthens the need for regulation and can create a kind of vicious cycle in market and regulatory incentives.

From an economist's perspective, such ex post financing should be viewed as a form of market failure. The federal government cannot credibly commit *not* to fund disasters after the fact: even if it says that it will not provide disaster relief ex ante, the political incentives to do so ex post are overwhelming. Given that this is the case, no one would have the incentive to buy a private-insurance contract at an actuarially fair price or greater since the government effectively subsidizes losses through these programs. Of course, taxpayers will pay for subsidized losses by some means. The government is unlikely to administer a disaster program and monitor disaster payments as well as a dedicated insurer would, so the size of the loss (net of processing costs) paid by taxpayers is likely to be that much greater. Also, there is no mechanism to discipline risk-taking incentives: population growth in high-flood-risk zones is not moderated by charging risk takers for the expected losses that they impose on the system.

How does ex post financing affect the price and quantity of reinsurance? Clearly, insurers have less incentive to provide insurance in the presence of ex post financing. One way of doing this is by not underwriting risk in the first place. A second way is to shift the actuarial costs of the risks onto others. Since insurers must pay for reinsurance but may obtain ex post financing at lower (even zero) costs, they have an incentive to substitute away from reinsurance.

As with explanation 6, ex post financing cannot explain why prices might be high. It can, however, explain why insurers perceive reinsurance prices as high. It can also explain low quantities of high-layer reinsurance and the cyclic downturns in quantities after major events.

Explanation 8: Behavioral Factors

A commonly cited reason for the low quantity of high-layer reinsurance is that the *perceived* likelihood that reinsurance will pay is too low to matter. This issue about perception is ubiquitous in insurance markets.

For economists who use a utility-based approach to understand behavior, insurance against severe but low-probability events is very valuable to consumers. Utility-type approaches argue that outcomes that lose twice as much are perceived by people as more than twice as bad. Yet, in contrast, people often do not insure against low-probability, severe outcome events. They often underpurchase insurance. They often do not take mitigation seriously, and, when they do, they require too high a return on mitigation expenditures (see Kleindorfer and Kunreuther, chap. 4 in this volume).

There are many potential reasons for this behavior. One is that people discount too heavily events that they cannot readily perceive. Famous studies from the 1970s (e.g., Tamerin and Resnik 1972) show that the rate of smoking is higher among the general populace than among general practitioners, higher among general practitioners than among internists, and higher among internists than among specialists who work directly with lung cancer patients. Even when the consequences and probabilities of bad outcomes are well known, the repeated hammering home of bad outcomes affects behavior (Diamond, comment on chap. 2 in this volume).

A second behavioral effect is that individuals often seem "ambiguity" averse. A lack of clarity about the risks and events being insured may lead insurers and reinsurers to set premiums high (see Kunreuther, Hogarth, and Meszaros 1993). Behaviorally, people distinguish between risk and uncertainty. With risk, the probabilities of different outcomes can be determined. Examples would be lotteries or card games. With uncertainty, however, the probabilities cannot be determined. What is the likelihood of an earthquake in Boston? How frequently is a well-built house on the Florida coast destroyed by wind? Uncertainty is inherently more ambiguous, and surveys suggest that individuals charge more to bear it.

A related behavioral argument is that big events do not generate enough "job risk" for people in charge of buying insurance and reinsurance. Studies of corporate insurance purchases, for example, tend to show that mid-layer risks are often insured more frequently than high-layer risks. The argument is that managers are off the hook if the event is large enough since many others will be in the same boat. For smaller events, insurance is easily available and purchased by others, which reinforces the desire for a manager to purchase (re)insurance. It is worth noting that this argument is another form of agency cost—"job risk" would not be an issue if people were buying insurance on their own behalf.

As under explanations 6 and 7, pricing may be fair under the behavioral hypothesis, but the quantity of risk transfer is nevertheless low.

Moving Ahead: Changing the Distribution of Risk through Capital Markets, Deregulation, and Alternative Risk Transfer

Many observers, practitioners, and academics have argued that bringing cat exposures directly to the capital market can help reduce reinsurance prices and increase risk transfer. Mechanisms include cat-linked bonds, swaps, exchange-traded options and futures, cat-linked issues of equity, etc. (see, e.g., Cummins, Lewis, and Phillips, chap. 3 in this volume).

Clearly, the degree of success that the capital markets can hope to bring depends on one's assessment of the explanations outlined above. If the problem is that catastrophe-risk-taking capital is insufficient (explanation 1), then the capital markets clearly represent a potential solution. Indeed, the $50–$100 billion events discussed earlier are equal in size to a normal day's fluctuation in the value of U.S. equities. With U.S. financial assets totaling over $12 trillion, a large catastrophic event represents only about fifty basis points of wealth.

Similarly, if the problem is that the corporate form of today's reinsurers is inefficient (explanation 3), capital market devices would seem to help. Cat bonds specifically collateralized in a special purpose trust to fund insurers' higher-layer cat risks would not be subject to the kinds of agency costs experienced by firms. Moreover, if the equity of these firms is costly because of its tendency to move up and down with the market, then these costs could also be eliminated by embedding the risk in a cat bond, which would be treated more as debt.

Certainly, these investments would at first need to provide an average return in excess of U.S. Treasury bills. Indeed, cat bonds were originally envisioned for the CEA reinsurance layer written by Berkshire Hathaway and were to be offered on terms not so different from the reinsurance. If these prices are to decline, it is clear that considerable infrastructure must first be laid. Investor education about cat risks, for example, is an important externality and will take time to build.

Another important piece of infrastructure is a means for standardizing risk. Simple securitization of existing reinsurance contracts is unlikely to lower costs or increase capacity. Reinsurance contracts have tailor-made features and cover company-specific exposures; they are, therefore, informationally intensive as investments. It makes little sense for individual investors, or their institutional investment agents, to analyze these instruments. Existing reinsurance conserves on analysis by concentrating the exposures in a few places. Clearly, if it is to be economical to spread cat risk more widely, more standardization will be required.

Catastrophe indexes are one way to accomplish this. Indexes help avoid the redundant analysis of distinct risks. They also help promote liquidity, which further lowers the cost of risk transfer. Furthermore, to the extent that moral hazard and adverse selection (explanation 5) are sources of high prices and low quantities, indexes can help. If insurers transfer risks that are linked to industrywide losses, they can reduce the problems of moral hazard and adverse selection faced by investors. Individual insurers may have control over their own losses and know more about those losses than reinsurers. However, they do not have control over, nor do they know more about, index outcomes. Thus, indexes can make risk transfer more efficient, regardless of whether it occurs through capital market devices or traditional reinsurers. Indeed, index-linked cat reinsurance is already gaining popularity as a way of reducing reinsurer capital costs.

Of course, the standardization of an index is, all else equal, a disadvantage from the perspective of the (re)insurance buyer. An insurer would like to protect itself against *its* losses, not insurance-industry losses. Thus, a critical issue in index design is that the index be flexible enough to keep down the "basis" between insurer-specific and index risk. An effective index must provide good hedging tools for cat-risk cedents.

Indeed, my own view is that existing indexes have not caught because they are poorly correlated with individual insurer losses, given a large event. Existing indexes aggregate industry losses at the statewide level. Unfortunately, however, insurer exposure as a percentage of total industry exposure varies considerably within a state. The right hedge ratio, therefore, varies considerably within the state. To see this, suppose that a company hedges on the basis of its 5 percent statewide market share and that a storm destroys a small portion of the state where the insurer's market share happens to be 10 percent of the market. Only half the insurer's losses will be covered by the index. In short, statewide blocks are too large to yield low-basis risk. To serve as good insurer hedges, indexes will need to report industrywide losses for smaller geographic blocks (i.e., zip codes).[17]

Much of this is now being tested as a new catastrophe exchange located in Bermuda has recently opened. The Bermuda Commodities Exchange (BCE), owned by AIG, Guy Carpenter, and Chase Manhattan, and involving the Chicago Board of Trade, will trade contracts based on a U.S. homeowner's catastrophe index developed by Guy Carpenter. The index aggregates losses at the zip-code level and can, therefore, match the exposure of certain insurer portfolios more precisely than statewide indexes can.

Clearly, however, whether capital market devices can work will depend on which of the eight explanations outlined above for the paucity of risk transfer are telling. For example, if the problem is purely reinsurer market power, then innovations in financing will lower prices and increase quantities only if new entrants come along and make the market more competitive. On the other hand, to the extent that market power is created by high reinsurer costs of capital, capital market solutions could help reduce the adverse effects of market power.

Lowering the costs of risk transfer may provide savings, but it cannot directly solve the problems that result from state regulation and insurance pricing (explanations 6 and 7). However, transparent pricing of catastrophe risks in the reinsurance market may have important benefits for the efficiency of regulation. The market pricing of electricity is forcing the rationalization of utilities across the United States. This process will result, not only in more efficient plants and equipment, but also in more rational pricing by utilities and their public commissions. Customers will benefit by having a transparent and observable market energy price to which to tie ratepayer contracts and service. By analogy, reinsurer and insurer financing costs can be useful benchmarks for a regulatory review of underwriting prices. However, pricing is only one of many regulatory hurdles that may prevent efficient distribution of catastrophe risk.[18]

Clearly, government regulation can facilitate or impede risk transfer outside

---

17. For an analysis of how hedge performance is affected by geographic aggregation, see Major (chap. 10 in this volume).

18. Another example of costly regulation is that financial instruments linked to catastrophe losses can in some cases be considered insurance contracts by state insurance commissioners. Because only licensed insurers are allowed to write such contracts, financial instruments that transfer premiums to investors in return for catastrophic risk bearing must seek exemptions and approval from commissioners.

traditional reinsurance channels. Regulation can also mandate reporting of loss and exposure information to authorities, thereby permitting easy aggregation. Much as with Fannie Mae, the government can pursue "market-enhancing" policies designed to jump-start broader market exchange of these risks.

Going forward, it is most likely that traditional reinsurance contracts will continue as the preferred risk-transfer vehicle even if capital market and other alternative-risk-transfer solutions take off. Insurers that are small and/or have less well-diversified exposures are likely to continue placing their risks with reinsurers. Indeed, it may well be that reinsurers, not insurers, will be the direct beneficiaries of capital market products. These products will simply allow reinsurers to place their risks with investors in many forms other than those of standard equity. The almost inevitable result is that the reinsurer cost of capital will decline and specialized capacity increase. As a result, more insured assets will be insurable than ever before. This will make risk sharing in society better, with better risk sharing being the fundamental goal of an insurance system.

References

Doherty, Neil, and Clifford Smith. 1993. Corporate insurance strategy: The case of British Petroleum. *Journal of Applied Corporate Finance* 6, no. 3:4–15.

Froot, Kenneth A., Brian S. Murphy, Aaron B. Stern, and Stephen E. Usher. 1995. *The emerging asset class: Insurance risk.* Special report. New York: Guy Carpenter & Co.

Guy Carpenter & Co. 1997. *Global reinsurance highlights.* Special report. New York.

Kunreuther, Howard, Robin Hogarth, and Jacqueline Meszaros. 1993. Insurer ambiguity and market failure. *Journal of Risk and Uncertainty* 7:71–87.

Moss, David. 1996. Government, markets, and uncertainty: An historical approach to public risk management in the United States. Working Paper no. 97-025. Harvard Business School.

Tamerin, J. S., and H. L. P. Resnik. 1972. Risk taking by individual option: Case study—cigarette smoking. In *Perspectives on benefit-risk decision making.* Washington, D.C.: National Academy of Engineering. (Reprinted in *Uncertainty in economics: Readings and exercises,* ed. P. Diamond and M. Rothschild [San Diego: Academic, 1989].)

1   Insurer Demand for Catastrophe Reinsurance

Anne Gron

The increasing role of risk management in corporate strategy can be seen in the development and use of new risk-management techniques. Two examples are the use of financial derivatives to manage interest rate exposure, foreign exchange risk, and commodity prices and the move away from insurance for managing commercial liability risks. One recent survey estimated that 65 percent of large, nonfinancial firms use derivatives to reduce risk exposure (Wharton School and Chase Manhattan Bank 1995).[1] Meanwhile, the substitution of such "nontraditional" risk-management practices as self-insurance, risk-retention groups, and captives for traditional insurance products has increased to an estimated 30–40 percent of the overall property-casualty insurance market and approximately 60–80 percent of the large casualty risks, where the trend is concentrated.[2]

An increasing academic literature has followed the increasing importance of corporate risk management, but the motivations for corporate risk management are not, as yet, well understood. The empirical studies of corporate risk management in particular are relatively few and the results inconclusive. The theoretical incentives for corporate risk management fall into three broad categories: reducing the cost of financial distress, reducing agency costs, and tax

Anne Gron is assistant professor of management and strategy at the J. L. Kellogg Graduate School of Management, Northwestern University.

The author thanks Anne Beatty, David Govrin, Nicholas Polson, and Raghu Rajan for helpful comments, suggestions, and advice as well as conference participants. Ken Froot, David Govrin, Paul O'Connell, Guy Carpenter & Co., and the Wharton Financial Institutions Center generously provided access to data and additional information. Data assistance from the Insurance Library Association of Boston is also greatly appreciated. Victoria Zuckerman provided able research assistance. Partial financial support for this paper was generously provided by the NBER Project on the Financing of Property-Casualty Risks.

1. Large firms are considered to be those with market value greater than $250 million.
2. For further details on this trend, see Murphy (1995) and Johnson and Higgens (1992).

motivations. While existing empirical studies have found some evidence consistent with each of these motivations, there is little consistency of results across studies.[3] This lack of consistency as well as data shortcomings indicate a need for further research on the topic.

This study adds to the literature by examining the determinants of insurer demand for catastrophe reinsurance. *Reinsurance* refers to insurance purchased by an insurer; *catastrophe reinsurance* is insurance for losses associated with natural hazards, such as hurricanes, earthquakes, and windstorms. Catastrophe reinsurance is well suited for this study because it is relatively homogeneous and well defined. This ensures that one insurer's catastrophe reinsurance is fairly similar to another insurer's and allows us to calculate good measures of firm exposure to risk, a feature lacking in studies of reinsurance more generally.[4] Also, unlike some financial engineering strategies, catastrophe reinsurance cannot be used both to speculate and to hedge risk. Thus, this study focuses directly on the determinants of corporate demand for a specific form of risk reduction.

Another advantage of this investigation is that the data include price as well as quantity measures. Previous studies either examine the quantity of risk-reduction activity or, in some cases, investigate whether firms engage in particular risk-management techniques. In both cases, the analysis is made without reference to cost because of data limitations. Ideally, one would like to examine the quantity of risk reduction given its cost. My data on catastrophe-reinsurance contracts, from the largest broker of catastrophe reinsurance, Guy Carpenter and Company, include both price and quantity measures for a large fraction of the U.S. catastrophe-reinsurance market for the period 1987–93. This allows me to examine insurers' willingness to trade off different quantity dimensions in response to changes in price. Since insurers are observed only if they purchase catastrophe reinsurance through Guy Carpenter, my estimation strategy corrects for sample selection.

I find that insurers do trade off quantity and price when purchasing catastrophe reinsurance: as prices increase, insurers increase retention levels, decrease total limits, and increase coinsurance rates. These findings support the notion

3. The empirical literature on corporate risk management includes studies that estimate insurer use of reinsurance (Mayers and Smith 1990; Garven 1994) and studies that examine corporate use of financial hedges (Nance, Smith, and Smithson 1993; Gezcy, Minton, and Schrand 1997; Tufano 1996).

4. As noted, *reinsurance* refers to an insurer buying insurance. This covers a wide range of financing and risk transfer. For example, diversification through swapping books of business between insurers and contracts requiring reimbursement if losses exceed a specified amount are both classified as *reinsurance*. Previous studies of reinsurance cannot distinguish among such contractual differences and do not distinguish between reinsurance transactions in property lines of business (e.g., automobile physical damage) and those in liability lines (e.g., medical malpractice). In addition, the value of reinsurance purchased by the insurer is netted against the reinsurance sold, even though the two may be very different types of transactions. The breadth of activity covered under the term *reinsurance* makes it more difficult to construct a representative measure of firm risk exposure.

that firms with greater probability of financial distress have greater demand for risk management and hence catastrophe reinsurance. The data also indicate that insurers with greater catastrophe exposure have significantly greater demand for catastrophe reinsurance. The data do not, however, indicate that smaller firms have greater demand for catastrophe reinsurance. In fact, I find that larger firms appear to have greater demand for catastrophe reinsurance. This finding suggests that the liquidity effect of catastrophe reinsurance dominates the solvency effect. Catastrophe reinsurance does two things: it decreases the probability of insolvency, and it increases liquidity after a large loss. Larger firms are likely to value the liquidity component more than smaller firms. My results suggest that the liquidity component dominates the solvency component in the data.

The purchase of catastrophe reinsurance is also important in its own right. The issue of funding catastrophic losses has come to the forefront in recent years with record catastrophe losses. In 1992, Hurricane Andrew caused $15 billion of insured losses, and, from July 1989 to July 1996, the insurance industry paid out over $35 billion from events with over $1.5 billion in insured losses (see Litzenberger, Beaglehole, and Reynolds 1996; and the sources therein). In the wake of Hurricane Andrew, prices for catastrophe reinsurance increased substantially, and availability declined. Studies suggest that exposure to catastrophe has greatly increased owing to migration and building patterns that have increased population and property exposure in the most catastrophe-prone regions. One consequence of these changes has been an increased interest in securitizing catastrophe exposure via futures, options, or bonds.[5] Reduced transactions costs and greater risk spreading are typically cited as the benefits derived from securitizing catastrophe risk. The results of this research suggest additional benefits. To the extent that insurers have lower leverage and hold more liquid assets as substitutes for catastrophe reinsurance, greater access to low-cost catastrophe reinsurance will free up insurer capital and reduce the need for liquidity.

The paper is organized as follows. Section 1.1 examines the relevant theories of corporate risk management and applies them to catastrophe reinsurance in particular. Section 1.2 presents the data, and section 1.3 reports the estimation results. A discussion of the results and their implications for corporate risk management and the catastrophe-reinsurance market is contained in section 1.4.

---

5. For example, trading in catastrophe-insurance options on the Chicago Board of Trade has increased steadily since the revised product was introduced in September 1995. October 1996 trading showed open interest and notional value at their highest points. Another instrument for trading catastrophe risk, the Catastrophe Risk Exchange (CATEX), allows subscribers to swap risks or exchange risks for cash or risk plus cash. It had five subscribers as of November 1996. Several bond issues linked to catastrophe exposure have also been considered. USAA plans to issue $500 million in catastrophe bonds, and the California Earthquake Authority may issue earthquake bonds in March 1997 (see Chookaszian, chap. 11 in this volume).

1.1   Corporate Risk Management and the Demand for Catastrophe Reinsurance

Catastrophe reinsurance is a contract whereby the reinsurer agrees to pay the insurer (purchaser) a specified amount in the event of a catastrophic event occurring within a defined time period causing large total property claims. The decisions to purchase insurance are motivated by the same basic forces that motivate other corporations to manage risk. The incentives for corporate risk management most relevant here fall into three categories: reducing the cost of financial distress, reducing agency costs, and tax motivations. Each of these is briefly described below.

1.1.1   Motivations for Corporate Risk Management

Purchasing catastrophe reinsurance can reduce the probability of financial distress and its associated costs by reducing the probability that the firm becomes insolvent as the result of a catastrophe. Research demonstrates that the costs of financial distress include increased cost of capital and reduced relationship-specific investment by suppliers and purchasers (see, e.g., the discussions in Mayers and Smith 1982; Smith and Stulz 1985; and Mayers and Smith 1990). These issues are particularly important for insurance companies where the product quality is inversely related to the probability of bankruptcy.[6] In the presence of capital market imperfections that make internal funds less costly than external funds, firms in financial distress will tend to underinvest because of lack of internal funds (see Froot, Scharfstein, and Stein 1993). This is likely to be particularly important in the insurance industry, where investment opportunities follow large industry losses. As demonstrated in Gron (1994a, 1994b) and Winter (1988, 1994), these types of capital market imperfections are associated with increases in industry profitability following large industry losses. Firms with greater leverage and lower liquidity are likely to have greater costs of financial distress.

Risk-averse individuals with large, undiversified stakes in a corporation will benefit from corporate risk management (Mayers and Smith 1982; Smith and Stulz 1985; Mayers and Smith 1990). This includes managers as well as owners when ownership is concentrated. The majority of insurance companies have one of two predominant ownership structures, stock or mutual. A substantial literature investigates the relative merits of stock and mutual ownership and their continued coexistence in the insurance and banking industries.[7] That liter-

---

6. While smaller buyers of insurance such as individuals and households may not be directly concerned with an insurer's solvency because of state guaranty funds, insurer solvency is important to larger purchasers such as corporations whose claims are typically only partially covered by the guaranty system because the size of losses is likely to be above guaranty-fund limits. Increased probability of financial distress is likely to reduce an insurer's financial rating, which may result in decreased demand from buyers, who use the ratings as a quality measure.

7. Lamm-Tenant and Starks (1993) provide a good summary of this literature.

ature suggests that the presence of both organizational forms is related to two agency conflicts: that between owners and policyholders and that between owners and managers. The mutual form removes the first conflict but exacerbates the second because there is no effective market for corporate control. Most of the theoretical literature implies that mutual insurers will tend to operate in types of insurance with lower risk and managerial discretion, and Lamm-Tenant and Starks (1993) provide empirical evidence of this. The tendency of mutual insurers to take on less risk than stock insurers is likely to persist with respect to catastrophe exposures. Mutual insurers will be more likely to purchase catastrophe reinsurance than will stock insurers because the firm owners are less diversified and risk-averse managers will benefit from the risk reduction.

Mayers and Smith (1982, 1990) and Smith and Stulz (1985) point out that the progressivity of the tax code provides incentives for hedging since it creates a convex tax function for low levels of income. Therefore, a firm with expected income in the convex range of the tax code can reduce expected tax payments by reducing the variance of income. After the Tax Reform Act of 1986 and the imposition of the alternative minimum tax, however, it has become quite difficult to determine how the tax code influences firm behavior. Still, tax-preference items such as tax-loss carryforwards will provide incentives to manage risk since their expected present value is decreasing in the variance of income.

The value of catastrophe reinsurance is also increasing in an insurer's exposure to catastrophic risk. The greater the exposure, the greater the benefit from reinsurance. Greater exposure can come from concentration in geographic areas where catastrophes are more common, such as coastal regions, or from concentration in property lines.

1.1.2   Insurer Demand for Catastrophe Reinsurance

Insurers have several methods for hedging catastrophic risk. An insurer can enter into a proportional agreement with another insurer, it can buy "pro rata" coverage, which reimburses a fixed percentage of losses, or it can buy "excess-of-loss" coverage, which reimburses losses above a specified level. A proportional reinsurance treaty is a contract between insurers where each agrees to finance a stated percentage of claims from a particular book of business. Such an arrangement is not aimed solely at reducing catastrophe risk, but it does so if the two insurers operate in separate geographic areas. If the insurer decides to purchase catastrophe coverage from a reinsurer, it can purchase either pro rata or excess-of-loss coverage. Pro rata coverage is typically purchased through a reinsurer that sells directly to insurers (a *direct* reinsurer), while excess-of-loss coverage is usually purchased from reinsurers that sell through brokers. The difference in the two approaches is in amount of coverage and access to reinsurers. Excess-of-loss programs purchased through a broker generally have greater amounts of coverage. The broker works with the insurer to construct a reinsurance program and then uses its contacts with many reinsurers to place layers of this program with several different reinsurers.

This paper investigates insurers' demand for catastrophe reinsurance purchased through reinsurance brokers. The insurance is excess-of-loss coverage; a typical catastrophe-reinsurance program may call for $90 million coverage with a $10 million retention. The broker then "places" the program in the market, selling different "layers" of the $90 million to reinsurers. For example, the contract might consist of five layers, each with its own retention and limit. The first layer covers the first $10 million after the insurer's initial retention of $10 million, the second the next $15 million, the third the next $20 million, the fourth the next $20 million, and the fifth the final $25 million. Together, they add up to $90 million in coverage. In addition to retention and limit, catastrophe-reinsurance programs have coinsurance rates that specify the percentage of the loss that the insurer will bear. If the coinsurance rate is 10 percent, then the insurer will pay 10 percent of any insured loss. In the example, a $50 million catastrophe will result in the reinsurers paying $36 million:

0.9 * $40 million (= $50 million less $10 million retention).

The amount of catastrophe reinsurance is increasing in the limit and decreasing in the retention and coinsurance rate.

The price of a catastrophe-reinsurance program is quoted as the premium paid divided by the amount of coverage, called the *rate on line*. If the premium in the example given above is $13.175 million, the "price" will be 0.146 (= 13.175/90). An insurer's willingness to pay for catastrophe reinsurance depends, not on the absolute retention level and limit, but rather on the retention level and limit relative to the insurer's exposure. The expected value of a particular retention level or limit depends on the frequency with which the insurer expects losses in that range to occur. This will be a function of the insurer's underlying property exposure. Therefore, the insurer demand for catastrophe reinsurance will be based on the retention level relative to the insurer's exposure and the limit relative to exposure, or relative retention and relative limit, respectively.

The demand for catastrophe reinsurance can be written as equation (1), where price (P) is a function of relative retention (RRET), the relative limit (RLIM), the coinsurance rate (COINS), and firm characteristics affecting the valuation of catastrophe reinsurance (Z):

(1) $P_{it} = \beta_0 + \beta_1 RRET_{it} + \beta_2 RLIM_{it} + \beta_3 COINS_{it} + \gamma Z_{it} + \varepsilon_{it}.$

Since this is a demand curve, we expect the estimated coefficients on relative retention and coinsurance to be positive, while the estimated effect of relative limit should be negative. That is, insurers are expected to respond to higher price with higher retentions, greater coinsurance rates, and lower total limits. Characteristics that affect an insurer's valuation of catastrophe reinsurance include factors that affect the costs of financial distress, agency costs, and tax motivations as well as firm exposure to catastrophe loss. These variables are discussed in the next section, which describes the data.

1.2   Data

The price and quantity data come from Guy Carpenter, a reinsurance broker, and cover those insurers who purchased catastrophe reinsurance through the brokerage. These data were supplemented with data on insurance-company operations and financial status from the A. M. Best Company. Guy Carpenter's data cover approximately 60 percent of the market for catastrophe reinsurance. Although the data include regional (smaller) companies and national (larger) companies, they are likely to be skewed toward larger companies for two reasons. First, many smaller companies purchase catastrophe reinsurance from a direct reinsurer or buy proportional reinsurance (or both). Second, Guy Carpenter has not traditionally served the majority of the smaller insurers who go to the broker market.

The Guy Carpenter data analyzed here include all the regional and national companies that purchased catastrophe reinsurance through Guy Carpenter from 1987 to 1993. The typical data entry for a company includes the number of layers, the retention for each layer, the limit, the premium, and coinsurance. Since the insurer decides to purchase the whole catastrophe-reinsurance program at the same time, the data are aggregated to the program, the relevant unit of observation. For each company year I calculate the program price (rate on line), program retention, coverage limit, and coinsurance rate. Price, or rate on line, is the total premium paid divided by total limit. Coinsurance was calculated as the average coinsurance rate for the contract.[8] The data consist of 327 observations covering fifty different insurers over the period 1987–93.[9]

To provide an overview of catastrophe-insurance prices, figure 1.1 graphs average price for national and regional insurers for the period 1974–94.[10] Both series display the same relative minima and maxima. Prices are at relative maxima in the middle of the 1970s and the 1980s, a feature common to many insurance-price or -profitability series. These periods coincide with the two most recent "insurance crises," when industry prices and profitability increased rapidly, accompanied by sharp declines in availability. Other research suggests that these episodes are related to temporary capacity shortages that are in part due to capital market imperfections (see, e.g., Gron 1994a, 1994b; Winter 1988, 1994; and the references therein). There is also a marked increase in

8. The coinsurance rate reported in the data is not likely to be the actual coinsurance rate; it is, instead, the minimum coinsurance rate that the selling reinsurers required. The actual coinsurance rate is not available but could be greater, depending on market conditions.

9. The actual estimation includes 298 observations, representing forty-five insurers. Observations were lost because of missing characteristic data.

10. The Guy Carpenter data do not include regional insurers until 1980.

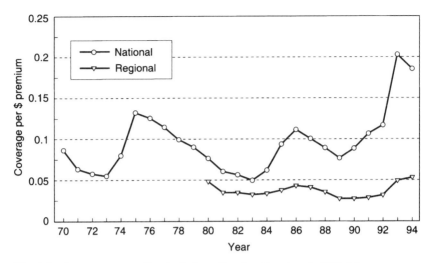

Fig. 1.1   Average rate on line (price), national and regional, 1974–94

price following 1992, when Hurricane Andrew produced record losses in Florida and Louisiana. Froot and O'Connell (chap. 5 in this volume) provide evidence that price increases in catastrophe reinsurance are also associated with temporary capacity shortages that are due to capital market imperfections.

Additional firm data for the years 1986–90 come from *Best's Insurance Tapes* and from *Best's Insurance Reports*.[11] Since I want firm characteristics prior to the purchase of catastrophe reinsurance, these values are lagged so that the data cover the period 1987–93. Firm exposure to catastrophe risk is measured by two variables: the percentage of premiums in property lines (PROP) and the percentage of premiums that are in property lines in coastal areas (COAST).[12] The relative retention and relative limit measures in the demand curve are measured as retention and limit divided by total property premiums just prior to purchase of the catastrophe-reinsurance program.[13]

11. Best's ratings and ownership structure are from *Best's Insurance Reports*.
12. The lines of insurance included as property exposure are fire, allied, farmer's multiple peril, homeowner's multiple peril, commercial multiple peril, inland marine, earthquake, glass, and automobile physical damage. Since the line of business data is at the national level, I assumed that that line's representation was the same at the state level as at the national level. Coastal property exposure is the sum of the property premium volume in the southern and eastern coastal states divided by total premium volume. The states included are Texas, Louisiana, Alabama, Mississippi, Florida, Georgia, South Carolina, North Carolina, Virginia, Washington, D.C., Delaware, Maryland, New Jersey, New York, Connecticut, Rhode Island, Massachusetts, New Hampshire, and Maine. Property premium in those states is total premium volume multiplied by the percentage of all premiums in the property lines.
13. All firm characteristics (except default ratings) are from insurers' statutory reports and reflect the status as of 31 December of that year. Firm characteristics are lagged one year and therefore represent the experience for the year prior to the catastrophe-reinsurance program. Since property policies are generally in force for a year, this provides a good measure of expected exposure. Almost 60 percent of reinsurance contracts begin on 1 January.

Other firm characteristics affect insurer demand through the probability of financial distress, agency costs, and tax motivations. Firm leverage (LEV), default risk (BRate), size (SIZE), the percentage of assets held in liquid assets (LIQ), diversification across lines of insurance (HHI), and geographic diversification (NUM) affect the probability of financial distress. Leverage is the ratio of insurer liabilities (loss reserve plus loss adjustment expenses) divided by assets. Default risk is measured as Best's rating, which varies from 13 (A++) to 1 (D). A rating of A++ or A+ is rated as "superior," while a rating of C or C− is "marginal" and a rating of D "below minimum standards" (*Best's Key Rating Guide,* 1993). I expect insurers with greater leverage and lower financial ratings to have a higher probability of financial distress. Insurer size, measured as net assets, is likely to be associated with a lower probability of financial distress, all else being equal, because the insurer has a greater ability to sustain a large loss. The liquidity measure is the percentage of assets held in liquid funds (the sum of short-term investments and cash on hand divided by net assets). Firms with greater liquidity are also less likely to suffer the costs of financial distress because they are more likely to have the required funds. Diversification across lines of insurance was measured as the sum of squared shares (a Hirschman-Herfindahl index). Geographic diversification was measured as the number of states in which the insurer sells insurance. I expect more diversified firms to have a lower probability of financial distress.

Tax-preference items (TAX) and insurer ownership (MUT) measure the effects of tax motivations and agency costs. I use federal taxes paid normalized by net assets to control for tax motivations.[14] Ownership is measured as an indicator variable that is one if the company is a mutual.

Table 1.1 reports the mean rate on line, relative retention, and relative limit by year for the companies in the sample, divided by whether the company is classified as national or regional. While there is substantial difference in the level of these variables between the two groups, the series behave quite similarly over time.[15] National insurers have lower relative retention and lower relative limits, on average, than smaller, regional insurers. The average price (premium divided by limit) is higher for national than for regional insurers, reflecting their greater exposure to catastrophe. Table 1.2 provides a summary of insurer characteristics for the insurers purchasing catastrophe reinsurance. Tables 1.3 and 1.4 provide comparison for insurers with positive property exposure as calculated from the Best data.[16] Companies in the sample of catastrophe-reinsurance purchasers are larger, on average, than other insurance firms,

14. Negative federal taxes paid on the cash-flow statement indicate taxes paid; positive amounts indicate a net operating loss carryback. A value of zero is consistent with a tax-loss carryforward.

15. The exception is relative retention. The correlation between the national and the regional annual means is above 60 percent for all series except relative retention, which is negatively correlated at −.18.

16. Since the catastrophe-reinsurance purchase is typically done for the whole insurance group, affiliated companies were dropped. The data include group and unaffiliated companies only.

Table 1.1   **Annual Averages: Price and Quantity Measures by Insurer Type**

Year	Price (Rate on Line)		Relative Retention		Relative Limit		Coinsurance	
	National	Regional	National	Regional	National	Regional	National	Regional
1985	.094	.039					.057	.040
1986	.112	.045					.058	.045
1987	.101	.044	.021	.051	.122	.733	.063	.044
1988	.090	.037	.021	.048	.128	.791	.062	.040
1989	.078	.029	.022	.056	.127	.924	.064	.036
1990	.089	.028	.024	.046	.138	.996	.060	.035
1991	.107	.030	.025	.046	.143	.972	.054	.035
1992	.118	.033	.029	.046	.150	.912	.049	.041
1993	.204	.049	.044	.049	.154	.939	.077	.050
1994	.187	.052					.074	.047

Table 1.2   **Summary Statistics of Insurer Data: Guy Carpenter Data**

Variable	Obs.	Mean	SD	Min.	Max.
SIZE	302	4,280,000,000	470,000,000	1,857,248	24,700,000,000
PROP	302	.653	.267	.143	.999
TAX	302	−.007	.015	−.062	.037
HHI	302	.285	.143	.110	.818
COAST	302	.378	.341	0	.997
LEV	302	.374	.195	.0185	.707
LIQ	302	.093	.086	−.0060	.599
RRET	302	.0395	.026	.0034	.174
RLIM	302	.586	.525	.025	1.921
COINS	302	.047	.024	0	.15
REGL	302	.593	.492	0	1
BRate	298	10.960	1.465	3	13
NUM	302	23.815	23.205	1	51
YEAR	302	89.944	1.993	87	93

Table 1.3   **Summary Statistics of Insurer Data: Full Sample**

Variable	Obs.	Mean	SD	Min.	Max.
GC sample	4,293	.070	.256	0	1
GC plus	4,293	.084	.277	0	1
SIZE	4,293	671,000,000	2,730,000,000	143,157	51,000,000,000
PROP	4,293	.587	.302	$1.23E-05$	1.178
TAX	4,293	−.0107	.024	−.417	.339
HHI	4,293	.415	.223	.102	1.807
COAST	4,293	.245	.313	0	1.137
LEV	4,293	.312	.187	$4.5E-05$	1.062
LIQ	4,293	.195	.208	−.036	1.315
NUM	4,293	15.242	18.794	0	51
YEAR	4,293	89.721	1.722	87	93

Note: GC = Guy Carpenter.

although the sample does include some relatively small companies. The purchasing sample also has slightly greater property and coastal exposure, a lower proportion of liquid assets, and slightly greater leverage. The Guy Carpenter sample is also slightly less concentrated across lines of business and, on average, licensed to write in eight more states.

1.3   Estimation

Before estimating equation (1), we need to deal with two estimation problems: sample selection and endogenous quantity measures. The first problem arises because the distribution of price in equation (1) is not observed for all

Table 1.4   Summary Statistics of Insurer Data: Sample without Guy Carpenter Insurers

Variable	Obs.	Mean	SD	Min.	Max.
GC sample	3,991	0	0	0	0
GC plus	3,991	.0143	.119	0	1
SIZE	3,991	398,000,000	1,960,000,000	143,157	51,000,000,000
PROP	3,991	.582	.304	1.23E−05	1.178
TAX	3,991	−.011	.0245	−.417	.339
HHI	3,991	.425	.225	.102	1.807
COAST	3,991	.235	.308	0	1.137
LEV	3,991	.307	.185	4.5E−05	1.062
LIQ	3,991	.203	.212	−.036	1.315
NUM	3,991	14.594	18.258	0	51
YEAR	3,991	89.704	1.699	87	92

Note: GC = Guy Carpenter.

insurers; instead, there is incidental truncation.[17] Estimating equation (1) without correction for incidental truncation is similar to calculating the mean of a normal distribution from a variable that is observed only if its value is above some threshold. In order to estimate the mean of the full distribution from a truncated variable, I include a correction factor for the truncation.[18]

The problem here is slightly different in that the truncation is not on price but on the valuation of catastrophe reinsurance. I observe a purchase (and therefore a price) only if the unobserved net value of catastrophe reinsurance is above zero. While I do not observe the net value of catastrophe reinsurance, I do observe the decision to purchase catastrophe reinsurance. The standard correction technique for this problem is to estimate a selection equation and include an estimated correction factor, known as the inverse Mills ratio or hazard rate, in the estimation. If V^* is the net value of catastrophe reinsurance and V is one if the insurer purchases and zero otherwise, then the underlying model can be written as

$$V^*_{it} = \delta_0 + \delta_1 W_{it} + \eta_{it},$$

A two-step estimation procedure where the first stage estimates the probability of purchase as suggested by Heckman (1979) is appropriate (see Greene 1993). The first stage uses a probit specification to estimate the probability of purchase:

$$\text{prob}(V_{it} = 1) = \Phi(\delta_0 + \delta_1 W_{it}),$$

17. For further discussion, see Greene (1993) and Maddala (1983).

18. For example, if the variable z is distributed normally with parameters (μ, σ^2) and we observe z only if $z > a$, then $E(z|z > a) = \mu + \sigma\phi(\alpha)/[1 - \Phi(\alpha)]$, where $\alpha = (a - \mu)/\sigma$. The second term corrects for the truncation, where $\phi(\cdot)$ is the standard normal probability density function, and $\Phi(\cdot)$ is the standard normal cumulative distribution function.

Table 1.5   **Summary Statistics of Insurer Data: Guy Carpenter Plus Additional Insurers**

Variable	Obs.	Mean	SD	Min.	Max.
GC sample	359	.841	.366	0	1
GC plus	359	1	0	1	1
SIZE	359	3,710,000,000	6,090,000,000	1,857,248	24,700,000,000
PROP	359	.632	.264	.143	1
TAX	359	−.0076	.0144	−.062	.037
HHI	359	.295	.157	.110	.999
COAST	359	.364	.326	0	.997
LEV	359	.385	.187	.018	.707
LIQ	359	.097	.109	−.0060	.948
NUM	359	24.529	22.820	1	51
YEAR	359	89.914	1.956	87	93

Note: GC = Guy Carpenter.

and

$$\text{prob}(V_{it} = 0) = 1 - \Phi(\delta_0 + \delta_1 W_{it}).$$

In the second stage, the estimated coefficients, $\hat{\delta}$, are used to construct the inverse Mills ratio, $\phi(\hat{\delta}w)/\Phi(\hat{\delta}w)$, and included in the estimation of equation (1). In this correction factor, $\phi(\cdot)$ is the standard normal probability density function, and $\Phi(\cdot)$ is the standard normal cumulative distribution function.

There is one additional caveat in this case: I observe purchases only for insurers with positive net value that purchase through the particular broker. In the sample selection equation, some of the firms that actually purchase catastrophe reinsurance will be misclassified as firms that do not. To partially correct for this, I augmented the data by searching annual reports on the Lexis-Nexis on-line service for insurers reporting catastrophe-reinsurance purchases. This yielded an additional fifty-seven (insurer-year) purchases that could be matched to the insurer data. (Sample statistics for this larger set of purchasers are reported in table 1.5.) I estimate equation (1) using correction factors generated from both samples.

Table 1.6 reports the results from estimation of the sample selection equation with buyers defined as only Guy Carpenter insurers in columns 1 and 2 and as both Guy Carpenter insurers and those reporting in their annual reports in columns 4 and 5. Columns 3 and 6 report the change in the probability of purchase, given a small change in the independent variable (evaluated at sample means). The results are qualitatively similar for both dependent variables, with the magnitude of a change in the independent variable slightly larger for estimation using the larger set of reinsurance purchasers. Somewhat contrary to theoretical predictions, but consistent with the institutional facts, large insurers are substantially more likely to purchase catastrophe reinsurance than smaller insurers are. Greater exposure to catastrophic losses, as measured

Table 1.6   **Estimation of Sample Selection Equation**

	Dependent Variable[a]		Change in Probability (3)	Dependent Variable[b]		Change in Probability (6)
	Coefficient (1)	z-Statistic (2)		Coefficient (4)	z-Statistic (5)	
SIZE	9.52E−11	13.37	4.82E−12	8.29E−11	11.99	6.67E−12
PROP	2.004	8.45	.101	1.590	8.23	.128
HHI	−1.725	−7.36	−.087	−1.294	−6.84	−.104
TAX	.208	.12	.011	−1.843	−1.15	−.148
LIQ	−1.513	−4.90	−.077	−1.329	−5.25	−.107
LEV	1.683	5.92	.085	2.009	8.09	.162
COAST	.556	5.22	.028	.565	5.64	.045
CONST	−2.906	−12.44		−2.756	−14.11	
Obs.	5,105			5,105		
Log likelihood	−872.24			−1,068.95		

[a]One if insurer in Guy Carpenter data.
[b]One if insurer in Guy Carpenter or additional data.

by the proportion of business in property lines and the proportion of premiums written for property exposures in coastal states, also substantially increases the probability of purchase. Contrary to expectations, firms with greater concentration by line of business are less likely to purchase catastrophe reinsurance. The estimated effects of the proportion of liquid assets and firm leverage are statistically significant and have the expected effect on the probability of purchase. The estimated effect of tax-loss carryforwards, as proxied by federal taxes paid, is not significantly different from zero and varies in sign across specifications.

A second estimation problem arises from the endogeneity of quantity measures. The usual estimation strategy for a demand curve would be to specify a reinsurance supply curve for the individual insurer and use the excluded variables in the supply curve to identify the demand curve. One particular problem in this case is that measurable factors that shift the demand for reinsurance will generally shift the supply of reinsurance as well. One variable that might affect the supply curve is the level of coverage. As noted by Smith and Doherty (1993), insurance markets generally become less competitive when the level of coverage is very high. Therefore, one instrument is the upper limit of the program, calculated as the sum of the limit and retention.

One possible source of instruments comes from the cross-sectional nature of the data. Relative retention, relative limits, and coinsurance rates are likely to be correlated across insurers owing to responses to supply conditions. Therefore, relative retention, relative limit, and coinsurance averaged over all other insurers for the year might produce acceptable instruments for estimating equation (1). The important assumption is that similarities reflect catastrophe-reinsurance supply conditions that all insurers face. I make this assumption in

Table 1.7   **Estimation of Catastrophe Reinsurance Demand**

Variable	A	B	C	D
RRET	−.161	33.961	30.103	30.343
	(−.138)	(3.169)	(3.075)	(3.066)
RLIM	−.469	−.246	−.380	−.350
	(−6.182)	(−.323)	(−.533)	(−.488)
COINS	1.814	25.822	26.850	26.977
	(1.642)	(2.257)	(2.552)	(2.525)
SIZE	1.54E−11	6.93E−12	5.28E−10	5.03E−10
	(2.613)	(.444)	(2.917)	(2.905)
PROP	−.786	.0828	10.197	9.458
	(−3.190)	(.107)	(2.660)	(2.627)
COAST	.329	1.255	4.820	5.262
	(3.493)	(3.571)	(3.522)	(3.449)
NUM	−.0049	.0336	.0272	.029
	(−1.005)	(1.328)	(1.147)	(1.222)
TAX	3.136	2.194	4.152	−8.543
	(1.882)	(.520)	(1.054)	(−1.524)
HHI	.798	−3.003	−10.713	−10.027
	(2.615)	(−2.420)	(−3.273)	(−3.288)
LEV	−1.171	−.916	6.960	10.431
	(−3.168)	(−.939)	(2.314)	(2.487)
LIQ	−.276	1.595	−9.951	−9.487
	(−.839)	(1.304)	(−2.540)	(−2.520)
REGION	−1.094	.104	−.406	−.357
	(−5.123)	(.134)	(−.550)	(−.480)
BRate	−.197	−.164	−.153	−.159
	(−1.013)	(−2.146)	(−2.155)	(−2.214)
Inverse Mill's ratio	[a]	[a]	7.947	8.766
			(2.868)	(2.851)

Note: Column A gives OLS estimation; column B gives instrumental variables (IV) estimation; column C gives IV with Mill's ratio based on the Guy Carpenter sample; and column D gives IV with Mill's ratio based on the augmented Guy Carpenter sample. The dependent variable is the natural logarithm of price, and t-statistics are presented in parentheses. Each regression has 298 observations and includes a constant term.

[a]The inverse Mill's ratio was not included in the estimation.

estimating equation (1) and provide OLS results to compare with the instrumental variables results.

Table 1.7 presents the results from estimation of equation (1). The logarithm of price was regressed on the explanatory variables because of its skewed distribution. Column A presents the results from OLS estimation, excluding the inverse Mills ratio. Column B displays results from instrumental variables (IV) estimation of equation 1, again excluding the Mills ratio. The estimated coefficients in columns C and D include two different measures of the inverse Mills ratio; the first is based on the selection equation classifying only Guy Carpenter insurers as purchasers, the second on the selection equation with the broader set of purchasing insurers.

The simple, OLS regression of price on quantity measures and firm characteristics does not perform particularly well. While the estimated effect of the relative limit is negative and the estimated effect of coinsurance is positive, as expected, the latter is not statistically significant at the 10 percent level. The estimated effect of relative retention is not different from zero. In addition, property exposure and leverage are statistically significant with the wrong signs. From the results in columns B–D, one sees that the coefficients on relative retention and coinsurance increase substantially (in magnitude and statistical significance) using instrumental variables, as one might expect if supply and demand effects were confounded in column A. The estimated effect of relative limit, however, decreases slightly in magnitude and remains negative but is not statistically different from zero. Estimation using instrumental variables causes the estimated coefficients on property exposure and leverage to be statistically insignificant. In addition, the estimated effects of diversification across lines is now negative and statistically different from zero.

Inclusion of the inverse Mills ratio in columns C and D improves the performance of the firm characteristics without substantially changing the estimated effects of the endogenous variables. In column C, the inverse Mills ratio is based on the Guy Carpenter data only, whereas, in column D, additional observations of catastrophe-reinsurance purchases are included. The results in both columns are quite similar, both quantitatively and qualitatively. The exception is the tax variable, which was also significantly different across specifications in table 1.6. The coefficient on the inverse Mill's ratio, correcting for sample selection, is positive and statistically significant, confirming the expected positive selection bias. Insurers with greater valuation of catastrophe reinsurance are more likely to be in our sample.

Increasing catastrophe exposure increases the demand for catastrophe reinsurance, as seen from the estimated effect of property and coastal exposure. Insurers with a higher probability of financial distress—those with higher leverage and lower Best's ratings—have a greater demand for catastrophe reinsurance as well. Insurers with a greater proportion of liquid assets have a lower demand for catastrophe reinsurance, also consistent with expectations. The estimated effect of insurer size is positive and statistically significant as well. Insurers writing in more states have a greater willingness to pay for catastrophe reinsurance, although the estimated effect is not statistically different from zero. The estimated coefficient of being a regional insurer is negative. This is contrary to the expected effect if these variables are measuring geographic diversification. The indicator variable for ownership structure (mutual or stock) was not included in the estimation because the variable was highly collinear with the regional indicator variable.[19]

Table 1.8 presents estimates of equation (1) with the default variable enter-

19. All but one of the mutual insurers are regional, and all but one of the regional insurers are mutuals.

Table 1.8   **Estimation of Catastrophe Reinsurance Demand with Categorical Default Variable**

Variable	A	B
RRET	32.864	33.228
	(3.077)	(3.059)
RLIM	−.282	−.248
	(−.345)	(−.300)
COINS	28.183	28.37
	(2.512)	(2.480)
SIZE	5.70E–10	5.36E−10
	(2.893)	(2.850)
PROP	10.977	10.047
	(2.650)	(2.585)
COAST	5.202	5.629
	(3.493)	(3.396)
NUM	.0352	.0374
	(1.258)	(1.320)
TAX	3.706	−9.927
	(.894)	(−1.634)
HHI	−12.042	−11.204
	(−3.269)	(−3.271)
LEV	7.303	10.928
	(2.262)	(2.421)
LIQ	−10.659	−9.994
	(−2.493)	(−2.441)
REGION	−.285	−.227
	(−.343)	(−.268)
BRate < 7	1.695	1.731
(B or below)	(2.473)	(2.486)
BRate 8 or 9	.589	.611
(B+, B++)	(1.675)	(1.716)
BRate 10 or 11	.0678	.0740
(A−, A)	(.461)	(.500)
Inverse Mill's ratio	8.640	9.410
	(2.864)	(2.818)

Note: Column A gives instrumental variables (IV) with Mill's ratio based on the Guy Carpenter sample, and column B gives IV with Mill's ratio based on the augmented Guy Carpenter sample. The dependent variable is the natural logarithm of price, and *t*-statistics are presented in parentheses. Each regression has 298 observations and includes a constant term.

ing as discrete categories rather than as a continuous variable. Four categories are included: rating of B or below, rating of B+ or B++, rating of A− or A, and rating of A+ or A++ (the excluded category). Insurers with lower ratings have significantly greater demand for catastrophe reinsurance, and the insurers with the lowest ratings have the highest demand, but there is no statistical difference between insurers in the two highest categories. The estimated effects of the other variables are qualitatively similar to those in columns C and D of table 1.7.

Table 1.9   **Estimation of Catastrophe Reinsurance Demand with Year and Firm Effects**

Variables	A	B	C	D
RRET	−.839	−.852	12.479	11.621
	(−.858)	(−.877)	(2.036)	(1.888)
RLIM	−.537	−.540	−1.371	−1.298
	(−7.969)	(−8.072)	(−3.639)	(−3.434)
COINS	.0526	.0769	15.909	16.676
	(.053)	(.079)	(3.297)	(3.369)
SIZE	2.02E−10	2.19E−10	5.69E−10	6.13E−10
	(3.942)	(4.452)	(3.341)	(3.567)
PROP	2.735	2.956	11.754	12.431
	(2.691)	(3.109)	(3.304)	(3.567)
COAST	1.700	2.0691	1.756	2.525
	(4.637)	(5.034)	(.860)	(1.181)
NUM	−.00246	−.0020	.101	.0956
	(−.602)	(−.514)	(1.111)	(1.063)
TAX	.671	−4.467	4.187	−9.500
	(.446)	(−2.446)	(2.038)	(−2.313)
HHI	−2.533	−2.651	−8.683	−8.737
	(−2.998)	(−3.398)	(−3.389)	(−3.625)
LEV	.809	2.651	9.107	13.911
	(.956)	(2.260)	(3.233)	(3.425)
LIQ	−3.760	−4.158	−11.190	−12.293
	(−3.229)	(−3.695)	(−2.998)	(−3.259)
REGION	−1.330	−1.340	−23.979	5.077
	(−7.358)	(−7.464)	(−.005)	(1.139)
BRate < 7	.219	.227	−.265	−.238
(B or below)	(1.560)	(1.626)	(−.906)	(−.819)
BRate 8 or 9	−.00196	.00362	−.131	−.111
(B+, B++)	(−.023)	(.043)	(−.568)	(−.487)
BRate 10 or 11	.0153	.0167	.0362	.0376
(A−, A)	(.338)	(.372)	(.304)	(.318)
Inverse Mill's ratio	2.863	3.613	7.548	9.578
	(3.668)	(4.169)	(2.950)	(3.210)

Note: Column A gives instrumental variables (IV) with Mill's ratio based on the Guy Carpenter sample with year fixed effects; column B gives IV with Mill's ratio based on the augmented Guy Carpenter sample with year fixed effects; column C gives IV with Mill's ratio based on the Guy Carpenter sample with firm fixed effects; and column D gives IV with Mill's ratio based on the augmented Guy Carpenter sample with firm fixed effects. The dependent variable is the natural logarithm of price, and t-statistics are presented in parentheses. Each regression has 298 observations and includes a constant term.

Table 1.9 investigates the robustness of the results when I control for year and firm effects. The results in columns A and B include year effects, those in columns C and D firm fixed effects. In contrast to the earlier results, the estimated effect of relative retention and coinsurance is not statistically different from zero when year fixed effects are added. The estimated effect of relative limit, however, is now statistically different from zero, although the estimated coefficient does not change as much as those of the other two quantity measures. This suggests that the time-series variation in the data is important for estimating the effects of relative retentions and coinsurance. The estimated coefficients for the other variables are generally much smaller in magnitude, but the qualitative results are largely similar to those in tables 1.8 and 1.9.

Columns C and D in table 1.9 report results including firm fixed effects. In this specification, all three quantity variables have the expected sign and are statistically different from zero. The magnitudes of the estimated effects of relative retention and coinsurance lie between those reported in columns A and B of tables 1.7 and 1.8, while the estimated effect of relative limit is much greater than in other specifications. The qualitative effects of the insurer characteristics are generally similar to those found in tables 1.7 and 1.8. One exception is the default variable, which is now statistically insignificant. Including both year and firm fixed effects (not reported) yields results similar to those of columns A and B in table 1.9.

1.4 Discussion

Although the estimated magnitudes of the coefficients vary across specifications, several interesting and robust findings emerge. Insurers with a greater probability of financial distress, as measured by higher leverage, lower liquidity, and lower ratings, have a greater willingness to pay for catastrophe reinsurance. Insurers with greater catastrophe exposure also have a higher demand for catastrophe reinsurance. Other results are more surprising. Larger insurers have a greater demand for catastrophe reinsurance. Demand by regional insurers was not statistically different from that of national insurers.

These results are less surprising if one considers the components of a catastrophe reinsurance contract in banking terms.[20] Each contract can be thought of as having two components: it creates a contingent liability that increases the probability that the firm remains solvent, and it acts like a loan commitment to provide liquidity. As argued earlier, larger insurers are less likely to become insolvent and so will value the contingent liability less than smaller insurers will.

However, the loan commitment has value only for solvent firms that lack liquidity. Larger insurers are less likely to be insolvent and therefore are more likely to be solvent but illiquid following a large loss. Larger firms value the liquidity component more than smaller firms. Therefore, the expected effect of insurer size is indeterminant. The results are consistent with liquidity effects dominating solvency effects in these data.

The specification of equation (1) is particularly important for the estimated quantity effects and tax effects. In specifications without time effects, relative retention and coinsurance had the expected, positive effects. In specifications with time effects, relative limit had the expected, negative effect, but the other

---

20. I am grateful to Raghu Rajan for this insight.

two quantity measures were statistically insignificant. The estimated effect of the tax variable appears to be very sensitive to the specification of the sample selection correction. The inconsistent performance of this variable may well come from its high correlation with firm profits, which are likely to be endogenous to other firm decisions.

This study complements other recent investigations of corporate risk management. Two of these, Mayers and Smith (1990) and Garven (1994), focus on insurers' use of reinsurance. Mayers and Smith (1990) find that the quantity of reinsurance used is increasing in the concentration across lines of ownership, increasing in default risk, decreasing in insurer size, and decreasing in concentration across lines of insurance and geographically. Garven (1994) extends the work of Mayers and Smith and relates the quantity of reinsurance to measures of investment and claims risk. The riskiness of investment returns is negatively related to the amount of reinsurance used, while geographic concentration and line-of-business concentration have similar estimated effects as in Mayers and Smith.

Three other studies—Nance, Smith, and Smithson (1993), Gezcy, Minton, and Schrand (1997), and Tufano (1996)—examine the use of hedging instruments in industries other than insurance. Nance, Smith, and Smithson (1993) and Gezcy, Minton, and Schrand (1997) examine the determinants of derivative use. These investigations are quite similar to the sample selection estimation presented in table 1.3 above. Both studies conclude that hedging with financial derivatives is more likely for firms with greater costs of financial distress (measured by low liquidity) and larger firms. Nance, Smith, and Smithson find evidence for tax motivations, while Gezcy, Minton, and Schrand find that firms with greater risk exposure and those that use other financial risk-management tools are more likely to use particular financial derivatives. Tufano (1996) finds that the managerial incentive measures are the major factor explaining the differences in risk management among the gold-mining firms in his study.

This study differs from previous studies in several important dimensions. The data include the cost of risk management as well the quantity. Unlike other studies of reinsurance more generally, this study allows us to generate better measures of exposure to risk since it examines catastrophe reinsurance specifically. Also, catastrophe reinsurance can be used only to hedge risk, unlike financial derivatives, which can be used to speculate. Like previous studies, this study shows that insurers with a higher probability of financial distress have greater demand for risk-management activities; however, I find that leverage as well as liquidity is important. I also find that larger insurers are more likely to purchase catastrophe reinsurance and have greater demand. This contrasts somewhat with previous research that finds that larger firms are more likely to employ financial derivatives or that smaller insurers purchase more reinsurance. Even after controlling for the fact that larger firms are more likely to purchase, larger firms still have greater demand for catastrophe reinsurance.

The findings indicate several directions for future research. Taken together with the results of previous studies, they show that the costs of financial distress are important determinants of corporate risk management but that the firm characteristics that best measure the costs of financial distress may vary across industries. For example, in this study, leverage and liquidity were associated with costs of financial distress, while, in Gezcy, Minton, and Schrand (1997), liquidity and research-and-development expenditures were particularly important. Further research investigating corporate risk management should be careful to allow for industry-specific effects of firm characteristics.

Further investigation into the liquidity and solvency components of insurance is also warranted. Are similar effects observed in other types of reinsurance, and do corporate purchasers of insurance exhibit similar behavior? It may be that the liquidity component dominates the solvency component for some, but not all, types of insurance and reinsurance. For types of insurance where the liquidity component is particularly important for large firms, financial products providing lines of credit may be reasonable substitutes for insurance. With respect to the alternative financing structures proposed for catastrophe risks, these findings suggest that risk financing may be as important, if not more important, than risk transfer for larger insurers. Indeed, large insurers are pursuing alternative financing instruments that provide financing at the time of a large catastrophe without risk transfer. For example, Nationwide Mutual and Morgan Guaranty have established an agreement whereby Nationwide can issue up to $400 million in debt instruments (called *surplus notes*) to a guaranteed buyer (see Chookaszian, chap. 11 in this volume).

References

A. M. Best Co. 1993. *Best's key rating guide.* Oldwick, N.J.
———. Various years. *Best's insurance reports.* Oldwick, N.J.
———. Various years. *Best's insurance tapes.* Oldwick, N.J.
Froot, Kenneth A., David S. Scharfstein, and Jeremy Stein. 1993. Risk management: Coordinating corporate investment and financing policies. *Journal of Finance* 48: 1629–58.
Garven, James R. 1994. The demand for reinsurance: Theory and empirical evidence. Working paper. Department of Finance, Graduate School of Business Administration, University of Texas at Austin.
Gezcy, Christopher, Bernadette Minton, and Catherine Schrand. 1997. Why firms use currency derivatives. *Journal of Finance* 52:1323–54.
Greene, William H. 1993. *Econometric analysis.* New York: Macmillan.
Gron, Anne. 1994a. Capacity constraints and cycles in property-casualty insurance markets. *Rand Journal of Economics* 25:110–27.
———. 1994b. Evidence of capacity constraints in insurance markets. *Journal of Law and Economics* 37:349–77.
Heckman, J. 1979. Sample selection bias as a specification error. *Econometrica* 47: 153–61.

Johnson and Higgens. 1992. *Self-insurance: Trends and perspectives, 1992.* Chicago.

Lamm-Tenant, Joan, and Laura T. Starks. 1993. Stock versus mutual ownership structures: The risk implications. *Journal of Business* 66:29–46.

Litzenberger, Robert H., David R. Beaglehole, and Craig E. Reynolds. 1996. *Assessing catastrophe-reinsurance-linked securities as a new asset class.* Fixed Income Research Series. New York: Goldman Sachs.

Maddala, G. S. 1983. *Limited dependent and qualitative variables in econometrics.* New York: Cambridge University Press.

Mayers, David, and Clifford W. Smith Jr. 1982. On the corporate demand for insurance. *Journal of Business* 55:281–96.

———. 1990. On the corporate demand for insurance: Evidence from the reinsurance market. *Journal of Business* 63:19–40.

Murphy, Michael. 1995. Alternatives devour a primary marketplace. *Best's Review P/C,* March, 44–47.

Nance, Deanna R., Clifford W. Smith Jr., and Charles W. Smithson. 1993. On the determinants of corporate hedging. *Journal of Finance* 48:267–84.

Smith, Clifford W., Jr., and Neil A. Doherty. 1993. *Journal of Applied Corporate Finance* 6, no. 3:4–15.

Smith, Clifford W., Jr., and Rene Stulz. 1985. The determinants of firms' hedging policies. *Journal of Financial and Quantitative Analysis* 20:391–405.

Tufano, Peter. 1996. Who manages risk? An empirical examination of risk management practices in the gold mining industry. *Journal of Finance* 51, no. 4 (September): 1097–1137.

Wharton School and Chase Manhattan Bank. 1995. *Survey of derivative useage among US non-financial firms.* Executive summary. Philadelphia: Weiss Center for International Financial Research, Wharton School.

Winter, Ralph A. 1988. The liability crisis and the dynamics of competitive insurance markets. *Yale Journal on Regulation* 5:455–500.

———. 1994. The dynamics of competitive insurance markets. *Journal of Financial Intermediation* 3:379–415.

Comment   Steven F. Goldberg

When I was asked to comment on Anne Gron's paper, my first inclination was to pull a Nancy Reagan and just say no. My presence at the conference was intended to be a one-way street: I would absorb all the academic raw intelligence on this subject and maybe in the process seek double or even triple credit for my actuarial continuing education.

I became chief actuary at USAA in 1989. That year turned out to be a major turning point for me and the industry. Prior to Hurricane Hugo in that year, the insurance industry had never suffered a loss of over $1 billion from any single disaster. Since that time, we have had ten disasters that exceeded that amount. As you might imagine, my watch has been dominated by this problem.

Catastrophes, of course, present a significant challenge to the U.S. economy

Steven F. Goldberg is senior vice president, chief property and casualty actuary, for USAA P&C Co. in San Antonio. He is a fellow of the Casualty Actuarial Society, a member of the American Academy of Actuaries, and a chartered property and casualty underwriter.

and to the U.S. property-casualty-insurance industry, posing financial solvency, capital accumulation, and insurance-availability issues. One of the principal tools used by insurers has been catastrophe reinsurance, but recent events have brought about many changes in demand for this product.

I am glad to see that the academic community is beginning to focus on these issues. I welcome Anne's paper and the others to be presented here in the next few days. I have to admit that the subject of Anne's paper was appealing to me. Having been part of the real demand for catastrophe reinsurance, I was wondering how this process could possibly be treated in an academic setting.

My personal view was that this market functioned in such a way that willing buyers would meet up with willing sellers in an environment that would have made Adam Smith proud. But, in 1992, following Hurricane Andrew, willing buyers became desperate buyers, while willing sellers vanished. Today, some of the old willing sellers have reappeared, a bit sobered. But, now, new willing sellers from an odd island known for a famous triangle have entered the picture as the invisible hand of competition once again seeks an equilibrium.

Those of us who are willing buyers are not fully satisfied with today's willing sellers. They just are not able to sell enough of the product at the full range of the buyers' needs. Thus, many of the buyers long for an additional source of sellers who can add more product at levels where the current sellers choose not to. Once again, it all follows the natural law that we call *economics*.

Anne's paper was quite interesting because she was able to assert conclusions empirically that those of us who are so-called practitioners observe anecdotally. I have chosen to accept the statistical methodology in Anne's paper at face value and leave to others the task of critiquing this aspect. I will note that there are a few practical areas that may bear some further analysis.

First, the data were derived from the period 1987–93. That is a little like examining the stock market from 1925 to 1930; it's a pretty mixed bag. The earlier part of the period was dominated by a paradigm of denial in the marketplace that went something like this: Since large catastrophes did not occur recently, they will never occur at all. I am not sure when we will be able to analyze this kind of data to find a typical pattern because this presupposes some sort of steady state.

Second, at the beginning of her paper, Anne asserts that not all insurers find it desirable to purchase catastrophe reinsurance that results in more accurate estimation. I think that, when we examine more closely why all insurers do not find it desirable to purchase catastrophe reinsurance, we find a circularity problem. That is, the very largest insurers need so much catastrophe reinsurance that their entry into the market itself substantially affects the demand. I have no idea how to adjust for that.

Finally, I fully agree with Anne when she says that insurers do trade off quantity and price when purchasing catastrophe reinsurance, that, as prices increase, insurers increase retention levels, decrease total limits, and increase coinsurance rates.

My empirical observation about the insurer demand for catastrophe reinsurance tends to be a bit simplistic, but it does agree with Anne's findings. A personal analogy would be my decision on purchasing my own car insurance. My personal equivalent of the market effect of Hurricane Andrew was last year when my son first got his driver's license. I always liked car insurance as a product (primarily because it was one product that I thought I understood). It protected my investment in my automobile and the obligation owed to society for my negligence in operating this automobile. I decided how much coverage to buy on the basis of an internal budget of about what I thought it would cost. Then came the shock of the sixteen-year-old male. All of a sudden, the demand for my insurance increased, but the price increased even more. I reevaluated what I wanted to pay for and thus increased my deductibles to the base level of pain. In other words, I had greater probability of financial distress and thus greater demand for insurance. I surely had greater personal catastrophe exposure.

While it may seem very crude, I approach the reinsurance buying decision in much the same way I approach my own personal insurance buying decision. What I need is a function of what I can afford, which is a function of what it costs. How high my retention is depends on how much pain I am willing to endure and what I am willing to pay. I may even be willing to change the original risk by increasing the risk that original policyholders take on themselves in highly risk-prone areas.

I do not want to suggest that these multimillion-dollar decisions are made frivolously. There is a lot more going on than I have suggested. In the case of USAA, we carefully examine our risk as modeled by the very best scientists, whom we employ as consultants through risk-modeling firms. We look at the wholesale cost of our reinsurance as if we were selling it to ourselves. Then we look at what the market is selling it for and make the best business decision under these circumstances. Sometimes, the price we choose to target governs the amount of capacity that we will achieve in the global marketplace. Our overall financial position and tax status go into making these final determinations. These decisions are important enough that our board of directors is frequently briefed about them.

I want to emphasize here some of the practical issues that may apply only to USAA's unique market. What we cannot do at USAA is walk away from our members. Our corporate mission obligates us to find a way to serve our members wherever they are. The level of service will have to be a function of a trade-off between the needs of individual members and the needs of the membership.

A critical new element is how to calculate the allocation of the cost of reinsurance to pass through to the ultimate consumer. This is a new dimension in the actuarial pricing equation because of the scale of the costs in the market. We want to charge only those members who are offered protection the ultimate cost of catastrophe reinsurance. Members with no such risk should not pay for it.

As a result of the sacred bond that we have with our members, we are going to work especially hard to find ways to provide this coverage fairly. Walking away from long-term commitments is the easy way out. The hard road is to hang in there, build up capital, seek additional sources of capacity, and thereby avoid the government inefficiently seizing another consumer need. I think that our industry would be in better condition in the long run if others were able to manage in a similar manner.

Insurers should be encouraged to engage in prudent risk-management behavior. We believe that one additional method of encouraging prudent risk behavior is to permit insurers to establish tax-deductible reserves for future catastrophes. Current tax laws and accounting principles discourage U.S. insurers from accumulating assets specifically to pay for future catastrophe losses. Instead, payments for catastrophe losses are made from unrestricted policyholder surplus after the losses are incurred. Because of their domestic tax laws and accounting principles, some non-U.S. insurers are able to deduct reserves for future catastrophes free of tax. That ability gives those non-U.S. insurers a competitive advantage over U.S. insurers, enabling them to attract insurance and reinsurance business that would otherwise be written by U.S. insurers. Such a change in the U.S. tax approach would complement, not diminish, existing risk-management methods like catastrophe reinsurance.

There is another important factor to consider in reinsurance demand. Looking back, the insurance industry is partially to blame for today's demand for original insurance in risk-prone areas. We unrealistically led consumers to believe that the cost of being in harm's way was very cheap. Now, their demand is high, but, while the supply of capacity is increasing, it cannot meet the full demand.

What will inevitably happen is that an equilibrium will be approached that will allow for adequate rates for the true risk. Rigid rate regulation can slow this process, but the underlying economics forces an eventual equilibrium. This will surely involve a change in the original risk in highly catastrophe-prone areas to include greater risk retention and improved damageability.

As an industry, we cannot look at this problem as one that is solely in the province of actuaries, accountants, and finance professors. A good part of the problem of demand for insurance and therefore reinsurance is a function of the physical quality of risks to withstand the natural hazards to which they are exposed. A group known today as the Insurance Institute for Property Loss Reduction has been formed and is now reinvigorated to address the physical aspects of the risk problem.

As I wrap up, I admit that I drifted away from a direct response to Anne's paper quite often. In my own defense, I wanted to make sure that the academic community gathered here understands that we practitioners need your creativity to address the many facets of this complex societal problem. I want to thank Anne for an interesting approach to measuring demand for catastrophe reinsurance.

Comment   Raghuram Rajan

This is a very nice, careful, paper that uncovers some interesting regularities about who buys catastrophe reinsurance. Since Anne has addressed most of my comments on an earlier draft, I will confine myself to interpreting the results.

I want to focus on two important theoretical reasons for buying reinsurance. The first is to assure potential policyholders that the insurer will be solvent in case of disaster and will be able to make good on claims. Here, reinsurance provides contingent capital to the insurer. With contingent capital, the same pool of capital sitting in a remote island can reinsure very diverse and, hence, uncorrelated risks around the world. By contrast, when capital is committed to an insurer via an equity infusion, the diversification possibilities are limited to the insurer's area of business. So contingent capital is cheaper. Another way of saying this is that the purpose of insurance is to produce confidence. With its access to the distribution systems of multiple insurers, the reinsurer can produce more confidence per dollar of capital than can a local insurer.

Of course, capital committed to an insurer can become contingent if the insurer enters into loss-sharing agreements with other distant insurers or if the insurer writes reinsurance contracts for others. In other words, a poorly capitalized, poorly diversified firm should have a high demand for buying reinsurance, while a well-capitalized, poorly diversified firm should sell a lot of reinsurance.

The paper provides some evidence consistent with at least part of this argument. It shows that low-rated and highly indebted insurers have a higher demand for reinsurance. However, it also shows that regional firms do not pay a higher price for reinsurance than national firms even though the benefits of contingent capital are probably the highest for the regional firms. Furthermore, larger firms pay more for reinsurance. It may be that we are seeing supply effects rather than demand effects here. Alternatively, small and regional firms may be better capitalized and make some of their capital contingent by effectively selling reinsurance.[1]

Before turning to the second role of reinsurance on which I think this paper sheds light, it is useful to ask the following question: If global diversification is so important, why do we not see more insurance companies across the world merging and displacing the need for reinsurers? While we see some trends in this direction, the political and tax barriers to such global companies may be high. But I also think that, for a reinsurer, being at arm's length from the insurer provides a degree of certification and credibility that a global insurer cannot

Raghuram Rajan is the Joseph L. Gidwitz Professor of Finance at the University of Chicago's Graduate School of Business and a research associate of the National Bureau of Economic Research.

1. It is also possible that the very small, undiversified insurers may be playing high-risk strategies where they make money for their stockholders at the expense of their core, unsophisticated policyholders by taking on more risk. This would show up as a lower demand for reinsurance.

provide. Every time an insurer buys reinsurance, the rating agencies, and consequently the customers, get the comfort that an independent third party has evaluated the insurer. When such transactions are brought in house, as with a global insurer, third-party certification is lost.

The second role that reinsurance plays is to provide the insurer with liquid funds when disaster strikes. The insurer may, in fact, be quite solvent, so the point of reinsurance here is not to provide assurance through contingent capital. Instead, reinsurance reduces the need for the insurer to raise capital at an unfavorable time, at potentially very unfavorable rates. Immediately after a catastrophe, financial markets may be very uncertain about how much loss an insurer has sustained. At that very moment, the insurer will need funds to pay policyholders. The issuance of equity to raise finance at that point would be viewed very negatively by the market. By securing contingent financing through reinsurance, the insurer alleviates potential liquidity problems.

The paper provides some evidence consistent with this role for reinsurance. Insurers with greater holdings of liquid assets buy less reinsurance. Insurers who have more debt (and, thus, who are likely to be forced to issue costly equity if disaster strikes) buy more reinsurance. The need for liquidity may also, as the paper suggests, explain the seemingly anomalous effect of size on the demand for reinsurance: perhaps large insurers have a greater concern for liquidity, and hence purchase more reinsurance, because they have to tap financial markets rather than potentially more sympathetic financial institutions for funds (small insurers may be able to obtain the needed liquidity from their banks, who are likely to be more informed about the extent of losses than financial markets). This is worth investigating in greater detail.

To summarize, the paper provides some valuable new evidence on the demand for reinsurance in particular and on the rationale for risk management in general. I am sure that it will stimulate further empirical and theoretical work on the subject.

2 Alternative Means of Redistributing Catastrophic Risk in a National Risk-Management System

Christopher M. Lewis and Kevin C. Murdock

Since 1989, the costs of natural disaster have risen dramatically. Combined insurance losses from Hurricane Andrew ($15.5 billion) and the Northridge Earthquake ($12.5 billion) alone totaled almost $30 billion. Insured and uninsured losses from these two events exceeded $40 billion. In fact, after adjusting for housing-price inflation, insured losses over the period 1989–95 totaled almost $75 billion, more than five times the average real insured losses during the prior four decades.[1]

The years 1989–95 by no means represent an unusual period of heightened disaster activity; new research shows that society's exposure to disaster risk is far greater than previously recognized. During 1995, more tropical storms were formed (nineteen) than at any time since 1933, foreshadowing a return to the higher tropical storm activity patterns experienced earlier this century (ISO 1996).[2] At the same time, geologic studies of earthquake recurrence intervals in the United States indicate that there is a very high probability of another Northridge-magnitude or larger earthquake occurring during the next decade.

Christopher M. Lewis is senior manager and risk management consultant at Ernst & Young LLP. Kevin C. Murdock is associate professor of strategic management in the Graduate School of Business, Stanford University.

The authors acknowledge helpful contributions made by Joseph Stiglitz, Ellen Seidman, and other members of the White House Working Group on Natural Disasters. Valuable insights were also provided by J. David Cummins, Richard Phillips, Howard Kunreuther, Kenneth Froot, and participants at the American Economic Association's Session on Catastrophic Risk at the 1995 annual meeting. The authors acknowledge partial financial support for this paper from the NBER Project on the Financing of Property-Casualty Risks. The views expressed in this paper are those of the authors and may not represent the views of Ernst & Young LLP or Stanford University. The authors retain responsibility for all errors and omissions.

1. Based on "PCS Catastrophe History Database," version 1.3, Property Claims Services, adjusted for housing-price inflation using owner-occupied housing-value information from the U.S. Bureau of the Census, Ser. HC80-1-A.

2. Most of these storms did not make landfall, but those that did contributed to the $8.5 billion in total insured catastrophe losses for 1995 (ISO 1996).

More significantly, the value of properties exposed to natural disaster risk has increased rapidly. From 1970 to 1990, the population density along the Southeast Atlantic Coast increased by nearly 75 percent, far in excess of the 20 percent increase experienced for the nation as a whole (ISO 1994). More troubling, insured coastal property values in the United States grew 69 percent from 1988 to 1993 to $3.15 trillion. Similarly, the average annual growth rates in the population per square foot in California (2 percent) and Florida (3.2 percent) over the past fifteen years have been double and triple the average national growth rate for the whole United States (U.S. Bureau of the Census 1994).

This increased recognition of disaster exposure has sent reverberations throughout the private-sector financial markets. In Florida, computer models of hurricane risk were reporting expected average annual hurricane losses of $1.4–$1.5 billion relative to total homeowner's premiums of just $1.2 billion (premiums earned on related lines totaled another $1.2 billion). In California, average annual earthquake exposures were quickly approaching $1 billion, compared with industry premiums of just $524 million (Insurance Information Institute 1994).

Reinsurance companies responded to this increased exposure quickly by raising rates. According to a study by Goldman Sachs, the average rate on line (ROL) for catastrophe covers jumped from 7.93 to 15.09 percent between 1985 and 1995, while the average attachment point for a single catastrophe increased from $1.14 to $2.57 billion in industry losses (Litzenberger, Beaglehole, and Reynolds 1996). Discussions with insurance-company executives indicate that reinsurance rates increased by as much as 150 percent from 1993 to 1995.

With a rise in reinsurance rates, an increased catastrophe-exposure retention, and a realization of their overexposure to disaster risk, primary insurers sought comparable rate increases. When these rate-increase proposals were pared down in the process of state insurance rate approval, insurers started to withdraw from the market, causing a drop in the availability of insurance coverage for individuals living in high-risk areas of the country. In response, states instituted new regulations restricting insurer exits, established new state insurance facilities, and approved modest increases in primary-insurance rates. The net result, however, was a continued overexposure of insurance companies to natural disaster risk. Similar disruptions occurred after the Northridge Earthquake.

The concern over natural disaster expenditures after Hurricane Andrew was not limited to the insurance industry. In 1994, the U.S. Congress raised concerns over the growth in long-term disaster-recovery expenses incurred by the federal government. Thus, at the same time as the insurance industry started seeking federal assistance in reducing its catastrophe exposure, the federal government was concerned with the budgetary implications of disaster-recovery expenses that were already being incurred.

As a result, homeowners, insurers, financial markets, and state and federal governments have started evaluating options for improving society's ability to finance disaster risk: New state programs have been developed in Florida (the Florida Catastrophe Fund), California (the California Earthquake Authority), and Hawaii to increase insurer capacity in these high-risk markets. New financial market instruments have been developed to help insurers hedge natural disaster risk (e.g., catastrophe options at the Chicago Board of Trade, surplus notes, and act-of-God bonds). An insurance swap market (CATEX, the Catastrophe Risk Exchange) has been developed to allow for enhanced geographic diversification of disaster risk. Finally, a federal excess-of-loss reinsurance program has been proposed to better diversify claims intertemporally.

These efforts to devise alternative means of financing disaster risk represent attempts to address the primary question gripping the U.S. economy with respect to catastrophic risk: How can catastrophic risk be more efficiently managed? This paper examines the current distribution of catastrophic risk in the United States and presents a general public-policy framework for evaluating the role that *federal* policy can play in improving this allocation of disaster risk. Within this framework, this paper then evaluates two major federal disaster reform initiatives.

First, the paper analyzes why a requirement for the purchase of natural disaster insurance on new structures could be an effective mechanism for reducing total societal losses from natural disasters. Currently, the system for allocating natural disaster risk in the United States is inefficient and allows individual propertyowners to ignore their disaster-risk exposure when making construction decisions—promoting inefficient construction location and design. A requirement for the purchase of all-hazards insurance on new construction could help promote more efficient construction and reduce the incentives for moving to high-risk areas of the country, mitigating the costs of future disasters.

Second, this paper suggests that the creation of a new financial instrument (an industry excess-of-loss contract) could provide the insurance industry with an important tool for intertemporally diversifying natural disaster risk. Intertemporal diversification is an important component of disaster-loss financing given the large variance in aggregate disaster claims and the large differentials between annual premium volume and annual disaster losses. This type of risk can often be best hedged through market-based securities. Hence, the paper also suggests that having the federal government provide the initial liquidity for the market (with sufficient mechanisms for the private sector to "crowd out" the public sector) could allow insurance and reinsurance companies to make the necessary investments in business systems to support this new market. The creation of this new mechanism would likely promote a gradual transition to a more efficient risk-allocation mechanism for natural disasters where insurance companies and reinsurance companies are able to better pool risks geographically and intertemporal risk is managed through private market–based mechanisms.

Section 2.1 reviews the existing mechanisms used to finance catastrophic risk in the United States. Section 2.2 highlights some of the weaknesses within the current system that have given rise to the disruption in insurance markets following the recent rise in disaster activity. A framework for analyzing federal policy options for addressing these weaknesses is discussed in section 2.3. Section 2.4 applies this framework in analyzing two specific policy options designed to improve the management of disaster risk in the United States. A conclusion follows.

2.1   Financing Natural Disaster Risk

In the aggregate, all losses from natural disasters are paid out of individual incomes, through either direct losses, insurance premiums, losses on insurance stocks, charity, or taxes. However, the magnitude of future disaster losses depends on the level of ex ante disaster mitigation, and these mitigation investments, in turn, depend on the manner in which disaster risks are allocated and financed. The primary objective of natural disaster policy is to reduce the effect on welfare of a given disaster event. This paper focuses on how the choice of ex ante financing mechanisms for disaster risk can directly affect the size of the welfare loss associated with natural disasters within a context of disaster-risk management.

2.1.1   Recent History

Historically, losses from natural disasters have been financed using one of six mechanisms: private insurance, capital market securities, federal taxpayer assistance, state taxpayer assistance, self-insurance, or charity. Figure 2.1 shows the allocation of financing sources (excluding self-insurance) for the two largest disaster events in the United States: Hurricane Andrew and the Northridge Earthquake. The allocation of disaster expenditures differs significantly between the two events. For example, as ground-movement events, earthquakes tend to cause far more extensive damage to infrastructure than do hurricanes. As such, government assistance for infrastructure reconstruction tends to cover a larger percentage of earthquake losses. Also, hurricanes can create far greater damage from flooding, leading to a larger percentage of losses being covered through the federal flood-insurance program. (The largest percentage of losses from Hurricane Hugo came from flood damage.) Finally, since only 35–40 percent of Californians carried earthquake-insurance coverage, a smaller portion of personal property losses in Northridge was covered by insurance, shifting more losses to individuals, taxpayer assistance, and, where the loss of property value resulted in a mortgage default, investors in mortgage securities.

Figure 2.1 also shows the magnitude of cross-subsidization of disaster risk from low-risk to high-risk areas. In the case of state taxpayer assistance, cross-subsidies exist between low-risk and high-risk properties within the state. At the federal level, cross-subsidies are broader, with taxpayers in low-risk states

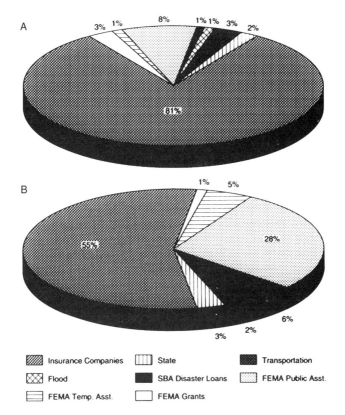

Fig. 2.1   Allocation of financing sources: *A,* **Hurricane Andrew ($18 billion);** *B,* **Northridge Earthquake ($23 billion)**

paying for losses in disaster-prone areas. To the extent that the federal or state governments borrow to cover disaster expenditures, disaster risk is also cross-subsidized intertemporally. Charity obviously represents a direct transfer from nonaffected parties to those who experienced a disaster loss.

In the case of purchased insurance and capital market instruments, however, the risk of loss should be incorporated in the purchase price of the coverage provided (assuming that the price of the instrument is efficient).[3] As such, the risk is internalized in the purchase decision. In the case of self-insurance, the degree of internalization is unclear. However, the buildup of property values in disaster-prone areas of the country and the lack of disaster-mitigation investment in these areas suggest an underrecognition of risk internalization.

Experience over the last six years has demonstrated that traditional channels

---

3. To the extent that state insurance commissioners impose price ceilings on insurance rates, the price of insurance will only partially internalize the disaster risk.

for financing disaster losses are adequate to cover losses of the magnitude of $10–$20 billion, but only with disruption in the market for disaster insurance and rapid increases in federal and state disaster spending. Fueling congressional and industry concerns is a recognition that, as disaster losses start to exceed $30–40 billion, the functioning of the entire insurance system may be at risk. While the probability of such an event occurring is relative small—1–2 percent according to some estimates (Cummins, Lewis, and Phillips, chap. 3 in this volume)—it is important to examine this contingency.

2.1.2   Efficient Market Allocation of Disaster Risk

The question of how to allocate disaster risks most efficiently is best understood by first examining the simple case in which all individuals have perfect knowledge concerning the joint distribution of claim amounts and others' attitudes toward risk. The basic theory for understanding the markets for risk bearing was initially developed by Arrow (1953, 1964) and Debreu (1959), with a specific extension to insurance markets by Borch (1974). Even after twenty-five years of advances in the theory of insurance and capital markets, the most fundamental propositions of these papers offer insights into the problem of managing catastrophic risk.

As concisely demonstrated in Lemaire's (1990) summary of Borch's theorem and in Arrow (1996), the basic risk-exchange model starts with a set of N individuals in the economy $N = \{c_1, \ldots, c_n\}$, each with an initial wealth of w_i and subject to a risk of loss characterized by distribution function $F_j(x_j)$. Then, assuming that each individual possesses a utility function $u_j(x)$ such that $u_j'(x) > 0$ and $u_j'(x) < 0$ (diminishing marginal utility), the expected utility of c_j's ex ante position is defined by

$$(1) \qquad u_j(x_j) = u[w_j, F_j(x_j)] = \sum_{i=1}^{n} u_j(w_j, x_j)\pi_j,$$

where π_j represents the probability that the state of the world x_j will occur. To maximize their ex ante utility, the n individuals will then enter into risk-sharing transactions to form a risk pool defined by

$$(2) \qquad [y] = [y_1(x_1, \ldots, x_n), \ldots, y_n(x_1, \ldots, x_n)],$$

where $y_j(x_1, \ldots, x_n) = y([x])$ is the sum that agent c_j has to pay if the claims for the different agents respectively amount to $x_1, \ldots, x_n$. Then, assuming that the market clears (a closed exchange),

$$(3) \qquad \sum_{j=1}^{n} y_j([x]) = \sum_{j=1}^{n} x_j = \text{total amount of all claims.}$$

Both Lemaire (1990) and Arrow (1996) show that, under mild assumptions, the Pareto-optimal risk-sharing treaty among the individuals depends only on the *sum* of individual claim amounts x_j, not on individual results. As Arrow

(1996) concludes, the probability-adjusted price for obtaining a wealth transfer contingent on the realization of a given state of the world depends *only* on the total of all endowments available in that state of the world, not on the wealth effect on the insured individual.[4]

Thus, in efficient Arrow-Debreu markets with perfect information, individuals can manage their exposure to contingent disaster liabilities by taking (long and short) positions in state-contingent risk-exchange securities. That is, individuals agree to enter into state-contingent risk-shifting contracts that allocate wealth from individuals who benefit from the realization of a specific state of the world to individuals who would suffer disaster losses in that state of the world. Thus, to construct a Pareto-optimal risk-sharing arrangement, agents simply need to form a pool of all claims and specify a formula for distributing the burden of such claims, independent of their origin (Lemaire 1990). This observation, which Debreu extended into a multigood, multiperiod model, launched an enormous body of research dedicated to specifying the optimal pool risk-sharing formulas for various risk preferences, utility-curve representations, individual versus collective rationality, and market structure (Lemaire 1990).

The efficiency of the Arrow-Debreu solution centers on the ability of individuals to share perfect knowledge over the probabilistic outcomes associated with future states of the world. As a result, through the operation of a price system, individuals can obtain an efficient ex ante allocation of risk bearing. While an efficient allocation of risk bearing does not eliminate the losses associated with a natural disaster, it makes the losses to society as small as possible. Of course, even in the Arrow-Debreu world, as the size of the disaster loss increases and the state-contingent endowments fall, the market for transfer payments decreases. Thus, for perfectly correlated catastrophic disaster events that universally affect society, the extent of transfer payments is relatively small.

Unfortunately, an examination of the market for risk bearing in the United States demonstrates that the conditions posed by the Arrow-Debreu model of allocating risk do not hold in today's markets. Instead, several real-world inefficiencies restrict the ability of the market for risk bearing to function efficiently. First of all, individuals do not have access to perfect information concerning their disaster-risk exposure. As a result, individuals cannot internalize an accurate assessment of their risk exposure in their decisions to purchase insurance or mitigate hazard losses (Kunreuther 1996).

Second, the process of managing individual insurance contracts entails considerable administrative costs associated with evaluating risks, processing claims, and monitoring risk (Epstein 1996). In addition, insurance must contend with the ability of the insured to influence his or her endowment (and

---

4. Thus, for two states with the same total of endowments, the prices (premiums) of payments conditional on those states are in proportion to their probabilities.

therefore the endowments of others through risk-shifting) in future states of the world without being observed. This ability to shift risk is the classic problem of moral hazard that introduces inefficiencies into the competitive insurance equilibrium (Arnott and Stiglitz 1990). Finally, the existence of ex post government subsidies imposes inefficiencies and disincentives for risk sharing (Priest 1996).

We now turn to a discussion of these factors to gain a better understanding of how risks currently are allocated in the U.S. economy. After examining problems associated with the process of internalizing risks at the individual level, we focus on the structure of existing mechanisms for risk financing. Finally, we demonstrate where the existing systems for financing disaster risks break down.

2.1.3   Internalization of Risk at the Individual Level

Associated with every property or structure in the United States is a probability of loss due to a natural disaster. Knowingly or unknowingly, buyers implicitly accept this liability to disaster risk when they build or purchase property. The value of this liability is given by a disaster-loss distribution derived from the product of two probability distributions—the probabilities of disaster occurrences on the property in question and the conditional distribution of loss severities associated with those disaster occurrences.

In a world of perfect information and efficient markets, propertyowners would accurately value the disaster liability associated with a property. As such, propertyowners could assess (*a*) the relative value of properties with or without the disaster liability included in the offer price, (*b*) how the risk of loss to a particular property can be reduced through mitigation actions (i.e., actions that lower disaster severities), and (*c*) the net benefits of alternative means of financing the losses that do occur. Essentially, propertyowners would recognize that they hold a long position in natural disaster risk and would incorporate the value of this exposure in their utility-maximization process—utilizing actions to reduce their disaster exposure when it proves a value-enhancing option.

First, mitigation measures that pass a benefit/cost test from the market's perspective—not just the individual's assessment—will be undertaken. When calculating the benefits derived from a mitigation action, propertyowners would incorporate the flow of benefits during and *after* their tenure of ownership since the value of all benefits would be reflected in the market price of the property. Of course, if mitigation generates positive externalities not captured in the market price, the socially optimal level of mitigation may still exceed the market's valuation of mitigation.

Also, propertyowners would have an incentive to purchase insurance to reduce their risk of loss from a disaster. By purchasing insurance, propertyowners can short a portion of their disaster risk exposure in exchange for a premium that, because of the diversification benefits offered by insurance, should be less than the value of continuing to hold the full position in disaster risk.

Finally, prospective propertyowners would incorporate the (negative) value of the disaster liability into the price that they are willing to pay for new property, increasing the return to lower-risk properties, and reducing the incentives for building new properties in disaster-prone areas.

Unfortunately, propertyowners do not appear to have a good assessment of their relative disaster exposure, and many individuals invest little in protective actions to reduce their exposure to disaster risk. In essence, propertyowners are not internalizing their risk of exposure in their decisions governing where they live, the extent of mitigation investment undertaken, or the decision to purchase insurance.

Kunreuther (1996) cites two possible reasons for this lack of investment— an underestimation of exposure to loss and high personal discount rates in valuing the benefits of disaster mitigation, possibly reflecting the attitude that "it won't happen to me." First, underestimating the value of the contingent disaster liability will create a disconnect between the price of insurance required by an insurer properly valuing the exposure of the property and the price the propertyowner is willing to pay. This disconnect will reduce the likelihood that the propertyowner will finance disaster losses through the purchase of insurance. Furthermore, understating the value of the disaster risk may raise the benefit/cost threshold for mitigation actions by understating the absolute reduction in loss associated with a given mitigation activity. Also, above-market personal discount rates reduce the present value of benefits derived from mitigation relative to the up-front cost incurred, reducing the likelihood that mitigation actions would be undertaken.

Another possible factor creating an underinvestment in mitigation is the large differential between the expected arrival time of disaster events and the expected length of ownership tenure for properties. If propertyowners incorporate only the value of benefits generated over the expected length of ownership tenure (six to seven years for homes based on a mobility rate of 10 percent per year), and if the residual benefits are not incorporated into the market price of the property, then propertyowners would have a disincentive to undertake potentially beneficial mitigation efforts that accrue benefits over a longer period of time.

On the other hand, it does appear that homeowners are willing to incorporate disaster risk into their calculations if given appropriate information on disaster risk. In a survey of Florida homeowners, the Institute for Property Loss Reduction found that nine of ten homeowners in coastal areas were willing to pay as much as $5,000 (or 5 percent) more for a house built to withstand hurricane damage (IPLR 1995). In fact, 91 percent of homeowners supported a requirement that builders follow stricter building codes to make dwellings less vulnerable to hurricane damage. At the same time, only 29 percent expressed a willingness to retrofit their existing homes if the cost exceeded $2,000, with another 18 percent indicating a willingness to spend between $1,000 and $2,000 (IPLR 1995).

Furthermore, Bernknopf, Brookshire, and Thayer (1990) studied the effect on property values of posting information on the relative threat of earthquake and volcano damage in the area of Mammoth Lakes, California. Their study showed that, while recreational visitation was largely unaffected by the posting of new information on the area's disaster exposure, the information created a significant and persistent drop in the value of properties in the region. Thus, the important question that must be addressed is whether individuals simply lack access to adequate data on their disaster exposure or simply do not incorporate this information into their decisions on where to live, how much insurance to purchase, and what level of mitigation to undertake.

2.1.4   Private Market Mechanisms for Financing Disaster Risk

Arrow-Debreu markets provide a context for viewing an "ideal" risk-exchange economy in which individuals, armed with perfect information, can purchase pure state-contingent securities that pay the holder after the realization of a particular state of the world and otherwise pay nothing. Once the assumptions of perfect and shared information are relaxed, however, one must contend with the difficulties involved in diversifying individual risks in an economy with transactions costs. At this point, the economic role of financial intermediaries as low-cost transactors in the financial markets becomes central. Currently, there are two principal methods of undertaking the financial intermediation of risk in today's financial markets—the purchase of private insurance and the trading of market-based securities.

The Role of Securities Markets in Diversifying Claims

Individuals living in a classic Arrow-Debreu world can purchase pure state-contingent securities that pay the holder only on the realization of a specified state of the world. In cases where the information about the underlying risk-generating process of an asset is public (or at least not asymmetrically distributed), today's securities markets function as an efficient mechanism for diversifying risks very much in the spirit of the Arrow-Debreu model. Securities markets in the United States are highly liquid, quickly incorporate new information in the value of securities, and have relatively low transactions costs.

Advances in the theory of derivatives over the past twenty-five years have reinforced the ability of the capital markets to optimize the allocation of financial resources in the economy. In 1973, Black and Scholes (1973) and Merton (1973) developed the general theory of options pricing for derivative securities—allowing for the valuation of untraded assets whose payoffs were a function of traded assets. A few years later, Ross (1976), Hakansson (1976), Banz and Miller (1978), and Breeden and Litzenberger (1978) linked this theory of options pricing to the Arrow-Debreu world of state-contingent securities by demonstrating that portfolios of options can be used to replicate pure securities and that these pure securities could be used to price derivative securities

(Merton 1990). Thus, in a world of no transactions costs, investors could efficiently diversify their risks by constructing optimal portfolios of derivative securities.

Once transactions costs are introduced, however, the role of low-cost financial intermediaries becomes important. Financial intermediaries are needed to provide individuals with financial instruments that cannot be traded directly in the capital markets, usually owing to information asymmetries that require the screening, monitoring, and pricing of individual risks. Financial intermediaries sell these individual financial products, aggregating their exposure from these products, and establishing positions in the secondary market to hedge their exposure. The role of a financial intermediary is to provide a bridge between the capital markets and the specific financial needs of individuals. As such, intermediaries can minimize the distortions created by transactions costs and accomplish an efficient allocation of resources in the economy by helping individuals diversify their financial positions.

Insurance Companies as Intermediaries

Property-casualty-insurance companies are the primary intermediary financing the insurance of natural disaster risk in the United States today. As mentioned above, individuals living in disaster-prone areas of the United States hold a long position in disaster risk. In providing disaster insurance, an insurance company offers to assume a portion (e.g., over a deductible) of the policyholder's disaster-risk exposure in exchange for a premium. After accumulating these policyholder positions, the insurance company can diversify its net disaster exposure through portfolio diversification and through the purchase of either reinsurance or capital market derivatives that directly hedge the insurer's exposure. Any remaining disaster exposure is borne by the stockholders of the insurance company. Therefore, insurance firms add value to the market for disaster risk through their role as a low-cost transactor in the capital market and their ability to diversify disaster risks through risk pooling (aggregation), risk identification and segregation, and risk monitoring (Priest 1996).

Diversification through risk pooling is achieved by creating a large portfolio of independent and identically distributed risks, the result being that (by the law of large numbers) the variance of the average expected loss in the portfolio becomes smaller. That is, for independent risks, the mean risk for an insurance pool, and for society in general, is less than the individual risks in the pool. Of course, for statistically correlated risks, the benefits of risk pooling are significantly reduced, and insurance becomes less attractive. The opportunities for risk diversification through pooling are more limited in the market for catastrophic risk, where risks are highly correlated. Even for a pool containing the entire U.S. market, the mean risk will have substantial variance, and the annual flow of insurance premiums will vary greatly from actual disaster losses.

Insurers also diversify through risk identification and segregation. Insurance companies serve an important function in the processing of information—assessing and pricing the risk inherent in the property being insured. For many risks covered by insurance contracts, information on the underlying insured risk is not generally available. As a result, insurance companies are needed to identify and segment risks into appropriate risk categories. This information-intensive evaluation process is accomplished through explicit insurer screening mechanisms, offering a menu of contracts that enable different risk groups to self-select the best available contract given their own private information and through a continuous monitoring of the underlying risk. By segregating risks into risk pools, insurers improve the predictive accuracy of the aggregate risk insured and reduce the mean risk to society in a manner analogous to risk aggregation. For example, the variance in expected losses of two independent risk pools with different expected losses will be less than the variance in expected losses associated with the combined pool.

Furthermore, by charging insurance premiums commensurate with risk, insurers relay valuable information to the insured concerning their relative risk exposure: information that will often influence the behavior of the insured. For example, if insurers provided premium discounts for hazard mitigation, high-risk properties would have an incentive to undertake cost-effective mitigation actions to reduce their insurance rates, thereby reducing the aggregate exposure. Similarly, higher-priced premiums increase the cost of undertaking riskier activities; and, to the extent that risk-taking activity is reduced, total risk in the economy is lower.

Insurance companies also control risk through the use of deductibles, coinsurance, and coverage exclusions to limit moral hazard and other forms of distributional risk shifting by the insured. By transferring a portion of the risk of loss back to the insured party, deductibles and coinsurance attempt to align the interest of the policyholder with the interest of the insurance company—to mitigate the risk of a claim. As a result, these provisions lower insurance costs and expand the availability of insurance to more of society.

Limited Liability and Default Risk

Insurance companies clearly serve a valuable role in identifying, monitoring, pricing, and controlling the individual risks associated with property coverage: risks that are too asymmetrically under the control of the insured to be effectively traded directly in the capital markets. However, as financial intermediaries, insurance companies suffer from a problem endemic to all intermediaries: the risk of financial insolvency. When a policyholder purchases an insurance policy from an insurer, he or she obtains an option to collect from the intermediary under certain states of the world. The policyholder's ability to collect on this contract, however, is contingent on the claims-paying ability of the intermediary under that state of the world. The claims-paying ability of the intermediary, in turn, depends on its entire structure of the insurer's assets and liabilities and its ability to hedge its aggregate exposure in the broader capital markets.

The problem with natural disaster risk (and any risk subject to catastrophic loss) is that the exposure to a catastrophic event has a substantial effect on the solvency of the insuring firm. Since customers often cannot diversify away this institutional exposure by taking positions in the market (given transactions costs), the premium levels that the customer is willing to pay for this insurance will be a function, not only of the pure financial instrument purchased, but also of the intermediary's financial condition.

Thus, it is interesting to note that, if there is an exogenous increase (decrease) in the perceived risk exposure of insurance companies owing to the arrival of new information on the nature of the risk being insured, and if this new information decreases (increases) the policyholders' perception of the financial solvency of the insurance firm, policyholders should decrease (increase) the amount that they are willing to pay in premiums for a given level of insurance. Ironically, this reduction in demand would occur exactly when insurance companies would be lobbying to raise rates to cover their overexposure to the insured risk—possibly compounding any perceived "availability" gap in the market for insurance coverage.

To enhance their claims-paying ability, reduce their disaster-risk exposure, and maximize franchise value, insurance companies attempt to hedge the net exposure of their portfolio in the capital market. In this regard, insurance companies have relied almost exclusively on stockholder capital and reinsurance.

While financial theory suggests that reinsurance is redundant in the conditions of capital market equilibrium for diversified firms, many companies and their stockholders do not have well-diversified portfolios and cannot diversify the residual nonsystemic risk inherent in an insurance company's portfolio (Doherty and Tinic 1981). Furthermore, factors such as taxes, bankruptcy costs, regulations, real service advantages, and overinvestment decisions make reinsurance an attractive option for insurance companies (for a review, see Lewis and Murdock [1996]).

Like all firms, insurance companies must hold capital as a buffer for losses. In 1995, the market value of capital and surplus in property-casualty lines was roughly $232 billion, with approximately $20 billion representing the capital in U.S. reinsurance firms (ISO 1994). However, this more than $200 billion in capital supports all property-casualty lines, with as little as one-tenth supporting property losses from disaster-related claims. Furthermore, while some insurance firms may hold sufficient capital to buffer disaster losses, many regionally concentrated firms do not.

While reinsurers provide a useful source of capital for regional and local insurance firms and play an integral role in expanding capacity in the primary-insurance market, the comparative advantage of reinsurers is to enhance spatial diversification. In terms of intertemporal diversification of disaster risk, reinsurance firms must also look to the capital markets to hedge their exposure there. As a result, stockholders in insurance and reinsurance companies bear significant exposure to catastrophic-disaster-insurance losses. After Hurricane

Andrew, firms in at-risk areas of Florida experienced a significant decline in their stock value as a result of their hurricane exposure (Lamb 1995).[5] Unfortunately, three factors inhibit the ability of disaster losses to be effectively diversified through capital market investments by stockholders in insurance companies: (*a*) Stockholders do not receive an ex ante premium on their investments associated with their catastrophic exposure, nor can they hedge their net exposure to disaster risk through other capital market securities. (*b*) Stockholders have had little information on the basis of which to assess the catastrophic exposure of the insurance company. (*c*) Stockholders have limited liability to cover the losses of an insurance firm: as a result, the residual losses of insolvent insurers can be pushed back to policyholders, solvent insurers, or state taxpayers through the state-guarantee system, creating an incentive for management to undertake higher-risk ("go-for-broke") investment strategies.

For the most part, insured losses from disasters have been covered within the insurance industry. In Florida, losses from Hurricane Andrew did result in the failure of twelve insurance companies, but these firms were relatively small, and claims owed under their policies were covered by shareholders and the state-guarantee system (ISO 1996). The prospect of larger disasters in the near future, however, has led to considerable concern over the ability of the insurance system to meet catastrophic disaster claims. In response, considerable attention has been focused on creating alternative market mechanisms for insurance companies to hedge their exposure to natural disaster risk.

The Development of a Secondary Market for Catastrophic Risk

After Hurricane Andrew and the Northridge Earthquake, insurance and reinsurance companies were concerned that a large catastrophic disaster would quickly exhaust the existing capital base in the insurance and reinsurance industry. As a result, insurers started looking for alternative forms of inexpensive capital. The natural place to look was the $19 trillion capital markets.

The prospect of finding a cheap source of capital through disaster derivatives or securitization was alluring to insurance and reinsurance firms because of the sheer size of the market. If financed through the capital markets, natural disaster losses of the magnitudes of the Northridge Earthquake and Hurricane Andrew would often be swamped in normal trading volatility in the market. Furthermore, insurers hoped that capital market instruments would provide a cheaper source of funding than reinsurance and, therefore, would be more supportable at given primary-insurance rates.

At the same time, catastrophe securities offer advantages to institutional investors. On the investor side, the attraction of securities in disaster risk is the ability to better diversify the investment portfolio by adding a nonredundant

---

5. Interestingly, property-casualty stocks appreciated following the Loma Prieta Earthquake, suggesting an investor anticipation of higher demand for insurance (Shelor, Anderson, and Cross 1992; Aiuppa, Carney, and Krueger 1993). Stock prices of real estate firms, however, fell after the earthquake (Shelor, Anderson, and Cross 1990).

security with a return that is largely uncorrelated with the returns associated with stock and bond portfolios (Litzenberger, Beaglehole, and Reynolds 1996). Furthermore, an examination of the reinsurance market suggests that the potential investor return from catastrophe securities could be significant. An industry analysis performed by J. P. Morgan estimated that, while investor returns on capital investments in reinsurance companies were volatile, the expected return over a three-year period was in the neighborhood of 18–22 percent per year (English 1996). Thus, it is likely that catastrophe securities can be structured to yield an attractive risk-adjusted rate of return for investors.

Prior to the advent of catastrophe bonds, the only way an investor could take a position in disaster risk was through ownership of a property-casualty insurance or reinsurance company, as demonstrated by the growth in the Bermuda reinsurance market. However, investing capital through a reinsurance or insurance company requires the assumption of a larger bundle of risks. For example, even if a reinsurer provided only catastrophic disaster coverage, the investor in the reinsurance firm would bear the credit risk associated with the reinsurer's investment policies. Thus, a capital market mechanism that allows a reinsurance company to evaluate, underwrite, and monitor the risks, but allows investors to invest directly in the catastrophe exposure, may be more efficient.

The private mortgage market for nonconforming loans provides a useful example of the effective role that a financial intermediary can play. Mortgage assets are underwritten, pooled, and serviced by a primary originator of mortgages. The originator then packages the assets into a pool and sells the pool to a private conduit. The conduit then sells securities in the capital markets representing direct or indirect rights in the package of assets. In this way, the risks inherent in the cash flows of the assets can be diversified through the capital markets. As a result, these securities transactions, which also provide tax and regulatory relief, are a valuable source of competitively priced capital for mortgage banks (Han and Lai 1995).

The mortgage market provides a direct analogue for the property-casualty insurance market. In the case of mortgages, an intermediary (e.g., a bank) evaluates and monitors the risk of loss to the mortgage pool from a mortgage default. In many cases, such a default is determined by a decline in the value of the property supporting the mortgage, giving the mortgagor the incentive to default on the mortgage. The cash flows associated with the mortgage pool are passed through to the pool and distributed to investors in mortgage-backed securities. In the case of property insurance, an intermediary (i.e., an insurance company) underwrites the risk of loss from an event (e.g., natural disaster) that could reduce the insured value of the property on which the policy is written. The cash flows associated with all property-casualty policies are then pooled internally within the insurance company, with residual earnings distributed to stockholders or, if the policies were securitized, the investor in the disaster-liability securities.

The first attempt to market a natural disaster–related security was made by the Chicago Board of Trade (CBOT) in 1992. After recent revisions, the CBOT now offers catastrophe futures and call-spread options based on nine catastrophe-industry-loss indices calculated by Property Claims Services. CBOT contracts are available to cover exposures on a national, regional, or high-risk-state basis. By basing the payout of the CBOT contracts on industry losses, the CBOT eliminates the ability of insurers to pass moral hazard and adverse-selection risk to the financial counterparty in the transaction. At the same time, the CBOT contracts force insurers to manage "basis" risk—the differences in claim patterns between an individual insurer's portfolio and the industry index (as well as any error introduced by discrepancies between the index and the actual loss experience).

Starting in 1997, insurance and reinsurance companies can enter into direct risk swaps through the Catastrophe Risk Exchange (CATEX) to enhance their diversification of disaster risk. A CATEX swap entails exchanging equal amounts of relative units of catastrophe exposure by peril. While not infusing new capital into the insurance market, CATEX leverages the existing capital resources of the industry by enhancing the ability of the insurance industry to diversify low to medium levels of catastrophic risk. However, since the CATEX market is operated outside a formal exchange with no counterparty risk controls, the catastrophe swap market has been slow in developing.

Other derivative markets that have developed during the past four years include contingent lines of credit, contingent equity financing, and credit-linked notes: (*a*) A contingent line of credit (CLOC) is a commitment by a bank to provide a revolving line of credit to an insurer in the wake of a prespecified range of catastrophe losses, subject to the insurer's continued financial solvency. While usually representing only a marginal source of additional funding, these CLOCs help insurers mitigate a run-up in debt-funding costs created by postevent financing. (*b*) Pioneered by AON's CatEPut, contingent equity financing represents the sale of an over-the-counter put option to an insurer that allows the insurer to "put" a portion of its catastrophic losses to the issuer in exchange for a transfer of equity shares. (*c*) Credit-linked notes or surplus share notes are closely akin to selling investors a credit derivative packaged in a standard debt-financing scheme. In exchange for bearing the credit risk of the insurer, the investors receive an additional interest spread (option premium). Examples of credit-linked notes include the Nationwide (1994), St. Paul Reinsurance (1997) and Hanover (1997) transactions.

Finally, several attempts have been made to "securitize" the catastrophic liability exposure of individual insurance companies or state reinsurance pools directly in the capital markets. For instance, Guy Carpenter, J. P. Morgan, and other capital market institutions have offered "act-of-God" bonds as a source of financing for insurance companies. Act-of-God bonds are debt instruments that are subject to principal reductions in the event of a disaster loss to the insurance firm. To compensate investors for the risks of lost principal, these bonds carry high coupon rates (e.g., 10 percent over Treasury securities).

While the success of these catastrophe bonds has been mixed over the past two years, the issuance of over $400 million in act-of-God bonds by USAA in 1997 and 1998 may represent a turning point in the evolution of these securities. Under these transactions, bondholders stand to lose interest payments (principal protected securities) or interest and principal payments (principal unprotected securities) if USAA's losses from a catastrophic hurricane over the next twelve to eighteen months exceed $1 billion. Investors cover a share of losses in excess of $1 billion up to a cap of $1.5 billion, with USAA maintaining a 20 percent share between the trigger and the cap to mollify concerns over moral hazard or adverse selection. In 1997, investors earned 273–576 basis points over the London Interbank Offered Rate (LIBOR) depending on whether they purchased a principal protected or a principal at-risk participation.

Thanks to an aggressive marketing campaign, the 1997 USAA transaction was actually oversubscribed by investors, and USAA was able to place $100 million in principal protected and $300 million in principal unprotected debt securities. Furthermore, the transaction demonstrated a willingness on the part of investors to bear a portion of the risk for events that, on an industrywide scale, would result in losses of $25–$35 billion. As such, the USAA transaction set the stage for several additional deals in late 1997 and 1998, including earthquake bonds covering California (Swiss Re) and Japanese (Tokio-Marine) earthquake exposure. In total, approximately $1 billion in cat bonds was issued in 1997, with a similar volume of deals in 1998.

Still, some pessimism remains concerning the capacity of the private capital markets to absorb a large number of USAA-type transactions. The problem for institutional investors appears to be the great deal of uncertainty concerning the assessment of catastrophic disaster risk, the lack of standardization in measuring disaster losses and exposures, and the absence of an institutional structure for disaster securities. For insurers, the current soft reinsurance market, the tax and accounting advantages of reinsurance, and the little leverage offered by the cat bonds provides additional hurdles. As a result, the ultimate fate of the catastrophe-securities market remains uncertain. (For a further summary of catastrophe-risk capital market instruments, see Lewis and Davis [1998].)

2.1.5   Government Assistance

Complicating the allocation of disaster risk in the United States is the provision of subsidized postdisaster assistance. Through postdisaster assistance, individuals can reduce their ex ante insurance coverage and shift losses to lower-risk individuals after a disaster occurs through a government reallocation of wealth through taxes and transfers.

Federal Postdisaster Assistance

For uninsured disaster losses, the federal government provides a wide variety of emergency relief and disaster reconstruction assistance.[6]

The Federal Emergency Management Agency (FEMA) provides emergency relief for individual disaster losses in the form of individual and family grants of up to $12,200 for renters and homeowners not eligible for Small Business Administration (SBA) loans (with a 75/25 percent cost share); $10,000 for minor home repairs (100 percent federal share); rental (or mortgage) assistance for the payment of rental costs (local fair market rent) for a period of up to eighteen months for individuals and families unable to occupy their homes; crisis counseling; and disaster-unemployment assistance.

At the state and local levels, FEMA provides cost-share grants, with at least 75 percent covered by the federal government, to fund debris removal; emergency work assistance; and the reconstruction of public buildings and facilities damaged in a disaster.

In the case of hurricanes, FEMA also provides direct insurance coverage for flood damage through the National Flood Insurance Program.

The SBA provides subsidized disaster loans of up to $200,000 for uninsured losses to property and up to $4,000 for uninsured losses of personal contents. For businesses, the SBA provides disaster loans of up to 100 percent of uninsured losses up to a maximum of $1.5 million. In determining the interest rate on the loan, the SBA differentiates on the basis of whether credit is available to the borrower from other sources, but both types of loans are heavily subsidized. (The loan rate is 3.63 percent when credit is determined not to be available and 7.25–7.7 percent when credit is available.) After the Northridge Earthquake, approximately $1.5 billion in SBA disaster loans was appropriated in disaster supplementals by Congress.

The Department of Transportation (DOT) bears a large portion of the financial responsibility for repairing damage to infrastructure (e.g., roads, bridges, etc.) through its emergency relief fund for disasters. For example, the DOT spent roughly $1.3 billion repairing infrastructure damage following the Loma Prieta Earthquake.

Funds appropriated under these programs come directly from federal taxes and, therefore, represent a form of social insurance that cross-subsidizes areas exposed to disaster risk. While Kunreuther (1996) finds little explicit evidence supporting the argument that individuals do not purchase insurance because of the existence of subsidized postdisaster assistance, federal assistance may still implicitly affect homeowners' incentives to purchase insurance. Consider the counterfactual. If no disaster aid had been provided after the Northridge Earthquake, large numbers of individuals would have suffered greater losses associated with their earthquake exposure. These losses would have generated infor-

---

6. Not including federal disaster programs for farmers (e.g., federal crop insurance).

mation (news stories) that would have informed a much wider population of the costs of not purchasing disaster insurance. It is reasonable to expect that, if this occurred, many more individuals would have the incentive to purchase disaster insurance today.

State Disaster Programs

Disaster losses are also financed through taxes levied on individuals within the state in which the disaster occurred. Given geographic constraints associated with state borders, state taxpayer assistance usually spreads the burden of disaster recovery intertemporally through deficit financing—imposing an intergenerational tax on future generations of state taxpayers. In addition, premium assessments levied by the state-guarantee system on surviving firms to cover the claims of an insolvent insurer can be deducted as a business expense and reduce premium taxes otherwise due. Thus, state taxpayers ultimately bear a portion of the cost of a disaster.

In recent years, however, high-risk states have taken a more active role in designing state programs for financing disaster risk. Just within the past two years, Florida, Hawaii, and California have established hurricane- and earthquake-financing facilities funded through a combination of insurance, reinsurance, and state taxes.

The Florida Hurricane Catastrophe Fund is a mandatory, state-sponsored catastrophe-reinsurance pool for property insurers writing business in Florida. Property insurers are required to maintain a retention against qualifying catastrophes (a hurricane as classified by the National Hurricane Center), but they may select to participate at one of three coverage levels: 45, 75, or 90 percent. The fund is financed through insurer premiums of approximately $500 million per year (ISO 1996). However, the fund also has emergency borrowing authority and the ability to assess insurers in the wake of a disaster. The catastrophe fund currently does not have the capacity to handle losses from large hurricanes like Hurricane Andrew. As a result, there is a concern among participating firms that the residual liability of the fund represents a growing liability against future earnings (Marlett and Eastman 1998).

The California Earthquake Authority (CEA) is a state-sponsored insurance facility designed to provide up to $10 billion in earthquake insurance in California. The fund is financed using a combination of up-front and contingent insurer contributions, traditional reinsurance, and revenue bonds (CEA 1996). The insurance policies provided under the CEA include a 20 percent deductible, cover only primary residential buildings, and provide limited coverage for building contents. As a result of the more limited earthquake-insurance policy, the CEA is expected to cover property losses from earthquakes at least as large as Northridge.

The Hawaii Hurricane Relief Fund provides limited hurricane-insurance coverage for the state. The fund is limited to just under $2 billion in coverage, with all residual risk shifting back to taxpayers in the state.

Of course, the advantage of these state-run facilities is that they are supported by institutions with taxing authority (the state). Therefore, unlike insurance companies, the risk of insolvency is much lower for state pools. In fact, if states could enforce a closed exchange of risk within their boundaries, state pools could theoretically be structured to replicate efficient risk-sharing pools—with disaster claims reallocated after a disaster in accordance with the ex ante provision of state-insurance contracts to all homeowners. This approach would clearly force homeowners within the state to internalize the risk of their disaster exposure and could lead to an optimal sharing of disaster risk within the state.

Unfortunately, the provision of federal assistance, the incentives to redistribute disaster losses to future generations, and the spreading of claims payments to other states through the state-guarantee system introduce leakages into the state pooling system that limit the ability of the states to create effective risk pools. Furthermore, state programs offer little benefits for larger-scale disasters where the in-state correlation in claims is high. The disaster risks of the individual states in the United States can be better diversified through the creation of larger risk pools on a national or an international level. Finally, politics at the state level could result in an underpricing of the true risk assumed by the state facility.

A recognition of this limitation has resulted in proposals for the creation of multistate pools. However, multistate pools must confront a serious problem of moral hazard. If a multistate pool is inadequately structured, any one state in the pool would have an incentive to suppress insurance rates within its boundaries for political gain while shifting additional liability to other states through the pool. As such, there is little incentive for lower-risk states to participate in such pools. Finally, research suggests that government-run insurance mechanisms have no comparative advantage over insurance and reinsurance firms in assessing, pricing, or controlling the risks in an insurance or reinsurance portfolio (Priest 1996).

2.2   Weaknesses in the Current System

The discussion in the previous section identified two major sources of inefficiency in the current allocation of disaster risk in the United States: (1) the failure of individuals to internalize the risk exposure of their properties, which results in a socially suboptimal level of disaster mitigation, and (2) the absence of any private funding mechanism for spreading disaster claims intertemporally. In this section, we discuss these two weaknesses in more detail.

2.2.1   Inappropriate Incentives for Mitigation in New Construction Decisions

As discussed in section 2.1.3, individuals do not appear to internalize the disaster-risk exposure of their properties when they decide where to live, whether to purchase insurance, or how much they should mitigate against future losses. At this point, it is not clear whether this failure to internalize disaster risk is caused by individuals' lack of adequate information about their disaster exposure or a divergence between individual and societal objectives in reducing disaster risk. In either case, the current system for managing natural disaster risks does not provide appropriate incentives for mitigation, especially with respect to decisions about new construction.

This absence of mitigation incentives has repercussions across a number of dimensions. First, buildings continue to be constructed in high-risk areas, actually increasing society's overall exposure to disaster risk. One example of such a situation would be when a new home is constructed on a soft foundation over a fault rather than in a safer location on more solid ground. Second, designs, building materials, and the nature of construction are held to a less rigorous standard than is efficient for society as a whole. This is particularly problematic because, once a building is constructed, it is far more costly to retrofit the building than it is to incorporate mitigation investments during construction. For example, once a building is completed, retrofitting against earthquake risk often requires tearing out interior walls to add new structural framing.[7] As such, owners may view the risk of loss from natural disaster as a "sunk cost." From the vantage point of society, a more efficient management of natural disaster risks would internalize the full cost of natural disaster risks in the construction process.

By examining the private market process by which new construction is built, we can gain a clearer understanding of why the present system fails to internalize these risks fully. For simplicity, we will consider the case of a new residential home—although a parallel analysis could be described for other types of construction as well. The incentive for the home builder is to maximize profits. This requires buying land, building a home that maximizes the difference between the perceived value by the customer and the cost of construction, and then selling the home to its first purchaser. If the first homeowner derives no perceived value from mitigation investments and these investments have a cost, the builder has little incentive to undertake mitigation investments. The builder's incentives to internalize natural disaster risk in the value of the home critically depend on the first customer's perceived value of these investments.

For the purchaser, most mitigation investments are hidden from view—built into the structural design and dependent on the quality of the workmanship (nail density, types of fasteners used, quality of framing materials, etc.). The design is somewhat observable—if the purchaser were to study the blueprints—but few homeowners have the ability or interest to study blueprints. Second, even if consumers could observe all mitigation investments, it is not

---

7. Of course, some mitigation actions can be completed with far less reconstruction (e.g., strapping down water heaters, bolting the walls to the foundation, and improving the structural integrity of the roof).

clear that they would value them at a socially efficient level. Large natural disasters occur infrequently, and it is well documented in the field of psychology that consumers have nonconvex preferences around small-probability, large-magnitude events (Tversky, Sattath, and Slovic 1988). Intuitively, because a 500-year-cycle earthquake is not expected to happen for another 250 years, a homeowner's children, grandchildren, and great-grandchildren will probably not even be alive when the earthquake hits. It may be difficult to internalize this kind of risk in decision making, especially since homeowners are often looking to move after a period of six to seven years.

Finally, we can look at the role of financing in property purchases. Under current underwriting rules for most mortgages, prospective home buyers are limited in the amount of housing that they can purchase by constraints that limit total monthly payments for the loan, taxes, insurance, etc. to a fraction of the purchaser's income. Included in these underwriting guidelines is a requirement that buyers have homeowner's insurance to protect the collateral supporting the mortgage. However, few lenders require the purchase of natural disaster insurance. Therefore, homeowners have little incentive to purchase additional disaster insurance because (*a*) it is not required by the lender and (*b*) the additional insurance payments would further limit the amount of housing that the home buyer could afford.

Thus, if we examine the new construction process as a whole, we see the following dynamic. Builders maximize their customers' (the first purchasers) perceived value of the property. Owing both to their inability accurately to monitor the value of mitigation investments and to the paucity of information on individual disaster exposures, these customers do not fully value disaster-mitigation investments. As a result, there are (from a societal viewpoint) too few incentives to incorporate mitigation in new construction decisions. Furthermore, because most lenders do not require the purchase of disaster insurance, a natural mechanism to create incentives for mitigation (one based on the monthly cost of disaster insurance) is not a part of the current private mechanism for managing natural disaster risk.

2.2.2   Lack of Reinsurance Coverage for Large (over $30 Billion) Risks

Although the magnitude of losses from natural disasters over the last decade has been significantly greater than it has been over any previous decade in the postwar period, there exists a significant risk that a disaster causing far greater damage may occur. As an example, if Hurricane Andrew had struck Miami, insured losses alone may have exceeded $40 billion (Van Anne and Larsen 1993). A loss of this magnitude would present a considerable strain on the solvency of the U.S. insurance industry.

Unfortunately, as discussed in section 2.1 above, neither the insurance nor the securities model is sufficient to diversify the risk of loss arising from a large-scale natural disaster. In the case of a natural disaster, losses occur mainly in traditional property lines, where information on the properties at risk is not generally publicly available and is asymmetrically distributed in favor of the insured (i.e., property maintenance, the quality of building construction, and the enforcement of building codes). As a result, protection against loss for property has traditionally been provided through insurance products.

The losses associated with a natural disaster, however, are not statistically independent within the affected region but geographically correlated within that risk pool. As a result, the larger the population area affected by the disaster, the less effective insurance is as a diversification tool. Furthermore, the losses arising from large natural disasters are idiosyncratic through time in the aggregate and hence not diversifiable through the creation of a large portfolio of like risks. This creates stress on an insurance-based risk-management mechanism because, as the size of the event increases beyond some level, the underlying loss characteristics of disaster risk diverge from the characteristics best served by the insurance model. On the other hand, the magnitude of loss that arises from a given event depends in large part on the quality of construction of individual property units—information that is not publicly available and that is asymmetrically distributed in favor of the insured. Thus, disaster risk cannot be solely diversified through the trading of securities.

Lewis and Murdock (1996) contend that the shortcoming of this system is that, given the infrequency and magnitude of losses from natural disasters, catastrophe risks need to be diversified intertemporally as well as spatially. For small and medium-sized disasters, the geographic diversification accomplished through traditional insurance and reinsurance markets is clearly adequate for financing disaster losses. However, the existence of limited liability and bankruptcy costs prevents insurance and reinsurance firms from fully diversifying disaster risk intertemporally. While growing, private securities markets (where private agents also have limited liability) currently lack the information, standardization, and institutional structure to support a high volume of catastrophe risk financing. Consequently, these markets have yet to fill the gap in the market for financing upper-middle layers of disaster risk.[8]

This lack of reinsurance capacity has significant repercussions in terms of the availability of primary insurance for homeowners, particularly in such disaster-prone states as California and Florida. When primary insurers cannot purchase reinsurance, they must pay claims after a large disaster out of their accumulated reserves. When their total (unhedged) exposure equals a significant fraction of their individual reserves, it is only prudent to stop writing policies. This results in a lack of availability of primary insurance. Therefore, any effort to expand insurance coverage for disaster risks must include a solution for improving the private sector's ability to spread disaster claims over time.

---

8. Clearly, the discussion in this paper is limited to disaster risks that can be estimated and priced with a certain degree of precision. Excluded from consideration are disaster risks for which the probability of occurrence is so uncertain that the estimation error swamps the estimates of loss, such as a $200 billion earthquake in New York City.

2.3   Framework of Government Policy

From the vantage point of society, it is important to understand the repercussions of the weaknesses identified in the previous section. If homeowners' decisions on where to locate, how much insurance to purchase, and what level of mitigation to undertake fail to reflect the natural disaster risk inherent in their properties, the aggregate exposure of the U.S. economy to disaster losses will increase. If the losses associated with these decisions implicitly to absorb more risk were completely borne by the individuals making these decisions, then the interests of the individuals and the interests of society would be aligned. However, the current system for financing disaster risk incorporates a significant degree of cross-subsidization. Thus, individual decisions to absorb disaster risk result in a shifting of risk to other members of society, creating a suboptimal level of hazard protection.

For society, disaster policy should look to increase the internalization of disaster risk in individual decisions, reducing the ability of individuals to increase (and shift) society's exposure to disaster events. At the same time, enhancing society's ability to finance disaster risk across time will allow for a greater degree of risk internalization in the economy. Thus, natural disaster policy should examine ways to encourage better coordination in the private sector's attempts to develop a new financing mechanism for diversifying large disaster claims over time. This section examines the role of federal policy in addressing these concerns.

As discussed above, a large portion of natural disaster risk management is performed by property-casualty insurance companies that are regulated at the state level. The system of state insurance regulation has evolved at the state and local level over the past two hundred years. However, the strict delegation of insurance regulation to the states (except in instances where federal law specifically supersedes state law) was formally codified in 1945 with the passage of the McCarren-Ferguson Act. However, the state insurance system, which focuses on the premiums, market practices, and solvency of insurance companies, remains in flux (Klein 1995).

Like that of regulation in other areas of the economy, the theory of regulation in the insurance industry generally falls into one of two camps: laissez-faire or government intervention. That is, the first group believes that the market equilibrium, even if second best, represents the most efficient outcome available. When asked to explain the existence of regulation in the insurance industry, members of this school often adopt a public choice interpretation of regulation: regulation reflects the special interests of the regulated entities setting rules to bolster their market power (Buchanan and Tullock 1966; Stigler 1971).

In contrast, supporters of government intervention in the market generally support a public interest theory of regulation (see Musgrave and Musgrave 1976). Public interest theory holds that the existence of market failures (e.g., imperfect competition, externalities, public goods, economies of scale, etc.) can lead to a suboptimal allocation of scarce resources in the economy and that government intervention designed to correct these market failures can be used to improve this market equilibrium. In this framework, government intervention is often seen as a *substitute* for coordination in the private markets.

In this paper, we introduce a different framework, one in which the goal of government policy is not to substitute for, or to replace, coordination in the private marketplace but rather to *facilitate* more efficient coordination in the private sector. This is the *market-enhancing view* of government policy (Aoki, Murdock, and Okuno-Fujiaara 1996). Underlying this framework is the presumption that decentralized decision making is, in general, more efficient than centralized control. Thus, private-sector coordination is preferable to significant government intervention. Therefore, the goal of this approach is to promote the creation of private-sector institutions that increase the efficiency of private-sector coordination.

2.3.1 "Traditional" Views of Government Action

First, let us examine the more traditional policy prescriptions, beginning with the laissez-faire policy. Here, the presumption is that, in the absence of distortion-inducing government interventions, the outcome from decentralized private-sector activity would be efficient (or at least more efficient than the alternative with government intervention). In many instances, this view has merit. For example, if state insurance commissioners suppress insurance rates to a "politically acceptable" level where insurers can no longer cover the variable cost of providing insurance or recoup their initial investments in providing service to that state, the market will withdraw capacity, creating an availability crisis (Harrington 1992). Attempts by insurance commissioners to impose exit restrictions to prevent this exodus from the market will only compound the misallocation of resources in the insurance market and provide strong disincentives for future entry into that state. In contrast, if price ceilings are not imposed, insurance premiums will rise to the point where natural disaster insurance will be available to all willing to pay the market-clearing price.[9]

Unfortunately, laissez-faire policy does not adequately address the weaknesses in the current system for internalizing natural disaster risk in new construction decisions or provide suggestions for filling the current gap in the lack of capacity to diversify claims over time. For example, with respect to upper tiers of disaster financing, the laissez-faire approach has a presumption that, in the absence of any price controls, primary and reinsurance capacity would appear and the market would clear. There is some evidence supporting this conclusion. Two years after the Northridge Earthquake, and four years after Hurri-

9. If the government were concerned about the real "affordability" of insurance, it could allow premiums to rise to market-clearing levels and then subsidize the purchase of insurance for those individuals whose budget constraint is binding at the market-clearing price.

cane Andrew, new capital started flowing into the reinsurance industry. By the end of 1997, industry experts estimated that over $5 billion in new risk capital had been accumulated in the Bermuda market alone, resulting in considerable downward pressure on reinsurance rates. When faced with large catastrophic claims, however, this new capacity may prove to be an unstable source of risk capital, especially given the rapidity with which reinsurance capital has exited the insurance market in the past (Berger, Cummins, and Tennyson 1992). Soft reinsurance markets are already causing many of these new reinsurers to look for alternative ways of leveraging their risk capital.

The other traditional policy alternative is to look to government intervention to "solve" these "market failures." With respect to the internalization of risk, the government could simply increase the requirements of building codes to a sufficiently high level so that disaster-risk protection is always incorporated into new construction. Again, there is some merit to this view. By providing some minimum base level of expectations, all participants in the construction process—architects, builders, inspectors, etc.—raise their standards for how buildings are constructed.

Unfortunately, this "command and control" policy has a number of flaws. Any building code is a rule book, and, even though these rules have some flexibility, a rule book has the effect of imposing a "one-size-fits-all" solution to any building problem. In reality, a huge variety of circumstances face any particular builder in any given location. In the case of earthquakes, the local geography, proximity to fault lines, the likely character of a given earthquake (whether the shaking is vertical or horizontal), etc. all differ widely for each project. It is simply not feasible for building codes to specify all possible contingencies.

More important, for codes to be effective, they must be enforced, and there are insufficient incentives, at present, to ensure proper enforcement of building codes. From a builder's perspective, building codes only impose costs. From the local government's perspective, building inspectors and more effective inspections cost money. Furthermore, cities have an incentive to remain lax on building-code enforcement when competing with neighboring cities for new developments, as seen in the experience of Florida after Hurricane Andrew. Even though very rigorous building codes were on the books, builders simply ignored the codes. As a consequence, homes suffered significant damage in the storm because their roofs were improperly attached to the rest of the structure.

In the case of reinsurance capacity, the government-intervention approach would simply call for the federal government to step in and provide disaster insurance. This approach has significant risks, as government agencies are notoriously unreliable at providing efficient, unsubsidized insurance (Priest 1996). Furthermore, there are significant political pressures to hold premiums at artificially low levels, and government bureaucrats may have less incentive to manage the risk exposure of the government than do the agents of private insurance companies (Kane 1996). A large-scale government program may succeed at providing disaster-insurance capacity, but at the cost of significant losses on claims paid out in the future and a worsening of the incentives to build new construction more efficiently (since arguably the government would be less apt to set risk-based insurance premiums properly).

Thus, neither traditional approach offers an attractive option for improving the market's allocation of disaster risk once the costs of intervention or inaction are assessed. Therefore, we turn to a discussion of a new framework for federal policy, a framework that we believe is appropriate for an industry regulated at the state level.

2.3.2   The Market-Enhancing View

The *market-enhancing view* of government policy is a fundamentally different approach than either the laissez-faire or the public interest theory. The market-enhancing approach looks for the role of government to facilitate more efficient private-sector coordination, complementing the market while respecting the advantages of decentralized information processing. In contrast to traditional government intervention, which centralizes decision making, the market-enhancing view promotes the decentralization of decision-making power in the market. At the same time, this view recognizes that there are potential inefficiencies associated with decentralized coordination that are left unaddressed under a laissez-faire approach to government policy. These inefficiencies arise when the decentralized agents have inefficient incentives that are not aligned with maximizing social welfare (e.g., individuals' failure to internalize disaster risk) or when there exists a need for significant coordination of a large number of these decentralized agents to promote a shift to a more efficient equilibrium (e.g., the need to develop new financial markets for catastrophic risk).

An important dimension of the market-enhancing view that distinguishes it from the public interest theory of regulation is the emphasis on the importance of local information. Whereas most government interventions require some kind of central agent to process information and make decisions that affect a large number of outcomes, an intervention designed to be market enhancing simply attempts to align the incentives of decentralized private agents with socially efficient incentives. Then the decentralized private agents can use the locally available information to come up with market-based solutions that are significantly more efficient than those that could be imposed by a central authority.

2.4   Applications of the Framework

In this section, we apply the framework of the market-enhancing view to analyze two of the many public policy proposals that have been suggested in the debate over managing catastrophic disaster risk. The first policy is to require the purchase of disaster insurance on all new construction (i.e., all new homes that are built after 1 January 2000). The purpose of this policy is to create a mechanism whereby private-sector agents (in this case, new home builders) internalize the risk of natural disasters into the construction decision. The second policy is to have the federal government develop a financing mechanism that enhances the intertemporal diversification of natural disaster risks and then have the government gradually cede the market to the private sector.

2.4.1   An Insurance Requirement on New Construction

In section 2.2 above, we identified the root cause of why there was insufficient incentive for builders to construct "disaster-safe" houses—because purchasers do not fully perceive the value of mitigation investments. Recognizing this issue as the central question, we ask whether there is any mechanism to overcome this market failure. In this section, we analyze one possible solution—instituting a requirement that all homeowners obtaining a mortgage from a federally related institution for new construction must obtain all-hazards insurance in addition to traditional homeowner's insurance.

If enacted as a government policy, this approach would result in a gradual "phase-in" of disaster insurance so that, ultimately, disaster-insurance capacity will be available to all homeowners. Once new home buyers are required to buy disaster insurance on new construction, the price of insurance will affect homeowners' decisions on where to locate and their desired level of investment in mitigation against future disaster losses. As a result, builders will have incentives to manage the cost of disaster insurance for their home buyers. If they can design a home that has a lower cost of disaster insurance, they will be able to capture a higher price for their homes. Thus, to the extent that there are differential rates on disaster insurance, builders will have incentives to design in mitigation measures that are cost effective.[10]

Equally important, builders and insurance companies will have incentives to work together to develop varying grades of certification for the new disaster-proof construction. This will allow the insurance companies to price the risk of natural disaster loss more accurately and will increase the builders' ability to reduce the cost of disaster insurance for homeowners (and thus allow the builders to capture higher profits). Thus, in their search for higher profits, these two industries will choose to work together to come up with mechanisms to reduce the risk of loss from natural disasters.

Once this policy of a disaster-insurance requirement for new construction has been put in place (and after an initial period of adjustment), new construction will be designed and built with a much higher level of investment in disaster mitigation. Moreover, these investments will be determined in a decentralized manner, by builders responding to a price mechanism, which in this case is the differential price of disaster insurance between varying grades of mitigation investment.

---

10. Of course, state regulations governing insurance pricing may interfere in the pricing of relative risks for new construction and thereby mute the effect of this proposal.

While this policy suggestion may seem overly intrusive, there are several arguments in its favor: (*a*) Mortgage lenders require the purchase of fire insurance to secure the value of the collateral underlying a mortgage loan. This policy simply extends that principle to include natural disaster risks. (*b*) Because the risk of disasters will be internalized in the cost of new buildings via the insurance premium, new structures will be built only in areas for which the home buyer is willing to pay for the risk associated with the property's location, reducing current incentives to build in high-risk areas to a more efficient level. (*c*) Individuals will have a greater incentive to undertake mitigation investments in order to lower their insurance premiums, again lowering the aggregate exposure of society (Kunreuther 1996). (*d*) A larger portion of the responsibility for funding the payment of disaster claims will be allocated to individuals with control over the disaster exposure being created—reducing the level of cross-subsidies in the market. (*e*) By linking the proposal to new construction, primary-insurance capacity will have to expand only at a rate equal to new construction in the United States to meet the increase in insurance demand generated by this proposal. Of course, the willingness of insurers to expand their supply of all-hazards insurance will be a function of state insurance regulation and insurers' current exposure. (*f*) By linking the provision of insurance to mortgages, this requirement will also provide additional protection to mortgage pools exposed to disaster-related mortgage defaults.[11]

As a result, this proposal would reduce the aggregate exposure of society to disaster losses and improve efficiency with respect to the way in which disaster claims are financed. Of course, the proposal does require an expansion of primary-insurance coverage for natural hazards. As such, this proposal would be most effective if linked to an expansion in financing capacity for upper layers of disaster risk—an issue to which we now turn.

2.4.2   An Industry-Level Excess-of-Loss Contract

The second market problem identified in section 2.2 above is the absence of any market mechanism for spreading large, idiosyncratic, and spatially correlated disaster claims intertemporally. As noted above, traditional property insurance diversifies claims through a pooling of risk, where the risk pool is held by a low-cost intermediary that specializes in assessing, monitoring, and pricing insurance risks. Once risks in an insurance pool become correlated, however, the value of insurance as a risk-diversification and financing mechanism is diminished.

For relatively high-probability, low-severity events, property insurance is a classic insurance risk. However, when natural disasters create widespread

---

11. A study by Duff and Phelps found that mortgage-backed security pools exposed to earthquake losses in California had special hazard-loss provisions equal to approximately 1 percent of the pool, four times the expected losses from the highest loan-to-value categories in those pools (Mandel and Hayssen 1995).

property damage within a region, claims on the pool are highly correlated, and the insurance mechanism breaks down. In this case, the risk of insolvency for the insurance company rises, the premium that homeowners are willing to pay for given a coverage level falls (premiums are discounted to reflect the solvency risk of the insurer), and the premiums that the insurance companies need to earn to capitalize against large losses increase. As a result, the insurance sector is thrown into disequilibrium.

An obvious avenue by means of which insurance intermediaries can reduce their exposure to natural disaster risk is the $19 trillion capital market. Theoretically, as a low-cost transactor in the market, insurance companies are in a good position to diversify any residual exposures from their insurance portfolio by taking positions in capital market securities. Unfortunately, the development of capital market securities remains in its infancy, leaving a financing gap for insurance companies. As a result, members of the insurance industry have raised the possibility of federal intervention in the provision of disaster insurance.

Lewis and Murdock (1996) argue that the federal government is in a unique position to utilize its ability to diversify claims intertemporally by designing a new risk-management mechanism for diversifying disaster risks intertemporally. However, taking a market-enhancing view of government policy, they argue against proposals for federalizing the provision of disaster insurance or reinsurance. Consistent with Priest (1996), they find that the federal government would have a comparative disadvantage in assessing disaster-risk exposures for individual properties or companies.

Instead, they offer a market-based proposal where the federal government would attempt to expand private-insurance capacity through the creation of a federal excess-of-loss reinsurance mechanism narrowly targeted to the missing market for the intertemporal diversification of large disaster losses. Specifically, the federal government would sell tradable per occurrence excess-of-loss (XOL) reinsurance contracts for insured disaster losses in the United States in the range of $25–$50 billion. These contracts, which are equivalent to call-spread options written on an industry index of disaster losses, would be auctioned to qualified insurance companies and would carry a maturity of one year.

The XOL program would be based on industry losses to minimize the moral hazard associated with providing company-specific reinsurance. Further, the program would be actuarially sound and would be designed to complement existing private-sector insurance and reinsurance mechanisms by covering only layers of reinsurance currently unavailable in the private market and by incorporating a cost-of-capital adjustment to offset the federal government's lower borrowing costs. As such, the program is designed to allow the "crowding out" of the federal government by private-sector institutions instead of the classic crowding out of the private sector by the government. Lewis and Murdock (1996) argue further that, by offering an efficient, nonredundant security, the XOL proposal actually enhances the ability of the private market to develop new financial instruments for financing lower levels of disaster risk in the private market. (For more information on the pricing of XOL contracts, see Cummins, Lewis, and Phillips [1997, chap. 3 in this volume].)

An important aspect of the excess-of-loss program not discussed in Lewis and Murdock (1996) is the institutional benefits that the program would bring to the private market. The natural question emerging from the debate over capital market disaster instruments is why the market has failed to fill this need for intertemporal risk diversification. We believe that a large portion of the answer to this question revolves around (*a*) the great deal of uncertainty that capital market institutions and institutional investors have concerning the evaluation of disaster risks, (*b*) the lack of standardization in measuring disaster risk or structuring catastrophe securities, (*c*) the lack of an institutional structure for a capital market in catastrophe risk, and (*d*) the high degree of risk aversion exhibited by investors when faced with a financial payoff that provides a high risk-adjusted return but carries a small probability of a large loss.

The model for the industry structure that would evolve with the XOL program is fundamentally different from the current industry model. At present, reinsurance companies provide reinsurance to a pool of primary insurance firms—diversifying the risk geographically. Since the occurrence of large disasters is highly idiosyncratic (and has a high variance), however, reinsurance companies cannot adequately diversify catastrophic disaster risk through insurance pooling and remain exposed to large losses. As a result, reinsurance companies limit their exposure to catastrophic risk by limiting supply, raising the price of catastrophe covers, or requiring a cross-selling of other products.

With the XOL mechanism, reinsurers would still assemble national pools of risk by providing an appropriate mix of reinsurance to primary insurers. However, the XOL program would provide reinsurers with a mechanism for transferring the responsibility of intertemporally smoothing large disaster claims to the federal government and, ultimately, to competing private market providers of similar instruments. As such, reinsurers could loosen supply constraints on the amount (or price) of catastrophe reinsurance being offered in the market. Then, as the reinsurers accumulated larger, national insurance pools, the correlation between their disaster exposure and the industry's exposure would rise, increasing the value of XOL-type contracts and encouraging the establishment of private-label XOL structures.

As noted above, however, the proper functioning of an XOL market requires a number of investments in institutional infrastructure before the market can flourish. First, someone must make the investment to create an audited value (on agreed-on terms and parameter assumptions) for total industry losses arising from a natural disaster and the probability of disaster events. Second, some agent must credibly provide a sufficient number of XOL contracts to allow the reinsurance and insurance industry to cede a significant portion of the upper-end catastrophe risk. Third, the reinsurance industry and the national primary insurers must make substantial adjustments to their internal policies and procedures and risk-management tools to support the purchase of XOL-type contracts.

For the industry, these last two issues present the classic "chicken-or-egg" problem. The reinsurance industry is not going to make large investments to integrate XOL contracts into their business system unless there is a credible multiyear commitment to supplying these XOL contracts. However, without the reinsurers making this investment, there will be insufficient demand to justify the investments required by potential suppliers of these contracts.

The temporary provision of these contracts by the federal government "solves" this coordination problem. First, the XOL contract will establish the standards on which all future XOL contracts (public or private) can be based. Second, the federal government commits to providing a sufficiently large supply of XOL contracts to allow reinsurers to justify the investment in changing their business systems. As the demand for these contracts is realized, however, the government continues to short the market for these contracts, allowing the private sector to serve a growing fraction of the market. Ultimately, the private sector will crowd out the federal government, and the XOL program will be ceded to the private sector.

Reinsurance companies and capital market firms could take a much more active role in providing this coverage today. However, private capital may be reluctant to flow into a market before the appropriate investments are made to establish institutions and standards for providing information on how to structure securities on the basis of this new asset class. The advantage of the XOL program is that it helps establish these institutions. The program can also serve as a conduit for information on assessing natural disaster risks in general. Then, once the market structure and standardization is accomplished, the private sector can simply "crowd out" the federal presence in the market.

Finally, the excess-of-loss program provides an immediate expansion in the capacity of the reinsurance and insurance markets, greatly reducing the exposure overhang felt by insurers in the wake of reassessing their disaster-risk exposures. As such, the program would relax the solvency concerns of policyholders and investors, which will aid the market in reaching a new equilibrium. Without such an expansion in capacity, it is possible that concerns over counterparty solvency will prevent the development of any private market institutions in this area.

2.5   Conclusion

In reviewing the existing state of catastrophic risk management in the United States, this paper examined whether *market-enhancing* public policy can be used to improve the financing of disaster risk in the United States. On the basis of weaknesses identified within the current system, the paper suggests that at least two public policy options being discussed publicly have the potential to generate improvements in the way in which the United States manages disaster risk: (*a*) requiring homeowners to purchase all-hazards disaster insurance as a condition of receiving a federally related mortgage and (*b*) establishing a federal reinsurance mechanism, as proposed by Lewis and Murdock (1996), that allows insurers and reinsurers to purchase protection against large industry losses from catastrophic disasters.

The objective of the all-hazards-insurance-purchase requirement is to establish a direct link between individuals' decisions to create disaster exposure and the recognition of the costs associated with that exposure—that is, to increase the internalization of disaster risk. The objective of the federal reinsurance facility is to provide an immediate expansion in the capacity of the insurance industry to finance existing disaster exposure while providing the institutional investments that will foster the development of more active private-sector mechanisms for financing these disaster risks.

However, it is important to recognize that any real solution to the natural disaster insurance problem in the United States requires a comprehensive set of policy reforms that address all aspects of disaster policy, including hazard mitigation, tax policy, and the removal of any inefficiencies or inappropriate incentives in the state or federal regulatory structure. In this context, the public policy framework developed in this paper will be a useful tool for analyzing the merits of alternative disaster-reform proposals.

References

Aiuppa, Thomas A., Robert J. Carney, and Thomas M. Krueger. 1993. An examination of insurance stock prices following the 1989 Loma Prieta Earthquake. *Journal of Insurance Issues and Practices* 16:1–14.

Aoki, Masahiko, Kevin Murdock, and Masahiro Okuno-Fujiaara. 1996. Beyond the East-Asian miracle: Introducing the market-enhancing view. In *The role of government in East Asian economic development: Comparative institutional analysis,* ed. Masahito Aoki, Hyung-Ki Kim, and Masahiro Okuno-Fujiwara. Oxford: Clarendon Press.

Arnott, Richard, and Joseph Stiglitz. 1990. The welfare economics of moral hazard. In *Risk information and insurance: Essays in the memory of Karl H. Borch,* ed. Henri Loubergé. Boston: Kluwer Academic.

Arrow, Kenneth J. 1953. Le rôle des valeurs boursiéres pour la répartition la meilleure des risques. *Econometrie* (Paris: Colloques Internationaux du Centre National de la Recherche Scientifique) 11:41–47.

———. 1964. The role of securities in the optimal allocation of risk bearing. *Review of Economic Studies* 31 (April): 91–96.

———. 1996. The theory of risk-bearing: Small and great risks. *Journal of Risk and Uncertainty* 12:102–111.

Banz, R. W., and M. H. Miller. 1978. Prices for state-contingency claims: Some estimates and applications. *Journal of Business* 51 (October): 653–72.

Berger, Lawrence A., J. David Cummins, and Sharon Tennyson. 1992. Reinsurance and the liability crisis. *Journal of Risk and Uncertainty* 5:253–72.

Bernknopf, Richard L., David S. Brookshire, and Mark Thayer. 1990. Earthquake and volcano hazard notices: An economic evaluation of changes in risk perceptions. *Journal of Environmental Economics and Management* 18:35–49.

Black, F., and M. Scholes. 1973. The pricing of options and corporate liabilities. *Journal of Political Economy* 81 (May–June): 637–54.

Borch, K. 1974. *The mathematical theory of insurance.* Lexington, Mass.: Heath.

Breeden, D. T., and R. Litzenberger. 1978. Price of state contingent claims in options prices. *Journal of Business* 51:621–51.

Buchanan, J., and G. Tullock. 1966. *The calculus of consent.* Ann Arbor, Mich.: University of Michigan Press.

California Earthquake Authority (CEA). 1996. *Summary of Plan of Finance I: Issuance of taxable securities.* New York: Morgan Stanley; Bear, Stearns; and Goldman, Sachs, January.

Cummins, J. David, Christopher M. Lewis, and Richard D. Phillips. 1997. Excess of loss reinsurance contracts against catastrophic loss. In *Alternative approaches to insurance regulation,* ed. Robert Klein. Kansas City, Mo.: National Association of Insurance Commissioners.

Debreu, J. 1959. *Theory of value.* New York: Wiley.

Doherty, N., and S. Tinic. 1981. Reinsurance under conditions of capital market equilibrium: A note. *Journal of Finance* 36:949–53.

English, James. 1996. Shareholder returns of catastrophe reinsurers. In *Insurance industry analysis.* New York: J. P. Morgan Securities, May.

Epstein, Richard A. 1996. Catastrophic responses to catastrophic risks. *Journal of Risk and Uncertainty* 12:287–308.

Hakansson, N. H. 1976. The purchasing power fund: A new kind of financial intermediary. *Financial Analysts Journal* 32:49–59.

Han, Li-Ming, and Gene C. Lai. 1995. An analysis of securitization in the insurance industry. *Journal of Risk and Insurance* 62:286–96.

Harrington, Scott E. 1992. Rate suppression. *Journal of Risk and Insurance* 59: 185–202.

Institute for Property Loss Reduction (IPLR). 1995. *Homes and hurricanes: Public opinion concerning various issues relating to home builders, building codes, and damage mitigation.* Boston.

Insurance Information Institute. 1994. *The fact book: 1994 property casualty insurance facts.* New York.

Insurance Services Office (ISO). 1994. *The impact of catastrophes on property insurance.* Insurance Services Issues Series. New York, May.

———. 1996. *Managing catastrophe risk.* Insurance Services Issues Series. New York, May.

Kane, Edward J. 1996. Difficulties in making implicit government risk-bearing partnerships explicit. *Journal of Risk and Uncertainty* 12:189–99.

Klein, Robert W. 1995. Insurance regulation in transition. *Journal of Risk and Insurance* 62, no. 3:363–404.

Kunreuther, Howard. 1996. Mitigating disaster losses through insurance. *Journal of Risk and Uncertainty* 12:171–87.

Lamb, Reinhold. 1995. An exposure-based analysis of property-liability insurer stock values around Hurricane Andrew. *Journal of Risk and Insurance* 62, no. 1:111–23.

Lemaire, Jean. 1990. Borch's theorem: A historical survey of applications. In *Risk, information, and insurance: Essays in memory of Karl H. Borch,* ed. Henri Loubergé. Boston: Kluwer Academic.

Lewis, Christopher M., and Peter O. Davis. 1998. Capital market instruments for financing catastrophe risk: New directions? Working paper. Research Project on Catastrophic Risk, Wharton School, University of Pennsylvania.

Lewis, Christopher M., and Kevin Murdock. 1996. The role of government contract in discretionary reinsurance market for natural disaster. *Journal of Risk and Insurance* 63, no. 4:567–97.

Litzenberger, Robert H., David R. Beaglehole, and Craig E. Reynolds. 1996. Assessing catastrophe-reinsurance-linked securities as a new asset class. In *Fixed income research*. New York: Goldman, Sachs, July.

Mandel, Brian K., and Henry Hayssen. 1995. *The Northridge Earthquake: Special report.* New York: Duff & Phelps Credit Rating, February.

Marlett, David C., and Alan D. Eastman. 1998. The estimated impact of residual market assessments on Florida property insurers. *Risk Management and Insurance Review* 2, no. 1 (Summer): 37–49.

Merton, Robert C. 1973. Theory of rational option pricing. *Bell Journal of Economics and Management Science* 4 (Spring): 141–83.

———. 1990. *Continuous-time finance.* Cambridge, Mass.: Blackwell.

Musgrave, R. A., and P. B. Musgrave. 1976. *Public finance in theory and practice.* Tokyo: McGraw-Hill.

Priest, George L. 1996. The government, the market, and the problem of catastrophic loss. *Journal of Risk and Uncertainty* 12:219–37.

Ross, S. A. 1976. Options and efficiency. *Quarterly Journal of Economics* 90 (February): 75–89.

Shelor, Roger M., Dwight C. Anderson, and Mark L. Cross. 1990. The impact of the California earthquake on real estate firms' sock value. *Journal of Real Estate Research* 5:335–40.

———. 1992. Gaining from loss: Property-liability insurer stock values in the aftermath of the 1989 California earthquake. *Journal of Risk and Insurance* 5:476–88.

Stigler, G. J. 1971. The theory of economic regulation. *Bell Journal of Economics* 2 (Spring): 3–21.

Tversky, Amos, Shmuel Sattath, and Paul Slovic. 1988. Contingent weighting in judgement and choice. *Psychological Review* 95:371–84.

U.S. Bureau of the Census. 1994. *Statistical abstract of the United States, 1994.* 113th ed. Washington, D.C.: U.S. Government Printing Office.

Van Anne, Craig, and Thomas Larsen. 1993. Estimating catastrophe losses with computer models. *Contingencies,* March/April.

Comment   Peter Diamond

This is an interesting paper, which does a good job of bringing existing theory to bear on these problems. I want to go over the same ground, organizing the material differently, and connecting with additional parts of the literature, especially the second-best literature.

The paper identifies two potential public policy issues, one relating to the behavior of individual propertyowners, the other to the behavior of insurers

Peter Diamond is professor of economics at the Massachusetts Institute of Technology and a research associate of the National Bureau of Economic Research.

and reinsurers. The paper argues that we can successfully disconnect these two problems, thinking about them separately. I agree, but, as has already been mentioned by Steve Goldberg, some ways of approaching insurance provision will make worse the problems with the behavior of individual insurees. I will consider the two problems separately, assuming such a disconnect.

Individual behaviors include decisions involving new construction (where to build, how to build), existing construction (whether to retrofit, whether to replace), and insurance (whether to smooth income across states of nature). There are three models of individual behavior presented in different places in the paper. Model A has rational consumers responding to incentives, such as the tax deductibility of large losses and disaster relief, that induce some inefficiency. Model B has rational consumers suffering from inadequate information (presumably resulting from a high cost of obtaining that information) and therefore making some decisions that are inefficient relative to a richer information set. Model C has irrational consumers in one of a variety of forms, such as those having very high implicit discount rates (coming from myopia, not just facing higher interest rates because of capital market imperfections) and those ignoring or undervaluing risks.

If all consumers satisfied model A, then the focus would be on the incentives, recognizing the second-best issue that, with asymmetrical information, it is impossible either to provide insurance or to redistribute income without some distortions. The focus would be on finding the balance between providing more insurance and more redistribution and inducing larger deadweight burdens. While I do believe that many people are responsive to these incentives, I do not think that this is the whole story.

If all consumers satisfied model B, then the focus would be on providing information. However, I think that the evidence is overwhelming that many people do not successfully incorporate risk information into their decisions without experiences that affect responses. This has been explored extensively in the work of Kunreuther (e.g., Kunreuther et al.). My first exposure to this was a presentation by two psychiatrists discussing decisions on smoking (Tamerin and Resnik 1972). In addition to laying out a perspective on individual decision making, they cited the result that, "among the medical specialties, the most successful in quitting smoking are internists and radiologists, who have repeated contact with the disease consequences of smoking, and those with poor records are psychiatrists, who have the least direct contact with the sequellae" (p. 82). Note that the presence of irrationality in assessing risks is compounded by a "winner's curse," the tendency for those with the least concern about the risks to value new construction most highly.

In order to address the issues raised by model C, we need to consider some forms of compulsion. Note also that, as long as we are not addressing all the issues raised by model C, we will have a need for institutional structures that will have to balance helping those satisfying model C with those satisfying model A, whose behavior is distorted by these measures. Note also that the issue arises, not only in high-risk areas, but also in low-risk areas and for problems with uniform risks. For example, a recurrence of a major earthquake in New England, as occurred in the eighteenth century, would cause major damage. So too would the impact of a meteor, such as the one that created the massive crater in Arizona. How society should respond to the occurrence of such events, which are "unpredicted" as far as insurance preparation goes, depends on one's view of society. With the American ethos, there is a strong sense that the government should help in such settings.

The proposed compulsion analyzed in the paper is mandating insurance for new construction. The paper does not indicate whether this is just in areas considered high risk or in all parts of the country. Part of the motivation for this approach is to allow time for insurance capacity to grow along with mandated coverage. The paper assumes that such a mandate would result in efficient price signals to builders. But this seems overly optimistic to me. There will be insurance-price variation with mitigation efforts, but the level may not be efficient. Some of this insurance cost will be bundled with the other costs of buying new housing. Some of it may generate market power and thus redistribution from home buyers. That in turn may be dissipated in overentry. A parallel with closing costs may be appropriate, with limited market discipline on levels. The paper contrasts assumed efficient pricing with the shortcomings of building codes, recognizing both the problems of high uniformity in codes and the tendency to underenforce some of them. Once one also recognizes inefficiencies in pricing, we may be in a setting best approached in the prices versus quantities framework of Weitzman (1974). Indeed, since we will have codes no matter what we do about pricing, it may be best to think about having both tools in effect and to consider how to coordinate them.

Another problem with Lewis and Murdock's approach is that it grandfathers existing construction. Given the presumed undervaluation of mitigation expenditures by the market, this results in an overvaluation of existing housing. This results in an inefficient incentive to build on vacant land rather than replace existing structures. How this relates to renovation depends on the rules covering grandfathering. A natural solution to this problem is to expand the mandate for insurance to existing buildings slowly. This can be done at transaction time, as, for example, is being done in Massachusetts relative to septic systems. Of course, this has a distortionary effect on transactions. Another approach might be to have an analogue to the draft lottery, picking counties at random and extending the mandate slowly throughout the country. That would produce a dream instrument for econometricians.

We might also consider more use of tort liability of builders along the lines of products liability, although such an approach will not solve this problem by itself.

I turn now to the second problem—that of the behavior of insurers and reinsurers. The discussion considers the cost of reserves—basically a cost of liquidity. Implicit in some discussions is an assumption that the social cost of liquidity differs from its private cost. This may well be the case, but we do not have good equilibrium models of liquidity, models with capital market imperfections, with which to evaluate the implications of this perspective for insurance. There are two implications of low reserves—an insolvency risk for insurees and guaranty funds and a slow growth of capacity after a catastrophe and therefore a limited availability of insurance during such an adjustment period, as has been examined in the work of Gron (1990). Again, we would need a model of capital market imperfections to examine how to respond to this problem. Intertemporal sharing of risks involves substituting consumption in one year for that in a later year, something that takes place through changes in the level of investment. The link between this and reserves runs primarily through atemporal distribution of risks. Analysis of this issue may parallel that of the national debt, where the intertemporal effects come from the effect of alternative decisions affecting the national debt on investment decisions.

There are two ways to go for tapping into conditional funds in order to speed the growth of capacity after a catastrophe. One is to have conditional payments (a form of insurance), and the other is to have conditional loans (a form of committed lines of credit). Which approach would do better at tapping additional sources of funds I do not know, but it would be good to analyze this formally. On the one hand, lines of credit involve putting less at risk by the new sources of funds. On the other hand, it may take having more at risk to create the incentives to get involved in supplying this market.

As a matter of equilibrium, it is also important to recognize that increasing the availability of conditional funds is likely to reduce the level of insurance-company reserves, so one needs to evaluate the net effect relative to whatever other incentives are associated with increasing such fund availability.

References

Gron, Anne. 1990. Property-casualty insurance cycles, capacity constraints, and empirical results. Ph.D. diss., Massachusetts Institute of Technology.

Kunreuther, Howard, et al. 1978. *Disaster insurance protection.* New York: Wiley.

Tamerin, J. S., and H. L. P. Resnik. 1972. Risk taking by individual option: Case study—cigarette smoking. In *Perspectives on benefit-risk decision making.* Washington, D.C.: National Academy of Engineering. (Reprinted in *Uncertainty in economics: Readings and exercises,* ed. P. Diamond and M. Rothschild [San Diego: Academic, 1989].)

Weitzman, Martin. 1974. Prices vs. quantities. *Review of Economic Studies* 41, no. 4 (October): 477–92.

Comment   Paolo M. Pellegrini

I read the Lewis and Murdock paper with great interest. My comments are in the spirit of stimulating further thought and research as they reflect limited data and analysis.

First, I would like to offer some introductory thoughts about the two proposals contained in the paper. Concerning Lewis and Murdock's first proposal, mandatory disaster insurance for new homes, I agree with their view that home buyers in disaster-prone areas need guidance to internalize risk. At a minimum, some form of disaster-hazard disclosure should be required. I doubt whether mandatory insurance is socially or politically viable. However, it would not be unreasonable to condition federal postdisaster assistance to ex ante insurance requirements. Also, the tax deductibility of disaster-insurance premiums could be a powerful incentive for individuals to make responsible risk-management decisions.

Concerning the second proposal in Lewis and Murdock, a federal government excess-of-loss (XOL) program, I believe that such a program is neither justified nor effective. The industry's $200 billion capital is subject to volatility far greater than its catastrophe exposure in the $25 billion excess of $25 billion layer covered by the proposed XOL program. Moreover, such exposure is unlikely to be significantly correlated to the industry's other sources of volatility, and, therefore, removing it would not reduce the industry's overall volatility by any noticeable amount.[1] Individual companies that do need catastrophe protection, perhaps as a result of sound strategies based on geographic focus, would benefit only marginally from the XOL program because, as discussed in Major (chap. 10 in this volume), index-based hedges (such as the XOL program would be) present unacceptable basis risk.

The insurance industry and the capital markets can address the nation's property-catastrophe risk-transfer needs without the direct involvement of the federal government. The only policy initiative that I would support is the transfer of regulatory authority from the states to the federal government. State insurance departments lack the degree of coordination required to regulate the inherently suprastate process of redistributing property-catastrophe risk. Con-

---

Paolo M. Pellegrini is president of Global Risk Advisors LLC, a New York firm that advises utility and insurance clients with respect to corporate finance and risk management. Until May 1998, Mr. Pellegrini served as president of Select Reinsurance Ltd., a Bermuda property-catastrophe reinsurance company.

1. As a hypothetical example, let us assume that the insurance industry's annual results have a standard deviation equal to 15 percent of the industry's $200 billion capital, or $30 billion (this is comparable to the volatility of the S&P 500 and lower than the volatility of many individual insurance stocks). By some estimates, the annual losses associated with the XOL program (the XOL losses) have an expected value of $125 million and a standard deviation of $1.25 billion. Assuming no correlation between XOL losses and industry results excluding XOL losses, the industry standard deviation excluding XOL losses would be $29.97 billion. Assuming a 50 percent correlation (a figure far above any reasonable expectation), the industry standard deviation excluding XOL losses would still be $29.66 billion.

sequently, they tend to impose market-inefficient constraints on insurance companies' risk selection and pricing as well as on their financial and investment policies.

I offer the following explanatory model for the current property-catastrophe-insurance- and reinsurance-capacity shortfall.

Because of regulatory constraints, primary insurers cannot control their risk exposure directly, through selective underwriting. Although they could control their risk exposure indirectly, through reinsurance, they cannot pass through the cost of reinsurance to policyholders. Therefore, they are forced to resort to market exit as their primary risk-management tool.

Reinsurers face their own constraints, as they lack opportunities to diversify geographically their concentrated exposures to zones such as Florida and California. Consequently, they can offer incremental coverage in such zones only at prices that primary insurers can hardly afford.[2] Lewis and Murdock advocate intertemporal diversification as a possible solution.[3] A much simpler solution is diversification through investments.[4] The obvious impediment to such a solution is that regulators and rating agencies would not allow it. Even more important, the syndicated, "consensus-pricing" structure of the property-catastrophe-reinsurance market would not allow it.

Despite much effort, the capital markets have failed to fill the gap so far. There is no obvious explanation. Perhaps the securities offered are too risky for the fixed-income buyers and too anemic for the hedge funds, the two primary marketing targets to date. Perhaps they are simply not attractive, given the market's current perception of potential risk and return. With respect to risk, investors are skeptical about the predictive power of simulation models, given their poor performance in events such as the Los Angeles Earthquake. With respect to return, investors perceive a capped upside that will not affect overall portfolio results substantially. Consequently, they are reluctant to make the intellectual investment required to understand the new securities. Although most industry observers agree that securitization will ultimately succeed, the timetable is unclear.

The following are possible suggestions to reduce dislocation in the property-catastrophe-insurance and -reinsurance markets.

---

2. As a hypothetical example, let us assume that a reinsurance company has a cost of capital of 25 percent, provided that the standard deviation of its return on capital not exceed 20 percent. Let us assume further that it can underwrite treaties with the same limit in n zones not subject to a common peril. In addition, let us assume that each treaty has an expected value and a standard deviation of losses equal to 3 and 12 percent of the treaty limit, respectively, and that investments yield a risk-free rate of 5 percent. The break-even rate on line (i.e., premium divided by limit) would be 15 percent for $n = 1$, 11.5 percent for $n = 2$, 9.0 percent for $n = 4$, and 7.2 percent for $n = 8$.

3. Assuming that losses in different years are independent of each other, underwriting n years (for a fixed multiyear premium) would have the same diversification effect as underwriting n zones.

4. Using the same assumptions as were used in n. 2 above, except for an investment yield of 20 percent with a standard deviation of 15 percent, the break-even rate on line for $n = 1$ would be 7.5 instead of 15 percent.

Since federal postdisaster assistance is a given, property-catastrophe insurance should be regulated by the federal government with the objective of reducing unintended cost shifting and cross-subsidization. Clearly, this is not an option that is available in the near future.

Most of what can be done immediately involves reinsurance and securitization, which are regulated only indirectly by individual states.

Reinsurers have already accomplished a lot in terms of underwriting methods and standards. However, there could be beneficial changes. The property-catastrophe reinsurance market should move beyond the syndicated, consensus-pricing format to accelerate further the process of underwriting-quality improvement. Even today, few treaties are underwritten on the basis of the best information already available, namely street address data, because few reinsurers have the capability to analyze such data. If individual reinsurers were able to underwrite treaties in their entirety, the pressure on the technology laggards would be much greater.

In addition, reinsurers should satisfy the risk/return equation, not by chasing marginally priced, nonaccumulating business, but by changing financing and investment policy. If a reinsurer's volatility is 15 or 20 percent as a result of underwriting property-catastrophe business, its cost of capital will be commensurate, perhaps also 15 or 20 percent or higher. A 5 percent yield on investments financed with equity creates enormous deadweight cost and imposes rate-on-line hurdles that cannot be sustained by the ceding companies. A focus on business with a low expected loss ratio, even at the expense of geographic diversification, is a superior strategy, provided that the reinsurer (1) maintains a conservative ratio of premiums and underwriting exposure to capital and (2) allocates its assets to higher-return, even though higher-volatility, investments.

The role of the capital markets needs to be reevaluated in the light of the experience of the last three years. Clearly, unlike securitization, the capital raising efforts on behalf of the Bermuda property-catastrophe-reinsurance specialists were an unqualified success.

The issue of whether there is a need for additional reinsurance capital is a conundrum. Reinsurers complain about their inability to write enough adequately priced business, an indication that there is too much capital. Yet insurers complain about their inability to buy enough reasonably priced coverage, an indication that there is too little capital.

The implication of my previous comments is that there is too much capital available to underwrite diversifiable risks and too little to underwrite undiversifiable risks. Investor-return requirements to underwrite undiversifiable risks, however, will be comparable to those for privately placed risky assets.

Therefore, the immediate focus of capital markets intermediaries should be to raise equity for a new class of highly capitalized, single-cedent reinsurers, able to achieve return enhancement and risk diversification internally, through a more aggressive investment policy.

The competitive advantages of these new entities are significant. They will be able to address any insurance risk, regardless of accumulation, and at any time (as opposed to the standard inception dates of 1 January, 1 April, and 1 July). They will be able to perform superior underwriting due diligence and, therefore, price risk more accurately. They will be able to offer transparent security—the reinsured will know as much about the reinsurer as the reinsurer itself (today, the security of property-catastrophe reinsurers, or the lack thereof, is difficult to assess).

Over time, single-cedent reinsurers could become increasingly debt financed, driving down the cost of capital and risk-transfer pricing to the theoretical level that would be demanded by risk-neutral investors, that is, expected value of losses with no premium for volatility. Initially, however, they will reap excess returns comparable to those reportedly enjoyed by Berkshire Hathaway in connection with its treaty with the California Earthquake Authority.[5]

5. According to some estimates, the California Earthquake Authority and Berkshire Hathaway have entered into a treaty providing, on an annual equivalent basis, for a rate on line of approximately 10 percent, against losses with an expected value of between 0.5 and 1 percent and a standard deviation of between 2.5 and 5 percent (the standard deviation estimate reflects the four-year intertemporal diversification inherent in the treaty).

3 Pricing Excess-of-Loss Reinsurance Contracts against Catastrophic Loss

J. David Cummins, Christopher M. Lewis,
and Richard D. Phillips

With the recent rise in catastrophic disaster losses and the resulting effect on insurance-company solvency, the insurance industry is increasingly calling for some form of federal assistance in meeting disaster claims. Most of these requests, including the industry-sponsored Natural Disaster Partnership Protection Act of 1995, incorporate some form of all-hazard federal reinsurance program or backstop. A recent paper by Lewis and Murdock (1996) argues that the lack of federal regulatory authority in the insurance industry, the prevalence of moral hazard, adverse selection, and other opportunities for risk shifting, and the well-documented inability of the federal government to set adequate premiums to control for these costs make any traditional federal reinsurance program problematic.

Instead, Lewis and Murdock propose an alternative form of federal reinsurance that provides targeted protection for the insurance industry against catastrophic events but limits the federal government's exposure to additional losses.[1] Under this alternative, the federal government would sell per occurrence excess-of-loss contracts to private insurers and reinsurers, where both

J. David Cummins is the Harry J. Loman Professor of Insurance and Risk Management at the University of Pennsylvania. Christopher M. Lewis is senior financial economist at Ernst & Young LLP. Richard D. Phillips is assistant professor in the Department of Risk Management and Insurance at Georgia State University.

The authors thank Jim Tilley and Sanjiv Das for providing helpful comments on earlier versions of this paper. In addition, the authors thank the various members of the White House Working Group on Natural Disasters for their insightful comments. Simulation data used in this study were provided by Weimin Dong of Risk Management Solutions, Inc. Historical data on U.S. catastrophes were provided by Gary Kerney of Property Claims Services. Financial support for this paper from the NBER Project on the Financing of Property Casualty Risks is also acknowledged.

The authors retain any responsibility for errors or omissions.

1. The operating assumption in this paper is that the establishment of a federal reinsurance program does not include the provision of a taxpayer subsidy, which is viewed as a political decision outside the realm of this analysis.

the coverage layer and the fixed payout of the contract are based on insurance-industry losses, not company losses. In financial terms, the federal government would be selling earthquake- and hurricane-catastrophe call options to the insurance industry to cover catastrophic losses in the range of $25–$50 billion. Lewis and Murdock argue that this type of contract would expand capacity and stability for the insurance industry while limiting the taxpayer's exposure to the insured event: namely, a catastrophic disaster.

The purpose of the present paper is to develop a methodology for pricing the catastrophic reinsurance contracts proposed in Lewis and Murdock (1996) and to present price estimates based on both historical catastrophe-loss experience and engineering simulations. After briefly discussing the need for a federal role and summarizing the key provisions of the proposed reinsurance contract, the paper proceeds by developing a statistical model of losses that would be covered under the contract. We then discuss how insurers could use the proposed contracts in hedging catastrophic risk. Finally, we provide estimates of catastrophe frequency, severity, and expected total losses based on two sources—the Property Claims Services (1994) database on insured catastrophe property losses covering the period 1949–94 and simulated catastrophe losses obtained from Risk Management Solutions—and use these estimates to illustrate prices of the reinsurance contracts.

3.1   The Proposed Reinsurance Contracts

3.1.1   The Need for a Federal Role

The proposed federal catastrophe-reinsurance contracts are needed because of dislocations in insurance and reinsurance markets resulting from growing catastrophic property losses. Combined, Hurricane Andrew in 1992 ($18.4 billion) and the Northridge Earthquake in 1994 ($12.5 billion) resulted in nearly $31 billion in insured industry losses and caused the failure of at least ten insurance companies (see Scism and Brannigan 1996). The magnitude of insurance-industry losses associated with these two recent disasters is unprecedented. The next largest insured catastrophe loss was the $4.2 billion in losses associated with Hurricane Hugo. Over the period 1988–94, insured industry losses exceeded $35 billion in 1992 dollars, more than the cumulative total over the previous twenty-one years.

More troubling is the fact that Hurricane Andrew and the Northridge Earthquake may not represent "outlier" events. Research on the frequency and magnitude of hurricanes and earthquakes, as measured by the Saffir-Simpson and Richter scales, respectively, indicates a strong potential for increased disaster activity over the next twenty years (Gray 1990). In addition, given the 69 percent increase in insured coastal property values in the United States since 1988 (to $3.15 trillion), the losses associated with hurricanes are likely to be more severe than historical experience. Thus, the probability of disasters with losses at least as large as those incurred as a result of Hurricane Andrew and the Northridge Earthquake over the coming years remains significant.

The realization of this increased risk exposure has sent reverberations through the insurance markets, especially in Florida and California. Reinsurance companies have raised rates rapidly, in many cases by as much as 150 percent. Following suit, primary insurers have submitted requests for large rate increases to state insurance commissioners. However, most of these rate increases have been pared down by states before being approved, allegedly creating a gap between the reinsurance premium for a given layer of coverage and the amount the insurer can recover from the buyer through the primary market premium.[2] Thus, the recent jump in expected disaster-claim severity and frequency and the resulting recognition of the inadequacy of insurance premiums have prompted the industry to look to the federal government for some form of assistance, typically through a reinsurance mechanism.

On the basis of the federal government's superior ability to diversify intertemporally, Lewis and Murdock (1996) contend that a targeted, risk-specific federal reinsurance program could expand the supply of reinsurance without imposing a large liability on the federal government. Typically, the cost-of-funds advantage of private reinsurers over a ceding insurer relates to an improved ability to diversify risk geographically and, for some levels of risk, intertemporally. However, the ability of a reinsurer to diversify catastrophic risk is limited by the reinsurer's access to capital and the costs associated with the risk of insolvency. The actuarially fair premium for a hundred-year disaster is meaningless if the hundred-year disaster occurs in year 2 and bankrupts the reinsurer. Thus, even if a differential exists between the reinsurer's targeted economic return and the ceding insurer's required return, the risk premium required by the reinsurer for high-risk lines may make reinsurance unaffordable for the primary insurer. This is especially true for very high-risk exposures where the uncertainty with respect to the loss is also high.

The federal government, on the other hand, carries a near zero default rate. Therefore, a federal reinsurer would not be subject to insolvency risk and the limitations that insolvency risk places on a private reinsurer's access to capital. As a result, the risk premiums required by a federal reinsurer for upper layers of catastrophic risk would be significantly below the premiums required by private reinsurers. If this cost-of-capital advantage exceeds any efficiency losses associated with the federalization of this form of reinsurance, the supply of reinsurance will expand, creating additional capacity in the primary-insurance market. In addition, since catastrophic reinsurance capacity is almost nonexistent for upper layers of loss, inefficiency costs will most likely be small

2. Testing the existence of state "rate suppression" or "rate stickiness" with respect to catastrophe loads is outside the scope of this paper. However, it should be noted that the existence of state "rate stickiness" can account only for the failure of insurance rates to adjust to higher levels in the postdisaster environment in California since rates in the state were not approved before 1990.

as long as the federal reinsurance program is adequately targeted to insuring catastrophic risk.

3.1.2   The Proposed Contract

The objective of catastrophic reinsurance is to provide per occurrence protection for losses (L) that exceed some trigger level (T) based on the level of losses that the insurer can absorb. By design, once an event exceeds this trigger, the reinsurance pays (some fixed proportion of) disaster losses (L) usually up to some predetermined cap C on the reinsurer's exposure. Therefore, if losses are less than the trigger, the contract pays nothing. If losses fall in the range between the trigger and the cap, the contract pays out $L - T$. If losses exceed the cap, the contract pays out the difference between the cap and the trigger, or $C - T$. Using this basic structure, one can specify the payout (P) of the reinsurance as follows:[3]

$$
\begin{aligned}
\text{(1)} \qquad P &= \text{Max}\,[0,\, \text{Min}\,(L - T,\ C - T)] \\
&= \text{Max}\,[0,\ L - T] - \text{Max}\,[0,\ L - C].
\end{aligned}
$$

As the expression following the second equals sign in (1) reveals, the reinsurance contract is simply the difference between two call options with different strike prices, that is, a call-option spread, written on the loss exposure of the underlying event. This specification corresponds directly with conventional per occurrence reinsurance and with the structure of the catastrophe call options being traded on the Chicago Board of Trade (CBOT) (see Cummins and Geman 1995) and thus provides a financial framework for structuring the federal reinsurance role.

Under the proposed reinsurance program, the federal government would directly write and sell contingent claims against the upper (capped) layers of catastrophic disaster losses on a per occurrence basis. These contingent claims, hereafter referred to as *excess-of-loss* (XOL) contracts, would be available for qualified insurance companies, pools, and reinsurers and would cover industry losses from a disaster in the $25–$50 billion layer of coverage—a layer currently unavailable in the private market.

Like private catastrophe covers, these XOL contracts would provide coverage for a single event, not an aggregation of losses over a fixed period. However, like the CBOT options, the reinsurance trigger and cap would be based on insured industry losses to minimize the moral hazard and adverse-selection problems associated with writing company-specific reinsurance.[4] The payout

---

3. This specification oversimplifies somewhat the actual contract payoff. For a more detailed discussion, see Lewis and Murdock (1996).

4. For a review of the problems of adverse selection and moral hazard in insurance markets, see Dionne and Doherty (1992). For recent discussions involving catastrophe reinsurance and futures markets, see D'Arcy and France (1992), Cummins and Geman (1994), and Lewis and Murdock (1996).

function on these XOL contracts would also be a function of industry losses and would be fixed at the time the contract is issued. Thus, the expected payout of the contract would be reexpressed as follows:

(2) $$P = \text{Max}\,[0,\,\delta(L - T)] - \text{Max}\,[0,\,\delta(L - C)],$$

where $\delta(\cdot)$ represents the payout function of the contract, which depends on the difference between the level of total industry losses and the contract trigger or strike price.

As mentioned above, the XOL contracts offered by the federal government would be analogous to writing a call option for the insurance industry that pays off when industry disaster losses exceed \$25 billion, along with a "short" call option such that industry losses in excess of \$50 billion are retained by the insurance industry (i.e., buyers of the contract would be "long" in the call option with strike price T and short in a call with strike price C).

Thus, the payout to insurers of the first (long) call-option component of the XOL contract rises as a fixed proportion of industry losses in excess of \$25 billion once the \$25 billion threshold is reached. However, once industry losses exceed \$50 billion, the second (short) component of the XOL contract provides an equal offset to any additional industry losses above \$50 billion. As a result, the federal government's exposure is limited to covering losses in the \$25–\$50 billion range. On the basis of this payout structure, insurance and reinsurance companies could decide on the optimal number of contracts to purchase in order to hedge their catastrophe-loss exposure.

Other aspects of the XOL contracts include the following:

a) As mentioned above, the contracts would cover insured property losses from hurricanes, earthquakes, and volcanic activity. Qualified lines of insurance for earthquake damage would include property losses in earthquake-shake policies (written separately or as part of a homeowner's policy), commercial multiperil, and commercial inland marine coverage associated with earthquakes. For hurricane damage, losses covered by homeowner's, wind (written separately or as part of a homeowner's policy), commercial multiperil, fire, allied, farmowner's, and commercial inland marine policies would be covered. For reporting purposes, estimates reported by the state insurance commissioner's office in each affected state would be used as an index of loss, with validation accomplished through year-end tax filings.

b) The XOL contracts would be sold annually with a maturity of one year. However, each contract would include a renewal provision that allows the holder of an exercised contract to purchase an additional contract to cover losses to the end of the original contract year at a cost of the original premium prorated to the remaining term on the exercised contract. An alternative form of the contracts, also under discussion, would cover the insurer for multiple events over a period of one year. This form would be equivalent to including an automatic renewability feature in the contract.

c) The trigger level of the contracts would be set at a level above the layers of reinsurance being provided in the private markets. On the basis of evidence provided by private reinsurers and the levels of coverage available in the CBOT market, the trigger (*T*) is set initially at $25 billion in industry losses. This trigger level of coverage would be adjusted or indexed annually to the rate of property-value inflation.

d) The fact that the actual distribution of catastrophic losses is unknown and must be estimated from imperfect data exposes the federal government to parameter-estimation risk as well as the risk of the underlying process. To place a cap on the government's exposure, the upper limit of the reinsurance contract is initially set at $50 billion. Again, the level of the cap can be adjusted annually to reflect property-value inflation.

e) The payout function of the XOL contract stipulates how much each individual contract will pay in the event the contract trigger is reached. As proposed, $\delta(\cdot)$ simply represents a scalar function relating industry losses to the desired denomination of each contract. That is, $\delta(\cdot)$ is set so that each contract pays out $1 million for every $1 billion by which industry losses exceeded the trigger:

$$(3) \qquad \delta(\cdot) \;=\; \frac{1}{1000}\,(L - T).$$

This simple payout function, which by construction includes a contract payout cap equal to $25 million, would provide a total capacity of one thousand contracts being sold annually. A more complicated specification for $\delta(\cdot)$ is, of course, possible, but we will assume that the contracts will be based on the simple linear structure given by (3).

f) Only insured losses paid during the eighteen-month period immediately following the disaster and reported to the federal government within twenty-one months of the event date will be covered to limit the tail on the contract payout and to prevent the accumulation of losses over a series of events. While helping protect against fraud and abuse, this provision has the additional advantage of encouraging insurance companies to expedite the processing of claims in the wake of a disaster—a social good from a policy standpoint.

g) Private reinsurance firms, primary insurance companies, and state, regional, and national pools would be eligible to purchase and exercise federal XOL contracts, as long as they are licensed to write property-casualty insurance or reinsurance in a state in the United States and are actively providing insurance/reinsurance for property located in the United States.

To accelerate the development of a private reinsurance market to "crowd out" the federal government in the provision of catastrophe-reinsurance coverage layers, these XOL contracts could be priced using a private market cost-of-capital adjustment. That is, the reservation price established for the XOL contracts could be based, not on the federal government's cost of borrowing, but on a private market discount rate or hurdle rate established by the federal government. For additional details regarding the contracts, see Lewis and Murdock (1996).

3.2 Pricing Methodology

Pricing the contracts involves two steps: (1) estimating the loss distribution and the expected value of loss and (2) incorporating a risk premium and expense loading in the contract price. These steps are discussed below, following a general discussion of the pricing rationale for the contracts.

3.2.1 Pricing Rationale

Ideally, an insurance risk pool would be able to diversify risk across time as well as across exposure units in the pool at a given point in time. Most discussions of risk diversification through pooling consider only the latter dimension (for a review, see Cummins [1991]). Adding the time dimension can significantly reduce the standard deviation of losses from a pool of risks, reducing the residual risk faced by pool participants. As a simple example, consider a pool consisting of N independent, identically distributed exposure units with expected loss μ and variance of loss σ^2. The mean of the pool loss is then $N\mu$, and the variance is $N\sigma^2$, yielding a coefficient of variation (a standard measure of the "insurer's risk") of $\sigma/(\mu\sqrt{N})$. If the pool can also diversify across time, the coefficient of variation becomes $\sigma/(\mu\sqrt{TN})$, where T = the number of time periods. Therefore, time diversification has the potential to reduce the insurer's risk significantly.

In a theoretical world, under the assumptions of perfect information, no transactions costs or contract-enforcement costs, and no probability of bankruptcy, time diversification would merely involve the pool's borrowing at the risk-free rate of interest when losses exceed the expected value of loss and lending (or repaying loans against the pool) when losses are less than their expected value. In principle, mutual insurers operate much like the theoretical risk pool, accumulating retained earnings when losses are less than expected and drawing down equity or borrowing to pay losses that are greater than expected. A stock insurer operates similarly except that the firm can raise funds by issuing equity as well as through borrowing and retaining earnings. Thus, at least in theory, both types of insurers diversify risk across time.

Because the assumptions underlying the pure risk pool hold only as approximations in the real world, however, insurance markets do not fully achieve time diversification. Time diversification fails most acutely in the case of very large losses, such as those resulting from catastrophes. Because capital is costly, insurers cannot maintain a sufficient equity cushion to guarantee the pool against bankruptcy. The possibility of bankruptcy, along with information imperfections in insurance and capital markets, is primarily responsible for the failure of time diversification for large losses.

The existence of these market imperfections implies that the cost of both debt and equity capital is likely to rise significantly following a large loss or an unusual accumulation of small losses. Prospective capital providers are concerned about the long-term viability of insurers that have suffered major loss shocks, and they are also worried that the insurers' reserves are not adequate to fund the losses from the catastrophe. The cost of capital reflects these information asymmetries, and, therefore, capital costs more following a loss shock than it would if the insurance and capital markets were frictionless and complete information were available. Thus, the insurer may not survive long enough to deliver a fair return on equity or repay loans needed to fund loss payments. The cost of capital would reflect these market imperfections, and capital would cost more than if the insurance and capital markets were frictionless and complete information was available. In the extreme, capital may not be available at any price to some insurers following a major loss shock.

The federal government is better able than the private-insurance market to diversify large losses across time efficiently. The principal reason is that the riskless borrowing and lending assumption required for time diversification that does not apply to private insurers applies to the federal government, allowing it to borrow at the risk-free rate to fund losses arising from a catastrophe and then to repay the loans out of subsequent premium payments in periods when no severe catastrophes occur. Implicitly, premiums paid into a catastrophe-reinsurance program in excess of accumulated losses go to offset federal debt arising from other programs, so the pool is in effect "lending" at the risk-free rate during these periods. The ability of the federal government to time diversify would ensure the availability of reinsurance at a cost of capital that does not include a margin for information asymmetries and other market imperfections. Even with a risk premium to encourage private market crowding out of the federal contracts, the cost of capital would be lower than if the reinsurance were provided privately.

The discussion of time diversification suggests the following basic principle for pricing the federal XOL contracts: The contracts should be self-supporting in expected value; that is, the expected costs to the government of operating the program should be zero, where the expectation is defined as including the expected value of losses and other program costs across time. In principle, the price should also reflect financing costs. However, the net financing costs of the program are expected to be zero if the premiums are retained by the government. This is the case because the costs of borrowing to pay catastrophe losses are offset in expectation by the proceeds gained by "lending" the premium payments to the federal government during periods when no losses occur.

As mentioned above, the proposal calls for adding a risk premium to the contracts so that their prices will approximate the price that would be charged in the private marketplace in the absence of severe information imperfections (i.e., a normal risk charge or cost of capital). The risk can be viewed as a way to ensure that there would not be any unintended consequences in the private insurance and reinsurance markets due to the proposed program. This risk charge can also be viewed as compensating the government for other unforeseen costs that could arise under the program. Thus, the final price will be the expected value of loss plus administrative expenses and a risk loading.

3.2.2 The Loss Distribution and Its Moments

We develop the pricing model under two alternative assumptions regarding the design of the reinsurance contracts: (1) that the contracts cover only one loss, with the option to purchase an additional contract covering one loss for the balance of the year based on a price equal to the original price times the proportion of the year remaining after the first loss, and (2) that the contracts cover a theoretically unlimited number of multiple losses during a period of one year.

(Renewable) Contracts Covering a Single Loss Event

Using generalizations of standard actuarial formulas, the loss distribution under the proposed contract can be written as follows:

$$F(L) = \sum_{N=0}^{\infty} p(N)q(L > T|N)S(L|L > T)$$
$$(4)$$
$$= S(L|L > T)\sum_{N=0}^{\infty} p(N)q(L > T|N),$$

where $F(L)$ = the distribution function of catastrophic losses; $p(N)$ = the probability that N catastrophes occur during the contract period; $q(L > T|N)$ = the probability that one catastrophe exceeds the trigger level of losses, conditional on the occurrence of N catastrophes; and $S(L|L > T)$ = the distribution function of the severity of catastrophic loss, conditional on losses from a catastrophe exceeding the trigger. Thus, payment under the contract requires the occurrence of some number N of catastrophes (an event with probability $p(N)$) such that one loss exceeds the trigger level (T) (an event with probability $q(L > T|N)$). Both $p(N)$ and $q(L > T|N)$ are discrete probability distributions. The severity of the loss (loss amount), given that the loss exceeds the trigger, is assumed to follow the continuous probability distribution function $S(L|L > T)$. Even though the contract terminates following the first catastrophe where losses exceed the trigger, the exposure to a catastrophe of this magnitude increases with the number of catastrophes that occur.

The summation on the right-hand side of the second line of equation (4) gives the unconditional (on N) probability of a loss above the trigger point. We call this probability $(p*)$. To obtain an expression for the unconditional probability $(p*)$, we first derive $q(L > T|N)$. For any one catastrophe, let $\Pr(L \leq T) = P_<$ and $\Pr(L > T) = P_>$, and observe that

$$q(L > T|N) = P_> + P_< P_> + P_<^2 P_> + \cdots + P_<^{N-1} P_>$$

(5)

$$= P_> \frac{1 - P_<^N}{1 - P_<} = 1 - P_<^N.$$

Intuitively, catastrophes are assumed to arrive sequentially throughout the year.[5] On the arrival of the first catastrophe, the reinsurance contract pays off if the losses from this catastrophe exceed T, an event that occurs with probability $P_>$. If the first catastrophe does not exceed the trigger level (an event with probability $P_<$), then the contract pays off if the second catastrophic loss exceeds T, with the result that the probability that the second catastrophe triggers the contract is $P_< P_>$, and so on.

The unconditional probability of a loss exceeding the trigger ($p*$) is then obtained as the expected value of $q(L > T|N)$ over N. The result is

(6) $p* = E_p[q(L > T|N)] = [1 - E_p(P_<^N)] = \{1 - M_p[\ln(P_<)]\}$,

where $M_p[\ln(P_<)]$ = the moment-generating function of the probability distribution $p(N)$. Thus, if claim arrivals are Poisson distributed,

(7) $p* = [1 - e^{\lambda(e^{\ln(P_<)}-1)}] = [1 - e^{\lambda(P_<-1)}] = [1 - e^{-\lambda P_>}]$,

where λ = the parameter of the Poisson distribution. And, if claims arrive according to a negative binomial distribution, then

(8) $p* = \left\{1 - \left[\dfrac{\rho}{1 - (1 - \rho)e^{\ln(P_<)}}\right]^\alpha\right\} = \left\{1 - \left[\dfrac{\rho}{1 - (1 - \rho)P_<}\right]^\alpha\right\}$,

where α and ρ are the parameters of the negative binomial distribution, which is

(9) $$p(k) = \binom{\alpha + k - 1}{k} \rho^\alpha (1 - \rho)^k$$

for $k = 0, 1, 2. \ldots$.

The moments of $F(L)$ can be derived from the moment-generating function

(10) $M_F(t) = (1 - p*) + p* \int_L^\infty e^{tL} s(L|L > T) dL$

$$= (1 - p*) + p* M_{S|L>T}(t),$$

where $M_F(t)$ = the moment-generating function of $F(L)$, and $M_{S|L>T}(t)$ = the moment-generating function of the distribution $S(L|L > T)$. The mean and variance of $F(L)$ are, respectively,

---

5. Equation (5) is the distribution function of the geometric distribution. As shown by the rightmost expression in (5), the probability of an event that exceeds the threshold is one minus the probability that none of the N events exceeds the threshold.

(11a) $E(L) = p^*\mu_1,$

(11b) $\mathrm{Var}(L) = p^*\mu_2 - p^{*2}\mu_1^2 = p^*(\mu_2 - \mu_1^2) + \mu_1^2 p^*(1 - p^*),$

where μ_i = the ith moment about the origin of the distribution $S(L|L > T)$.

We next consider the severity distribution $S(L|L > T)$. We derive the expected severity under the assumption that the catastrophic loss distribution is shifted from the origin to point $0 < d \leq T$. This allows for the possibility of defining catastrophes as being events of some minimal size d, with the result that the support of the distribution is the interval $[d, \infty]$ rather than the usual support interval for loss severity of $[0, \infty]$.[6] Thus, L is distributed as $S(L - d)$, $L \geq d$; and the expected severity for a call option on L with strike price T is then given by

(12)
$$E(L - T|L > T) = \mu_{1T} = \int_T^\infty (L - T)dS(L - d|L > T)$$
$$= \int_T^\infty [1 - S(L - d|L > T)]dL,$$

where μ_{1T} = the expected severity of loss under a call with trigger T. The second moment about the origin for the call-option severity is

(13)
$$E[(L - T)^2|L > T] = \mu_{2T} = \int_T^\infty (L - T)^2 dS(L - d|L > T)$$
$$= 2\int_T^\infty (L - T)[1 - S(L - d|L > T)]dL,$$

where μ_{2T} = the second moment about the origin of the severity of loss under a call with trigger T.[7]

The corresponding moments of the severity of loss for the call spread can then be written conveniently as

(14)
$$\mu_{1CT} = \int_T^C (L - T)dS(L - d|L > T)$$
$$+ (C - T)[1 - S(C - d|L > T)]$$
$$= \int_T^C [1 - S(L - d|L > T)]dL,$$

(15)
$$\mu_{2CT} = \int_T^C (L - T)^2 dS(L - d|L > T)$$
$$+ (C - T)^2[1 - S(C - d|L > T)]$$
$$= 2\int_T^C (L - T)[1 - S(L - d|L > T)dL,$$

6. Shifting the distribution enables us to deal with data such as that on catastrophes collected by Property Claims Services (PCS), an insurance-industry statistical agent. PCS defines catastrophes as losses from catastrophic perils that cause insured property damage of $5 million or more. This database is analyzed in detail later in the paper.

7. The right-most expressions in (12) and (13) are obtained by integrating by parts.

where μ_{1CT} = the first moment about the origin of the severity of loss for a call spread with trigger T and cap C, and μ_{2CT} = the second moment about the origin of the severity of loss for a call spread with trigger T and cap C. The mean and variance of the call spread are then given by respectively,

(16a) $E_F(L; T, C) = p^*\mu_{1TC}$,

(16b) $Var_F(L; T, C) = p^*\mu_{2TC} - p^{*2}\mu_{1TC}^2$

$$= p^*(\mu_{2TC} - \mu_{1TC}^2) + \mu_{1TC}^2 p^*(1 - p^*),$$

where p^* is given by expression (6), and μ_{1CT} and μ_{2CT} are from (14) and (15).

Contracts Covering Multiple Losses

If the contracts cover multiple losses during a specified period, the frequency distribution becomes

(17) $$p_k(k; L > T) = \sum_{N=k}^{\infty} p(N)p_k(k; L > T|N),$$

where $p_k(k; L > T)$ = the probability that the XOL contracts are triggered k times during the coverage period, unconditional on the total number of catastrophes; and $p_k(k; L > T|N)$ = the probability that the XOL contracts are triggered k times during the coverage period, conditional on the occurrence of N total catastrophes. The distribution $p_k(k; L > T|N)$ is a binomial distribution with parameters $P_>$ and N. If $p(N)$ is Poisson with parameter λ, then it can be shown that $p_k(k; L > T) = p_k(k)$ is Poisson with parameter $\lambda P_>$. Similarly, if $p(N)$ is negative binomial with parameters ρ and α (see eq. [9]), $p_k(k)$ is also negative binomial with parameters α and $\beta = (\rho'P_>)/(1 - P_<\rho')$. The mean and variance of the call spread are then given by

(18a) $E_F(L; T, C) = E_k(k)\mu_{1TC}$,

(18b) $Var_F(L; T, C) = E_k(k)(\mu_{2TC} - \mu_{1TC}^2) - Var_k(k)\mu_{1TC}^2$,

where $E_k(k)$ = the expected value of frequency based on the distribution $p_k(k; L > T)$, and $Var_k(k)$ = the variance of frequency based on the distribution $p_k(k; L > T)$.

3.2.3   Risk and Expense Loadings

There are two primary approaches to incorporating risk loadings into prices of insurance and reinsurance contracts—the actuarial approach and the financial approach. An extensive literature exists on actuarial pricing principles (e.g., Goovaerts, de Vylder, and Haezendonck 1984; Buhlmann 1984; Wang 1995). The actuarial pricing principles usually imply that prices should have some desirable mathematical properties such as value additivity or that firms behave as if they were risk averse so that prices can be derived using utility functions. Although the lack of theoretical foundation for most additive risk-loading formulas and the assumption of firm utility functions would seem to rule out the actuarial approach, these approaches may provide some useful information in solving the pricing problem, under the interpretation that they provide a way to incorporate judgmental risk premiums in option prices on nonhedgeable stochastic processes. However, in this role, they should be considered subordinated to financial pricing approaches.

Financial pricing models are the most appropriate way to price the catastrophe-reinsurance contracts. Financial pricing models incorporate risk loadings that are based on an asset-pricing model or, minimally, avoid the creation of arbitrage opportunities. The classic paper on the pricing of options on jump processes is Merton (1976). More recent extensions are Naik and Lee (1990), Heston (1993), Aase (1993), and Chang (1995). The principal problem in applying option-pricing methodologies to options on catastrophes is that these methodologies are based on arbitrage arguments that do not apply in general to jump processes. The problem is one of market incompleteness when jumps in asset prices are possible. Market incompleteness implies that jump risk cannot be hedged, and therefore arbitrage arguments generally do not apply.

Because of the market-incompleteness problem, some additional assumptions are needed to price options on jump processes. Merton (1976) circumvents the problem by assuming that assets are priced according to the capital asset–pricing model (CAPM) and that jump risk is nonsystematic, that is, not correlated with the market portfolio of securities. If the risk of catastrophes is unsystematic, catastrophe risk can be diversified away by investors, and thus the return on the catastrophe reinsurance option is equivalent to the risk-free rate. Merton derives the formula for option prices on jump processes under these assumptions, with the magnitude of jump risk assumed to follow a lognormal distribution.[8]

If the assumption that jump risk is nonsystematic is not viewed as satisfactory—for example, because market prices respond to large catastrophes or because federal borrowing to fund the reinsurance contracts increases market interest rates—then other assumptions can be used to price the options. One approach is to assume that jumps can assume only a finite number of constant magnitudes and that a sufficient number of traded securities exist that are correlated with the jumps to permit the formation of portfolios to hedge the jump risk (see, e.g., Cummins and Geman 1995). This is equivalent to breaking up the severity of loss distribution applicable to catastrophes into a finite sequence of mass points. Gerber (1982) shows how this can be done while preserving

---

8. Chang (1995) shows that Merton's assumption of diversifiable jump risk is consistent with no arbitrage only when the aggregate consumption flow is not subject to jumps. If that assumption does not hold, Merton's formula underprices hedging assets and overprices cyclic assets. Cyclic assets are defined as assets subject to jumps that are negatively correlated with jumps in aggregate consumption, while hedging assets are defined as assets subject to jumps that are positively correlated with aggregate consumption jumps.

the moments of the severity distribution. If only the first few moments (such as the mean and the variance) of severity are of interest, this approach could prove to be effective. However, the moments do not uniquely characterize most probability distributions, including the lognormal (Johnson and Kotz 1970). Thus, if the first two or three moments are not sufficient for pricing the contracts, this approach may not be satisfactory.

An alternative approach that does not require constant jump sizes is to make an assumption about investor preferences. In a recent paper, Chang (1995) derives pricing formulas for traded and nontraded options under the following assumptions: (1) aggregate consumption follows a jump-diffusion process, and (2) preferences can be incorporated using the assumption that there exists a representative investor whose utility function is of the constant relative risk aversion type. Chang presents an option-pricing model that is "distribution free" in the sense that it places no restrictions on the probability distributions of the magnitudes of jumps in the value of the underlying asset or the "market portfolio," which in this case is aggregate consumption. Chang (1995) gives formulas for the option price in the case where jump sizes in aggregate consumption and in the strike price are jointly lognormal. However, it would also be possible to calculate option prices using other multivariate distributions that sometimes provide better models of catastrophic losses, such as the multivariate Burr 12 distribution (see Johnson and Kotz 1972). The approach could be implemented through numerical integration, based on Chang's pricing formulas.

We decided not to attempt to parameterize an option-pricing model for two primary reasons: (1) the option-model adjustment in the expected value price obtained from our pricing model is likely to be a second-order effect, and (2) the data available to parameterize the option-pricing model are likely to be inadequate to yield reliable parameter estimates. The problem is that the value of the underlying asset (property subject to insured catastrophe loss) is not available except at the time of the decennial U.S. Census. Thus, the calculation of essential quantities such as the instantaneous volatility parameter would have to rely on data that may be unreliable proxies for the actual value of insured property. Since option values are very sensitive to the key parameter estimates, this could introduce potentially serious error into the premium estimates.

Relying on the argument that the risk of loss from hurricanes and earthquakes is likely to be largely unsystematic, we propose using the expected-loss values based on our formulas as the basis for the price of the XOL options. This is essentially equivalent to using Merton's approach except that we substitute the loss estimates derived below for the lognormal distributions on which the Merton jump-option-pricing formula is based. As in our prices, no explicit market-risk premium is included in Merton's option-pricing formula. However, his formula does recognize the time value of money by discounting the anticipated payout under the option at the risk-free rate of interest. Our formula could also incorporate a discount factor for the time value of money. The appropriate period would be the expected time of the payment under the renewable option. However, under the multiple-claim option, technically it would be appropriate to discount each expected payment for its specific expected time of arrival. This could be done under the Poisson distribution using the duality between the Poisson process and the exponential distribution of the time of arrival between events. However, this, too, is an adjustment of second order in importance and probably not worth the extra effort.

Consequently, the final step in pricing is to incorporate expenses into the price of the contracts using the usual actuarial formula,

$$(19) \qquad G(S, \ \tau) \ = \ \frac{F(S, \ \tau)}{(1 \ - \ e)(1 \ + \ r)^{t}},$$

where $G(L; T, C, d)$ = the expected loss loaded for expenses and discounted, e = the expense ratio (ratio of expenses to the gross premium), r = the risk-free rate (e.g., the ninety-day Treasury bill rate), and t = expected time of arrival of the first event that triggers the contracts. The price based on (19) should be viewed as the federal government's *reservation price,* that is, the minimum price at which the contracts should be sold. If a higher price results when the contracts are auctioned, they should be sold at the auction price. The contracts should not be issued if the reservation price is not realized because that is likely to expose the government to an expected loss from issuing the contracts.

3.3   Hedging Catastrophe Risk with Federal XOL Reinsurance

This section illustrates how the proposed federal excess-of-loss (XOL) reinsurance contracts could be used by an insurer to hedge its exposure to the risk of hurricanes, earthquakes, and volcanic activity. It is assumed that the insurer's objective is to protect its equity capital and achieve other business objectives by optimally reducing the variance of its loss ratio.[9] This objective is consistent with the literature on insurance futures and options (e.g., Buhlmann 1995; Niehaus and Mann 1992). More general discussions of the rationale for managing firm risk are provided in Froot, Scharfstein, and Stein (1994), Mayers and Smith (1982), and Shapiro and Titman (1985). Insurers may find it advantageous to manage their net income risk in order to minimize taxes (Cummins and Grace 1994), protect franchise values, reduce regulatory costs, and avoid being penalized in the insurance market for changes in insolvency risk.

To model the insurer's loss ratio and hedging strategy, let L_{CA} = catastrophe losses of insurer A, L_{NA} = noncatastrophe losses of insurer A, L_{CI} = catastrophe

---

9. Because premiums can be treated as nonstochastic, it is not necessary to work with loss ratios. Loss ratios are used here because they provide a familiar and convenient framework for evaluating hedging strategies in insurance.

losses of the insurers included in the catastrophe loss index, P_A = premiums of company A in lines affected by catastrophes, and P_I = premiums for insurers reporting data to the catastrophe loss index. Insurer A's loss ratio is then defined as

$$(20) \qquad R_A = \frac{L_{NA}}{P_A} + \frac{L_{CA}}{P_A}.$$

Assuming that the company buys some number N_A of XOL contracts, its loss ratio will be

$$(21) \qquad R_A = \frac{L_{NA}}{P_A} + \frac{L_{CA}}{P_A} - \frac{N_A}{P_A}\left\{\frac{\text{Max}[L_{CI} - T, \; 0]}{1,000} - \frac{\text{Max}[L_{CI} - C, \; 0]}{1,000}\right\}.$$

It is assumed that L_{NA} is independent of L_{CA} and L_{CI} but that L_{CA} and L_{CI} are not independent.

As a first example, we assume that the company's objective is to cap its loss ratio due to catastrophes at the industrywide loss ratio represented by the trigger point of the XOL contract. Assume that industrywide premiums from policies covering perils included in the XOL contracts equal $100 billion.[10] Then the federal XOL contracts can be viewed as providing a twenty-five/fifty loss ratio call spread, that is, as providing protection for loss ratios due to catastrophes ranging from 25 to 50 percent of premiums. The number of contracts that the insurer would purchase to implement this strategy is given by

$$(22) \qquad N_A = \left(\frac{C - T}{P_I}\right)\frac{P_A}{S},$$

where S = contract size = $25 billion/1,000 = $25 million.

A numerical example based on this hedging strategy is provided in Table 3.1. We assume that company A's share of the market for coverages affected by catastrophes is 1.2 percent and that its premium volume from policies covering perils included in the XOL pool is therefore $1.2 billion.[11] We focus first on case A of table 3.1. This case assumes a catastrophic loss of $40 billion, giving an industry loss ratio from catastrophic losses of 40 percent. It is also assumed that company A's catastrophic losses are perfectly correlated with the industry's catastrophic losses, with the result that company A's catastrophe-loss ratio is also 40 percent. Given company A's premium volume, this implies that company A suffers catastrophe losses of $480 million. Equation (19) implies that the insurer purchases twelve XOL reinsurance contracts. The payoff per

10. Actual industry premiums for fire, allied lines, inland marine, farmowner's, homeowner's, commercial multiple peril, and auto physical damage, the coverages included in the federal XOL contracts, totaled $94.5 billion in 1994 (A. M. Best Co. 1995).

11. The fifteenth largest property-liability insurer in the United States has a market share of 1.3 percent, and the twentieth largest has a market share of 1 percent (A. M. Best Co. 1995).

Table 3.1   **Hedging Example Using Federal XOL Reinsurance**

	Case A	Case B	Case C	Case D
Industry data				
Industry premiums ($)	100,000,000	100,000,000	100,000,000	100,000,000
Company A data				
Company A's				
market share (%)	1.20	1.20	1.20	1.20
Company A's				
premiums ($)	1,200,000	1,200,000	1,200,000	1,200.000
Federal XOL contracts				
Trigger expressed as loss				
ratio (%)	25.00	25.00	25.00	25.00
Cap expressed as loss				
ratio (%)	50.00	50.00	50.00	50.00
Contract size ($)	25,000	25,000	25,000	25,000
Hedging strategy				
Number of contracts	12.00	12.00	12.00	12.00
Evaluating the hedge				
Catastrophe size ($)	40,000,000	40,000,000	40,000,000	55,000,000
Industry catastrophe-loss				
ratio (%)	40.00	40.00	40.00	55.00
Company A's catastrophe				
losses ($)	480,000	504,000	444,000	660,000
Return per contract ($)	15,000	15,000	15,000	25,000
Company A's gain on cat				
contracts ($)	180,000	180,000	180,000	300,000
Company A's catastrophe-				
loss ratio:				
Without XOL				
reinsurance (%)	40.00	42.00	37.00	55.00
With XOL				
reinsurance (%)	25.00	27.00	22.00	30.00

Note: Case A = company A's and industry loss ratios perfectly correlated, loss less than $50 billion. Case B = company A's loss ratio greater than industry ratio, loss less than $50 billion. Case C = company A's loss ratio less than industry ratio, loss less than $50 billion. Case D = company A's and industry loss ratios perfectly correlated, loss greater than $50 billion. All dollar figures reported in thousands.

contract for a $40 billion loss is $15 million, so company A's gain from the reinsurance contracts is $15 million × 12, or $180 million. Company A's net loss from the catastrophe is $300 million ($480 million − $180 million), for a loss ratio of 25 percent. Thus, by purchasing the reinsurance contracts, company A has been able to cap its catastrophe-loss ratio at 25 percent.

Cases B and C of table 3.1 illustrate the effects of hedging when insurer A's losses are not perfectly correlated with industrywide losses. In case B, insurer A's loss ratio exceeds the industry loss ratio, and, in case C, insurer A's ratio is less than the industry ratio. In these cases, the hedge is not successful in holding the catastrophe-loss ratio to 25 percent, but the loss ratio is still substantially less than if no XOL contracts had been purchased. Case D shows the effects of a catastrophic loss ($55 billion) that exceeds the cap on the XOL contracts ($50 billion). Assuming that insurer A's losses are perfectly correlated with industry losses, insurer A's loss ratio under the XOL hedge is 30 percent, that is, the 55 percent unhedged-loss ratio minus the layer of XOL reinsurance coverage (25 percent).

The hedging strategy illustrated in table 3.1 is not necessarily optimal. To derive an optimal strategy, we consider the variance of the loss ratio. To simplify the notation, we disregard the upper limit in the XOL contracts and assume that the insurer can buy a call option with a strike price of $T = \$25$ billion. The loss-ratio variance is given by

$$(23) \quad \mathrm{Var}(R_A) = \sigma_A^2 = \frac{1}{P_A^2}(\sigma_{NA}^2 + \sigma_{CA}^2 + N_A^2\sigma_{CIT}^2 - 2N_A\sigma_{CA,\,CIT}),$$

where σ_A^2 = the variance of insurer A's loss ratio, σ_{NA}^2 = the variance of insurer A's noncatastrophe losses, σ_{CA}^2 = the variance of insurer A's catastrophic losses, σ_{CIT}^2 = the variance of losses included in the XOL reinsurance-contract pool, and $\sigma_{CA,CIT}$ = the covariance of insurer A's catastrophe losses with the losses included in the XOL pool. To find the number of contracts that minimizes the loss-ratio variance, we differentiate equation (20) with respect to N_A and set the resulting expression equal to zero, obtaining

$$(24) \quad N_A = \frac{\sigma_{CA,\,CIT}}{\sigma_{CIT}} = \frac{\rho_{CA,\,CIT}\sigma_{CA}}{\sigma_{CIT}},$$

where $\rho_{CA,CIT}$ = the correlation coefficient of L_{CA} and $\mathrm{Max}[L_{CI} - T, 0]/1,000$. Thus, to estimate the optimal number of contracts, the insurer would have to estimate the variance of its catastrophe losses, the variance of the losses in the XOL pool, and the correlation coefficient between its losses and the pool losses. The optimal number of contracts is increasing in the insurer's variance and the correlation coefficient and decreasing in the variance of the pool's losses.

3.4 Empirical Estimates of Catastrophic Losses and XOL Premiums

Two principal methods exist that could be used to develop empirical estimates of catastrophic losses: (1) fitting probability distributions to historical catastrophe-loss-experience data and (2) engineering simulation analysis. Both methods are utilized in this paper. Our historical catastrophe-loss-experience data are the insured catastrophic property losses reported to Property Claims Services (PCS), an insurance-industry statistical agent, for the period 1949–94. The engineering simulation analysis is based on catastrophe-loss simulations provided to us by Risk Management Solutions (RMS), a private firm that conducts research on the economic effects of catastrophes for insurance companies and other interested parties. The RMS analysis utilizes engineering and statistical techniques to simulate the probability and severity of catastrophes. This information is then merged with the firm's extensive database on insured-property exposures to estimate insured losses. Conducting the estimates on the basis of two sources of data provides a reasonableness check on the results and should provide the government and industry with a higher degree of confidence in the results than if only one source of data were used.

3.4.1   Loss-Severity Models

In modeling loss severity, it is important to fit a probability distribution to the observed data as well as evaluating the observed data directly. By fitting a probability distribution to the data, it is possible to model loss expectations in the tail of the loss distribution for ranges of losses larger than those contained in the data set. This is especially important when the sample size is small and/or very large events are possible but have low probabilities of occurrence.

On the basis of prior experience with modeling severity-of-loss distributions, we utilize four probability distributions as possible models for loss severity, the Pareto, the lognormal, the Burr 12, and the generalized beta of type 2 (GB2) (see Cummins et al. 1990; and Cummins and McDonald 1991). The density functions for these distributions are given below:

(25)   Lognormal: $s(L) = \dfrac{1}{(L - d)\sigma\sqrt{2\pi}} e^{-\left[\frac{\ln(L - d) - \mu}{\sigma}\right]^2}, \ L > d,$

(26)   Pareto: $s(L) = \alpha d^\alpha L^{-(1 + \alpha)}, \ L > d,$

(27)   Burr 12: $s(L) = \dfrac{|a|q(L - d)^{a-1}}{b^a\left[1 + \left(\dfrac{L - d}{b}\right)^a\right]^{q+1}}, \ L > d,$

(28)   GB2: $s(L) = \dfrac{|a|(L - d)^{ap-1}}{b^{ap}B(p, \ q)\left[1 + \left(\dfrac{L - d}{b}\right)^a\right]^{p+q}}, \ L > d,$

where $B(p, q)$ is the beta function. Because catastrophic losses are often defined as losses that exceed some monetary threshold, the probability distributions have been shifted so that they are defined for losses in excess of some threshold $d > 0$.

3.4.2   Loss Estimates Based on PCS Data

PCS defines a property catastrophe as a single event that gives rise to insured property damages of at least $5 million (the limit was $1 million prior to 1983). PCS obtains loss estimates by state for each catastrophe from individual insurers. The catastrophes reported include hurricanes, tornadoes, windstorms, hail, fires and explosions, riots, brush fires, and floods.[12]

It is important to be cautious in using historical loss data because systemic changes may have occurred such that prior catastrophes may not be representative of those that will occur in the future. Systemic changes may involve both frequency and severity of loss. For example, climatological changes may have occurred that increase either the frequency or the severity of various catastrophic perils. Economic and demographic changes can also affect catastrophe losses.

Fortunately, it is possible to adjust for most of the important systemic changes involving the frequency and severity of catastrophes. The two major factors affecting the severity of catastrophes are price-level changes (i.e., changes in construction costs and other factors that affect the prices of property exposed to loss) and changes in the amount of property exposed to loss. The latter adjustment is particularly important because several of the states with the highest exposure to catastrophe risk (such as California, Florida, and Texas) have been among the fastest-growing states over the past several decades.

We use two alternative approaches to adjust for changes in price and exposure levels. The first approach is to adjust for price-level changes affecting property values by using the U.S. Department of Commerce census fixed-weighted construction-cost index (taken from various years of the *Statistical Abstract of the United States*) to restate all catastrophe-loss values in 1994 dollars. To adjust for changes in the exposure base, we use data on population by state obtained from the U.S. Bureau of the Census. This approach assumes that the amount of property exposed to loss is highly correlated with population. Each catastrophe is adjusted to 1994 price and housing-value levels using the following formula:

$$(29) \qquad L_{ijt}^{94} = L_{ijt} \frac{c_{94}}{c_t} \frac{v_{j,94}}{v_{jt}},$$

where L_{ijt}^{94} = loss from catastrophe i in state j in year t, restated in 1994 dollars and exposure levels; L_{ijt} = loss from catastrophe i in state j in year t in year-t dollars; c_{94} = construction-cost index for 1994; c_t = construction-cost index for year t; $v_{j,94}$ = population of state j in 1994; and v_{jt} = population of state j in year t. In the discussion to follow, we refer to loss data based on equation (29) as *population-adjusted (PA) losses*.

As a second approach to adjusting for changes in price levels and the amount of property exposed to loss, we use data on the value of owner-occupied housing obtained from the U.S. Census of Housing, series HC80-1-A. This series provides the value of urban and rural owner-occupied buildings in each state

---

12. The catastrophe-insurance call spreads traded on the Chicago Board of Trade (CBOT) are also based on the PCS loss data.

at ten-year intervals based on the U.S. Census.[13] The series implicitly incorporates both changes in the price of housing and changes in the physical stock of property. Thus, no price indices are needed when adjusting catastrophes using the housing-value data. We refer to the data adjusted for changes in the value of owner-occupied housing as *value-adjusted (VA) losses.*

We consider the VA losses to be the primary data series for the estimation of XOL reinsurance premiums. Accordingly, most of the summary tables and graphs given below are based only on the VA series. However, the premium and loss-layer estimates are reported on the basis of both the PA and the VA series.

The insured VA catastrophe losses from 1949 through 1994 are shown in figure 3.1. The largest losses were attributable to Hurricane Andrew, which caused $18.4 billion in insured losses in 1992, and the Northridge Earthquake, which accounted for $12.5 billion in insured losses in 1994. Value adjustment has a substantial effect on some of the earlier catastrophes. For example, after adjusting for property values, a windstorm loss in 1950 that affected eleven northeastern and Middle Atlantic states is the third most severe catastrophe. This loss ranks *much* lower in terms of the unadjusted data.

Summary statistics on VA catastrophe losses by cause of loss are shown in table 3.2. On the basis of the loss experience since 1949, earthquakes and hurricanes have been the most serious type of catastrophe, with by far the highest mean and standard deviation of loss. Earthquakes and hurricanes also have among the highest coefficients of variation and skewnesses.

In estimating potential catastrophe losses in the $25–$50 billion range, it is clear that one should focus on catastrophes that are sufficiently severe to cause damage in this layer. Relatively minor catastrophes, such as hailstorms in the Midwest, for example, have a negligible probability of ever generating a loss of $25 billion or more (the largest such loss to date was $443 million). Although windstorms other than hurricanes clearly have caused very large losses, most of the 864 windstorms in the sample were relatively minor storms, such as tornadoes, that likely did not have the potential to cause losses in the loss layer covered by the proposed reinsurance contracts.

Accordingly, we focus the remainder of the analysis on the catastrophic losses most likely to be representative of those that would generate covered losses under the reinsurance contracts—hurricanes and earthquakes. The number of events in these two categories from 1949 to 1994 was seventy-one, fifty-seven hurricanes and fourteen earthquakes (including the Northridge Earthquake). These hurricane and earthquake losses are graphed in figure 3.2. Four of the seventy-one hurricanes and earthquakes did not exceed the PCS defini-

13. Values for years in between the census years were based on the average growth rate in property values over each ten-year period. Comparable data on the value of rental properties and commercial and industrial buildings were not available. However, this should not cause a problem as long as the values of these types of properties are highly correlated with values of owner-occupied dwellings.

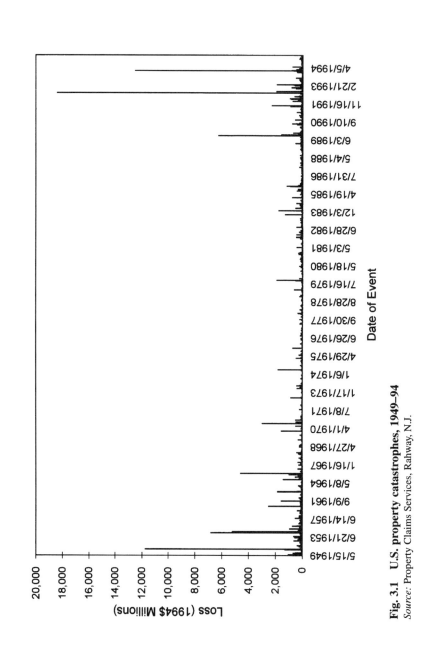

Fig. 3.1 U.S. property catastrophes, 1949–94
Source: Property Claims Services, Rahway, N.J.

Table 3.2   Summary Statistics, U.S. Property Catastrophes, 1949–94

Type of Catastrophe	N	Mean	SD	Coeff. of Var.	Skewness	Minimum	Maximum
Earthquake	14	1,079,919,991	3,313,558,418	3.07	3.64	11,852,852	12,500,000,000
Brush fire	27	228,427,389	434,833,689	1.90	4.44	3,769,473	2,296,609,302
Flood	14	73,110,934	117,528,364	1.61	2.20	7,022,724	356,502,769
Hail	53	82,098,301	90,209,509	1.10	2.11	7,992,680	443,331,807
Hurricanes	57	1,222,680,792	2,763,012,070	2.26	4.76	5,278,321	18,391,014,407
Ice	1	20,625,310	0			20,625,310	20,625,310
Snow	11	102,884,340	194,752,240	1.89	3.07	7,167,945	677,636,717
Tornado	21	74,586,127	116,138,156	1.56	3.67	3,246,349	546,706,772
Tropical storm	8	73,889,334	58,915,748	.80	1.81	19,991,072	204,946,131
Volcanic eruption	1	69,870,633	0			69,870,633	69,870,633
Wind	864	95,987,693	429,832,971	4.48	23.50	2,827,037	11,746,275,284
All other	66	108,959,698	191,921,889	1.76	3.25	3,777,433	983,118,263
Total	1,137	166,981,831	849,081,766	5.08	14.85	2,827,037	18,391,014,407

Source: Property Claims Services, Rahway, N.J.

Note: Losses were adjusted to 1994 exposure and price levels using U.S. Census of Housing's series HC80-1-A.

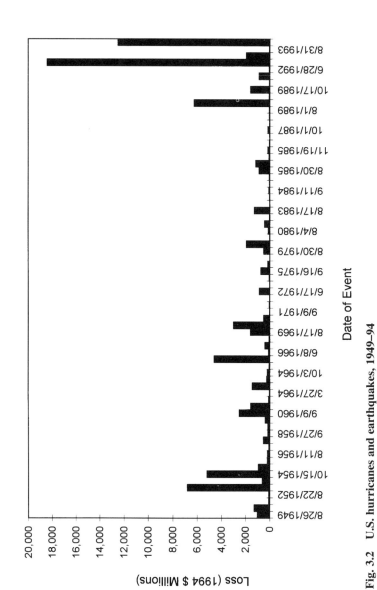

Fig. 3.2   U.S. hurricanes and earthquakes, 1949–94
Source: Property Claims Services, Rahway, N.J.

tion of a catastrophe ($12.04 million in 1994 dollars) when inflated to 1994. Consequently, these four events were dropped from the sample for the purposes of estimating severity distributions and XOL contract premiums. The final sample thus consists of sixty-seven events.

The next step is to estimate severity of loss distributions for the hurricane and earthquake data. As our value of d, the threshold that must be exceeded in order for a loss to be defined as a catastrophe, we use $12.04 million, which is the PCS lower-bound definition of a catastrophe ($5 million) inflated to 1994 price and exposure levels using the value of owner-occupied housing (i.e., the VA adjustment). Based on the PA adjustment, $d = $6.85 million.[14]

We use maximum-likelihood-estimation techniques to estimate the parameters of the various probability distributions that we employed in this study. The parameters and log-likelihood function values are shown in table 3.3, along with the RMS parameters, which are discussed later.[15] Parameter estimates are shown for both PA and VA losses. The estimated probability distributions based on the VA losses are graphed in figure 3.3. Also shown in the graph is the empirical distribution function, calculated as $i/(n + 1)$, where $i = 1, 2, \ldots,$ n, and $n =$ the number of observations. Both the lognormal and Burr 12 distributions provide excellent fits to the observed data. The GB2 (not shown) also fits well and is about the same as the Burr 12. However, the Pareto distribution tends to overestimate the amount of probability in the tail of the distribution. This is shown more clearly in figure 3.4, which graphs the tails of the estimated distribution functions, where the tail is defined somewhat arbitrarily as the largest third of the observations. From figure 3.4, it is clear that both the lognormal and the Burr 12 provide an adequate fit to the tail of the loss distribution. The tail of the Pareto is too heavy to represent the observed data. However, it is important to keep in mind the possibility of sampling error in a sample of this size, particularly if our adjustments for exposure are not sufficiently precise. Thus, we believe that the results based on the Pareto should also be considered when setting the premiums for the XOL contracts. In this sense, the Pareto can be viewed as providing a conservative upper bound for the premiums. However, on the basis of goodness of fit, we recommend basing the premiums on the lognormal, the Burr 12, or the GB2.

Analysis of the PA losses reveals that the Burr 12 and GB2 provide the best model for this data series. The lognormal underestimates the tail of the PA loss

14. Prior to 1983, PCS defined a catastrophe as any single event that generated insured losses greater than $1 million. Therefore, we also investigated an alternative threshold for catastrophic losses of $1 million inflated to 1994 dollars from the first year in the analysis, 1949. Using the housing-value index, this would have set the lower-bound definition of a catastrophe at $57.7 million. Reworking the analysis using this definition of a catastrophic event did not substantially change the results. Thus, they are not reported here.

15. The log-likelihood function values for the PCS and RMS samples are not directly comparable because the sample sizes differ—the PCS sample has sixty-seven events, and the RMS samples each have one thousand events.

Table 3.3 Parameter Estimates Summary

Distribution and Parameter	PCS Housing Value (VA)	PCS Population (PA)	RMS Nation	RMS California	RMS Florida	RMS Southeastern United States
Lognormal:						
μ	5.396	4.586	4.403	3.703	5.654	5.337
σ	2.064	2.168	2.195	2.059	2.259	2.211
$-\log(L)$	471.667	426.964	6,108.236	5,344.295	7,388.235	7,049.331
Pareto:						
α	.328	.343	.431	.564	.296	.323
d	12.040	6.850	12.040	12.040	12.040	12.040
$-\log(L)$	430.041	470.040	6,653.261	5,834.966	8,087.477	7,712.696
Burr 12:						
a	.659	.804	.910	1.099	.689	.760
b	874.302	95.780	44.600	18.006	690.888	308.502
q	1.991	.999	.737	.619	1.507	1.215
$-\log(L)$	502.537	461.542	6,609.184	5,813.172	7,889.142	7,539.407
GB2:						
a	.150	.078	.405	1.842	.179	.491
b	291,488,438.71	.001	23.515	21.847	1,349,162.97	469.254
p	10.970	121.909	3.816	.498	7.988	1.886
q	88.975	50.199	2.491	.335	34.485	2.590
$-\log(L)$	501.438	460.476	6,604.769	5,811.365	7,882.308	7,537.281
Frequency	2.20	2.20	6.67	3.60	.83	1.35

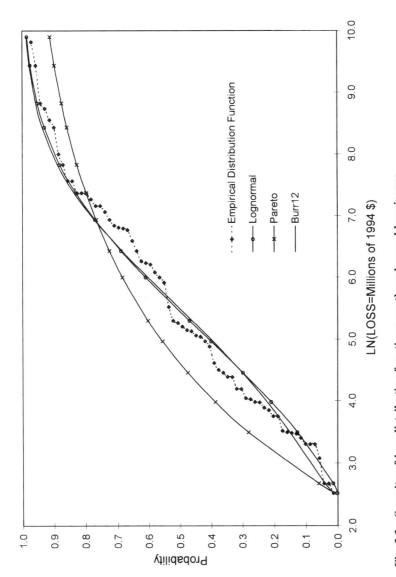

Fig. 3.3 Severity-of-loss distribution functions: earthquakes and hurricanes

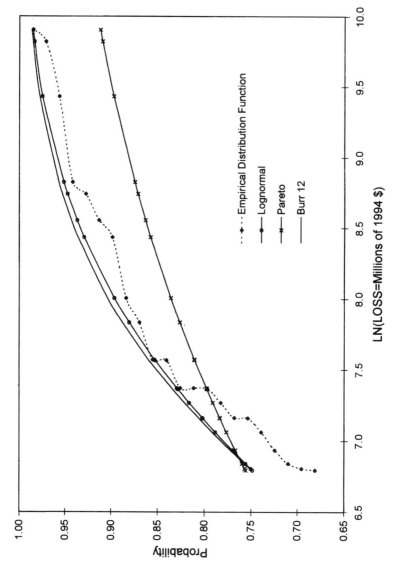

Fig. 3.4 Severity-of-loss distribution function tails: earthquakes and hurricanes

distribution, and the Pareto overestimates the tail, although not by as much as in the VA analysis.

The annual frequency of earthquakes and hurricanes is graphed in figure 3.5. The graph reveals a high degree of volatility in the frequency series. Frequency has been trending upward, as shown by the least-squares line and ten-year-moving-average lines in the figure. The variance of frequency also increased near the end of the period, as shown by the ten-year-moving-average variance line. On the basis of these apparent trends in the average number and variance of catastrophic events, we estimate the average number of events at 2.2 and use this estimate as the parameter of the Poisson frequency distribution in estimating $p*$).[16]

Expected loss severities were calculated for various policy limits on the basis of the estimated severity distributions. For the VA loss data, these expected severities represent the expected value of loss for a policy that covers catastrophes in excess of $12.04 million up to the specified policy limit (e.g., $10 billion). For the PA data, the expected severities cover catastrophes in excess of $6.85 million up to the specified policy limits. Reinsurance-layer prices are obtained as differences between the expected policy limit severities. The results are presented in table 3.4 for both the PA and the VA data.

The Pareto distribution clearly gives the largest estimate of expected severity in the $25–$50 billion layer, $1.806 billion based on the VA data and $1.319 billion based on the PA data. For the lognormal, the expected severities in the $25–$50 billion layer are $170.2 based on the VA data and $81.0 million based on the PA data. The corresponding expected severities in the $25–$50 billion layer given by the Burr 12 and GB2, respectively, are $162.4 million and $112.0 billion, based on the VA data, and $211.0 million and $97.1 million, based on the PA data.

Table 3.4 also shows the overall expected loss for the four severity distributions, based on equations (11a) and (16a), and a Poisson frequency parameter of 2.2 events per year.[17] Based on the Pareto distribution, the expected loss is $3.636 billion for the VA data and $2.719 billion for the PA data. The lognormal gives expected losses of $370.0 million and $177.2 million based on the VA and PA series, respectively. The corresponding estimates based on the Burr 12 are $353.4 million (VA data) and $458.5 million (PA data), and those based on the GB2 are $244.2 million (VA data) and $212.1 million (PA data).

Overall, considering the goodness of fit to both data series, we recommend using either the Burr 12 or the GB2 model to calculate the XOL premiums. Taking the average of the Burr 12 estimates based on the VA and the PA data, one obtains an estimate of $405.9 million, or $405,900 for each $25 million

16. Our frequency estimate is based on a linear least-squares trend line fitted to the annual frequency observations and used to project trend to 1995.

17. The Poisson parameter is used in conjunction with eq. (7) to obtain an estimate of the loss probability $p*$. The negative binomial results are very close to the Poisson results and hence are not shown.

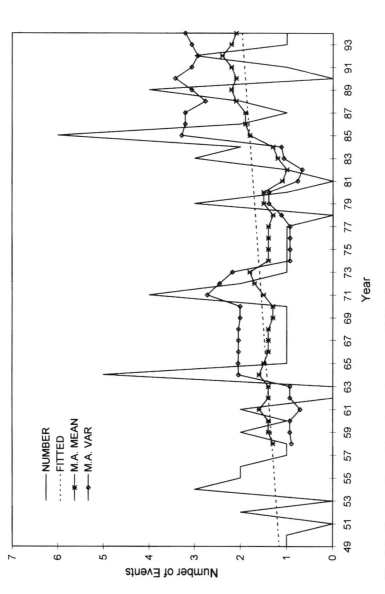

Fig. 3.5   Earthquake and hurricane frequency, 1949–94

Table 3.4   **Expected Loss Severities for Various Layers, Total Expected Loss for $25–$50 Billion Layer**

	Lognormal	Pareto	Burr 12	GB2
Losses inflated by housing values:				
E(L)	1,869.96M	Undefined	2,209.63M	1,511.32M
SD(L)	15,520.12M	Undefined	Undefined	55,723,965M
E(L; $12.04M, $5B, $12.04M)	864.75M	1,025.95M	841.38M	854.45M
E(L; $12.04M, $10B, $12.04M)	1,092.08M	1,637.97M	1,043.37M	1,059.38M
E(L; $12.04M, $15B, $12.04M)	1,220.31M	2,152.84M	1,156.47M	1,166.37M
E(L; $12.04M, $20B, $12.04M)	1,306.34M	2,613.28M	1,233.12M	1,233.67M
E(L; $12.04M, $25B, $12.04M)	1,369.34M	3,037.06M	1,290.16M	1,280.27M
E(L; $12.04M, $30B, $12.04M)	1,418.04M	3,433.75M	1,335.10M	1,314.54M
E(L; $12.04M, $35B, $12.04M)	1,457.10M	3,809.24M	1,371.88M	1,340.81M
E(L; $12.04M, $40B, $12.04M)	1,489.29M	4,167.49M	1,402.81M	1,361.57M
E(L; $12.04M, $45B, $12.04M)	1,516.37M	4,511.31M	1,429.37M	1,378.38M
E(L; $12.04M, $50B, $12.04M)	1,539.54M	4,842.81M	1,452.55M	1,392.24M
E(L; $25B, $50B, $12.04M)	170.20M	1,805.75M	162.39M	111.97M
Prob[L > $25|event occurs] =				
$P_>$ (%)	1.10	8.18	1.00	.79
Prob [L > $25] = p* (Poisson				
param. = 2.2)	.0238	.1647	.0218	.0172
E (L; $25B, $50B, $12.04M|				
L > $25B)	15,518.11M	22,073.58M	16,194.72M	14,179.08M
Total E(L): $25–$50B layer	369.97M	3,635.69M	353.35M	244.21M
Losses inflated by population:				
E(L)	1,036.65M	Undefined	Undefined	1,150.19M
SD(L)	10,733.19M	Undefined	Undefined	415,863,130M
E(L; $6.85M, $5B, $6.85M)	551.51M	789.43M	541.34M	550.52M
E(L; $6.85M, $10B, $6.85M)	670.09M	1,247.59M	691.79M	675.25M
E(L; $6.85M, $15B, $6.85M)	734.59M	1,629.95M	790.83M	745.46M
E(L; $6.85M, $20B, $6.85M)	776.99M	1,970.14M	866.40M	792.87M
E(L; $6.85M, $25B, $6.85M)	807.62M	2,282.06M	928.20M	827.89M
E(L; $6.85M, $30B, $6.85M)	831.06M	2,573.14M	980.85M	855.23M
E(L; $6.85M, $35B, $6.85M)	849.71M	2,847.98M	1,026.92M	877.37M
E(L; $6.85M, $40B, $6.85M)	864.98M	3,109.64M	1,068.01M	895.79M
E(L; $6.85M, $45B, $6.85M)	877.76M	3,360.28M	1,105.19M	911.44M
E(L; $6.85M, $50B, $6.85M)	888.65M	3,601.54M	1,139.21M	924.95M
E(L; $25B, $50B, $6.85M)	81.03M	1,319.49M	211.01M	97.06M
Prob[L > $25|event occurs] =				
$P_>$ (%)	.53	6.01	1.13	.61
Prob[L > $25] = p* (Poisson				
param. = 2.2)	.0116	.1239	.0246	.0134
E(L; $25B, $50B, $6.85M|				
L > $25B)	15,286.12M	21,950.14M	18,617.91M	15,839.40M
Total E(L): $25–$50B layer	177.20M	2,719.11M	458.48M	212.06M

Note: E(L; T, C, d) = expected value of loss severity (L) for a shifted distribution beginning at *d* for a reinsurance contract beginning at point of attachment *T* and having upper limit *C*. M = million; B = billion. The total E(L) is based on the Poisson frequency distribution with mean of 2.2. Figures are dollar values unless otherwise specified.

contract. The corresponding estimate based on the GB2 is $228.1 million, or $228,100 for each $25 million contract. These premiums translate into *rates on line* for the $25–$50 billion layer of 1.62 percent and 0.91 percent, respectively.[18] The most conservative estimate of the premium is provided by the Pareto distribution, which gives a premium estimate of $3.177 billion or a 12.7 percent rate on line based on an average of the VA and PA results.

3.4.3 Loss Estimates Based on RMS Data

Risk Management Solutions supplied ten thousand simulated catastrophe losses for each of several geographic areas for use in this study. The geographic areas included the entire United States, the southeastern United States, California, and Florida. Preliminary analysis indicated that it is not necessary to work with all ten thousand observations when estimating the loss-severity distributions. Accordingly, we randomly selected subsamples of one thousand losses for each geographic-area definition to form the primary basis for the following discussion.[19] We use the full samples of ten thousand claims to provide empirical estimates of the premiums for comparison with the estimates based on the loss-severity distributions.

The RMS estimates also differ from the PCS estimates in the choice of the loss-frequency parameter. For the PCS data, loss frequency was estimated by fitting a trend line to a time series of observed annual catastrophe frequencies. However, RMS estimates frequency on the basis of engineering and meteorologic models that are used to predict the probabilities and severities of hurricanes and earthquakes. It is important to analyze the RMS frequency estimates because no catastrophe causing insured property damage in the $25–$50 billion range has been observed during the period covered by the PCS data (1949–present), but such events are possible and can be simulated using the RMS approach.

Summary statistics for the PCS sample and the national RMS sample are shown in table 3.5. The mean severities for the two samples are quite comparable, $1.284 billion for the PCS sample and $1.048 billion for the RMS sample. However, the coefficient-of-variation, skewness, and kurtosis estimates are considerably higher for the RMS sample, and the maximum loss in the RMS sample is about six times as large as the maximum in the PCS sample. The simulated RMS frequency of events larger than $12.04 million is also considerably higher than the corresponding PCS estimate (6.7 as opposed to 1.5). And the RMS estimate of frequency is about three times as large as our fre-

18. The rate on line is defined as the premium divided by the width of the layer, $25 billion in this case.

19. Estimation of the parameters of the loss distributions was very slow when all ten thousand observations were used. Preliminary analysis based on ten thousand and several random samples of one thousand revealed that the parameter estimates are very stable, i.e., not sensitive to the choice of sample. Accordingly, the remainder of the analysis was based on one-thousand-observation samples.

Table 3.5 Summary Statistics: Actual Loss Experience and Simulated Loss Experience, Hurricanes and Earthquakes

	Obs.	Mean ($)	SD ($)	Coeff. of Var.	Skewness	Kurtosis	Minimum ($)	Maximum ($)
Severity of losses reported by PCS, 1949–94, losses > $12.04 million	67	1,283,998.7	2,942,996.6	2.292	4.198	20.124	12,434.3	18,391,014.4
Severity of losses simulated by RMS:								
All losses	95,182	736,533.4	3,790,455.6	5.146	12.126	199.853	5,007.2	107,546,261.0
Losses > $12.04 million	66,138	1,047,983.0	4,493,486.8	4.288	10.193	141.061	12,058.2	107,546,261.0

	Obs.	Mean	SD	Coeff. of Var.	Skewness	Kurtosis	Minimum	Maximum
Frequency of losses reported by PCS, 1949–94	67	1.543	1.312	.85	1.477	2.539	0	6
Frequency of losses simulated by RMS:								
All losses	95,182	9.518	3.056	.321	.333	.152	0	23
Losses > $12.04 million	66,138	6.668	2.559	.384	.399	.195	0	19

quency estimate based on linear time trending (2.2 events per year). As discussed further below, the primary reason for the difference in frequencies is that RMS is simulating a larger number of earthquakes per year than have been observed historically.

The national loss estimates based on the RMS empirical and fitted probability-of-loss distributions are shown in table 3.6. It is noteworthy that the estimated loss severities in the $25–$50 billion layer are quite comparable to our PCS estimates presented in table 3.4. The lognormal and Pareto PCS estimates in table 3.4 are actually larger than their RMS counterparts in table 3.5. The severity estimates based on the Burr 12 and GB2 distributions fitted to the RMS data (table 3.5) are somewhat larger than the corresponding estimates based on the PCS data (table 3.4). For example, the Burr 12 loss-severity estimate for the $25–$50 billion layer is $279.2 million, whereas the PCS estimate is $162.4 million (based on the VA adjustment).

The comparability of the fitted PCS and RMS loss estimates in the $25–$50 billion layer shows that using probability distributions to model the tails of loss distributions on the basis of relatively small samples can yield accurate estimates of expected values of large losses even if no losses in this range have been observed. This is also illustrated by figures 3.6 and 3.7, which show, respectively, the empirical distribution functions for the RMS and PCS data and the tails of the empirical distribution functions along with GB2 distributions fitted to the PCS and RMS data. Figure 3.6 shows that the tail of the PCS distribution is actually somewhat heavier than that of the RMS distribution for relatively small losses and is comparable for larger losses. Figure 3.7 shows that the GB2 distributions are also quite comparable for large losses, although the RMS distribution has a somewhat heavier tail.

Table 3.6 also shows the estimates of the total expected loss (i.e., the expected loss component of the XOL premiums) in the $25–$50 billion layer based on the RMS data. The expected loss estimates in table 3.6 are considerably larger than those based on the PCS data (table 3.4), primarily because of the difference between the RMS and the PCS loss-frequency estimates. The RMS-based estimates of the expected loss range from $453.4 million (or a 1.8 percent rate on line) for the lognormal distribution to $4.635 billion (or an 18.5 percent rate on line) for the Pareto. Again, however, the Pareto does not provide a very good fit to the data. The best fit is provided by the Burr 12 and GB2, and the premiums based on those models are $1.758 billion (7 percent rate on line) and $1.020 billion (4.1 percent rate on line), respectively.

Expressed per XOL contract, the expected-loss estimates from table 3.6 imply a price of $1,758,000 per $25 million national contract based on the Burr 12 and $1,020,000 per contract based on the GB2. These are much larger than the $405,900 per contract (Burr 12) and $228,100 per contract (GB2) based on the PCS data. Whether the RMS or the PCS sample gives more reasonable estimates depends on the accuracy of the RMS prediction that 6.6 events will occur per year. A practical approach to resolving the uncertainty would be to

Table 3.6   Expected RMS Loss Severities for Various Layers for the United States, Total Expected Loss for $25–$50 Billion Layer

	Empirical	Lognormal	Pareto	Burr 12	GB2
Losses simulated by RMS					
E(L)	987.67M	922.63M	Undefined	132,471,003.8M	36,766.2M
SD(L)	4,433.98M	10,082.30M	Undefined	Undefined	Undefined
E(L; $12.04M, $5B, $12.04M)	538.44M	492.68M	646.72M	498.66M	496.29M
E(L; $12.04M, $10B, $12.04M)	669.39M	595.84M	963.60M	662.15M	628.83M
E(L; $12.04M, $15B, $12.04M)	736.27M	651.67M	1,215.96M	776.88M	712.49M
E(L; $12.04M, $20B, $12.04M)	780.90M	688.28M	1,433.83M	868.19M	774.28M
E(L; $12.04M, $25B, $12.04M)	820.30M	714.68M	1,629.19M	945.26M	823.48M
E(L; $12.04M, $30B, $12.04M)	850.34M	734.87M	1,808.30M	1,012.61M	864.44M
E(L; $12.04M, $35B, $12.04M)	872.29M	750.92M	1,974.94M	1,072.81M	899.59M
E(L; $12.04M, $40B, $12.04M)	882.29M	764.06M	2,131.60M	1,127.49M	930.39M
E(L; $12.04M, $45B, $12.04M)	892.29M	775.05M	2,280.03M	1,177.78M	957.82M
E(L; $12.04M, $50B, $12.04M)	902.29M	784.41M	2,421.50M	1,224.45M	982.56M
E(L; $25B, $50B, $12.04M)	81.99M	69.73M	792.32M	279.19M	159.08M
Prob[L > $25\|event occurs] = P$_>$ (%)	.70	.46	3.73	1.43	.89
Prob [L > $25] = p* (Poisson param. = 6.7)	.0451	.0297	.2182	.0903	.0571
E (L; $25B, $50B, $12.04M| L > $25B)	11,713.10M	15,266.03M	21,246.44M	19,477.90M	17,847.16M
Total E(L): $25–$50B layer	528.84M	453.36M	4,635.46M	1,758.16M	1,019.66M

Note: E(L; T, C, d) = expected value of loss severity (*L*) for a shifted distribution beginning at *d* for a reinsurance contract beginning at point of attachment *T* and having upper limit *C*. M = million; B = billion. The total *E(L)* is based on the Poisson frequency distribution with mean of 6.7. Figures are dollar values unless otherwise specified.

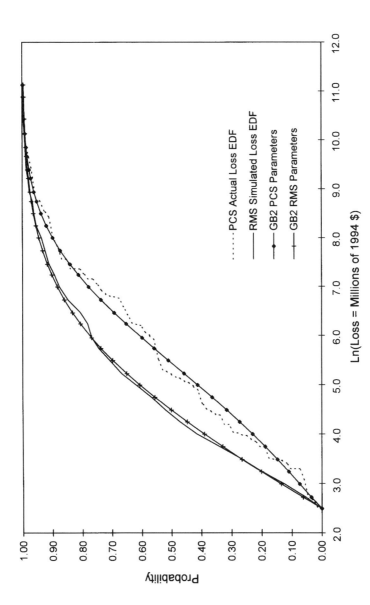

Fig. 3.6 Severity-of-loss distribution functions: GB2 hurricanes and earthquakes, PCS reported actual losses vs. RMS simulated losses

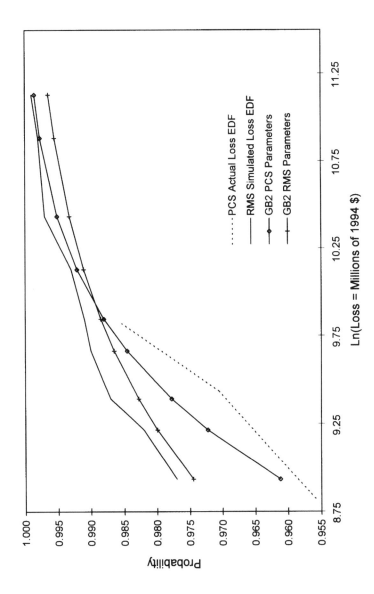

Fig. 3.7 Severity-of-loss distribution function tails: GB2 hurricanes and earthquakes, PCS reported actual losses vs. RMS simulated losses

set the reservation price as the average of the RMS and the PCS estimates. This would give a reservation price of $1.082 million (4.3 percent rate on line) based on the Burr 12 and $624,000 (2.5 percent rate on line) based on the GB2.

On the basis of the RMS data, we also estimated conditional and unconditional loss severities for California, Florida, and the southeastern region of the United States. Tables comparable to table 3.6 and based on these three samples are presented in appendix B. We also had enough PCS data on losses in the southeastern region of the United States to provide PCS estimates for this region. The results are summarized in table 3.7, which shows the conditional expected severity of losses in the $25–$50 billion layer, the probability of a loss in this layer based on the severity distribution (i.e., $P[L > \$25 \text{ billion}|\text{an event occurs}] = P_>]$), and the unconditional expected severity in the layer (the product of the conditional severity and $P_>$). For purposes of comparison, the table also shows the comparable national statistics based on the PCS and RMS samples.

The RMS conditional loss severity is highest in California, $16.6 billion (table 3.7). The comparable conditional loss severities are $15.0 billion for Florida and $13.9 billion for the Southeast. However, the unconditional severities are higher in Florida and the Southeast than in California. The chance of breaching the $25 billion trigger is larger in Florida and the Southeast, but, given that a loss breaches the trigger, expected severity is higher in California. Graphic analysis (not shown) reveals that the GB2 is the best model for the RMS California severity data, while the Burr 12 and GB2 are the best models for Florida and the Southeast. Comparison of the PCS and RMS data for the Southeast reveals that the PCS data imply lower conditional severity, a lower probability of a loss exceeding the trigger, and lower unconditional severity than the RMS data, where these comparisons are based on the best-fitting GB2 distribution. This is likely due to the reduced PCS sample size and the absence of large events, such as the Northridge Earthquake, from the southeastern PCS sample.

The total expected-loss components of the PCS reservation-price estimates and their corresponding rates on line are summarized in table 3.8. The first panel of the table is based on historical loss-frequency estimates, while the second panel is based on the RMS frequency estimates. The differences between the results in the first two panels of the table can be attributed primarily to the loss-frequency estimates generated by RMS, which are higher than the historical averages nationally and those for California, Florida, and the Southeast. For example, the historical average number of events per year in California is 0.22, whereas the RMS estimate is 3.6. To see the effect that the higher-frequency estimates has on the reservation price, consider the best-fitting distributions—the Burr 12 and the GB2. Using the PCS VA (housing value) severity estimates and the historical frequencies for the national contracts, the estimated reservation rates on line are 1.41 percent for the Burr 12 and 0.98 for the GB2. However, using the corresponding RMS-provided frequency data

Table 3.7   Summary: Expected Loss Severities and Expected Losses, $25–$50 Billion Layer

Region	$E(L; \$25B, \$50B, \$12.04M\|L > \$25B)$ ($)				
	Empirical	Lognormal	Pareto	Burr12	GB2
PCS housing value (VA)	...	15,518.11M	22,073.58M	16,194.72M	14,179.08M
PCS population (PA)	...	15,286.12M	21,950.14M	18,617.91M	15,839.40M
RMS, United States	11,713.10M	15,266.03M	21,246.44M	19,477.90M	17,847.16M
RMS, California	16,601.38M	13,739.22M	20,229.10M	19,402.25M	19,844.63M
RMS, Florida	14,974.47M	16,839.55M	22,339.15M	17,514.89M	15,414.08M
PCS, Southeastern United States (VA)	...	16,677.02M	21,966.54M	15,853.33M	14,356.77M
RMS, Southeastern United States	13,867.94M	16,276.46M	22,111.64M	17,963.53M	16,776.73M

Region	Prob $[L > \$25B\|\text{Event Occurs}] = P_>$ (%)				
	Empirical	Lognormal	Pareto	Burr12	GB2
PCS housing value (VA)	...	1.10	8.18	1.00	.79
PCS population (PA)	...	.53	6.01	1.13	.61
RMS, United States	.70	.46	3.73	1.43	.89
RMS, California	.60	.09	1.34	.73	.92
RMS, Florida	1.70	2.39	10.44	2.13	1.70
PCS, Southeastern United States (VA)	...	1.57	7.41	.77	.59
RMS, Southeastern United States	1.20	1.52	8.47	1.66	1.33

Region	$E(L; \$25B, \$50B, \$12.04M)$ ($)				
	Empirical	Lognormal	Pareto	Burr12	GB2
PCS housing value (VA)	...	170.20M	1,805.75M	162.39M	111.97M
PCS population (PA)	...	81.03M	1,319.49M	211.01M	97.06M
RMS, United States	81.99M	69.73M	792.32M	279.19M	159.08M
RMS, California	99.61M	12.46M	271.42M	141.86M	182.84M
RMS, Florida	254.57M	402.06M	2,333.02M	372.95M	262.73M
PCS, Southeastern United States (VA)	...	261.57M	1,626.79M	122.47M	84.17M
RMS, Southeastern United States	166.42M	246.64M	1,873.72M	297.76M	223.63M

Note: M = million; B = billion.

Table 3.8 **Reservation-Price Estimates of Federal XOL Contracts**

Region	Historical Frequency Estimates	Severity Distribution Assumption ($)			
		Lognormal	Pareto	Burr12	GB2
PCS housing value	2.2	369.97M	3,635.69M	353.35M	244.21M
(VA)		(1.48)	(14.54)	(1.41)	(.98)
PCS population	2.2	177.20M	2,719.11M	458.48M	212.06M
(PA)		(.71)	(10.88)	(1.83)	(.85)
RMS, United	2.2	152.64M	1,673.51M	604.63M	346.57M
States		(.61)	(6.69)	(2.42)	(1.39)
RMS, California	.217	87.02M	500.57M	80.74M	56.91M
		(.35)	(2.00)	(.32)	(.23)
RMS, Florida	.378	4.71M	102.34M	53.55M	68.99M
		(.02)	(.41)	(.21)	(.28)
PCS, Southeastern	.844	219.31M	1,330.98M	103.03M	70.86M
United States (VA)		(.88)	(5.32)	(.41)	(.28)
RMS, Southeastern	.844	206.84M	1,526.20M	249.56M	187.68M
United States		(.83)	(6.10)	(1.00)	(.75)
	RMS Frequency Estimates				
PCS housing value	6.7	1,083.66M	9,209.22M	1,037.08M	720.08M
(VA)		(4.33)	(36.84)	(4.15)	(2.88)
PCS population	6.7	525.46M	7,188.55M	1,341.85M	627.69M
(PA)		(2.10)	(28.75)	(5.37)	(2.51)
RMS, United	6.7	453.36M	4,635.46M	1,758.16M	1,019.66M
States		(1.81)	(18.54)	(7.03)	(4.08)
RMS, California	3.6	44.61M	950.54M	502.23M	645.12M
		(.18)	(3.80)	(2.01)	(2.58)
RMS, Florida	.83	331.61M	1,861.27m	307.93M	217.31M
		(1.33)	(7.45)	(1.23)	(.87)
PCS, Southeastern	1.35	349.41M	2,089.95M	164.48M	113.18M
United States (VA)		(1.40)	(8.36)	(.66)	(.45)
RMS, Southeastern	1.35	330.30M	2,395.22M	398.38M	299.86M
United States		(1.32)	(9.58)	(1.59)	(1.20)

Note: The rates online, given in percentages and shown in parentheses, are obtained by dividing the reservation prices by $25,000 million. M = million.

increases the estimates to 4.15 and 2.88 percent, respectively. A similar pattern can be observed for the other severity estimates reported in table 3.8 and across each of the different regions.

Whether the reservation price should be based on the historical data or on the RMS projections depends on the degree of credibility that should be assigned to the RMS projections. This is difficult to gauge in the absence of a full-scale engineering analysis or a few more years of historical experience. However, the difference between the two approaches provides a reasonable range that government officials could use when setting the reservation price. Also, as indicated above, these rates should be loaded for the expenses of administering the program and discounted to reflect the time lag between the premium payment and expected-loss-payment dates.

3.5 Conclusions

This paper analyzes a proposal for federal excess-of-loss (XOL) reinsurance contracts to assist insurers in hedging the risk of property catastrophes. Under the proposed reinsurance program, the federal government would directly write and sell per occurrence excess-of-loss reinsurance contracts protecting against catastrophe losses. These XOL contracts would be available for qualified insurance companies, pools, and reinsurers and would cover industry losses from a disaster in the $25–$50 billion layer of coverage—a layer currently unavailable in the private market.

The rationale for government provision of these contracts is that the capacity of the private insurance and reinsurance markets is presently inadequate to provide coverage for losses of this magnitude. The unavailability of capacity for large catastrophes has a number of serious effects on the viability of insurance markets and the ability of society to respond to a major disaster. The lack of capacity has led to shortages in the supply of insurance, with the resulting potential for higher federal disaster-relief expenditures as a result of a major catastrophe. The unavailability of high-limits reinsurance also increases the probability of insolvency for insurers participating in the property-insurance market, thus posing further risk to the stability of insurance markets.

Private market capacity for large losses is limited because the possibility of bankruptcy, along with information asymmetries in insurance and capital markets, constrains the ability of private insurers and reinsurers to diversify risk across time. Time diversification requires that insurers be able to raise debt and/or equity capital at reasonable rates following a large loss. However, the cost of capital to insurers tends to increase following a loss shock, and capital may be unavailable at any price for certain lines of coverage. Private insurance markets tend to function effectively in diversifying the risk of relatively small losses, but they are not very efficient in dealing with extremely large losses.

The federal government, on the other hand, has a superior ability to diversify risk across time through the exercise of federal borrowing power. While it is costly for private insurers to raise additional capital following a loss shock, federal debt is viewed as default-risk free, and thus the federal government would not find its cost of capital increasing significantly following a catastrophe. Thus, the federal government's superior financing and time-diversification capabilities would permit the federal XOL contract program to bypass the imperfections in the insurance, reinsurance, and capital markets that impede the private provision of disaster insurance.

The proposed XOL contracts would help solve the problems in insurance markets while potentially reducing the federal government's role in providing disaster-relief payments to propertyowners following a catastrophe. The contracts do not provide a subsidy to insurers but instead are designed to be self-supporting in expected value; that is, the contracts are to be priced so that the expected cost to the government is zero. If a loss occurred that exceeded the amount of premiums that had been paid into the program, the federal government would use its borrowing power to raise funds to pay the losses. During periods when the accumulated premiums paid into the program exceeded the losses that had been paid, the buyers of the contracts implicitly would be lending money to the Treasury, reducing the costs of government debt. The expected interest on these "loans" offsets the expected financing (borrowing) costs of the program as long as the contracts are priced at the expected value of loss plus program administrative expenses.

A risk premium could be added to the price of the contracts to provide an incentive for private market crowding out of the federal program. This could imply that the expected return to the government from the program would be positive rather than zero, but this would not necessarily be the case if the risk premium compensates the government for parameter-estimation risk or unforeseen program risk.

A methodology was developed for calculating premiums for the XOL contracts. The first step is to estimate the expected value of loss. This involves fitting severity distributions to catastrophe losses. We estimated loss-severity distributions on the basis of two samples—the historical data on hurricane and earthquake losses maintained by Property Claims Services (PCS) and a sample of simulated loss based on engineering analysis provided by Risk Management Solutions (RMS). Four severity-of-loss distributions were used, the lognormal, the Pareto, the Burr 12, and the generalized beta of type 2 (GB2) distributions. The Burr 12 and GB2 distributions generally provided the best fit to the data. Using our severity distributions, we estimated the expected-loss component of the government's reservation price for proposed XOL contracts covering the entire United States, California, Florida, and the Southeast. The reservation prices were computed using historical frequency data and using the frequency projections developed by RMS. The RMS frequency estimates are considerably higher than the historical averages. Thus, we suggest that the reservation price should be set using the range of PCS and RMS price projections based on the best-fitting Burr 12 and GB2 distributions as the expected-loss component of the reservation price as a guide for policymakers. The expected loss should be loaded for administrative expenses and discounted to obtain the final reservation price. The ultimate price for the contracts would be determined by auction, but the contracts should not be issued for less than the reservation price.

Future research is needed to explore the full implementation of the option model. In addition, the premium estimates could be improved by obtaining more comprehensive estimates of the value of property by state (e.g., to include rental, commercial, and industrial property) and physical measures of the severity of catastrophes. The incorporation of physical projections of the predicted frequency of major catastrophes would also improve the estimates.

Appendix A
Derivation of $p_k(k; L > T)$ When $p(N)$ Is Negative Binomial

Recall that the unconditional distribution of the number of catastrophes that breach the trigger T is

$$(A1) \qquad p_k(k; L > T) \; = \; p_k(k) \; = \; \sum_{N=k}^{\infty} p(N) p_k(k; L > T|N).$$

Assume that $p(N)$ is negative binomial, that is, that

$$(A2) \qquad\qquad p(N) \; = \; \frac{\Gamma(\alpha + N)}{\Gamma(\alpha)N!} \rho^{\alpha}(1 - \rho)^{N}.$$

Given N events and $P_> = S(L > T)$, $p_k(k; L > T|N)$ is binomial:

$$(A3) \qquad p_k(k; L > T|N) \; = \; \frac{N!}{(N - k)!k!} P_>^k(1 - P_>)^{N-k}.$$

Substituting (A2) and (A3) into (A1) and collecting terms yields

$$p_k(k; L > T) \; = \; p_k(k)$$

$$= \; \sum_{N=k}^{\infty} \frac{\Gamma(\alpha + N)}{(N - k)!k!\Gamma(\alpha)} P_>^k(1 - P_>)^{N-k} \rho^{\alpha}(1 - \rho)^{N}.$$

Changing the index of summation from N to $h = N - k$, setting $\rho' = (1 - \rho)$, and moving terms that do not involve h outside the summation sign, we obtain

$$(A4) \qquad p_k(k) = \frac{(\rho'P_>)^k\rho^{\alpha}\Gamma(\alpha + k)}{k!\Gamma(\alpha)(1 - P_<\rho')^{\alpha+k}} \sum_{h=0}^{\infty} \frac{\Gamma(\alpha + h + k)}{h!\Gamma(\alpha + k)} (P_<\rho')^h(1 - P_<\rho')^{\alpha+k}.$$

The expression to the right of the summation is a negative binomial distribution, so the summation equals one. Rearranging the expression to the left of the summation yields

$$(A5) \qquad p_k(k) = \frac{\Gamma(\alpha + k)}{k!\Gamma(\alpha)} \left(\frac{\rho' P_>}{1 - P_< \rho'} \right)^k \left(\frac{\rho}{1 - P_< \rho'} \right)^\alpha .$$

This is a negative binomial distribution with parameters α and $\beta = \dfrac{\rho' P_>}{1 - P_< \rho'}$.

Appendix B

Table 3B.1   Expected RMS Loss Severities for Various Layers for California, Total Expected Loss for $25–$50 Billion Layer

	Empirical	Lognormal	Pareto	Burr 12	GB2
Losses simulated by RMS					
$E(L)$	682.41M	351.29M	Undefined	Undefined	Undefined
$SD(L)$	3,889.86M	2,796.35M	Undefined	Undefined	Undefined
$E(L;$ \$12.04M, \$5B, \$12.04M$)$	322.04M	255.66M	367.81M	288.45M	299.39M
$E(L;$ \$12.04M, \$10B, \$12.04M$)$	423.61M	285.60M	502.45M	373.19M	398.19M
$E(L;$ \$12.04M, \$15B, \$12.04M$)$	492.21M	299.42M	602.25M	432.21M	469.34M
$E(L;$ \$12.04M, \$20B, \$12.04M$)$	536.57M	307.57M	684.55M	478.98M	526.95M
$E(L;$ \$12.04M, \$25B, \$12.04M$)$	570.97M	313.01M	755.88M	518.34M	576.22M
$E(L;$ \$12.04M, \$30B, \$12.04M$)$	599.37M	316.90M	819.53M	552.66M	619.71M
$E(L;$ \$12.04M, \$35B, \$12.04M$)$	619.95M	319.83M	877.43M	583.28M	658.93M
$E(L;$ \$12.04M, \$40B, \$12.04M$)$	639.95M	322.12M	930.83M	611.05M	694.83M
$E(L;$ \$12.04M, \$45B, \$12.04M$)$	655.58M	323.96M	980.58M	636.56M	728.05M
$E(L;$ \$12.04M, \$50B, \$12.04M$)$	670.58M	325.46M	1,027.30M	660.20M	759.06M
$E(L;$ \$25B, \$50B, \$12.04M$)$	99.61M	12.46M	271.42M	141.86M	182.84M
Prob[$L >$ \$25|event occurs] $= P_>$ (%)	.60	.09	1.34	.73	.92
Prob [$L >$ \$25] $= p^*$ (Poisson param. = 3.6)	.0213	.0032	.0470	.0259	.0325
$E(L;$ \$25B, \$50B, \$12.04M| $L >$ \$25B)	16,601.38M	13,739.22M	20,229.10M	19,402.25M	19,844.63M
Total $E(L)$: \$25–\$50B layer	353.48M	44.61M	950.54M	502.23M	645.12M

Note: $E(L; T, C, d)$ = expected value of loss severity (L) for a shifted distribution beginning at *d* for a reinsurance contract beginning at point of attachment *T* and having upper limit *C*. M = million; B = billion. The total $E(L)$ is based on the Poisson frequency distribution with mean of 3.6. Figures are given in dollar values unless otherwise specified.

Table 3B.2   **Expected RMS Loss Severities for Various Layers for the Southeastern United States, Total Expected Loss for $25–$50 Billion Layer**

	Empirical	Lognormal	Pareto	Burr 12	GB2
Losses simulated by RMS					
E(L)	975.63M	2,408.49M	Undefined	Undefined	3,032.44M
SD(L)	4,433.98M	27,495.06M	Undefined	Undefined	Undefined
E(L; $12.04M, $5B, $12.04M)	900.14M	901.68M	1,047.91M	845.30M	861.95M
E(L; $12.04M, $10B, $12.04M)	1,156.90M	1,172.45M	1,678.27M	1,089.65M	1,096.86M
E(L; $12.04M, $15B, $12.04M)	1,302.95M	1,334.42M	2,209.87M	1,244.13M	1,236.16M
E(L; $12.04M, $20B, $12.04M)	1,390.10M	1,447.72M	2,686.02M	1,358.52M	1,334.13M
E(L; $12.04M, $25B, $12.04M)	1,452.58M	1,533.46M	3,124.78M	1,449.86M	1,409.07M
E(L; $12.04M, $30B, $12.04M)	1,502.66M	1,601.58M	3,535.86M	1,526.15M	1,469.39M
E(L; $12.04M, $35B, $12.04M)	1,538.50M	1,657.53M	3,925.29M	1,591.80M	1,519.61M
E(L; $12.04M, $40B, $12.04M)	1,568.99M	1,704.61M	4,297.07M	1,649.49M	1,562.49M
E(L; $12.04M, $45B, $12.04M)	1,593.99M	1,744.97M	4,654.10M	1,701.02M	1,599.78M
E(L; $12.04M, $50B, $12.04M)	1,618.99M	1,780.10M	4,998.50M	1,747.62M	1,632.70M
E(L; $25B, $50B, $12.04M)	166.42M	246.64M	1,873.72M	297.76M	223.63M
Prob[L > $25|event occurs] = P $>$ (%)	1.20	1.52	8.47	1.66	1.33
Prob [L > $25] = p* (Poisson param. = 1.35)	.0161	.0203	.1083	.0222	.0179
E(L; $25B, $50B, $12.04M| L > $25B)	13,867.94M	16,276.46M	22,111.64M	17,963.53M	16,776.73M
Total E(L): $25–$50B layer	223.34M	330.30M	2,395.22M	398.38M	299.86M

Note: E(L; T, C, d) = expected value of loss severity (L) for a shifted distribution beginning at d for a reinsurance contract beginning at point of attachment T and having upper limit C. M = million; B = billion. The total E(L) is based on the Poisson frequency distribution with mean of 1.35. Figures are given in dollar values unless otherwise specified.

Table 3B.3 Expected RMS Loss Severities for Various Layers for Florida, Total Expected Loss for $25–$50 Billion Layer

	Empirical	Lognormal	Pareto	Burr 12	GB2
Losses simulated by RMS					
E(L)	987.67M	3,675.52M	Undefined	132,471,003.80M	2,557.73M
SD(L)	4,433.98M	46,828.08M	Undefined	Undefined	234,918,436.58M
E(L; $12.04M, $5B, $12.04M)	1,135.33M	1,099.92M	1,189.12M	1,066.08M	1,104.32M
E(L; $12.04M, $10B, $12.04M)	1,509.92M	1,480.25M	1,940.19M	1,397.98M	1,445.22M
E(L; $12.04M, $15B, $12.04M)	1,704.34M	1,718.89M	2,582.86M	1,604.34M	1,642.39M
E(L; $12.04M, $20B, $12.04M)	1,832.49M	1,891.23M	3,163.90M	1,754.58M	1,775.82M
E(L; $12.04M, $25B, $12.04M)	1,929.21M	2,024.88M	3,703.04M	1,872.77M	1,873.74M
E(L; $12.04M, $30B, $12.04M)	2,002.29M	2,133.18M	4,210.97M	1,970.17M	1,949.35M
E(L; $12.04M, $35B, $12.04M)	2,060.75M	2,223.63M	4,694.35M	2,052.98M	2,009.83M
E(L; $12.04M, $40B, $12.04M)	2,103.77M	2,300.85M	5,157.65M	2,124.98M	2,059.48M
E(L; $12.04M, $45B, $12.04M)	2,143.77M	2,367.91M	5,604.09M	2,188.66M	2,101.07M
E(L; $12.04M, $50B, $12.04M)	2,183.77M	2,426.94M	6,036.06M	2,245.72M	2,136.47M
E(L; $25B, $50B, $12.04M)	254.57M	402.06M	2,333.02M	372.95M	262.73M
Prob[L > $25|event occurs] = P> (%)	1.70	2.39	10.44	2.13	1.70
Prob [L > $25] = p* (Poisson param. = .83)	0.0141	0.0197	0.0833	0.0176	0.0141
E(L; $25B, $50B, $12.04M|					
L > $25B)	14,974.47M	16,839.55M	22,339.15M	17,514.89M	15,414.08M
Total E(L): $25–$50B Layer	210.56M	331.61M	1,861.27M	307.93M	217.31M

Note: E(L; T, C, d) = expected value of loss severity (L) for a shifted distribution beginning at d for a reinsurance contract beginning at point of attachment T and having upper limit C. M = million; B = billion. The total E(L) is based on the Poisson frequency distribution with mean of 0.83. Figures are given in dollar values unless otherwise specified.

References

Aase, Knut K. 1993. A jump/diffusion consumption-based capital asset pricing model and the equity premium puzzle. *Mathematical Finance* 3:65–84.

A. M. Best Co. 1995. *Best's aggregates and averages: Property-casualty, 1995 edition.* Oldwick, N.J.

Buhlmann, Hans. 1984. The general economic premium principle. *ASTIN Bulletin* 14: 13–21.

———. 1995. Cross-hedging of insurance portfolios. Paper presented at the 1995 Bowles Symposium "Securitization of Insurance Risk," Georgia State University, Atlanta.

Chang, Carolyn W. 1995. A no-arbitrage martingale analysis for jump-diffusion valuation. *Journal of Financial Research* 18:351–81.

Cummins, J. David. 1991. Statistical and financial models of insurance pricing and the insurance firm. *Journal of Risk and Insurance* 58:261–302.

Cummins, J. David, Georges Dionne, James B. McDonald, and Michael Pritchett. 1990. Applications of the GB2 family of distributions in modeling insurance loss processes. *Insurance: Mathematics and Economics* 9:257–72.

Cummins, J. David, and Hélyette Geman. 1994. An Asian option approach to the valuation of insurance futures contracts. *Review of Futures Markets* 13:517–57.

———. 1995. Pricing catastrophe insurance futures and call spreads: An arbitrage approach. *Journal of Fixed Income* 4:46–57.

Cummins, J. David, and Elizabeth Grace. 1994. Tax management and investment strategies of property-liability insurers. *Journal of Banking and Finance* 18 (January): 1–228.

Cummins, J. David, and James B. McDonald. 1991. Risky probability distributions and liability insurance pricing. In *Cycles and crises in property/casualty insurance: Causes and implications for public policy,* ed. J. D. Cummins, S. E. Harrington, and R. Klein. Kansas City, Mo.: National Association of Insurance Commissioners.

D'Arcy, Stephen P., and Virginia Grace France. 1992. Catastrophe futures: A better hedge for insurers. *Journal of Risk and Insurance* 59:575–601.

Dionne, George, and Neil Doherty. 1992. Adverse selection in insurance markets: A selective survey. In *Contributions to insurance economics,* ed. Georges Dionne. Norwell, Mass.: Kluwer Academic.

Froot, Kenneth A., David S. Scharfstein, and Jeremy C. Stein. 1994. A framework for risk management. *Harvard Business Review* 72 (November–December): 91–98.

Gerber, Hans U. 1982. On the numerical evaluation of the distribution of aggregate claims and its stop-loss premiums. *Insurance: Mathematics and Economics* 1:13–18.

Goovaerts, M. J., F. de Vylder, and J. Haezendonck. 1984. *Insurance premiums: Theory and applications.* New York: North-Holland.

Gray, William J. 1990. Strong association between West African rainfall and U.S. landfall of intense hurricanes. *Science* 249:1251–56.

Heston, Steven L. 1993. Invisible parameters in option prices. *Journal of Finance* 48:933–47.

Johnson, Normal L., and Samuel Kotz. 1970. *Continuous univariate distributions—1.* New York: Wiley.

———. 1972. *Continuous multivariate distributions.* New York: Wiley.

Lewis, Christopher M., and Kevin C. Murdock. 1996. The role of government contracts in discretionary reinsurance markets for natural disasters. *Journal of Risk and Insurance* 63:567–97.

Mayers, David, and Clifford W. Smith Jr. 1982. On the corporate demand for insurance. *Journal of Business* 55:281–96.

Merton, Robert C. 1976. Option pricing when underlying stock returns are discontinuous. *Journal of Financial Economics* 3:125–44.

Naik, V., and M. Lee. 1990. General equilibrium pricing of options on the market portfolio with discontinuous returns. *Review of Financial Studies* 3:493–521.

Niehaus, Greg, and Steven Mann. 1992. The trading of underwriting risk: An analysis of insurance futures contracts and reinsurance. *Journal of Risk and Insurance* 59: 601–27.

Property Claims Services. 1994. *The catastrophe record.* Rahway, N.J.

Scism, Leslie, and Martha Brannigan. 1996. Florida homeowners find insurance pricey, if they find it at all. *Wall Street Journal,* 12 July.

Shapiro, Alan C., and Sheridan Titman. 1985. An integrated approach to corporate risk management. *Midland Corporate Finance Journal* 3:41–56.

U.S. Department of Commerce. Various years. *Statistical abstract of the United States.* Washington, D.C.: U.S. Government Printing Office.

Wang, Shaun. 1995. The price of risk: An actuarial/economic model. Working paper. Department of Statistics and Actuarial Science, University of Waterloo.

Comment   Sanjiv Ranjan Das

Catastrophic losses ensue from large acts of God, such as earthquakes, hurricanes, etc. The insurance industry uses the term *cats* to describe these events and the contracts underwritten for these events. The paper by Cummins, Lewis, and Phillips is a paper on what I will denote *bigcats*. Bigcats are single events that result in losses exceeding $25 billion. The objective of this paper is to price one-year reinsurance contracts on bigcats. These are underwritings on single events on loss magnitudes that we have not as yet experienced. The motivation is simple: losses of this size will eventually occur, and, without a good mechanism to handle them, the reinsurance industry as well as consumers of insurance will suffer severe economic crises.

Cummins, Lewis, and Phillips offer the following in the paper: (i) a proposal that the government write these bigcat insurance covers and (ii) a mathematical exposition of what these contracts will cost. By examining the past distribution of large losses, they develop a methodology to price these contracts and then provide indicative prices. Using, for example, the Burr 12 distribution, they arrive at a severity-of-loss estimate of about $17 billion on average, and multiplying this by a 2 percent probability of occurrence results in an expected loss of about $350 million.

My review of the paper falls into four categories: (1) the need for these contracts; (2) an examination of the proposed mechanics of these contracts; (3) an examination of the pricing method; and (4) a proposal for binary contracts.

Sanjiv Das is assistant professor of finance at the Harvard Business School and a faculty research fellow of the National Bureau of Economic Research.

Necessity of the Bigcat Contract

Is the bigcat contract much ado about nothing? Should the government expend costly resources on this proposal? It may be akin to the development of the superheavyweight category in world boxing tourneys when people were satisfied with the heavyweight version. A little probability work shows, however, that the proposal is not only justified but timely as well.

Consider some of the data in the paper. The expected number of cats per year is $\lambda = 2.2$ (Poisson arrival rate parameter λ). A simple back-of-the-envelope calculation from the data in table 3.3 of the paper will show that the probability of the loss exceeding \$25 billion is 0.005. Thus, the probability of occurrence of a bigcat is on the order of 1 percent per year. On average, we will see one bigcat every one hundred years. This does not sound like a cause for concern. However, this is not the correct way to look at this question. What we need to examine is the probability of at least one occurrence in one hundred years, not the average number of occurrences:

N	Poisson Probability
0	.1108
1	.3679
2	.1839
3	.0613

This turns out to be 89 percent! Hence, it is clearly a matter requiring attention. Similar analysis for twenty-five years gives a probability of at least one bigcat as 23 percent, and for ten years the probability is 10 percent. It is clear that, if the numbers hold, we will see a bigcat in the near future.

The issue is, can we live with it? In assessing this matter, we must consider whether allowing a certain number of reinsurance firms to go down will have a detrimental effect on the insurance industry. On balance, it probably will. On another tack, discussion with industry representatives suggests that the pricing at lower levels of coverage seems to be affected by the difficulty of reinsuring bigcat risk. The paper argues in addition that the government is better placed to provide the time diversification needed to hedge these contracts and that the provision of this contract will provide better assessment of this risk as well as formalizing a system where the participants pay for the coverage rather than relying on endgame government bailouts.

Eventually, cross-sectional diversification will overtake time diversification as the means to manage this risk. Cross-sectional pooling of risk also offers a better market in that there will likely exist larger numbers of buyers and sellers of the risk (i.e., a two-way market), as opposed to the current proposal, which envisages one seller and many buyers. In sum, there is a clear need for this type of contract, as a starter to a full-fledged market in bigcat risk.

Contract Mechanics

The toughest issues to be dealt with in any proposal arise from the implementation mechanics. This proposal is no exception. There are several issues that need attention.

1. The first is delayed settlement: the contract is written on losses aggregated over eighteen months after the date of the event. Given this, buyers of the contract must wait to obtain the proceeds from the government. With what is almost certainly a badly eroded capital base, the reinsurance firms may not be able to wait that long. Of course, they may securitize their expected claim against the government, but this will mean taking a discount on the value of the claim, which may be quite large, given both the "distress" nature of the sale and the uncertainty of the true value of the claim.

2. The contract with one seller who sets a reservation price may actually distort the fair value of the insurance in this market.

3. The third issue is auction design: here several issues need addressing, especially in the light of the fact that both price and quantity risk are severe. The winner's curse would be large, making the setting of the reservation price critical, to ensure not only that the government achieves a fair reserve but also that the reservation price offers a good signal of value. The likelihood of one firm garnering a disproportionate amount of this cover appears high as well.

4. The fourth issue is the rollover version of the contract: the contract envisages a rollover option that allows the buyer to renew the contract for the rest of the year if within the year a bigcat occurs. The renewal is made for the remaining part of the year at a time-prorated value of the original contract. This rollover design has two flaws: (i) If the analogy of options is used, the time value of the contract is not equally distributed over the life of the option and tends to decay rapidly at times closer to maturity. If this is the case, the rollover would be overpriced. (ii) If the arrivals of cats are not independently and identically distributed but positively autocorrelated, as is surely the case with hurricane risk, then the rollover is underpriced. Hence, a more careful specification of the rollover contract is called for.

One possible suggestion may be to write contracts on the change in the price of insurance within a short period immediately after the cat. We observe that the price of insurance rises when a catastrophic event occurs and is correlated with the size of the event. This happens because the insurance industry needs to raise prices to cover higher costs of capital given capital erosion, and the rise in prices is partly demand driven since people seem to rush out and buy insurance when alarmed by a large catastrophe. This has the advantage of (i) being directly and immediately measurable, (ii) being traded, (iii) avoiding the delayed-settlement problem, all of which would make for a more liquid market. However, this assumes that prices react to cat size with a high degree of correlation (i.e., low-basis risk). It is not clear that this is so, and it calls for further empirical investigation.

Pricing Approaches

The paper makes a difficult evaluation problem appear easy. The approach examines the fit of several statistical distributions to the data on loss severity and finds that the Burr 12 and GB2 distributions provide a good fit. While an options approach may also be used to come up with the insurance value of the contracts, it is hard to justify it, given that risk-neutral valuation does not apply in the absence of an ability to replicate the option with an underlying security/asset.

Pricing these contracts requires three separate analyses: (1) a scheme to develop a distribution of loss severity; (2) estimation of the hazard or event rate; and (3) use of an appropriate cost-of-capital or discount rate to compute the present value of the losses. These three are clearly in descending order of complexity, and the paper rightly focuses on the most complex analysis, developing a satisfactory and pleasing methodology.

If one has to raise a red flag, it is about what is often called the "Star Trek" problem. Since we have never seen a bigcat as yet, we are employing statistical analysis to make forecasts about a zone where we have never been before! The degree of confidence in this exercise must perforce be weak.

Finally, one suggestion about the modeling: we do know that the standard deviation of losses tends to increase as we go into higher and higher layers of risk; that is, volatility of loss severity $\sigma(T)$ is increasing in the trigger level (T), or $\partial\sigma(T)/\partial T > 0$. Use of this fact may bring more structure to the modeling method and sharpen the confidence levels in the pricing results.

Binary Contracts

In some cases, loss occurrence is easier to forecast than loss severity. A good example of this is hurricanes, where advances in weather-forecasting technology have made the prediction of hurricane arrivals more facile. By writing binary contracts that pay off a fixed amount only on the occurrence of the bigcat, not on the severity, the writer of the contract will be able to price it more accurately. While this increases basis risk substantially, at the bigcat level, with triggers of $25 billion, the reinsurer is more concerned with credit risk than basis risk. There are several advantages of the binary contract, and, indeed, several participants in the market already trade such instruments. The benefits are the following: (1) The binary contract avoids the "Star Trek" problem. (2) The per contract risk can be quantified by the writer of the contract. (3) The market is forced to forecast severity but now has an available instrument to trade it. (4) It is easier to offer multiple maturities of contracts. (5) Implied hazard rates can be traded, just the way the market for equity options trades implied volatilities. (6) It will be easier to make a market, and demand and supply will therefore set price in a liquid two-way market. It avoids the paradigm of one seller and many buyers. (7) Pure jump-process option-pricing technology may be used. (8) Plenty of physical forecasting expertise now exists for these risks.

Conclusion

The paper makes an important contribution in highlighting the urgent need for bigcat contracts. While there are several mechanics and pricing issues that need sorting out, the authors should be pleased that their work will provide a first benchmark for contracting in this area and set a standard of quality for future work. With the establishment of indexes on cat risk, a new generation of pricing models such as this one will soon be spawned. It is truly an exciting time for modelers in this industry—this paper is the tip of the iceberg.

Comment   James A. Tilley

One thing that is becoming clear is that it is easier to be a discussant the later in the conference one speaks because some of the good points one wants to make have already been very well expressed by others. It is too difficult for me to resist making comments about the role of the federal government and the proposed manner of federal government involvement in the catastrophic loss problem, but I will also live up to my assigned task of commenting on the pricing methodology proposed by the authors.

The first key question is, Does the federal government need to be involved at all—can the private sector handle the problem by itself? Many advocates of leaving it to the private sector base their view on the huge capital base of the insurance/reinsurance industry, the ability of the industry to diversify across risks other than property-catastrophe, the possibility of adopting more aggressive investment strategies that have high returns and high volatilities but little if any correlation with the insurance risks underwritten, and the hope that constraints on the state regulation of premium rates for personal lines can be eased or eliminated. Still, I have not seen any thorough, definitive analysis to suggest that the private sector alone can cope with the financial consequence of mega-disasters, either now or in the future.

The second key question is, If the federal government should participate, are the proposed $25–$50 billion excess-of-loss (XOL) contracts the best way? Several participants have made good points already. I will repeat them briefly and then add a few points not yet raised.

1. The fundamental issue is whether federal government involvement should be on a basis of *risk transfer* or *risk financing*. An associated issue is

James A. Tilley is managing director and chief information officer of information technology at Morgan Stanley.

whether the involvement should be ex ante (risk transfer) or ex post (risk financing). Chris Milton of AIG has already argued in discussion here for the use of "transitory capital" in lieu of permanent capital. I think that that is consistent with a financing view; that is, the federal government should be ready to lend when required.

2. I agree completely with Aaron Stern's comment that, if the proposed federal XOL contracts are used, they should cover losses on an aggregate basis rather than a per occurrence basis. An aggregate basis is consistent with the notion of the federal government serving an industry "backstop" role, whereas an occurrence basis is not.

3. If the federal XOL contracts are utilized, how high should the attachment be? Should it be set at a twenty-five-, fifty-, or one-hundred-year return likelihood, or should the probability of attachment be even more remote? Again, this is a question of private- versus public-sector involvement and underscores the role of the federal government as providing a backstop to the industry.

4. Should there be more than one layer of federal XOL contracts so that even higher caps can be provided, thus enhancing the value of the federal government backup to the insurance industry?

5. Is the basis risk imposed on the purchasers of the call-spread contracts so great as to largely negate the hedging value of the contracts? To what level of geography would the contracts have to be refined to deal satisfactorily with basis risk?

6. One idea that may bear fruit is the *mandatory* purchase of the federal XOL contracts by the industry, assuming that the attachment point were high enough and the price low enough (e.g., the reservation price). Such mandatory purchase could mitigate basis risk greatly because the federal government would in essence be underwriting the entire industry. If the issue of individual insurer attachment points could be dealt with satisfactorily, each insurer could make recovery in proportion to underwritten net losses (UNL) in lieu of a predetermined market share of industry losses. This approach is equivalent to the use of federal XOL contracts in combination with intercompany swaps of industry-based recovery in return for UNL-based recovery.

Let me now turn to my explicit assignment of commenting on the authors' proposed pricing methodology for the federal XOL contracts. A good starting point is the fundamental actuarial formula:

$$\text{reinsurance premium} = \text{"pure premium" to cover expected losses}$$
$$+ \text{ expense loading } + \text{ risk loading.}$$

The risk-loading component is usually developed from notions of required capital to support the risks underwritten via the contract and the reinsurer's cost of that capital. The concept *required capital* should account for the spread of risk in the reinsurer's entire portfolio, both cross-sectionally and over time.

The variance of the reinsurer's loss distribution and more particularly, the risk of ruin underpin the calculation of the risk loading.

The problem posed by catastrophic losses is that the ratio of the standard deviation to the mean of the loss distribution applying to an XOL contract increases dramatically as the attachment for the XOL cover increases, actually rendering risk transfer uneconomical at some point. That is, at such a point, there is no price acceptable to both reinsurer and cedent.

The authors point out that the federal government is in a unique position to take a nearly *infinite time horizon* and thus fully exploit the benefit on intertemporal spreading to reduce the risk loading to *zero*. However, the authors seem to advocate building a risk load into the XOL contract pricing in order to avoid "crowding out" the private sector. My question to the authors is, If the federal government backstop of the insurance industry triggers only at a very high level, and if the federal government has a critical competitive advantage due to long-run intertemporal spreading, why would the private sector even consider playing the game? The industry has more than enough to worry about without taking on the megacatastrophic problem as well.

As a final point, I would like to comment on the calibration of the pure-premium component of the pricing formula. The authors' work demonstrates that distribution assumptions matter a great deal, as one expected they would— RMS versus PCS, GB2 versus lognormal, etc., all make a difference. It is difficult to see how the federal government would be able to gauge, even over the very long run, whether the reservation price has been established properly. Moreover, would federal politicians be able to resist the "payback" mentality of the reinsurance industry following a megacatastrophe? Would the prices for federal XOL contracts then be jacked up? The notions of infinite-horizon intertemporal spreading and "here-and-now" political decision realities seem to conflict.

In summary, I think that the product structure and pricing concepts advanced in the authors' paper merit serious attention, but, as always for proposed solutions to vexing issues, early work often raises even more questions—that is its essential value, after all. The authors are to be congratulated for their contributions.

4 Challenges Facing the Insurance Industry in Managing Catastrophic Risks

Paul R. Kleindorfer and Howard C. Kunreuther

The private insurance industry feels that it cannot continue to provide coverage against hurricanes and earthquakes as it has done in the past without opening itself up to the possibility of insolvency or a significant loss of surplus. This concern stems from a series of natural disasters in the United States since 1989 that have resulted in unprecedented insured losses.

Figure 4.1 depicts the magnitude of the catastrophic losses experienced by the insurance industry in the United States from 1961 to 1995. The graphic change from 1989 is obvious. Prior to the occurrence of Hurricane Hugo in 1989 (insured losses in that year were over $4 billion), the insurance industry had never suffered any losses from a single disaster of over $1 billion. Since that time, it has had ten disasters that have exceeded this amount ("Catastrophes" 1996).

Hurricane Andrew was the most severe disaster that the insurance industry has experienced to date. It swept ashore along the Florida coastline in August 1992, causing insured losses from wind damage that topped $15 billion.[1] Had

Paul R. Kleindorfer is the Universal Furniture Professor of Decision Sciences and Economics and professor of public policy and management at the Wharton School, University of Pennsylvania. Howard C. Kunreuther is the Cecilia Yen Koo Professor of Decision Sciences and Public Policy at the Wharton School, University of Pennsylvania.

Special thanks go to Risk Management Solutions of Menlo Park, California, for providing the authors with the data to construct the model city and analyze the effect of earthquakes on property damage. Weimin Dong, Pierre Lemaire, and Christopher Warren were extremely helpful in constructing the different modules that characterize the earthquake-simulation model. They and Rick Anderson also provided valuable assistance in data analysis. Jacqueline Meszaros, Gilbert White, and Peter Zweifel provided helpful comments on an earlier draft of the paper. The authors are especially grateful to our discussants, James Garven and Dwight Jaffee, and to the conference participants for their comments on the paper. The authors acknowledge partial financial support for this paper from National Science Foundation grant 524603. They acknowledge partial financial support for this paper from the NBER Project on the Financing of Property/Casualty Risks.

1. Water damage to insured property is covered by the government-based National Flood Insurance Program.

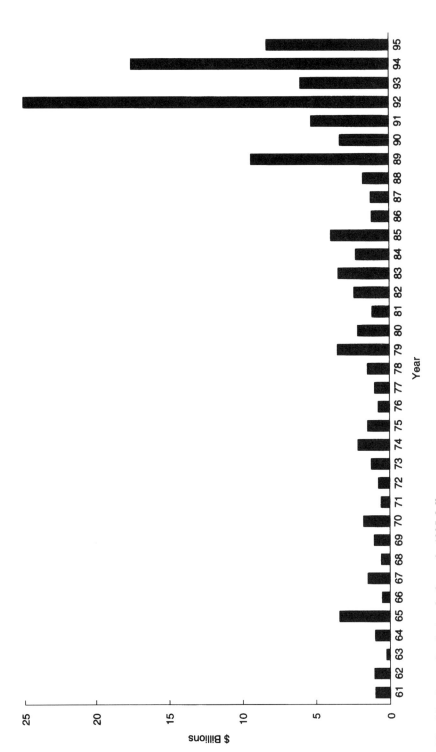

Fig. 4.1 Insured catastrophe losses in 1995 dollars
Source: Insurance Services Office (1996, 4).

the storm taken a more northerly track and hit downtown Miami and Miami Beach, total insured damage could have approached $50 billion. The storm forced the insurance industry to recognize that it might be subject to losses in the future way beyond any figures previously imagined.[2]

On the West Coast of the United States, insured damage from the Northridge Earthquake of January 1994 exceeded $12 billion. Had a similar quake hit central Los Angeles, the insured bill could have been over $50 billion. The Kobe Earthquake in Japan, which occurred exactly one year after Northridge, caused substantially more damage, with estimates of the costs of repair at well over $100 billion. Since very few structures were insured, the cost to the insurance industry was relatively small ($1 billion) (Scawthorn, Lashkari, and Naseer 1997). A repeat of the earthquake that destroyed Tokyo in 1923 could cost between $900 billion and $1.4 trillion today (Valery 1995).

The change in the character of these disasters in recent years and the specter of megacatastrophes in the future raise two fundamental questions: (1) What steps can be taken to reduce the losses from future disasters? (2) Who can and should pay for the costs of these events when they occur?

This paper suggests an approach to evaluating the role of insurance and other policy instruments for managing the catastrophic risk problem. The next section provides an overview of why traditional reinsurance mechanisms are limited in their ability to cover recent losses. It also indicates how pooling arrangements at the state and federal levels have attempted to fill this void as well as the need for new sources of funds from the capital markets.

Section 4.2 stresses the importance of understanding the decision processes of the key interested parties concerned with catastrophic losses and their interaction with each other. On the basis of this descriptive characterization of the problem, section 4.3 proposes a conceptual framework for examining a set of alternative strategies by taking advantage of information technology, expanded databases, and modeling approaches now being used to analyze catastrophic risks. Section 4.4 utilizes this framework to examine the role that two policy instruments, reinsurance and mitigation, can play in dealing with catastrophic losses for a "model city" in California. The concluding section suggests ways to expand these analyses to include alternative decision rules and policy instruments in structuring and evaluating new approaches to managing catastrophic risks.

4.1 Need for New Funding Sources

Insurers have traditionally protected themselves through private reinsurance contracts whereby portions of their losses from a catastrophic disaster are cov-

---

2. Six years prior to Andrew, an industry-sponsored study had been published, indicating the effect of two $7 billion hurricanes on property-casualty insurance companies. The report indicated that no hurricane of that magnitude had ever occurred before but that "storms of that dollar magnitude are now possible because of the large concentrations of property along the Gulf and Atlantic coastlines of the United States" (AIRAC 1986, 1).

ered by some type of treaty or excess-loss arrangement. To illustrate, consider an excess-of-loss protection policy between a private insurer and a reinsurer where a 300/100 excess-loss layer was provided. This arrangement means that, if losses from a specific earthquake exceed $300 million, the reinsurer will cover the next $100 million in losses. The insurer is responsible for covering losses above $400 million. The $300 million is designated as the *attachment point,* and the other end of the range, $400 million, is specified as the *limit.* The difference between these two points defines the amount of reinsurance in force. In return for this protection, the insurer pays the reinsurer a prespecified premium.

4.1.1   Role of Reinsurance

Following the recent catastrophic disasters, insurers have been demanding more reinsurance coverage, but they are having a difficult time obtaining the layers that they require at prices that they consider affordable. If insurers were allowed to charge higher premiums on their own policies, many would need less reinsurance and would accept higher attachment points. However, regulatory constraints, such as obtaining prior approval by the state insurance commissioner of rate changes, limit insurers' ability to raise premiums to levels that they feel reflect the risk. For example, in Florida, restrictions have been placed on rates that can be charged on homeowner's coverage (which covers wind damage) in areas of the state affected by hurricanes (Lecomte and Gahagan 1998).

Given the limitations on the amount of reinsurance that insurers can afford to purchase, they have been greatly concerned with the maximum probable losses that they may experience from a severe hurricane or earthquake with their current book of business. This concern is *not* unfounded. Nine insurance companies were insolvent as a result of Hurricane Andrew, adding to the financial burden of other insurers who were assessed for the claims of the insolvent firms by the Florida Insurance Guarantee Fund. In fact, these post-Andrew assessments led to a tenth company becoming insolvent (Conning & Co. 1994).

Many insurers writing earthquake coverage in California have also been concerned with the possibility of insolvency or a significant loss of surplus following another major earthquake. Although there are no formal rate restrictions by the state Insurance Department, companies feel constrained on how high a rate they can charge and still maintain their credibility with the public. Furthermore, they have been limited in the amount of reinsurance that they have been able to obtain owing to the capacity limits of the worldwide reinsurance market (Insurance Services Office 1996). In fact, shortly after the Northridge Earthquake, Standard and Poor's Insurance Rating Service identified ten insurance companies that would be in danger of failing if another major natural disaster occurred in California (Insurance Services Office 1994).

The U.S. Congress is now considering proposals for providing federal excess-loss reinsurance. The National Economic Council has recommended that the federal government offer *catastrophe-reinsurance contracts* that would be auctioned annually. The proposal would establish a program in which the Treasury would auction a limited number of excess-of-loss contracts covering industry losses between $25 and $50 billion from a single natural disaster. Insurers, reinsurers, and state and national reinsurance pools would be eligible purchasers (Lewis and Murdock 1996).

4.1.2   Emergence of State Pools

During the past five years, several states have established pools to provide either coverage or additional capacity following disasters. The first such arrangement was in Hawaii, where a hurricane relief fund was established after Hurricane Iniki (1992) to provide windstorm coverage for residential and commercial property. In Florida, a joint underwriting association was established in 1992 following Hurricane Andrew to issue policies to those homeowners who were refused coverage by private insurers. Today, this residual market mechanism is the state's third-largest property insurer, having underwritten almost 900,000 policies and exposing itself to $100 billion in potential losses, much of that in southern Florida (Scism 1996).

The Florida Hurricane Catastrophe Fund was created in 1992 with trust funds reimbursing insurers for a portion of their losses from future severe hurricanes. Above a predetermined retention level, insurers are provided with reinsurance benefits from the fund following a future catastrophic disaster. The current cash balance of the fund will *not* enable it to provide adequate protection to insurers for hurricanes as costly as Hurricane Andrew (Insurance Services Office 1996).

Since 1985, insurers in California have been required to offer earthquake coverage to anyone who has a homeowner's policy with them. This created few problems until after the Northridge Earthquake, when many insurers felt that they could not risk selling any more earthquake policies in the state. In 1995, the California Insurance Department surveyed insurers and learned that up to 90 percent of them had either placed restrictions on the sale of new homeowner's policies or stopped selling these policies completely (Roth 1998).

As a result of this lack of availability of homeowner's insurance following the Northridge Earthquake, a state-run earthquake-insurance company was proposed. In September 1996, the state legislature approved the formation of the California Earthquake Authority (CEA), which provides coverage to homeowners with a 15 percent deductible. The CEA is an innovative arrangement that reflects a combination of both private and public funding to cover the insured losses from a catastrophic disaster.

Table 4.1 depicts the different layers of coverage to finance the $10.5 billion funding requirement, assuming that all licensed insurance companies in the market participated. *Insurers' liability* is limited to $6 billion ($1 billion in start-up assessments, $3 billion for the first layer of coverage to pay claims

Table 4.1   Structure of the California Earthquake Authority:
Capacity Participation

Layer		Total ($ billion)
$2 billion	Industry-contingent assessment (after the earthquake)	$10.5
$1.5 billion	Berkshire Hathaway	8.5
$1 billion	Policyholder-contingent assessment	7
$2 billion	Reinsurance (no reinstatement)	6
$3 billion	Industry-contingent assessment (after the earthquake)	4
$1 billion	Industry assessment (to start the program)	1

Source: Roth (1998).

after an earthquake, and another $2 billion if the insured damage exceeds $8.5 billion). The other layers are funded by either *reinsurance* ($2 billion); *policyholder assessment* ($1 billion), to cover a loan from the bond market; or Berkshire Hathaway ($1.5 billion) (Roth 1998).

4.1.3   Potential Role of the Capital Markets

In the past few years, considerable interest has been shown by investment banks and brokerage firms in developing new financial instruments for providing protection against catastrophic risks (Jaffee and Russell 1996). Their objective is to find ways in which investors will be as comfortable trading new securitized instruments covering catastrophic exposures as they would the securities of any other asset class. In other words, catastrophe exposures would be treated as a new asset class.

Litzenberger, Beaglehole, and Reynolds (1996) have simulated ten thousand scenarios for a hypothetical ten-year catastrophe bond where the investor receives a coupon of 14.57 percent (nine hundred basis points above Treasury bonds) over the life of the bond. If the loss ratio exceeds 20 percent in any calendar year, the bond expires, and the investor receives half the principal. The average rate of return for these bonds under these simulations was 7.47 percent when random samples were taken from a lognormal distribution. This compares with an average return of 5.61 percent for a ten-year high-yield bond. Froot et al. (1995) computed the returns that an investor would have earned by providing capital to fund excess-of-loss reinsurance contracts during the period 1970–94. They found that an investor would have earned returns of 224 basis points above the Treasury bill rate during this entire period. In the best and worst years over this time horizon, the *excess return* would have been 7.5 percent and −22.1 percent, respectively.

Until 1997, there has been relatively little interest by the investment community in these new instruments. But the picture appears to changing. Recently, USAA successfully floated a catastrophe bond that has two layers of debt: one layer is subject to interest forgiveness should USAA suffer a loss in excess of

$1 billion from a class 3, 4, or 5 hurricane; the other layer has both principal and interest at risk.[3] The $400 million targeted capacity was oversubscribed, partly because investors are now more familiar with these types of instruments, but also because of the very high return on the investment. Another catastrophe bond based on California industry losses has been put together by Swiss Re, Credit Suisse, and First Boston for dealing with catastrophic earthquake losses (Doherty 1997).

We feel that there are several reasons why the investment community has been slow to embrace these new capital market instruments. For one thing, the risks of catastrophic losses from natural disasters are highly uncertain, causing investors to focus on the high variance in losses. This concern has been heightened by the recent projections of future losses from hurricanes and earthquakes, which far exceed any disasters that have occurred until now. In addition, these are risks with which the investment community has no prior history or experience. Hence, there are currently no standards or ratings for evaluating the quality of a particular instrument. Finally, and perhaps most important, any innovation takes time to be adopted. There is generally a long process between the time a new product is introduced and the time there is a market for it, particularly if there are long-standing relationships between the two key interested parties—insurers and reinsurers (Wind 1982).

4.2   Understanding Decision Processes of the Key Stakeholders

In order to develop a strategy for managing catastrophic risks, one must characterize the nature of the hazards as well as understand the behavior of the interested parties concerned with the consequences of these events. The risks associated with earthquakes and hurricanes fall into the class of low-probability, high-consequence (LP-HC) events. There is considerable ambiguity and uncertainty associated with predicting both the *probability of the event* occurring at a specific time and place and the *resulting losses* to the affected community (Hanks and Cornell 1994). Experts often disagree on these risk estimates. There is not sufficient evidence from past events or scientific models to reconcile these differences.

Hazard-risk maps have been drawn for both earthquakes and hurricanes, but they provide only rough guidelines as to the likelihood and potential damage from specific events. A case in point is the medium-intensity Northridge Earthquake, where the actual losses were considerably more than what was predicted by experts. Certain structures, notably steel-framed buildings with moment-resisting frames, failed even though they had been considered outstandingly good at handling earthquakes prior to Northridge (Valery 1995).

3. The interest rate was 273 above LIBOR for the first layer of debt and 576 for the more risky second layer.

4.2.1   Simplified Decision Rules

The ambiguity associated with these events, coupled with the limited information-processing capabilities of individuals, has led potential disaster victims and insurers to utilize simplified decision rules that differ from such normative models of choice as expected-utility theory or cost-benefit analysis (Camerer and Kunreuther 1989). These choice processes need to be taken into account in designing strategies for managing catastrophic events.

Residents in hazard-prone areas often exhibit one of two reactions with respect to LP-HC events. If they have not experienced the specific disaster and do not know friends and neighbors who have been in these events, then many believe that "it will not happen to me." This perception of the risk is equivalent to treating the probability of the hurricane or earthquake as if it were zero. These residents will have no interest in voluntarily purchasing insurance or investing in mitigation measures (Kunreuther 1996).

Individuals who have experienced a disaster or are concerned about the possibility of severe losses in the future because of the media and/or personal knowledge are likely to purchase insurance voluntarily and/or invest in mitigation measures. One factor that restrains propertyowners from incurring the upfront costs of loss-reduction measures is their unusually short time horizons. This may be due to the inability of people to project benefits over a long period of time and/or budget constraints that preclude large investments unless they pay off rapidly. For example, if it costs \$1,000 to bolt a structure to its foundation and the expected annual reduction in losses is \$300,[4] then, even with an annual discount rate as high as 15 percent, the investment will pay off in five years.[5] However, if a homeowner compares the \$1,000 investment with the one-year saving of \$300, then he will not want to invest in this measure.

Insurers are also concerned with ambiguity and uncertainty in determining whether they want to offer coverage and, if so, what premiums to charge against particular risks. For earthquakes and hurricanes, where the insurer is likely to have a portfolio of policies concentrated in one area, then the insurer will experience either feast (no hurricanes) or famine (a hurricane hitting the area where it has sold many policies). For such correlated risks, the insurer is concerned, not only with the uncertainty of the probability of a loss, but also with the magnitude of claims should a single disaster occur.

In fact, a series of interviews conducted with insurers following Hurricane

---

4. The expected annual loss is determined by multiplying the probabilities of disasters of different magnitudes by the resulting damage. For example, if the annual probability of an earthquake affecting one's home was one in fifty and the savings in damage from bolting the house to the foundation was \$15,000, then the expected annual reduction in losses is \$300 (i.e., $1/50 \times$ \$15,000), assuming that this was the only earthquake that could damage the house.

5. The expected benefit from the mitigation measure over a period of five years is Σ \$300/$(1 + d)^t$, or \$1,005, using an annual discount rate of $d = 15$ percent.

Andrew and the Northridge Earthquake indicated that a key factor influencing their decision-making process regarding how many policies to write is their probable maximum loss (PML) should a catastrophic disaster occur.[6] In many hazard-prone regions, a number of insurers would like to reduce their current PMLs, in part because the A. M. Best Company has begun to include PML exposures as a part of its rating of insurer capability ("Catastrophes" 1996).

One of the questions that every insurer asks is whether earthquake risks are insurable. In his definitive study, which sheds light on this question, Stone (1973) indicated that firms are interested in maximizing expected profits subject to two constraints, representing the survival of the firm and the stability of its operation. The insurance underwriter operationalizes the survival constraint by choosing a portfolio of risks so that the estimated probability of insolvency is less than p_1. The stability constraint focuses on the combined loss and expense ratio (LR) for each year. Insurers define a target level (LR*) that represents an upper limit on this ratio and requires the probability that LR exceed LR*) to be less than p_2.[7]

A simple example illustrates how these two constraints would be utilized by an insurer in determining whether the earthquake risk is insurable. All houses in the earthquake area are assumed to be identical, and the insurance premium on each structure is therefore set at P. Suppose that the Shaker Insurance Company had A dollars in current surplus and wanted to determine the number of policies it would be able to sell and still satisfy the above two constraints. The maximum number of policies (n_1) that would satisfy the *survival constraint* is determined by

$$\text{probability}[(\text{total losses} > n_1 P + A)] < p_1.$$

The maximum number of policies (n_2) satisfying the *stability constraint* is determined by

$$\text{probability}[(\text{total losses} + \text{expenses})/n_2 P > LR^*] < p_2.$$

Whether the Shaker Company will view the earthquake risk as insurable depends on whether the fixed cost of developing the product is sufficiently low that it can make a positive expected profit. This in turn depends on how large the values of n_1 and n_2 are for any given premium P. Note that Shaker also has the freedom to change its premium. A larger P for any prespecified loss structure will increase the values of n_1 and n_2 but will lower the demand for coverage. Shaker will decide *not* to offer earthquake coverage if it believes that it

---

6. These interviews were conducted by Jacqueline Meszaros as part of a National Science Foundation study (see Meszaros 1997).

7. In their analysis of insurance pricing of catastrophic risks, Dong, Shah, and Wong (1996) modify the stability constraint by formulating it as the probability that LR exceeds LR* by x percentage points (e.g., 4 percent) is less than p_2.

cannot attract enough demand at any premium structure to make a positive expected profit using the survival and/or stability constraints as restrictions on how many policies it is willing to offer.

The decision rules utilized by insurers in setting premiums for coverage are a function of how ambiguous and correlated the risks are. Studies of actuaries and underwriters of primary insurers and reinsurers reveal that both these factors play a key role in their premium-setting decisions. A survey of 463 actuaries concerning a defective-product scenario where the probability of loss was varied and there was a perfectly correlated risk revealed that the median premium that they would charge was anywhere from two to ten times larger if the probability was ambiguous than if it was well specified (Hogarth and Kunreuther 1992). In another survey, when underwriters in primary and reinsurance companies were given scenarios of an earthquake risk with well-specified probabilities and losses as well as scenarios where the risk was ambiguous and uncertain, the responses were similar to those of the actuaries. The mean premium was 50 percent higher for primary underwriters and 40 percent higher for reinsurer underwriters for the case where the probability of a loss was ambiguous and the magnitude of the loss was uncertain than when the risk was well specified (Kunreuther et al. 1993).

4.2.2   Nested Decision Structures

Another feature of the choice process that needs to be taken into account when developing strategies is the interconnectedness between the different policy instruments and the stakeholders associated with the management of catastrophic risks. To illustrate how policy instruments are nested, consider the relation between mitigation and insurance. If building codes are enforced for all structures in hazard-prone areas, future disaster losses are likely to be reduced significantly. This will have several desirable effects. First, it will reduce the magnitude of the losses from future disasters and hence enable insurers to provide additional coverage to propertyowners. This will decrease the need for reinsurance and for funds from other sources, such as the capital market and state pools. If rates are based on risk, it will also enable insurers to offer propertyowners coverage at lower premiums for the same amount of coverage.

The National Flood Insurance Program (NFIP), created by Congress in 1968 in response to mounting flood losses and increasing costs to the general taxpayers through disaster relief, illustrates the interaction of a set of policy tools for dealing with this hazard. To encourage communities to participate in the program, and to maintain the property values of structures, those residing in the area prior to the issuance of a flood-insurance rate map had their premiums subsidized. New construction was charged an actuarial premium reflecting the risks of flood (Interagency Flood Plain Management Review Committee 1994).

To prevent development of structures in highly hazard-prone areas, communities can remain in the NFIP only if they develop certain ordinances restricting the construction of houses in high-hazard areas or if residents are required to meet standards according to which they are protected against floods with an annual probability of one in one hundred or greater. As a condition for receiving grants or loans for the acquisition, construction, or improvement of structures located in the one-hundred-year floodplain, the propertyowner must purchase flood insurance. However, evidence from a U.S. General Accounting Office study indicates that this requirement has not been routinely enforced. A survey in Texas following a major flood in 1989 revealed that 79 percent of the damaged properties that had been required to purchase flood coverage were uninsured at the time of the disaster (U.S. General Accounting Office 1990).[8]

Turning to the stakeholders, the decision processes of one interested party will affect the behavior of another group, which will influence the choices of a third party, etc. A change in a given policy or program must be carefully structured to reflect this nested decision structure (Kleindorfer, Kunreuther, and Schoemaker 1993). The challenges associated with reducing disaster losses through mitigation measures illustrate this point. There is considerable empirical evidence that relatively few homeowners adopt loss-reduction measures even if they are relatively inexpensive and promise to yield sufficient benefits to justify the cost (Palm 1995). One solution to this problem is to inform individuals of the dangers of living in specific areas and to develop building codes that are well enforced.

Other stakeholders have good financial reasons not to implement these measures. *Real estate agents* have no reason to provide prospective buyers with information on the hazards associated with living in a particular structure that does not meet the building code. They are supported implicitly by the *current owner,* who wants to sell his property at as high a price as possible. Furthermore the potential buyer may have little interest in knowing about the design of the structure if he does not think about the risks associated with future disasters.

The problem is compounded by *developers and contractors,* who want to build structures as cheaply as possible so that they can sell them more easily and remain competitive. Until recently, *insurers and reinsurers* have generally not been sensitive to the design of structures when they issue coverage against wind or earthquake damage. Hence, inspections are not required as a condition for insurance. In setting premiums for structures in hazard-prone areas, insurers do not know whether specific mitigation measures have been put in place. To the extent that local and state governments do *not* enforce codes through inspections of individual structures,[9] this represents a type of ex ante moral hazard.

One might expect *banks and financial institutions* to be sensitive to the

---

8. More details on proposals for linking alternative policy instruments for dealing with the flood hazard can be found in the Interagency Floodplain Management Review Committee (1994) report.

9. For a more detailed discussion of ex ante moral hazard, see Pauly (1974), Marshall (1976), Shavell (1979), and Dionne and Harrington (1992).

structural design of the property when issuing a mortgage, but they generally do not require any certification that the property meets current building codes. In informal discussions, one hears the comment that a bank cannot remain competitive if it is the only one demanding that the property be inspected. One can also speculate that managers employed by financial institutions do not worry about the possibility of a future disaster or are convinced that victims will receive sufficient disaster assistance to maintain their mortgage payments. In addition, most banks send their mortgages to the secondary market, where the new lending institution may have limited knowledge of the hazard in question.

The upshot of this set of dynamics is that many homes are likely to be constructed in such a way that they do not meet code. Insurance experts have indicated that 25 percent of the insured losses from Hurricane Andrew could have been prevented through better building-code compliance and enforcement (Insurance Information Institute 1995). One question that naturally arises is whether insurers working closely with financial institutions and public-sector agencies can encourage propertyowners to adopt cost-effective mitigation measures by offering premium reductions for safer houses and requiring that homes be inspected before a policy is issued. The effect of such a strategy could significantly reduce future losses from natural disasters.

4.2.3 Summary

Given the nature of the decision processes and the degree of nestedness between the different stakeholders, there may be new roles for the private market and the public sector to play in helping manage the problems of catastrophic risk. For example, if individuals are reluctant to incur up-front costs of mitigation measures that promise to be cost effective in the long run, there is an opportunity for insurers and banks to join forces to alleviate this concern. One way to do this is for the insurer to lower premiums, reflecting the expected reduction in future losses, and for banks to provide the propertyowner with a low-interest loan over the life of the mortgage for financing mitigation expenses. It is very likely that the annual loan payments will be less than the premium reduction, thus guaranteeing that every knowledgeable homeowner will want to adopt cost-effective mitigation measures.

Different stakeholders can also join forces in promoting new financial instruments to supplement reinsurance for protecting insurers against catastrophic losses. Here, the challenge is to convince investors that their chances of suffering large losses are relatively small compared to the expected return on their investment. This process is not an easy one, particularly if the investment community is unfamiliar with the types of risks against which they would be providing protection. The ambiguity associated with estimating future losses and the conflicts between experts on their assumptions for developing catastrophe models leave investors somewhat confused about what they are getting themselves into if they decide to commit funds to some of these new financial instruments. As we will indicate in the next section, there are opportunities for examining expert differences in a systematic manner. Such analyses may alleviate some of the concerns of potential investors.

4.3   A Conceptual Framework for Analyzing Alternative Programs

4.3.1   New Advances in Risk Assessment, Information Technology, and Catastrophe Modeling

There is now an opportunity to evaluate alternative strategies for managing the risks from natural disasters by taking advantage of a set of new developments in the areas of risk assessment (RA), information technology (IT), and catastrophe modeling (CM). Turning first to RA, by merging information derived from past records of earthquakes and hurricanes with an increased understanding of the characteristics of these hazards, scientists have been able to reduce our uncertainty about forecasting future events. With respect to damage estimation, engineers can now better characterize the performance of different types of structures during hurricanes of different wind speeds and earthquakes of different magnitudes and intensities.[10]

On the IT side, the development of faster and more powerful computers enables us to examine extremely complex phenomena in ways that were impossible even five years ago. Large databases can easily be stored and manipulated so that large-scale simulations of different disaster scenarios under alternative policy alternatives can now be undertaken.

Finally, new advances in CM provide an opportunity to combine scientific risk assessments with historical records to estimate the probabilities of disasters of different magnitudes and the resulting damage to the affected region. A catastrophe model is the set of databases and computer programs designed to analyze the effect of different scenarios on hazard-prone areas. The information can be presented in the form of *expected annual losses* based on simulations run over a long period of time (e.g., ten thousand years) or the effect of *specific events* (e.g., worst-case scenarios). Several firms have developed catastrophe models and provide detailed analyses of their databases to the various parties concerned with these risks (e.g., insurers, reinsurers, government agencies, and disaster-prone communities).

4.3.2   Nature of Modules

These new advances in RA, IT, and CM provide the impetus for constructing a framework for examining alternative approaches to managing catastrophic risks. Below, we describe the different modules that are depicted graphically in figure 4.2.

---

10. For a more detailed discussion of new advances in seismology and earthquake engineering, see FEMA (1994) and Office of Technology Assessment (1995).

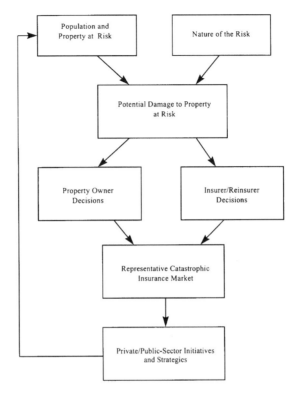

Fig. 4.2   Framework for analyzing catastrophic risks

One must first characterize the *population and property at risk.* For the natural hazards problem, this involves constructing a community or region consisting of homes, businesses, and other properties that are subject to future disasters. More specifically, we want to know the design of each structure, whether specific mitigation measures are in place or could be utilized, the precise location of the structure in relation to the hazard (e.g., distance from an earthquake fault line or proximity to the coast in a hurricane-prone area), and other risk-related factors.

The second module consists of the elements that characterize the *nature of the risk,* namely, the probability that disasters of specific magnitudes will occur and the resulting losses to structures in harm's way. These first two modules provide the ingredients for a module labeled *potential damage to property at risk,* which characterizes the potential damage to individual structures and the model cities from a specific type of hazard.

The *propertyowner decisions* module consists of a set of decision rules utilized by propertyowners in making choices regarding the purchase of insurance and the adoption of loss-prevention measures. The module will build on our understanding of the decision processes of individuals with respect to LP-HC events. For example, if homeowners consider purchasing insurance only if they perceive the probability of the event to be greater than some critical value $p*$), then one must incorporate risk perceptions as part of the decision-process module and determine how these perceptions are formed. In addition, one will need information on residents' and businesses' income and assets, their attitudes toward risk, and their expectations of public subsidies and assistance following a disaster.

The *insurer/reinsurer decisions* module characterizes the decision processes utilized by insurers and reinsurers in underwriting residential and commercial property by building on recent empirical studies of the decision processes of underwriters, actuaries, and other insurance executives. In particular, there is a need to understand the factors that encourage or inhibit the insurance industry from providing coverage against losses due to hurricanes, earthquakes, and other natural disasters.

A module characterizing a *representative catastrophic insurance market* will be developed consisting of propertyowners, prototypical insurance companies (e.g., small, medium, large), and reinsurers. Books of business for each company will be generated under various assumptions about the supply of and demand for insurance and alternative regulatory policies and risk-management strategies of insurers and reinsurers.

By constructing large, medium, and small *representative* insurers with specific balance sheets, types of insurance portfolios, premium structures, and a wide range of potential financial instruments, one could examine the effect of different disasters on the insurer's profitability, solvency, and performance. Such analyses may also enable one to price the costs of different types of financial instruments on the basis of simulated loss experience over time. This information could be translated into prices of these financial instruments reflecting both the expected loss and the variance in these estimates. One could also examine the role of the public sector in regulating rates and providing protection against catastrophic losses.

Finally, the *private/public-sector initiatives and strategies* module will evaluate alternative programs and institutional arrangements between the private and the public sectors. These strategies, which range from information, incentives, and insurance to building codes and land-use regulations, will be important inputs to the modules characterizing propertyowner and insurer/reinsurer decisions. For example, if banks and financial institutions require certain mitigation measures as a condition for a mortgage, this has implications for the way in which propertyowners make decisions and also affects insurer/reinsurer decision processes.

In examining these measures, one must consider the agendas and decision processes of the concerned interested parties in the private and public sectors. What values and agendas do these stakeholders bring to the table? How do they interact with each other? What programs and policies do they favor for reducing future losses and paying for disasters that occur, and why?

The analyses of these issues often involve questions of equity and efficiency. Who should pay for the costs of natural disasters? What is the appropriate level and nature of regulatory oversight of catastrophe-insurance markets? Are other regulatory measures needed to encourage mitigation and prefinancing? Should we restrict individuals from residing in hazard-prone areas or require them to adopt mitigation measures? How do we deal with low-income families who cannot afford the costs of insurance and prevention measures? These and other related questions need to be addressed in developing a strategy for managing catastrophic risks.

4.4   Prototype Analysis Using the Conceptual Framework

To provide insight into the interaction of policy instruments and outcomes, we have constructed a "model city" in California that is subject to possible damage from earthquakes. Four prototypical insurance companies provide coverage to the propertyowners in the city. In this community, we assume that all residents and businesses would like to purchase earthquake insurance but that not all of them can obtain coverage. If the insurer is concerned with the possibility of insolvency, it will limit the amount of coverage that it provides, and some propertyowners will be unprotected. For this analysis, we are assuming that the insurer will determine how much coverage it offers by focusing on a survival constraint similar to the one characterizing insurers' behavior in section 4.2 above.

Two policy options will be examined in this analysis: *the availability of reinsurance for and effect of reinsurance on* primary underwriters and *the adoption of mitigation measures* by propertyowners. The amount and pricing of available reinsurance are, of course, likely to be the result of complex market and regulatory interactions that are not explored explicitly here. Our interest is in understanding the aggregate effect of reinsurance on expected and worst-case results for various classes of propertyowners in the model city and for insurance companies operating there. Similar comments apply for mitigation in that we do not study the pricing, the detailed decision processes, or the regulatory requirements associated with mitigation, only the aggregate effects of several exogenously imposed scenarios for mitigation adoption. More detailed models for both reinsurance and mitigation are the subjects of ongoing research using the model city framework introduced here.

4.4.1   General Model Structure

The structure of the prototype analysis is shown in figure 4.3. First, the structure of the model city is specified. Then scenario variables are set. These variables, together with a model characterizing the earthquake hazard (i.e., the RWP model described below), give rise to a loss distribution, $F(L) = \Pr\{\text{loss} \leq L\}$, and the associated exceedance probability (EP) function, $EP(L) = \Pr\{\text{loss} > L\} = 1 - F(L)$. For a given insurance company, the EP function is,

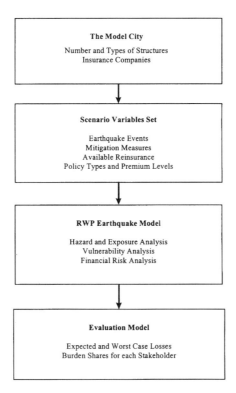

Fig. 4.3   General structure of the model

of course, a function of the number and type of properties insured, mitigation levels, coverage limits, amount of reinsurance, and events (location, number, and severity of earthquakes) that are used to generate loss exposures. The EP functions for all insurance companies and for uninsured properties provide the foundation for evaluating expected and worst-case consequences of the assumed scenario. The structure of the model is depicted in figure 4.3. Let us consider each of its elements in more detail.

4.4.2   Construction of Model City

The model city is a virtual mirror of Oakland, California, in terms of number, types, and mix of structures. As noted above, the insurance market consists of four hypothetical companies: company LG (large), company M (medium), company S (small), and company O (other or none of the above). All properties are initially assigned to precisely one of these companies, on a random basis, but matching some prespecified criteria for the book of business in question. Hence, the books of business of companies LG, M, S, and O cover every property in the city.

One may think of these initially assigned books of business as the maximum

Table 4.2   Composition of Books of Business by ATC Classification

	Small	Medium	Large	Other	Model City
Wood frame	3,077	6,214	0	53,154	62,445
Light metal	1,384	2,778	0	23,144	27,306
Unreinforced masonry wall	10	25	0	147	182
Reinforced concrete (RC) shear wall with frame	50	230	1,192	882	2,354
RC shear wall without frame	22	93	456	380	951
Reinforced masonry shear wall	3	9	82	59	153
Reinforced masonry shear wall with frame	38	211	1,031	775	2,055
Braced steel frame	6	35	114	115	270
Moment steel frame (perimeter)	9	38	180	149	376
Moment steel frame (distributed)	6	38	137	110	291
Ductile RC frame (distributed)	0	15	28	77	120
Nonductile RC frame (distributed)	0	136	282	919	1,337
Precast concrete (non-tilt-up)	0	0	0	2	2
Precast concrete (tilt-up)	0	0	2	2	4
Total number of structures	4,605	9,822	3,504	79,915	97,846

(or full-coverage) book of business that each of the four companies can write in the city. As we will note below, however, companies may cover only a fraction of their "full-coverage" book of business, depending on the amount of coverage they wish to offer in the city. Let $P(x)$ = the probability that a structure will be assigned to company x. To construct the initial or full-coverage books of business, each structure of the model city was randomly assigned to a specific book of business according to the following rules: (a) If the structure is classified as *commercial*, it is assigned as follows: $P(LG) = .50$, $P(M) = .10$, $P(S) = .02$, and $P(O) = .38$. (b) If the structure is classified as *industrial*, it is assigned as follows: $P(LG) = .20$, $P(M) = .10$, $P(S) = .00$, and $P(O) = .70$. (c) If the structure is classified as *residential*, it is assigned as follows: $P(LG) = .00$, $P(M) = .10$, $P(S) = .05$, and $P(O) = .85$. Tables 4.2 and 4.3 provide information on the specification of the model city and of the insurance companies' initial books of business (by ATC [Applied Technology Council] class and occupancy type).

Levels of Mitigation. Alternative types and levels of mitigation are assumed as part of the model scenario. The level of mitigation can vary from 0 to 100 percent of applicable structures for each type of mitigation. We will be examining three levels in our analysis: 0, 50, and 100 percent. Full (100 percent) mitigation assumes that every structure in the model city is rehabilitated to the level of the current code, with lower levels of mitigation (e.g., 50 percent) having costs proportional to the full mitigation costs (e.g., 50 percent of these full costs). For older structures, rehabilitation can be quite expensive. For those

Table 4.3   **Composition of Books of Business by Occupancy Type**

	Small	Medium	Large	Other	Model City
Permanent dwelling: family housing	3,149	6,383	376	54,259	64,167
Retail trade	33	78	187	539	837
Professional, technical, and business services	5	20	80	76	181
Entertainment and recreation	1	6	34	43	84
Unspecified	1,417	3,335	2,827	24,998	32,577
Total number of structures	4,605	9,822	3,504	79,915	97,846

already at current code, no further expense is required. Mitigation costs are based on those of a sample of rehabilitated structures (of the various types outlined in tables 4.2 and 4.3) in Los Angeles, which are then revised to take account of construction methods, materials, labor, and building-permit fees in other locales.[11]

Availability and Type of Reinsurance. We assume that excess-loss reinsurance is available that requires the primary insurer to retain a specified level of risk and covers all losses between the attachment points of the reinsurance policy. Thus, reinsurance policies are of the following form: the reinsurer pays all losses in the interval L_0 to L_1, where $L_1 - L_0$ is restricted to be no greater than some maximum reinsurance coverage.[12] As explained in more detail in appendix A, we assume that each insurance company is required to retain a certain percentage of its risk, where the retention level is defined as a percentage of worst-case losses.

Insurance and Reinsurance Premium Levels. We assume that full earthquake coverage is available, with a prespecified deductible, at a rate proportional to the expected loss of the property covered. The same premium structure is assumed for reinsurance rates, that is, proportional to the expected loss associated with the reinsurance contract in question. The proportionality or loading factors for primary coverage and for reinsurance may be different, of course.

4.4.3   The RWP Model and EP Functions

In appendix B, we describe the structure of the RWP software that was used to obtain probabilistic damage estimates from earthquakes of different magni-

---

11. These figures were provided to us by Risk Management Solutions. We will use the midpoint (or average) of the sample estimates of mitigation costs in our analysis. Low estimates (corresponding to the .1666 fractile of the sample distribution) of mitigation costs run about 25 percent of the midpoint values, and high estimates (corresponding to the .8333 fractile of the sample distribution) of mitigation costs run about double the midpoint values.

12. For additional details on the structure of reinsurance policies, see app. A.

Table 4.4   Base-Case Parameters

Parameter	Base-Case Value ($ million)
Company S assets	100
Company M assets	200
Company LG assets	400
Deductible (%)	10
Worst-case probability	.01
Target ruin probability	.01
Insurance loading factor (%)	100
Reinsurance loading factor (%)	150
Maximum reinsurance available for company S	50
Maximum reinsurance available for company M	100
Maximum reinsurance available for company LG	200
Required burden (b) (%)	10

tudes and intensity for structures in the model city. Essentially, the probability distribution of losses (and the associated EP function) for any given book of business is determined by simulating the effects of the set of earthquake events that could effect the model city over a specified interval of time, a single year for our analysis. Such events are differentiated by location, magnitude, and type of earthquake. The losses from the assumed set of earthquake events can then be stochastically summed to obtain a histogram and cumulative distribution of losses arising from these events, together with the associated EP function. These loss distributions can be derived for any specific set of properties and, in particular, for the books of business of the prototypical insurance companies of interest to us in the model city. Note that a separate model run is required whenever the characteristics (e.g., mitigation levels or building type) of the properties underlying the EP function are changed.

4.4.4 Evaluation

The evaluation phase considers the total expected and worst-case losses for each stakeholder group, where worst-case losses are computed for an EP value of .01, with the result that *worst case* here means that the probability of exceeding these losses is .01. Of course, insurers and reinsurers may use "target ruin probabilities" that are considerably smaller than .01 in computing needed reserves and coverage limits. For insured propertyowners, losses include expenses prior to a disaster (premiums and mitigation costs) as well as repair costs that they must incur personally (i.e., deductibles on their insurance policy). The losses of uninsured propertyowners consist of mitigation costs plus repair costs. For society as a whole, total losses include the cost of mitigation plus total property losses from the disaster as well as any transactions costs resulting from insolvencies and their consequences.

The base-case parameters for the analyses that follow are given in table 4.4. Note that we have varied the asset levels of the small, medium, and large com-

Table 4.5   **The Effect of Mitigation Level on Expected and Worst-Case Losses ($millions)**

	Mitigation Level		
	0%	50%	100%
Small-pool losses:			
Expected losses	25.9	22.4	18.9
Total worst-case loss	369.9	323.5	277.1
Insurer's worst-case loss	264.2	225.0	187.0
Mitigation costs	.0	6.9	13.8
Medium-pool losses:			
Expected losses	67.0	58.0	49.0
Total worst-case loss	912.3	800.4	688.4
Insurer's worst-case loss	654.8	559.9	467.2
Mitigation costs	.0	16.3	32.5
Large-pool losses:			
Expected losses	133.6	115.4	97.2
Total worst-case loss	1,549.9	1,362.2	1,174.6
Insurer's worst-case loss	1,139.7	977.0	816.2
Mitigation costs	.0	30.2	60.5
Other-pool losses:			
Expected losses	280.4	242.6	204.9
Total worst-case loss	4,576.8	3,996.9	3,416.9
Insurer's worst-case loss	3,195.1	2,714.9	2,246.3
Mitigation costs	.0	81.6	163.3
Model city losses:			
Expected losses	506.9	438.4	369.9
Total worst-case loss	7,408.9	6,438.0	5,557.1
Insurer's worst-case loss	5,253.8	4,476.8	3,716.7
Mitigation costs	.0	135.0	270.1

panies. Premiums are determined by calculating the expected annual losses from earthquakes and adding a loading factor of 100 percent. If reinsurance is available to companies, the maximum amount varies depending on the size of the insurer. The lower attachment point is determined for each company by requiring that the company be able to take on 10 percent of the losses from a worst-case event for the company's insured book of business.

To begin, let us consider the effect of the level of mitigation on total losses. These results are shown in table 4.5 for the full book of business for each of our four insurance companies and for levels of mitigation of 0, 50, and 100 percent; where 100 percent means that all model city properties have been rehabilitated to current code for each structural type. To make mitigation costs comparable with insurance costs and losses (all of which are annual), we annuitize total mitigation costs, using an interest rate of 10 percent.[13] Note in partic-

13. Thus, for the small company pool, which consists of 4,605 structures of various types, the (typical or midpoint) total mitigation cost to bring these all to current code was $137.5 million. With a discount rate of 10 percent, this leads to an annuity of $13.8 million, as shown in table

ular that we do not check each structure to determine whether particular mitigation measures are cost effective. Rather, the analysis assumes that structures
in a particular class adopt mitigation measures appropriate to that class on a
random basis, with the percentage of adoption (0–100 percent) being specified
in the scenario. A structure-by-structure cost-effectiveness approach would, of
course, yield significantly lower total costs than our one-size-fits-all approach.

In table 4.5, we have tabulated the expected and worst-case losses for the
four respective insurance pools (the first two entries under each heading) and
for the entire model city. We have also listed the insurer's worst-case loss. This
is different from the total worst-case loss since we assume as our base case
(see table 4.4) that there is a 10 percent deductible on each policy. The consequence of this is that total worst-case losses will contain both the insurer's
worst-case loss as well as the first risk layer, deductible losses, assumed by the
propertyowners. Thus, the difference between the second and the third entries
under each heading (total worst-case loss minus insurer's worst-case loss) represents worst-case deductible losses for the respective full insurer pool (actual
worst-case deductible losses will be less if the insurer does not offer coverage
to the whole pool).

We see from table 4.5 that, as the level of mitigation increases, both expected and worst-case losses decrease. Note that the expected losses and the
worst-case losses tabulated here are simply the total losses in the indicated
insurance pool (small, medium, large, or other) and do not include mitigation
costs, which are tabulated separately in table 4.5.

Neglecting the costs of insolvencies, we see that, for this scenario, total social cost (the sum of gross costs plus mitigation costs) increases in expected-
value terms as mitigation increases but decreases significantly in terms of
worst-case losses. This suggests that purely random prioritization of mitigation
or total rehabilitation will not be effective in expected-value terms. However,
even random prioritization may have significant benefits in avoiding insolvencies and in reducing worst-case losses. Put differently, assuming the usual convex shape of mitigation cost effectiveness, these initial results suggest that the
social optimum will require less than 100 percent mitigation and some prioritization of mitigation targets to assure cost effectiveness. Other aspects of reducing the tail losses through mitigation will be discussed below.

Let us now examine in a bit more detail the consequences of mitigation for
companies LG, M, and S, with and without reinsurance available. The results
for these cases are given in tables 4.6–4.8. Each of these tables analyzes one
of the companies LG, M, and S under three mitigation levels assumed (0, 50,
and 100 percent) and under two reinsurance scenarios (no reinsurance and reinsurance levels as specified in table 4.4 above). (Note that the prefix E means

---

4.5. This annuitization will be a good approximation to annual costs if the structure and the mitigation undertaken enjoy a long life into the future. Shorter lives of the property or the mitigation or
higher discount rates would imply higher effective annual mitigation costs.

Table 4.6   **Small Company Case ($millions)**

	0% No Reins	0% Reins	50% No Reins	50% Reins	100% No Reins	100% Reins
	Mitigation Level					

	0%		50%		100%	
	No Reins	Reins	No Reins	Reins	No Reins	Reins
Insurance outcomes:						
% insured	40.4	59.8	47.3	70.0	56.7	84.1
Insurance premiums	6.8	10.0	6.4	9.5	5.9	8.8
E-cost of claims	3.4	3.8	3.2	3.6	3.0	3.5
Worst-case loss for S	106.8	158.0	106.4	157.5	106.0	157.3
Limits (L_0 and L_1) of	N.A.	15.8	N.A.	15.8	N.A.	15.7
reinsurance policy		65.8		65.8		65.7
Reinsurance premiums	N.A.	2.1	N.A.	1.8	N.A.	1.5
Expected outcomes:						
Cost of mitigation	.0	.0	6.9	6.9	13.8	13.8
E-deductible loss for insured						
propertyowners	7.1	10.5	7.4	10.9	7.7	11.5
E-cost to insured						
propertyowners	13.9	20.5	17.1	25.2	21.4	31.9
E-cost to uninsured						
propertyowners	15.4	10.4	15.4	8.8	14.2	5.2
E-cost to all propertyowners	29.3	30.9	32.5	34.0	35.6	37.1
Worst-case outcomes:						
WC-deductible loss for						
insured propertyowners	42.7	63.2	46.6	69.0	51.1	75.8
WC-cost to insured						
propertyowners	49.5	73.2	56.3	83.3	64.8	96.2
WC-cost to uninsured						
propertyowners	220.4	146.8	174.1	99.1	126.0	46.3
WC-cost to all propertyowners	269.9	222.0	230.4	182.5	190.8	142.5

Note: N.A. = not applicable.

"expected"—e.g., E-cost of claims is the expected cost of claims for those who are insured—and that the prefix *WC*-means "worst case.") As the results are similar for each company, we focus in table 4.7 on company M results (see tables 4.2 and 4.3 above for the book of business that M covers). In table 4.9, we also provide "per capita figures" corresponding to company M. These were obtained by noting from table 4.2 that there are a total of 9,822 properties insured in M's total pool. Since at each level of coverage we are assuming that a random portfolio of these properties is chosen, we can provide per capita results simply by dividing the respective quantities (e.g., expected losses) by the fraction of the 9,822 properties involved in generating the quantity in question (e.g., dividing by the number of properties represented in the aggregate expected-loss figure). For example, consider the E-cost of claims with no reinsurance and 50 percent mitigation. The total expected losses for this are shown

Table 4.7   **Medium Company Case ($millions)**

	Mitigation Level					
	0%		50%		100%	
	No Reins	Reins	No Reins	Reins	No Reins	Reins
Insured outcomes:						
% insured	32.7	47.6	38.1	55.6	45.5	66.4
Insurance premiums	14.1	20.6	13.3	19.4	12.4	18.1
E-cost of claims	7.1	5.0	6.7	4.7	6.2	4.3
Worst-case loss for M	214.1	311.7	213.3	311.3	212.6	310.2
Limits (L_0 and L_1) of	N.A.	31.2	N.A.	31.1	N.A.	31.0
reinsurance policy		131.2		131.1		131.0
Reinsurance premiums	N.A.	8.9	N.A.	8.3	N.A.	7.8
Expected outcomes:						
Cost of mitigation	.0	.0	16.3	16.3	32.5	32.5
E-deductible loss for insured						
propertyowners	14.8	21.6	15.4	22.5	16.1	23.5
E-cost to insured						
propertyowners	28.9	42.2	34.9	51.0	43.3	63.2
E-cost to uninsured						
propertyowners	45.1	35.1	46.0	33.0	44.4	27.4
E-cost to all propertyowners	74.0	77.3	80.9	84.0	87.7	90.6
Worst-case outcomes:						
WC-deductible loss for						
insured propertyowners	84.2	122.6	91.6	133.6	100.6	146.9
WC-cost to insured						
propertyowners	98.4	143.2	111.1	162.1	127.8	186.6
WC-cost to uninsured						
propertyowners	613.9	478.0	505.5	362.6	392.9	242.2
WC-cost to all propertyowners	712.3	621.2	616.6	524.7	520.7	428.8

Note: N.A. = not applicable.

as $6.7 million in table 4.7 (row 3). The percentage of full coverage offered under the no-reinsurance, 50 percent mitigation scenario is (see row 1 of table 4.7) 38.1 percent, or 3,742 of the 9,822 properties at risk. Hence, the per capita figure for E-cost of claims is $6.7 million/3,742 = $1,790, as shown in table 4.9 (row 3).

Now consider the results under each heading in tables 4.7 and 4.9.

Percentage Insured. As the level of mitigation increases, the EP function shifts downward. Thus, company M, which is assumed to operate under a PML rule, is able to expand its coverage while still keeping within its target ruin probability. Similarly, with increased availability of reinsurance, company M can expand its coverage (even though M is paying a reinsurance premium of 150 percent times the expected value of the losses covered by the reinsurance).

Table 4.8   **Large Company Case ($millions)**

			Mitigation Level			
	0%		50%		100%	
	No Reins	Reins	No Reins	Reins	No Reins	Reins
Insurance outcomes:						
% insured	38.1	56.3	44.3	65.5	52.6	78.1
Insurance premiums	34.5	51.0	32.1	47.5	29.4	43.7
E-cost of claims	17.3	19.8	16.0	19.0	14.7	18.1
Worst-case loss for LG	434.2	641.7	432.8	639.9	429.3	637.5
Limits (L_0 and L_1) of	N.A.	64.2	N.A.	64.0	N.A.	63.7
reinsurance policy		264.2		264.0		263.7
Reinsurance premiums	N.A.	9.4	N.A.	7.9	N.A.	6.2
Expected outcomes:						
Cost of mitigation	.0	.0	30.2	30.2	60.5	60.5
E-deductible loss for insured						
propertyowners	33.7	49.7	35.0	51.8	36.4	54.1
E-cost to insured						
propertyowners	68.2	100.7	80.5	119.1	97.6	145.1
E-cost to uninsured						
propertyowners	82.7	58.4	81.1	50.2	74.7	34.5
E-cost to all propertyowners	150.9	159.1	161.6	169.3	172.4	179.6
Worst-case outcomes:						
WC-deductible loss for						
insured propertyowners	156.4	230.9	170.4	252.2	188.5	279.9
WC-cost to insured						
propertyowners	191.0	281.9	215.9	319.5	249.7	370.9
WC-cost to uninsured						
propertyowners	958.9	677.4	774.2	480.4	585.4	270.5
WC-cost to all propertyowners	1,149.9	959.3	990.1	799.9	835.2	641.3

Note: N.A. = not applicable.

Insurance Premiums and Expected Cost of Claims. As the level of mitigation increases, both premium income and the expected cost of claims decline. These reductions occur in spite of the fact that M is offering greater coverage in the model city. Clearly, the lower losses due to mitigation more than compensate for the risks of increased coverage.

Worst-Case Loss for M. This is the worst-case loss for insurer M for its full book of business times the percentage of that book (see row 1 of table 4.7) that M insures. Per capita figures simply divide this loss by the number of insured properties. Let us illustrate the links between various quantities in tables 4.5 and 4.7. We do this for the case of 0 percent mitigation and no reinsurance, where the worst-case loss for the entire medium pool (see table 4.5) is 912.3. And this sum contains deductible losses of 257.5, leaving M with a worst-case

Table 4.9   Medium Company Case Per Capita Outcomes ($)

	0%		50%		100%	
	No Reins	Reins	No Reins	Reins	No Reins	Reins
Number of insured properties	3,212	4,675	3,742	5,461	4,469	6,522
Insurance outcomes:						
Insurance premiums						
($/structure)	4,390	4,406	3,554	3,552	2,775	2,775
E-cost of claims	2,211	1,069	1,790	861	1,387	1,549
Worst-case loss for M	66,661	66,670	56,999	57,004	47,572	47,563
Reinsurance premiums	N.A.	1,904	N.A.	1,520	N.A.	1,196
Expected outcomes for property-owners:						
Cost of mitigation per structure	0	0	1,660	1,660	3,309	3,309
E-deductible loss for insured propertyowners	4,608	4,620	4,115	4,120	3,603	3,603
E-cost to insured propertyowners	8,998	9,026	9,326	9,339	9,689	9,691
E-cost to uninsured propertyowners	6,820	6,820	7,567	7,567	8,300	8,300
E-cost to all propertyowners	7,534	7,870	8,237	8,552	8,929	9,224
Worst-case outcomes for property-owners:						
WC-deductible loss for insured propertyowners	26,216	26,223	24,478	24,464	22,511	22,524
WC-cost to insured propertyowners	30,637	30,629	29,689	29,683	28,597	28,612
WC-cost to uninsured propertyowners	92,875	92,875	85,147	85,147	77,394	77,394
WC-cost to all propertyowners	72,521	63,246	62,777	53,421	53,014	43,657

Note: N.A. = not applicable.

insured loss of 912.3 − 257.5 = 654.8 (again shown in table 4.5) under the assumption that M insures the entire medium pool. But, as we see from row 1 of table 4.7, M insures only 32.7 percent of this full book of business, leading to a worst-case loss for M's actual book of business of .327 × 654.8 = 214.1 and a worst-case deductible loss of .327 × 257.5 = 84.2, as shown in table 4.7.

Reinsurance Premiums and Limits. Reinsurance premiums also decline as the level of mitigation increases, owing to the downward shifting of the EP function. Note that we have assumed that maximum reinsurance coverage is not reduced as mitigation is increased (and expected losses are reduced). Note that the reinsurance limit of $100 million is always attained, a result of the fact that M is insuring less than its full book of business (and would prefer to insure more, save the PML constraint).

Cost of Mitigation. The cost of mitigation naturally increases as the level of mitigation increases. Note that the cost figure given here is the total cost for the entire initial book of M's business, only a fraction of which (see the first row of table 4.7) is actually insured.

Deductible Losses (either Expected or Worst Case) for Insureds of M. As the level of mitigation increases and the level of insurance coverage offered increases, so will deductible losses (the first risk layer) arising from this expanded coverage (see table 4.7). Reinsurance will further increase coverage and therefore increase deductible losses for insureds.

Cost to Insured Propertyowners (either Expected or Worst Case). Neglecting any costs of insolvency, the cost to insured propertyowners is their deductible loss plus their premium plus mitigation costs. These expected costs increase, and the worst case costs decline, as the level of mitigation increases. This is the result of the random prioritization of mitigation; that is, mitigation has not been applied here in a cost-effective manner for the structures in this book of business. Availability of reinsurance expands coverage dramatically and causes total expected costs to all insured propertyowners to increase. The reader may note from table 4.9 that on a per capita basis total expected costs increase with the availability of reinsurance.

Costs to Uninsured Propertyowners (either Expected or Worst Case). The cost to uninsured propertyowners is just the sum of their mitigation cost plus their losses. For example, in the case with 50 percent mitigation and no reinsurance, we see from table 4.5 that the E-cost of medium-pool losses is 58.0 and that mitigation costs are 16.3. We can determine from row 1 of table 4.7 that the percentage of uninsured propertyowners in M's pool is $100 - 38.1$ percent = 61.9 percent. Thus, the E-cost to uninsured propertyowners is $.619 \times 16.3 + .619 \times 58.0 = 46.0$, as shown in table 4.7.

Costs to All Property Owners (either Expected or Worst Case). This is just the sum of all costs to insured and uninsured propertyowners in company M's pool. For this pool, expected costs are minimized at no mitigation and no reinsurance, while the opposite is true of worst-case costs. The key here is that expected costs increase as insurance coverage increases since there is a significant loading factor on expected losses to obtain premiums charged. The optimal mitigation and reinsurance level for social welfare will, of course, depend on the degree of risk aversion of propertyowners.

While we have discussed only company M in detail, the results for the other companies and for the total losses and the overall portfolio of insurance offered in the model city are quite similar. The analysis presented above considers only the effects of mitigation and the availability of reinsurance. It is straightforward to consider other effects as well, by explaining the effect of decision parameters or scenarios variables on outcomes, for example, the effect of changing any of the base-case assumptions and parameter values given in table 4.4. As it turns out, many of these results are quite intuitive. For example, if target ruin probabilities are reduced, indicating more conservative behavior of insurance companies, insurance coverage will be reduced in the model city. Again, if reinsurance rates are increased, or if the terms of reinsurance are made otherwise less favorable (e.g., a larger retention rate is required), then direct insurance coverage will be reduced. Finally, if additional reinsurance is made available, for example, because of new government guarantee programs, then additional insurance coverage will be offered.

A key driver for the specific results obtained above is the set of earthquake events that underlie the probabilistic structure of annual losses through the resulting exceedance probability function. More generally, our assumptions on pricing, on mitigation adoption, and on other aspects of the decision processes of the economic agents involved are central factors in determining the outcomes of our analysis. Many of these are the focus of ongoing studies based on the model city framework developed here.

The results of this prototypical analysis highlight the basic points made earlier in this paper. It is critical to understand the nestedness that exists between various policy instruments and scenario variables and the decision processes of the economic agents involved. If, for example, cost-effective mitigation is available, it has a double effect. First, it will be attractive for propertyowners to adopt. Second, because of its effect on both expected losses and the tail of the exceedance probability function, it will lead to increased availability and affordability of insurance and reinsurance. This will yield significant efficiency gains in both an expected (ex ante) sense as well as in the worst case (ex post). The complexity of this nestedness supports reliance on decentralized decision making and market forces where possible. It should also be clear, however, that science-based and credible risk-assessment procedures are critical to the outcome of this process. Otherwise, one or more of the economic actors involved could be significantly biasing decisions that have nested consequences. The ultimate outcome could undermine the market or the viability of the agents involved.

4.5   A Proposed Program for Dealing with Catastrophic Risks

In this concluding section, we describe a strategy for managing catastrophic risks that builds on the analysis in the previous section and suggests the types of analyses that can be undertaken using the conceptual framework outlined above. One must involve other stakeholders and policy instruments to complement the use of insurance in reducing losses while providing protection once a disaster occurs. The program consists of the following four elements: improving risk estimates, evaluating alternative mitigation measures, encouraging the adoption of mitigation measures, and broadening protection against catastrophic losses.

4.5.1   Improving Risk Estimates

There are two principal reasons why insurers will benefit from improved estimates of the risks associated with catastrophes. By obtaining better data on the probabilities and consequences of these events, insurers will be able to set their premiums more accurately and tailor their portfolio to reduce the chances of insolvency. Providing more accurate information on the risks also reduces the asymmetry of information between insurers and other providers of capital, such as reinsurers and the financial investment community. Investors are more likely to supply capital if they are more confident in the estimates of the risks provided to them by the insurers.

Today, there are a growing number of catastrophe models that have been utilized to generate data on the likelihood of and expected damage to different communities or regions from disasters of different magnitudes or intensities. Each model uses different assumptions, different methodologies, different data, and different parameters in generating its results. These conflicting results make it difficult for investors to feel comfortable investing their money in financial instruments associated with catastrophic risk. In order to better understand why these models differ, we must attempt to reconcile these differences in a more scientific manner than has been done until now. For example, bringing the leading modelers together with financial institutions to discuss how their data are generated may reduce the mystery that currently surrounds these efforts.

Another way to make the investment community more comfortable is to be as conservative as possible in estimating future losses when developing an exceedance probability (EP) curve. This will make it highly likely that the actual damage will be less than the predicted amounts. By simulating a number of different loss scenarios using an EP curve, one can determine the prices that would have to be charged to the insurer or reinsurer purchasing specific financial instruments in order to yield an attractive rate of return to investors. This type of analysis should enable one to contrast the relative benefits and costs of act-of-God bonds with traditional reinsurance and other ways of financing catastrophic losses, such as purchasing options on the Chicago Board of Trade, purchasing federal reinsurance, or negotiating finite risk arrangements.

4.5.2   Evaluating Alternative Mitigation Measures

Mitigation is a desirable way to manage catastrophic risks because it alleviates the problem at the source. If experts were able to design a completely hurricane-proof structure, there would be no need for insurance against this risk. This is a desirable objective, but one highly unlikely to be achieved in practice.

The first step is to determine which mitigation measures are likely to be cost effective. This is not easy to do in practice, as illustrated by the case of shutters. Storm shutters can be an effective measure to protect a building during a hurricane; however, someone must close and secure them prior to the hurricane. Furthermore, they must meet current wind-resistance standards and be properly installed. Finally, by themselves, shutters may reduce losses slightly, but, if combined with complete wall protection, an aerodynamic roof structure, and good roof-to-wall and wall-to-foundation connections, the benefits could be substantial.[14]

The second step is to examine the effect of specific mitigation measures on the reduction in losses through simulations similar to the ones described above. One can then undertake sensitivity analyses by examining the effect of a specific mitigation measure on different EP curves and other design features of the property. Such analyses will then translate into estimated reductions in expected losses. This should enable insurers to pass on the savings to the property-owner in the form of reduced premiums, lower deductibles, and/or higher limits of coverage.

4.5.3 Encouraging the Adoption of Mitigation Measures

It is often necessary to undertake audits and inspections in order to avoid problems of moral hazard and adverse selection. With respect to properties at risk, one way to encourage the adoption of cost-effective loss-reduction measures is to have them incorporated in building codes and provide a seal of approval to each structure that meets or exceeds these standards. To institutionalize such a procedure, financial institutions could require an inspection and certification of the facility against natural hazards as a condition for issuing a mortgage. This process would be similar in concept to termite and radon inspections normally required when property is financed.

The success of such a program requires the support of the building industry and a cadre of well-qualified inspectors to provide accurate information as to whether existing codes and standards are being met. To reduce their losses from disasters, insurers may want to limit coverage only to those structures that are given a seal of approval. If budget constraints prevent propertyowners from investing in these mitigation measures, then the bank can provide funds through a home-improvement loan with a payback period identical to the life of the mortgage.

4.5.4 Broadening Protection against Catastrophic Losses

New sources of capital from the private and public sectors have the possibility of providing insurers with guaranteed funds against losses from catastrophic events so as to alleviate their concerns that they may be insolvent from

---

14. We are indebted to George Segelken of CIGNA for providing us with this example.

the next major disaster. Some instruments provide funds to the insurer should they suffer a catastrophic loss. J. P. Morgan and Nationwide Insurance successfully negotiated such a transaction, Nationwide borrowing $400 million from J. P. Morgan. This money was placed in a trust fund composed of U.S. Treasury securities. Nationwide pays a higher than normal interest rate on these funds in return for having the ability to issue up to $400 million in surplus notes to help pay for the losses should a catastrophe occurs (Kunreuther 1998). As pointed out above, such instruments as the USAA act-of-God bonds have recently been floated, and other catastrophic bonds are now being initiated (Doherty 1997).

The multiyear catastrophic bonds that have recently been proposed promise a relatively high rate of return compared to high-yield bonds. Other financial arrangements such as *catastrophic insurance futures contracts* and *call spreads* introduced by the Chicago Board of Trade in 1992 enable an insurer to hedge against underwriting risk by attracting capital from insurance and noninsurance segments of the economy (Cummins and Geman 1995; Harrington, Mann, and Niehaus 1995).[15] The Catastrophic Risk Exchange (CATEX) creates a marketplace where insurers, brokers, and the self-insured can swap units of their catastrophe risks by region and peril. For example, an insurer could swap units of California earthquake for Florida windstorm (Insurance Services Office 1996).

The evaluation of these instruments through the simulations described above may provide an understanding of the opportunities of using a combination of insurance, reinsurance, financial instruments, and government-related programs to encourage cost-effective mitigation and infuse new capital into the system. Insurers could supplement traditional reinsurance with these guaranteed sources of funding when their losses exceed a certain level. This would relax (implicit or explicit) solvency constraints and stimulate additional coverage in high-risk areas.

Finally, we note that simulation modeling of the sort proposed here must rely on solid theoretical foundations in order to delimit the boundaries of what is interesting and implementable in a market economy. Such foundations will apply, not only to the traditional issues of capital markets and the insurance sector, but also to the decision processes of insurance and reinsurance companies, public officials, and propertyowners in determining levels of mitigation, insurance coverage, and other protective activities. Achieving an integrated understanding of the aggregate effect of these decision processes and the underlying hazards has been our central focus. We have argued that better risk-assessment tools, including the advances in the micromodeling of hazards and

---

15. To date, the Chicago Board of Trade has not had much success in selling these futures contracts. Recently, it introduced a new option based on the value of an index compiled by Property Claim Services. For more details on these options, see Culp (1996, 31–42).

mitigation measures described in the present paper, hold considerable potential for increasing our understanding of these issues and promoting the design of better programs for catastrophic risk management.

Appendix A
Decision Rules for Insurance and Reinsurance

This appendix describes the rules used for making insurance and reinsurance decisions in the simulation studies undertaken for the model city. We focus first on the insurance companies in the model city and describe how these companies are assumed to decide on the size of their book of business (the extent of the coverage they offer in the model city) and the amount of reinsurance they purchase. Premium levels are assumed to be set on the basis of a fixed loading on expected losses. We consider two basic approaches: a safety-first approach based on a specified probable maximum loss (or PML) rule and a related expected-utility-maximization rule.

Assumptions concerning the Book of Business for Insurers

We assume that each insurer begins with a base-case book of business, which is a set of properties that it might consider insuring in the model city. For the small, medium, large, and other insurer, this base-case book of business serves as the reservoir of risks that the insurer may take on. If the insurer can take on its full book of business, it is assumed to do so (i.e., it is assumed that the loading factors associated with premiums provide a fair return on reserves invested to cover the associated risks). If, however, the insurer chooses not to offer this full coverage in the model city (e.g., because it cannot meet its target ruin probability or PML at the full book of business), then we assume that the insurer reduces its coverage until its desired coverage limit is reached.

To compute various quantities of interest, we need the distribution of the random variable of losses for an insurance company as its book of business changes. For analytic convenience, we assume that coverage reduction is accomplished in a random order in each category of property insured: if the insurer is insuring a book of business of "size" $\alpha\varepsilon[0, 1]$ and its original or full book of business faced a loss distribution of L, then the random variable of losses $L(\alpha)$ when its book of business is of size $\alpha\varepsilon[0, 1]$ is just $L(\alpha) = \alpha L$. Thus, denoting the cumulative probability distribution function (cdf) of $L(\alpha)$ by $F(x; \alpha) = \Pr\{L(\alpha) \leq x\}$, we see that $\Pr\{L(\alpha) \leq x\} = \Pr\{\alpha L \leq x\} = \Pr\{L \leq x/\alpha\}$, with the result that $F(x; \alpha) = F[(x/\alpha)]$, where F is the cdf of the original full book of business for the insurer. Naturally, F will depend on a number of factors, including mitigation, amount of deductibles, and other policy provisions. The key point is that, once F has been derived for the original full book of business for an insurer, the cdf for any other size book of business is analytically available.

PML Rule without Reinsurance

Define the exceedance probability (or EP) curve for losses for a particular insurer with book of business of size $\alpha\varepsilon[0, 1]$ as $EP(x; \alpha) = \Pr\{L(\alpha) > x\} = 1 - F(x; \alpha) = 1 - F[(x/\alpha)]$. Thus, interpreting the PML rule as taking on the maximum-size book of business that does not produce an exceedance probability in excess of a given "target ruin probability," we determine the size of the book of business offered by a PML insurer when no reinsurance is available as the solution α^* to

$$1 - F\left[\frac{A + \alpha\rho_0}{\alpha}\right] = p^*,$$

where A = initial reserves; ρ_0 = premium income from the full book of business for the insurer in question, or $(1 + l_I) \times$ expected losses of the full book of business (so $\alpha\rho_0$ is the premium income for the book of business of size α); l_I = insurance-policy loading factor; and p^* = target ruin probability.

PML Rule with Reinsurance

A number of assumptions will be made in this case: (*a*) Reinsurers will offer a limited amount of coverage $\Delta = L_1 - L_0$, where L_0 is the lower attachment point and L_1 is the upper attachment point of the reinsurance contract. (*b*) The reinsurer makes the added stipulation that the insurance company retains some fraction b of the worst-case-scenario event. In other words, the lower attachment point $L_0(\alpha) = bL^{WC}(\alpha)$, where $L^{WC}(\alpha)$ is the loss associated with the worst-case event, and $b\varepsilon[0, 1]$ is the required retention level. We take the worst-case event to be the loss associated with $EP(x; \alpha) = p^{WC}$ (e.g., $EP[x; \alpha] = .00001$). Thus, $L^{WC}(\alpha)$ is the loss that solves $1 - F[L^{WC}(\alpha); \alpha] = p^{WC.}$

In choosing the amount of reinsurance and the size of the book of business it wishes to purchase (at a fixed loading above expected losses in the reinsurance layer), the insurer will make one of the following choices: (*a*) If the cap on Δ is not binding, $EP[(L_0 + \Delta)/\alpha; \alpha] = 1 - F[(L_0 + \Delta)/\alpha] < p^*$, then the insurer is assumed to purchase a reinsurance contract with attachment points L_0 and L_1^*, where L_1^* solves $1 - F(L_1^*) = p^*$; that is, the insurer will then take on the entire portfolio, $\alpha = 1$. (*b*) If the cap on Δ is binding, then the insurer will adjust α until its PML is satisfied. This amounts to finding α^* solving

$$1 - F\left[\frac{A + \alpha\rho_0 - R_{\text{Premium}} + R_{\text{Payoff}}}{\alpha}\right] = p^*,$$

where A = initial reserves; ρ_0 = premiums = $(1 + l_I) \times$ expected losses; R_{premium} = reinsurance premium = $(1 + l_R)\int_{L_0}^{L_1}[1 - F(L/\alpha)]dL$, where $L_0 = L_0(\alpha) = bL^{WC}(\alpha)$ and $L_1 = L_1(\alpha) = L_0(\alpha) + \Delta$; R_{payoff} = reinsurance payoff; and p^* = target ruin probability. This may be rewritten as

$$1 - F\left[\frac{A + \alpha\rho_0 - (1 + l_R)\int_{L_0(\alpha)}^{L_1(\alpha)}\left[1 - F\left(\frac{L}{\alpha}\right)\right]dL + \Delta}{\alpha}\right] = p^*.$$

Note that the integral determining the reinsurance premium determines expected losses between the two attachment points $L_0(\alpha)$ and $L_1(\alpha)$. Once the cdf of losses $F(x)$ is known for the full book of business, it is straightforward to solve the above for the optimal size α for the PML insurer. Note that $L_0(\alpha) = \alpha L_0$, and define L^* by $1 - F(L^*) = p^*$. Then, changing the variable of integration above to $x = L/\alpha$, we can rewrite this expression in the form:

$$A + \alpha\rho_0 - \alpha(1 + l_R)\int_{L_0}^{\frac{L_1(\alpha)}{\alpha}} [1 - F(x)]dx + \Delta = \alpha L^*.$$

In particular, if $L_1(\alpha) = L_0(\alpha) + \Delta = \alpha L_0 + \Delta$ so that all available reinsurance is purchased, then the upper limit of integration becomes $L_0 + (\Delta/\alpha)$.

Expected Utility Rules

If, instead of a PML choice rule, an insurance company uses an expected-utility rule, similar results to the above are attained. For example, when reinsurance is not available, an expected-utility maximizer would solve for the optimal book of business by solving the following problem:

$$\text{Maximize}\{E[U(A_0 + \alpha\rho_0 - \alpha L)]|\alpha\varepsilon[0, 1]\},$$

where the expectation is with respect to the underlying random variable of losses L. If we assume a CARA utility function, $U(W) = -e^{-\lambda W}$, then the task becomes solving the first-order condition below for α:

$$\int_0^\infty (\rho_0 - L)e^{\lambda\alpha L}dF(L) = 0,$$

where $\rho_0 = (1 + l_I)\int_0^\infty[1 - F(L)]dL$. Intuitively, the expected-utility rule mimics the PML rule in that, as risk aversion increases, the optimal book of business α^* decreases, corresponding to an equivalent PML insurer with lower target ruin probability p^*.

The case where reinsurance is available is modeled similarly. Here, the insurer would solve for the optimal α and the optimal amount of reinsurance to purchase by solving

$$\underset{\alpha\varepsilon[0,1]}{\text{Max}} \ EU[A_0 + \rho_0\alpha - \tilde{L}_I(\alpha) - P(\alpha)],$$

where $P(\alpha) = (1 + l_R)\int_{L_0/\alpha}^{L_1/\alpha}[1 - F(L)]dL$ is the reinsurance premium, and where $L_I(\alpha)$ is the loss exposure for the insurance company given its reinsurance decision, so that

$$L_1(\alpha) = \alpha L \quad \text{for} \quad \alpha L < L_0(\alpha),$$

$$L_1(\alpha) = L_0(\alpha) \quad \text{for} \quad L_0(\alpha) \leq \alpha L \leq L_1(\alpha),$$

$$L_1(\alpha) = L_0(\alpha) + \alpha L - L_1(\alpha) \quad \text{for} \quad L > L_1(\alpha),$$

$L_0(\alpha)$ is constrained by the retention-level requirement that $L_0(\alpha) = bL^{\text{WC}}(\alpha)$, and $L_1(\alpha)$ is constrained by the maximum coverage offered, that is, $L_1(\alpha) \leq L_0(\alpha) + \Delta$. Again here, the expected-utility-maximizing rule gives rise to similar behavior as for a corresponding PML rule: as risk aversion increases, the size of the optimal portfolio decreases, and the amount of reinsurance purchased increases.

Appendix B
The RMS-Wharton (RWP) Software

RWP Earthquake is a refined model originally developed at Stanford University and licensed exclusively to Risk Management Solutions (RMS) in 1988. The model simulates earthquakes and the transfer of energy from a rupture to a site and then calculates the damage to insured properties. The RMS modeling framework from which RWP Earthquake is derived is quite general and has been adapted in RWP to study a particular city, the model city, described in the text. RWP assesses three factors when it analyzes earthquake risks: (1) hazard and exposure data; (2) vulnerability; and (3) financial risk.

Hazard and Exposure Data

To calculate loss, RWP must first determine the modified Mercalli intensity (MMI), or the intensity of shaking at a site due to an earthquake. There are three factors in determining the amount of shaking at a site: (1) the earthquake's source; (2) attenuation of seismic energy; and (3) local soil conditions (see fig. 4B.1). The first three items are enough for "what if" types or deterministic types of analyses that do not consider the element of time. To answer the question "How much am I likely to lose in X years?" the fourth factor, recurrence relationship, is needed to estimate how often earthquakes occur.

Earthquake Sources. The first questions that need to be answered in a loss calculation are, Where is the earthquake? and, How big is the earthquake? RWP provides these answers in the form of a database of seismic sources. Each seismic source contains geographic information about a region or geologic structure with the potential to generate earthquakes. It also stores the maximum credible magnitude for an earthquake on that source as well as recurrence

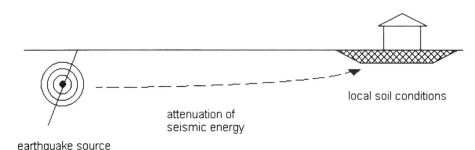

local soil conditions

attenuation of
seismic energy

earthquake source

Fig. 4B.1   Determinants of earthquake intensity at a remote site

parameters indicating average occurrence intervals for each event magnitude. This information comes primarily from public data expanded by proprietary sources and research by RMS engineers.

RWP models a seismic source as either a line or an area. Line sources are used when seismicity is associated with a well-defined geologic structure, usually shallow faults with a surface expression. Area sources cover a broader geographic region and treat that area as one unit. These sources assume that earthquakes can occur anywhere within the region with equal probability and are used when seismicity is associated with many faults that individually are too poorly characterized to be modeled by themselves. Area sources are also used when seismicity occurs along a dipping plane (rather than vertically) or when seismicity is not clearly associated with a geologic structure.

Attenuation of Seismic Energy. Once the size of an earthquake and its distance from a location are determined, RWP must calculate how much energy is released at the rupture and, of that energy, how much actually reaches the site. RWP calculates this level of ground shaking using attenuation relations that estimate the drop in energy with distance from an earthquake. These attenuations can differ by the type of earthquake or by region.

An earthquake of a particular magnitude generates ground motion. Peak ground acceleration (PGA) is a measurement of the maximum ground movement at a location. As the distance from an earthquake source increases, the ground movement, or PGA, decreases. RWP calculates the PGA for a location on the basis of the seismic sources and the attenuation of seismic energy.

Local Soil Conditions. The third factor in determining the amount of shaking at a site is the potential amplification of ground motion by soil conditions present at the site. After geocoding a location, RWP retrieves data on the local conditions and potential hazards for that site. The local geology can have a major effect on ground motion. Buildings standing on bedrock will usually sustain less damage than those on water-saturated alluvial deposits or on artificial fill. There are four "soil" classes used in RWP: (1) bedrock; (2) shallow alluvium; (3) deep alluvium; and (4) bay mud/artificial fill. The names given these classes do not always reflect the true geology at the site but refer to the relative amplification potential of the underlying material.

A simplified analogy helps illustrate how different materials can amplify ground motion. Imagine a plate with a thick chocolate cake on it. Imagine a second, identical plate with a block of Jello of the same size as the cake. Put a box of matches on top of each and then slide the plates back and forth at the same speed. Even though the initial motion is the same, the matchbox on the Jello will shake more violently.

Measures of Ground Shaking. When a fault ruptures, it causes waves of ground motion. One way of measuring the strength of this motion is the PGA, the maximum pulse of ground shaking at a location. Instrumental records from past earthquakes have provided enough data to define PGA-based attenuations for many regions. RWP uses established PGA attenuations wherever possible.

In some regions, however, the limited (or nonexistent) PGA data are not sufficient to define a reliable attenuation. In these cases, ground shaking is given in terms of a subjective scale, the MMI. The MMI is a subjective measure of how severe the damage from an earthquake is on a scale of I–XII. For example, an MMI of II is defined as being felt by few persons at rest, especially on upper floors of tall buildings. An MMI of VI is defined as being felt by all, except drivers of cars, where some heavy furniture moves and there is slight damage to poor-quality masonry, particularly chimneys. Ground shaking in RWP is defined in terms of MMI. RWP converts the level of PGA for a site to MMI and modifies the intensity based on amplification by the local soil conditions. The ultimate outcome of the hazard portion of the earthquake model is the MMI experienced by each location.

Vulnerability Assessment

In the second step of an earthquake analysis, RWP uses information about several factors to assess potential damage resulting from local ground shaking (MMI): the structural characteristics of a location; the type of contents; and the social function of the building. The potential damage is first expressed as the class mean-damage ratio. The class mean-damage ratio is then used to calculate the building mean-damage ratio, the content damage ratio, and the business-interruption-damage ratio. The ultimate outcome of the vulnerability assessment is a determination of the damage distribution or damage curve for a particular building.

Class Mean-Damage Ratio. First, given a particular MMI and a construction class for a specific building, RWP retrieves a class mean-damage ratio. A class damage ratio is the average damage expected for a specific construction class given a particular MMI. A 10 percent class damage ratio means that the cost of repair will be 10 percent of the cost to replace the building completely. The actual losses to individual buildings may be very different than the class damage ratio. For example, a class damage ratio of 10 percent for a population of one hundred buildings could equate to ten buildings that are total losses and ninety that sustained no damage. Other factors that often help determine the class damage ratio are the number of stories and the occupancy type. The damage ratios are determined by the damage table selected in RWP during an analysis. RWP utilizes the PML table for this purpose.

The PML methodology as expressed in RWP is based on published work performed by Karl Steinbrugge (1982). Dr. Steinbrugge's work has formed the foundation of generally accepted earthquake expected-loss analysis, including the regulatory filings required by the state of California. RMS has used Steinbrugge's intensity versus damage relations as the core of the PML computation performed by RWP. Note that, as defined in RWP, the PML methodology represents a significant improvement over the traditional PML methodology. PML is a more conservative approach; estimated losses will be higher for all construction classes except wood frame.

Building Mean-Damage Ratio. RWP's next step is to modify the class damage ratio according to four additional types of information to calculate the building mean-damage ratio, or the average damage expected for a specific building. The four additional types of information are the following: (1) secondary building characteristics, such as ornamentation, which can increase or decrease the damage; (2) year of construction or upgrade, information that helps determine building-code requirements and can also increase the damage ratio; (3) landslide and liquefaction, which can increase damage ratios if ground shaking is sufficient to trigger them; and (4) distance to fault, since surface rupture may contribute to the mean-damage ratio if a location lies very close to the fault.

Content Damage Ratio. RWP calculates the content damage ratio by multiplying the building damage ratio by the content modifier. For each class of construction, there are four content modifiers, referred to as *rate grades.* The rate grades range from 1 to 4, with 1 being fragile and 4 being least damageable. Depending on the type of construction entered, RWP multiplies a specific number by the building damage ratio to calculate the contents damage ratio.

Financial Risk Assessment

The final step of the earthquake analysis is to estimate financial risk. RWP used the building mean-damage ratio and the total level of uncertainty to create a damage curve for the building. The uncertainty is determined by the quality of the location data: Is the construction class provided? How many secondary building characteristics are known? At what level is hazard data available? and so on. As the quality of the location data improves, the uncertainty decreases, resulting in a narrower range of loss estimates. High uncertainty, such as not knowing the construction class of a building, results in a broad damage curve with a wide range of potential losses.

Out of four modes that can be used to determine the financial risk, RWP uses the distributed mode. The distributed mode is the most sophisticated mode that combines the damage curve with the financial structure to produce a weighted average for each layer of the financial structure (e.g., deductible, primary insurance, coinsurance layer, and so forth). In essence, it distributes the potential losses to each layer of the financial structure on the basis of the probability that the loss may penetrate a specific layer. The total specified loss when using the distributed mode equals the total specified loss when using the expected mode, but the loss per layer may differ. The greater the difference, the more uncertainty in the estimation of financial risk.

The distributed mode considers the probability of loss for each particular layer. This mode can produce results that are at first glance confusing. For example, consider the distributed-loss calculation of a $100,000 deductible in the event of an expected loss equal to $200,000. Using the expected mode, the loss to the insured would be the full value of the $100,000 deductible. Using the distributed mode, the loss to the insured may be slightly lower than the $100,000 deductible after the probabilities of loss have been factored in. Factoring in the probabilities of loss allows the model to reflect the chance, even if it is slight, that the loss may be under the $100,000 deductible. This causes the probabilistic loss to the insured to be slightly lower than the full amount of the deductible.

As another example, consider a policy with a 10 percent deductible. If the expected loss to the policy were 9 percent, no loss to the policy would be calculated in the expected mode or the percentile mode. However, the distributed mode would factor in the probability that the loss would exceed the expected loss of 9 percent and may show a small loss to the policy. The distributed mode of financial loss assessment allows RWP users to understand the statistically predicted losses for various layers of a policy.

References

All-Industry Research Advisory Council (AIRAC). 1986. *Catastrophic losses: How the insurance industry would handle two $7-billion hurricanes.* Oak Brook, Ill.

Camerer, Colin, and Howard Kunreuther. 1989. Decision processes for low probability events: Policy implications. *Journal of Policy Analysis and Management* 8:565–92.

Catastrophes: A major paradigm shift for P/C insurers. 1996. *BestWeek: Property-Casualty Supplement,* 25 March, 1–18.

Conning & Co. 1994. *Candles in the wind.* Hartford, Conn.: Conning & Co.

Culp, Christopher. 1996. Relations between insurance and derivatives: Applications from catastrophic loss insurance. Paper presented at the conference "Rethinking Insurance Regulation" sponsored by the Competitive Enterprise Institute, Washington, D.C., 8 March.

Cummins, David, and Hélyette Geman. 1995. Pricing catastrophe insurance futures and call spreads: An arbitrage approach. *Journal of Fixed Income* 4:46–57.

Dionne, Georges, and Scott Harrington, eds. 1992. *Foundations of insurance economics.* Boston: Kluwer.

Doherty, Neil. 1997. Financial innovation for financing and hedging catastrophe risk. Paper presented at the Fifth Alexander Howden Conference on Disaster Insurance, Gold Coast, Australia, August.

Dong, Weimin, Haresh Shah, and Felix Wong. 1996. A rational approach to pricing of catastrophe insurance. *Journal of Risk and Uncertainty* 12:201–18.

Federal Emergency Management Agency (FEMA). 1994. Assessment of the state-of-the-art earthquake loss estimation. Washington, D.C.: National Institution of Building Sciences.

Froot, Kenneth, Brian Murphy, Aaron Stern, and Stephen Usher. 1995. *The emerging asset class: Insurance risk.* New York: Guy Carpenter & Co., July.

Hanks, Thomas, and C. Allin Cornell. 1994. Probabilistic seismic hazard analysis: A beginner's guide. Paper presented at the Fifth Symposium on Current Issues Related to Nuclear Power Plant Structures, Equipment and Piping, North Carolina State University.

Harrington, Scott, Steven Mann, and Greg Niehaus. 1995. Insurer capital structure decisions and the viability of insurance derivatives. *Journal of Risk and Insurance* 3: 483–508.

Hogarth, Robin, and Howard Kunreuther. 1992. Pricing insurance and warranties: Ambiguity and correlated risks. *Geneva Papers on Risk and Insurance Theory* 17:35–60.

Insurance Information Institute. 1995. *Insurance issues update.* New York, November.

Insurance Services Office. 1994. The impact of catastrophes on property insurance. New York.

———. 1996. Managing catastrophic risk. New York.

Interagency Flood Plain Management Review Committee. 1994. *Sharing the challenge: Floodplain management into the 21st century.* Washington, D.C.: U.S. Government Printing Office.

Jaffee, Dwight, and Thomas Russell. 1996. Catastrophe insurance, capital markets, and uninsurable risks. Paper presented at the Wharton Financial Institutions Center Conference "Risk Management in Insurance Firms," May.

Kleindorfer, Paul, Howard Kunreuther, and Paul Schoemaker. 1993. *Decision sciences: An integrative perspective.* New York: Cambridge University Press.

Kunreuther, Howard. 1996. Mitigating disaster losses through insurance. *Journal of Risk and Uncertainty* 12:171–87.

———. 1998. A program for reducing disaster losses through insurance. In *Paying the price: The status and role of insurance against natural disasters in the United States,* ed. Howard Kunreuther and Richard J. Roth Sr. Washington, D.C.: Joseph Henry.

Kunreuther, Howard, Jacqueline Meszaros, Robin Hogarth, and Mark Spranca. 1993. Ambiguity and underwriter decision processes. *Journal of Economic Behavior and Organization* 26:337–52.

Lecomte, Eugene, and Karen Gahagan. 1998. Hurricane insurance protection in Florida." In *Paying the price: The status and role of insurance against natural disasters in the United States,* ed. Howard Kunreuther and Richard J. Roth Sr. Washington, D.C.: Joseph Henry.

Lewis, Christopher M., and Kevin C. Murdock. 1996. The role of government contracts in discretionary reinsurance markets for natural disasters. *Journal of Risk and Insurance* 63:567–97.

Litzenberger, Robert, David Beaglehole, and Craig Reynolds. 1996. *Assessing catastro-phe-reinsurance-linked securities as a new asset class.* New York: Goldman Sachs, July.

Marshall, John. 1976. Moral hazard. *American Economic Review* 66:880–90.

Meszaros, Jacqueline R. 1997. The cognition of catastrophe: Preliminary examination of an industry in transition. Working Paper no. 97–02–01. Wharton Center for Risk Management and Decision Processes, University of Pennsylvania.

Office of Technology Assessment. 1995. *Reducing earthquake losses.* Washington, D.C.: U.S. Government Printing Office.

Palm, Risa. 1995. *Earthquake insurance: A longitudinal study of California homeown-ers.* Boulder, Colo.: Westview.

Pauly, Mark. 1974. Overinsurance and public provision of insurance: The role of moral hazard and adverse selection. *Quarterly Journal of Economics* 88:44–62.

Roth, Richard, Jr. 1998. Earthquake insurance protection in California. In *Paying the price: The status and role of insurance against natural disasters in the United States,* ed. Howard Kunreuther and Richard Roth Sr. Washington, D.C.: Joseph Henry.

Scawthorn, Charles, Ben Lashkari, and Amjad Naseer. 1997. What happened in Kobe and what if it happened here? In *Economic consequences of earthquakes: Preparing for the unexpected,* ed. Barclay Jones. Buffalo, N.Y.: National Center for Earthquake Engineering Research.

Scism, Leslie. 1996. Florida homeowners find insurance pricey if they find it at all. *Wall Street Journal,* 12 July, 1.

Shavell, Steven. 1979. On moral hazard and insurance. *Quarterly Journal of Econom-ics* 93:541–62.

Steinbrugge, Karl V. 1982. *Earthquakes, volcanoes, and tsunamis: An anatomy of haz-ards.* New York: Skandia American.

Stone, James. 1973. A theory of capacity and the insurance of catastrophe risks. *Journal of Risk and Insurance* 40:231–43, 337–55.

U.S. General Accounting Office. 1990. *Flood insurance: Information on the mandatory purchase requirement.* Washington, D.C., August.

Valery, Nicholas. 1995. Fear of trembling. *Economist,* 22 April, 11.

Wind, Yoram. 1982. *Product policy: Concepts, methods and strategy.* Reading, Mass.: Addison-Wesley.

Comment   James R. Garven

Kleindorfer and Kunreuther provide a very useful and insightful approach to evaluating the role of insurance and other policy instruments for managing catastrophic risk. Their findings derive from a sophisticated and highly detailed modeling process that stochastically generates earthquake scenarios for a model city, which in turn specifies the probabilistic structure of losses and corresponding implications for insurer solvency and stability. The Kleindorfer and Kunreuther model does a superb job of capturing the interdependencies that exist between various policy instruments, scenario variables, and decision processes of firms and consumers. Consequently, their model provides a useful

James R. Garven holds the William H. Wright Jr. Endowed Chair for Financial Services, Depart-ment of Finance, E. J. Ourso College of Business Administration, Louisiana State University.

framework that can be readily expanded to consider the potential role of alternative approaches to funding and mitigation.

In what follows, I will offer some suggestions concerning how the present analysis could be usefully modified and perhaps even extended. Specifically, I will offer comments concerning mitigation incentives, insurer objectives, and an interesting "real-world" application of the Kleindorfer and Kunreuther model.

Incentives for Mitigation

The apparent disregard shown historically by banks and insurers when funding and insuring properties located in catastrophe-prone areas is appalling. As the authors point out, this has increased the severity of losses when catastrophes have actually occurred.

It may be that regulatory complicity (in the form of rate suppression and cross-subsidies) causes consumers to not fully consider the risks associated with investing in catastrophe-prone properties. Consequently, insurance prices may falsely convey the nature of the risks that consumers assume in deciding to build in such areas. The fact that the Florida joint underwriting authority acquired so much market share in so short a period of time is clear evidence of severe adverse selection and obviously very bad news from a mitigation perspective.

Insurance-Company Objectives

The paper takes as given the notion, advanced originally more than two decades ago by Stone (1973), that insurers will seek to maximize the expected return on capital, subject to complying with (arbitrarily parameterized) solvency and stability constraints. Such an approach is logically consistent with recent findings that insurers apparently factor in the probable maximum loss associated with a catastrophe when they determine how many policies to write. Kleindorfer and Kunreuther also show in an appendix that their results are apparently qualitatively robust to alternative specifications of the firm's objective function; for example, one could apply the expected-utility hypothesis without any apparent loss of generality.

I would encourage the authors to consider as well a financial market setting as an alternative framework for modeling insurer decisions. The adoption of a financial market setting would afford a number of analytic advantages. For example, it would provide an internally consistent framework for introducing such alternative financial instruments as act-of-God bonds and insurance derivatives directly into the analysis. Furthermore, a financial market setting also makes it much easier to consider important incentive effects associated with taxation and solvency. Studies based on financial market models (e.g., Mayers and Smith 1990; Garven and Lamm-Tennant 1997) have shown that insurer willingness to bear risk may be significantly influenced by factors such as asymmetries in the tax code and variation in ownership structure as well as the risk of insolvency. Furthermore, limited liability and tax asymmetries create "kinky," option-like payoffs that also convey systematically different risk incentives for stock versus mutual organizations (see Garven 1992). The incentive effects documented in these studies become even more pronounced in the face of catastrophic risks.

An Interesting "Real-World" Application

A very interesting "out-of-the-box" application of the Kleindorfer and Kunreuther model would involve the evaluation of the optimality (or lack thereof) of the California Earthquake Association financial structure (see their table 4.1). Given the conceptual framework provided by the Kleindorfer and Kunreuther model, does the CEA financial structure make sense? If not, would there be better ways to parameterize it from the perspectives of funding and mitigation?

References

Garven, J. R. 1992. An exposition of the implications of limited liability and asymmetric taxes for property-liability insurance. *Journal of Risk and Insurance* 59:34–56.

Garven, J. R., and J. Lamm-Tennant. 1997. The demand for reinsurance: Theory and empirical tests. Working paper. Louisiana State University/Genre Corp.

Mayers, D., and C. W. Smith Jr. 1990. On the corporate demand for insurance: Evidence from the reinsurance market. *Journal of Business* 63:19–40.

Stone, J. 1973. A theory of capacity and the insurance of catastrophe risks. *Journal of Risk and Insurance* 40:231–43.

Comment   Dwight Jaffee

Catastrophe insurance in the United States (and other countries) is, generally speaking, not provided by private companies operating in free markets. Instead, government entities and regulators (state or federal) have become major players in virtually all such markets. This is perplexing since standard theory would suggest that insurance for low-probability, high-consequence events should create an active demand (by consumers and business firms seeking to reduce their catastrophe risk) and an aggressive supply (by profit-seeking insurance companies) that would support such a market. An accurate understanding of why private insurance markets for catastrophes fail to operate is critical for evaluating how best to deal with this failure. Otherwise, we cannot know whether the government-based solutions, now adopted for hurricanes in Flor-

Dwight Jaffee is professor of real estate and finance at the Haas School of Business, University of California, Berkeley.

ida and Hawaii, for earthquakes in California, and for floods across the United States, are the best available solutions.

This paper, by Paul Kleindorfer and Howard Kunreuther, provides important advances in understanding some of the important elements that are creating the market failure. In particular, the paper makes important contributions in two primary areas. First, it focuses on the decision processes of the key stakeholders and on how the interaction of these processes has made it difficult for private firms to manage catastrophe-insurance risks. Second, it focuses on new methods for modeling catastrophe-risk management. I discuss these in turn.

Behavioral Insurance: The Decision Processes of Stakeholders

Kleindorfer and Kunreuther focus on how the behavior of various stakeholders in the catastrophe-insurance market—the insurance companies, insured individuals, and government regulators—might vary from that implied by expected-utility theory. This research area might be called *behavioral insurance,* in parallel with the new field of behavioral finance. Indeed, insurance market anomalies, such as the failure of private markets for catastrophe insurance, can be as interesting and challenging to explain as the well-known financial market anomalies.

Kleindorfer and Kunreuther on Behavioral Insurance

The authors are persuasive in arguing that behavioral factors may play an important role in explaining the catastrophe market anomaly. For example, they point out that consumers may understate the probability of a catastrophe ("it will not happen to me") while insurers may operate under a "probable-maximum-loss" constraint to limit their risk of ruin. These factors reduce both the demand for and supply of catastrophe insurance. These factors may also explain why consumers can complain that insurance is too expensive and the companies unfair while at the same time failing to carry out economically sensible mitigation investments.

Kleindorfer and Kunreuther also emphasize that further effects can arise owing to interconnections on a systemwide basis. They point out, for example, that construction firms, local building-code inspectors, homeowners, insurance companies, real estate agents, and mortgage lenders (including Fannie Mae and Freddie Mac) have all chosen to overlook important cases in which homes have not been built to code. This was clearly revealed during Hurricane Andrew as improperly constructed roofs blew away.

The Government and Behavioral Insurance

The authors indicate that the government can be a constructive force in reversing some of the problems of the catastrophe-insurance industry, which is certainly true. On the other hand, it is important to recognize that most government disaster-relief programs create highly adverse incentives both for catastrophe insurance and for the ex ante mitigation of the effects of catastrophes. In the extreme case, if the government pays for all uninsured losses, then there is a positive incentive to place activity in risky locations and not to carry private catastrophe insurance. This is not an easy problem to fix since it is difficult for a government to claim, with credibility, that it will not provide disaster relief in the future.

It is interesting in this regard that the Italian government is currently attempting to reduce the budgetary effect of disaster relief by making catastrophe insurance mandatory for all homeowners. Under current proposals, the premiums will be paid through a surtax on other casualty insurance. In this case, the Italian budget may benefit, but, since the premiums will not vary by specific location, the incentive to locate in hazardous areas will continue. On the other hand, different problems are created when individuals are forced to pay directly for mandatory insurance, as illustrated by the number of uninsured motorists and the assigned risk pools in U.S. auto-insurance markets. This all reinforces the authors' basic point that it is important to consider behavioral factors when determining the proper role for government in insurance markets.

New Methods for Modeling Catastrophe-Risk Management

The second primary contribution of the Kleindorfer and Kunreuther paper is a prototype model for managing catastrophe risk, one based on recent developments in risk assessment and information technology. The model measures the exposure to earthquake risk of a city that is a virtual mirror, in terms of the number and mix of structures, of Oakland, California. The model includes an insurance industry (with firms of differing size), reinsurance in alternative amounts, and mitigation in alternative amounts. Model results are generated by Monte Carlo simulations, which determine expected and worst-case losses for each stakeholder group.

Model Results

The model provides reasonable results in terms of the effect of varying the amount and cost of reinsurance available to the insurance companies. In particular, as the cost of reinsurance rises or its availability falls, the insurance companies reduce the amount of primary coverage that they are willing to offer.

The model also provides intriguing results concerning the benefits of mitigation. As expected, the model shows that the worst-case losses decline as the degree of mitigation is improved. However, the model also shows no benefits to mitigation on average, which is surprising. This result arises because mitigation is measured in the model by the degree of adherence to the building codes. In particular, the model ignores potential mitigation that is not code related while including the cost of code-based retrofits that have no mitigation benefits. In other words, properly interpreted, the model is showing that *inefficient* mitigation is not cost effective, certainly a reasonable result. It must remain for future work, however, to measure the potential benefits of *efficient* mitigation.

Further Comments on the Model

This model is really a remarkable feat, and my hat is off to the authors. Nevertheless, there are features that could be and probably should be improved. I will focus on two key areas, the role of prices in the model and certain missing model features.

The model determines the premium prices for both insurance and reinsurance as a markup over the expected loss for each property. The loading factor for the markup is exogenously determined to be 100 percent. In particular, the premium prices do not necessarily clear the market, and it seems that they are generally below the market-clearing level. It is hard to know how much this affects the model's results for reinsurance and mitigation. In any case, it would be useful to have a version of the model with market-clearing prices. As a related matter, it might also be useful to allow new entry into the insurance market to occur as a function of the profit margins being earned by the current participants.

There are several other features of earthquake-insurance markets that might be useful to incorporate in future versions of the model. I simply list these briefly: (*a*) As already mentioned, government disaster relief programs create an incentive to locate activity in hazardous areas and not to buy earthquake insurance. (*b*) Fraud can be an important part of the cost of settling claims. (*c*) Alternative contracts can provide more or less coverage and be more or less subject to fraud. These ideas illustrate the range of questions that can be potentially answered by such models. I look forward to more results from Kleindorfer and Kunreuther as they continue their research in this area.

5   The Pricing of U.S. Catastrophe Reinsurance

Kenneth A. Froot and Paul G. J. O'Connell

The price of catastrophe reinsurance in the United States has fluctuated markedly in recent years. These fluctuations are commonly associated with the pattern of catastrophe occurrences. For example, catastrophe losses during the period 1992–94 totaled $38.6 billion in 1994 dollars, exceeding the cumulative total of losses during 1949–91 of $34.6 billion. During this three-year period, prices on catastrophe-reinsurance cover more than doubled and then began to decline thereafter. What drives such changes in price? Does the demand for reinsurance shift, does the supply of reinsurance capital change, or do both occur?[1]

If catastrophe losses lead to a decrease (leftward shift) in supply, then we would expect to see increases in price coupled with declines in quantity after an event. Of course, a decline in supply is possible only in the presence of some form of capital market imperfection. If capital markets were perfect, the supply curve for reinsurance would be perfectly elastic. In this case, regardless of losses, the price of reinsurance would be fixed, where the "price" of a con-

Kenneth A. Froot is the Industrial Bank of Japan Professor of Finance and director of research at the Harvard Business School and a research associate of the National Bureau of Economic Research. Paul G. J. O'Connell is president of Emerging Markets Finance, LLC.

The authors are grateful to Peter Diamond, Chris Milton, Julio Rotemberg, Jeremy Stein, Rene Stulz, and conference participants for helpful comments; to David Govrin, Chris McGhee, Denis Medvedsek, Brian Murphy, and Barney Schauble for help in obtaining and understanding reinsurance data; and to the NBER and the Division of Research at Harvard Business School for generous research support. All errors are the authors'.

1. A number of papers have investigated these cycles, attempting to identify supply and demand shocks in insurance markets. Cummins and Outreville (1987) show that lags in data collection or price regulation can generate cycles in property-casualty underwriting margins. Gron (1994) presents evidence that, assuming that there are no marketwide demand shocks, the cycles in property-casualty margins are due to variation in the supply of insurance capacity rather than institutional lags or reporting practices. Gron and Lucas (1995) investigate why these cycles appear to be so persistent. They find that, when the net worth of insurers declines, the total amount of capital raised through security issues is small. See also Winter (1988) and Cummins and Danzon (1991).

tract is best thought of as the ratio of premiums to actuarially expected losses covered under that contract. Capital market imperfections would imply that the marginal cost of producing reinsurance is increasing in the quantity supplied. Thus, these imperfections lead to an upward-sloping supply curve, which (all else equal) can shift back as a result of reinsurer losses. Such a supply shift increases price and reduces quantity. As with price, it is best to think of this "quantity" as the actuarially expected loss covered by reinsurance.

On the other hand, catastrophe losses may lead to increases in demand. Rightward demand shifts can be thought of as the result of an actual or perceived increase in actuarial losses covered by a given contract. We call this *probability updating*. Naturally, it would seem possible to identify such demand shifts from the fact that they lead to an increase in price *and* quantity. Thus, conditional on a loss, an absolute decline in the quantity of reinsurance purchased would be evidence of important leftward shifts in supply even if there were also positive increases in demand.

We look for such absolute declines in quantity, but, in addition, we pursue the probability-updating hypothesis further. While it is impossible to distinguish between probability updating and capital market imperfections on the basis of the behavior of aggregate price indices over time, it is possible to distinguish between them on the basis of the behavior of *cross-sectional* changes in reinsurance prices. Specifically, probability updating ought to vary across contracts, with larger price increases associated with contracts for which more probability updating occurs. We therefore examine cross-sectional price increases in response to an event and determine the extent to which they are explained by relative contract exposures.

To see how this works, consider a catastrophe loss caused by a winter freeze in New England. We might expect such a loss to affect strongly (and positively) the distribution of prospective losses due to freeze and/or the distribution of prospective losses due to other perils in New England. After all, the event may cause people to recognize how much damage a freeze can do or to learn about the replacement costs of certain physical assets in New England. However, such updates in knowledge would have little or no import for the distribution of catastrophe losses outside New England, where freezes do not occur. Specifically, little would be learned about loss exposures in California (which faces primarily earthquake risk), the Southeast (which faces primarily hurricane risk), or Texas (which faces primarily windstorm risk). Under probability updating, it follows that contracts with relatively little exposure to freeze and/or to the Northeast region ought to have relatively small price increases. In this way, we are able to further distinguish between capital market imperfections and probability updating.

Our identification strategy is made possible through the use of a unique and detailed data set from Guy Carpenter and Company, by far the largest catastrophe-reinsurance broker for U.S. catastrophe exposures. These data include all U.S. catastrophe-reinsurance contracts brokered by Guy Carpenter between

1970 and 1994. They allow us to measure prices and contract losses and to go about the complex process of estimating each contract's exposure to different event types and regions.

To preview our results, we find that supply, rather than demand, shocks are more important for understanding the effect of losses on reinsurance prices and quantities. Capital market imperfections therefore appear to be the dominant explanation. There is limited evidence for probability updating, and what evidence there is suggests that the effect is of a small magnitude. The magnitudes of the supply effects are large: after controlling for relative contract exposure, a $10 billion catastrophe loss raises average contract prices by between 19 and 40 percent and reduces quantity of reinsurance purchased by between 5 and 16 percent.

The rest of the paper is organized as follows. Section 5.1 sets out our identification strategy and the structure of our empirical tests. Section 5.2 describes our data sources. In section 5.3, the calculation of contract exposure and price is discussed in detail. We devote considerable attention to the calculation of exposure, which requires a number of involved steps. Section 5.4 provides a brief graphic analysis. The empirical testing is carried out in section 5.5. Section 5.6 summarizes and offers our conclusions.

5.1   The Price and Quantity of Reinsurance

We examine the equilibrium prices and quantities of single-event excess-of-loss reinsurance contracts. These contracts help reinsure insurance companies against losses resulting from natural catastrophes in the United States, such as windstorms or earthquakes.

To understand how such contracts work, consider an insurer that purchases a layer of reinsurance covering $100 million of losses in excess of $200 million. These terms imply that, if the insurer's losses from a single catastrophic event during the contract year exceed $200 million (the "retention"), the layer is triggered. The reinsurer pays the insurer the amount of any losses in excess of $200 million, with the maximum payment—the "limit"—capped at $100 million.[2] By purchasing this contract, the insurer cedes its exposure to single-event catastrophe losses in the $200–$300 million range. In return for assuming this exposure, the reinsurer receives a payment, known as the "premium." If the insurer wishes to cede a broader band of exposure, it could purchase additional layers—$100 million in excess of $300 million, $100 million in excess of $400 million, and so on.

The price of a reinsurance contract is best measured as the premium per unit of exposure. In the marketplace, premium is usually expressed relative to limit (the ratio is called *rate on line*). However, limit is a poor proxy for contract

---

2. To guard against moral hazard, excess-of-loss reinsurance contracts typically require coinsurance. In practice, this effectively means that the insurer provides 5–10 percent of the reinsurance.

exposure—it ignores the level of the contract's retention, for example. To remedy this, we measure price by premium per unit of actuarially expected loss. Indeed, we use actuarially expected loss as our measure of the "quantity" of reinsurance purchased.

In section 5.3, we describe how historical data on catastrophe losses and company-specific market-share information can be used to measure the actual exposure of each reinsurance contract. It is important to emphasize that we measure actuarially expected loss from a loss distribution that is *time invariant*. We cannot condition our measures of expected loss on previous losses. To the extent that loss distributions shift in response to recent loss history, we measure both quantity and price with error. These potential mismeasurements are important for the way we specify our tests and hypotheses.

5.1.1 Identifying Capital Market Imperfections

As noted above, we investigate two channels by which catastrophe losses affect reinsurance prices and quantities. First, "capital market imperfections" may impede the flow of capital into the reinsurance sector. There may be several sources of such imperfections. One is that existing reinsurers may find it costly or undesirable to *raise* additional external capital. These costs could result from information asymmetries between managers and owners (which implies that equity-sale announcements drive down share prices) or from dilution of managerial control (which implies that managers are averse to expanding the capital base). Another potential source of imperfection is that it is costly to *carry* equity capital. These costs may accrue from forgone tax shields, agency problems, or, in the case of reinsurers, frictional collateral costs.[3]

If we could accurately measure, at each point in time, the distribution of one-year-ahead losses conditional on all information, then it would be relatively simple to test the capital market imperfections story. In the presence of such imperfections, capital depletion associated with event losses constricts the supply of reinsurance, driving up the price of all contracts. If, for example, the event were a hurricane, the supply of hurricane-reinsurance capacity would fall. So would the supply of nonhurricane-reinsurance capacity since both exposures are borne by the same capital base. Figure 5.1 shows the effect on equilibrium prices and quantities for contracts that are exposed to hurricane risk (fig. 5.1A) and those that are not (fig. 5.1B). Note that the exposure supply curves are upward sloping. This is due to the capital market imperfections, which raise the marginal cost at which reinsurers are able to offer successively greater exposure protection to insurers.[4]

Figure 5.1 suggests that capital market imperfections generate a negative correlation between prices and quantities since loss shocks lead to shifts in the

---

3. For a survey of these costs and their effect on financing patterns, see Froot (1995). Froot and Stein (1998) study the implications for financial intermediaries of costly equity finance.

4. For a model of the reservation price that a financial intermediary such as a reinsurer is willing to offer marginal units of risk exposure, see Froot and Stein (1998).

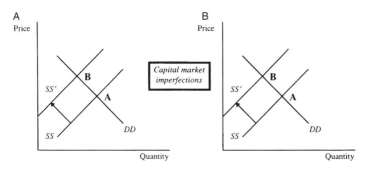

Fig. 5.1   Capital market imperfections: *A,* **Hurricane-exposed contracts;** *B,* **Non-hurricane-exposed contracts**

Fig. 5.2   Real quantity of catastrophe exposure ceded, 1975:1–1993:4
Note: In any quarter, the series is the sum of the contract exposure that is ceded by four major insurers in that quarter. The four companies represent approximately 10 percent of the market.

supply curve. If losses lead to demand-curve shifts, on the other hand, a positive correlation between price and quantity results.

Since negative correlation would seem to be evidence in favor of supply shifts (and, therefore, capital market imperfections), it seems useful to ask whether prices and quantities are in fact negatively correlated. Figures 5.2 and 5.3 show our measures of quantity and price, respectively, for the sample period for which we have contract data.[5] More specifically, figure 5.2 shows an

---

5. For a description of our data and the computation of prices and quantities, see sec. 5.2 below.

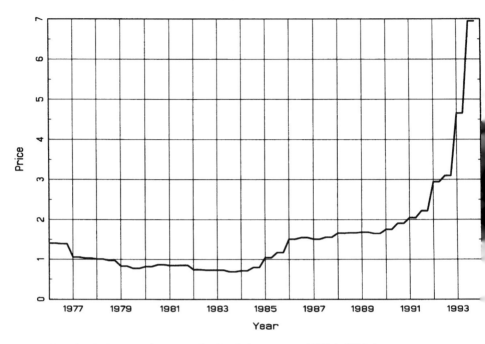

Fig. 5.3   Industry price per unit of ceded exposure, 1975:1–1993:4

index of the total quantity of catastrophe exposure that was ceded in the U.S. reinsurance market from 1975:1 to 1993:4. The series is calculated by summing all the exposure embodied in the excess-of-loss contracts in each quarter and dividing it by the total market share represented by the contracts. Figure 5.3 plots the industry price series quarterly from 1975:1 to 1993:4. Each observation is the exposure-weighted average of the price of all contracts that are in force in that quarter.[6]

A number of features of these figures are noteworthy. First, it appears that quantities rose and prices fell for much of the late 1970s and 1980s. Second, a startling rise in prices and decline in quantities took place beginning in the mid-1980s through the end of the sample period. Indeed, in 1993, price was between five and seven times its historical average. This will come as no surprise to industry observers. It is common to relate this price rise to the occurrence of a number of large events during this period, notably Hurricane Andrew ($20 billion in losses) in August 1992, Hurricane Hugo in 1989, and several windstorms in 1985–86. Figure 5.4, which plots total catastrophe losses by quarter from 1970:1 to 1994:4 as measured by Property Claims Ser-

---

6. These industry series are based on the contract prices and exposures for four insurers that purchased reinsurance through Guy Carpenter in every year from 1975 to 1993. The series are representative of the behavior of prices and quantities for the other insurers in our database.

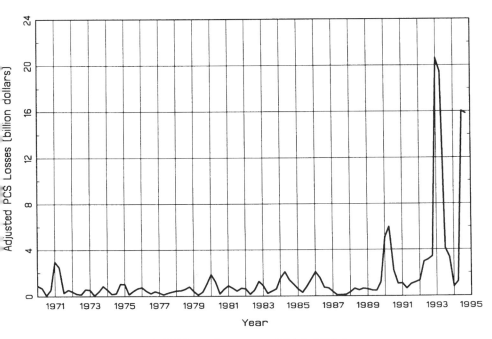

Fig. 5.4   Total adjusted PCS losses by quarter, 1970:1–1994:4

vices, lends support to this view.[7] In the period since 1994 (for which we have no data), the price of reinsurance has declined and quantity increased somewhat, notwithstanding the occurrence of the Northridge Earthquake in January 1994. From these observations, it is clear that there is considerable negative correlation between prices and quantities at frequencies of several years.

Figures 5.5 and 5.6 provide further evidence of the apparent negative correlation between equilibrium prices and quantities. Figure 5.5 plots industry price-quantity pairs. It is interesting because it suggests the existence of two regimes in catastrophe-reinsurance pricing. The 1970s and early 1980s saw strong expansion in the quantity of risk ceded coupled with a moderate decline in per unit prices. The late 1980s and early 1990s were characterized by ballooning prices coupled with quantity declines. One interpretation of these patterns is that the 1970s and 1980s were a period of expanding reinsurance demand while the 1990s exhibit a contraction of reinsurance supply. Figure 5.6 plots each contract's price against its exposure. Both variables have been demeaned by insurer. As indicated by the linear fit to the plot (slope -0.32, standard error 0.04), when a contract embodies less-than-average exposure, it tends to be priced above average. Taken at face value, the points appear to lie on firm-specific reinsurance-demand schedules. Or, put another way, strong

7. For a description of this loss series, see sec. 5.2 below.

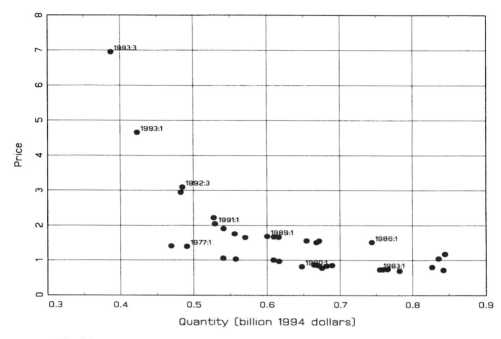

Fig. 5.5   Industry price-quantity pairs, 1975:1–1993:4

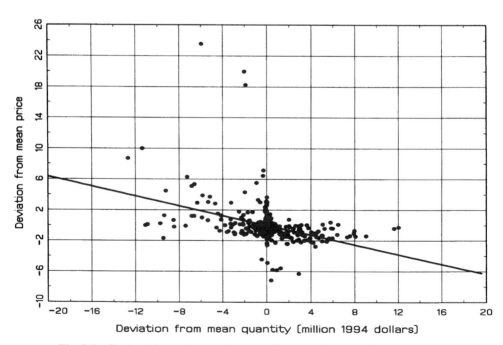

Fig. 5.6   Contract-by-contract price-quantity pairs, demeaned by company, 1970–94 (linear fit estimated by OLS)

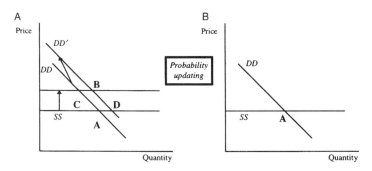

Fig. 5.7   Probability updating: *A*, Hurricane-exposed contracts; *B*, Non-hurricane-exposed contracts

evidence of negative correlation between price and quantity suggests that shifts in the reinsurance supply curve have been important.

Taken by itself, this evidence would seem to support the hypothesis of capital market imperfections. However, it is important to see the implications of demand shocks, or what we call *probability updating*. Probability updating holds that the occurrence of a catastrophe may raise the real or perceived distribution of losses above what we measure with our time-invariant loss distribution. For example, after Hurricane Andrew in 1992, some insurers were surprised that the construction methods used for houses in Homestead, Florida, performed so poorly in high winds. Andrew might also have led to upward shifts in agents' subjective distributions.

To see the effects of probability updating, suppose that, after a particular event, say, a hurricane, agents update positively about the likelihood of hurricane losses. Then, even if the premium per unit of actual exposure stays constant, the ratio of premium to *observed* exposure rises. This is because we measure exposure from a time-invariant loss distribution. Figure 5.7 traces this effect on supply and demand. Suppose that capital markets are perfect—the supply of capital to the reinsurance sector is infinitely elastic at a given price. In the aftermath of the hurricane, the observed supply curve shifts upward, as shown in figure 5.7A. To understand what happens to the demand schedule, consider an insurer that, at a given price, wants to cede the same amount of exposure before and after the hurricane. Since the perceived risk of hurricanes increases, the terms of this insurer's contract must be rewritten to keep exposure constant. For example, the retention on the contract could be raised. Any such change that keeps *actual* ceded exposure constant causes *measured* exposure to fall and, concomitantly, *measured* price to rise. Thus, the entire observed demand schedule shifts upward and to the left. All this assumes that there is no actual change in demand. However, the demand curve may exhibit further changes as agents alter the amount of reinsurance they are willing to demand at a *given* price. For example, the demand schedule may shift out if

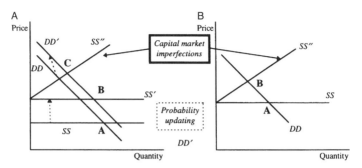

Fig. 5.8   Capital market imperfections and probability updating: *A*, **Hurricane-exposed contracts;** *B*, **Non-hurricane-exposed contracts**

homeowners learn from the hurricane that they are underinsured. Alternatively, the schedule may shift in if coastal homeowners who sustain severe damage from the hurricane elect to move to a less-exposed inland region rather than to rebuild in the same place.

Consequently, the overall effect on the observed demand curve is ambiguous. If the observed *DD* curve experiences no net shift at all, the equilibrium moves from point *A* to point *C*, which results in an increase in price and a decrease in demand. Thus, demand shifts combined with probability updating can duplicate the finding that prices increase while quantities decrease. We therefore cannot conclude that such negative correlation is evidence of capital market imperfections. On the other hand, if the observed *DD* curve shifts out on net, as shown in the figure, the equilibrium shifts from point *A* to point *B*.

Probability updating, then, complicates the process of identifying capital market effects. To overcome this problem, consider the following identification strategy. Assume that hurricane losses may lead to probability updating for hurricanes but not for other types of events in other regions. The idea here is simple: if a hurricane occurs, it may not alter the perceived frequency or severity of nonhurricane events. Accordingly, probability updating from a hurricane should produce no change in prices or quantities of contracts that have little or no hurricane exposure. However, if there are capital market imperfections, then prices tend to increase and quantities decrease on nonhurricane-exposed contracts.

Figure 5.8 illustrates. A hurricane loss that raises the perceived likelihood of future hurricane losses will simultaneously shift the observed demand and supply curves upward and to the left. These effects are shown as movements in the schedules from *DD* to *DD'* and from *SS* to *SS'* in figure 5.8A, which together produce an increase in price. There are no such probability-updating effects for the contracts that are not exposed to hurricane risk in figure 5.8B. However, if the catastrophe loss depletes the pool of capital that is available to the industry for all types of reinsurance, then the supply schedule for both types of contracts shifts back to SS''. In these circumstances, we can expect the price of both to increase.

A natural way to implement this identification scheme is to regress changes in price and quantity on lagged losses by type and lagged losses by type interacted with contract exposure by type. If there are K types of catastrophe, the conditional expectation functions takes the form

$$(1) \qquad \Delta \ln(p_{j,t}) = \alpha + \sum_{k=1}^{K} \beta_k \theta_t(l_k) + \sum_{k=1}^{K} \gamma_k w_{j,k,t} \theta_t(l_k) + \varepsilon_{j,t},$$

$$(2) \qquad \Delta \ln(q_{j,t}) = \alpha + \sum_{k=1}^{K} \delta_k \theta_t(l_k) + \sum_{k=1}^{K} \phi_k w_{j,k,t} \theta_t(l_k) + \varepsilon_{j,t},$$

where $p_{j,t}$ and $q_{j,t}$ are the price and quantity, respectively, of insurer j's contract at time t, $\theta_t(l_k)$ is a distributed lag of losses of event type k, $w_{j,k,t}$ is the exposure of insurer j to catastrophes of type k at time t, and $\varepsilon_{j,\tau}$ is a disturbance term. The relative exposure term, $w_{j,k,t}$, is defined as

$$(2) \qquad \Delta \ln(q_{j,t}) = \alpha + \sum_{k=1}^{K} \delta_k \theta_t(l_k) + \sum_{k=1}^{K} \phi_k w_{j,k,t} \theta_t(l_k) + \varepsilon_{j,t},$$

where $q_{j,k,t}$ is the absolute exposure (the actuarially expected loss) of insurer j to catastrophes of type k at time t. $\beta_k(\delta_k')$ measures the response of contract prices (quantities) to losses of type k independent of contract exposure. The parameter γ_k (ϕ_k') detects the exposure sensitivity of the price (quantity) responses. In estimating (1) and (2), we restrict attention to simple lag structures, such as[8]

$$(4) \qquad \theta_t(l_k) = l_{k,t-2} + l_{k,t-3} + l_{k,t-4} + l_{k,t-5}.$$

To the extent that capital market imperfections are responsible for price and quantity changes, we expect $\beta_k > 0$ in (1) and $\delta_k < 0$ in (2), with the null hypothesis of perfect capital markets being $\beta_k = 0$ and $\delta_k = 0$. Conditional on a loss from a particular event type, prices tend to rise and quantities to fall equally across all contracts if there are capital market imperfections. The composition of contract exposure matters for price changes only if probability updating is present. Thus, with no probability updating, $\gamma_k = 0$ for all k, and, with probability updating, $\gamma_k > 0$ for all k. Of course, if both capital market imperfections and probability updating are important, we expect $\beta_k > 0$ and $\gamma_k > 0$.

It is of interest to consider several modifications of the basic specifications (1) and (2). For instance, if the average effect of a dollar of losses is the same across catastrophe types, as the capital market imperfections view would suggest, then we expect $\beta_1 = \beta_2 = \ldots = \beta_K$. This restriction can readily be im-

---

8. Losses in the quarter immediately preceding contract inception appear to have no influence on prices. The most likely reason for this is that there can be a delay in assessing the extent of catastrophe losses. Accordingly, losses lag prices by two or more quarters in all our analyses.

posed in the estimation. A second worthwhile modification is to allow the average and marginal effects of losses to differ. If the supply schedule is nonlinear, for example, then it may be true that large losses have proportionately bigger effects than small losses. Indeed, this is true in most models of capital market imperfections, as discussed in Froot and O'Connell (1997). A convenient way to allow for this possibility is to include higher-order terms in the distributed lag of losses.

5.1.2   Differentiating among Catastrophe Types

We differentiate exposure along two dimensions: by geographic region and by catastrophe type. Distinguishing events across regions is appealing because regional market-share data are available for many reinsurance contracts. These market-share data provide a ready measure of relative contract exposure. Thus, $w_{j,k,t}$ can be defined as

$$(5) \qquad w_{j,k,t} = \frac{m_{j,k,t}}{\left(\dfrac{1}{K}\right)\displaystyle\sum_{k=1}^{K} m_{j,k,t}},$$

where $m_{j,k,t}$ is the market share of insurer j in region k. We estimate (1) and (2) using this measure of exposure in the empirical analysis in section 5.5 below.

There are two drawbacks to this approach, however. First, market shares are typically built up from the share of total catastrophe premiums in a region that go to insurer j. To the extent that premiums are a poor proxy for true exposure, $w_{j,k,t}$ will be subject to measurement error. Second, it is clear that the catastrophe occurrences in one region may reveal important information about the distribution of losses in other regions. For example, hurricane losses in the Southeast are likely to lead to probability updates in the distribution of hurricane losses in both the Northeast and the Southeast. As a result, price increases (and quantity decreases) in the Northeast in the aftermath of a Florida hurricane could be due to either probability updating or inelastic capital supply to the industry, and identification may be tenuous.

These two shortcomings motivate us to differentiate catastrophes by type as well. Here, the exposure of each contract to distinct classes of events, such as earthquakes, hurricanes, and winter storms, is calculated. This strategy avoids the second shortcoming noted above. Losses from a particular type of event (e.g., a windstorm) are likely to generate little updating in the distributions of other event losses (e.g., an earthquake). Thus, separate identification of probability updating and capital market imperfections is more dependable. The cost is that calculating exposures' catastrophe type *and* region entails considerable computational effort. First, the frequency and severity of each type of catastrophe must be estimated *by region*. Then these distributions must be used to derive the distribution of losses on each contract by simulation. The calculation of contract exposure by catastrophe type is taken up in section 5.3 below, after a discussion of the data and the construction of our main variables.

5.2   Data

Our data are built up from four sources. The basic information on catastrophe-reinsurance pricing is provided by Guy Carpenter. Information on the regional market share of insurers is developed from A. M. Best data on insurance premiums written by company. Our estimates of catastrophe frequency and severity are based on Property Claims Services (PCS) data on U.S. catastrophe losses since 1949. Finally, interest rate and CPI data are collected from Ibbotson and Associates and the IMF, respectively.

5.2.1   Guy Carpenter Catastrophe Treaty Data

Our basic data come from Guy Carpenter's proprietary database of catastrophe-reinsurance contracts. Guy Carpenter is by far the largest U.S. catastrophe-reinsurance broker, with a market share of between 30 and 80 percent during our sample period. The contracts brokered by Guy Carpenter cover a variety of natural perils, including earthquake, fire, hurricane, winter storm, and windstorm.

We examine a total of 489 contracts brokered for eighteen national and nineteen regional insurers over the period 1970–94.[9] The duration of coverage is typically one year. Most contracts have a single mandatory-reinstatement provision.[10] Data on contract inception date, retention (i.e., the retention of the lowermost layer in the contract), limit (i.e., the sum of the limits of all the layers in the contract), and premium (i.e., the sum of the premiums paid for the layers in the contract) are employed. All the contract inception dates are at the start of a quarter.

5.2.2   A. M. Best Market Share Data

To determine the catastrophe exposure of each contract, we must calculate the distribution of contract losses, a random variable for each contract. To do this, we assume that, within each region, each company's exposure is proportional to insurance-industry exposure within the region. We therefore first determine a distribution for insurance-industry losses for each region (by event type) and then multiply this aggregate distribution by an individual insurer's market share to determine the distribution of insurer-specific exposure faced by that company. Using this information, we can calculate the company-specific distribution of losses under each contract.

---

9. Seven very small regional insurers were dropped from the original Guy Carpenter data. In some of the computations presented below, we focus on a smaller number of national reinsurers, for whom data are available in every year.

10. The reinstatement provision stipulates that, conditional on an event that triggers losses on the contract, the limit is to be mandatorily reinstated (one time only) by the reinsurer after payment of a reinstatement premium by the cedent. It appears that this provision has had only a modest effect on prices, and we ignore its effects. Conversations with brokers suggest that observed prices are approximately 10 percent *lower* than they would have been without the reinstatement premium. This seems surprising (forward contracts are usually priced at zero) but, if anything, leads us to underestimate what premiums would be in the absence of a reinstatement provision.

Our estimates of insurer market shares are developed using data from A. M. Best on insurance premiums written by company, by line of business, by state, and by year. We reduce these multiline market shares to regional catastrophe market shares by applying a modified Kiln formula, which assigns regional weights to premiums in each line of business on the basis of exposure to catastrophes of that line in that region.[11] For example, depending on the region, anywhere between 50 and 95 percent of homeowner's premiums are considered as funding catastrophe exposure. The five U.S. regions used for insurer market shares are the Northeast, the Southeast, Texas, the Midwest, and California.[12] We apply this market-share data to all 489 reinsurance contracts selected from the Guy Carpenter treaty database.

5.2.3 Historic Catastrophe-Loss Data from Property Claims Services

As mentioned above, we must determine the distribution of industrywide losses to calculate the catastrophe exposure of each contract. To do this, we estimate the distributions of catastrophe frequency and severity using data from Property Claims Services (PCS). PCS has cataloged all catastrophe losses on an industrywide basis since 1949 by type and U.S. region. The PCS data are widely used as an industry standard.

Prior to estimating the parameters of the frequency and severity distributions, two adjustments are made to the PCS data. First, the losses are converted to 1994 dollars using the CPI. Second, they are modified to take into account shifts in the portfolios of property exposed to loss over the period. A key component of the latter adjustment is the demographic shift toward California, Florida, and Texas that has characterized recent decades. These two adjustments are carried out by Guy Carpenter. Both adjustments are important. Indeed, the second adjustment implies that the same-size event in *real* dollars causes damages that have grown on average by 5 percent per year over the sample period.

5.2.4 Interest Rate and CPI Data

For the purposes of calculating the net present value of payment flows, we use Ibbotson Associates' index of the return on thirty-day U.S. Treasuries. This is collected monthly from 1970:1 to 1995:4. The U.S. CPI is taken from the IMF's *International Financial Statistics*. The frequency is monthly, from 1970:1 to 1995:3.

---

11. This is a common industry practice. The specific weights used in our Kiln formula are from Guy Carpenter.

12. The regions are constituted as follows: The Northeast comprises Connecticut, Delaware, Maine, Maryland, Massachusetts, New Hampshire, New Jersey, New York, Pennsylvania, Rhode Island, and Vermont. The Southeast comprises Florida, Georgia, Mississippi, North Carolina, South Carolina, Virginia, and West Virginia. Texas comprises Texas. The Midwest comprises Illinois, Indiana, Kentucky, Missouri, and Tennessee. California comprises California.

5.3   Calculation of Exposure and Price

5.3.1   Exposure

In this section, we describe our method of estimating the catastrophe exposure embodied in each excess-of-loss contract. The estimation is carried out in three stages. First, the frequency and severity of each type of event and region are estimated by maximum likelihood for particular families of distributions. Second, a simulated event history is generated by repeatedly drawing from the fitted frequency and severity distributions. Finally, the payouts under each contract in each year of event history are calculated. The mean of the distribution of these payouts is our estimate of the "quantity" of reinsurance, $q_{j,k,t}$, embedded in that particular contract.

The Frequency and Severity of Catastrophes

The first step toward calculating contract exposure is to estimate the frequency and severity of catastrophes using the adjusted PCS loss data. Altogether, there are over eleven hundred catastrophes recorded by PCS. These events are classified into ten categories: earthquake, fire, flood, freeze, hail, hurricane, snowstorm, tornado, thunderstorm, and windstorm.[13] Many of these events are relatively minor: only 557 have adjusted losses in excess of $15 million, and only 107 have losses in excess of $100 million. Four categories of losses are well represented in the set of large losses: earthquake, fire, hurricane, and windstorm.[14] As our primary interest is in exposure to large losses, we confine our attention to these types. Examination of the data reveals that there is some heterogeneity in the losses that arise from windstorms. In particular, a number of the windstorms refer to winter storms ("Nor'easters") in New England. Accordingly, we split the windstorm category into two subcategories: winter storm, defined to be a windstorm in New England in either the first or the fourth quarter, and windstorm, defined to be all other occurrences of a windstorm.[15]

Having defined these five categories of events, we need to make some assumption about regional effects before we can estimate frequency and severity distributions. The simplest assumption would be that, for each catastrophe

13. PCS classifies many events into more than one category. For instance, winter storms in New England, which have on occasion caused substantial damage, are classified first as windstorm and then as hail, freeze, or snowstorm.

14. During the 1949–94 sample period, there were no floods, snowstorms, or thunderstorms with losses in excess of $100 million. Only one freeze had losses in excess of $100 million, a $307 million freeze in Texas in 1989. Three hailstorms and three tornadoes did produce losses in excess of $100 million, but these are all dated prior to 1970 and so do not appear in our regression analysis below.

15. The assumption that winter storms do not afflict the Midwest may seem strange. The reason is that our regional market-share data are calculated for the Midwest using only five states: Illinois, Indiana, Kentucky, Missouri, Tennessee. The Dakotas, Michigan, Minnesota, Wisconsin, and other characteristically midwestern states are excluded.

Table 5.1   **Frequency and Severity Assumptions by Catastrophe Type**

| | | Assumptions | | |
| | Description of PCS data | Regions | Frequency[a] | Severity[a] |
Type	(1)	(2)	(3)	(4)
Earthquake	10 events, all in CA. Frequency appears throughout year.	CA	1: uniform across quarters	1
Fire	19 events: 12 in CA, 2 in MW, 3 in NE, 2 in SE. Frequency higher in quarter 4 and different for CA. Severity comparable across events.	NE, MW, CA	2: CA and NE/SE/MW/TX. Both uniform across quarters	1
Hurricane	48 events: 26 in SE, 22 in NE and TX. Most in third quarter. More severe in Southeast.	NE, SE, TX	8: SE (4 quarterly) and NE/TX (4 quarterly)	2: SE, NE/TX
Winter storm	35 events: in NE in quarters 1 or 4.	NE	1: uniform across quarters 1 and 4	1
Windstorm	352 events: all regions. Frequency differs across regions, but severity is comparable.	NE, SE, TX, MW, CA	20: one for each region and quarter	1

Note: Assumptions for catastrophe frequency and severity distributions are based on catastrophe experience 1949–94. A catastrophe is defined as an event that gives rise to $15 million or more in insured losses. Column 1 gives a description of catastrophe occurrence by type, 1949–94. NE denotes Northeast, SE Southeast, TX Texas, MW Midwest, and CA California. Columns 2–4 give the assumptions concerning the frequency and severity distributions. The number in the frequency and severity columns represents the number of separately estimated distributions for that type. For example, the number "1" implies that all regions are pooled and that a single, nationwide distribution is estimated.

[a]Number of regional distributions.

type, event occurrences are drawn from a single nationwide frequency distribution while loss sizes are drawn from a single nationwide severity distribution. Given the relative paucity of loss information, this approach helps by pooling the available data. However, the assumption of equal regional distributions is likely to be incorrect. For instance, hurricanes are much less likely to occur in California than in Florida, and the majority of earthquakes occur in California.

As a result, we make specific assumptions regarding frequency and severity on the basis of a careful examination of the 1949–94 catastrophe data. These assumptions are summarized in table 5.1. A catastrophe is defined as an event that gives rise to $15 million or more in insured losses. Column 1 summarizes the event history for each type. Column 2 reports the regions in which each event type is assumed to occur. Columns 3 and 4 indicate the number of regional frequency and severity distributions estimated for each type. Some of the constraints, such as the assumption that winter storms do not strike California, seem entirely reasonable. Others, such as the assumption that earthquakes do not strike outside California or that winter storms do not hit the Midwest, are less tenable (although see n. 15) and are dictated largely by data availability.

With the assumptions described in table 5.1, there are thirty-three frequency distributions to estimate. We assume that the frequencies are Poisson distributed and estimate the Poisson parameters by maximum likelihood (the estimates are equal to the mean number of events that occur per quarter). Table 5.2 presents the frequency results in four quarterly arrays, by type and region. The estimated frequencies accord with what one might expect. For example, hurricanes are most likely to occur in the third quarter.

We next consider severity. There are six severity distributions, one for each of the catastrophe types identified in table 5.1. We fit two alternative density functions to the empirical severity distribution of each type. The first is a lognormal distribution, with density function for losses l given by $f(l) = \exp\{-[\ln(l) - \mu]^2/2\sigma^2\}/[l\sigma\sqrt{(2\pi)}]$, $l > 0$. The second is a Pareto distribution, with density function $f(l) = \alpha\beta^\alpha/l_{(1+\alpha)}$, $l > \beta$. Once again, the estimation is carried out by maximum likelihood. The fitted distributions are reported in table 5.3. For earthquake, winter storm, and windstorm events, the likelihood ratio test selects the Pareto distribution as the better fit, while, for fire and hurricane events, the lognormal distribution is preferred. However, because the Pareto distribution tends to place a large amount of probability in the righthand tail of the distribution, it does not perform well in attaching reasonable probabilities to large losses. For example, using the estimated Pareto density, the probability that a hurricane in the Southeast generates $15 billion in losses (given that a hurricane occurs) is almost 10 percent, which appears somewhat high.[16] It might be preferable, therefore, to use the lognormal fit as the baseline severity distribution for all event types. This is the strategy that we adopt. The fitted lognormal distributions are shown in figure 5.9 for losses in the $0–$3 billion range.

Simulated Event History

Using these frequency and severity distributions, we are able to simulate an "event history" of catastrophes. From this event history, the distribution of payments under each excess-of-loss contract can be obtained.

Of course, it is not necessary to simulate the distribution of contract payments. In principle, it is possible to determine contract payments analytically. However, analytic solutions are complicated because a contract's payment is triggered by only a single event, even though that event could be one of five

---

16. Using PCS data, Cummins, Lewis, and Phillips (chap. 3 in this volume) argue that the Pareto distribution tends to overestimate the probability in the tail of catastrophe severity distributions and that the lognormal fit is to be preferred on these grounds.

Table 5.2   Frequency of Catastrophes, Measured by Their Poisson Parameters, by Quarter, Type, and Region, 1949–94

	NE	SE	TX	MW	CA	NE	SE	TX	MW	CA
	January–March					April–June				
Earthquake					.054					.054
Fire	.031	.031	.031	.031	.125	.031	.031	.031	.031	.125
Hurricane (SE)		.000					.043			
Hurricane (NE/TX)	.000		.000			.033		.033		
Winter storm	.380									
Windstorm	.174	.652	.326	.500	.304	.196	.457	1.109	.935	.000
	July–September					October–December				
Earthquake					.054					.054
Fire	.031	.031	.031	.031	.125	.031	.031	.031	.031	.125
Hurricane (SE)		.370					.130			
Hurricane (NE/TX)	.283		.283			.033		.033		
Winter storm						.380				
Windstorm	.174	.065	.152	.326	.000	.174	.283	.326	.370	.130

Note: Poisson parameter is equivalent to the mean number of catastrophe occurrences per quarter by type and region. If the frequency of each catastrophe type in each region is Poisson distributed—$f(n) = e^\lambda \lambda^n / n!$, where n is the number of events that occur—then the numbers in the table are the maximum likelihood estimates of λ. NE denotes Northeast, SE Southeast, TX Texas, MW Midwest, and CA California. Blank elements of the arrays are 0 by assumption (see table 5.1).

Table 5.3   Fitted Severity Distributions by Catastrophe Type, 1949–94

Distribution and Parameter	Earthquake	Fire	Hurricane (SE)	Hurricane (NE/TX)	Winter Storm	Windstorm
n	10	19	26	22	35	352
Lognormal:						
μ	−2.100	−2.350	−1.233	−1.454	−2.440	−3.039
σ	1.964	1.196	1.610	1.454	1.166	.859
Mean log-likelihood	.006	.752	−.662	−.340	.867	1.772
Pr(l > $5 billion)%	2.915	.046	3.870	1.760	.025	.000
Pr(l > $15 billion)%	.684	.001	.718	.211	.000	.000
Pareto:						
α	.476	.541	.337	.364	.568	.862
β	.015	.015	.015	.015	.015	.015
Mean log-likelihood	.358	.735	−.854	−.556	.875	1.891
Pr(l > $5 billion)%	6.288	4.327	14.110	12.057	3.684	.670
Pr(l > $15 billion)%	3.727	2.389	9.743	8.082	1.973	.260

Note: Results from fitting of lognormal and Pareto distributions to PCS event losses. PCS losses have been adjusted for inflation and population movements by Guy Carpenter. A catastrophe event is defined as one giving rise to insured losses in excess of $15 million. The density function for the lognormal is $f(l) = \exp\{-[\ln(l) - \mu]^2/2\sigma^2\}/[l\sigma\sqrt{(2\pi)}]$, $l > 0$, while the density function for the Pareto is $f(l) = \alpha\beta^\alpha/l^{(1+\alpha)}$, $l > \beta$. The parameters μ, σ, and α (not β, which is a fixed scale parameter set equal to $15,000,000) are estimatd by maximum likelihood. For a given catastrophe type, estimated mean log likelihoods for the two distributions are comparable and provide a means for choosing between them. The table also shows the probability that an event produces insured losses in excess of $5 billion and $15 billion, respectively.

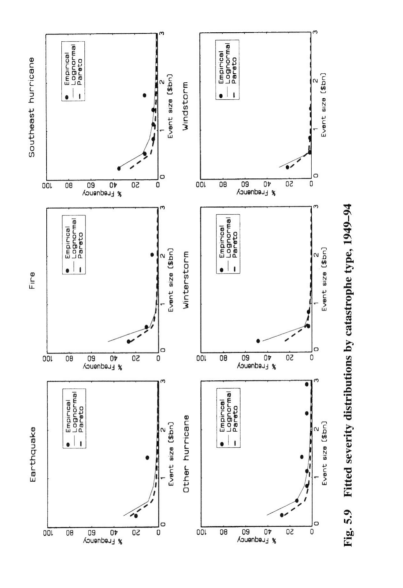

Fig. 5.9 Fitted severity distributions by catastrophe type, 1949–94

different peril types. The single-event clause is in effect a knockout provision, allowing the contract to mature following the first event that generates losses in excess of the retention. For example, it may be that earthquakes are the major large risk for a contract to trigger, but a large freeze in the Northeast in early January could trigger the contract, thereby knocking out the earthquake risk for the remainder of the year.

This knockout provision gives the contract a payment distribution that is very different from that which would apply if the contracts were instead written to cover aggregate losses (i.e., the sum of losses across events). It can also give rise to some paradoxical effects. For example, an increase in the frequency of winter storms may actually *reduce* the total exposure embodied in a single-event contract since it may increase the probability that it matures following a winter storm rather than a devastating hurricane. We look briefly at the value of the knockout provision in the appendix.

We simulate a 1,250-year event history. For each quarter, the following steps are performed: (1) The number of events of each type that occur in each region is randomly drawn from the relevant Poisson frequency distribution (table 5.2). (2) For each event that occurs, a loss amount is randomly drawn from the relevant severity distribution (table 5.3). (3) Finally, all the events that occur in the quarter are randomly sequenced in time. The random sequencing of the events throughout the quarter is an approximation, at best. It is likely, for example, that winter storms occur more frequently in January than March. While it would be preferable to sequence the events on a time scale finer than quarterly, too few events have occurred since 1949 to allow the estimation of this.

Contract Exposure

The exposure of each excess-of-loss contract in our data can be calculated by examining its loss experience in each year of the simulated event history. To take an example, suppose that we are considering a contract brokered by a national insurer with an inception date of 1 April. Let L and R be the contract's limit and retention, and let $m_{j,k}$, $k \in \{NE\ SE\ TX\ MW\ CA\}$ be the jth insurer's market share in each of the five regions. The contract's exposure is measured as follows:

1. Split the event history into 1,249 year-long periods measured from 1 April to 31 March.
2. Consider each period in turn. If no event occurs in a period, move to the next period. Otherwise, consider each event in sequence.
   a) Let the first event be in region k, and let insured losses from this event be l.
   b) If $m_{j,k}l > R$, the contract is triggered. Measure the reinsurance payment for this period as $\min(L, m_{j,k}l - R)$, and move on to the next period. The contract is no longer in force.

c) If $m_{j,k}l < R$, no payment takes place, and the contract remains in force. Move on to the next event or to the next period if there are no more events.

This algorithm generates 1,249 observations on the distribution of payments under the contract. The first moment of this distribution is the expected exposure to catastrophe losses. It is easy to derive various conditional loss distributions from the unconditional distribution, such as the distribution of hurricane losses or the distribution of losses from events in the Northeast.

5.3.2 Contract Quantity and Price

We label the expectation of the unconditional distribution $q_{j,t}$, the exposure embodied in company *j*'s contract at time *t*. This is interpreted as the quantity of reinsurance purchased. By considering only those reinsurance payments that occur following particular types of catastrophes, it is possible to use the same algorithm to calculate the contract's exposure to each of the catastrophe types listed in table 5.1 above. These exposures by type form the inputs to the calculation of loss weightings in equation (3).

To calculate contract price, we begin with the premium paid for each contract. This is measured simply as the sum of the premiums paid for each layer. Typically, the premiums are paid on a quarterly basis over the duration of the contract. We discount these premium flows back to the contract inception date using the three-month Treasury bill rate. By using the riskless rate, we are equating actuarial present values with true value. Strictly speaking, this assumption holds only under risk-neutral pricing and in the absence of insurer credit risk. However, given that catastrophe losses are uncorrelated with total wealth, risk-neutral pricing is not easily rejected. Furthermore, the use of a risk-adjusted discount rate would, in practical terms, have little import for our results.

Once the net present value (NPV) of the premiums is calculated, it is converted to 1994 dollars using the CPI deflator. Our measure of price is the net present value of premiums divided by contract exposure. Thus, the price of company *j*'s contract at time *t* is

$$(6) \qquad p_{j,t} = \frac{\text{NPV(premiums)}}{q_{j,t}}.$$

5.4 Graphic Analysis

We are now in a better position to understand the data and computations behind figures 5.2 and 5.3 above. They plot, respectively, the industry quantity and price series quarterly from 1975:1 to 1993:4. The quantity series is the simple sum of exposure across companies. The price series is the exposure-weighted average of the prices of all contracts in force in that quarter.[17] Note that figure 5.3 shows that risk was sometimes ceded at less than actuarial value (i.e., $p_{j,t} < 1$) during the 1970s and early 1980s.

Hurricane Andrew is responsible for the largest catastrophe loss during our sample period. In the light of this, it is of interest to look at the time series of prices around the time of this event. In particular, we can differentiate between the price-quantity reactions of those contracts heavily exposed to hurricane risk/Southeast risk and those with relatively less exposure. Table 5.4 contrasts the price and quantity responses. From panel A, we see that even those contracts with zero market share in the Southeast show large increases in price in the wake of Andrew. This is supportive of the capital market imperfections view. However, as already discussed, even if there are no other losses occurring at this time, these price responses may be the result of probability updating if the Andrew loss experience revealed new information about hurricane exposure in other regions. Panel B investigates this by sorting contracts according to their hurricane exposure. It turns out that it is those contracts least exposed to hurricane losses that exhibit the largest increase in price. Taken at face value, this suggests that capital market imperfections, and not probability updating, are the most important determinant of the price responses. In order to shed more light on this question, we need to estimate the conditional expectation functions (1) and (2).

5.5   Estimation

5.5.1   Exposure Measured by Regional Market Share

In this subsection, we differentiate events by region and estimate (1) and (2) using regional market shares as proxies for regional exposure. Eight variants of the base specification are estimated, corresponding to different assumptions about the functional form through which losses affect prices. The results are shown in tables 5.5 and 5.6.

Turning to the price regressions first, the β_k are positive and statistically significant in all specifications. The γ_k are positive but generally not very significant. This is prima facie evidence that both capital market imperfections and probability updating play some role in determining the response of price to catastrophe losses. However, in all cases, the coefficient on unweighted losses is larger and more statistically precise than that on exposure-weighted losses. This suggests that the supply-side capital market channel is the more dominant of the two.

---

17. This industry series is based on the contract prices for four insurers that purchased reinsurance through Guy Carpenter in every year from 1975 to 1993. It is representative of the behavior of prices for the other insurers in our database.

Table 5.4   Event Study of Hurricane Andrew

	A. Southeast Exposure			B. Hurricane Exposure		
	Mean Exposure	Mean $\Delta \ln(p_{j,t})$	Mean $\Delta \ln(q_{j,t})$	Mean Exposure	Mean $\Delta \ln(p_{j,t})$	Mean $\Delta \ln(q_{j,t})$
5 most-exposed insurers	.707	.310	.085	.654	.270	−.030
5 least-exposed insurers	.000	.334	−.011	.218	.557	−.138

Note: Comparison of price responses in the year after Hurricane Andrew (20 August 1992–19 August 1993) for different insurers. Panel A contrasts insurers that have high and low exposure to the Southeast (as measured by market share). Panel B contrasts insurers that have high and low exposure to hurricanes. The table shows the mean exposure and the mean price change of the five most extreme contracts in each case. The mean price change for the insurers with lesser exposure to the Southeast is calculated using all fourteen of the insurers that have zero market share in that region.

Table 5.5   The Response of Price and Quantity to Losses, Exposure Measured by Regional Market Shares

	$\sum_{s=1}^2 l_{k,t-s-1}$		$\sum_{s=1}^2 l^2_{k,t-s-1}$		$\sum_{s=1}^4 l_{k,t-s-1}$		$\sum_{s=1}^4 l^2_{k,t-s-1}$	
	$\Delta\ln(p_{j,t})$	$\Delta\ln(q_{j,t})$	$\Delta\ln(p_{j,t})$	$\Delta\ln(q_{j,t})$	$\Delta\ln(p_{j,t})$	$\Delta\ln(q_{j,t})$	$\Delta\ln(p_{j,t})$	$\Delta\ln(q_{j,t})$
$\sum_k \theta(l_k)$	1.865	−.518	.103	−.028	1.736	−.284	.109	−.019
	(.449)	(.300)	(.027)	(.018)	(.326)	(.202)	(.020)	(.011)
$\sum_k w_k \theta(l_k)$	.372	−.039	.014	−.001	.519	−.169	.021	−.006
	(.261)	(.160)	(.013)	(.009)	(.249)	(.149)	(.013)	(.008)
R^2	.140	.012	.096	.008	.263	.019	.230	.015
N	435	435	435	435	435	435	435	435

Note: OLS estimates of price- and quantity-response regressions. The dependent variables are 100 times the change in the natural logarithm of contract price and 100 times the change in the natural logarithm of quantity. Losses are measured in billions of dollars. Exposure to each type of regional losses (w) is measured by regional market shares, as in eq. (5). Each column corresponds to a separate regression. Four different assumptions are made about the functional form of distributed lag of losses that affects prices. In cols. 1 and 2, the loss variable is simply the sum of two lagged quarterly losses; in cols. 3 and 4, it is the sum of squared losses from two lagged quarters; in cols. 5 and 6, it is the sum of four lagged quarterly losses; and, in cols. 7 and 8, it is the sum of squared losses from four lagged quarters. OLS standard errors are given in parentheses.

Table 5.6 The Response of Price and Quantity Losses, Exposure Measured by Regional Market Shares

	$\sum_{s=1}^{2} l_{k,r-s-1}$		$\sum_{s=1}^{2} l^2_{k,r-s-1}$		$\sum_{s=1}^{4} l_{k,r-s-1}$		$\sum_{s=1}^{4} l^2_{k,r-s-1}$	
	$\Delta \ln(p_{j,t})$	$\Delta \ln(q_{j,t})$	$\Delta \ln(p_{j,t})$	$\Delta \ln(q_{j,t})$	$\Delta \ln(p_{j,t})$	$\Delta \ln(q_{j,t})$	$\Delta \ln(p_{j,t})$	$\Delta \ln(q_{j,t})$
$\sum_{k} \theta(l_k)$	1.759	−.468	.103	−.029	1.164	−.148	.054	−.005
	(.447)	(.286)	(.028)	(.018)	(.345)	(.212)	(.023)	(.013)
$w_{NE}\theta(l_{NE})$	6.621	−1.272	4.681	−0.835	4.514	−.670	3.037	−.592
	(1.490)	(.645)	(1.228)	(.433)	(1.057)	(.624)	(.959)	(.439)
$w_{SE}\theta(l_{SE})$	.175	.116	.009	.006	.463	.023	.024	−.000
	(.215)	(.140)	(.012)	(.008)	(.221)	(.118)	(.012)	(.006)
$w_{TX}\theta(l_{TX})$	3.830	.895	2.622	.404	4.595	.241	3.293	−.078
	(2.606)	(1.287)	(2.199)	(.763)	(2.105)	(1.101)	(1.833)	(.590)
$w_{MW}\theta(l_{MW})$	53.052	−45.808	95.048	−135.190	34.090	−14.479	72.853	−12.393
	(37.846)	(25.460)	(110.627)	(84.527)	(30.153)	(21.793)	(66.278)	(53.118)
$w_{CA}\theta(l_{CA})$	8.982	−12.595	3.943	−5.589	6.589	−8.817	2.659	−2.978
	(4.599)	(4.813)	(2.444)	(2.754)	(2.571)	(2.678)	(.961)	(1.116)
R^2	.220	.048	.197	.035	.306	.060	.283	.047
N	435	435	435	435	435	435	435	435

Note: OLS estimates of price- and quantity-response regressions. The dependent variables are 100 times the change in the natural logarithm of contract price and 100 times the change in the natural logarithm of quantity. Losses are measured in billions of dollars. Exposure to each type of regional losses (w) is measured by regional market shares, as in eq. (5). Each column corresponds to a separate regression. Four different assumptions are made about the functional form of distributed lag of losses that affects prices. In cols. 1 and 2, the loss variable is simply the sum of two lagged quarterly losses; in cols. 3 and 4, it is the sum of squared losses from two lagged quarters; in cols. 5 and 6, it is the sum of four lagged quarterly losses; and, in cols. 7 and 8, it is the sum of squared losses from four lagged quarters. NE denotes Northeast, SE Southeast, TX Texas, MW Midwest, and CA California. OLS standard errors are given in parentheses.

To get a sense of magnitudes, suppose that a $10 billion event occurs in a particular region. Using the first price specification (which uses two quarters of lagged losses), the $10 billion loss increases all contract prices in the next year by an average of about 19 percent. Notice that this price increase is independent of contract exposure to the region. Higher exposure to the affected region leads to further, but much smaller, increases in price. A firm that increases its share of the market in the affected region from 0 to 100 percent sees its reinsurance price increase by an average of 4 percent. Thus, much of the increase in price appears to be due to a decline in the supply of reinsurance (or to increases in expected losses *outside* the affected region). Probability updating and capital market imperfections both help, but the capital market effects seem much larger.

Table 5.5 also reports results from equation (2), where quantity reinsured is the dependent variable. The results here are consistent with those presented above: the coefficients on unweighted losses provide strong evidence of capital market imperfections. The δ_k coefficients are negative and statistically less than zero at the 10 percent level in all cases. As we expect from figure 5.1 and figures 5.7 and 5.8, the ϕ_k coefficients on market-share weighted losses are ambiguous in sign.

To calibrate, the first quantity specification suggests that a $10 billion loss in a particular region leads to a 5.2 percent *decline* in quantity on average over the next year. Meanwhile, for the same size loss, a company that has 100 percent market share in the affected region on average purchases 0.4 percent less reinsurance than if it had a 0 percent market share. Note, however, that this latter effect is neither economically nor statistically significant. In other words, we cannot reject the hypothesis that *relative-exposure* levels have no effect on quantity purchased. But we can reject the hypothesis that purchases do not decline on average subsequent to an event. The quantity results are therefore most consistent with the capital market imperfections story.

In table 5.6, we relax the restriction that all the γ_k and ϕ_k coefficients are equal. This allows the probability-updating effect to differ by region. Indeed, there is some evidence for this in the coefficient estimates, which differ substantially across regions. Here, there is somewhat stronger evidence of probability updating. The cumulative sum of regional losses over the last four quarters appears to affect price positively in all cases. Nonetheless, unweighted losses in each region continue to affect price positively and quantity negatively. All but two of these estimates are statistically significant.

5.5.2 Exposure Measured by Actuarially Expected Loss

The specifications in tables 5.7 and 5.8 are analogous to those in tables 5.5 and 5.6. However, here we use actuarial exposures to weight losses. As discussed earlier, probability updating may occur across, rather than within, regions, and this complicates the identification of capital market effects using regional market shares. By distinguishing losses by type rather than by region,

Table 5.7   The Response of Price and Quantity to Losses, Exposure Measured Directly by Catastrophe Type

	$\sum_{s=1}^{2} l_{k,t-s-1}$		$\sum_{s=1}^{2} l^2_{k,t-s-1}$		$\sum_{s=1}^{4} l_{k,t-s-1}$		$\sum_{s=1}^{4} l^2_{k,t-s-1}$	
	$\Delta \ln(p_{j,t})$	$\Delta \ln(q_{j,t})$	$\Delta \ln(p_{j,t})$	$\Delta \ln(q_{j,t})$	$\Delta \ln(p_{j,t})$	$\Delta \ln(q_{j,t})$	$\Delta \ln(p_{j,t})$	$\Delta \ln(q_{j,t})$
$\sum_k \theta(L_k)$	4.143	−1.644	.172	−.070	3.161	−1.617	.180	−.081
	(1.097)	(1.031)	(.056)	(.055)	(1.004)	(.858)	(.052)	(.045)
$\sum_k w_k \theta(L_k)$	−.897	.505	−.033	.021	−.418	.523	−.025	.024
	(.445)	(.393)	(.023)	(.021)	(.448)	(.344)	(.021)	(.016)
R^2	.136	.018	.101	.013	.238	.023	.222	.022
N	435	435	435	435	435	435	435	435

Note: OLS estimates of price- and quantity-response regressions. The dependent variables are 100 times the change in the natural logarithm of contract price and 100 times the change in the natural logarithm of quantity. Losses are measured in billions of dollars. Exposure to each type of catastrophe loss (w) is calculated directly by simulation. Each column corresponds to a separate regression. Four different assumptions are made about the functional form of distributed lag of losses that affects prices. In cols. 1 and 2, the loss variable is simply the sum of two lagged quarterly losses; in cols. 3 and 4, it is the sum of squared losses from two lagged quarters; in cols. 5 and 6, it is the sum of four lagged quarterly losses; and, in cols. 7 and 8, it is the sum of squared losses from four lagged quarters. OLS standard errors are given in parentheses.

Table 5.8 The Response of Price and Quantity Losses, Exposure Measured Directly by Catastrophe Type

	$\sum_{s=1}^{2} l_{k,t-s-1}$		$\sum_{s=1}^{2} l^2_{k,t-s-1}$		$\sum_{s=1}^{4} l_{k,t-s-1}$		$\sum_{s=1}^{4} l^2_{k,t-s-1}$	
	$\Delta \ln(p_{j,t})$	$\Delta \ln(q_{j,t})$	$\Delta \ln(p_{j,t})$	$\Delta \ln(q_{j,t})$	$\Delta \ln(p_{j,t})$	$\Delta \ln(q_{j,t})$	$\Delta \ln(p_{j,t})$	$\Delta \ln(q_{j,t})$
$\sum_k \theta(l_k)$	1.491	-.771	.091	-.045	.535	.025	-.035	-.006
	(1.137)	(1.097)	(.055)	(.053)	(1.126)	(1.060)	(.089)	(.073)
$w_{EQ}\theta(l_{EQ})$	65.826	-30.015	44.099	-17.720	24.265	-35.153	26.740	-29.059
	(50.672)	(17.103)	(37.030)	(10.130)	(16.375)	(16.931)	(11.852)	(12.808)
$w_{FI}\theta(l_{FI})$	-26.137	-8.489	6.451	-11.843	-36.406	13.440	-3.873	-1.220
	(28.439)	(20.256)	(11.162)	(6.311)	(32.047)	(21.315)	(15.906)	(7.531)
$w_{HR}\theta(l_{HR})$	-.218	.307	-.015	.016	.266	.010	.028	.004
	(.446)	(.410)	(.022)	(.020)	(.459)	(.410)	(.031)	(.026)
$w_{WS}\theta(l_{WS})$	51.084	13.796	27.597	12.133	21.862	10.452	-5.706	10.512
	(25.298)	(9.816)	(20.651)	(8.235)	(21.868)	(12.211)	(21.304)	(14.074)
$w_{WD}\theta(l_{WD})$	9.273	-3.362	5.912	-1.883	5.905	-2.918	2.726	-.881
	(1.771)	(1.200)	(.762)	(.399)	(1.226)	(1.088)	(.622)	(.415)
R^2	.249	.038	.264	.032	.301	.056	.291	.039
N	435	435	435	435	435	435	435	435

Note: OLS estimates of price and quantity response regressions. The dependent variables are 100 times the change in the natural logarithm of contract price and 100 times the change in the natural logarithm of quantity. Losses are measured in billions of dollars. Exposure to each type of catastrophe loss (w) is calculated by simulation. Each column corresponds to a separate regression. Four different assumptions are made about the functional form of losses that affects prices. In cols. 1 and 2, the loss variable is simply the sum of two lagged quarterly losses; in cols. 3 and 4, it is the sum of squared losses from two lagged quarters; in cols. 5 and 6, it is the sum of four lagged quarterly losses; and, in cols. 7 and 8, it is the sum of squared losses from four lagged quarters. EQ denotes earthquake, FI fire, HR hurricane, WS winter storm, and WD windstorm. OLS standard errors are given in parentheses.

we can separately identify capital market and probability-updating effects on prices.

The results presented in tables 5.7 and 5.8 are in line with what we found in the previous two tables. First, the unweighted losses in the price equations enter positive and significantly, the coefficients having even larger signs. Specification 1, for example, reveals that a $10 billion event tends to increase prices by over 40 percent in the following year. Moreover, the aggregated γ coefficient on event-exposure-weighted losses is not positive in the price equations, suggesting that the unweighted losses account for *all* explainable price increases subsequent to events. Second, the unweighted losses in the quantity regressions enter negatively and statistically significantly in three of the four regressions. This is again consistent with capital market imperfections. Indeed, the coefficient is large, suggesting that a $10 billion event reduces the quantity of reinsurance purchased by between 8 and 16 percent. There is no evidence supporting the presence of event-specific probability updating in table 5.6.

Table 5.7 provides similar results. Unweighted losses influence prices positively and quantities negatively (although not significantly). Squared losses do not seem to have the expected effects, suggesting that large losses may not have proportionately as large effects as smaller losses in the data.

Taken together, these results provide evidence to support the existence of both imperfections in capital supply and probability updating. However, it is the former that accounts for the bulk of price movements in the wake of losses.

5.6   Conclusion

There are at least two candidate explanations for the sharp rise in catastrophe-reinsurance prices and retentions that occurred in the 1990s, a time of unprecedented catastrophe losses. The first holds that capital market imperfections impeded the flow of capital into the reinsurance sector. In the presence of these imperfections, prices are bid up, and quantities fall, owing to the supply contractions that accompany losses. The second explanation is that the changes in prices and quantities have largely been the result of an increase in the perceived frequency or severity of catastrophes. If, after a loss, neither supply nor demand shifts but actuarial probabilities of losses tend to increase, then we would observe price increases and quantity reductions since our quantity measure is derived from time-invariant loss distributions.

To separate out the effects of capital market imperfections and probability updating, we consider two specifications of how loss distributions are updated. First, we assume that probability updating occurs on a region-specific basis and that event losses in a given region may therefore increase perceived future losses within that region but not in other regions. Second, we assume that probability updating occurs within (but not across) event types and that event losses associated with a particular peril may therefore increase perceived future losses from that peril but not losses associated with other perils.

We estimate these specifications using detailed reinsurance contract data from Guy Carpenter. Our findings suggest that, subsequent to losses, price increases and quantity declines are more pervasive across contracts than they should be on the basis of contract-specific exposures to event types and regions. Since cross-sectional variation in exposures should explain changes in prices and quantities but does not, it appears that price shocks are highly correlated across all forms of catastrophe exposure. This lends support to the view that aggregate price and quantity shocks stem from shifts in the supply of capital to the industry. Since reinsurers are financial intermediaries with relatively few fixed factors besides financial capital, the existence of such shifts in supply is evidence of capital market imperfections.

Appendix
The Value of the Knockout Provision in Single-Event Contracts

Using the simulated event history, it is possible to measure the value of the knockout provision that is implicit in single-event contracts. This knockout feature stems from the fact that it is the first event occurrence that triggers the contract.[18] Table 5A.1 illustrates how the knockout feature affects expected payouts under various contract provisions. Columns 1–6 of the top panel consider contracts whose payouts are contingent on the occurrence of particular types of catastrophes. For example, in column 1, the contract can be triggered only by earthquake losses in excess of the retention. Column 8 gives the expected payout on a contract that is structured in the same way as the Guy Carpenter treaties—that is, it pays out on the first event of any type that generates losses in excess of retention. The table shows that the sum of the expected payouts on event-specific contracts (col. 7) exceeds the expected payout on the all-type contract. This is the familiar result that, with imperfectly correlated risks, it is cheaper to buy insurance on a portfolio than it is to buy a portfolio of insurance policies. The bottom panel of the table is structured in the same way, except that it distinguishes events by region rather than by type. Once again, the sum of the expected payouts on the region-specific contracts exceeds that on the all-region contract.

It is noteworthy that, in both cases, the inception date of the contract has only a minor influence on the distribution of payouts.

---

18. The complexities introduced by the knockout provision form part of the reason why the catastrophe options that trade on the Chicago Board of Trade are written as aggregate rather than single-event contracts.

Table 5A.1 Value of Knockout Provision in Single-Event Excess-of-Loss Contracts

Inception Date	(1)	(2)	(3)	(4)	(5)	(6)	(7)	(8)
	Quake	Fire	Hurricane (SE)	Hurricane (NE/TX)	Winter Storm	Wind-storm	Sum	All Type
1 January	1.9	2.7	6.5	7.8	1.7	9.8	30.4	22.3
1 July	1.9	2.7	6.5	7.8	1.7	9.9	30.4	22.9
	NE	SE	TX	MW	CA		Sum	All Region
1 January	6.1	8.9	7.8	3.7	3.9		30.4	22.3
1 July	6.3	8.9	7.7	3.8	3.9		30.5	22.9

Note: Expected reinsurance payments (in millions of dollars) for a $100 million excess-of-$500-million contract under various contract payment provisions. In the top panel, the contract is single event, but payment is contingent on the type of catastrophe. Thus, in col. 1, the contract matures on the occurrence of the first earthquake event that produces $500 million in insured losses. Column 7 gives the sum of the expected payments from the contracts in cols. 1–6. Column 8 is the value of expected payments under an all-event contract that matures on the occurrence of any event producing $500 million in insured losses. The difference between col. 7 and col. 8 is the value of the event knockout provision implicit in single-event, all-event contracts. The bottom panel is structured in exactly the same fashion, except that it distinguishes events by region rather than type. The five regions are Northeast (NE), Southeast (SE), Texas (TX), Midwest (MW), and California (CA).

References

Cummins, J. D., and P. Danzon. 1991. Price shocks and capital flows in liability insurance. In *Cycles and crises in property/casualty insurance: Causes and implications for public policy,* ed. J. D. Cummins, S. E. Harrington, and R. W. Klein. Kansas City, Mo.: National Association of Insurance Commissioners.

Cummins, J. D., and J. F. Outreville. 1987. An international analysis of underwriting cycles in property-liability insurance. *Journal of Risk and Insurance* 54:246–62.

Froot, K. A. 1995. Incentive problems in financial contracting: Impacts on corporate financing, investment, and risk management policies. In *The global financial system.* Cambridge, Mass.: Harvard Business School Press.

Froot, K. A., and P. G. J. O'Connell. 1997. On the pricing of intermediated risks: Theory and application to catastrophe reinsurance. Working Paper no. 6011. Cambridge, Mass.: National Bureau of Economic Research, April.

Froot, K. A., and J. Stein. 1998. Risk management, capital budgeting and capital structure policy for financial institutions: An integrated approach. *Journal of Financial Economics* 47 (January): 55–82.

Gron, A. 1994. Capacity constraints and cycles in property-casualty insurance markets. *Rand Journal of Economics* 25, no. 1:110–27.

Gron, A., and D. Lucas. 1995. External financing and insurance cycles. Working Paper no. 5229. Cambridge, Mass.: National Bureau of Economic Research.

Winter, R. A. 1988. The liability crisis and the dynamics of competitive insurance markets. *Yale Journal on Regulation* 5:455–500.

Comment   Jeremy C. Stein

"The Pricing of U.S. Catastrophe Reinsurance," by Kenneth A. Froot and Paul G. J. O'Connell, is an excellent paper. It poses a clear-cut and very interesting question, comes up with an extremely clever empirical approach to tackle the question, and delivers quite compelling results. The question is, To what extent do the dramatic variations in the price of catastrophe reinsurance reflect shifts in reinsurers' supply curves? In a world of imperfect capital markets, one would naturally expect supply shifts to be associated with large disasters— for example, Hurricane Andrew or the Northridge Earthquake—which badly deplete reinsurers' existing capital bases.

The question is interesting, not only from the narrow perspective of the catastrophe-insurance market, but to anyone concerned with the economics of financial intermediation. For example, in the context of commercial banking, there has recently been a great deal of interest in the analogous question, Can shocks to banks' capital influence their willingness to make loans? Although there is by now a large literature that seeks to address this "bank capital

Jeremy C. Stein is the J. C. Penney Professor of Management at the Sloan School of Management, Massachusetts Institute of Technology, and a research associate of the National Bureau of Economic Research.

crunch" issue, it is in many cases plagued by the fundamental identification problem of separating out movements in supply and demand. It is clear that banks lend less when their capital is reduced. It is less clear that this is because of a loan-supply effect—it might instead be that reduced capital is indicative of a deterioration in the lending environment and hence a decline in the demand for new loans. Froot and O'Connell are able to use the unique nature of the catastrophe-reinsurance market to largely get around this type of identification problem and thereby say something more definitive about the role of capital in the supply of intermediation services.

My comments are organized as follows. I will first review the intuition behind the Froot-O'Connell identification scheme. Since I am ultimately quite convinced by their approach, I will only briefly quibble with the details of its implementation. Instead, I will save a little bit of space to discuss some further implications of their results.

The Froot-O'Connell Approach to Identifying Supply Shocks

The Basic Idea

How would one know whether disasters lead to an inward shift in the supply of reinsurance? One obvious thing to do is to look at whether the price of reinsurance rises in the wake of a large disaster. In fact, it typically does, but this is not decisive. There are two potentially confounding factors. First, it may be that the demand for reinsurance also rises after a disaster, as insurers seek more cover. Second, there is the "probability-updating" effect that Froot and O'Connell stress: "price" is measured relative to a static estimate of actuarial value, with the result that, if a big hurricane causes market participants to update their estimates of the actuarial exposure of a given contract, this will incorrectly be interpreted as an increase in "price."

As a next simple step, one might jointly consider information on both prices and quantities. For example, if prices rise and quantities fall after a disaster, this looks more like an inward shift in the supply of reinsurance than an increase in demand. Indeed, this approach is probably all that would be needed if the only confounding factor were demand shifts. But it does not by itself get around the probability-updating problem, as Froot and O'Connell are careful to point out. Because of the way their price and quantity measures are constructed, there can be a "hardwiring" effect where an increase in the perceived probability of a hurricane simultaneously raises the measured price and lowers the measured quantity of reinsurance. Thus, to get convincing identification, one must tackle the probability-updating problem head-on.

This is where the key insight of the paper comes in: while a bad hurricane like Andrew might be expected to change market participants' expectations about the likelihood and costs of future hurricanes, it should not cause similar updating about earthquakes. Thus, if one could somehow document that a bad hurricane leads to an increase in the price and a decrease in the quantity of earthquake policies, and vice versa, this would be convincing evidence of a supply effect driven by capital constraints. Quite literally, we would have an ideal natural experiment.

Implementation

Unfortunately, the data are not quite as cooperative as one might like. The main problem is that one never actually observes separate prices for earthquake and hurricane policies. Rather, all we know about a given contract is the layer of protection and the regional market shares of the insurer involved. Thus, the exposure of a contract to a given type of peril must be imputed. Froot and O'Connell do this imputation in two ways. The first, simplest method uses only information on insurers' regional market shares. Thus, for example, two insurers who both have 50 percent of their market share in California would be deemed to be equally exposed to earthquakes (since earthquakes are assumed to happen only in California). Obviously, this entails some measurement error since it may be that, in reality, one of the two insurers is more heavily exposed to properties that lie near a fault line. The second method of imputing exposure is substantially more complicated, but it is fair to say that, while it may attenuate this sort of measurement error, it cannot hope to eliminate it.

The measurement error is significant because of the kind of regression specifications that Froot and O'Connell use. For example, in their contract-price equation (1), if the contract exposures (the w's) are only noisy proxies, this will lead to a downwardly biased estimate of their γ coefficient and most likely an upwardly biased estimate of β. In other words, the method will be biased toward overrejecting the null hypothesis of perfect capital markets. I should say that, as a practical matter, I would be very surprised if measurement error can completely explain away the very strong rejections of the null that show up in their tables 5.5–5.8. Nonetheless, it would be nice if there were some way to demonstrate this point more convincingly.

It should be possible to take some steps in this direction. The idea would be to examine a subset of the data where we know a priori that measurement error is less likely to be an issue. Let me give a concrete example. Suppose we can find some insurers who have literally *zero* market share in California. In this case, we can say fairly confidently that they are completely free of earthquake exposure. (In contrast, once there is some nonzero market share in California, it becomes much harder to say *just how large* the earthquake exposure is.) One could focus in on just these earthquake-free insurers and see how the prices of their contracts respond to an earthquake. If they go up a lot, I would be totally convinced.

It should be noted that this approach is very much in the spirit of what is done in the Hurricane Andrew "event study" in table 5.4, where Froot and O'Connell look at the five insurers with the smallest (albeit still nonzero) exposure to hurricanes and find that their contract prices rose markedly after Andrew. I found this event study to be perhaps the most compelling piece of evidence in the paper, and I would have liked to have seen more in a similar vein.

Implications: What Are the Underlying Capital Market Frictions?

If one accepts Froot and O'Connell's conclusion that the large swings in reinsurance prices seen in recent years are indeed a capital related phenomenon, the natural next question to ask is, What exactly are the underlying primitive frictions that cause reinsurers to become so capital constrained? Without a coherent answer to this question, it would be difficult to evaluate either policy proposals or potential financial innovations that hold the promise of "fixing" the capital scarcity problem.

A simple but important point—one that strikes me as underappreciated in this context—is that capital constraints can have an important effect in steady state only if *two* necessary conditions are both met. First, there must be *flow* costs of adding new external capital. These flow costs might come, for example, from information asymmetries between managers and shareholders that create adverse-selection problems and discourage seasoned equity offerings. In addition, however, there must be *stock* costs of simply holding a large capital buffer on the balance sheet. Were it not for the stock costs of holding a capital buffer, the flow costs of raising new external finance could be rendered irrelevant. In the extreme, a reinsurer could set itself up ex ante with a huge capital buffer, so large that, no matter the disaster, it could be assured of never having to seek new external finance under adverse-selection conditions.[1] Thus, the fact that there appear to be persistently binding capital constraints in the reinsurance industry strikes me as indirect evidence that, in addition to any adverse-selection frictions, there must also be important stock costs of holding capital.

Where do the stock costs come from? The two obvious candidates are taxes and agency. On the tax side, with a U.S.-style code, it is obviously inefficient to set up an equity-financed entity that raises billions of dollars from investors and then parks the proceeds in Treasury bills until there is a major disaster— the interest income will be subject to double taxation. Of course, if one takes the view that taxes are the dominant friction, then the ultimate financial innovation is the offshore reinsurance corporation, exemplified by the number of reinsurers that, by setting up in Bermuda, have been able to realize substantial tax advantages.

---

1. By *ex ante* I mean that it should be possible to raise a large amount of funding to start (and overcapitalize) a new reinsurance company at some initial date before any policies have been written and, hence, before managers have any informational edge over investors. Thus, at this ex ante date, there should be no adverse-selection problem in raising the money. Alternatively, a large capital buffer could be accumulated by retaining earnings over a long period of time.

My own guess is that agency considerations are at least as important as taxes in discouraging large buffer stocks of capital.[2] Put simply, in the standard corporate form, where managers have wide discretion over how to spend internal resources, it can be scary to think about setting them up with a multi-billion-dollar cushion that is not needed for day-to-day operations. The obvious worry is that the money will find a way to get spent, perhaps on writing negative-net-present-value policies in a misguided effort to grow the business.

If agency is indeed the key problem, this suggests thinking about contractual measures that restrict the discretionary uses to which the excess capital can be put. In the extreme, one might think of setting up a "lockbox" arrangement: the money can be used only to pay off the losses on reinsurance contracts that have already been written. But, of course, this extreme lockboxing solution is tantamount to securitization—that is, it completely eliminates managerial discretion and effectively takes the reinsurance out of the corporate form.

While securitization may be helpful in some regards, one should not jump to the conclusion that it can easily "solve" the capital problem. Taking discretion out of the hands of reinsurer management undoubtedly has costs as well as benefits since management presumably is better able to evaluate and price complex risks than would be diffuse capital market investors. Thus, the right question is, *How much* of what is currently done via intermediaries can be usefully taken out of the corporate form? The presence of significant agency problems implies that the corporate form for reinsurance should be used sparingly, only for those particular risks where the ability to exercise managerial discretion is on net beneficial.

---

2. I do not have any direct evidence to back up this guess. One way to gain some insight might be to study the relative behavior and performance of U.S.-domiciled and Bermuda-based re-insurers over time, as more data become available.

6 Reinsurance for Catastrophes and Cataclysms

David M. Cutler and Richard J. Zeckhauser

> Insurance has done more than all gifts of impulsive charity to foster a
> sense of human brotherhood and of common interests. It has done more
> than all repressive legislation to destroy the gambling spirit. It is impos-
> sible to conceive of our civilization in its full vigour and progressive
> power without this principle, which unites the fundamental law of practi-
> cal economy, that he best serves humanity who best serves himself, with
> the golden rule of religion, "Bear ye one another's burdens."
> —William Gow, "Insurance," *Encyclopedia Britannica* (11th ed., 1910)

This paper examines the optimal design of reinsurance—insurance for insurers. Reinsurance enables insurers to lay off concentrated positions in idiosyncratic risks and places risks that are large for society as a whole in the hands
of those best able to bear them. We examine how reinsurance can be designed
to meet these purposes. Although our focus is on reinsurance, much of what
we discuss is widely relevant to primary-insurance markets as well.

Reinsurance is valuable for insurers because it allows them to reduce their
risk levels. If an insurance company is concentrated in a risk in a particular
geographic area, for example, then a disaster affecting everyone in that area
may severely reduce the insurance company's reserves. We term a situation of
threatened or actual insurer insolvency in the event of an adverse risk a *catastrophe*.

The first question that we address is, How should reinsurance premiums
and reimbursement be designed to address the potential for catastrophes? This
question is complicated because the primary insurer is likely to know much
more about the true loss distribution than will the reinsurer. As a result, adverse
selection is a concern. We show that optimal policies in the face of adverse
selection depend on the nature of the information asymmetry. When the asym-

David M. Cutler is professor of economics at Harvard University and a faculty research fellow
of the National Bureau of Economic Research. Richard J. Zeckhauser is the Frank P. Ramsey
Professor of Political Economy at the Kennedy School of Government, Harvard University, and
a research associate of the National Bureau of Economic Research.

The authors are grateful to Roy Astrachan and Sandra Favlukas for research assistance; to David
Cummins, Christopher Lewis, and Richard Phillips for making available their value-adjusted loss
data; and to Chris Avery, John Cochrane, Ed Glaeser, Bill Hogan, Louis Kaplow, Jeff Liebman,
John Pratt, Aaron Stern, Ray Vernon, and both academic and industry conference participants for
helpful discussions. The authors acknowledge partial financial support for this paper from the
National Institutes on Aging, the Herrnstein Fund, and the NBER Project on the Financing of
Property/Casualty Risks.

metry is on the probability of a loss but not its magnitude, the optimal reinsurance contract is a standard "excess-of-loss" policy—the primary insurer is responsible for small risks, and the reinsurer is responsible for large risks. When the asymmetry is over the magnitude of the loss, the optimal reinsurance policy covers smaller losses as well as large losses but leaves the primary insurer exposed for some large losses. The striking difference between these policies suggests that one cannot make broad statements about the optimal form of reinsurance policies.

As the size of catastrophes increases, a second difficulty with reinsurance markets emerges. If the underlying risk is large in aggregate, the reinsurance industry as a whole may not be able to provide sufficient capital to cover a loss. Hence, wide-scale insolvencies may be threatened, and insurance may become unavailable or excessively priced. We term an event that strains worldwide insurance and reinsurance industry reserves—arbitrarily defined as an event with $5 billion or more of insured losses—a *cataclysm*.[1]

The second question that we address is, Who should provide reinsurance for cataclysmic events? By definition, the reinsurance industry will be poor at reinsuring cataclysms. We argue that cataclysms must be reinsured either in broader financial markets or by the government, or both. The second part of the paper explores these options.

The paper is structured as follows. We begin in the next section by outlining the nature of the problem. In the second section, we consider quantitatively the size of property-casualty insurance and reinsurance markets. In the third section, we deal with the problem of reinsuring catastrophes. In the fourth section, we consider reinsurance of cataclysms. The last section concludes.

6.1   The Nature of the Problem

To understand the nature of our analysis, consider a particular example: the market for homeowner's insurance. Fire damage is one risk facing insurers underwriting homeowner's policies. If the insurer is sufficiently big, given that the risks being insured are for the most part uncorrelated, internal diversification will provide sufficient diversification for this risk. Reinsurance is internal.

Other risks will not be diversifiable in this fashion, however. For example, a large hurricane or earthquake will affect all the houses in a broad geographic area. If insurers are concentrated in particular areas, for example, because of differences in sales-force concentration or underwriting knowledge,[2] they may be overly exposed to particular risks. Thus, insurers concentrating in California may find themselves with excessive amounts of earthquake risk, while insurers predominantly in Florida may be overly exposed to hurricane risk. Adding ad-

---

1. More generally, a cataclysm occurs when the size of a loss is large relative to the insurance pool for that category of risk.
2. With insurance, as opposed to most other goods, characteristics of the purchaser matter. Hence, knowledge of local conditions provides for local economies of scale.

ditional houses in California or Florida to the pool will not help diversify risk if an earthquake or a hurricane will damage all houses.

This excessive concentration will be undesirable for the insurance company's shareholders if the firm is a stock company and the shareholders' portfolios are not otherwise diversified,[3] or for its policyholders if the firm is a mutual. Such concentration may even risk the insurer's bankruptcy, putting recovery for its insureds at risk.[4]

Reinsurance can help insurers diversify their excessive concentration in particular markets. For example, insurers in California and Florida can swap earthquake and hurricane risk, or both sets of insurers could sell risks to third companies, including specialty reinsurers, perhaps in other countries. We term this role for reinsurance the *catastrophe role*. A catastrophe is bigger than any one insurer can handle but not big enough to upset the entire insurance market. A catastrophe is defined as an event with at least $5 million in insured damages that affects the policyholders of many different insurance companies (Insurance Information Institute 1996a).[5] A $10 million loss at one company, for example, may be large for that company, but for the industry as a whole it is a minor event. Pooling of catastrophic losses is the traditional role for reinsurance.

A major difficulty with catastrophic reinsurance is adverse selection. An insurer who is buying risk protection for his portfolio will have superior information about the risks he holds, partly because he was more knowledgeable at the time the risk was written and partly because of his subsequent experience. If diversification is the goal, the ideal seller would be a company whose own book is quite different in its holdings;[6] naturally, such a seller is likely to be poorly informed about true risk levels. Both seller ignorance and buyer superiority of information suggest that adverse selection will be a problem (Akerlof 1970).

Moral hazard may also be a concern with reinsurance. Insurers that have purchased reinsurance may have differing incentives to sign up particular insureds, monitor the precautions that their insureds take, or fight potential litigation. We leave these issues of moral hazard for later analysis.

Until recent years, adverse selection was compounded because reinsurance was transacted more on a relationship basis—insurers and reinsurers dealt frequently on a business and social level—than on a scientific basis. In such a market, it is easy to see how private information may be exploited. Reinsurers

3. If shareholders have well-diversified portfolios, a good deal of risk spreading can be achieved by having companies bear the risk of losses and passing them on, in turn, to their shareholders. We suspect that this is how a large amount of risk is ultimately diversified.

4. Insurance managers are in an agency relationship with policyholders. Bankruptcy in response to a massive loss is probably a larger relative loss for policyholders. If, as seems likely, policyholders cannot monitor sufficiently, insufficient reinsurance purchases may result. For related reasons, states impose solvency requirements on insurers.

5. The loss threshold for a catastrophe was raised to $25 million in 1997.

6. This is why reinsurance at the international level is an important phenomenon.

today rely much more on statistical methods, risk models, etc.[7] No matter how hard reinsurers try to learn about the relevant information, however, adverse selection remains a concern. Consider an extreme case—where reinsurers know more about the underlying risk being insured than does the primary insurer. Suppose that the risk being insured is commercial liability. The insurer may still have relevant private information—how likely the particular company being underwritten is to file for a claim; how aggressive it will be in legal actions; how competent the executives are; etc. Reinsurer information will be reflected in competitive market prices for the risks being insured, but, within that risk class, private information possessed by the primary insurer may still influence when reinsurance is purchased.

Often, the risk being insured is so large that the aggregate risk exposure of the worldwide insurance industry is dangerously high, even if risks were fully reinsured. Hurricane Andrew, the largest U.S. catastrophe on record, cost insurers $15.5 billion. Had Andrew hit Miami rather than less densely populated parts of South Florida, the losses could have been at least three times as large. The second largest catastrophe on record was the Northridge Earthquake of 1994, with insured losses of about $12.5 billion. Had the earthquake hit Los Angeles or San Francisco, the damage could well have been over $50 billion. If a major earthquake hit Tokyo, the losses could approach $1 trillion. Beyond natural disasters, the cost to insurers of toxic waste cleanup may reach as high as $30–$50 billion (Insurance Information Institute 1996b). The potential for cataclysms to strike insurance markets is very real.

When cataclysms strike, insurers may be undercapitalized, and widespread insolvencies may result. To avoid such a situation, insurers might decide not to underwrite particular risks. For example, some insurers—such as Nationwide—no longer write hurricane insurance in Florida. Others may refuse to cover various environmental, product safety, or other risks that stretch years into the future (long-tailed risks). When terrorist bombings struck London in 1992, for example, reinsurers and insurers immediately stopped insuring terrorism damage. Less drastic measures to curtail exposure to cataclysms would be to switch from occurrence to claims-made policies (from year of the accident to year of the lawsuit) and to write policies for short periods of time. The net result of such actions would be to limit or dry up reinsurance markets, which in turn would dry up insurance and thus stifle economic activity.

Why do insurers and reinsurers not merely raise rates when new risks emerge or old risks appear to be greater in magnitude? There are two answers. First, implicit and explicit regulatory constraints may prevent this. Second, insurers appear to be extremely risk averse about open-ended risks, and the risk premium required for them to continue bearing this risk would therefore be prohibitively expensive.

---

7. We are grateful to participants at the conference for discussing the actual operation of reinsurance markets with us.

By definition, the reinsurance market cannot provide coverage for cataclysms. Reinsuring such risks requires new institutional forms. While $10 billion is large relative to the insurance markets, it is tiny relative to asset markets as a whole. The total value of stocks traded on the New York Stock Exchange, for example, is over $6 trillion, and the aggregate value of assets in capital markets in the United States is estimated at more than $10 trillion. Thus, one possibility would be to diversify cataclysms through broader capital markets, and some recent steps have been taken in that direction. Cataclysms can also be dealt with through government reinsurance—and have been in many nations. The government has the advantage that it can diversify losses over time and over broader groups of people than the investors in asset markets. Section 6.4 below explores the role of reinsurance for cataclysms, looking in particular at publicly provided reinsurance.

6.2   Reinsurance Markets and Potential Losses

Before considering the design of reinsurance policies, we start with a discussion of reinsurance markets and the potential for cataclysmic losses.

6.2.1   The Size of Reinsurance Markets

Property-casualty insurance—ranging from fire insurance to products liability—is a $300 billion per year industry. Reinsurance is a much smaller but still significant feature of property-casualty insurance. In 1994, about $140 billion of insurance was reinsured to an affiliate of the primary insurer, and $47 billion was reinsured to nonaffiliates (A. M. Best 1996).

Reinsurance is written by reinsurance departments of primary insurers as well as specialty reinsurers (the most famous of which is Lloyd's of London). Specialty reinsurers account for about $12 billion of premium income annually. While primary insurers tend to write primarily in their own country, reinsurance is a much more international business. Nearly half the reinsurance ceded by U.S. insurers to nonaffiliates is ceded to international reinsurers. The leading reinsurance markets are the United States, London, and, increasingly, Bermuda (Giles 1994; Insurance Information Institute 1996c).

Table 6.1 shows which lines of insurance are reinsured most heavily. The first column shows direct premiums written. The second column shows all premium cedings to both affiliates and nonaffiliates.[8] The third column shows cedings to nonaffiliates only. The largest property-casualty categories are auto liability (direct premiums of $81 billion) and automobile physical damage (direct premiums of $43 billion). Reinsurance for automobile losses is comparatively rare; less than 10 percent of the premiums are ceded to nonaffiliates.

---

8. The amount of reinsurance can be greater than direct insurance written since risk may be ceded to affiliates and then further ceded to nonaffiliates. This transaction would be counted twice in the table.

Table 6.1   Size of the Property-Casualty Insurance and Reinsurance
            Industries, 1995

| | | Reinsurance Ceded as a Percentage of Direct Business | |
Line of Business	Direct Business ($ billion)	Affiliates and Nonaffiliates	Nonaffiliates Only
Automobile liability	81	54	9
Automobile physical damage	43	48	8
Workers' compensation	28	88	16
Home/farm multiple peril	27	61	11
Products and other liability	25	89	30
Commercial multiple peril	21	86	16
Special property[a]	19	98	45
Other[b]	11	60	18
Medical malpractice	6	42	22
Special liability[c]	4	112	53
Fidelity/surety	4	64	21
Financial/mortgage guaranty	2	22	11
Total	273	67	16

Source: A. M. Best.

[a]Fire, allied lines, inland marine, earthquake, glass, burglary, and theft.
[b]Credit, accident and health, international, other.
[c]Ocean marine, aircraft (all perils), boiler and machinery.

This makes sense; automobile losses result from thousands of independent accidents, so diversification is accomplished internally. The one major risk associated with automobile accidents is that the litigation climate will change. Under our present system, where premiums are set annually, this risk is primarily borne by drivers, who incur any yearly variability in expected losses. Reinsurance is most common for special liability (ocean marine, aircraft, boiler and machinery), special property (fire, earthquake, etc.), and products and other liability. With some exceptions, these risks tend to be more correlated across individuals or over time than is automobile liability.

Most reinsurance is written on a "treaty" basis—reinsurance is provided for all exposures for a specific class or multiple classes of business.[9] Treaty reinsurance is generally of two types. The first type is *proportional reinsurance;* the reinsurer agrees to assume a share of the risk in exchange for a share of the premiums. Typically, the ceding company retains 30 percent or less of the original risk. The second type of reinsurance is *excess-of-loss reinsurance;* the ceding company retains risk up to some amount, and then reinsurance pays above that. Excess-of-loss reinsurance is often purchased in layers. For ex-

9. For more discussion of reinsurance policies, see Conning & Co. (1993).

ample, a company might purchase a layer of reinsurance for $1.5 million in excess of $500,000—that is, the reinsurer assumes risks between $500,000 and $2 million. Excess-of-loss reinsurance has a greater orientation toward catastrophe protection than does proportional reinsurance. We analyze both these forms of insurance below.

6.2.2   The Potential for Cataclysms

We term events that would exhaust the reserves of worldwide insurers in a particular risk market *cataclysms*. We arbitrarily call a loss *cataclysmic* if it exceeds $5 billion. Much of the concern about reinsurance markets is related to the potential for cataclysmic losses. It is useful to understand how these potential losses might arise and what their magnitudes might be.

Cataclysmic losses can arise in two ways. The first is "single-event" cataclysms, such as a major earthquake in San Francisco or Tokyo that imposes sufficiently large losses to exhaust insurer capital. The second is what we label a *common-risk* cataclysm—a relatively small adverse change in a risk that affects large numbers of people and thus imposes large expected losses on insurers as a whole. Changes in climatic conditions that increase the probability of a hurricane but not the damage per hurricane are an example of a common-risk cataclysm; increases in tort-liability judgments for a given accident size and type are another.[10] With either type of cataclysm, unfolding events may provide significant information about underlying, possibly changing, risk levels. If so, as we shall see in section 6.4 below, risks about future premiums levels may be significant.

Single-Event Cataclysms

We consider the potential for single-event cataclysms using data from 1949 to 1994 compiled by Property Claim Services (PCS). Damages should naturally increase over time as the value of the asset being insured—generally house prices—rise. To express losses on a consistent basis over time, we follow Cummins, Lewis, and Phillips (chap. 3 in this volume) and inflate losses to 1994 dollars using the growth of aggregate house values in each state and year.[11]

PCS has raised the threshold for a catastrophe over time; we cannot adjust for this, but we suspect that threshold changes do not have a major effect on the time series of losses. Cataclysmic losses are dominated by several large events. In 1992, losses were almost $25 billion, largely because of Hurricane Andrew. Losses were nearly $20 billion in 1994, with a substantial share from the Northridge Earthquake. Losses were nearly $10 billion in 1989 (Hurricane Hugo).

---

10. Common risk from changing liability rules is sometimes referred to as *social inflation*.

11. Updating by aggregate house values factors in three terms: population growth, overall price inflation, and the growth of real house values. We are grateful to David Cummins, Christopher Lewis, and Richard Phillips for supplying us with their data.

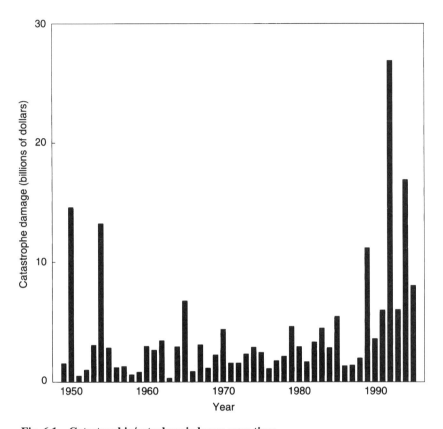

Fig. 6.1   Catastrophic/cataclysmic losses over time
Note: Data are from Property Claim Services as adjusted by Cummins, Lewis, and Phillips (chap. 3 in this volume).

Cataclysmic damages have increased over time. There were two large losses in the 1950s (windstorm damage in the Northeast and Middle Atlantic in 1950 and two hurricanes hitting the Northeast and Middle Atlantic in 1954) but no losses of even $7 billion between 1955 and 1988. Since 1989, however, cataclysmic losses have been much larger. On the basis of figure 6.1, an insurer thinking about pooling cataclysmic losses over many years could not be confident of setting appropriate premiums since past losses do not seem to be a reliable indicator of future losses.

The nature of the risk greatly affects the potential for cataclysms. We compare losses from two types of events—windstorms and hurricanes.[12] Wind-

12. Data on losses by catastrophe are available only through 1994. In some years, there are no catastrophic losses from hurricanes. We assume that catastrophe losses for hurricanes were $500,000 in those years.

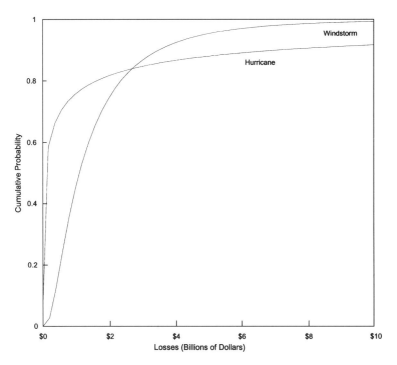

Fig. 6.2   Cumulative probability of damage from windstorms and hurricanes
Note: Data are from Property Claim Services as adjusted by Cummins, Lewis, and Phillips (chap. 3 in this volume).

storm damage averages $1.2 billion annually; hurricane damage is substantially less, with an average of $97 million annually. The variance of hurricane damage is much greater, however. The standard deviation of windstorm damage is 90 percent, compared to 340 percent for hurricane damage.

To determine what these different variances imply, figure 6.2 graphs the cumulative probability of loss for each type of risk on the basis of a lognormal model of expected losses.[13] For windstorms, the probability of only minimal damage (less than $500 million in aggregate) is only 25 percent, and the probability of a $10 billion loss—twice our cataclysmic level—is about 0.5 percent. In contrast, the probability of minimal hurricane damage is nearly two-thirds, while the probability of $10 billion of losses is about 8 percent. Indeed, the loss distribution from hurricanes has an extremely wide tail; the probability of a $20 billion hurricane, for example, is over 5 percent. Thus, while cataclysmic

13. Clearly, we have very little information about major cataclysms, so the lognormal might not be the best approximation to the true distribution in the tails, which is the primary concern. Cummins, Lewis, and Phillips (chap. 3 in this volume) show that the lognormal model fits the tails of the distribution nearly as well as do more flexible distributions.

windstorm damage does not appear to be a major concern, the possibility of a cataclysmic hurricane is very real.

Common-Risk Cataclysms

The probability of common-risk cataclysms is more difficult to judge, in part because common-risk cataclysms may result from a number of small events rather than one large event. For example, knowledge about which chemicals are dangerous is formed only over time. Similarly, legal rulings regarding insurer liability for hazardous products do not change all at once but are refined gradually in a series of judicial and appellate decisions. The cumulative effect of such small events can be very large. Indeed, it has been widely argued that legal changes in the 1970s and 1980s represented a cataclysmic change (see, e.g., Huber 1988; Viscusi et al. 1993).[14] The likelihood of a common-risk cataclysm is also hard to project because common-risk cataclysms tend to be unique events. We do not expect new liability revolutions such as we have seen in recent decades.

Not all common-risk cataclysms develop slowly, however. For example, when the first terrorist incident happened in London in 1992, insurers and reinsurers were quick to perceive this as a major area of potential loss.

Often, common-risk cataclysms evolve over time, with a significant component of risk relating to the insurance coverage itself. For example, an insurance company might insure any malpractice claim in the future filed against its insured physicians in the policy year—termed an *occurrence-based* policy. Or insurers could underwrite protection from the financial consequences of leakage over the next twenty years from hazardous waste disposed this year. These types of long-tailed risks are particularly susceptible to the arrival of damaging new information or changes in legal and judicial interpretations. For example, we may learn that products previously thought safe actually damage humans—as with asbestos or the Dalkon shield—or are effectively treated that way by the legal system.[15] Or legal rulings could expand an insurer's liability beyond what it thought it had committed to—as with environmental liability.

It is not even clear that these long-term risks can be measured by insurers, let alone priced. *Risk,* as it is conventionally defined, assumes that insurers know the probability of a loss and its expected size. As the period of insurance

---

14. It is important for policy purposes to differentiate between two factors. One thing that we learned over recent decades is that many things once thought safe—e.g., asbestos in buildings—are not in fact safe. Coupled with that is the assignment of liability once we have discovered damages. For insurance losses, the distinction between these two is irrelevant. The distinction is important for public policy purposes, however, because, while assigning risk ex post is just a transfer from one person to another, discovering a new set of toxic chemicals is a net cost to society that *someone* must pay. By definition, one group of people or another will be worse off.

15. For a discussion of legal and scientific evaluations of the safety of silicone-gel breast implants, see Angell (1996). Despite the lack of scientific evidence of risk from breast implants, there are likely to be multi-billion-dollar recoveries.

coverage increases, however, each of these values becomes more uncertain. Zeckhauser (1991) distinguishes between *risk,* the common basis for insurance, Knightian *uncertainty,* in which insurers know the events they are insuring but not their probability, and *ignorance,* in which even the events themselves are not well defined.

Fire insurance is overwhelmingly risk based. An example of Knightian uncertainty might be insurance against workplace accidents. The fact that workplace accidents may occur is well known, but the potential medical cost for workplace accidents several years in the future is not well known. Thus, the costs associated with work accidents several years in the future are uncertain. The potential for legal or legislative changes in liability is an example of ignorance. The provisions of the Superfund legislation, for example, are not something that insurers in the 1950s and 1960s could reasonably have had much idea about. Insurers are also ignorant about potential losses from terrorist risk. (In the life-insurance domain, we are ignorant about the risks of a future AIDS-type epidemic.)

Insurers and reinsurers are reluctant to provide protection against uncertainties and extremely reluctant to do so against events about which they are ignorant. To provide coverage in such a situation would entail high risk and would allow for significant adverse selection since others could know much more. Beyond this, the decision maker—say a manager as agent for shareholders—would be open to blame from shareholders: "Knowing nothing about it, how could you write insurance against that type of event?"

Changes in common risk can be significant when the time between when the losses occur and when the damages are paid is greater. This is a period when additional knowledge about true risks is learned and expected damage awards can change the most. The time lag varies substantially for different lines of insurance. Table 6.2 shows the share of losses incurred in 1986 that were paid within a given amount of time for different lines of property-casualty insurance. (Since data do not exist past 1995, we assume that all claims are paid within nine years.) For example, the first row shows that, for home/farm and commercial multiple-peril policies, 75 percent of the claims that are paid within the first nine years of the policy are paid within the first year (by the end of 1987) and 96 percent of the claims are paid within five years (the end of 1991). These claims tend to be paid very quickly; common-risk problems may thus not be particularly severe.

For other types of risks, however, there is a much longer time between loss and recovery, creating greater risk. For example, only half of workers' compensation claims are paid within the first year and only 91 percent within five years. Falling in between home/farm and commercial insurance and workers' compensation are special liabilities (aircraft, ocean marine, and the like) and automobile liability. As a rough rule of thumb, losses involving personal injury impose a much greater common-risk problem than losses involving damage to

Table 6.2   Cumulative Share of Losses by Payment Period (%)

	Years		
Line of Business	1	5	9
Home/farm/commercial multiple peril	75	96	100
Special liabilities	63	95	100
Automobile liability	61	97	100
Workers' compensation	50	91	100
Medical malpractice, occurrence	6	67	100
Medical malpractice, claims made	20	85	100
Products liability, occurrence	9	74	100
Products liability, claims made	20	94	100
Other liability, occurrence	21	81	100
Other liability, claims made	18	85	100

Source: A. M. Best.

Note: Data are for incurred losses in 1986. Year 1 extends through 1987; year 5 extends through 1991; and year 9 extends through 1995. There are assumed to be no losses after year 9.

property since both risk levels and ultimate compensation arrangements are harder to judge.[16]

We know of no estimates of the aggregate cost of common risks for insurers, but data are available for one such risk, real medical malpractice premiums from 1968 to 1993 (see fig. 6.3). Medical malpractice represents a small share of total property-casualty coverage—about $5 billion in premiums annually. It is clear that malpractice premiums vary substantially over time. Between 1968 and 1976, real premiums quintupled. Over the next decade, they nearly doubled again. Premium increases were followed by periods of real premium reductions. To the extent that these extreme premium fluctuations are the result of common-risk changes, they represent an enormous problem for insurers and the firms they are insuring.

Summary

For both single-event and common risks, the probability of a cataclysm seems quite real. Indeed, both single-event and common-risk cataclysms appear to have become more likely over time, and not merely because of the growth of coverage. In the case of single-event risks, natural disasters appear to have increased in frequency and severity since the late 1980s. In the case of common risks, the past several decades have seen an explosion of liability in areas where insurers generally did not expect it, although some reforms have ameliorated the situation.

16. With personal injuries, it is often difficult to determine what event led to the injury—hence, whether there is liability—and whether compensation will depend on casualty. The breast implant case (see n. 15 above) is one example. Malpractice is a second. Studies suggest that many errors go unpunished and that many awards do not relate to negligence (Weiler et al. 1993).

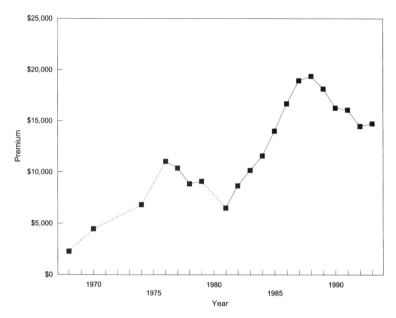

Fig. 6.3   Real malpractice premiums
Note: Data are from the American Medical Association. Dashed lines are interpolated.

6.3   Reinsurance for Catastrophes

This section investigates how reinsurance premiums for catastrophic risks should be set and policies designed in the light of potential adverse selection. Although cast in reinsurance terms, our analysis applies immediately to any situation of adverse selection and insurance, including the classic one-stage insurance transaction between an insurer and a potential insured who possesses private information. Our goal in this analysis is efficiency. We seek the policy that is optimal for the insurer, given that the risk-neutral reinsurer breaks even. Our treatment allows for a single policy with a single premium.[17]

We formalize the relationship between the primary insurer (buyer) and the reinsurer (seller) by assuming that there is a common prior probability distribution on the likelihood of an occurrence but that the primary insurer has special knowledge about losses since he underwrote the original risk and has a more intimate relationship with the insured. We summarize this as a signal that the buyer of reinsurance receives about the likely distribution of losses. Obviously, the buyer is more likely to seek reinsurance protection—what is often termed *ceding insurance*—when he suspects that either the probability of the insured event is high or the magnitude of a given loss occurrence is high. Such behavior is the source of the adverse selection.

---

17. Thus, we avoid Rothschild-Stiglitz (1976) types of difficulties—e.g., do all policies need to break even?—when there are multiple contracts in a world with multiple types.

Before turning to our second-best solutions, we should observe that a fully optimal reinsurance contract could be drawn if payoffs were made contingent on objectively observable and verifiable conditions, such as the magnitude and path of a hurricane. Beyond any problems agreeing ex post on what occurred, such arrangements would suffer from "basis risk"—the risk that a particular insurer's losses would differ from average losses and thus that the insurer could not receive full reinsurance. If basis risk is significant or adverse happenings difficult to verify, we would expect reinsurance arrangements to depend on the experience of particular companies.[18]

There are many strategies to ameliorate adverse selection. The contractual solution is to have the insurer provide the reinsurer with detailed and accurate statistical information on the insured risks. But more will be required if asymmetries remain, for example, about the tenacity with which a claim will be pursued. One approach is to arrange in advance (before the buyer receives his private information) for the buyer to pay the seller should a risk not be sold. Such a payment would make the buyer more willing to sell, thereby reducing adverse selection. More generally, reinsuring risks shortly after they are written makes it less likely that the buyer of reinsurance has superior information.

A second strategy is nonlinear pricing depending on the proportion of the portfolio that is sold. The larger the portion of the buyer's portfolio that he is reinsuring, the less opportunity for him to buy coverage for his worst prospects, what we term *lemon shedding* to contrast with the standard *cherry picking*. Thus, adverse selection would be discouraged if we simply reduce the per unit charge for reinsurance as a greater percentage of the portfolio is sold.

A third approach is to use proportional reinsurance to ensure that the bad risks are not the only risks reinsured.[19] But adverse selection will remain a problem: insurance companies that wrote bad risks in general will be more eager to buy reinsurance than insurance companies that underwrote solid risks.

Asymmetries may cut in the opposite direction. That is, reinsurers with broader experience may be able to assess some information more precisely than are the insurers for whom they are providing coverage. This suggests that they may selectively accept policies. Whatever reinsurers may know, private information will remain on the buy side and adverse selection will persist as a problem. Moreover, if reinsurers as a group know information not known to insurers, a competitive market would prevent them from exploiting this differential knowledge. The model that follows considers only adverse selection on the buy side.[20]

---

18. We are grateful to Louis Kaplow for highlighting this point.

19. Proportional reinsurance has the further advantage that, if the insured purchases multiple contracts with the same proportion, possibly from different parties, his insurance will address his total risk, which is his major concern. This is not true with nonlinear forms of reinsurance.

20. In ongoing work, we are exploring the problem of bilateral adverse selection in health care markets.

We examine nonlinear pricing mechanisms as a means to ameliorate adverse selection.[21] We start with the observation that the losses that an insurer realizes for insured asset i will be $L_i = p_i \cdot m_i$, where p_i is the probability of a loss, and m_i is the magnitude of the loss if there is one. Both p_i and m_i may vary in the population. We denote the prior distribution of p as $f(p)$ and the prior distribution of m as $g(m)$. The means of the two distributions are $\bar{p}$ and $\bar{m}$. For simplicity, we assume that p and m are independent risks, with the result that the expected loss is $E[L] = \bar{p} \cdot \bar{m}$.

Our mechanisms recognize the possibility that asymmetries may be greater on one of these components than on the other. If differential knowledge is greater on p than it is on m, or vice versa, a significantly nonlinear scheme of risk sharing is required to achieve a second-best solution. We do not expect to observe either pure case in the real world, but we do expect some cases to be characterized by asymmetry on the probability of a loss and others to be characterized by asymmetry on the magnitude of a loss. Unfortunately, the nature of the schemes in the two pure cases are quite different. This suggests that, when the buyer of reinsurance has superior information about both p and m, the second-best optimum may be relatively poor.

We develop our results by employing a simple model with a risk-averse buyer of reinsurance and a risk-neutral seller (the buyer if often said to "cede insurance" to the seller). The buyer's utility function is $u(w) = -e^{-aw}$, where w is wealth. The seller has utility function $v(w) = w$. If we think of sellers as the reinsurance market as a whole, risk neutrality may be a reasonable assumption provided that losses are below cataclysmic levels.

6.3.1 Asymmetry on Probabilities

Consider the situation where both buyer and seller have the same subjective distribution of the size of a loss should there be a loss, $g(m)$. The buyer and the seller differ in their knowledge of p; the seller knows only the prior probability distribution on p, $f(p)$, while the buyer has more specialized knowledge of the loss probability. For example, the seller of reinsurance may know the flood risk in a particular city, but the buyer may know it for particular houses in the city. The insurer will choose to purchase reinsurance if his houses at risk are in particularly high-risk areas. We denote the buyer's posterior probability of a loss as p_b.[22]

Since the buyer is risk averse, he is eager to lay off his loss, even at actuari-

---

21. Essentially, we are engaged in a process of mechanism design for a situation of asymmetric information. Our risk-sharing arrangements in effect invoke the revelation principle: the optimal second-best mechanism can always be one that makes truth telling (in this case, by the insurer) optimal. To do this, the reinsurer must commit in advance how it will use the information it secures. We are grateful to John Cochrane for reminding us of this equivalence. For more discussion, see Myerson (1979).

22. Since the asymmetry relates to a probability, it is only the mean of the buyer's posterior distribution that matters.

ally unfair rates. Since the size of the loss is a random variable, the seller can deter the buyer from putting unfavorable risks up for sale by making him bear a disproportionate share of small losses.

The buyer has initial wealth w, which includes the premium that he has already collected. In the absence of reinsurance, his terminal wealth will be $w - m$ if there is a loss and w if there is not one. His expected utility, assuming no reinsurance, can be written as

$$(1) \qquad E[U] = p_b \int -e^{-a[w-m]} g(m) dm + (1 - p_b) - e^{-aw}.$$

Ceding the Entire Risk

Since the buyer is risk averse and the seller is risk neutral, it might seem that the buyer should purchase reinsurance for the entire risk at some preestablished price. However, when p_b is low enough, the primary insurer would rather bear the risk than pay the premium for reinsurance.

Represent the price of reinsurance as r. If the payment were the ex ante actuarial value of the loss, $r = \bar{p} \cdot \bar{m}$. The buyer would purchase for values of p_b such that expected utility of being uninsured is below the expected utility of purchasing insurance, $-e^{-a[w-r]}$.

This policy may not be feasible in the market, as a simple calculation reveals. Let us say that $a = 1$, $g(m)$ is uniform on $[0, 1]$, and $f(p)$ is uniform on $[0, .1]$, implying $\bar{m} = .5$, $\bar{p} = .05$, and the ex ante actuarial premium would be .025 (.5 × .05). The buyer would purchase reinsurance whenever $p_b \geq .0352$. But, for this value, the expected loss is .0388,[23] which significantly exceeds the payment. No seller would take on the policy at the price of .025.

As the premium is increased, the buyer will be more reluctant to sell his risks. The dashed curve in figure 6.4 shows the value p_b above which the buyer will reinsure the risk, as a function of the premium for reinsurance.[24] The solid line is the actuarially fair premium as a function of the buyer's cutoff probability.[25] The point where the curves intersect is an equilibrium—the seller breaks even given the degree of adverse selection and the buyer gains from the reduction in risk.

Table 6.3 shows information about possible equilibria for various insurance schemes for the parameters described above. For comparison, the first column shows the equilibrium with no reinsurance, and the last column shows the equilibrium with perfect reinsurance. The second column shows the equilibrium when the entire risk is ceded (whole reinsurance). The risk is assumed by the

---

23. Since p is distributed uniformly, $E[p \mid p \geq p_b] = .0676$. The expected loss is therefore .0676 × .5 = .0338.

24. The curve is slightly convex to the origin; a straightedge can assist the naked eye to demonstrate this.

25. We assume that the premium for the reinsurance, conditional on its being purchased, is established before the seller learns his p_b.

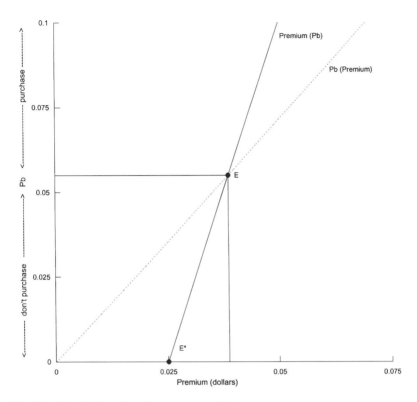

Fig. 6.4   Equilibrium in reinsurance market

reinsurer 45 percent of the time, and, because of adverse selection, the equilibrium price (.039) is well above the expected loss in the population as a whole (.025).

Whole reinsurance is quite inefficient. For values of p below p', which occurs 55 percent of the time, there is no risk spreading even though risk spreading is socially desirable. The second row shows the percentage gain in the primary insurer's certainty equivalent, where 100 percent is the gain from perfect reinsurance. Whole reinsurance provides only two-thirds of the benefit of perfect reinsurance.

Risk aversion plays a critical role in determining when reinsurance will be purchased. Increased (diminished) risk aversion—an increase in a—tilts down (tilts up) the dashed curve and thus increases (decreases) the range over which reinsurance is purchased. If we double the degree of risk aversion locally ($a = 2$), for example, reinsurance will be purchased 69 percent of the time, and the realized gains will be 90 percent of the potential gains from perfect reinsurance.

Table 6.3   Comparison of Policies with Asymmetry on Probability of Loss

	Form of Reinsurance				
Measure	None	Whole	Proportion[a]	Excess of Loss[b]	Perfect
Percentage of time risk is assumed by reinsurer	0	45	50	52	100
Percentage gain in primary insurer's certainty equivalent	0	68	71	72	100
Premium ($)	. . .	.039	.031	.027	.025

Note: Certainty equivalent is scaled to 0 percent in the no-reinsurance case and 100 percent in the perfect-reinsurance case.

[a]Reinsurer bears 81 percent of risk.

[b]Reinsurer bears loss above .152, where potential losses range from zero to one.

As a contrast with whole reinsurance, we investigate nonlinear reinsurance arrangements. Two such arrangements are common: proportional reinsurance and excess-of-loss reinsurance.

Proportional Reinsurance

We begin by considering proportional risk sharing. We assume that the buyer pays the seller to take on a fraction b of the risk. This fraction must be such that, with adverse selection, the premiums just cover expected payouts. For the example given above, we find that the optimal fraction is for the reinsurer to assume 81 percent of the losses ($b^* = .81$), charging a premium of .031 (see table 6.3).[26] The premium is closer to the population average in this case than in the whole reinsurance case because the proportional policy induces less adverse selection. The buyer's utility is greater under proportional reinsurance than under no reinsurance or whole reinsurance; 71 percent of the potential gains to the buyer are realized. The superiority of proportional reinsurance to whole reinsurance is to be expected since the latter is a special case of proportional reinsurance where $b = 1$.

Excess-of-Loss Reinsurance

Risk-averse buyers particularly want reinsurance for large losses, while risk-neutral sellers are indifferent to the size of the losses that they reinsure. This fact can be used to limit adverse selection. By reinsuring only large losses, the most important risk spreading can be achieved, with adverse selection held to a minimum.

26. The optimal policy, as with those considered later, is found by computer simulation. Some of our differences in performance across policies are small. We did not engage in the modeler's equivalent of data mining: reworking parameters and functional forms to produce bigger differences. The specific gains associated with different policies will depend on functional forms; the ranking of policies will not.

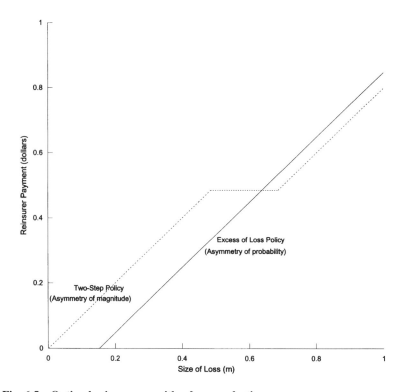

Fig. 6.5   Optimal reinsurance with adverse selection

We consider arrangements for nonproportional, or excess-of-loss, reinsurance. As noted above, this is a common form of reinsurance in current markets. We constrain such policies (and all policies in this paper) in two ways: the buyer's share of the loss can never exceed 100 percent; and, at the margin, the buyer's share of losses can never exceed 100 percent.

The optimal reinsurance arrangement subject to these constraints is shown in figure 6.5 and described in table 6.3. The policy has the buyer of reinsurance assume all risks up to $m = .152$. Beyond this point, the reinsurer assumes all losses (hence the title *excess-of-loss*). Premiums are only slightly above the no-selection level, and 72 percent of the potential gains from reinsurance are realized. Indeed, we can demonstrate that, when there is asymmetry about the probability of a loss, excess-of-loss reinsurance is optimal.[27]

PROPOSITION 1. When the buyer has no special knowledge of m but knows more than the seller about the probability of a loss, the optimal reinsurance

27. An excess-of-loss policy will also be optimal when there is moral hazard on the probability of a loss (i.e., having insurance affects the loss probability) but not on the magnitude of a loss. In ongoing work, we are exploring optimal reinsurance with moral hazard.

policy charges the risk-averse buyer for all losses up to a point, with the risk-neutral seller responsible for losses beyond that point.

PROOF. See the appendix.

Given the theoretical merits of excess-of-loss reinsurance and its common occurrence in the real world, it might be logical to conclude that it is always the most-preferred arrangement. This would be a startlingly inappropriate conclusion.

6.3.2 Asymmetry on Size of Loss

We now consider situations where the primary asymmetry is on the magnitude of loss, not its probability. For example, the insurer understanding the litigation climate for toxic torts may have expectations about punitive damages that are not available to more distant reinsurers. Asymmetry about size of loss may apply as well for natural disasters. For example, a Korean insurance company will likely have superior information relative to an overseas reinsurance about whether its clients' buildings would survive an earthquake, whether fire services would be sufficient should there be one, etc.

To simplify discussion, we assume that both the buyer and the seller of reinsurance believe in common that the probability of a loss is p. However, assessments of damage conditional on loss are asymmetrical. Specifically, we assume that the buyer knows the damage from a loss exactly, m_b,[28] and that the reinsurance seller has loss distribution $g(m)$. Thus, the buyer knows everything, while the seller knows nothing.

Table 6.4 shows a variety of policies, each optimized for a different structure, given this type of information asymmetry. For excess-of-loss reinsurance, it is optimal for the reinsurer to start to pay at zero. In effect, the optimal excess-of-loss plan offers whole insurance. This in turn makes it more attractive to buy insurance when losses will be small, helping deter adverse selection. If there were a threshold for reinsurance coverage, the buyer would not purchase reinsurance for any losses below the cutoff, indeed, for some amount above it. Adverse selection would be severe. Even with the optimal plan of this type, risks are not laid off 60 percent of the time.

Interestingly, when information asymmetry is about the magnitude of a loss, proportional reinsurance is superior to excess-of-loss reinsurance. The optimal policy has the reinsurer assume 89 percent of the risk, and the policy is purchased 42 percent of the time. Even with proportional reinsurance, however, adverse selection has a large effect, as indicated by the substantial difference between premiums and average losses.

---

28. In the case of asymmetry about probabilities, a sufficient statistic for the buyer's superior knowledge is the mean of his distribution, p_b. That is because rational decision makers are not risk averse on uncertainties about probabilities. With uncertainty about expected losses, we would need to summarize the entire probability distributions of the buyer and seller to characterize the market accurately. For simplicity, we assume that the buyer knows the actual value of a loss should it occur.

Table 6.4   Comparison of Policies with Asymmetry on Magnitude of Loss

			Form of Reinsurance			
Measure	None	Whole/ Excess of Loss[a]	Proportion[b]	Whole with Cap[c]	Two Step[d]	Perfect
Percentage of time risk is assumed by reinsurer	0	40	42	49	54	100
Percentage gain in primary insurer's certainty equivalent	0	80	81	85	87	100
Premium ($)	. . .	.040	.035	.037	.029	.025

Note: Certainty equivalent is scaled to 0 percent in the no-reinsurance case and 100 percent in the perfect-reinsurance case.

[a] Optimal excess-of-loss reinsurance is whole reinsurance.

[b] Share of time risk borne by reinsurer is 89 percent.

[c] Primary insurer starts paying at .686.

[d] Primary insurer starts paying .486 and stops paying at .686, where potential losses range from zero to one.

The next two columns show alternative reinsurance designs. The fourth column examines a "whole-with-cap" policy—a policy that has the reinsurer fully assume small losses and the primary insurer pay for all losses above a cutoff (the optimal cutoff is .686). This is the opposite of an excess-of-loss policy. The whole-with-cap policy is superior to the excess-of-loss policy; it is purchased 49 percent of the time, and 85 percent of the potential utility gains are realized.

The last column considers a reinsurance arrangement where the reinsurer bears all small losses, the primary insurer bears a layer of losses, and the reinsurer then reassumes the risk. We term this a *two-step* policy.[29] This policy outperforms all the other policies examined; it is purchased 54 percent of the time, and 87 percent of the potential utility gains are realized. Our simulations suggest that the two-step policy is the optimal reinsurance arrangement, although we do not currently have a formal proof that it is always best.

Figure 6.5 compares the reimbursement structure of the optimal two-step policy and the optimal excess-of-loss policy from table 6.4. The optimal policies for these two cases are strikingly different. While these results may appear puzzling, the intuition is readily grasped. Optimal reinsurance makes the buyer bear more of the risk on the dimension about which he has superior knowledge. If the buyer knows more about the probability of a loss than its magnitude, reinsurance should exclude coverage for the common small risks that are the source of exploitable adverse selection; this is exactly the "deductible-style"

29. The optimal two-step policy has the first layer of no reinsurance up to losses of .486, full reinsurance up to losses of .686, and then no reinsurance above that point.

policy that characterizes excess-of-loss insurance. If the buyer knows more about the magnitude of loss than its probability, however, it is optimal to make it costly for him to buy reinsurance when he knows that the magnitude of loss is high. This is why the capped and two-step policies are desirable when the asymmetry is on the size of loss.

6.3.3   Summary

Optimal reinsurance policies differ significantly depending on the form of information asymmetry. If the asymmetry in information is solely about the probability of a loss, the traditional excess-of-loss reinsurance contract is optimal. If the asymmetry is only about the size of a loss, however, it is preferable for the buyer to assume extreme losses as well as ordinary losses. Most real-world situations will involve elements of both asymmetries; hence, they will require future analysis to define the optimal policy structure.

Current reinsurance arrangements predominantly use proportional or excess-of-loss reinsurance. If most of the asymmetry between buyers and sellers is about the probability of a loss, our results suggest that this is reasonable. However, if asymmetry is primarily about the magnitude of a loss rather than its probability—as seems reasonable for many catastrophes—these types of insurance arrangements may be far from optimal. Thus, reinsurance arrangements might be considerably improved. Indeed, since our analysis carries through to markets for primary insurance coverage as well, such contracts also might be improved.

6.4   Reinsurance for Cataclysms

Many important risks are common to all insurers. For example, an earthquake in California will affect all insurers that provide coverage in that area. Similarly, changes in automobile-accident rates or tort-liability judgments for accidents will affect all insurers underwriting automobile insurance. Reinsurance can help diversify losses for any one insurance company, but, if the aggregate loss is sufficiently large, the capital of the worldwide insurance and re-insurance industries may not be large enough to cover the losses.

Cataclysms resulting from some common-risk changes are already spread relatively widely. If automobile-liability costs in the United States go up by 10 percent in a year, for example, that may be serious for the automobile-insurance industry, but the risk will be widely spread since the geographic basis is wide and many different insurers will be involved. Far more significant would be an event with the same total damage but in a geographic region where some insurers are concentrated, such as an earthquake. Of course, diversification across areas of the country is less effective when a common risk happens and losses escalate.

Both single-event and common-risk cataclysms have far-reaching implications. The Insurance Services Office, for example, estimates that a cataclysm on the order of $50–$100 billion could bankrupt one-third of all insurers. Un-reimbursed citizens will lose, and the government will almost certainly incur high costs in reconstructing public facilities, offering disaster aid to uncom-pensated victims, and suffering losses in tax revenues.

6.4.1 Market-Based Responses to Cataclysmic Risk

The market appears to have perceived the increase in cataclysmic risk in recent years and has taken steps to limit coverage for it. Often, this is accomplished by withdrawing from the market. In the past few years, for example, insurers and reinsurers have withdrawn from homeowner's insurance in Florida (as Nationwide did recently) and California. Insurers and reinsurers also dropped coverage for terrorism risk in the United Kingdom after bombings in the early 1990s. These actions can make it impossible for people to buy insur-ance even for noncataclysmic losses. When insurers withdraw from the Florida homeowner's market, for example, homeowners cannot insure themselves against even relatively minor losses.

With many common-risk problems, insurers have responded by effectively shortening the life of the policies they sell. Medical malpractice and environ-mental liability are two common examples. In both these markets, traditional insurance was occurrence based. As the nature of long-term risk became more apparent in the 1970s and 1980s, insurers switched to a claims-made insurance policy, one that covers the policyholder only for claims filed in a particular period of time for damages occurring during that time.

Insurers may prefer such mechanisms to raising their premiums to cover cataclysmic risk. Political or social considerations, for example, may prevent insurers from increasing premiums to the level required to insure against in-creasingly important cataclysms. In addition, the managers of the insurance company may not want to risk insolvency even though the expected profits may be great.[30]

Table 6.2 above shows some evidence of how the market's response to grow-ing cataclysmic risk affects firms and individuals seeking insurance. Under an occurrence-based malpractice-insurance policy, only 6 percent of losses are realized in the first year, and only two-thirds are realized within five years. In contrast, under a claims-made malpractice policy, 20 percent of the losses are borne in the first year, and 85 percent of the losses are borne within five years.[31] Hence, a claims-made policy has less long-tailed risk. Ignorance or uncertainty

30. In theory, shareholders might like charging actuarial prices for risks that would not pay off in case of occurrence. Their losses on the downside are capped, raising the expected value of their investment.

31. This ignores any differences in the types of policies that are sold on a claims-made or an occurrence-based basis. Because the longer-risk types of medical care are more likely to be sold as claims-made policies, this should reduce the loss difference in the two policies.

about the losses incurred will be reduced, and premiums can be set on a sounder basis. Claims-made policies have had a similar effect on product-liability coverage, although not other liability coverage. Curtailing the life span of insurance coverage returns the risk to insureds, whose premiums will rise and fall with estimates of coverage costs. This risk falls on the insured in part because most of the events covered by new-insurance purchases will have already happened but not yet been compensated.

The potential losses from common-risk cataclysms thus seem substantial. The market's response to date has been largely to increase premiums for insurance, to reduce the extent of coverage, and to limit exposure to long-tailed losses. The net result of these actions is to put much more risk back on the purchasers or insurance. The risk of premium variability over time thus becomes a concern. The rest of this section examines other actions that could be taken to increase financial protection against cataclysmic losses.

6.4.2   Reserves and Borrowing Capacity

Typically, insurers build reserves so that they can pay for very large damages. However, reserves are unlikely to be an effective means to deal with cataclysms.

It is a challenge for mutual insurance companies to build up substantial reserves. Current policyholders, who may not be insured in the future, are likely to think that the reserves are their monies. Saving them for future policyholders who may suffer cataclysms is hardly in their interest. Beyond this, when reserves are significant, there is tremendous pressure on companies to demutualize and thereby distribute them.[32]

For-profit insurers or reinsurers could build reserves because the money comes from and belongs to their shareholders. But the primary reason to build up reserves would be to reassure policyholders that the company will survive the cataclysm. Given the difficulty of communicating information on the soundness of one's company to policyholders, we would expect for-profit companies to have inadequate reserves for outlier losses.

The government could regulate reserve levels to be adequate to meet a cataclysm, but it might be a quixotic quest. If we wish an insurance company today to build up reserves against losses that are ten times an ordinary year's losses— as, for example, a major hurricane might impose—then it would have to charge an extra premium of 50 percent a year for twenty years to have enough money on hand. Not much is accomplished if the event occurs in year 7. And, while a regulator could require a for-profit reinsurer to raise enough capital to be prepared for a cataclysm, the reserves required may simply be too large to be practicable.

---

32. Demutualization has been widely observed for savings banks and could be an increasing phenomenon for insurance companies. Some mutuals have large reserves.

An alternative approach to protecting against cataclysms is to have deep-pocket parties post bonds or their equivalent. This was the approach of Lloyd's of London. Rich people essentially placed their whole net worth at risk to cover potential future claims. The great advantage of this "pledge" system for reserves is that monies are kept working in high-valued uses until needed. The system proved less effective when it was called on severely, as Lloyd's was when the rapid escalation of costs for asbestos and other changing liabilities exhausted its borrowing capacity. Even people who have made large amounts of money over many years, as many of the Lloyd's names did, get upset when a substantial portion of their net worth is lost. Lloyd's is now reconstituting itself, but with more restricted obligations of outside investors; presumably, this has diminished the security of its reinsurance capacity.

Outside Lloyd's-type pledge arrangements, it may be possible for reinsurers to borrow to pay out cataclysmic losses, with the promise of future premiums as collateral. However, such borrowing might not be repaid for up to a century or more (in the case of a major earthquake) and would presumably be offered only at a substantial risk premium.

In sum, traditional methods of diversification are unlikely to work well in the case of cataclysms. The next subsections discuss two alternatives that might be more effective.

6.4.3 Securitization of Cataclysmic Risk

Cataclysms may be large for the reinsurance industry but are generally small for the world's capital markets as a whole. A $100 billion earthquake loss, for example, would bankrupt a fair share of the reinsurance industry but would represent only 2 percent of the New York Stock Exchange asset value and less than 1 percent of the value of the U.S. capital market. Movements of this magnitude in net asset value in a month are the norm. Further, many cataclysms will be uncorrelated with economic conditions, and investments in cataclysmic risk could therefore help market investors diversify their portfolios.

Thus, it seems promising to diversify cataclysmic risk in broader securities markets, much as is now done for home mortgages. Such diversification for risks is beginning to occur.[33] Perhaps the best-known examples of the securitization of sizable risks are the catastrophe options that have been traded on the Chicago Board of Trade since 1992. For example, reinsurers can buy a call option that pays off if aggregate losses are above a given level—perhaps $5 billion. The size of the payment would be directly proportional to the losses above $5 billion. The call could be sold by firms that would do well in the event of a catastrophe—home builders, for example—or by general investors looking for a chance to diversify outside traditional securities markets.

---

33. For a discussion of securitization of cataclysmic risk, see Borden and Sarkar (1996) and Litzenberger, Beaglehole, and Reynolds (1996).

Other instruments for trading cataclysmic risks have been introduced, but they have been less popular than options. Contingent surplus notes, for example, guarantee the insurer buyers for its debt in the event of a cataclysmic loss. Typically, money is taken up front and invested in Treasury securities, which can be exchanged for company bonds at the insurer's discretion if a cataclysm occurs. Nationwide Mutual completed such a transaction recently. Investors purchased $400 million in U.S. Treasury bonds, and Nationwide can convert the Treasury bonds to company notes in the event of a catastrophe. Thus, Nationwide has access to a ready source of cash in the event of a catastrophe. Investors are compensated by getting a higher return than a normal Treasury bond would yield.

Catastrophe bonds (also termed *act-of-God bonds*) also yield cash from catastrophes for insurers. These bonds have coupon payments that depend on the level of the insurer's losses. As losses increase, insurers are not required to pay out as much and can use interest on the initial principle (and sometimes the principle itself) to pay out the unusually high claims.

One concern with all these financial instruments for offering reinsurance protection is whether the triggering event should be company specific or marketwide. Insurers and reinsurers would naturally want to have company-specific securitization, other factors equal. Basis risk is an important issue for insurers, and diversification against that risk would bring substantial value (Major 1996). But company-specific securities make both adverse selection and moral hazard more likely. For example, insurers that know that they have financial market reinsurance might pay less attention to the loss probabilities or magnitudes of their insureds. A likely scenario is that securitization will be based on marketwide losses and that intermediaries will pool particular companies into smaller groups approximating the market average, where risk spreading can be achieved but moral hazard and adverse selection minimized.

To date, securitization of cataclysmic risk has been limited. Catastrophe options, for example, trade less frequently than do most other options on the Chicago Board of Trade, and contingent-surplus notes and act-of-God bonds trade relatively infrequently. This relative illiquidity has probably led to a higher required return for investors than would be required if trading were more fluid. It is unclear whether the market will ultimately become large enough to support true cataclysmic diversification or whether other forms of reinsurance will be required.

6.4.4   The Government as Reinsurer

The government has a deep credit capacity: it can borrow by issuing debt far more readily than can private insurers or reinsurers, and it can raise resources rapidly through its ability to tax.[34] The ability to borrow or tax to meet

---

34. The government might also build up reserves to pay for potential cataclysms, but such build-ups are rare in the public sector, as the examples of social security and Medicare demonstrate.

cataclysmic obligations depends only on political capabilities. This puts the government in a natural position to be a reinsurer. The government can also compel reinsurance to solve the adverse-selection problems noted above. This is one of the traditional rationales for mandatory participation in social security, Medicare, and other public-insurance programs.

The government is also a natural reinsurer because it is often called in to cover cataclysmic losses after they have occurred, whether it has contracted for them or not.[35] In the recent past, the government has bailed out many savings-and-loan institutions; these efforts will cost taxpayers money for many years to come.[36] The government will pay the cost of cleaning up its atomic-weapons waste sites, estimated at well above $100 billion. The Price-Anderson Act, which is no longer in effect, insured nuclear utilities against severe losses from individual accidents; the cutoff of private loss was $560 million. Governments also run insolvency funds that bail out policyholders when their insurance company goes bankrupt. And, when hurricanes or floods occur, the government often provides disaster aid.

Formal government reinsurance programs are often established when primary-insurance markets break down. For example, the U.K. government decided to provide terrorism insurance following the breakdown of insurance and reinsurance markets when the bombings in London began in 1992. High-risk homeowners' pools in the United States typically get under way when the premiums that the private market would charge are above the levels that are socially acceptable.

Establishing a formal reinsurance system, and thus collecting at least some money, may be preferable to waiting until the event occurs and spreading the costs more broadly. Selling insurance in advance of a disaster also makes people aware of the social cost of their actions and thus limits moral hazard—for example, discouraging excessive building on floodplains.

The government could price reinsurance at its expected cost or, alternatively, provide a subsidy to purchasers. A subsidy might be appropriate if the government is worried that people will not purchase insurance appropriately or if the government wants to share in the losses from a catastrophe the same way it shares when it receives additional tax revenue when there are not catastrophes. Flood insurance, for example, is heavily subsidized. Savings-and-loan insurance, pension-plan insurance (PBGC), and state insurance-guarantee funds offer a more subtle subsidy: they charge premiums but typically fail to differentiate the premiums on the basis of risk. For example, savings-and-loan premiums were the same for all institutions. As we saw, this encouraged risky activity for institutions near default. Similarly, the PBGC used to provide pension insur-

---

35. Indeed, the probability of government involvement in certain cases may explain why insurance is only rarely purchased for some events (Kaplow 1991).

36. The government also has the authority to order other parties to pay for damages, as it did with Superfund. The government's unique capability to pass and enforce legislation—up to the limits of constitutionality—puts it in a position to get someone else to pay for removing a risk.

ance at $19.00 per participant plus $9.00 per $1,000 in vested but unfunded benefits. However, there was a cap of $53.00 per participant. This created an incentive to defund a plan once the cap was approached or passed. Many insurance-guarantee funds charge the same rate for all insurers, thus encouraging insurers to gamble with state funds if they are near bankruptcy and eliminating the need for individuals to think about the solvency of the company from which they purchase insurance.

Because of these moral hazard problems, the government might want to provide insurance at an actuarially fair cost. Indeed, if the government is providing reinsurance solely because its size allows it to better diversify cataclysmic risks, that is a function that the market should be willing to pay full cost for. Some insurance has been proposed along these lines. The Treasury Department, for example, recently proposed public reinsurance for natural disasters with aggregate losses from $25–$50 billion. Reinsurance would be auctioned to insurers in amounts ranging from $1 to $25 million. Although this proposal has somewhat of a market flavor, there are significant questions: Would the amount auctioned be too great to secure the government at least actuarial prices? Would such insurance be pitched at too low a range, given the government's inevitable financial responsibilities when losses exceed $50 billion?

In other cases, government insurance is moving closer to actuarial pricing. For example, the Retirement Protection Act of 1994 eliminated any cap on PBGC per participant costs starting in 1997. As a result, the PBGC should come closer to risk-based pricing.

One might question how the government will know enough about appropriate pricing to sell actuarially fair insurance when the government is the only insurance seller. The recent experience of the California Earthquake Authority (CEA) does not suggest that government authorities are well equipped to secure low prices for reinsurance. The CEA was seeking to purchase reinsurance for the layer between $7 and $8.5 billion over a four-year period. Its best estimate (based on scientific information) was that the layer would be reached with probability 1.2 percent, implying a fair market premium of $18 million. In the end, Warren Buffet sold the CEA this layer of reinsurance for $161 million per year. This is roughly ten times the estimated actuarial cost.

To learn what prices the government ought to use in selling reinsurance, the government may wish to inject a sliver of private-sector pricing of cataclysmic risk to indicate how much it costs to provide. For example, the government could sell off a small portion of its book, say a total of 1 percent in 0.1 percent units. Then, if the government were responsible for $100 billion of risk, investors could set prices for accepting risks up to $100 million. If the market price for a 0.1 percent share turned out to be $10 million, this amount would be paid to the investors, who would then take on the responsibility for this portion of the risk. Equally important, this rate would be charged to insurers who are reinsured by the government. Depending on administrative complexities, these prices could be auctioned to the private sector on a basis that reflected the risks involved, the specific insurer, or both.

The issue of basis risk adds complexity to such an auction scheme. Demand for reinsurance is likely to vary with the risk exposure of the particular company. Companies with a broad nationwide exposure will find a claim based on aggregate losses well suited to its needs. Companies with concentrated risks in a particular area or type of catastrophe, however, will find such reinsurance policies less suitable. This variation in the ability to obtain hedging suggests that the price of the reinsurance policy may vary with total sales. The equilibrium price will be high if little reinsurance is offered but low if a lot of reinsurance is offered. Determining how much reinsurance the government should provide in such a situation is a difficult issue.

Many countries use public insurance to address cataclysmic risk (although, to our knowledge, the private sector has not been involved in setting prices). Table 6.5 shows examples of public-sector reinsurance programs for catastrophic risk: France, the Netherlands, Japan, Spain, New Zealand, Norway, South Africa, and the United Kingdom. Most of the reinsurance programs cover natural disasters. In France, for example, flood losses that are particularly large are paid for by the national reinsurance company. The company collects premiums from a mandatory assessment on insurance premiums for property damage, business interruption, multirisk policies, and automobile insurance. Other countries cover events such as terrorism or political risk.

Public-reinsurance systems have three advantages beyond their ability to address cataclysmic risk. First, if the government provides reinsurance for cataclysms, it might allow a private market to develop for smaller aggregate losses. Second, public-sector reinsurance may address a moral hazard problem concerning government behavior. Many cataclysms can be ameliorated or magnified by government policy. Legal judgments, for example, vary with legislative and judicial actions. Decisions about where houses can be built will affect hurricane and earthquake losses. By making the government the reinsurer for

Table 6.5   **Public-Sector Catastrophic Reinsurance Programs**

Country	Year Began	Coverage
New Zealand	1944	Earthquake; war damage
Spain	1954	Natural disasters; terrorism; peacetime acts of armed forces
Japan	1966	Natural disasters
South Africa	1979	Political riots
Norway	1980	Natural disasters
France	1982	Natural disasters
The United Kingdom	1992	Terrorism
The Netherlands	1996	Natural disasters

these risks, the government may internalize some of the costs of its actions. Third, if government is the insurer of last resort anyway, a formal public-reinsurance system may raise revenues for this service. Of course, if insurance would be provided without the government, government involvement may just lead to a subsidy of risky activities that is not warranted.

6.4.5   Cataclysms and Learning about the Future

The occurrence of a cataclysm may affect our predictions about the magnitude of losses in the future. On one side, a cataclysm may eliminate the highest-risk situations; an earthquake may bring down the weakest buildings and release stress in a fault. Moreover, once society is alerted to the risk, it may take actions, say, reinforcing buildings, that will make the risk less likely or less costly in the future.

Cataclysms may also portend greater future losses if they result in an updating of event probabilities or the distribution of loss magnitudes. If we think the weather may be changing, then a hurricane this year may suggest additional hurricanes in future years. And, if losses are surprisingly high given a hurricane, we may conclude that future hurricane losses will be greater than we had anticipated.[37] This is anecdotally what occurred after Hurricane Andrew in Florida.

When cataclysms lead to updating in this fashion, a second major risk arises—the risk that premiums will rise in the future (Cochrane 1995; Cutler 1996). For example, the liability crisis of the 1970s and 1980s was caused much more by a rapid escalation in premiums than by any set of events that in themselves imposed substantial costs.[38] Just as costs escalated dramatically for insureds, so too did they for insurance companies seeking to reinsure risks. Insurers, presumably being more risk averse than those selling reinsurance, would probably have liked to have insured their future premiums as well.[39] But this insurance was not provided.

Indeed, reinsurance to protect against future premium increases is rarely issued, for three reasons. First, the insured has a quantity choice to make (the amount of insurance to purchase), which would be distorted if rates were not equal to current actuarial costs. Second, no reinsurer could bear the risk associated with protecting its customers against future increases in premiums. It would be offering protection against common-risk cataclysms. The exposure would be monumental. Third, a large up-front payment would be required to

---

37. For most statistical models, the more extreme the event, the more significant is the updating of future probabilities. Thus, the occurrence of a $25 billion hurricane will increase estimates of future event likelihoods and costs more than the occurrence of a $5 billion hurricane.

38. Macroeconomic factors such as inflation and high interest rates were also important in the liability crisis.

39. This is analogous to having future health-insurance premiums guaranteed even if the person contracts a chronic, expensive disease.

prevent insurance purchasers from leaving the contract if insurance premiums decline. Charging in this fashion seems impractical.

Current insurance arrangements generally put the buyer of insurance at risk for premium increases and decreases over the period of the policy, usually one year or (in a claims-made policy) somewhat longer. If there is little movement in expected costs from year to year, say, because there is little learning, this risk is minimal. However, experience over the past several decades suggests that expectations of future costs change substantially, and thus variability in premiums is large.

To determine how important learning about future losses is, we use the PCS data to determine how predictions of losses should be updated over time. We assume that expected losses in any year are a function of expected losses in the previous year and the actual loss experience in the previous year:

$$(2) \qquad E[L_{t+1}] = \alpha \cdot L_t + (1 - \alpha) \cdot E[L_t].$$

The coefficient α is the weight on the previous year's losses.[40] Therefore, α will be greater than zero if the world changes fundamentally over time in a way that insurers had not predicted. For example, if the underlying cause of North American hurricanes (perhaps weather conditions in sections of Africa) changes in such a way that more hurricanes are likely, this would be represented first as an increase in current hurricane losses, which then feeds back into expected future hurricane damage.

Actual damages in any year are expected damages times an error term:

$$(3) \qquad L_{t+1} = E[L_{t+1}] \cdot e^{\varepsilon_{t+1} - .5\sigma^2},$$

where ε is normally distributed with variance σ^2. The second term in the error term is an adjustment to make the mean of actual losses equal to the mean of expected losses.

Equations (2) and (3) can be estimated for α and σ^2 and expected losses in the first year of the data. Combining all the catastrophes, our estimate of α is .02, with a standard error of .01.[41]

To understand what this implies about premium variability, we simulate premiums and losses using equations (2) and (3). We simulate thirty thousand separate three-hundred-year time-series paths. We exclude the first one hundred years of the simulation to avoid start-up effects, with the result that we have effectively 6 million years of data.

Table 6.6 summarizes these simulations. The first columns show results for $\alpha = .02$; the second column shows results for $\alpha = .20$. The higher level of α

40. Estimates using average losses in the previous few years instead of just the past year yielded very similar results.
41. We attempted to estimate the model separately for different types of risks (particularly hurricanes) but found the estimates of α imprecise for risks with large variability.

Table 6.6   **Simulated Losses from Premium Variability ($ million)**

| | Weight Placed on Current Year's Losses | | | |
| | $\alpha = .02$ | | $\alpha = .20$ | |
Loss Distribution	Premium	Actual	Premium	Actual
Overall distribution:				
Mean	2,651	2,652	2,724	2,725
Standard deviation	876	3,273	73,433	100,258
Percentiles of average values:				
10th percentile	1,801	1,666	13	11
Median	2,509	2,471	159	144
90th percentile	3,670	3,856	2,539	2,416
99th percentile	5,230	5,756	33,326	33,231
Average of percentiles:				
Mean 10th percentile	2,256	559	392	188
Mean 90th percentile	3,084	5,739	7,127	7,049

Note: Based on 30,000 simulations each of 200 years' duration. The degree to which expected losses change with current-year losses is given by α. The second block shows the distribution of the average premium or loss across the 30,000 simulations. The third block shows the distribution of the 10th percentile premium or loss within each simulation and the 90th percentile premium or loss within each simulation.

is meant to proxy for a market with a greater degree of persistence in innovations. The first rows of the table show the mean premiums and losses across all years of the simulation. Not surprisingly, mean premiums match mean losses for each value of α.[42]

Our first measure of premium variability is the distribution of the average premium. That is, if an insurer cares only about the average premium over a two-hundred-year period, how variable is that average premium? This would be the relevant measure of variability for an insurer that was able to borrow and lend costlessly but was worried about what its average repayment over a long period of time would be.

We show the distribution of average premiums and losses for each two-hundred-year simulation in the second block of the table. Over a two-hundred-year period, average premiums are distributed essentially the same as average losses. For each value of α, the tenth percentile of average premiums is essentially the same as the tenth percentile of average losses, and the same is true at other points in the distribution. Thus, for a given level of α, insurance helps spread the risk that actual losses in a year will substantially exceed the mean, but it offers little benefit in reducing the spread in average losses for the two-hundred-year period. There are large differences in the variability of premiums as α changes, however. The ninety-ninth percentile average premium for the

---

42. The mean loss for $\alpha = .20$ is above the mean loss for $\alpha = .02$ because of sampling variability.

case of $\alpha = .20$ is over six times greater than the ninety-ninth percentile premium for the case of $\alpha = .02$.

Not all insurers are risk neutral over a two-hundred-year horizon, however. Bankruptcy fears or agency costs may make insurers care about losses at a greater frequency than the long-run average. Our second measure of variability captures this issue. We show the average value of premiums or losses across simulations. That is, if one thought about the ninetieth percentile premium *within* the two-hundred-year period, what is the average value of that number? To the extent that the average value of the ninetieth percentile premium is substantially above the average value of the average premium, the within-time-period risk will be substantial.

We show the distribution of these percentiles in the lower panel of the table. It is clear that insurance has an important role to play in this case. For the case of $\alpha = .02$, the average value of the ninetieth percentile premium is 45 percent below the average value of the ninetieth percentile actual loss. But the ninetieth percentile premium is 16 percent above the premium that would be required if insurers could reinsure the risk associated with variation in expected losses (the premium for this would be the overall average loss, \$2.7 billion). For the case of $\alpha = .20$, the ninetieth percentile premium is 160 percent above the unconditional mean loss. The losses to an insurer from premium variability due to changing loss processes may be substantial.

While current insurance arrangements generally either fix premiums over time or vary them fully with annual changes in expected losses, respectively placing all risk on the insurer or insured, other arrangements are possible. Some would share the burden of premium increases between the insurer and the insured. This type of "premium sharing" could perform a function much like insurance and risk sharing. The optimal form of premium sharing, of course, will depend on the utility function of the insured and insurer. If the two parties have exponential utility, albeit with different parameters, then they should bear local and global risks in proportion to those parameters. Side payments at the outset provide for movements along the Pareto frontier. By contrast, if both parties have utility functions where wealth is raised to a power, the logarithm being a special case, then they should proportionally share the total pie, including initial wealths. Movements along the Pareto frontier are achieved by varying the sharing percentage. In both situations, once a division of welfare is agreed on, all risks are shared in the same proportion (see Wilson 1965).[43] In our model, the risks are experienced as expected costs per period and in variability about those expected costs.

In theory, if firm contracts could be drawn for such situations, the parties would share increases and decreases in premiums in the same percentage that they shared any actual losses. In practice, it will not be possible to work out

---

43. Pratt and Zeckhauser (1989) show that this is the only case for which sharing is proportionate.

such sharing arrangements owing to the insecurity of premium promises. But we should recognize that the present situation, where insureds pay a small proportion of losses when period losses are great but bear virtually all the variability in premiums, is far from optimal.

6.5   Conclusion

Catastrophic and cataclysmic losses are an increasing concern for insurance companies, reinsurers, and society. In recent years, losses have escalated because of both unpleasant surprises in natural disaster magnitudes and a changing liability game. Some major insurers have become insolvent; many have been restructured or sold under duress. Insurance difficulties impinge on the public through premium boosts and the disappearance of insurance in some markets. Ultimately, economic activity suffers.

Such developments suggest that it is important to insure the insurers. Reinsurance markets are booming, but past reinsurance structures may be inadequate to today's markets. Reinsurers are likely to be less familiar with the risks that they are insuring than their insureds, both because the reinsurance market is increasingly globalized and because new risks, such as those related to technology or terrorism, need to be insured and reinsured. As a result, asymmetrical information and adverse selection are likely to be problems. If the asymmetry is on the magnitude of the loss, standard reinsurance frameworks—such as excess of loss or proportional—are inappropriate.

Cataclysmic losses—those that overwhelm insurance markets—are more common than they used to be. Cataclysms can stem from both single events and common risks. While new financial instruments are bringing additional liquidity to insurance markets, the government has substantial advantages as a reinsurer given its deep credit capacity. Although putting government insurance on a sound financial basis, say, by taking guidance from private transactions, is perhaps an unlikely step, it would contain the dangers of bureaucratic optimism and political interference.

Nature and the economy, not to mention government processes, are throwing risks at us on a grand scale. Significant innovation will be required if insurance and reinsurance markets are to make a sufficiently grand response.

Appendix
Proof of Proposition 1

The insurer can choose to purchase reinsurance or not. Denote utility if the insurer does not purchase reinsurance as U_N and utility if the insurer purchases reinsurance as U_I. These utility functions are given by

(A1)
$$U^N = (1 - p_b)U(Y) + p_b E_m[U(Y - m)],$$

$$U^I = (1 - p_b)U(Y - \pi) + p_b E_m[U(Y - \pi - \theta(m))],$$

where Y is premium income, π is the reinsurance premium, p_b is the probability (known to the insurer) of experiencing a loss, m is the realized loss, and $\theta(m)$ is the insurer's payment if he has purchased reinsurance. E_m signifies that the expectation is taken with respect to the random variable m. The first term in each utility function is utility if there is no loss. The second term is utility when there is a loss.

Let p_b^* be the probability where the insurer is indifferent between purchasing and not purchasing reinsurance ($U^N = U^I$). We can express the difference in utility $U^I - U^N$ as the sum of two terms: the difference in utility when there is no loss, $\{(1 - p_b)[U(Y - \pi) - U(Y)]\}$, and the difference in utility when there is a loss, $\{p_b E_m[U(Y - \pi - \theta(m)) - U(Y - m)]\}$. Notice that, if there is no loss, utility is lower if insurance has been purchased than if it has not been purchased since a premium was paid with no recovery. If there is a loss, however, expected utility will be greater with insurance than without. The insurer with $p_b = p_b^*$ is the firm where these two terms exactly balance each other.

Now consider any $p_b > p_b^*$. For each of these firms, the weight placed on expected utility when there is a loss is greater, and the weight placed on utility without a loss is smaller, than for the firm with $p_b = p_b^*$. Thus, each of these firms will find reinsurance more attractive than does the firm with $p_b = p_b^*$. Therefore, all firms with $p_b > p_b^*$ will purchase reinsurance, and all firms with $p_b < p_b^*$ will not purchase reinsurance.

Combining equations (A1), p_b^* is determined as

(A2) $$p_b^* = \frac{U(Y) - U(Y - \pi)}{U(Y) - U(Y - \pi) + E_m[U(Y - \pi - \theta(m)) - U(Y - m)]}.$$

The reinsurance premium π^* is the average reinsurance payment conditional on having a loss (the loss less the primary insurer's payment) times the probability that a firm purchasing insurance has a loss. This is given by

(A3) $$\pi^* = \{E_m[m] - E_m[\theta(m)]\} \cdot E[p_b | p_b > p_b^*].$$

The optimal reinsurance policy maximizes expected utility over p_b. If there were only one p_b, full insurance would be optimal ($\theta[m] = 0$). With differing values of p_b, however, only the firms with higher p_b will purchase insurance.

To combat adverse selection, think about increasing $\theta(m)$ on the first dollar of losses. As this is done, the premium falls by the expected primary-insurer payment. Starting from the point of full insurance, this reduction in coverage has no welfare cost for firms already purchasing reinsurance. For firms at the margin of purchasing reinsurance, however, the reduction in reinsurance coverage is attractive; reinsurance is actuarially overpriced for this group. Thus, some additional firms will choose to purchase reinsurance. This reduces the reinsurance premium by even more, benefiting the firms that were already purchasing insurance. Thus, incomplete reinsurance will be optimal.

To design the optimal reinsurance policy, consider a given amount of total cost sharing in the reinsurance policy, $E_m[\theta(m)]$. The direct effect of this cost sharing on the reinsurance premium (eq. [A3]) is independent of where in the distribution of m this cost sharing occurs. But selection and welfare of insurers purchasing reinsurance depends on how this cost is determined. Note that firms purchasing reinsurance want to design cost sharing to maximize $E_m[U(Y - I - \theta(m)]$. Maximizing this value also reduces p_b^* the most (eq. [A2]).

Thus, the goal is to design the reinsurance policy that maximizes $E_m[U(Y - I - \theta(m))]$ over all the policies with the same level of total cost sharing $E_m[\theta(m)]$. Given risk aversion, the most valuable insurance to provide is that for the greatest risks; the next most valuable insurance is that for the next highest risk; and so forth. Thus, the optimal policy must insure all the high risks up to the point where the budget constraint is met. This is exactly the excess-of-loss policy described in the text.

References

Akerlof, George. 1970. The market for lemons. *Quarterly Journal of Economics* 84: 488–500.
Angell, Marcia. 1996. *Science on trial: The clash of medical evidence and the law in the breast implant case.* New York: Norton.
A. M. Best Co. 1996. *Best's aggregates and averages—property-casualty.* New York.
Borden, Sara, and Asani Sarkar. 1996. Securitizing property catastrophe risk. *Current Issues in Economics and Finance* (Federal Reserve Bank of New York) 2 (August): 1–6.
Cochrane, John. 1995. Time consistent health insurance. *Journal of Political Economy* 103:445–73.
Conning & Co. 1993. *Reinsurance: Too little or too much?* New York.
Cutler, David M. 1996. Why don't markets insure long-term risk? Harvard University, Economics Department. Mimeo.
Giles, Martin. 1994. A survey of insurance. *Economist,* 3 December, suppl., 3–22.
Huber, Peter. 1988. *Liability: The legal revolution and its consequences.* New York: Basic.
Insurance Information Institute. 1996a. *Catastrophes: Insurance issues.* New York.
———. 1996b. *Environmental pollution: Insurance issues.* New York.
———. 1996c. *Reinsurance.* New York.
Kaplow, Louis. 1991. Incentives and government relief for risk. *Journal of Risk and Uncertainty* 4:167–75.
Litzenberger, Robert H., David R. Beaglehole, and Craig E. Reynolds. 1996. *Assessing catastrophe-reinsurance-linked securities as a new asset class.* New York: Goldman Sachs.
Major, John. 1996. Basis risk and catastrophe reinsurance. Guy Carpenter & Co. Mimeo.

Myerson, Roger. 1979. Incentive compatibility and the bargaining problem. *Economet-rica* 47:61–73.

Pratt, John W., and Richard J. Zeckhauser. 1989. The impact of risk sharing in efficient decision. *Journal of Risk and Uncertainty* 2:219–34.

Rothschild, Michael, and Joseph Stiglitz. 1976. Equilibrium in competitive insurance markets: An essay on the economics of imperfect information. *Quarterly Journal of Economics* 90:629–50.

Viscusi, W. Kip, Richard J. Zeckhauser, Patricia Born, and Glenn Blackmon. 1993. The effect of 1980s tort reform legislation on general liability and medical malpractice insurance. *Journal of Risk and Uncertainty* 6:165–86.

Weiler, Paul C., Howard H. Hiatt, Joseph P. Newhouse, William G. Johnson, Troyen A. Brennan, and Lucian L. Leape. 1993. *A measure of malpractice: Medical injury, malpractice litigation, and patient compensation.* Cambridge, Mass.: Harvard University Press.

Wilson, Robert B. 1968. On the theory of syndicates. *Econometrica* 36:119–32.

Zeckhauser, Richard J. 1991. The strategy of choice. In *Strategy and choice,* ed. Richard J. Zeckhauser. Cambridge, Mass.: MIT Press.

Comment   John H. Cochrane

This paper is an ambitious survey. It is full of interesting anecdotes, facts about reinsurance, and speculations about forces that might move reinsurance contracts in one direction or another. While much time could pleasantly be spent going through the paper and discussing each issue that it raises, instead I will concentrate on the central analytic point. Here's the setup: m denotes the size of the loss if there is one, with probability $g(m)$. The probability that any loss occurs is p. This probability is random, too, and $f(p)$ is the "probability of probability" p. The original insurer may have better information about the probability of loss $f(p)$ or about the distribution of the size of losses $g(m)$.

I emphasize that the issue here is, not the probability structure itself, but *differences* between the insurer's knowledge and the reinsurer's knowledge. The fact that we are all uncertain about what probabilities to attach to cataclysmic events has nothing to do with adverse selection.

The central point is stated right up front: "When the asymmetry is on the probability of a loss [$f(p)$] but not its magnitude [$g(m)$], the optimal reinsurance contract is a standard 'excess-of-loss' policy [deductible]. . . . When the asymmetry is over the magnitude of the loss [$g(m)$], the optimal reinsurance policy covers smaller losses as well as large losses but leaves the primary insurer exposed for some large losses [risk sharing]." I think that this proposition is a misleading summary of what we learn from the analysis in the paper.

John H. Cochrane is the Sigmund E. Edelstone Professor of Finance at the Graduate School of Business, University of Chicago; a consultant at the Federal Reserve Bank of Chicago; and a research associate of the National Bureau of Economic Research.

All that can matter to the optimal contract is each player's probability distribution over final outcomes—losses m in this case. Since there are no intermediate moves, the sequence of signals must be irrelevant. Thus, suppose that you get to distributions over final outcomes by different values for p. You obtain *exactly the same optimal contract* if you get to those distributions over final outcomes by different values for $g(m)$. The labels *uncertainty over probabilities* and *uncertainty over losses* must be meaningless in terms of the optimal contracts that they generate.

What about Cutler and Zeckhauser's examples?

Both the "asymmetric information about probability" example and the "asymmetric information about losses" example generate situations in which the reinsurer knows that he faces an original insurer that has one of two probability distributions over final events. He has to design a clever schedule of payments as a function of losses to separate out original insurers with one versus the other type of probability distribution.

The examples differ in what the two types of final distributions over outcomes are. It should not be a surprise that contracts designed to separate people with one pair of probability distributions over final outcomes are different from contracts that separate people with much different pairs of such distributions. In fact, the paper has a very nice exposition of the intuition for this result: "If the buyer knows more about the probability of a loss than its magnitude, reinsurance should exclude coverage for the common small risks that are the source of exploitable adverse selection; this is exactly the 'deductible-style' policy that characterizes excess-of-loss insurance. If the buyer knows more about the magnitude of loss than its probability, however, it is optimal to make it costly for him to buy reinsurance when he knows that the magnitude of loss is high."

This intuition is right on the money, but notice that it concerns only the uncertainty that reinsurers have about the original insurers' probabilities over *final outcomes,* not how one gets there. Another way to put the point is that, in general, the uncertainty over probabilities and the uncertainty over distributions are not separately identified by the uncertainty over distributions over final outcomes. One can tell the difference between these two only in highly structured and stylized examples. In this case, the crucial "identifying assumption" is that $g(m)$ places no weight on $m = 0$. Absent that identifying assumption, we can rewrite the uncertainty in probability example as an uncertainty in distribution example, and you would never know the difference between the two.

These are also perfectly standard results in the theory of insurance—for example, Rothschild and Stiglitz (1976) or Kreps (1990, 668). These days, one usually finds optimal contracts with the "revelation principle" rather than by the supply-and-demand methods used in this paper (or at least the conference draft). A risk-neutral insurer offers a contract to a risk-averse consumer. The consumer is one of two or more "types" with different probability distribution of losses. To find the optimal contract—the optimal payment given each possible loss—we maximize the insurer's profits subject to the constraints that each type of consumer will accept the contract he is offered and that each type of consumer will correctly reveal his type. In equations, one solves problems like the following:

PROBLEM. Choose state-contingent payment to maximize insurer profit

$$\max_{\{q(m_i,\cdot)\}} \text{Pr}(A)\sum_i \pi_i^A q(m_i, A) + \text{Pr}(B)\sum_i \pi_i^B q(m_i, B)$$

(where $\text{Pr}[A]$ = insurer's probability that consumer is type A, m_i = loss in state i, π_i^A = type A probability of loss m_i, and $q[m_i, A]$ = net payment if consumer says type A and loss is m_i) subject to (1) type A consumers accept the contract:

$$\sum_i \pi_i^A u[w - m_i - q(m_i, A)] \geq \sum_i \pi_i^A u(w - m_i);$$

(2) type B consumers accept the contract:

$$\sum_i \pi_i^B u[w - m_i - q(m_i, B)] \geq \sum_i \pi_i^B u(w - m_i);$$

(3) type A consumers do not pretend that they are type B:

$$\sum_i \pi_i^A u[w - m_i - q(m_i, A)] \geq \sum_i \pi_i^A u[w - m_i - q(m_i, B)];$$

(4) type B consumers do not pretend that they are type A:

$$\sum_i \pi_i^B u[w - m_i - q(m_i, B)] \geq \sum_i \pi_i^B u[w - m_i - q(m_i, A)].$$

We know how to solve problems like this and how to find *optimal* contracts. The optimal contracts behave just as Cutler and Zeckhauser find in their examples. There will be less insurance—deductibles, caps, copayments, etc.—in the range of outcomes where the possible probabilities differ the most or "odds ratios" are highest. In fact, one can reverse engineer problems like this to find an assumption about the nature of private information to generate any desired sharing rule or contract.

In sum, these examples are perfectly standard insurance theory. They have nothing special to do with reinsurance or cataclysms, and the results—the degree to which different sizes of loss are covered—depend only on probability distributions over final outcomes, not in any fundamental way whether those distributions are generated by "uncertainty over probabilities" or "uncertainty over losses given there is a loss." If one wants to avoid revelation-principle constructions, then either one has to find a new, restricted definition of optimal contract, or one is just showing a different implementation mechanism for a revelation-principle contract.

I do not mean to sound critical. I think that it is a good thing that the analysis in this paper comes down to perfectly standard theory. Thousands of papers have been written on optimal contracting with asymmetric information. It would be astounding if this paper came up with an original theory. I much *prefer* papers that apply standard theory to interesting practical situations. It gives me comfort as an economist that we do not have to invent a new and clever theory for every situation. I am in the same boat. The paper I wrote (Cochrane 1995) that got me invited to this conference applied contract theory so old-fashioned there was not even private information. The point of the above forest of equations is constructive. It is a suggestion for how Cutler and Zeckhauser can actually compute optimal contracts in the situation that they analyze, rather than analyzing the relative merits of arbitrary contracts.

But, while there have been thousands of papers working out the theory, there have been almost no papers that try to see whether this beautiful theory has anything to do with our world. Is there really any asymmetric information, and what form does it in fact take? *Let us* reverse engineer-observed real-world contracts and see if the required uncertainty about insurer's probability distributions over losses makes any sense. *Let us* examine what information we have on actual insurer's probability distributions. Along this path, completing the marriage of theory and detailed industry knowledge toward which I see this paper working, I think that Cutler and Zeckhauser can end up with something really useful.

This said, I must voice my skepticism. Of the standard textbook problems with insurance contracts, of all the impediments to cataclysm reinsurance, is adverse selection—asymmetric information over the probability distribution of losses—really the most important?

Adverse selection is already not so obvious for people. Do you really know more about your health on the basis of your aches and pains than a doctor armed with your medical history and actuarial tables? For institutions—insurance companies selling to reinsurers—asymmetric information seems even more tenuous. Anything that an institution knows and can act on is written down somewhere and can be shared with a reinsurer.

Furthermore, the uncertainties about the probability of cataclysmic losses that many of us have commented on during this conference argue to me against asymmetric information as a serious problem. The heart of asymmetric information problems is that the reinsurer does not want to offer a contract and have only those original insurers who *know* the probabilities are a lot worse than it thinks they are take the contract. It is not enough that the insurers happen to *believe* that the probabilities are a lot worse: so long as the insurers do not *know* a lot more than the reinsurer does, the reinsurer will not discover ex post a surprisingly large exposure, and contracts will work fine. If nobody knows the right probabilities, there will be little information and lots of confusion as to correct pricing. But there will not be *asymmetric* information and adverse selection.

We can think of testing for adverse selection rather than intuiting or investigating the extent of asymmetric information. I just read an interesting paper (Cawley and Phillipson 1996) that tested whether asymmetric information is important in life insurance. The theory, like that presented here, predicts that it should be cheaper to buy a little insurance than a lot of insurance, to keep really sick people from loading up on insurance. Insurers should make sure that consumers do not undo this size premium by getting insurance from several different companies. But, in fact, there are volume discounts, and insurers do not care if you take out multiple policies! Cawley and Phillipson also find that insurers, with good actuaries and models, have *better* information than customers on likely life spans!

So bring on the empirical work. Cutler and Zeckhauser seem ideally ready to do a similar exploration of the catastrophe-reinsurance market. But, as with life insurance, let us be prepared to find that, although adverse selection fascinated a generation of theorists, it might not have much to say about many actual insurance contracts.

A word of caution, however. Adverse selection leads to nonlinear risk sharing, but not every nonlinear contract means adverse selection. For example, consider a company that is hedging oil-price or interest rate risk in derivatives markets. It will sign many contracts with highly nonlinear payouts, payouts that look like "deductibles," "caps," "slices," and so forth. But, obviously, the structure of these securities has *nothing* to do with adverse selection. Analogously, I think that it could be very dangerous to jump to an adverse-selection interpretation of nonlinear contracts in an increasingly securitized reinsurance market.

Of the textbook asymmetric information stories, I would guess that asymmetric information about how big the losses really are *once they have happened* is a far bigger problem. You do not just call up your reinsurer and say, "It rained a bit. Send us that check for $100 billion." The contracts must be carefully written and triggered on events that can be easily verified and not subject to manipulation. Currently, reinsurance and even the exchange-traded cat options are triggered on reports of industry losses. To a cynic like me, this places an extraordinary amount of faith in accountants, adjusters, and reporting services. But, by focusing attention on this issue and giving an incentive for the production of good indices, the process of securitization seems likely to help.

I would also follow much of the discussion here and guess that loss reserves, liquidity, capital, etc. are crucial issues. David Cutler asked the question, "Who should pay?" The answer is that we all should pay. The (Pareto-)optimal response to a large shock is that everyone should pitch in a bit. The question is, What institutions or securities best implement this result?

We worry that cataclysms, although trivial compared to national wealth, nonetheless can exhaust reserves, setting off a chain of bankruptcies. Yet tying up more reserves in liquid assets—building up capital to cover the largest cataclysm—is obviously inefficient.

The central problem is limited liability. The answer, it seems to me, is more widespread use of securities that allow some liability. Each $10,000 of a pension fund should include a security, or just a contractual arrangement, that costs nothing, gets, say, $5.00 per month premium, but exposes the fund to a liability of up to, say, $100 in cataclysm or calamity events. The current pricing of catastrophe reinsurance means that these securities earn very large expected returns even though they are uncorrelated with other security returns. One could come close to this arrangement with the cat options that are already traded.

This arrangement allows us all to share in the risk, which is still, after all, a small fraction of total wealth. It does so without the need for huge inefficient loss reserves or the distortions and inefficiencies of implicit government catastrophe insurance by ex post taxation. The design, implementation, and marketing of such securities seems to me the most promising response to the issue of cataclysm reinsurance. Of course, pension funds must be allowed to hold such securities, so, in the end, regulation may be the reason that we do not already all share in catastrophe risk, and regulatory change may be an important step in allowing us to do so.

References

Cawley, John, and Tomas Phillipson. 1996. An empirical examination of information barriers to trade in insurance. Working Paper no. 5669. Cambridge, Mass.: National Bureau of Economic Research.

Cochrane, John H. 1995. Time-consistent health insurance. *Journal of Political Economy* 103:445–73.

Kreps, David M. 1990. *A course in microeconomic theory.* Princeton, N.J.: Princeton University Press.

Rothschild, M., and J. Stiglitz. 1976. Equilibrium in competitive insurance markets: An essay on the economics of imperfect information. *Quarterly Journal of Economics* 90:630–49.

7 The Influence of Income Tax Rules on Insurance Reserves

David F. Bradford and Kyle D. Logue

One of the most important components of the balance sheet of a property-casualty insurance company is the *loss reserve.* In spite of what the term may suggest, a loss reserve is not a pot of funds set aside for the uncertain future. It is an accounting entry, a liability on the balance sheet. More precisely termed the *unpaid-losses account,* the loss reserve expresses the amount the company expects to pay out in the future to cover indemnity payments that will come due on policies already written for losses that have already been incurred and to cover the costs of dealing with the associated claims. The latter category of costs, which includes, for example, the litigation costs associated with settling claims, is called *loss-adjustment expenses.*[1]

If loss reserves were determined solely on the basis of pure insurance-accounting theory, they would reflect only those factors that affect the size, frequency, and pattern of future claim payments and loss-adjustment expenses. Such factors would include changes in patterns of actual claim payments; changes in inflation rates, weather patterns, and technology; and, particularly

David F. Bradford is professor of economics and public affairs at Princeton University, a research associate of the National Bureau of Economic Research, and adjunct professor of law at New York University. Kyle D. Logue is professor of law at the University of Michigan.

During his work on the paper, Bradford enjoyed the hospitality of the Center of Economic Studies at the University of Munich and helpful discussions there with Michael Reiter, Christian Thimann and Richard Arnott. Logue's work on this project benefited from numerous conversations with his colleagues at the University of Michigan Law School. He gives special thanks to Jeffrey Lehman, who provided both useful substantive suggestions and wise counsel throughout this project. He also thanks Stuart Thiel for several helpful discussions. In addition, helpful comments and suggestions were received from David Cummins, James Hines, Sean Mooney, Ralph Winter, and Mark Wolfson. James Bohn was helpful on matters of aggregation. Ryan Edwards and Ning Zhang provided exceptionally able research assistance. Financial support was provided by the Woodrow Wilson School, Princeton University, and the NBER Project on the Financing of Property/Casualty Risks. The usual caveats apply.

1. Our discussion of insurance accounting and solvency regulation draws primarily from Mooney and Cohen (1991), Salzmann (1974), Peterson (1981), and Troxel and Bouchie (1990).

significant in the context of liability insurance, trends in tort doctrines and jury awards. In practice, however, loss reserves are influenced by other considerations as well, considerations such as how the reported reserves will affect the likelihood of regulatory scrutiny, the perceptions of investors, and the firm's income tax liability. In this paper, we begin to examine the effects of income tax rules on property-casualty reserving practices.

Although insurers can choose from a number of different approaches to calculating their loss reserves, all these approaches share some common characteristics. The insurer generally begins by collecting information about its own loss experience as well as information about the rest of the industry's loss experience. With respect to the latter, industrywide data are collected and distributed to insurers through rating bureaus such as the Insurance Services Organization. These data include information about the severity, frequency, and timing of past claim payments and claim-expense payments as well as information about changes in trends and patterns of payments.

Once these data have been collected, the insurer's actuarial department applies various statistical techniques designed to generate predictions about the insurer's future loss claim payments and loss expenses. Typically, the actuarial department will recommend a range of loss reserves. Then, from within this range, someone in management (e.g., the chief financial officer) will choose the actual number that will be reported on the insurer's books. In any event, the choice of the reported loss reserve inevitably rests with management, and it is undisputed that management has some measure of discretion in setting those reserves (Peterson 1981).

In thinking about the role played by reserves as liabilities in the financial, regulatory, and tax accounting of the insurance company, it is useful to keep in mind the generic connection between a balance sheet and an income statement. In general terms, *income,* a flow concept, equals the sum of the increase in an associated stock concept, which is *net worth,* and amounts distributed to the company's owners during a given period. And net worth is the excess of a company's total assets over its total liabilities at a given time. For reporting purposes, the flow concept (income) is recorded on the income statement, and the stock concept (net worth) is recorded on the balance sheet. Thus, in theory, a company's reported income for a given period is simply the increase in the company's net worth during the period. (If there is a distribution to owners during the period, this statement is modified in an obvious way.) As for the specialized case of insurance accounting, the concept of net worth is called *surplus,* and it is reported on the insurer's year-end balance sheet as the difference between total assets and total liabilities. Likewise, net changes in surplus are reflected on the insurer's income statement as an operating gain or loss.

This is where an insurer's loss reserves come into the picture. Loss reserves are typically the largest single liability on an insurer's balance sheet. Therefore, owing to their sheer magnitude, even relatively small percentage changes in loss reserves can significantly affect an insurer's surplus (i.e., the company's stock picture) and its operating results or income (i.e., the company's flow picture).

State insurance regulators specify the accounting conventions that insurance companies must use in the reports that they file for purposes of regulatory oversight. Collectively, these conventions are known as *annual statement* or *statutory accounting*. Statutory accounting has traditionally required—and, in most states, still requires—that loss reserves be reported on an undiscounted basis, both on the balance sheet and on the income statement. That is, despite the fact that an insurer's loss reserves represent the insurer's expected future claim payments and loss expenses, which one might expect to be discounted to a present-value equivalent, statutory accounting requires the insurer to calculate the balance-sheet entry using the simple sum of those future outlays.

In addition, until 1986, insurers were required to use statutory accounting—including undiscounted loss-reserve calculations—for the purpose of calculating their federal income tax liability. As part of the Tax Reform Act of 1986 (TRA86), however, insurers were required to discount their loss reserves for federal tax purposes. The details and the importance of this change are discussed below.

In the modern view of the firm, managers are modeled as making managerial decisions that serve their own interests. These interests will coincide with the interests of the firm's owners if the managers are appropriately socialized or if appropriately structured compensation schemes are in place (Fama 1980; Jensen and Meckling 1976). The management of an insurance company has an interest in the results reported on the company's balance sheet and income statement. Additionally, with respect to some elements of the balance sheet and income statement, management has considerable discretion. That is, for such accounting elements, the information that is available to management regarding the company's performance and financial position does not translate automatically into accounting data that can be reported. For these elements, the exercise of managerial judgment is not only feasible but necessary. The insurer's loss reserve is one such accounting variable, the setting of which can be understood as a managerial decision.

In addition to playing an essential role in determining the insurer's annual financial and tax-accounting income, loss reserves are used in measuring an insurer's overall financial strength. All else equal, including a fixed and positive relation between reported loss reserves and a "best estimate" of future payment liabilities, a larger loss reserve is associated with an increased risk of the insurer's insolvency. If this risk becomes sufficiently large, state insurance regulators may increase their level of surveillance or intervene in some way. State regulators monitor specifically the insurer's ratio of surplus to premiums written. If this ratio falls below a given threshold, the regulator will require that steps be taken by the company to improve its financial position. In the extreme case, if the insurer is on the brink of insolvency, the regulator may take over the company and run it. For obvious reasons, the financial condition of the insurer is also important to investors and to policyholders. In fact, from the point of view of insurance-company management, perhaps the most important consumer for the company's accounting data is the commercial rating agencies, such as A. M. Best and Standard & Poor's, whose ratings regarding a company's financial condition can be critical to the company's future prospects.

In sum, because loss reserves play an important role in determining insurers' reported income and surplus, one would expect management's reserving discretion to be affected by all the external factors mentioned above.

The exercise of discretion in reporting reserves has been studied by a number of previous researchers. Within this literature, perhaps the most commonly tested question is the extent to which insurers deliberately manipulate loss reserves to "smooth" (i.e., to reduce the variability in) earnings over time (see, e.g., Forbes 1970; Balcarek 1975; Ansley 1979, and Harrington 1988). This question was studied, for example, by Smith (1980) and Weiss (1985) in the context of automobile-liability lines of insurance. Both concluded that their findings were consistent with the smoothing hypothesis; both also suggested other possible causes of the reserving errors observed in their data, for example, unanticipated inflation. Grace (1990) carried out a similar study of loss-reserving errors. Grace hypothesized that management would choose loss reserves that maximize the company's discounted after-tax cash flow subject to smoothing constraints and uncertainty. Looking at automobile-liability lines from the period between 1966 and 1979, Grace, too, concluded that the results of her study were largely consistent with her hypothesis. More recently, Petroni (1992) explored the hypothesis that the incentive to underestimate loss reserves is a decreasing function of the financial strength of the insurer. The results of this study suggest that insurance companies that are close to receiving regulatory scrutiny tend to understate their reserves by a larger amount than other insurance companies.

Our interest in loss-reserving practices began with our realization that major changes in the federal income tax laws enacted in 1986 altered dramatically (although temporarily) the loss-reserving incentives of property-casualty insurers. Specifically, TRA86 changed the tax treatment of property-casualty insurance companies in ways that greatly increased the tax advantage of "conservative" loss reserving during the transition period from the pre-TRA86 world to the post-TRA86 world. (Conservative loss reserving is the reporting of loss reserves that fall systematically on the high end of the distribution of possible outcomes.) Thus, we were interested in exploring empirically how responsive insurers' loss-reserving discretion is to tax incentives.

Our study of the effect of taxes on loss reserving can be located within two established lines of inquiry. First, in the accounting literature, several researchers have attempted to determine the extent to which external incentives affect management's use of its accounting discretion in reporting earnings. For example, important contributions to the study of income management include

White (1970), Dascher and Malcolm (1970), Koch (1981), Lambert (1984), Moses (1987), McNichols and Wilson (1988), and Scholes, Wilson, and Wolfson (1990). Second, our research contributes to the study of the effect of tax law and tax-law changes on business decisions more generally. For a sampling of the enormous literature on this subject, see Slemrod (1992), which includes a collection of empirical studies of the effects of TRA86 on various types of business decisions.

Section 7.1 describes the relevant tax-law history and sketches out some of our hypotheses concerning reserving behavior. Section 7.2 gives some descriptive statistics on the industry. Section 7.3 develops a quantitative measure of the tax incentives bearing on the reserving decision. Section 7.4 looks at the time-series evidence in industrywide data. There is a brief concluding section.

7.1 Income Tax Treatment of Property-Casualty Insurance Companies

The tax treatment of property-casualty insurance companies is governed by a special set of rules that are found in subchapter L of the Internal Revenue Code. Under these rules, property-casualty insurers are required to calculate their taxable income using essentially the same accounting conventions required by state insurance regulators, referred to, as we have noted, as *statutory* or *annual statement accounting.* The statutory approach requires an insurer to calculate its annual income by taking into account both its net underwriting profit (or loss) and its net investment income (or loss) for the year. To determine its underwriting profit or loss, the insurer starts with the premiums accruing during the year and then takes a number of deductions, the largest of which is typically the increase in the insurer's incurred losses account, which, in turn, includes any increases in unpaid loss reserves. Note also that annual statement accounting requires insurers to treat loss-reserve *increases* and loss-reserve *decreases* symmetrically. Thus, if an insurer has a net decrease in its loss reserves during the course of the year, the insurer must include the amount of that decrease in its underwriting profits for the year. (An increase in the estimated total of losses incurred and loss-adjustment expenses for policies that were written before the current reporting year is known as a *reserve strengthening.* A downward adjustment in those estimates is known as a *reserve weakening* or *release.*

Given the availability of the loss-reserve deduction for federal income tax purposes, an insurer will often have a tax incentive to overstate its loss reserves. This is because overstating the reserve will increase the deduction and reduce the insurer's taxable income for the year. To be sure, that reduction comes at the cost of an equal increase in a future year's taxable income; nevertheless, in the meantime, the insurer will have benefited from the time value of the excess deduction. (As we explain below, owing to the transition provisions of TRA86, there was an extra advantage for reserves in 1986 and 1987 and possibly for reserves in earlier years as well.) Of course, tax effects are not the only source of incentives operating on the reserving decision. In some years, for example, management may have an interest in understating the insurer's loss reserves so as to boost reported financial earnings. In addition, any tendency to overstate reserves will be constrained to some extent by the threat of increased scrutiny by state regulators or by the Internal Revenue Service. (If a loss-reserve deduction is unreasonably large, the unreasonable amount of the deduction can be disallowed by the IRS [Treas. Reg. sec. 1.832-4(b)].)

TRA86 contained at least three provisions that should have significantly affected management's incentives with respect to loss reserving: First, TRA86 enacted the largest reduction in corporate income tax rates ever. Under the act, the corporate rate was scheduled to decline from 46 percent in 1986, to 40 percent in 1987, and, finally, to 34 percent in 1988. Second, TRA86 introduced the requirement that, in calculating loss-reserve deductions and inclusions for federal income tax purposes, insurers must discount loss reserves to present value.[2] Third, TRA86 included a special "fresh-start" transitional rule that applied to pre-1987 loss reserves, under which insurers were permitted to write down their end-of-1986 reserves to the discounted amount. Reserve increases due to *strengthening* in 1986 of *pre-1986* reserves were, however, not eligible for the fresh start.

The opportunities that were created by the tax rate changes to reduce effective tax burdens are straightforward. Overstating loss reserves (i.e., reporting "conservative" reserves) is a method of postponing taxable income. Thus, any dollar of taxable income that was postponed from 1986 to 1987 or from 1987 to 1988 would have generated $.06 in tax savings (not including the usual benefit of deferral).

The fresh-start rule enacted in conjunction with the discounting requirement also created possibilities for reducing taxes by adjusting reserves. Under the fresh-start provisions, insurers could take loss-reserve deductions in pre-1987 tax years at their undiscounted value, while the corresponding *inclusions* in income in post-1987 tax years were on a *discounted* basis. The net effect was to provide a second deduction (deferred in time to a degree depending on the length of the payout tail on the line in question) for the difference between the discounted and the undiscounted total of reserves carried into the new regime on 1 January 1987. (The length of the tail of an insurance policy is the span of time from issue until all payments have been made.) Congress recognized that the fresh-start provision would give insurers an incentive to exercise their loss-reserving discretion so as to increase the amount of their loss reserves eligible for the fresh start. That is why the law expressly disallowed the application of

2. The discount rate and loss-payment pattern that insurers must use in discounting their reserves are promulgated by the Treasury Department. Under certain circumstances, an insurer may elect to use its own historical loss-payment pattern. TRA86 also contained several other changes that specifically altered the tax treatment of property-casualty insurers. For a discussion of some of these changes and an investigation of their effects on insurers' investment strategies, see Cummins and Grace (1992).

the fresh-start rule to reserve strengthening that occurred in the 1986 tax and reporting year. (For most insurers, the concepts *tax year* and *reporting year* coincide.) Under this rule, to the extent that an insurer increased its loss reserves in the 1986 tax year in a way that was deemed to be a reserve strengthening by the IRS, the insurer would in effect be required to treat that reserve strengthening as if it had been made in 1987, under the new discounting rules. To be more precise, the insurer would be permitted to deduct the undiscounted value of the reserve strengthening in the 1986 tax year, but it would also be required to return the amount of the discount into income in the 1987 tax year (Treas. Reg. 1.846-3[e]). Thus, insurers could increase the amount qualifying for the fresh-start advantage by increasing reported reserves on new policies written in 1986 and by increasing reserves on all other policies in 1985 or earlier. For example, if an insurer overstated its loss reserves in the 1986 tax year for policies written in 1986 and corrected the overstatement in some post-1986 reporting year, the initial loss-reserve deduction would have been taken at the larger, undiscounted value, and the later loss-reserve inclusion (resulting from the corresponding weakening of the overstated reserve) would have occurred at the smaller, discounted value. The fresh-start rule implied a similar incentive to overstate loss reserves in pre-1986 tax years, to the extent that companies anticipated the enactment of the discounting requirement.[3]

7.2   The Industry: Descriptive Statistics

The lines of insurance that are offered by property-casualty insurance companies can be described in a number of different ways. For the purposes of this paper, we use the five lines set out in table 7.1, which are the categories that were used by the industry before 1989.

3. The requirement that property-casualty loss reserves be discounted for federal income tax purposes was first proposed in June 1983 in a hearing before the Senate Finance Committee. The proposal was put forward both by the Treasury Department (see Chapoton 1983) and by the General Accounting Office (see Mavens 1983). Comments on the proposal were received at the same hearing from members of the insurance industry, including representatives of the American Insurance Association, the National Association of Independent Insurers, and the Alliance of American Insurers and representatives of a number of large insurance companies. The discounting requirement appeared then in 1984 as part of the Treasury Department's report to the president ("Treasury I"; see U.S. Treasury Department 1984). Subsequently, in President Reagan's 1985 tax-reform proposal ("Treasury II"; see U.S. Treasury Department 1985), a proposal was included that would have had the same effect as the discounting requirement proposed by the Treasury Department and by the General Accounting Office. Earlier in 1985, the GAO had published its report calling for, among other changes, the introduction of the discounting requirement (see U.S. General Accounting Office 1985). Finally, a provision quite similar to the Treasury Department and GAO proposals was enacted as part of TRA86. The proposal to reduce the top marginal corporate income tax rate from 46 percent ultimately to 33 percent also appeared in both Treasury I and Treasury II.

In related research, Logue (1996) examines the extent to which, in the period leading up to TRA86, the news of these two tax-reform proposals—the discounting requirement and the reduction in corporate tax rates—may have affected insurers' loss-reserving decisions and, in turn, the pricing and availability of some lines of insurance. This period roughly corresponded in time with the so-called liability-insurance crisis of the mid-1980s.

Table 7.1   Line Abbreviations

MI	"Miscellaneous": farmowner's, homeowner's, and commercial multiple peril, ocean marine, aircraft (all perils), and boiler and machinery
AL	Automobile liability
WC	Workers' compensation
OL	Other liability
MM	Medical malpractice

Note: In the pre-1989 statements, data for these lines were reported in the following parts of Schedule P: 1A (automobile liability), 1B (other liability), 1C (medical malpractice), 1D (workers' compensation), and 1E (farmowner's multiple peril, homeowner's multiple peril, commercial multiple peril, ocean marine, aircraft [all perils], and boiler and machinery) (our "miscellaneous" line). After 1988, the same lines were reported as follows: 1A (homeowner's/farmowner's), 1B (private passenger automobile liability/medical), 1C (commercial automobile/truck liability/medical), 1D (workers' compensation), 1E (commercial multiple peril), 1F (medical malpractice), 1G (special liability [ocean marine, aircraft (all perils), boiler and machinery]), 1H (other liability). To put the later data in the same categories as the earlier data, lines 1B (privage passenger automobile liability/medical) and 1C (commercial automobile/truck liability/medical) of the 1989 form were added together to match the pre-1989 line 1A (automobile liability). Lines 1A (homeowner's/farmowner's), 1E (commercial multiple peril), and 1G (special liability [ocean marine, aircraft (all perils), and boiler and machinery]) from 1989 were added together to match the pre-1989 line 1E (farmowner's multiple peril, homeowner's multiple peril, commercial multiple peril, ocean marine, aircraft [all perils], and boiler and machinery). The remaining lines of insurance (workers' compensation, medical malpractice, and other liability) were the same for both years, differing only by part designation within the schedule. Before 1989, the part designations were 1B (other liability), 1C (medical malpractice), and 1D (workers' compensation). In 1989, the designations were 1D (workers' compensation), 1F (medical malpractice), and 1H (other liability).

The lines are arranged in order of length of tail. Thus, the shortest-tailed line is the category *miscellaneous,* and the longest-tailed line is the category *medical malpractice.* We have used these line designations to organize the descriptive statistics in table 7.2, which is meant to provide a general picture of the total property-casualty market, specifically, of how much of the overall market is represented by each line of insurance.

Another way of illustrating the differing tail lengths, and the actual pattern of loss payments, for various lines is to use loss profiles. In table 7.3, we provide the standard loss profiles, for all five lines, that have been promulgated by the Treasury Department to be used in computing discounted loss reserves, as required by TRA86. The columns show, for each line, the assumed percentage of the incurred losses (and loss expenses) that have been paid by the end of the year specified in the row, relative to the accident year. The figures in boldface type indicate the years in which the year-to-year change in paid losses exceeds 4 percent of the total. Thus, table 7.3 displays clearly the different lengths of tails of the five lines. Table 7.4 shows the implied average time to payout for each line.

Table 7.5 shows the "loss ratios" for the industry, by line by accident year. The loss ratio is simply the ratio of incurred losses (including loss-adjustment expense) to earned premiums. Because of the deferral of payout under the long-tailed lines, one would expect their equilibrium loss ratios to be higher

Table 7.2 Property and Casualty Insurance, Aggregate Statistics for 1993 (amounts reported in thousands)

Line	Premiums Earned (RY 1993)	% Distribution of Premiums	Total Losses and Loss Expenses Incurred (AY 1993 reported in 1993)	Ratio of Losses to Premiums	Unpaid Loss Reserves for All Accident Years	% Distribution of Reserves
MI	41,502,943	25	33,299,942	80	36,522,008	14
AL	69,735,926	43	62,136,202	89	83,733,227	32
WC	30,311,809	19	24,733,279	82	67,077,085	26
OL	17,018,772	10	14,104,169	83	53,819,285	21
MM	4,278,988	3	5,316,464	124	19,560,549	8
Total	162,848,438	100	139,590,056	86	260,712,154	100

Source: Authors' calculations based on *Best's Aggregates and Averages* (various years).

Note: RY = reporting year. AY = accident year.

Table 7.3   **Treasury-Specified Loss Profiles, 1988, by Line**

	MI	AU	WC	OL	MM
AY + 0	**56**	**34**	**26**	**9**	3
AY + 1	**79**	**65**	**55**	**25**	**13**
AY + 2	**86**	**80**	**68**	**40**	**23**
AY + 3	**91**	**89**	**76**	**55**	**36**
AY + 4	94	**94**	**80**	**66**	**45**
AY + 5	97	97	84	**75**	**54**
AY + 6	98	98	85	**80**	**61**
AY + 7	98	98	87	**84**	**67**
AY + 8	99	99	89	87	**72**
AY + 9	99	99	89	88	75
AY + 10	99	99	90	89	78
AY + 11	100	100	91	90	81
AY + 12	100	100	91	91	83
AY + 13	100	100	92	92	86
AY + 14	100	100	92	93	89
AY + 15	100	100	100	100	100

Source: Treasury Department regulations. Table extended beyond AY + 10 according to Treasury rule of thumb and truncated at AY + 15.

Note: Figures given in boldface type indicate the years in which the year-to-year change in paid losses exceeds 4 percent of the total. AY = accident year.

Table 7.4   **Average Time to Payout, by Line**

Line	Average Time to Payout (years)
MI	1.2
AU	1.6
WW	3.1
OL	4.4
MM	6.3

Source: Authors' calculations on data from *Best's Aggregates and Averages* (1988).

than those of the short-tailed lines.[4] (The reference in the table to the "post-1988" lines relates to the way the statistics are presented in the annual reports; the aggregation of policies used in this table differs from the standard described in table 7.1 in that automobile liability is split into two lines, private passenger and commercial automobile.)

We should point out that there is an element of apples and oranges in table 7.5. For the earlier accident years and especially the shorter-tailed lines in those years, the loss ratios are effectively the final result. That is, the loss ratios can be understood to be no longer an estimate or prediction of future loss pay-

4. For an extended discussion of the determinants of equilibrium premiums, see Bradford and Logue (1998).

Table 7.5   **Loss Ratios by Accident Year (using post-1988 lines of insurance)**

Accident Year	Homeowner's/ Farmowner's (MI)	Private Passenger	Commercial Automobile	Workers' Compensation (WC)	Other Liability (OL)	Medical Malpractice (MM)
1980	.76	.78	.84	.72	.83	1.47
1981	.69	.83	.91	.73	.99	1.68
1982	.75	.85	.97	.82	1.21	1.70
1983	.76	.88	1.09	.93	1.45	1.71
1984	.74	.95	1.20	1.07	1.66	1.47
1985	.79	.97	1.04	1.04	1.22	1.21
1986	.67	.92	.79	.95	.64	.81
1987	.65	.91	.75	.91	.56	.72
1988	.68	.91	.79	.93	.62	.75
1989	.83	.93	.84	.94	.70	.82
1990	.78	.92	.81	.93	.75	.98
1991	.86	.87	.80	.89	.78	1.13
1992	1.24	.88	.80	.86	.80	1.21
1993	.83	.90	.83	.82	.83	1.24
1994	.89	.90	.84	.80	.84	1.23

Source: Best's Aggregates and Averages (various years).

outs over premiums earned but rather an accounting of past payouts over premiums earned. For the later accident years, however, especially the longer-tailed lines in those years, the loss ratios continue to have a substantial element of uncertainty; thus, those ratios continue to be, to a substantial extent, in the nature of forecasts.

7.3   Tax Incentives Bearing on Reserves

As discussed above, when an insurance company writes a policy, it acquires, in addition to a right to receive a premium payment or series of such payments, an obligation to make a stream of future loss payments (dependent on contingencies). For the purpose of computing its annual underwriting income, the insurer starts with premiums accrued during the year. From this amount is deducted the amount of accrued premiums not yet earned (because they are for coverage to be provided in the next year); these accrued premiums are added to the "unearned premium reserve account," and to this amount is added the amount of premiums accrued in the past but earned in the current year, which premiums are subtracted from the unearned-premium-reserve account. (The details of the treatment of the unearned-premium-reserve account in the derivation of taxable income were changed by TRA86. For a discussion, see Bradford and Logue [1998].) The net result is the "earned-premium" income. The second major step in determining underwriting income for a given reporting period is the deduction for "losses incurred" during the period. This deduction consists of two parts: a deduction for the losses that were actually paid during the period and a deduction for the increase in the unpaid-losses account (i.e., the loss reserves). (Recall that the loss reserves are the losses that the company has reason to believe have been incurred but have not yet been paid.)

With the passage of time, that is, as the insurer moves from one reporting year to the next, the insurer accumulates information about the policies that it has written in each accident year. As indemnity payments are made under those policies, the insurer shifts losses from the "unpaid" to the "paid" accounts. In addition, the insurer updates its estimates of total losses incurred under those policies. These two changes are implemented in the accounts by a combination of a deduction for the losses paid during the year and a deduction for any increase in loss reserves during the year. The latter is simply the difference between the end-of-current-reporting-year reserve and the end-of-previous-reporting-year reserve.

To see how this works, consider the case in which, in the current reporting year, there is no change in the estimate of the total losses incurred for a given past accident year—call it "accident year X." In such a case, the unpaid loss account (loss reserves) will be reduced by the amount of loss expense paid during the year. Therefore, the deduction for losses paid during the current reporting year with respect to accident year X will be exactly offset by a *negative* deduction for the change in reserves. Because the end-of-current-reporting-year reserve for accident year X will be lower than the end-of-previous-reporting-year reserve for that accident year *by exactly the amount of losses paid during the year,* accident year X will have no underwriting-income consequences for the current reporting year.

Now consider the case in which, in the current reporting year, there is a change in the estimated total loss incurred with respect to a past accident year—again, call it accident year X. Such a change will result in a *further* change in the end-of-current-reporting-year loss reserve for that accident year, that is, a change in addition to the normal reduction in that reserve to account for paid losses. The point can be put more generally. If, in the current reporting year, an insurer increases its estimate of total incurred losses for a given accident year (i.e., the insurer strengthens that accident-year reserve), there will be a corresponding deduction from income in that reporting year in precisely the amount of the strengthening, holding all else constant. The flip side is also true. If the insurer reduces its estimate of total incurred losses for a given accident year (a reserve weakening), there will be a corresponding inclusion in income for that reporting year.

Thus, the sequence of deductions and inclusions in income that must be made by an insurer with respect to the loss side of any insurance policy is identical to the sequence of adjustments to the losses-incurred account for that policy—which, recall, represents the estimated total loss (paid and unpaid) with respect to that policy. Of course, the first time that the losses incurred for a given accident year in a given line show up in the insurer's accounts is at the end of the accident year. That would be the only year in which the accident year and the reporting year overlap. After that, any net deduction or inclusion in a given reporting year with respect to a given accident year would be the result of a revision in the total incurred losses for that accident year. If there is a fixed point in this sequence of adjustments, it would be when enough time has passed so that all liabilities with respect to an accident line and year are finally settled and the final losses-incurred number is known. Working back from that point, any variation in the incurred-loss estimate at the end of the previous reporting year results in offsetting changes in the income in the two adjoining reporting years.

So, whether intentional or not, an overstatement of total incurred losses at the end of the next-to-last reporting year results in a deduction from that year's income that is balanced by an equal extra inclusion in income in the last reporting year. This is the mechanical result of the income calculation: deduction of the sum of losses paid during the year and the excess of the end-of-year loss reserve (zero in the last year) over the end-of-previous-year loss reserve. The same reasoning applies as one works back from year to year. A decision to overstate loss reserves by one dollar in one year implies—other things, including future loss reserves, equal—a reduction in this year's income by a dollar and the addition of a dollar to the following year's income.

To this point in the analysis, we have assumed that loss reserves are not discounted to present value. In the case of discounted reserves, the analysis is slightly different. In this case, a one-dollar overstatement of reserves in one reporting year produces an extra deduction of less than a dollar in that year, namely, the discounted value of the future payment implied by the addition to total estimated payouts.[5] Consequently, adding a dollar to the total incurred-loss estimate in a year results in a deduction from income in that year of some amount less than a dollar. As in the undiscounted case, however, a reduction in this year's income by a dollar implies—other things, including future loss reserves, equal—the addition of a dollar to the following year's income. The deferral effect of overstatement is the same, but the deferral per dollar of overstatement is reduced, relative to the undiscounted case.

The tax and accounting-income consequences of the choice of stated reserves in a given reporting year can thus be fully summarized by the implications for the income calculations in that year and in the next year. To determine the tax incentive to add a dollar to the incurred-loss estimate in a year, we therefore need to know the tax rate applicable in the adjacent years as well as an estimate of the discount rate applied by companies to variation in the cash flow due to changes in the tax liabilities in the adjacent years.

The incentive bearing on the reserving decision depends on the company's anticipation of future tax rates. The rate applicable to a given company will

5. The factor by which undiscounted reserves are multiplied to get discounted reserves depends on the profile of remaining payments to be made under a policy. It will tend to be larger the later in the life of a policy. However, if the payment profile is "humped," the factor applicable to a given line and accident year could actually decline from one year to the next.

Table 7.6   Anticipated Federal Income Tax Rates

	Tax Rates in	
Anticipated in	Current Year	Next Year
1976	.48	.48
1977	.48	.48
1978	.48	.46
1979	.46	.46
1980	.46	.46
1981	.46	.46
1982	.46	.46
1983	.46	.46
1984	.46	.46
1985	.46	.46
1986	.46	.40
1987	.40	.34
1988	.34	.34
1989	.34	.34
1990	.34	.34
1991	.34	.34
1992	.34	.34
1993	.35	.35
1994	.35	.35

Source: Commerce Clearing House (1996, vol. 1, sec. 3265.0129–.0139).

depend on its particular circumstances as well as the tax law. For the case of a company that is continually subject to tax at the full tax rate, the variation in taxes depends on the statute. Statutory corporate tax rates have changed from time to time. Sometimes tax legislation specifies the future course of tax rates. For purposes of this exercise, we assume that companies know the tax rate applicable in the current reporting year and for future years believe the tax rates specified in legislation as of the end of the current reporting year. Table 7.6 sets out the tax rates used in our calculations for each year.[6]

To calculate the net benefit from deferral, we require a discount rate. In table 7.7, we have used the yield, after taxes, on one-year Treasury bonds to determine the addition to the after-tax bottom line in a given year of adding a dollar to loss reserves (holding future reserves constant). Thus, the tax payoff to insurers of overstating reserves has generally been a function of prevailing interest rates and of anticipated reductions in tax rates. The overstatement payoffs in 1986 and 1987, for example, were notably high by historical standards ($0.07 and $0.06 per dollar, respectively) owing to the anticipated reduction in corporate tax rates.

Given the assumptions about insurers' expectations regarding tax rates and

6. Logue (1996) explores the possibility that tax-rate changes may have been anticipated by insurers before 1986 and so influenced their behavior at an earlier point.

Table 7.7   Tax Deferral Gain Due to One Extra Reserve Dollar

Reporting Year	Discount Factor	Tax Saving This Year	Extra Tax Next Year	Before-Tax Interest Rate	After-Tax Interest Rate	Current Value of Next Year's Extra Tax	Present-Value Payoff per Extra Dollar of Reserves
1976	1.00	.48	.48	5.88	3.06	.47	.01
1977	1.00	.48	.48	6.09	3.17	.47	.01
1978	1.00	.48	.46	8.34	4.50	.44	.04
1979	1.00	.46	.46	10.65	5.75	.43	.03
1980	1.00	.46	.46	12.00	6.48	.43	.03
1981	1.00	.46	.46	14.80	7.99	.43	.03
1982	1.00	.46	.46	12.28	6.63	.43	.03
1983	1.00	.46	.46	9.58	5.17	.44	.02
1984	1.00	.46	.46	10.91	5.89	.43	.03
1985	1.00	.46	.46	8.42	4.55	.44	.02
1986	1.00	.46	.40	6.46	3.87	.39	.07
1987	.80	.32	.27	6.77	4.47	.26	.06
1988	.80	.27	.27	7.65	5.05	.26	.01
1989	.80	.27	.27	8.53	5.63	.26	.01
1990	.80	.27	.27	7.89	5.21	.26	.01
1991	.80	.27	.27	5.86	3.87	.26	.01
1992	.80	.27	.27	3.89	2.57	.27	.01
1993	.80	.28	.28	3.41	2.22	.27	.01
1994	.80	.28	.28			.28	.00

Source: Interest rates, Federal Reserve Board data, gopher://gopher.town.hall.org/other/fed/h_15; discount factors as described in Bradford and Logue (1998).

Note: One-year interest rates are the simple arithmetic means of one-year Treasury bond yields during the year. The 1986 row refers to strengthening of past years. The factor for 1985 ignores the fresh-start rule (see the text). The discount factors after 1986 are the simple average of the 1987 factors for AY + 0 to AY + 10. (AY = accident year.)

interest rates in table 7.6, the overstatement payoff described in table 7.7 would apply to any reserving decisions *except those affected by the fresh-start rule.* The fresh start changes the story. For those reserves to which the fresh start was expected by insurers to apply, the reserve-overstatement payoff was increased beyond the amounts described in table 7.7. To what reserves might insurers have plausibly expected the fresh start to apply? TRA86 specifically provides that the fresh start applies to all property-casualty reserves outstanding as of the end of 1986, with the following exception: it does not apply to any reserve strengthening reported in 1986. Thus, for any reserve strengthening made in 1986, the analysis in table 7.7 would apply. But the analysis is different for any new policies written in 1986 and (to the extent that companies anticipated TRA86's introduction of discounted reserves and of the fresh-start rule) any new policies written in (or strengthening reported in) 1985 or earlier.

Under the fresh-start rule, for example, the present value of one dollar of reserve overstatement in the 1986 tax year for the 1986 accident year depends on the line of insurance. This is because the effect of the rule is to offset a deduction of a dollar in 1986 with an inclusion of the discount factor in 1987. The discount factor is larger the longer the tail of the insurance in question (because the payments are more distant in the future). Therefore, the tax-reducing value of an extra dollar of reserves is larger for the longer-tailed lines. Table 7.8 spells out the details. The fresh-start rule substantially increased the incentive to overstate reserves in 1986 (for policies covering 1986), compared with the incentives resulting from the declining tax-rate effect taken by itself. For medical malpractice, for example, an extra dollar of reserves on a new policy, holding constant the end-of-1987 reserves, was worth the equivalent of $0.19 in after-tax income in 1986. A comparable incentive applied to reserves for accident years 1985 and earlier at the end of the 1985 reporting year, to the extent that the fresh-start rule was anticipated then.

It is easy to become confused about the various tax incentives. To review, the incentive effect of the change in tax rates applied to all reserves at the end of 1986 and 1987. Strictly speaking, the rate reductions for 1987 and 1988 did not imply any extra incentive to add to reserves in 1985 since the same benefit could be obtained by strengthening reserves in 1986. (If strengthening reserves is itself costly, for example, if it attracts extra regulatory scrutiny, then the extra payoff to reserves at the end of 1986 would have an *indirect* incentive effect on reserving in 1985 or even earlier.) The incentive effect owing to the fresh-start rule (combined with the rate-change effect) applied to new reserves established during 1986 (i.e., to reserves for policies covering accident year 1986). The fresh-start effect also had a *direct* effect on the incentive to add to reserves (for all accident years) at the end of 1985 to the extent that the new tax policy was anticipated. In this case, the extraordinary tax benefit was the result of carrying the higher reserves into 1987.

Table 7.9 gives an idea of the magnitudes involved in the fresh-start rule as it affected losses incurred in 1986. (For a discussion of the predicted effect of

Table 7.8   Gain from an Extra Dollar of Reserves of New Policies in 1986: The Effect of the Fresh-Start Rule

Line	Discount Factor	Tax Saving This Year	Extra Tax Next Year	Before-Tax Interest Rate	After-Tax Interest Rate	Current Value of Next Year's Extra Tax	Payoff per Extra Dollar of Reserves
MI	.89	.46	.36	6.46	3.87	.34	.12
AL	.89	.46	.36	6.46	3.87	.34	.12
WC	.81	.46	.32	6.46	3.87	.31	.15
OL	.77	.46	.31	6.46	3.87	.30	.16
MM	.69	.46	.28	6.46	3.87	.27	.19

Sources: Interest rates, Federal Reserve Board data, gopher://gopher.town.hall.org/other/fed/h_15; discount factors as described in Bradford and Logue (1998).

Note: One-year interest rates are the simple arithmetic means of one-year Treasury bond yields. The discount factors are the simple average of the 1987 factors for AY + 0 to AY + 10. (AY = accident year.)

Table 7.9   Losses Incurred in 1986 and Fresh Start (loss reserves for accident year 1986, reported in 1986, amount reported in thousands)

Line	Reserves for AY 1986 at Year-End 1986 (1)	Premiums Earned for AY 1986 (2)	Loss Incurred in AY 1986 Reported in 1986 (3)	Payoff to Extra Dollar of Reserves (%) (4)	Estimated Saving Due to Fresh-Start Rule (col. 1 × col. 4) (5)	Estimated Saving from 10% Increase in Incurred-Loss Estimate (10% of col. 3 × col. 4) (6)
MI	9,705,812	32,284,313	19,206,091	12	1,144,212	226,419
AL	23,500,447	41,133,219	33,550,013	12	2,740,056	391,179
WC	12,019,927	19,039,001	15,376,597	15	1,779,845	227,688
OL	11,841,432	16,188,897	12,262,955	16	1,946,029	201,530
MM	3,450,089	3,509,158	3,500,588	19	671,926	68,176
Total	60,517,707	112,154,588	83,896,244		8,282,068	1,114,993

Source: Authors' calculations based on *Best's Aggregates and Averages* (various years).

Note: AY = accident year.

the fresh-start rule on premiums, assuming no variation in any tax-induced bias in reported loss reserves, see Bradford and Logue [1998].)

An implication of this analysis of the tax incentives bearing on the reserving decision is that, apart from 1986 and possibly for strengthening in 1985, the marginal payoff to an extra dollar of reserves is the same for all lines and accident years. That is, with the exception of the fresh-start effect, any difference in tax-motivated reserving behavior from line to line or accident year to accident year must be related to the differences in the regulatory, financial, and other nontax consequences of variation in the reported loss reserves.

7.4   Reserving Seen in Industry Data

Industry aggregate data are suggestive of behavior consistent with tax-influenced reserving. Figures 7.1–7.5 attempt to capture the pattern of reserve strengthening that occurred in the various lines (running from short to long tailed). The graphs show the ratio of (*a*) the incurred loss estimate at the end of each year after the accident year to (*b*) the estimate at the end of the accident year (i.e., the first reported figure). All the curves start at one. A rising link in a curve indicates that the reserve for the given accident year was strengthened in the reporting year in question. In that sense, it means that the accident-year reserve was understated in the prior year. A falling link in a curve indicates reserve weakening for that accident year in the reporting year in question. In that sense, it means that the accident-year reserve was overstated in the prior year. The augmented tax incentive to bias reserves would imply, for pre-1985

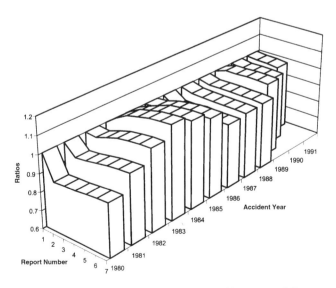

Fig. 7.1   Incurred-loss estimates by years since accident year: MI
Source: Authors' calculations based on data from *Best's Aggregates and Averages* (various years).

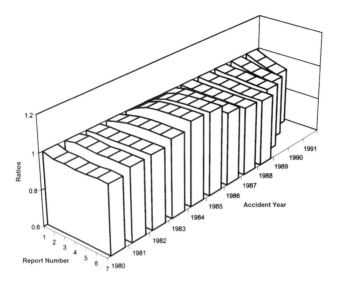

Fig. 7.2 Incurred-loss estimates by years since accident year: AL
Source: Authors' calculations based on data from *Best's Aggregates and Averages* (various years).

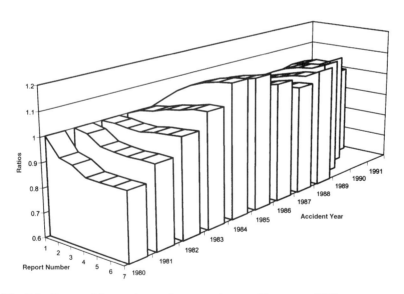

Fig. 7.3 Incurred-loss estimates by years since accident year: WC
Source: Authors' calculations based on data from *Best's Aggregates and Averages* (various years).

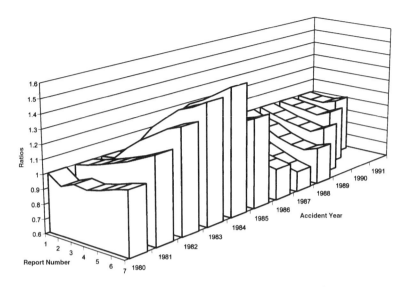

Fig. 7.4   Incurred-loss estimates by years since accident year: OL
Source: Authors' calculations based on data from *Best's Aggregates and Averages* (various years).

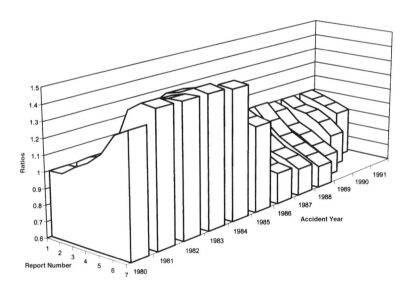

Fig. 7.5   Incurred-loss estimates by years since accident year: MM
Source: Authors' calculations based on data from *Best's Aggregates and Averages* (various years).

accident years, rising links corresponding to reporting years 1985 and later. For the 1986 and 1987 accident years, and for 1985 to the extent that the restriction on the fresh-start rule was anticipated, one would expect that a tax-induced overstatement of initial reported losses incurred, followed by subsequent reserve weakening (downward links) as the policies matured toward their ultimate payout. For accident years 1988 and later, one might expect a reversion to something like the pattern of earlier years.

Since the incurred losses are subject to considerable uncertainty, it is not possible to draw conclusions from the industry data with great confidence. The pictures, however, appear broadly consistent with the description just given. In the 1986 accident year, especially in the long-tailed lines (see figs. 7.4 and 7.5), there is a substantial shift in the downward direction in the curves—suggesting overstatement of the initial 1986 reserves that subsequently required weakening. Note also the 1985 accident year for the long-tailed lines. That is the first accident year to show a substantial change in reserving direction; that is, although the 1985 reserves ultimately had to be strengthened, they had to be strengthened by considerably less than the 1984 accident-year reserves. Until 1985, the degree of strengthening in the long-tailed lines had been increasing for several years.

The picture after 1987 is less obviously consistent with our hypothesis. We would have expected the reserves in those years, when the tax incentive was no longer so strong, to return to the pre-1986 patterns. But that did not happen. The post-1987 accident-year reserves were, like the 1986 reserve, initially overstated (thus the downward character in the curves). There is no obvious tax-related explanation for this trend. For some reason, over the course of one or two years, the property-casualty insurance industry became more conservative in its reserving decisions, and, what is difficult to explain (at least from a tax-avoidance perspective), the change in this tendency stuck. One possible explanation is that, putting aside the temporary tax incentive to overstate reserves created by the fresh-start rule, there was generally a greater incentive to overstate reserves after TRA86 than before simply because, after the act, property-casualty insurers had more taxable income. That is, before the act, because of the undiscounted reserving, among other things, the insurance industry in the aggregate had relatively little taxable income anyway, whereas, after the act, the industry had considerably more income that was potentially taxable.[7] Another possibility, of course, is that—for reasons unrelated to taxes—insurers became more conservative in their estimates of loss reserves.

Table 7.10 attempts to capture the extent of conservatism in the initial incurred-loss report in the form of the ratio of the report five years later to the initial report. So, for example, according to the table, the incurred loss figure for automobile liability for accident year 1985 was up by 7 percent at the end of 1990, relative to the initially announced level. Relatively high numbers mean

7. For further discussion of this possibility, see Logue (1996).

Table 7.10   **Incurred-Loss Estimates Five Years Out (summary: ratio of losses, report 5 to report 1)**

Accident Year	MI	AL	WC	OL	MM
1980	.88	.98	.88	.99	1.18
1981	.97	1.01	.94	1.12	1.39
1982	1.05	1.01	1.00	1.24	1.40
1983	1.11	1.04	1.06	1.36	1.41
1984	1.08	1.07	1.14	1.38	1.27
1985	1.05	1.07	1.13	1.16	1.21
1986	.96	1.02	1.07	.87	.86
1987	.98	.99	1.04	.81	.85
1988	.98	.98	1.07	.85	.83
1989	1.03	.98	1.08	.90	.79
1990	.99	.95	1.09	1.00	.81

Source: Authors' calculations based on data from *Best's Aggregates and Averages* (various years).

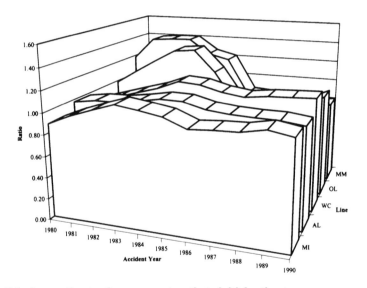

Fig. 7.6   Loss estimates five years out: ratio to initial estimates
Source: Authors' calculations based on data from *Best's Aggregates and Averages* (various years).

relatively low initial reserves. Particularly for the long-tailed lines, there appears to be a break at 1986. Figure 7.6 displays the same information graphically.

Table 7.11 presents data on the extent of reserve strengthening (relating to past accident years) in reporting years 1983–94. Each cell reports, for that reporting year, the average over the five most recent accident years of the ratio of

Table 7.11   **Average Year-to-Year Increase in Incurred-Loss Reports, Reporting Years 1983–94**

Line	1983	1984	1985	1986	1987	1988	1989	1990	1991	1992	1993	1994
MI	.02	.12	.13	.09	.08	.04	.04	.00	.00	.00	–.01	–.05
AL	–.01	.00	.05	.01	.02	.01	.01	.00	–.01	–.04	–.04	–.05
WC	–.05	.00	.01	.04	.04	.06	.03	.04	.06	.05	.00	.05
OL	.01	.08	.11	.10	.09	.04	.03	.00	–.03	–.05	–.04	.08
MM	.03	.06	.26	.08	.02	.02	.08	–.08	–.08	–.05	–.08	–.09
Average	.00	.05	.11	.06	.05	.03	.04	–.01	–.01	–.02	–.03	–.01

Source: Authors' calculations based on data from *Best's Aggregates and Averages* (various years).

Note: Cells show average for the five most recent accident years of the fractional increase in the sum of paid and unpaid losses. (For 1983, three accident years are included and, for 1984, four accident years.)

the increase in the total incurred loss estimate (i.e., the sum of paid and unpaid losses) to its previous level. (Because the data extend back only to 1980, for 1983 three past years are accounted for, and for 1984 four past years are accounted for.) Finally, we have noted that the incentive to *strengthen* reserves on past accident years was strongest in 1985 to the extent that the fresh-start rule was anticipated. Otherwise, the incentive effects of the tax-rate changes from 1985 to 1986 and from 1986 to 1987 reflected in table 7.7 above apply. The bottom line of the table presents the simple averages of the averages. Here, one sees a pattern generally consistent with the influence of the tax incentives, including something of a reversion to roughly zero strengthening in the more recent years.

7.5 Concluding Comments

In this paper, we have explained how the federal income tax rules, and especially changes in those rules, have combined with financial market circumstances (interest rates) to create incentives bearing on property-casualty insurers' decisions regarding the level of loss reserves to report. We find that these incentives have varied substantially over time. In particular, transition effects due to the Tax Reform Act of 1986 created unusually large incentives to overstate reserves in reporting years 1985–87. We would emphasize that, because they amount to forecasts of quite variable quantities, reserves are inevitably subject to correction over time. Furthermore, taxes are not the only sources of biasing incentives that may vary from time to time. Still, the picture in aggregate industry data that we have assembled is broadly consistent with the tax-motivated reserving hypothesis. In work in progress, we hope to tease additional insights about reserving from the quantitative record.

References

Ansley, Craig F. 1979. Automobile liability insurance reserve adequacy and the effect of inflation. *Chartered Property and Casualty Underwriters Journal* 31:105–12.
Balcarek, Rafal J. 1975. Loss reserve deficiencies and underwriting results. *Best's Review-Property Casualty* 76:21–22.
A. M. Best Co. Various years. *Best's aggregates and averages.* Morristown, N.J.
Bradford, David F., and Kyle D. Logue. 1998. The effects of tax-law changes on property-casualty insurance prices. In *The economics of property-casualty insurance,* ed. David F. Bradford. Chicago: University of Chicago Press.
Chapoton, John E. 1983. Statement of John E. Chapoton, Assistant Secretary for Tax Policy, Hearing on the Taxation of Property Casualty Insurance Companies, Senate Finance Committee. *Congressional Record,* 98th Cong., 1st sess., 13 June, 53–54.
Commerce Clearing House. 1996. *Standard federal tax reporter.* Chicago.
Cummins, J. David, and Elizabeth Grace. 1992. Tax management and investment strategies of property-liability insurers. *Journal of Banking and Finance* 18:43–72.

Dascher, Paul E., and Malcolm, Robert E. 1970. A note on income smoothing in the chemical industry. *Journal of Accounting Research* 8:253–59.

Fama, Eugene F. 1980. Agency problems and the theory of the firm. *Journal of Political Economy* 88:288–307.

Forbes, Steven W. 1970. Loss reserving performance within the regulatory framework. *Journal of Risk and Insurance* 37:527–36.

Grace, Elizabeth V. 1990. Property-liability insurer reserve errors: A theoretical and empirical analysis. *Journal of Risk and Insurance* 51:28–46.

Harrington, Scott E. 1988. Price and profits in the liability insurance market. In *Liability: Perspectives and policy,* ed. Robert E. Litan and Clifford Winston. Washington, D.C.: Brookings.

Jensen, Michael C., and William H. Meckling. 1976. Theory of the firm: Managerial behavior, agency costs and ownership structure. *Journal of Financial Economics* 3:305–60.

Koch, Bruce. 1981. Income smoothing: An experiment. *Accounting Review* 56:574–86.

Lambert, Richard A. 1984. Income smoothing as rational equilibrium behavior. *Accounting Review* 59:604–18.

Logue, Kyle D. 1996. Toward a tax-based explanation of the liability insurance crisis: A case study in the collateral effects of tax reform. *University of Virginia Law Review* 82:895–959.

Mavens, Harry S. 1983. Statement of Harry S. Mavens, Assistant Comptroller General for Program Evaluation, Hearing on the Taxation of Property Casualty Insurance Companies, Senate Finance Committee. *Congressional Record,* 98th Cong., 1st sess., 13 June, 68.

McNichols, Maureen, and G. Peter Wilson. 1988. Evidence of earnings management from the provision of bad debts. *Journal of Accounting Research* 26:1–40.

Mooney, Sean, and Larry Cohen. 1991. *Basic concepts of accounting and taxation of property/casualty insurance companies.* New York: Insurance Information Institute Press.

Moses, O. Douglas. 1987. Income smoothing and incentives: Empirical test using accounting changes. *Accounting Review* 62:358–77.

Peterson, Timothy M. 1981. *Loss reserving: Property-casualty insurance.* Cleveland: Ernst & Whinney.

Petroni, Kathy R. 1992. Optimistic reporting in the property-casualty insurance industry. *Journal of Accounting and Economics* 15:485–508.

Salzmann, Ruth. 1974. Estimated liabilities for losses and loss adjustment expenses. In *Property-liability insurance accounting,* ed. R. W. Strain. Kansas City, Mo.: Insurance Accounting and Statistical Association.

Scholes, Myron J., G. Peter Wilson, and Mark A. Wolfson. 1990. Tax planning, regulatory capital planning, and financial reporting strategy for commercial banks. *Review of Financial Studies* 3, no. 4:625–50.

Slemrod, Joel. 1992. *Do taxes matter?* Cambridge, Mass.: MIT Press.

Smith, Barry D. 1980. An analysis of auto liability loss reserves underwriting results. *Journal of Risk and Insurance* 47:305–20.

Troxel, Terri, and George Bouchie. 1990. *Property-liability insurance accounting and finance.* 3d ed. Malvern, Pa.: American Institute for Property and Liability Underwriters.

U.S. General Accounting Office. 1985. Congress should consider changing federal income taxation of the property/casualty insurance industry. GAO/GGD-85-10. Washington, D.C.: U.S. Government Printing Office, March.

U.S. Treasury Department. 1984. Tax reform for fairness, simplicity, and economic growth. Washington, D.C.: U.S. Government Printing Office, November.

———. 1985. The president's tax proposals to the Congress for fairness, growth, and simplicity. Washington, D.C.: U.S. Government Printing Office, May.

Weiss, Mary. 1985. A multivariate analysis of loss reserving estimates in property-liability insurance companies. *Journal of Risk and Insurance* 52:199–221.

White, Gary. 1970. Discretionary accounting decisions and income normalization. *Journal of Accounting Research* 8:260–73.

Comment   Ross J. Davidson Jr.

When Ken Froot asked me to discuss this paper, I was quick to remind him that I am neither a reserving actuary nor a tax expert. He was either desperate for another discussant or thought that my involvement in capital management, financial exposure management, and insurance regulatory capital issues over the past few years could add a unique perspective to this topic.

But I must admit to an agenda in agreeing to discuss this paper. I am currently coordinating the Technical Advisory Group to the National Association of Insurance Commissioners (NAIC) Catastrophe Reserve Subgroup. This group is composed of approximately forty individuals who represent insurers, insurance brokers, catastrophe-modeling firms, investment banks, accounting, legal, and actuarial firms, and federal government agencies. They are a collection of very talented people, with broadly ranging expertise in actuarial science, tax, accounting, economics, capital markets, and state and federal regulatory affairs. We are charged with advising a group of state regulatory officials who represent the NAIC on the rationale, appropriate design, economic effects, and implementation of a reserve for future catastrophes. Annual additions to this reserve would be deductible for federal tax purposes, and drawdowns against the reserve would flow into taxable income, allowing smoothing of insurer results. Since this reserve is intended to provide insurers with incentives to write catastrophe coverage in hazard-prone areas while improving the financial strength of such insurers, I have more than a casual interest in any study that seeks to gauge the effect of changes in tax law on insurance reserving practices. The question is, Will the desired market and capital retention behavior be induced by tax incentives? Alternatively, if a reserve is mandated, can it be designed to be an efficient mechanism?

In fact, before I read Bradford and Logue's paper, I expected that it might be an answer to my prayers. The fundamental premise that income tax rules could influence reserving practices is closely related to the premise that reserving requirements that include tax incentives could influence an insurer's decisions to write hazard insurance. In fact, the very techniques by which Bradford

Ross Davidson is vice president of industry affairs at the United Services Automobile Association in San Antonio, Texas.

and Logue sought to ferret out past behaviors induced by tax-law changes could form the basis of predictive behavior models that could help shape and direct the debate on reserving practices that include tax incentives. What's more, maybe after our discussion more of you will want to develop a method to predict the influences on market behavior and financial strength of tax-deductible catastrophe reserves. As we have seen, Howard Kunreuther and the Wharton school are beginning to build some of the infrastructure models for such a project.

Now, more to the topic of the paper, I will not seek to comment on the elegance of the formulas or the correctness of the statistical analysis or even the authors' attempts to deal with imperfections in or paucity of the data, but I will attempt to address the relevance of the paper and its conclusions to insurance management and regulation and will point out some dimensions of the paper that, if broadened, might be useful to practitioners.

Occasionally, I look at the last page of a book before I begin reading it. This has the risk of being like eating dessert first. It can stimulate the taste buds, but the rest of the meal may seem somewhat pedestrian. But I must say that, when I read the conclusion of this paper first, I did not have that experience. In fact, I found the reading of the paper, the main course if you will, to be far more satisfying than the conclusion (the hoped-for dessert). Remember the feeling you get when you're engrossed in an intense television program (maybe your favorite soap or "Star Trek" mutant) that seems to be approaching the climatic scene, only to see *to be continued* appear on the screen. I relived that feeling as I read the conclusion of this paper. To paraphrase, while from an industrywide perspective some tax-induced reserving behavior can be detected, other influences may in fact be causing the observed behavior. Moreover, the jury is still out on how to adequately measure the tax-incentive-influenced behavior of industry sectors or individual insurers with different tax characteristics. Admittedly, this is a very complicated subject that must be simplified. However, any tax-motivated behavior must be evaluated in balance with other important nontax factors that influence management decisions. As the authors continue their exploration, I encourage them to evaluate the influence and correlation of some of the following factors on past and future reserving behavior.

Effect of Alternative Minimum Tax (AMT)

This change in the tax law had a profound effect on property and casualty insurers and may even have modulated any reserving behavior influenced by tax incentives. Before AMT, varying the mix of taxable and tax-exempt investment income was a dominant tax-minimization strategy. After AMT, property and casualty insurers could no longer use investment mix as a dominant tool to minimize taxable income. With the AMT, many property-casualty insurers became taxpayers for the first time, and, having their options limited, they may have looked more carefully at reserving practices to modulate their taxable income.

The Uncertainty Factor

As I collected comments on the paper from USAA's reserving actuary, she reminded me that her job is not all science. A significant amount of uncertainty is involved in reserve estimation, especially for the long tail lines that seem to have demonstrated some evidence of change in the target period. New developments in cost and litigation can often dramatically change perceptions and give the impression that someone may have been cooking the books when in fact more information had led to a different expectation of loss development.

Changes in development of claims on other liability, especially environmental and asbestos claims during the 1980s, are a good example. Around the same time as the 1986 tax act, there were dramatic changes in the perception of insurers writing these coverages as to the development of claims. Many insurers were adding massive amounts to their reserves as the specter of increased costs of litigation and recovery loomed. Another example is the effect on medical malpractice claims of recent lower health care costs and a trend to a less litigious environment.

The Effect of the Competitive Cycle and Interest Rates and Inflation on Underwriting

The early to mid-1980s were years of dramatic change in interest rates and inflation, both of which greatly affect profitability. The transition out of high inflation and interest rates to lower rates caused many insurers to reevaluate the role of underwriting results in the profitability equation. If insurers were prone to use the underwriting component to smooth earnings, they would have found the mid-1980s to be an especially tempting time to do so.

The Limited Opportunity for Undetected Reserve Manipulation in Short-Tail Lines like Automobile Liability, Homeowner's, and Marine

Because of their relatively short development life cycle, these lines may not have allowed for enough flexibility for undetected tax-incentive-influenced reserving variations. Longer tail lines do, owing to the sheer larger number of years that it takes you or others to know if you were wrong.

The Complex and Dynamic Regulatory Scene

Regulators use many more tools than the premium-to-surplus ratio to determine the financial health of their regulated companies. In fact, they look carefully at the development of reserves, believing that most insurers are habitually underreserved. The fact that an insurer strengthened reserves may play more heavily on a regulator's view of the financial strength of an insurer than is credited by the authors. The NAIC has a couple of sets of ratios, some of which more directly go to the point of reserve adequacy. Financial hazardous condition laws use the so-called ratios to provide regulators with the authority to intervene in a company's management if negative trends develop in income, surplus, liabilities, etc.

More recently, the advent of risk-based capital has become more important than the surplus liquidity ratio, although its effect may be relatively similar to the premium-to-surplus ratio.

Rating Agency and Stock Analysts' Perceptions Are Not Exclusively Based on Earnings

Like regulators, rating agencies and stock analysts are just as interested and were maybe uniformly more sophisticated in the 1980s in assessing the adequacy of reserves in the capital sufficiency equation.

While the authors note in their conclusion that the measures they explored and the data set that they used did not lend themselves well to effective in-sector analysis, nonetheless there are fairly significant differences in how segments of the property-casualty industry might behave. Some of those include the following:

Stock and Nonstock Insurers. Insurers organized as stockholder-held entities are driven by different motives. They seek to please Wall Street, are more inclined to shorter-term tactical decisions, and may view reported earnings with a higher priority than nonstocks. Having worked for both types of organizations in my career, I can testify to the vast difference.

Capital Rich and Capital Poor Insurers. This can be a major motivator since those insurers that may be perceived as having too much capital will tend to try to reserve robustly and be less sensitive to tax-law changes.

Large and Small Insurers. Some insurers write only in one state and as a result are not affected as much by national insurance regulatory schemes such as the NAIC.

Another effect to be considered is *the dominance of one or a few* insurers in the data. In industry studies, we have found that State Farm and several other insurers dominate the outcome of any industry trends. Techniques to normalize for size of insurers seem to yield vastly different results.

Back to "As the World Turns"

I believe that the exploration done here may form the basis of very important research as the national debate on catastrophe management begins to consider tax-incentive-influenced reserving for catastrophes. The foundation of that effort is that tax incentives will produce behavior on the part of insurers and other capital providers that will help deal with solvency and availability issues in the hazard-insurance market.

Several points may give us perspective on this issue. While catastrophe risk can be managed in a number of ways, the bottom line is that the capital to cover these risks must come from somewhere—ultimately either current or future policyholders (the primary risk takers) or current or future taxpayers. Tax policy can either support or work against appropriate accumulation and allocation of that capital. The current taxation of profits or losses from catastrophe coverage works against the optimal allocation of capital. Even the carryback and carryforward rules intended to allow for temporal variation of results are inadequate to deal with the time frames that we encounter in managing exposures to megacatastrophes. Catastrophe reserves must fit into the overall framework of capital for catastrophe-management tools. A good balance must be struck with other capital resources.

One implication of these points is that tax policy must be used very carefully when attempting to modify capital accumulation and allocation behavior.

If the techniques explored in this paper for ferreting out tax-motivated historical behavior can be refined and applied prospectively to predict future tax-incentive-influenced behavior, the nation will have been well served in the upcoming debate on tax-deductible catastrophe reserves. I hope that the script of the next episode in this to-be-continued development will address these issues. I also hope that many of you will be similarly inspired to explore this new and exciting frontier. It may help us practitioners carry the catastrophe-management ball a little farther down the field.

Comment   James R. Hines Jr.

This paper offers a very readable description of the U.S. tax treatment of insurance loss reserves, which is a significant accomplishment, and goes on to analyze the industry's reactions to the incentives introduced by the Tax Reform Act of 1986. The evidence is consistent with an important effect of tax incentives on loss-reserve accounting, although the available data are so limited that it is difficult to measure precisely the magnitude of the effect. Nevertheless, the notion that insurers adjust their loss reserves in response to changes in tax incentives is consistent with other well-documented aspects of firm behavior and is of sufficient importance to be worthy of careful investigation.

The nature of the insurance industry makes income measurement particularly challenging, which in turn makes the taxation of its income a very difficult exercise. The arcane and somewhat arbitrary tax rules that Bradford and Logue describe are required in order to implement a system that attempts to tax the annual flow of income in a line of business in which one year's activities

James R. Hines Jr. is associate professor of business economics and public policy at the University of Michigan Business School and a research associate of the National Bureau of Economic Research.

generate a stream of future liabilities the present value of which is highly uncertain. Since the 1977 publication of *Blueprints for Basic Tax Reform,* David Bradford has been a leading proponent of replacing the income tax with a consumption tax, maintaining that the consumption tax is not only more efficient than an income tax but also easier to administer. Bradford's recent work includes careful descriptions of various complex parts of the Internal Revenue Code that are always to the point but that also always subtly remind the reader of the tangled web that an income tax represents (see, e.g., Bradford 1986; and Ault and Bradford 1990). This paper falls squarely in that tradition.

It is instructive to consider the incentives facing those in the insurance industry who select loss-reserve levels for their firms. Firms generally have tax incentives to overstate their loss reserves even in the absence of legislative transitions such as those introduced by the 1986 act. Increasing reserves reduces present taxable income by the same amount that it increases future taxable income. This is a profitable exercise as long as there is a positive time value to money. The uniformly positive numbers that appear in the rightmost column of Bradford and Logue's table 7.7 in part reflect this incentive. In an extreme case, a firm with carte blanche to select its loss reserve level can, by increasing the loss reserve sufficiently each year, reduce to zero its tax liability in every period.

What prevents taxable firms from greatly increasing their loss-reserve levels and enjoying the accompanying tax benefits? It is probably the case that several considerations conspire to prevent them from doing so. The first of these is oversight by the Internal Revenue Service, which can disallow unwarranted deductions and which can make life unpleasant for taxpayers deemed to have taken unwarranted deductions. The second is oversight by shareholders and bondholders, who may have difficulty distinguishing tax-motivated reserve increases from those that reflect true economic risks to the firm. As a result, share values, bond ratings, and managerial compensation may fall in reaction to announcements of higher loss-reserve levels. The third is oversight by state regulators, who are concerned about the relative magnitudes of assets and liabilities and who may also interpret higher loss-reserve levels as reflecting greater liabilities. The fourth consideration is professional custom and other human habits that prevent firms from optimizing on all margins all the time.

Consequently, the responsiveness of reserve levels to tax changes appears against a background in which firms do not fully optimize against the tax system owing to one or more nontax frictions. The inability or unwillingness of insurers to adjust their reserve levels to minimize tax liabilities is analogous to widely observed behavior in which firms fail to take full advantage of their opportunities to overstate their expenses or understate their incomes in order to reduce tax liabilities. One example is the choice of inventory-accounting method. In the presence of any amount of inflation, firms reduce their tax liabilities by substituting last-in, first-out for first-in, first-out inventory accounting. In spite of this incentive, a significant number of firms persist in using first-in, first-out accounting. A second example concerns the choice of depreciation method for tax purposes. Accelerated depreciation schedules, when available, generally enhance the present value of depreciation allowances—but, in spite of this advantage, they are not universally employed. The case of depreciation allowances is all the more thought provoking in that there is no requirement (as there is in the case of inventory accounting and loss-reserve accounting) that the same methods must be used for both tax calculations and financial statements.

In spite of the likely presence of nontax frictions, the loss-reserve behavior documented by Bradford and Logue is broadly consistent with the tax incentives introduced by the 1986 act. Loss reserves rise at the same time that incentives to overstate them rise, doing so most visibly in the long-tailed lines of business in which one would expect to see the strongest reaction. It is, however, impossible to draw any strong statistical inferences from the behavior of a sample of just five lines of business around one event date (1986). Furthermore, the changing legal environment of the mid-1980s that was responsible for rising liability awards may itself have encouraged insurers to expand their loss reserves in a way that could appear to have been tax motivated. While the evidence is highly suggestive of tax-motivated behavior, it simultaneously reflects all other secular changes that influence insurance reserves.

Part of the attraction of studying the industry's reaction to events around 1986 is that doing so affords insight into the extent to which tax and nontax considerations influence reserve levels during unspectacular periods. A finding that reserve levels respond dramatically to tax changes in turn suggests that reserves are significantly overstated on a chronic basis owing to the tax incentive that arises from discounting. Since the paper in fact reports evidence that reserves react significantly to tax transitions, it follows that reserves in normal years typically overstate expected future liabilities. This inference in turn carries any number of implications for tax and regulatory policy as well as implications for the way in which financial markets should react to announcements of changes in loss reserves. So there is quite a bit of interesting work to be done in addition to this very useful analysis of reactions to the Tax Reform Act of 1986.

References

Ault, Hugh J., and David F. Bradford. 1990. Taxing international income: An analysis of the U.S. system and its economic premises. In *Taxation in the global economy,* ed. Assaf Razin and Joel Slemrod. Chicago: University of Chicago Press.

Bradford, David F. 1986. *Untangling the income tax.* Cambridge, Mass.: Harvard University Press.

Bradford, David F., and the U.S. Treasury Tax Policy Staff. 1977. *Blueprints for basic tax reform.* Arlington, Va.: Tax Analysts.

8   Courting Disaster?
The Transformation of Federal
Disaster Policy since 1803

David A. Moss

8.1   Introduction: Disasters in America, 1543–1993

Natural catastrophes have always plagued the residents of what are now the United States. One of the earliest disasters on record dates to 1543, when the explorer Hernando de Soto witnessed the full fury of the Mississippi River. According to Garcilaso de la Vega (1951, 554), who chronicled de Soto's voyage, "That which previously had been forests and fields was converted now into a sea, for from each bank the water extended across more than twenty leagues [about sixty miles] of terrain. All of this distance was navigable in canoes and nothing was visible except the pine needles and branches of the highest trees." The flood of 1543 surely affected the Native Americans who lived and hunted in the Mississippi valley at that time. But the human significance of this type of disaster was transformed as the density of population and settlement increased sharply with the arrival of the Europeans, the founding of a new nation, and the rapid economic growth seen in the nineteenth century. As a congressional task force subsequently observed, "Floods are an act of God; flood damages result from acts of men" (*Unified National Program* 1966, 14).

David A. Moss is associate professor at the Harvard Business School.

Much of the material in this chapter, particularly the sections summarizing disaster history through 1993, is excerpted with permission from the Harvard Business School case study, "The Great Mississippi Flood in 1993," no. 797-097, prepared by David Moss and Julie Rosenbaum. Copyright © 1997 by the President and Fellows of Harvard College; all rights reserved.

Generous financial support was provided by the NBER and by the Division of Research at the Harvard Business School. The author benefited greatly from the suggestions of Alexander Dyck, Ken Froot, Julio Rotemberg, and Bruce Scott as well as from the comments of the two reviewers at the conference, Clement Dwyer and R. Glenn Hubbard. The author owes special thanks to Julie Rosenbaum for her superb research on U.S. disaster policy and to Jean-Marc Dreyfus for his careful work on disaster policy in France.

By 1927, the year of another massive flood in the lower Mississippi valley, the region was crowded with homes, farms, and other businesses. Once again, the river swelled to about sixty miles in width, inundating over 16.5 million acres of land in 170 counties (a land area roughly the size of Ireland). Several hundred people lost their lives as a result of the 1927 flood, over half a million were left temporarily homeless, and damages were estimated at $300 million, or almost $3 billion in 1993 dollars (American National Red Cross 1929, 10, 120–21; Daniel 1977, 10).[1]

When the next great flood struck the upper Mississippi region in 1993, the economic effect was even greater. An estimated 20 million acres flooded or were too waterlogged to support crops, leading the Soil Conservation Service to state with only some exaggeration that "it was as though a sixth Great Lake, centered around northern Iowa, had sprung up in the Midwest" (Phillips 1994, 18). The 1993 flood inflicted considerably less human misery than its predecessor in 1927: thirty-eight lives were lost and fifty-five thousand persons displaced. Yet the economic effect of the 1993 flood was much greater. Analysts estimated overall damages at between $12 and $16 billion (National Oceanic and Atmospheric Administration 1994, pp. 1.4–1.5; Facts on File 1993; Freivogel 1993; Sheets 1993, 67; *Sharing the Challenge* 1994, 16).

Of course, floods are only one type of natural disaster. Those organizations—both public and private—charged with aiding disaster victims must also address hurricanes, tornadoes, earthquakes, mudslides, and numerous other calamities. But the great Mississippi floods just described provide an ideal baseline against which to measure changes in public expectations and government responsibilities in the United States in time of disaster.

In response to the massive Mississippi Flood of 1927, the federal government and the American National Red Cross organized the biggest disaster-relief effort in U.S. history to that time. As was customary, Calvin Coolidge, president of the United States, was also president of the American National Red Cross.[2] On 22 April 1927, he announced:

> The Government is giving such aid as lies within its power. Government boats that are available are being used to rescue those in danger and carry refugees to safety. The War Department is providing the Red Cross with tents for housing refugees. The National Guard, State and local authorities are assisting. But the burden of caring for the homeless rests upon the agency designated by Government charter to provide relief in disaster—The American National Red Cross. For so great a task additional funds must be obtained immediately.
>
> It therefore becomes my duty as President of the United States and President of the American National Red Cross to direct the sympathy of our

---

1. There is some dispute over the number of flood-related fatalities in 1927. At the time, officials insisted that fatalities numbered fewer than 10, but Daniel has since estimated the number at between 250 and 500 (see also Koenig 1993).

2. See the discussion below of the founding and evolution of the American National Red Cross.

people to the sad plight of thousands of their fellow citizens, and to urge that generous contributions be promptly forthcoming to alleviate their suffering. (American National Red Cross 1929, 13)

As Coolidge suggested, the federal government and the Red Cross worked together in the relief effort, but the latter carried most of the financial burden. Federal assistance remained limited mainly to the lending of government equipment and personnel and to placing the bully pulpit of the presidency at the disposal of private fund-raising efforts. Although Coolidge refused to call a special session of Congress as some representatives from the affected states urged, he did direct his commerce secretary, Herbert Hoover, to help run the relief effort and ordered the rest of his cabinet to assist when necessary. Through various agencies, the federal government spent about $10 million (or 3.3 percent of total damages) on relief. The Red Cross, by comparison, collected $17.5 million in cash donations as well as another $6 million in in-kind contributions. It also provided emergency services, including food and shelter, to more than 600,000 flood victims over a fourteen-month period (see Lohof 1968, esp. 122, 169–70, 185; American National Red Cross 1929, 10–13).[3]

Herbert Hoover viewed the efforts of the Red Cross in 1927 as enormously successful. By today's standards, the dollar amounts were minuscule and the reimbursement rates small. Together, the states, the federal government, and the Red Cross covered only about 13 percent of total damages. But, by the standards of the time, the effort appeared herculean. Hoover declared that the Red Cross had "become the one guarantee to the American people that loss of life shall be prevented in calamity and that suffering shall be mitigated to the utmost degree" (quoted in American National Red Cross 1929, 145). Writing his memoirs a decade later, Hoover recalled with pride the relief efforts of 1927. Obviously dismayed by President Franklin D. Roosevelt's expansionary New Deal policies, Hoover noted that private sources had provided the bulk of assistance in 1927. "Those were the days," he wrote nostalgically, "when citizens expected to take care of one another in time of disaster and it had not occurred to them that the Federal Government should do it" (Hoover 1952, 2:126).

By 1993, however, Hoover's worst fears appeared to have been realized since just about everyone expected the federal government to bail out the victims of that year's Great Mississippi Flood. By late July, President Clinton had declared all of Iowa and multiple counties in eight other midwestern states federal disaster areas. With the passage in August of Public Law (PL) 103-75 (*Emergency Supplemental Appropriations* 1993), a large emergency supplemental appropriation, a host of federal agencies ranging from the Army Corps of Engineers to the Federal Highway Administration swung into action. Most important of all was the Federal Emergency Management Agency (FEMA), which oversaw much of the relief effort.

3. The affected states added roughly another $10 million in relief appropriations.

As the emergency requests made their way through Congress beginning in July, there was no significant disagreement about whether the federal government should undertake a massive relief effort. Instead, legislators mainly debated how the bailout should be financed. "What is at stake here," Representative Gerald Solomon (R-New York) stated, "is a very important principle, and that is whether we are willing to find other means to pay for these disaster assistance costs or whether we will simply let them add to the deficit. That is how we got in this awful sea of red ink that we are in today" (*Congressional Record* 139 [22 July 1993]: H5001).

Three House members sponsored "pay-as-you-go" amendments to the Midwest aid bill that sought to offset disaster spending with cuts to other government agencies. Representative Jim Slattery (D-Kansas) proposed a 1 percent across-the-board reduction in fiscal 1994 discretionary spending, while Representatives Timothy Penny (D-Minnesota) and Jim Nussle (R-Iowa) suggested trimming roughly $3 billion from the budgets of a variety of federal agencies, including the FBI, the Coast Guard, OSHA, and NASA (*Congressional Record* 139 [22 July 1993]: H5002, H5006). In support of cost-offsetting measures, Representative Mac Collins (R-Georgia) declared, "At a time of tight budgets, spending Federal dollars to help those flood victims is more important than spending 900-plus million dollars on direct aid to Russia or spending $1.9 [billion] on a space station or $300 million on additional health care benefits to illegal aliens and spending millions of taxpayer dollars on the National Endowment for the Arts" (*Congressional Record* 139 [20 July 1993]: H4783). But, as other members of Congress maintained, these were not necessarily programs that the government should sacrifice just because a flood had struck unexpectedly in the Midwest.

Stalled on 22 July by a bipartisan coalition of fiscal conservatives, the aid bill came again to the House floor the following week. This time, members from flood-stricken districts helped push it through without any pay-as-you-go provisions. The human tragedy that was unfolding simply overwhelmed arguments about fiscal responsibility. Said one congressman, "If you ask the American in the Midwest who is paddling towards his living room or watching his business go down the drain whether he wants us to sit here today and have a budget discussion or whether he wants to pass disaster aid, I submit he would say, 'I want disaster aid'" (Albert R. Wynn [D-Maryland], quoted in Krauss 1993). Cognizant of mounting public pressure, the Senate quickly followed the House and approved the disaster-aid bill on 4 August.

By this point, the package had swelled from President Clinton's initial $2.5 billion request to $6.3 billion, or about half of total estimated damages. Representatives from the affected states sympathized with President Clinton's concerns about the deficit but insisted that their constituents were in the midst of a crisis and that $2.5 billion was not nearly enough to help them (see Hegger 1993; "Clinton Pressed for Additional Flood Aid" 1993; Freemantle 1993).

The increase to $6.3 billion resulted from a long list of additional pleas for assistance, most of which seemed perfectly reasonable under the circumstances. Senators Tom Harkin (D-Iowa) and Christopher Bond (R-Missouri), for example, succeeded in changing the formula for calculating crop-loss payments to farmers. Their more generous provisions added nearly $1 billion to the package. Said Senator Harkin, "Now I say it's time to quit letting OMB twist our tails. . . . Agriculture is all there is."[4]

Although no serious opposition to the relief appropriation ever emerged, the congressional debate nonetheless revealed considerable discomfort with the direction of federal disaster policy. As has been mentioned, some lawmakers expressed concern that the cost of federal disaster relief was becoming unmanageable. Robert C. Byrd, chair of the Senate Appropriations Committee, repeatedly cautioned his colleagues against fiscal excess, asserting that "disasters are not spending opportunities" (quoted in Dewar 1993).

Others worried that a knee-jerk federal policy was rewarding personal irresponsibility on the part of home- and business owners in floodplains and other disaster areas. As Representative Fred Grandy (R-Iowa) observed, "We're basically telling people, 'We want you to buy insurance, but if you don't, we'll bail you out anyway'" (quoted in Benenson 1993). By this logic, the federal government was contributing to a potentially enormous moral hazard problem. Representative Patricia Schroeder (D-Colorado) asked on the House floor, "As we watch this tremendously awful flood scene unravel in the Midwest . . . and we look at the terrific debt, we are going to have to make some very difficult choices. One of the main choices will be: Do we help those who took responsibility, got flood insurance, put up levees, tried to do everything they could; or do we help those who did not do that, who risked it all and figured if all fails, the Federal Government will bail them out?" (*Congressional Record* 139 [19 July 1993]: H4760).

Politicians from the affected states showed little patience with such questions. "This is not a time for debating the fine points of long-term policy," exclaimed Governor Mel Carnahan of Missouri. "We have acted in other disasters, whether they be hurricanes, whether they be earthquakes, whether they be other floods. We even acted to help Kurdistan and the savings and loans" (quoted in Hegger 1993). Victims of the Mississippi Flood, he maintained, deserved no less. Echoing these sentiments, Governor Jim Edgar of Illinois

---

4. Originally, Senators Thad Cochran (D-Mississippi) and Robert J. Dole (R-Kansas) had sought to win support in Congress for a much bigger increase in farm payments by agreeing to make the changed formula retroactive to 1990. Farm disaster assistance had been cut from forty-two to twenty-one cents per dollar lost in 1990 in order to address budget constraints. The Clinton administration rejected the Cochran-Dole initiative on the grounds that it would cost an additional $3.4 billion. According to the *Washington Post,* Harkin and Bond won administration support for their less costly proposal, which included no retroactive payments, "after phone calls to the White House" (Dewar 1993, A19; see also "$5.7-Billion Disaster Relief Bill Is Approved" 1993; "Senate Committee OKs Aid Bill" 1993).

asserted that the Great Flood was "just as serious a problem for the country as war. I don't think anyone is expecting 100 percent reimbursement, but it has to be adequate" (quoted in Freemantle 1993).

In the end, warnings about fiscal excess and moral hazard proved no match for the politics of relief in the middle of a catastrophe. The massive appropriation was passed overwhelmingly in both houses of Congress, and President Clinton did not hesitate when given the opportunity to sign it.[5]

The key question now, in the aftermath of the 1993 flood and several other record-breaking catastrophes of the last few years, is whether federal disaster policy can be rationalized or, alternatively, whether the politics of relief will remain as uncontrollable in the future as they have been in the recent past. With federal disaster spending since the mid-1970s averaging about $7 billion annually (in constant 1993 dollars), and with every indication that the figure will rise in the years ahead, policymakers in Washington have good reason to be concerned. The remainder of this paper will offer some perspective on the problem by examining the history of federal disaster relief, surveying how disaster policy actually works today, and suggesting a practical proposal for reforming the system.

8.2 A Brief History of Federal Disaster Policy

8.2.1 Ad Hoc Relief, 1803–1947

The first known instance of the federal government providing relief to disaster victims dates to 1803, when Congress granted the victims of a fire in Portsmouth, New Hampshire, an extension on the repayment of customhouse bonds. Between 1803 and 1947, various floods, earthquakes, and fires prompted at least 128 specific legislative acts offering ad hoc relief. In most cases, the acts authorized the purchase and distribution of provisions and medical supplies (see *Congressional Record* 96, pt. 9 [7 August 1950]: 11900–11902). Despite the frequency of such legislation, the federal government did not view disaster relief as an ongoing federal responsibility. More often than not, the federal government provided no assistance at all in the aftermath of a disaster.[6] In the mid-1880s, for example, President Grover Cleveland vetoed a bill that would have appropriated $10,000 for the distribution of seed to the victims of a severe drought in Texas. He explained:

5. The House of Representatives passed the emergency supplemental appropriation bill by a vote of 400 to 27 on 27 July. The bill was then favorably reported to the full Senate by a unanimous 29 to 0 vote of the Senate Appropriations Committee on 30 July. The full Senate passed the bill by a voice vote on 4 August, and President Clinton signed it into law (as PL 103-75) eight days later.

6. Whereas between 1803 and 1947 the federal government provided disaster relief, on average, less than once per year, between 1977 and 1993 it provided assistance, on average, for thirty-four disasters per year (see *Federal Disaster Assistance* 1995, table 1.1, p. 5).

I can find no warrant for such an appropriation in the Constitution; and I do not believe that the power and duty of the General Government ought to be extended to the relief of individual suffering which is in no manner properly related to the public service or benefit. A prevalent tendency to disregard the limited mission of this power and duty should, I think, be steadfastly resisted, to the end that the lesson should be constantly enforced that though the people support the Government, the Government should not support the people. . . . Federal aid in [cases of misfortune] encourages the expectation of paternal care on the part of the Government and weakens the sturdiness of our national character, while it prevents the indulgence among our people of that kindly sentiment and conduct which strengthen the bonds of a common brotherhood. ("President Cleveland's Veto Statement" 1887)

Clara Barton, who traveled to Texas during the drought and reported that relief efforts there could be handled out of local resources, supported Cleveland's position (Barton to Cleveland 1887; see also Hurd 1959, 77–78). Barton, then in her sixties, was herself a major figure in the history of American disaster relief. She had founded the American National Red Cross in 1881 and, more than anyone else, was responsible for transforming it into a quasi-public disaster agency.[7]

In 1905, Congress passed a bill designating the American National Red Cross the official agent of the federal government in providing disaster relief. Ever since its founding, the Red Cross had raised and distributed private funds to aid the victims of disasters. But, after 1905, these services became the organization's legal responsibility. Congress had appropriated no new funds but simply assigned to this volunteer association the task of raising relief aid through private means (see Hurd 1959, 111–12). The biggest test of America's quasi-public system of disaster relief came twenty-two years later, during the Great Mississippi Flood of 1927. As has been mentioned, the Red Cross carried most of the burden in a large-scale cooperative relief effort that included state and federal agencies.

8.2.2   Flood Control

Although Congress appropriated only $10 million for relief and reconstruction associated with the 1927 flood, it spent nearly $300 million the following year on flood-control projects along the lower Mississippi (Lohof 1968, 243–44). Indeed, it was at this point in time that flood control began to be accepted primarily as a job for the federal government.

Communities had historically employed flood-control works such as levees to protect low-lying property. Through most of the eighteenth and nineteenth centuries, individual proprietors, towns, and states had assumed responsibility for levee construction and maintenance. But their uncoordinated efforts some-

---

7. Barton spelled out her understanding of the role of her organization in Barton to Cleveland (1886).

times worked at cross-purposes and frequently made the situation worse: in channeling floodwaters away from one person's land, a levee usually pointed it in the direction of a neighbor's. By 1879, the need for improved navigation and flood control on the Mississippi had prompted the federal government's direct involvement. Established that year as a permanent agency of the War Department, the Mississippi River Commission focused specifically on regulation and coordination of private-sector efforts.[8]

Over subsequent decades, a series of devastating floods sparked debate over the extent to which the federal government should assume responsibility for providing protection. Local Midwest businessmen, among others, lobbied for a sustained financial commitment.[9] Congress passed the first flood control act (PL 64–367) in 1917 and a second six years later. Both acts authorized flood control as part of the Mississippi River Commission's work, appropriating roughly $10 million annually for such projects. Still, the legislation emphasized local responsibility.[10] The Mississippi River Commission worked with the U.S. Army Corps of Engineers to repair and strengthen levee systems. As early as 1926, the Corps' chief of engineers had claimed that these improvements made for a safe navigation channel and could now "prevent the destructive effects of floods" (quoted in Daniel 1977, 6). The historic Mississippi River Flood of 1927 may have proved him wrong, but it did not shake confidence in the efficacy of flood control. Indeed, it spurred increased federal participation and the building of ever bigger and better works.

Following the $300 million appropriation in 1928, Congress formally declared flood control a federal responsibility in the Flood Control Acts of 1936 and 1938. The 1938 act authorized 100 percent federal financing of dams and reservoirs. Focused on the reclamation of land for agricultural and commercial enterprises, the Army Corps of Engineers concentrated its efforts on structural approaches to flood protection such as reservoirs, levees, channels, and the diversion of major rivers.[11]

8.2.3   Toward a Permanent Federal Role in Disaster Relief, 1947–93

Meanwhile, the federal government had begun taking more responsibility for disaster relief. In the wake of several natural catastrophes during the 1930s, the Federal Relief Administration and the Federal Civil Works Administration

8. On the history of flood-control efforts, see Daniel (1977, 5–7), Lohof (1968, 214–44), and Hoyt and Langbein (1955, 138–61).

9. In 1913, e.g., Midwest businessmen presented their case for federal involvement at a congressional hearing on the subject. "There is not now any question," they declared, "as to the right and duty of the National Government to make necessary appropriations for the care and regulation of the water highways of the country—its own property" (see *Mississippi River, Hearings on H.R. 1749* 1913, 31).

10. Local authorities were to contribute not less than one-third of the cost of construction and repair (see "A Brief Chronology" 1928).

11. By 1993, the Army Corps of Engineers maintained about 275 levees in the Mississippi region alone (see Facts on File 1993, 624 E3; see also Koenig 1993, 1A).

received authority from President Franklin Roosevelt to distribute surplus federal property to state and local governments and to repair damaged roads and bridges. Congress formalized this practice in 1947 when it passed the first general disaster relief act. In the event of a disaster, local governments could turn to the War Assets Administration or the Federal Works Administration. These agencies processed requests and arranged for the delivery of surplus federal property.

The major turning point in government involvement, however, came in 1950 with the passage of PL 81-875. (For a chronology of federal disaster legislation, see table 8.1.) Known as the Disaster Relief Act of 1950, the law created a permanent relief fund and gave the president broad discretionary power to decide what constituted a disaster eligible for federal aid. While the Red Cross continued to manage the distribution of relief to private citizens and businesses, the federal government now assumed responsibility for the repair and restoration of local government facilities.[12]

Through the 1950s and early 1960s, the federal government broadened and refined the contours of the 1950 law—in most cases with little debate or controversy. The 1951 Kansas-Missouri Flood, for example, led Congress to authorize emergency housing for disaster victims. Several years later, rural communities, unincorporated towns, and state facilities became eligible for federal assistance, as did Guam, American Samoa, and the Trust Territory of the Pacific Islands. Relief acts passed in 1964 and 1965 in response to disasters in multiple states (including a severe earthquake in Alaska, floods in the Pacific Northwest, and Hurricane Betsy in the Southeast) increased federal contributions to highway reconstruction and expanded federal loan programs, such as those of the Small Business Administration (SBA) and the Farmers Home Administration (FmHA) (see Office of Emergency Preparedness 1972, 1:168–70).[13] A proposed 1966 disaster relief bill to expand the range of federal assistance prompted a number of congressmen to declare that the time had come for the federal government to provide relief on a "uniform, nationwide basis" (*Congressional Record* 112, pt. 20 [17 October 1966]: 27096–27097). Indeed, step by step, the federal role in disaster relief had been transformed. Whereas in 1953 Red Cross assistance outpaced federal spending on disasters by a ratio of 1.6 to 1, by 1965 federal disaster aid exceeded Red Cross spending on disasters by nearly 8 to 1 (Dacy and Kunreuther 1969, table 2-1, p. 32).[14]

12. On the legislative history of federal disaster relief, see esp. May (1985, 17–47); Popkin (1990); *Federal Disaster Assistance* (1995, 99–102); Office of Emergency Preparedness (1972, 1:167–73); and Kunreuther (1973, 3–21).

13. Kunreuther (1973, 9) maintains that the earthquake in Alaska "marked a turning point in the federal government's role in disaster relief. The severity of the damage caused concern that, unless the SBA liberalized its [loan] policy, many individuals would not qualify for a disaster loan because of their inability to pay off their old mortgages and other debts and still make monthly payments to the SBA."

14. In calculating total federal spending on disasters in 1953 and 1965, a subsidy rate on SBA loans of 33 percent was assumed.

Table 8.1	Federal Disaster Legislation, 1950–94

1950, PL 81-875	Disaster Relief Act:
	  Created permanent relief fund; authorized federal funding for repair
	    of local government facilities

1951, PL 82-107	Amendment to 1950 law: Authorized federal emergency housing

1953, PL 83-134	Amendment to 1950 law:
	  Permitted donation of federal surplus property such as cots,
	    hardware, lumber, and plumbing supplies to state and local
	    governments for distribution to individuals

1962, PL 87-502	Amendment to 1950 law:
	  Extended federal assistance eligibility to state facilities in addition to
	    Guam, American Samoa, and the Trust Territory of the Pacific
	    Islands

1966, PL 89-769	Disaster Relief Act:
	  Extended federal assistance eligibility to rural communities,
	    unincorporated towns, and villages
	  Federal funding for damage to higher-education facilities
	  Affirmed authority of Office of Emergency Preparedness to
	    coordinate all federal disaster relief programs
	  Special loan provisions

1968, PL 90-448	National Flood Insurance Act:
	  Provided for federally subsidized insurance along with federal
	    reinsurance provisions
	  Permitted sale of policies by private-insurance agents

1969, PL 91-79	Disaster Relief Act (limited to 15 months):
	  Funding for debris removal from private property
	  Distribution of food coupons
	  Unemployment benefits for disaster victims
	  Temporary housing for disaster victims
	  SBA, FHA, VA loan revisions

1970, PL 91-606	Disaster Assistance Act:
	  Codified existing disaster legislation and added the following:
	    Grants to individuals for temporary housing/relocation
	    Funding for legal services
	    Community payments for tax loss

1974, PL 93-288	Disaster Relief Amendment:
	  Distinguished emergencies from major disasters
	  Emphasized disaster-mitigation programs

1980, PL 96-365	Federal Crop Insurance Act:
	  Made all commercial crops part of the program
	  Introduced premium subsidy
	  Permitted private-insurance companies to sell federal crop insurance

1988, PL 100-707	Stafford Act:
	  Constituted principal federal authority for providing disaster relief
	    (expansion of original 1950 authorization)

1994, PL 103-325	NFIP Reform Act:
	  Tightened flood-insurance purchase requirements
	  Expanded mitigation incentives

1994, PL 103-354	Federal Crop Insurance Reform Act:
	  Offered catastrophic coverage for a $50.00 administrative fee per
	    crop, per county
	  Provided additional coverage at subsidized rates

Source: Adapted from Office of Emergency Preparedness (1972, vol. 1, table 1) and May (1985, tables 2.1, 2.3).

The trend of growing federal involvement accelerated further during the early 1970s. In a presidential message on disaster assistance in April 1970, Richard Nixon announced: "As we move into a new decade, one of the nation's major goals is to restore a ravaged environment. But we must also be ready to respond effectively when nature gets out of control and victimizes our citizens" ("Message from the President" 1970, 6). The country had experienced twenty-nine major disasters in 1969, requiring an allocation of roughly $150 million from the President's Disaster Relief Fund. It was the largest appropriation for disaster relief since the enactment of PL 81-875 nineteen years earlier ("Message from the President" 1970, 1).

Responding to the devastation of Hurricane Camille and other catastrophes of 1969, Congress passed the 1970 Disaster Relief Act (PL 91-606). This legislation aimed to establish a permanent and comprehensive program of federal assistance, one that covered both private and public losses. Through the 1960s, federal disaster relief had gradually expanded to include funding for the repair of damaged higher-education facilities, debris removal from private property, and unemployment compensation and food coupons for hard-pressed disaster victims. The federal government had also increased the availability of SBA and FmHA disaster loans. The 1970 act not only codified this diverse disaster legislation but also charted new territory. Strongly emphasizing relief for individual victims, it mandated grants for temporary housing and legal services. Authorization for the permanent repair of public facilities (as opposed to the earlier restriction to temporary repair) and a focus on hazard mitigation constituted other key features of the act. An amendment that followed in 1974 established a two-tiered system distinguishing emergencies from major disasters and stepped up incentives for disaster-mitigation efforts. It expanded the president's authority to provide immediate relief and enlarged the category of public facilities eligible for repair and restoration. The 1974 amendment also made available a wider range of assistance for states and individuals.[15]

By the mid-1970s, federal disaster legislation provided an overall structure for public and private assistance. It did not, however, mandate a detailed agenda for response. Issues such as the division of responsibility among federal, state, and local authorities, or even among agencies within the federal government, remained open-ended and loosely organized. Successive administrations therefore focused on streamlining relief efforts as well as on implementing mechanisms for cost containment. In 1978, President Carter established the Federal Emergency Management Agency (FEMA) to coordinate disaster programs distributed across a host of government agencies, including the Departments of Agriculture, Commerce, Labor, and Housing and Urban Development.[16]

---

15. On legislative developments through 1974, see Office of Emergency Preparedness (1972) and Kunreuther (1973) as well as the key federal acts: PL 81-875 (1950), PL 89-769 (1966), PL 91-79 (1969), PL 91-606 (1970), and PL 93-288 (1974).

16. On the origins of FEMA, see *Federal Disaster Assistance* (1995, 94–97).

Table 8.2   **Federal Dollars Obligated for Disaster Assistance, Fiscal Years 1977–93 (in millions of constant 1993 dollars)**

Fiscal Year	Number of Disasters[a]	Comprehensive Emergency Management Component				Total[b]
		Preparedness	Mitigation	Response	Recovery	
1977	53	176	2,004	175	5,592	7,947
1978	40	189	2,102	211	14,849	17,351
1979	53	313	2,136	507	10,262	13,218
1980	30	220	1,818	38	7,748	10,167
1981	16	380	1,644	31	13,181	15,235
1982	26	81	1,567	31	4,247	5,926
1983	20	109	1,525	42	1,787	3,463
1984	40	105	1,565	48	2,368	4,086
1985	19	93	1,466	28	1,329	2,916
1986	30	78	1,368	82	1,733	3,261
1987	25	77	1,424	55	1,515	3,072
1988	17	77	1,415	28	743	2,262
1989	29	72	1,431	252	6,327	8,082
1990	35	66	1,447	282	4,792	6,586
1991	39	69	1,425	70	1,230	2,794
1992	48	65	1,450	678	4,461	6,654
1993	58	62	1,290	476	4,828	6,656
Annual average	34	131	1,593	199	5,117	7,040

Source: Federal Disaster Assistance (1995, table 1.1, p. 5).

Note: Table excludes civil defense preparedness expenditures and federal disaster-insurance-program costs, except for flood-hazard-mapping activities of the NFIP. Complete fiscal year 1977–93 obligation data were not available for every disaster-related program/activity.

[a]Number includes both major disasters and emergencies.

[b]Totals may not add because of rounding.

From 1977 to 1993, federal disaster spending varied from year to year but averaged about $7 billion in constant 1993 dollars (see table 8.2). Although disaster relief looked very much like an entitlement, it did not technically qualify as one. Unlike mandated AFDC or Medicaid programs, federal disaster assistance depended almost entirely on discretionary year-to-year and emergency congressional appropriations (see table 8.3).

8.2.4   Federal Flood and Crop Insurance

As the federal role in disaster relief expanded in the 1960s and 1970s, so did interest in federal disaster insurance, specifically against flood and crop damage. Policymakers emphasized the self-financing nature of such programs and their potential to curb expensive supplemental relief allocations each time a disaster struck. Flood insurance was of particular interest since most private insurers excluded flood damage from their general property and casualty policies. Knowing that individual flood risks in a given geographic area were often highly correlated, insurers feared that catastrophic flooding could wipe them

Table 8.3   **Supplemental Appropriations for Disasters, Fiscal Years 1970–94 (millions of dollars)**

Fiscal Year	Current Dollars	Constant 1993 Dollars	Fiscal Year	Current Dollars	Constant 1993 Dollars
1970	305	1,098	1983	25	36
1971	485	1,659	1984	153	210
1972	61	198	1985	419	553
1973	2,805	8,682	1986	547	702
1974	384	1,105	1987	109	136
1975	32	345	1988	55	66
1976	242	588	1989	1,207	1,388
1977	904	2,033	1990	2,850	3,143
1978	3,308	6,924	1991	0	0
1979	1,452	2,793	1992	6,063	6,224
1980	2,797	4,935	1993	3,474	3,474
1981	233	373	1994	8,412	8,245
1982	131	195			
Average					2,204

Source: Federal Disaster Assistance (1995, table 5.1, p. 77).

out. William G. Hoyt and Walter B. Langbein wrote in 1955 that floods "are almost the only natural hazard not now insurable by the home- or factory-owner, for the simple reason that the experience of private capital with flood insurance has been decidedly unhappy" (p. 104).

Reformers argued that a federally backed insurance program would succeed where private insurers had failed by spreading flood risks nationwide and providing the necessary financial reserves. It would also strike a better balance between the need for federal assistance in large-scale disasters and private responsibility. As disaster experts Douglas Dacy and Howard Kunreuther remarked in the late 1960s when Congress was debating this issue, "It is our hope that the flood insurance bill before Congress will be swiftly passed and eventually extended to cover other natural hazards, enabling the federal government to withdraw from its paternalistic role in relation to the private sector" (1969, 235).

The National Flood Insurance Act of 1968 (PL 90-448) offered coverage for residential and business properties. It particularly emphasized preventive efforts such as zoning regulations and building codes in order to minimize potential flood damage. For the most part, premiums corresponded to actual risk. Exceptions were made for structures erected before an area's identification as a flood zone, in which case subsidized rates applied. Over the years, the National Flood Insurance Program (NFIP) successfully encouraged better flood protection. But it did not entirely meet the goals of its original proponents. The program suffered from low subscription—except among those at highest risk. Because there were few mechanisms to require homeowners in floodplains to purchase insurance, many chose to remain uninsured and simply hope for the best. According to Benenson (1993, 1861), as few as one in five mortgageholders in flood-zone areas participated in the NFIP.

Repetitive-loss cases for buildings erected before the cutoff date of 1974 presented another serious problem. As long as damage from a single flood never exceeded 50 percent of the property's value, owners qualified for subsidized insurance. Such a provision allowed the Rulos family in Grafton, Illinois, to file four flood-insurance claims after buying a home in 1978. According to the Senate Task Force Report, repetitive-loss cases as of 1993 amounted to 2 percent "of the properties covered by flood insurance policies but accounted for 53 percent of the claims paid and about 47 percent of the dollars paid from the Flood Insurance Fund" (*Federal Disaster Assistance* 1995, 63).[17]

Federal crop insurance marked another significant attempt by lawmakers to take up the slack of private-insurance companies as well as to reduce the effect of natural disasters on the nation's farm economy. After a number of private companies failed trying to provide multiperil crop insurance during the first two decades of the twentieth century, Congress began to show interest in sponsoring a federal initiative. The idea came and went until the mid-1930s, when severe droughts transformed public crop insurance into a potent political issue. At President Roosevelt's initiative, federal crop insurance was finally enacted in 1938 under the Agricultural Adjustment Act. Part of a larger agricultural stabilization plan, the insurance program initially proved quite limited, covering only selected crops in selected counties. Over the years, however, Congress broadened the crop-insurance program and also supplemented it with substantial ad hoc farm-disaster payments. These ad hoc payments, which seemed to reward the uninsured, came under increasing fire in the 1970s.

Like the earlier flood-insurance legislation, the Federal Crop Insurance Act of 1980 (PL 96-365) attempted to eliminate ad hoc disaster payments by stressing coverage under a public-insurance program. To encourage higher levels of participation, the 1980 act introduced a premium subsidy as well as coverage for all commercial crops in all agricultural counties. But these changes did not have the desired results. After 1980, fewer than half of eligible farmers purchased crop insurance. Since generous ad hoc payments continued to be made to the uninsured in the aftermath of disasters, many farmers must have reasoned that even a subsidized insurance policy made little sense for them. As a result, the crop-insurance program was plagued by low participation and high costs. In 1993, farmers' premiums ($563 million) covered only 30 percent of total program costs (i.e., indemnities of $1.514 billion plus administrative costs of $355 million). The difference constituted a large federal subsidy to farmers. (See tables 8.4 and 8.5.)[18]

---

17. "On the Disaster Dole" (1993) cites slightly different figures. It states that, although "repetitive loss cases" amount to only 3 percent of all claims, "they account for more than a third of all payments."

18. For details on federal crop and flood insurance, see *Federal Disaster Assistance* (1995, 13–15, 112–15, 118–20). On crop insurance, see also Goodwin and Smith (1995, esp. chap. 3).

Table 8.4   **National Flood Insurance Program Income and Costs, Fiscal Years 1977–93 (in millions of constant 1993 dollars)**

| Fiscal Year | Total Income[a] | Insurance Program Expenses | | Administrative Expenses[c] | Total Government Cost[d] |
		Loss and Loss Adjustment	Other[b]		
1977	200	157	107	182	182
1978	221	307	98	194	194
1979	263	767	127	187	187
1980	272	517	280	138	138
1981	365	189	172	96	995
1982	416	243	167	69	559
1983	431	647	103	90	146
1984	501	488	148	88	140
1985	476	230	150	73	336
1986	536	354	192	67	115
1987	601	183	137	66	0
1988	544	73	188	63	0
1989	701	614	195	59	0
1990	710	353	217	58	0
1991	698	240	219	59	0
1992	728	488	207	53	0
1993	763	985	226	58	0
Average	$496	$402	$173	$94	$176

Source: Federal Disaster Assistance (1995, table 1.8, p. 13).

[a]Total income includes premiums, investment income, other income, and federal policy fees.

[b]Includes underwriting expense, interest expense, and adjustments and deferrals.

[c]Includes salaries and expenses and floodplain-management expenses.

[d]Figures represent appropriations for NFIP expenses. For fiscal years 1977–86, government costs consisted of administrative expenses and repayments of past loans from the Treasury. Beginning in fiscal year 1986, the NFIP has been required to pay all program and administrative expenses from the insurance fund.

8.3   Disaster Policy in Perspective: The Transformation of Public Risk Management in the United States since 1960

As should be clear from the brief history just offered, federal disaster policy represents an intricate patchwork of disparate programs and commitments. The first major piece was the Disaster Relief Act of 1950, which committed the federal government to a permanent role in disaster assistance. The patchwork grew most rapidly, however, during the late 1960s and early 1970s as program after program was added and expanded. This was the time when the federal government extended its standard coverage to include not only public casualties of disasters (such as schools, town halls, and so on) but private businesses and individuals as well. To cite just one example of the change, the number of subsidized home loans provided by the Small Business Administration (SBA) to disaster victims rose from only 11 in 1953 to 1,540 in 1963 to a peak of 195,762 in 1973 (data courtesy SBA). The average size of an individual disas-

Table 8.5   **Crop-Insurance Program Income and Costs, Fiscal Years 1977–93 (in millions of constant 1993 dollars)**

Fiscal Year	Premium Paid By: Farmer	Government	Indemnities[a]	Excess Losses[b]	Administrative Cost	Total Government Cost[c]
1977	204	0	319	117	45	162
1978	213	0	311	98	48	146
1979	181	0	92	−88	46	−42
1980	277	0	538	263	67	330
1981	532	75	763	155	168	398
1982	462	136	505	−94	192	234
1983	323	93	632	215	176	484
1984	463	134	893	295	244	673
1985	453	132	873	289	270	691
1986	382	115	771	273	255	643
1987	369	91	516	56	224	371
1988	385	124	1,261	751	280	1,155
1989	654	220	1,308	434	407	1,061
1990	697	235	1,142	212	396	843
1991	585	207	1,010	217	348	772
1992	581	202	1,003	219	341	762
1993	563	198	1,514	753	355	1,306
Average	431	115	791	245	227	588

Source: Federal Disaster Assistance (1995, table 1.9, p. 14).

[a]Indemnities are the costs of payments to farmers for crop losses.

[b]Excess losses are indemnities minus total premiums (figures may not add because of rounding).

[c]Total of premiums paid by the government, excess losses, and administrative costs (figures may not add because of rounding).

ter loan (in constant dollars) remained remarkably stable from the 1950s to the 1990s. What increased—and increased dramatically—beginning in the late 1960s was the number of citizens covered by such federal disaster policies as the SBA loan program (see figure 8.1).

In fact, the dramatic expansion of federal disaster relief after 1960 was part of a broader transformation of risk-management policy in the United States. As I have argued elsewhere (see Moss 1996, 1998), the state and federal governments had always engaged in various forms of risk management. Until about 1900, most risk-management policies provided security for businesspeople against risks that were thought to discourage investment and trade. Limited liability for corporate shareholders and bankruptcy law are two notable examples of what I have labeled *Phase I* risk-management policies. Beginning mainly after 1900, a new set of risk-management policies emerged, offering security to the American worker against a variety of industrial hazards, including on-the-job accidents, unemployment, and loss of income in old age. Social insurance legislation and countercyclic fiscal policy stand out as the primary policy innovations of *Phase II. Phase III* commenced around 1960

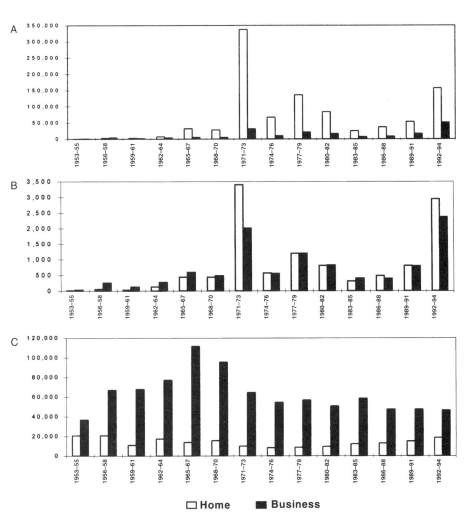

Fig. 8.1   Historical profile of SBA disaster loans: *A*, Number of SBA disaster loans; *B*, Total value of SBA disaster loans (in millions of constant 1987 dollars); *C*, Average size of SBA loans (in constant 1987 dollars)

Source: David Moss and Julie Rosenbaum, "The Great Mississippi Flood of 1993," case no. 797-097. Boston: Harvard Business School, 1997. Copyright © 1997 by The President and Fellows of Harvard College. Reprinted by permission. Data courtesy the Small Business Administration.

and involved an extension of risk-management policy to protect not only business and labor but also citizens more generally. The expansion of federal disaster relief after 1960 represents one of the many changes associated with Phase III. Some of the others include a transformation of product-liability law, the rapid growth of consumer protection and environmental regulation, and an explosion of federal financial guarantees (see table 8.6).

Table 8.6   The Three Phases of Risk-Management Policy in the United States

	Phase I: Creating a Secure Environment for Business	Phase II: Creating a Secure Environment for Workers	Phase III: Creating a Secure Environment for All Citizens
Period 1, prior to 1900	Property rights Common internal currency Deposit insurance (state legislation) Limited liability Bankruptcy law Fixed exchange rate		National defense[a] Local poor relief[a]
Period 2, 1900–1960	Deposit insurance (federal legislation)[b] Crop insurance[b] Foreign-investment insurance	Workplace safety regulation Workers' compensation Old age insurance Unemployment insurance Macroeconomic stabilization policy[b] Disability insurance	Product-safety laws (esp. foods and drugs) Federally insured mortgages (FHA and VA)
Period 3, since 1960	Company bailouts Country bailouts	Occupational safety and health regulation Pension regulation and insurance	Dramatic expansion of: Federal disaster relief[b] Health, safety, and environmental protection Federal insurance[b] Other federal financial guarantees[b] Means-tested "welfare" programs[a] Liability law

Source: Moss (1996, exhibit 1).

[a]Status as a "risk-management" policy uncertain.

[b]May fit into more than one phase.

The transitions from Phase I to Phase II to Phase III were, in my view, primarily a consequence of the rapid rise in income that industrialization generated. The primary objectives of Phase I risk-management policies were heightened economic activity and resource mobilization, two important sources of economic growth. Once national income had increased sufficiently, however, the goal of economic security—at first just for workers but ultimately for everyone—began to rival economic growth as a dominant social objective. That is, rising incomes induced a relative change in social priorities, which in turn drove the transformation of risk-management policy (Moss 1996).

A broad consideration of public risk management and its historical evolution in the United States helps explain not only why the federal government became so deeply involved in disaster relief but also why it did so in particular during the second half of the twentieth century. One part of the explanation has to do with the nature of disaster risk. While the public sector has historically managed many different types of risk, those that threaten victims with financial devastation have always proved especially attractive to lawmakers. Indeed, the vast majority of risk-management policies address relatively low-probability, high-consequence events. A short list of such policies includes limited liability for corporations, bankruptcy discharge, workers' compensation, unemployment insurance, deposit insurance, and pension insurance. Of course, disaster policy also addresses the threat of low-probability, high-consequence events. Howard Kunreuther (1993) has suggested that private markets deal poorly with such risks (see also Camerer and Kunreuther 1989). It may be that this market weakness accounts, at least in part, for policymakers' notable interest in them—and in disaster relief in particular.

A second part of the explanation for the federal government's increased role in disaster relief relates to the nature and pressures of Phase III. The enactment of new risk-management policies, and the expansion of existing ones, accelerated sharply after 1960. Between 1966 and 1980, Congress enacted a broad array of health, safety, and environmental legislation.[19] Over the same years, the maximum insured bank deposit under federal deposit insurance was increased tenfold, from $10,000 to $100,000 (U.S. Department of the Treasury 1991, table 2). In 1968, the same year that federal flood insurance was established, Congress also created federal crime insurance (ostensibly for areas

---

19. Some of the highlights include the National Traffic and Motor Vehicle Safety Act of 1966, which created the National Highway Transportation Safety Administration (NHTSA); the National Environmental Policy Act of 1969; President Nixon's 1970 Executive Order creating the Environmental Protection Agency (EPA); the Occupational Safety and Health Act of 1970, which established the Occupational Safety and Health Administration (OSHA); the Clean Air Act of 1970; the Clean Water Act of 1972; the Consumer Product Safety Act of 1972, which established the Consumer Product Safety Commission; and, several years later, the Comprehensive Emergency Response, Compensation, and Liability Act (CERCLA) of 1980, which has come to be known as Superfund. Between 1960 and 1980, the number of pages in the *Federal Register*—a favorite index of the regulatory explosion publicized by critics—increased more than fivefold, from 14,479 to 87,012 pages. On the increase in pages, see Koepp (1987, 50).

inadequately served by private carriers) and federal riot reinsurance (Greene 1976, 1979; *Federal Disaster Assistance* 1995, 112–21). The following year, Congress set up the Overseas Private Investment Corporation (OPIC), which offered political risk insurance to American businesses investing abroad (Robin 1984, 936–37). The Pension Benefit Guaranty Corporation, which insured workers against pension-fund failures, was established in 1974; and between 1970 and 1973 most states created insurance-guaranty funds to protect property and casualty policyholders against insurance-company insolvencies. Meanwhile, total public spending on social welfare in the United States surged, jumping from 11.5 percent of GDP in 1965 to 19.1 percent of GDP ten years later. The share of public social welfare spending in national income has remained roughly stable since then (Bixby 1993, esp. table 2, p. 74).[20] Many other examples could be provided, ranging from the transformation of product-liability law during the 1960s and early 1970s to the establishment of Fannie Mae, Freddie Mac, and Sallie Mae over roughly the same period (see Moss 1996, esp. 36–70).

The critical point here is that the rush of new risk-management policies after 1960 reflected a fundamental shift in public expectations about the role of government. Americans increasingly expected protection against an ever-widening array of hazards and, at the same time, were becoming more and more comfortable with federal insurance and other forms of public risk management.

What was distinctive about Phase III from the policymakers' standpoint was that security for the individual had become an end in itself—an apparent consequence of the nation's extraordinary postwar affluence.[21] During Phase I, policies that protected businesspeople against adverse risks no doubt advanced the security of some individuals. Bankruptcy-discharge provisions, for example, were often justified in the nineteenth century as relief measures for overextended debtors. But the primary purpose of these policies was to encourage those receiving protection to engage in trade and investment and thus to advance economic growth for the whole society. Although security for the individual was certainly an important motivation for worker-protection policies during Phase II, there nonetheless remained a broader objective as well—namely, social stability. Particularly after the First World War and during the

---

20. Total public spending on social welfare includes expenditures on social insurance (including Medicare), public aid (including Medicaid), other health and medical programs, veterans' programs, and housing as well as child nutrition and a number of other small categories. Social insurance and public aid, which experienced the most dramatic increases, accounted for 44 percent of the total in 1965 and over 56 percent of the total in 1975.

21. Indeed, John Kenneth Galbraith's *The Affluent Society* appeared in 1958. In it, he articulated much of the logic that would define Phase III. With only a touch of hyperbole, he explained that "the notion, so sanctified by the conventional wisdom, that the modern concern for security is the reaction to the peculiar hazards of modern economic life could scarcely be more in error. Rather, it is the result of improving fortune—of moving from a world where people had little to one where they had much more to protect" (Galbraith [1958] 1984, 87).

Great Depression, many social reformers worried that worker insecurity threatened the very existence of democratic capitalism.[22] Only in Phase III did protection of the individual against adverse risks become, by itself, a primary and sufficient justification for far-reaching security legislation (see Moss 1996, esp. 72–74).

The path of federal disaster policy over the last thirty to forty years is thus entirely consistent with broader developments associated with Phase III. The takeoff period in federal disaster spending came in the late 1960s and early 1970s, as Congress began for the first time to assume ongoing responsibility for assisting individual victims of natural disasters. In the absence of long-term public opinion polls on this subject, it is impossible to offer direct empirical evidence regarding changes in public expectations about the government's role in time of disaster. But it seems clear that public expectations increased enormously. As shown in figure 8.2, the federal government covered 6.2 percent of total damages after Hurricane and Flood Diane in 1955, 12.8 percent of damages after the Pacific Northwest Floods of 1964, and 48.3 percent of damages after Tropical Storm Agnes in 1972.[23] Since then, it has been common for the federal government to cover roughly half of uninsured losses stemming from major disasters.

The dramatic shift in public expectations is also evident in the politics of disaster relief. As we have seen, the massive bailout of 1993—which would have been inconceivable forty years earlier—faced almost no opposition whatsoever when it was passed in the wake of a calamity.[24] Americans had come to expect and demand public compensation for the victims of natural disasters just as they had come to expect and demand public compensation (or at least publicly mandated compensation) for a wide range of man-made hazards, from workplace accidents to pension-fund failures. Indeed, rising expectations drove the transformation of public risk management under Phase III, which involved, among other things, a transformation of federal disaster policy after 1960.

---

22. For example, the economist John R. Commons declared at a convention of government officials in 1919, "[U]nless the capitalistic system begins to take care of the security of the laborer, begins to make jobs as secure as investments, then there is a serious question, with the growing number of wage earners who have no capital of their own, whether that system can continue to exist" (see Commons 1919, p. 4, frame 818).

23. In none of these disasters were privately insured losses as a fraction of total estimated losses very large. The ratio of privately insured to total losses was 0.6 percent in the case of Hurricane and Flood Diane in 1955, virtually zero in the case of the Pacific Northwest Floods of 1964, and 4.9 percent in the case of Tropical Storm Agnes in 1972. These particular disasters were selected in part to allow a comparison of federal coverage across time for events in which private-insurance coverage was low (see Dacy and Kunreuther 1969, table 2-4, p. 46, and table 2-2, p. 35; Kunreuther 1973, table 3, p. 16).

24. In fact, public expectations regarding disaster relief have increased to such an extent that FEMA now feels compelled to instruct citizens that the federal government's responsibility in this area is not unlimited. In its *Citizen's Guide to Disaster Assistance* (1993), e.g., the agency highlights six common misconceptions about federal disaster policy. The first two misconceptions are that "the Federal government has total responsibility for disaster recovery" and that "the objective of Federal disaster assistance is to 'fix everything'" (see pp. 1–7).

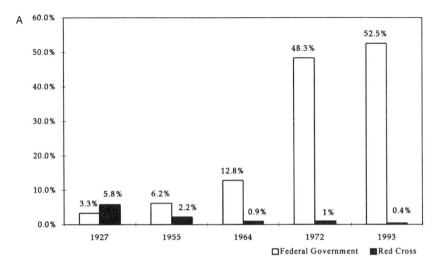

Fig. 8.2   Federal coverage of major natural disasters: *A*, Coverage rates—ratio of disaster spending to total estimated damages (in percentages)—on five major disasters, federal government and the Red Cross; *B*, Federal spending on major natural disasters, millions of 1993 dollars (1973 and 1993 fiscal years, not calendar years)

Source: David Moss and Julie Rosenbaum, "The Great Mississippi Flood of 1993," case no. 797-097. Boston: Harvard Business School, 1997. Copyright © 1997 by The President and Fellows of Harvard College. Reprinted by permission.

Panel A: The 1927 data pertain to the Mississippi floods of 1927. For estimates of total damages ($300 million), federal spending ($10 million), and Red Cross spending ($17.5 million), see Lohof (1968, 122, 185, 169). The 1955 data pertain to Hurricane and Flood Diane, and the 1964 data pertain to the Pacific Northwest Floods. For estimates of total damages ($832 million, $462 million), federal spending ($51.8 million, $59.4 million), and Red Cross spending ($18.3 million, $4.2 million), see Dacy and Kunreuther (1969, table 2-4, p. 46, and table 2-2, p. 35). The 1972 data pertain to Tropical Storm Agnes. For estimates of total damages ($2 billion), federal spending ($965 million), and Red Cross spending (1 percent of damages), see Kunreuther (1973, table 3, p. 16) and May (1985, table 7.7, p. 149). The 1993 data pertain to the Mississippi floods of that year. For estimates of total damages ($12 billion) and federal spending ($6.3 billion), see Facts on File (1993) and *Emergency Supplemental Appropriations* (1993). Data on Red Cross spending courtesy of the American Red Cross.

8.4   Federal Disaster Policy in Action: The Great Midwest Flood of 1993

Once federal lawmakers committed themselves to meeting high public demands in the area of disaster relief, how exactly did they go about assisting the victims? As a rule, major catastrophes overwhelmed the annual budgets allocated to government agencies providing relief. In such cases, after declaring a federal disaster, the president made an official request for supplemental appropriations (see table 8.3 above). In 1993, the record flooding in the Midwest triggered an enormous flow of funds (see table 8.7). Although numerous federal agencies took part in the relief effort, FEMA oversaw much of the operation and alone administered over $1 billion in disaster assistance. FEMA ac-

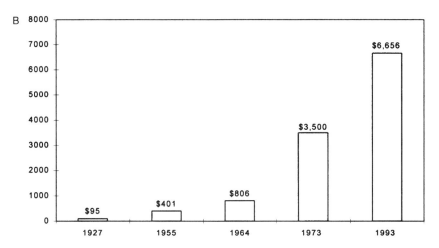

Panel B: In estimating federal spending on all major disasters in 1927, it was assumed that the amount expended on the Mississippi floods that year accounted for the vast majority of all federal disaster spending. Estimates of total federal spending on major disasters for 1955 ($73.9 million) and 1964 ($180.8 million) are based on Dacy and Kunreuther (1969, table 2-1, p. 32). Estimates of total federal spending for fiscal year 1973 ($1,170.1 million) are based on Kunreuther (1973, table 2, p. 14). Estimates of total federal spending for 1993 are from *Federal Disaster Assistance* (1995, table 1.1, p. 5). GDP deflators were used to convert these nominal figures into 1993 dollars.

Note: In estimating federal spending on individual disasters (panel A) and total federal spending on all major disasters (panel B) for 1955, 1964, 1972, and fiscal year 1973, only the subsized portion of federal loans was included. It was assumed that the approximate subsidy on loans equaled one-third of their face value. Naturally, the full value of federal grants was included in each calculation. There was no need to estimate the subsidized portion of federal loans in either 1927 or 1993. Little if any of the federal spending in 1927 was devoted to loans, and by fiscal year 1993 the federal government had changed its accounting system for disaster spending so as to include only the subsidized portion of federal loans.

cepted applications for cash grants of up to $11,900 each from individuals and families without access to other disaster aid. It also provided temporary housing assistance, unemployment compensation, food, legal services, and crisis counseling (see *Federal Disaster Assistance* 1995, 152–53).

Housing grants, which covered rent and minor repairs to flood-damaged homes, helped Shirley Bornman deal with her extensive property loss. Made homeless when waters rose to the roof of her house, she received from FEMA $240 per month, guaranteed for eighteen months or until she was better settled. Bornman relied as well on payments from her NFIP policy, administered by FEMA. She had paid roughly $400 per year to insure her house for $45,000 and the contents for $12,000. Bornman, however, was not typical of most floodplain residents. Only about 11 percent of the Midwest flood victims had flood insurance, and claims payments from the NFIP totaled only $297.3 million (see Sheets 1993, 67; *Sharing the Challenge* 1994, 27).[25]

25. For 1993 participation rates, see *Federal Disaster Assistance* (1995, 160).

Table 8.7 Federal Disaster Spending for the Midwest Flood of 1993 (millions of dollars)

Federal Department/Agency	Resources Provided in Emergency Supplemental 1 (August 1993)	Additional Assistance for This Disaster from Base Appropriations	Total Resources Available			Obligations by Fiscal Year		
			Amount	% Public[a]	% Private[b]	1993	1994	1995
USDA	3,117.2	1,021.7	4,138.9	0	100	677.1	2,203.1	1,024.0
Commerce Department	201.0	0.0	201.0	100	0	6.3	27.6	167.1
HUD	500.0	0.0	500.0	0	100	125.0	353.6	21.4
Transportation Department	212.0	0.0	212.0	100	0	42.0	133.7	36.3
Army Corps of Engineers	305.0	12.0	317.0	100	0	71.2	178.3	67.5
SBA[c]	398.7	294.9	693.6	0	100	301.5	234.8	0.0
FEMA	1,233.5	0.0	1,233.5	75	25	322.3	680.4	230.8
Other	332.8	49.1	381.9	67	33	92.7	234.0	54.9
Totals	6,300.2	1,377.7	7,677.9	24.9	75.1	1,638.1	4,045.5	1,602.0

Source: Data courtesy of the Office of Management and Budget. Also consulted: Agriculture Department, Commerce Department, HUD, Transportation Department, Army Corps of Engineers, SBA, and FEMA.

[a] Proportion of "Total Resources Available" targeted at public-sector recipients. Estimated by author.

[b] Proportion of "Total Resources Available" targeted at private-sector recipients. Estimated by author.

[c] Amounts for the SBA refer to the face value of its disaster loans. The subsidy rate for 1993 SBA flood loans was estimated at approximately 20 percent of face value.

Local communities also turned to the federal government. FEMA's public assistance programs helped rebuild infrastructure, including state and local government buildings, roads, and water-treatment plants. States and municipalities were also eligible for debris removal and emergency-work funds as well as community disaster loans in the event of substantial tax-base loss. Overall, public-sector relief accounted for one-quarter of federal spending on the 1993 flood (see table 8.7).

In Des Moines, the municipal waterworks suffered $12 million in physical damages and restoration expenses as a result of the flooding. Through the Fireman's Fund insurance company, the waterworks had added an endorsement to its general policy to provide $10 million in flood coverage. This extra insurance, which was not available for residential properties, had cost $2,000 per year. It proved critical that summer in restoring the plant. For expenses not covered by the insurance policy—such as the cost of sandbagging the levee and rent for temporary office space—the waterworks relied on FEMA's cost-sharing program for local governments. Although the standard cost-sharing arrangement obliged states to pick up 10 percent and local communities 15 percent of the cost of rebuilding public facilities, President Clinton waived these requirements in 1993, insisting on a combined state and local contribution of only 10 percent. In the case of the Des Moines waterworks, the state of Iowa picked up the entire 10 percent not covered by the federal government. With nearly all the direct property damage and restoration expenses covered through a combination of public and private sources, the only significant cost to the waterworks was $2 million in lost revenue.[26]

Another large chunk of federal disaster aid in 1993 went to farmers in the form of Department of Agriculture crop payments, FmHA loans, and Soil Conservation Service grants. Initial estimates set agricultural damage from direct flooding at over $2.5 billion, but, in the end, agricultural damage probably ran considerably higher than that. Those farmers with federally subsidized crop insurance qualified for compensation once their losses exceeded 35 percent of expected production. Those without insurance, however, collected almost as easily, qualifying for aid when losses were greater than 40 percent (*Sharing the Challenge* 1994, 16, 22; *Emergency Supplemental Appropriations* 1993, 1697). Technically, a farmer could combine a price-support payment, a crop-disaster payment, and a crop-insurance payment to recoup as much as 90 percent of the value of his crops (Freivogel 1993; Sheets 1993, 67). Congress's emergency appropriation allocated almost $2.5 billion to the Commodity Credit Corpora-

---

26. Telephone interview with Tamera Mason, Des Moines Water Works, May 1996. On cost-sharing arrangements between federal, state, and municipal governments, see "More Aid Arranged" (1993, A10). Once again, after the Northridge Earthquake of 1994, President Clinton increased the federal share for rebuilding state and local facilities from the standard 75 percent to 90 percent. Even that increase left California governor Pete Wilson disappointed since Wilson wanted the federal government to fund 100 percent of public reconstruction efforts (see Reeves 1994, 15A).

tion to relieve stricken farmers. Because ruined land from sand and debris compounded crop loss, Congress also appropriated $400 million to the Soil Conservation Service for soil repair. Ultimately, over half of all federal disaster spending on the 1993 flood covered agricultural losses (see table 8.7).

Tom Waters was one of the many farmers hit hard by the Midwest Flood of 1993, which stormed through the network of levees that usually protected his farmland near the river. That year he had planted twelve hundred acres of corn, soybeans, and wheat. By the end of the flood, only nine acres remained above water. Not only did Waters lose his crop, but sand deposits and holes filled his fields. Because federal all-peril crop insurance for floodplain farms was very expensive, Waters had opted against it. He was eligible for federal crop-disaster payments, however, which covered over three-fourths of the approximately $35,000 in material expenses that he incurred planting his 1993 crops. (In a typical year, he would have received roughly $80,000 after harvesting and selling them.) For help with his damaged fields, Waters turned to the Soil Conservation Service's cost-sharing program. The agency awarded just over $17,500, which covered 64 percent of the cost to remove debris, plow under sand, and level farmland. The remaining 36 percent Waters had to provide out of his own savings.[27]

The Small Business Administration's (SBA) loan program for both individuals and businesses constituted yet another important component of federal disaster relief. To ease the effect of flood loss, businesses small and large could apply for two types of disaster loans: one covered property damage and the other economic injury resulting from lost profits. In the wake of the flooding, Congress raised the disaster-loan limit from $500,000 to $1.5 million. By 15 November, seventy-five businesses had been approved for loans over $500,000 (*Small Business Administration Disaster Assistance* 1994, 7). Although the SBA charged a 4 percent interest rate in most cases, companies with substantial liquid assets or other available credit paid 8 percent. Individuals, too, were entitled to SBA loans for help in repairing damaged homes and recovering property. Like businesses, they simply needed to show ability to repay. The cost to the government of these subsidized interest rates was substantial—perhaps as much as one-third the face value of the loans (see, e.g., *Budget of the United States Government* 1996, 927).

One recipient of an SBA disaster loan in 1993 was Jeff Weber of Iowa, who lost both his home and his business to floodwaters. Inundation was so severe that for almost fifteen days he had to travel six-tenths of a mile by boat to reach the structures. Weber owned and ran a small business rebuilding automobile parts. Because of the number of waterways and the network of dams and levees in the region, government floodplain agencies had considered the area a low-risk zone for flooding. Relying on that information, Weber had not seen it necessary to take out flood insurance on the business. To satisfy the mortgage

27. Telephone interviews with Tom Waters, May 1996.

company when he bought his home, however, he had been required to purchase minimal flood insurance on that structure. This ultimately covered about 50 percent of the damage to his home. To stretch the insurance dollars, Weber had done almost all the rebuilding on his own. Like other individuals in the region, he also relied on help from private charitable organizations. While these organizations did not provide actual funds, their volunteers offered moral support and badly needed manpower to clean away the layers of sludge and dirt deposited by churning floodwaters. FEMA entered the scene early on to make preliminary damage estimates. Determining that Weber was not eligible for grant-in-aid programs, FEMA officials passed his file onto the Small Business Administration for a disaster loan. He qualified for both a home and a business loan. Concerned about going into debt, he took only a small loan for the house to cover approximately 10 percent of the damage; but he accepted a much larger one for his business. The SBA loaned the money in installments and required receipts to ensure that payments were spent in accordance with the loan terms. Because of serious structural damage, Weber ended up erecting a new building to house his office. Again, he did most of the work himself to avoid heavy labor costs. He subsequently took out flood-insurance policies on both his business and his home.[28]

On top of SBA loans, allocations for levee repair, health and environmental hazards, and highway and rail reconstruction rounded out federal relief expenditures. In addition, the federal government forwent revenue by permitting disaster-related tax write-offs—although much smaller ones than it had allowed in the 1970s. Prior to 1982, individuals could deduct damaged property minus salvage value and insurance or other reimbursements. The tax-code revision of 1982, however, instituted the $100/10-percent rule, which held that the only nonbusiness casualties qualifying for deductibility were unreimbursed losses exceeding $100 *and* 10 percent of one's adjusted gross income. The 1982 rule meant that a propertyowner with, for example, an adjusted gross income of $40,000 could deduct only $900 on an uninsured loss of $5,000 (i.e., $5000 minus $100 minus 10 percent of $40,000).

8.5   Federal Disaster Policy: Problems, Prospects, and Proposals

8.5.1   Problems

As should be clear from the discussion presented above, disaster policy represents a sizable federal commitment—and one that has begun to set off a few alarm bells in Washington. Just about everyone agrees that disaster victims deserve some sort of public help in their time of need. But there is considerable disagreement over just how far the federal government should go. Soon after the Northridge Earthquake of early 1994, which brought forth at least $12

---

28. Telephone interview with Jeff Weber (a pseudonym), December 1995.

billion in federal disaster expenditures (Critzer 1995), the U.S. Senate established a task force to study federal disaster policy. In a letter accompanying their final report, the task force's cochairs, Senators John Glenn and Christopher Bond, suggested that the nation's disaster policy, though serving an important public purpose, had finally begun to run up against real budgetary constraints: "In creating this Task Force, the Senate found that the policy underlying such federal disaster assistance was rooted in historical precedent and the American tradition of helping friends and neighbors who have been plagued by these unfortunate tragedies. At the same time the Senate noted that the growing cost of disaster assistance—six major emergency supplemental appropriations Acts totaling over $17 billion since fiscal year 1988—must be reconciled with the current budgetary restraints imposed on discretionary spending and our budget reduction goals" (*Federal Disaster Assistance* 1995, vii).[29] The senators might have mentioned that the amount that Congress appropriated for relief and reconstruction in the aftermath of the Northridge Earthquake just about equaled what the federal government spent annually on the AFDC program. Clearly, disaster relief had become a significant budget item.

Looking forward, it appears that budget pressures stemming from federal disaster policy are likely to intensify in the future. There are two basic reasons for this. First, high public expectations about the federal government's disaster responsibilities contribute to a powerful political dynamic in Congress while dampening personal responsibility among citizens. Second, growing uncertainty about the likelihood and potential costs of future natural disasters threatens to drive many private insurers away from catastrophe coverage, thus leaving the federal government with a larger potential pool of uninsured losses to address.

As this paper has attempted to demonstrate, public expectations about federal disaster relief have strengthened considerably since the 1960s. Indeed, public expectations are now so elevated that few politicians dare raise objections to a massive appropriation in the aftermath of a catastrophe. Disaster spending has become a political sacred cow. According to a survey conducted in 1995 for the Insurance Research Council, 87 percent of Americans either strongly approved (51 percent) or moderately approved (36 percent) of the federal government providing disaster relief (Insurance Research Council 1995, 63–67). The political dynamic evident in Congress in the wake of the 1993 flood demonstrated the power of these attitudes at a moment of crisis. Again and again in the aftermath of disasters, representatives from the affected states have insisted that their constituents deserve no less than what other vic-

29. A subsequent passage in the same letter reads: "There is no question Americans traditionally, and selflessly, have given themselves, their time, and their support to help fellow citizens who have suffered as a result of these catastrophes. That indeed is a hallmark of this country. And we should expect—and deserve—as much from the federal government. But just as our response to disasters must be swift, it must also be cost-effective, especially in an age where federal dollars are increasingly hard to find" (*Federal Disaster Assistance* 1995, x).

tims received in the past and that the particular nature of their disaster might justify even more. Federal catastrophe coverage has thus been subject to a ratcheting-up process from disaster to disaster, whereby coverage rates occasionally increased (particularly in the late 1960s and early 1970s) and only very rarely declined (see fig. 8.2 above and fig. 8.3).[30]

One important consequence of all this is that the federal government now lacks credibility when it threatens to withhold relief ex post from those individuals who fail to follow certain rules or meet particular criteria ex ante. At the time of the 1993 flood, for example, many farmers in the affected area were upset about a federal rule that denied soil-repair grants to anyone involved in three or more disasters over the previous twenty-five years. They proceeded to petition their representatives for help. In the end, Congressman Harold Volkmer (D-Missouri) persuaded the Agriculture Department to rescind the disqualification and make all farmers eligible. The failure of federal policymakers credibly to commit obviously generates a moral hazard problem. Citizens who feel confident that the government will pay are more likely to forgo insurance coverage and to live in more hazard-prone areas.[31] By increasing the level of uninsured disaster losses that the federal government will find itself politically bound to compensate in the future, the credible-commitment and moral hazard problems together form a vicious circle that ought to alarm federal policymakers.

Federal lawmakers also have reason to worry about new disaster-related findings within the scientific community that could lead to dramatically increased federal expenditures in the years ahead. Traditionally, it had been assumed that disaster experience over the recent past constituted a reasonable basis for assessing the likelihood of disasters in the future. If a particular region experienced four major hurricanes over the previous twenty years, then the probability of a major hurricane hitting the region in any future year was thought to be about one in five. But, according to Anthony H. Knap, director of the nonprofit Bermuda Biological Station for Research, "Assessing the historical frequency of natural catastrophes has certain inherent weaknesses. For example, the cycle of natural processes may be longer than the time period in

30. In 1993, e.g., one representative from Illinois reminded his colleagues on the House floor what he had done to support the victims of other disasters in the past: "Let me also tell my colleagues that when this gentleman was asked to come to the aid of California in their disaster, for the disaster in Florida and the disaster in Texas, I marched up that Hill to help American people in need. Today what we get are theories about how to pay for it" (*Congressional Record* 139 [22 July 1993]: H5005). Of course, disaster relief has always been subject to logrolling in Congress. In 1965, in an effort to assure disaster relief for his constituents, Senator Long remarked on the floor of the Senate, "[A]s I have told the senator [Proxmire] privately, if his State should ever be visited with a similar disaster, he could count on my vote to help provide for his people" (quoted in May 1985, 21).

31. In fact, the most hazard-prone states (such as California, Florida, Hawaii, and Texas) have, for quite some time, experienced much faster population growth than has the nation as a whole. Florida, e.g., experienced a population growth rate of 43 percent between 1980 and 1994, as compared to only 15 percent nationally (see Dunleavy et al. 1996, 5).

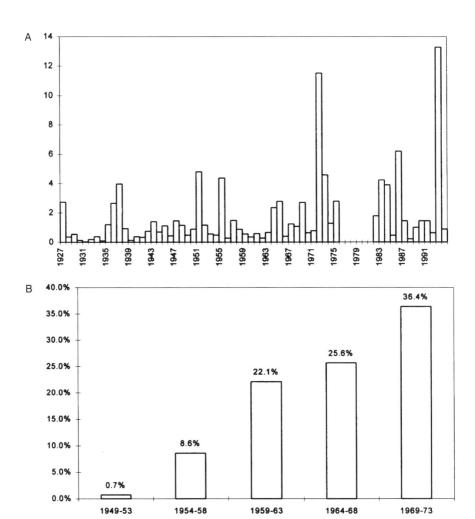

Fig. 8.3   Flood damage and federal relief: *A*, **Flood damages in the United States, 1927–94 (in millions of 1987 dollars);** *B*, **Federal flood relief subsidies as a fraction of total flood damages in the United States, 1949–73**

Sources: David Moss and Julie Rosenbaum, "The Great Mississippi Flood of 1993," case no. 797-097. Boston: Harvard Business School, 1997. Copyright © 1997 by The President and Fellows of Harvard College. Reprinted by permission.

Flood-damage estimates for 1927–75 are from *Climatological Data* 28, no. 13 (1977): 117. Flood-damage estimates for 1982–92 are from U.S. Army Corps of Engineers, *Annual Flood Damage Report to Congress for Fiscal Year 1992* (1993, fig. 2, table 10); data for 1993 and 1994 are from U.S. Army Corps of Engineers, *Annual Flood Damage Report to Congress for Fiscal Year 1994* (1995, table 4). A GDP deflator was used to convert nominal dollars to 1987 dollars. Data on the subsidized portion of federal flood-relief spending for 1949–73 are from Abeles, Schwartz (1978, table 4, pp. 9–10).

Note: In panel A, data are not available for 1976–81.

which they were observed. In addition, the past record may be inaccurate because of technical limitations at that time. Finally, human activity perturbs the global climate, perhaps changing the course of the cycles" (quoted in Banham 1995, 27). Richard T. Gordon, an applied physicist and scientific consultant to Chubb, offers a similar warning: "Insurers are making huge assumptions that the past will be the key to the future. We have at hand about 110 years of recorded observations of global climate activity. I can tell you with certainty that we have not seen the range of climate variation in that time. When you talk geologic time scales, 110 years just does not register. That means there are hurricanes out there that we have not seen in the past 110 years" (quoted in Banham 1995, 27).

Although a clear consensus has yet to form within the scientific community, many researchers are now suggesting that natural catastrophes are likely to come more frequently and strike with greater intensity in the years ahead. William Gray, a Colorado State University meteorologist, is predicting dramatically increased hurricane activity. Believing that we are now coming out of a twenty-year cycle of relative calm, Gray maintains, "Inevitably, long stretches of destruction will return. . . . Florida and the East Coast will see hurricane devastation as they have never experienced before" (quoted in Catalano 1995, 66; see also Cowen 1994). Meanwhile, several groups of seismologists have recently announced the existence of an "earthquake deficit" in California. Because the Los Angeles basin experienced many fewer earthquakes over the past two hundred years than would have been expected on the basis of geological science, these seismologists are anticipating increased earthquake activity in the future (see "Grievous Faults" 1995; Monastersky 1995). Finally, the biggest scientific question mark of all, global warming, threatens to generate more floods, droughts, and fires as well as hurricanes and other windstorms over the very long term. Gerhard Berz, a meteorologist who runs the technical research division at Munich Re, offers an almost apocalyptic warning: "The increased intensity of all convective processes in the atmosphere will force up the frequency and severity of tropical cyclones, tornadoes, hailstorms, floods and storm surges in many parts of the world, with serious consequences for all types of property insurance" (quoted in Leggett 1993, 29).[32]

Naturally, such scientific predictions have enormous implications for private insurers. And, since the federal government tends to pick up a large portion of uninsured disaster losses, any change in insurance coverage necessarily has significant implications for federal policy as well.

Before 1989, no natural disaster in the United States had ever caused more than $1 billion in insured losses. Hurricane Hugo shattered that record, increasing it by a factor of four. Even after Hugo, however, U.S. insurers tended to

32. Many analysts also cite demographic shifts—namely, domestic migration into coastal states, which are generally more prone to disasters than inland states—as another factor that will contribute to increased natural catastrophe losses in the years ahead (see, e.g., Dunleavy et al. 1996, 4–5; Durham, Johnson, and Winston 1995, 20).

assume that the worst possible windstorm would not cause damages to insured property in excess of $8 billion. Hurricane Andrew, which struck on 24 August 1992, transformed those expectations literally overnight. In the words of Phillip Longman, "This one storm alone blew apart Florida's private insurance market and even much of its fail-safe regulatory apparatus" (1994, sec. 1). The most costly disaster in American history, Andrew inflicted $15.5 billion in insured losses, which was about 50 percent more than all the premiums collected for property coverage in Florida over the previous 22 years. Estimates vary, but Andrew probably caused at least another $10 billion in uninsured losses (see Murphy 1995; Gastel 1996a; Longman 1994, sec. 1; Leggett 1993, 28; Ferrara 1995). Less than a year and a half later, insurers were blindsided once again when the Northridge Earthquake in southern California generated claims totaling $12.5 billion—a figure over three times larger than what the insurers had received in earthquake premiums over the previous twenty-five years (Quackenbush 1996; see also Gastel 1996b).

The one-two punch of Andrew and Northridge forced insurers to reassess their exposure to catastrophes nationwide and to begin taking a closer look at the newly emerging scientific research on natural disasters. Says Richard Gordon, "If in fact the past is not a good guide to what will happen in the future, the entire underwriting basis of what insurers are doing is flawed. That's a scary thought when you think of the billions of dollars that are at stake" (quoted in Banham 1995, 27).

Indeed, growing doubts about their ability to predict future catastrophic events on the basis of past experience has frightened quite a number of insurers. Many property and casualty companies, including the two biggest providers of homeowner's insurance, Allstate and State Farm, began to control their exposure in states like Florida and California by sharply limiting new coverage. Beginning in the fall of 1995, for example, State Farm stopped writing any new policies at all in Florida and worked to limit its operations in California and North and South Carolina as well as selected areas in Texas and Louisiana. In October 1996, Nationwide (the nation's fifth largest home insurer) announced a dramatic reduction of new sales of homeowner's insurance across the entire eastern seaboard and down through the Gulf of Mexico. Explaining the policy, which would affect sales from Maine to Texas, Nationwide's president declared, "Prudence requires us to diligently manage our exposure to catastrophic losses." Said the chief financial officer, "Nationwide Insurance possesses great financial strength—and we intend to keep it that way" (quoted in Treaster 1996).

The dramatic rise in disaster losses after 1989, along with mounting questions about the validity of predicting the incidence and severity of natural catastrophes on the basis of recent experience, had clearly shaken private insurers. Indeed, many simply decided to get out before it was too late. Reacting to Nationwide's announcement in October 1996, Jack Weber of the insurance industry's Natural Disaster Coalition acknowledged, "Finding companies that will write policies in coastal areas is becoming increasingly more difficult. And the trend appears to be accelerating" (quoted in Treaster 1996).[33]

8.5.2 Prospects and Proposals

Proposals for reform have emerged at both the state and the federal levels. For their part, legislators in the most disaster-prone states have attempted to assure an adequate supply of catastrophic insurance coverage for their citizens. In the immediate aftermath of Hurricane Andrew, officials in Florida imposed a moratorium on insurance-policy nonrenewals and cancellations, thus frustrating the plans of most insurers to reduce coverage sharply in the state. In order to accommodate the demand for new policies, Florida lawmakers also established the Residential Property and Casualty Joint Underwriting Association (JUA), which became an insurer of last resort. On 30 June 1996, the JUA was servicing over 910,000 policies, making it the second largest property insurer in the state. Florida's insurance commissioner, Bill Nelson, insisted at that time that the state's strategy for solving the insurance problem was "going in the right direction" but nonetheless acknowledged, "We're in a crisis" (Navarro 1996). Since Andrew, Florida homeowners had experienced a 72 percent increase in insurance premiums, and most property insurers were still trying to limit coverage in the state wherever possible ("American Insurance" 1993; Navarro 1996; Gastel 1996a; Longman 1994).

A similar drama unfolded in California after the Northridge Earthquake of early 1994. The Northridge catastrophe convinced most insurers that providing earthquake coverage in California was simply too risky. Because of a state law requiring all home insurers to offer earthquake policies to their customers, many insurers felt compelled to get out of the homeowner's market altogether. California's insurance commissioner, Chuck Quackenbush, announced in 1995 that the "entire insurance industry . . . is engaged in a panic run for the border" (quoted in Keohe 1995).[34]

In order to address the mounting insurance crisis, California officials initially authorized the state's FAIR (Fair Access to Insurance Requirements) Plan to offer residential property and earthquake insurance. Originally created to provide insurance in "underserved" areas, such as inner-city communities, the FAIR Plan was transformed after the Northridge Earthquake into a property insurer of last resort, analogous to Florida's JUA. Insurance Commissioner Quackenbush, however, was uncomfortable with the idea of allowing the FAIR

33. In a recent article, Jaffee and Russell (1997) attributed the reluctance of private insurers to cover natural catastrophe risk to their unwillingness "to hold large amounts of liquid capital." This unwillingness, in turn, is attributed to a variety of "institutional factors," including accounting requirements, taxes on reserves (retained earnings) as well as on the interest income that they generate, and the threat of takeover that generally comes with large holdings of cash.

34. In the fall of 1995, Quackenbush explained to lawmakers in Washington, "The threat of earthquakes has resulted in a virtual shutdown of the market for new homeowners insurance policies. Companies representing 93 percent of the market have either stopped or restricted the sale of new homeowners policies" (quoted in Phinney 1996; see also Wood 1996, 4).

Plan to become, by default, one of California's largest insurers. Like the JUA in Florida, the FAIR Plan in California was funded in large measure on a post-assessment basis. In the event of a major catastrophe, losses in excess of premium revenue would be imposed on the state's private insurers according to their share of the residential market. As an alternative, Quackenbush advocated the creation of a specialized earthquake-insurance pool that would be funded primarily by the state's insurers. When he scaled back the FAIR plan to its original mission on 1 June 1996, many critics charged that he was playing politics, trying to create a crisis in order to force the enactment of his proposals for a new state agency. Whatever Quackenbush's true motivation, his decision certainly increased the pressure on lawmakers, and they quickly fell into line.

At the beginning of September 1996, state lawmakers approved the establishment of the California Earthquake Authority (CEA) and authorized it to sell earthquake policies. The legislation allows insurers willing to commit funds to the CEA to discontinue their own earthquake coverage. Commissioner Quackenbush expects that, if necessary, the CEA would be able to cover even a major disaster through a combination of premiums and insurance-company contributions. Individual claims would likely be less than they would be under traditional earthquake coverage since CEA policies (known by some as "minipolicies") have high, 15 percent deductibles and cover very little beyond structural damage to the home itself. Damage to pools, driveways, patios, and so on would no longer be covered. Most of the big insurance companies doing business in California supported the legislation because it would cap their liability. An analyst at Merrill Lynch, for example, estimated that the creation of the CEA would limit Allstate's earthquake exposure to $900 million. Of course, the state of California has implicitly accepted responsibility for losses that cannot be paid for out of both CEA premiums and the ex ante commitments of private insurers (Kersnar 1996; Scism 1996; Quackenbush 1996).

In addition to these state efforts, three distinct reform initiatives have emerged at the federal level. One of the three, and the only one on which Congress has already taken action, aims at increasing participation in the federal government's flood- and crop-insurance programs. Legislation enacted in 1994 to reform the National Flood Insurance Program (NFIP) increased incentives for flood-mitigation efforts and tightened enforcement of flood-insurance requirements. Among other things, it prohibited federal disaster relief to persons living in flood-prone areas who had failed to maintain required insurance. It also established penalties for banks and other regulated lenders that extended loans to borrowers without flood insurance. The law changed as well the NFIP's waiting period for new flood-insurance policies from five to thirty days. The old provision had allowed homeowners during the 1993 Midwest Flood to purchase insurance even when danger proved imminent.[35] Congress also

---

35. See *Congressional Quarterly Weekly Report* 51 (30 October 1993): 2985; 51 (6 November 1993): 3053; 51 (11 December 1993): 3371; and 52 (7 May 1994): 1130. See also the outline of PL 103-25 in *United States Code Congressional and Administrative News* 5 (1994): 2025–35.

sought to reduce the need for large emergency-disaster payments to farmers by enforcing participation in the federal crop-insurance program. The 1994 reform act required a minimum level of participation while providing lower premium rates and better coverage to farmers. At the same time, it made enactment of future supplemental disaster appropriations by Congress much more difficult. In addition to repealing the authorizing legislation for farm-disaster payments, the act restricted Congress's ability to circumvent budget-control regulations by designating farm-disaster appropriations as emergency spending (*Federal Disaster Assistance* 1995, 14–15, 120–21).[36]

A second approach to reform, originally advocated by the insurance industry's Natural Disaster Coalition and considered by Congress in 1995, would have established a national equivalent to the California Earthquake Authority. The new private entity, to be known as the Natural Disaster Insurance Corporation (NDIC), would be financed and administered by a consortium of private insurance companies. The NDIC would sell disaster coverage through these private insurers and would bear all the associated risk. Much like the CEA, the NDIC would effectively cap the disaster liability of private insurers. In the event of a major catastrophe or series of catastrophes that exhausted the NDIC's available resources, the NDIC would (under the original proposal) be authorized to borrow from the U.S. Treasury. Unlike the law that established the CEA, however, the proposed NDIC legislation would require all homeowners with federally assisted mortgages and living in earthquake- and hurricane-prone regions to purchase a minimum level of catastrophic coverage. Currently, over 90 percent of homeowners have mortgages that are in one way or another federally assisted (see Phinney 1996; Emerson and Stevens 1995; Lochhead 1995).

A third reform initiative at the federal level, put forth by the Clinton administration, aims to strengthen and expand the catastrophe reinsurance market by having the U.S. Treasury sell disaster-contingent claims on the open market. These contracts would pay off in the event of natural disasters causing at least $25 billion in insured damages. Once the $25 billion trigger was reached, each contract would pay $1 million for every additional billion dollars in damages, up to a maximum of $25 million. Presumably, insurers and reinsurers would buy these contracts to cover their exposure in the event of a megacatastrophe like Andrew or Northridge. Administration officials insisted that the contracts

---

36. Many farmers became aware of the full significance of these changes only after another Midwest flood struck in 1995. The 1994 legislation compelled the farmer Tom Waters to pay an annual registration fee amounting to a few hundred dollars for the minimum required level of crop insurance. Although the 1995 flood took about half his corn acreage, he received no federal disaster payments that year—a notable departure from previous years. Nor did he receive any crop insurance since his overall yield remained just above the level that would have triggered benefits. While in theory he could have purchased additional crop insurance from the federal government (i.e., beyond the minimum level required), he had chosen not to do so because he regarded the premiums as exorbitant. In fact, Waters insisted that the legislative change of 1994 had constituted a major step in the wrong direction. "I pay $200 [in compulsory registration fees] every year for basically no coverage," he said. "It just makes me sick" (telephone interview with Tom Waters, May 1996).

would carry no federal subsidy (see Brostoff 1996; Gastel 1996a; see also D'Arcy and France 1992).

Unfortunately, all these initiatives, at both the state and the federal levels, are plagued by serious problems. The main interest of the state governments at this point is to assure the availability of homeowner's insurance, which is essential to the maintenance of healthy real estate markets. One approach, adopted by legislators in both Florida and California, has been for the states to provide insurance directly. But the simple fact is that each of the various states is poorly positioned to diversify catastrophic risks. In addition, each lacks the financial wherewithal to cover the losses stemming from a megacatastrophe, such as a $75 billion hurricane in Florida, a $70 billion earthquake in Los Angeles, or a $100 billion earthquake in the New Madrid region of the Midwest. Even California's Chuck Quackenbush acknowledges that, in the event of a megadisaster, federal support would be necessary (see Phinney 1996).

On the federal level, Congress's attempts in 1994 to increase participation in the government's flood- and crop-insurance programs certainly represented steps in the right direction. But there remains a serious question about the credibility of the federal government's threat to withhold assistance from victims lacking federal insurance. The politics associated with disaster relief highlighted earlier in this paper suggest that federal commitments are often abandoned in the midst of major crises, when public sympathy for victims is high. The true test of the 1994 reforms will come only after the next major flood.

The proposed Natural Disaster Insurance Corporation (NDIC) suffers from at least three significant flaws. First, any attempt to charge actuarially fair rates will likely mean prohibitively high rates in several regions of the country particularly prone to disaster activity. The historical record suggests that the NDIC will face enormous pressure to cross-subsidize rather than charge prohibitively high rates in certain regions, such as southern California. From a public policy standpoint, however, it would seem that such cross-subsidization should properly be left to lawmakers. Second, the NDIC will almost surely have to rely on federal financial support in the event of a megacatastrophe. But, again, prudence would suggest that, if the federal government is going to back the NDIC and implicitly underwrite its activities, then the federal government ought to have substantial control over its operations. Third, the NDIC proposal suffers from a credible-commitment problem comparable to that facing the flood- and crop-insurance reforms enacted in 1994. According to the NDIC's chief legislative sponsors, "Those who refuse to buy [insurance] coverage would no longer be eligible for federal assistance to rebuild their homes should a natural disaster strike" (Emerson and Stevens 1995). As we have seen, however, such a threat could well prove empty in the wake of a major disaster.

When asked to review the NDIC proposal, policy analysts at the Congressional Budget Office (CBO) drafted a memo on 2 February 1996 warning in the strongest possible terms about the first two problems noted above. On the issue of rate setting, the CBO analysts observed that "the goal of pricing policies at rates that are both affordable and (as required in the bill) actuarially sound might be incompatible." In fact, they questioned whether it was possible to identify actuarially sound rates at all, given the enormous uncertainties regarding disaster forecasting. They also expressed a great deal of concern that the NDIC's obligations would become contingent liabilities of the federal government. "While we cannot estimate the exact budgetary impact of H.R. 1856," the analysts wrote, "we are concerned that this bill could obligate the federal government to cover the costs of a major natural catastrophe. Tens of billions of dollars of insurance company liabilities could be shifted onto the federal government with highly uncertain prospects of repayment." Although the federal government would not be legally obligated to assume these liabilities, the memo noted, federal lawmakers would likely feel compelled to do so given the NDIC's federal charter and obvious public purpose. Unlike Fannie Mae and other government-sponsored enterprises, however, the NDIC "would be completely unregulated. That could require the federal government to assume responsibility for the NDIC's actions without the ability to regulate its rates and underwriting standards" (Congressional Budget Office 1996).[37]

Finally, the Clinton administration's recommendation that the Treasury Department offer disaster-contingent-claims contracts addresses only one part of the overall problem. The biggest advantage of the proposal is that it would allow insurers and reinsurers to hedge their bets on megacatastrophes. If, as has sometimes been argued, insurers and reinsurers are risk averse to high-consequence, low-probability events such as natural disasters, then the proposed contract would increase overall market efficiency by allowing the insurers and reinsurers to manage their extreme downside risk. Thus, to the extent that private markets for natural catastrophe risks are failing on account of risk aversion among insurers and reinsurers, the administration's proposal represents a valuable solution.

There is, however, another important reason for the failure of this market. The widespread perception that disaster activity is likely to increase and intensify in the years ahead has led insurers to demand catastrophe premiums—particularly in the most disaster-prone areas—that both policyholders and regulators view as prohibitive. If the high prices that insurers wish to charge are the result, not primarily of risk aversion on their part, but rather of their assigning high probabilities to the likelihood of major disasters, then the administration's proposal would be of little help.[38] It may well be that insurers are exiting the market for natural catastrophe risks simply because they are unable,

---

37. As a result of this and many other strong criticisms of the NDIC proposal, the Natural Disaster Coalition withdrew it in early 1996 and has since put forth a number of more modest reforms (see, e.g., Gettlin 1996, 8, 112).

38. The fact that only a very small volume of instruments similar to those proposed by the administration trade privately on the Chicago exchange represents further evidence that there may not be much of a market for nonsubsidized contracts of this kind. On disaster futures and options traded on the Chicago Board of Trade, see Zolkos (1996), Petch (1996), and "Disastrous Bonds" (1996).

for political reasons, to charge what they believe to be actuarially fair prices for these risks. Clearly, the introduction of disaster-contingent-claims contracts would affect neither the actual likelihood of major catastrophes occurring nor the actuarially fair premium rate for catastrophe insurance.

The broader problem is that many propertyowners living in disaster-prone areas would probably choose not to insure against catastrophe risks if faced with actuarially fair premiums. State officials have attempted to address this problem by regulating prices and restricting the opportunities of insurance companies to exit the market. But, even if regulators permitted actuarially fair premiums to be charged and the market were thus allowed to work, many people would end up without insurance because they would view the price as unaffordable. And the government, for its part, would remain liable for a large share of these uninsured catastrophe losses because of high public expectations about federal disaster coverage. The primary limitation of the administration's proposal to introduce disaster-contingent-claims contracts, therefore, is that it fails to address the inherent conflict between actuarial fairness and the affordability of catastrophe premiums in disaster-prone areas.

A secondary limitation concerns the issue of revenue neutrality, which the program's proponents insist is both possible and necessary. Given that a natural disaster causing over $25 billion in insured damages has never occurred, it is difficult to believe that anything but the roughest or most fanciful of probability estimates could be assigned to the likelihood of such a disaster actually striking. As a result, policymakers would probably come under intense political pressure to accept low-end risk estimates in setting the government's reservation price in order to make the contracts more affordable.[39]

So long as it is understood that a government subsidy would likely be involved, the proposal to create disaster-contingent-claims contracts should be seen as a constructive reform initiative. By affording insurers and reinsurers a means of protecting themselves against megacatastrophes, the proposed financial instrument might encourage increased private coverage of natural disaster losses. It would do this by addressing the inherent risk aversion of insurers and reinsurers to a particular set of high-consequence, low-probability events. However, unless the subsidies were quite large, private insurers would probably continue to find it impossible to offer catastrophe premiums that were both actuarially fair and economically affordable in the most disaster-prone regions of the country. The proposed contracts obviously would not be very efficient vehicles for cross-subsidizing disaster risks. But, since the politics of disasters in the United States appear to demand a significant degree of cross-

---

39. Congressional Budget Office (1996) suggests a similar critique: "While the Administration intends to price the contracts so that the net cost to the taxpayers over time is zero, CBO is uncertain whether it would be possible to establish a premium rate to an options contract that would have no present-value cost to the federal government. A triggering event must hit $25 billion before the contracts pay out; however, there has never been a catastrophe of that size, and it is extremely speculative to predict the likelihood of that which has never occurred."

subsidization, the administration's proposal cannot be viewed as anything like a complete remedy. Indeed, the ideas developed in this paper would suggest that a more comprehensive reform is required.

8.5.3 The French System of Catastrophe Coverage: A Model for the United States?

Perhaps the most successful national disaster policy in the industrialized world belongs to the French. Unlike the United States, which suffers many different types of natural catastrophes every year, France is plagued mainly by floods. But, much like their American counterparts, the French have come to expect a substantial state role in disaster relief. In fact, as early as 1946, the French Constitution established the principle of "solidarity and equality of all French towards the burden resulting from natural disasters." The same clause was incorporated into the Constitution of 1958. Until 1982, private insurers in France offered precious little coverage of natural catastrophe risks, but the government typically provided ad hoc assistance in the aftermath of disasters. Although concerns mounted in the 1970s about the rising expense of public disaster relief, it was not until major floods struck southern France in late 1981 that lawmakers were driven to overhaul the system and introduce a comprehensive natural disaster policy.[40]

The 1982 disaster law mandated that every non-life-insurance policy in France include comprehensive disaster coverage along with a corresponding surcharge fixed as a percentage of the base premium. Except for automobile insurance, property and casualty insurance is not compulsory in France; but, since 1982, every policy sold has had to include legally specified disaster provisions. The surcharge was originally set at 5.5 percent but increased to 9 percent the following year. The 9 percent surcharge remains in effect today on all policies except automobile insurance, for which the surcharge has been fixed at 6 percent since 1985. The 1982 law also permitted private insurers to pass on, at their discretion, between 40 and 90 percent of their catastrophe risk (and, of course, the corresponding premiums) to a state-guaranteed reinsurer, the Caisse Centrale de Réassurance (CCR). A stop-loss provision of the reinsurance contract, covering the retained portion of the risk, is triggered when the private insurer's annual losses from covered catastrophes reach 150 percent of the annual catastrophe premiums that the insurer chose to retain. Although private insurers are not required to reinsure their catastrophe risks through the CCR, most have opted to do so. In recent years, private insurers in France have chosen to retain approximately 60 percent of catastrophe risk and pass on the remainder (along with all the risk above the stop-loss trigger) to the CCR.

As the relatively high private retention levels suggest, the system has, so far at least, performed remarkably well. Except for the first year of operation (be-

---

40. Most of the material presented here on French disaster policy is drawn from Dreyfus (1995). See also Kielmas (1996).

fore the surcharge was increased to 9 percent) and 1994 (a year of exceptionally high disaster activity in France), catastrophe-reinsurance premiums paid
to the CCR have always exceeded the CCR's catastrophe payments. In fact,
annual payment-to-premium ratios of under 50 percent are typical for the
CCR's catastrophe-reinsurance program. To date, the state guaranty on CCR
reinsurance has never been triggered. The French government still appropriates
emergency funds in the aftermath of many large disasters to cover an assortment of uninsured damages, but the private-public insurance system now covers the vast majority of losses. Overall, the system established in 1982 enjoys
broadly based support—notably from policyholders, private insurers, and public policy makers. "While both the French direct insurers and the CCR agree
that there is room to improve the program," reports one business publication,
"no one challenges the basic tenets that led to the plan." The report adds that
the system "is considered an unqualified success by both buyers and insurers"
(Kielmas 1996).

The analysis of U.S. disaster coverage provided in this paper suggests that a
system similar to that now working in France could be established with some
benefit in the United States. Under such a system, the federal government
would require that specific coverage against natural catastrophes be included
in every property-insurance policy; it would mandate a premium surcharge to
pay for the additional coverage; and it would establish a federally guaranteed
reinsurance program allowing private insurers to cede most of the risk and the
associated premiums to the federal government.

Because the United States suffers, on average, from more natural catastrophes and from a wider assortment of them than does France, such a policy
would require several modest departures from the French model so as to better
suit the American context. Instead of fixing the natural catastrophe surcharge
at a flat percentage of base premiums (e.g., 9 percent in France), the U.S. system might provide for some variation across regions. Citizens living in the
most disaster-prone areas would pay the highest surcharge and citizens living
in the least disaster-prone areas the lowest. Some cross-subsidization would
still be necessary to make catastrophe insurance affordable in disaster-prone
areas, but there would be no need to establish a single, flat-rate surcharge as in
France. The basic surcharge could vary, for example, between 5 and 20 percent
and average about 13 percent of base premiums. The surcharge on automobile
insurance might be set at two-thirds of the basic surcharge, as in France. Presumably, the catastrophe surcharge would not be applied at all to unrelated
property and casualty lines, such as liability (both automobile and nonautomobile), workers' compensation, and accident and health.

If this schedule of surcharges had been applied between 1977 and 1993
to the relevant lines of property insurance, annual receipts would have been
enough to cover all private insurance payments for natural catastrophes as well
as all federal disaster payments and still leave a cumulative surplus of nearly
$2 billion at the end of the period. If these surcharges had been applied to all

property and casualty lines, the surplus at the end of 1993 would have totaled $148 billion. Indeed, if only half the basic surcharge (i.e., 6.5 percent for non-automobile insurance and 4.33 percent for automobile insurance) had been applied to all property and casualty lines, the cumulative surplus would have reached nearly $4 billion at the end of 1993 (see table 8.8). Clearly, a basic surcharge could be selected that would pay for catastrophe losses in the United States. Federal policymakers would have to decide which lines to include in the tax base and how much of a buffer they wished to build against potential megacatastrophes.[41]

American policymakers might also consider requiring private insurers to reinsure through the federal reinsurance agency with little if any flexibility on private-retention levels. For example, the U.S. law might require private insurers to retain 30 percent of natural catastrophe risk and to obtain reinsurance coverage for the next 70 percent, along with stop-loss protection on the retained risk, from the designated federal reinsurance agency. This departure from the French model would help prevent American insurers from capturing the program's implicit cross-subsidies for themselves. Given the much greater variation in disaster vulnerability across regions in the United States as compared to France, a flexible public-reinsurance program would offer American insurers enormous opportunities for gaming the system and cherry picking risks.

Naturally, a number of disadvantages would be associated with the adoption of even a modified version of the French system. For one thing, the federal government would be explicitly assuming yet another large contingent liability. But, since the federal government already stands as the implicit guarantor of both insurance companies and state-guarantee funds in the event of a megacatastrophe, it may be reasonable to offer an explicit guaranty in return for some steady revenues in the form of premiums. Another apparent disadvantage is that cross-subsidization benefits those living in dangerous areas and penalizes those living in safe areas, thus creating a significant moral hazard problem. But, again, since some level of cross-subsidization (and, in turn, moral hazard) is inevitable given public expectations about federal bailouts of disaster victims, it seems reasonable for the government to move from ex post to ex ante subsidies in return for revenues.

Perhaps the most serious problems associated with the proposed plan involve administrative issues. For example, how exactly would the federal government build a reserve fund? It is quite possible that annual surpluses in the proposed reinsurance fund would simply be raided rather than saved. Alternatively, democratically elected lawmakers might view reinsurance-fund surpluses as evidence that premiums were too high rather than as an indication

---

41. As has been mentioned in the text, the French system allows only one exception to the general rule of a flat 9 percent catastrophe surcharge on all non-life-insurance policies. The exception relates to the surcharge on automobile-insurance policies, which is 6 percent, or two-thirds of the basic surcharge.

Table 8.8 Financing Options for a French-Type Catastrophe System in the United States: Three Possible Scenarios (in millions of current dollars)

Year	Private-Insurance Loss Payments for Natural Catastrophes (1)	Federal Disaster Payments (2)	Total Public and Private Disaster Payments (3)	Revenues from 13% Basic Surcharge Applied to Property Lines Only[a] (4)	Revenues from 13% Basic Surcharge Applied to All Property and Casualty Lines[a] (5)	Revenues from 6.5% Basic Surcharge Applied to All Property and Casualty Lines[a] (6)
1966	111	N.A.	N.A.	1,151	2,403	1,201
1967	327	N.A.	N.A.	1,237	2,593	1,297
1968	135	N.A.	N.A.	1,362	2,839	1,419
1969	256	N.A.	N.A.	1,545	3,195	1,597
1970	450	N.A.	N.A.	1,741	3,582	1,791
1971	173	N.A.	N.A.	1,976	3,857	1,928
1972	215	N.A.	N.A.	2,237	4,274	2,137
1973	376	N.A.	N.A.	2,443	4,648	2,324
1974	696	N.A.	N.A.	2,611	4,977	2,488
1975	513	N.A.	N.A.	2,826	5,538	2,769
1976	271	N.A.	N.A.	3,398	6,744	3,372
1977	423	3,536	3,959	3,996	8,089	4,044
1978	646	8,311	8,957	4,601	9,180	4,590
1979	1,703	6,873	8,576	5,072	10,128	5,064
1980	1,177	5,765	6,942	5,428	10,727	5,364
1981	714	9,507	10,221	5,682	11,123	5,561
1982	1,529	3,976	5,505	6,023	11,599	5,800
1983	2,255	2,420	4,675	6,334	12,095	6,048
1984	1,548	2,983	4,531	6,955	13,109	6,555

1985	2,816	2,210	5,026	8,465	16,086	8,043
1986	872	2,544	3,415	9,943	19,772	9,886
1987	946	2,463	3,409	10,563	21,603	10,802
1988	1,409	1,882	3,291	10,955	22,519	11,259
1989	7,642	7,031	14,673	11,065	23,140	11,570
1990	2,825	5,974	8,799	11,435	24,185	12,092
1991	4,723	2,640	7,363	11,745	24,685	12,343
1992	22,970	6,481	29,451	11,902	25,049	12,525
1993	5,620	6,656	12,276	12,763	26,649	13,325
1994	17,010	N.A.	N.A.	13,493	27,665	13,833
1995	7,795	N.A.	N.A.	14,423	28,596	14,298
Cumulative surplus, 1977–93[b]				1,861	148,672	3,802

Sources: Data courtesy of Property Claim Services; *Federal Disaster Assistance* (1995, table 1.1, p. 5); *Best's Aggregates and Averages—Property-Casualty* (1996, 191–94).

Note: N.A. = not available.

[a]The basic surcharge applies to nonautomobile policies. Automobile policies are assessed at two-thirds of the basic surcharge.

[b]Sum of potential revenues (in cols. 4, 5, or 6) minus sum of actual payments (col. 3), assuming no interest charges or receipts.

of prudent preparation for large future catastrophes. After all, the American electorate has consistently demonstrated its interest in having both high benefits and low taxes.

Nonetheless, the proposed system offers sufficient advantages over the current system to justify serious consideration. Most important, it would stabilize what is now a dangerously unstable system of natural disaster coverage—one in which insurance companies are running for cover, individual states are setting up financially fragile funds of their own, and the federal government is finding itself unable to resist costly bailouts of the uninsured.

As has been argued throughout the paper, this instability stems from two sources—one associated with the economics and the other with the politics of natural disasters. On the economics side, growing uncertainty about disaster forecasting combined with a vague perception that disaster activity is likely to increase in the future has left private insurers skittish. Presumably, insurers would be willing to sell plenty of natural catastrophe coverage in disaster-prone areas at some price, but a sufficiently high price would, in all likelihood, not only offend state regulators but also lead many propertyowners to dismiss catastrophe coverage as simply unaffordable. As a result, the markets for catastrophe risks in disaster-prone areas are contracting. On the political side, powerful public expectations have forced the federal government to cover a large fraction of uninsured disaster losses. The federal burden seems likely to increase in the future as a result of both the inherent moral hazard problem and a contracting private market for natural catastrophe risks. Since public subsidization of propertyowners in disaster-prone areas represents a political reality in the United States, the relevant question is not how to eliminate subsidies but rather how to cross-subsidize most efficiently.

A modified version of the French system would be well suited to address this complex web of economic and political problems. First, it would rationalize the market for disaster risk. By requiring disaster coverage to be a part of every property-insurance policy and establishing a federal reinsurance program, the proposed policy would not only make insurance against natural catastrophes available to all (or nearly all) propertyowners but also eliminate the need for market-distorting regulations at the state level, such as those found in Florida and California. Equally important, the stop-loss feature of the proposed reinsurance contract would transform what is now paralyzing uncertainty into manageable risk by shifting the liability for potential megacatastrophes from private insurers to the federal government. In this sense, the stop-loss provision represents a substitute for the proposed disaster-contingent-claims contracts because both address the problem of risk aversion on the part of insurers and reinsurers. The federal government is best positioned to reinsure the extraordinary risks associated with megacatastrophes because it boasts the deepest of all financial pockets.

The second basic advantage of the proposed system is that it would streamline what is now a rather chaotic federal disaster policy. An earmarked source of funds would become available to the federal government to compensate disaster victims, and cross-subsidization, which already exists, would become far more transparent and predictable. As has been noted, such cross-subsidization would necessarily create a moral hazard problem. But it is hoped that a substantial (say, 30 percent) retention requirement would lead private insurers to refuse coverage altogether for property in extremely hazardous areas. Perhaps most important, once a publicly sponsored program to make disaster insurance widely available was in place, the federal government might find itself more credible when it threatened to withhold relief from those relatively few who remained uninsured.

Clearly, the proposed system would not be perfect. Nor would it completely address the problem of natural disasters. The state and federal governments would still have to provide emergency assistance to disaster victims outside the reinsurance framework, and some particularly disaster-prone sectors of the economy—such as agriculture—probably would have to be dealt with separately, or at least on different terms. But I believe that the system proposed here would address many of the key problems highlighted throughout this paper. Above all, it would provide a framework for managing the two factors that have contributed most to a chaotic federal disaster policy: high and rising public expectations about automatic federal disaster relief, on the one hand, and the insurance industry's mounting uncertainty about (and fear of) mega-catastrophes, on the other.

References

Abeles, Schwartz & Assoc. 1978. *History of federal expenditures on pre- and post-disaster assistance relating to property acquisition: A report submitted to the Department of Housing, Policy Development and Research.* New York, March.

American insurance; still waters. 1993. *Economist,* 16 October, 93.

American National Red Cross. 1929. *The Mississippi Valley Flood disaster of 1927: Official report of the relief operations.* Washington, D.C.

Banham, Russ. 1995. A changing world: Science, business and risk prediction. *Risk Management* 42, no. 4 (April): 21–31.

Barton, Clara. Letters to Grover Cleveland, 13 November 1886 and 19 February 1887. Grover Cleveland Papers (microfilm ed., ser. 2, reel 41), Presidential Papers Microfilm, Library of Congress.

Benenson, Bob. 1993. Insurance finds few takers. *Congressional Quarterly Weekly Report* 51, no. 29 (17 July): 1861.

Best's aggregates and averages—property-casualty. 1996. Oldwick, N.J.: A. M. Best Co.

Bixby, Ann Kallman. 1993. Public social welfare expenditures, fiscal year 1990. *Social Security Bulletin* 56, no. 2 (Summer): 70–76.

A brief chronology of what Congress has done since 1824 to control the floods of the Mississippi. 1928. *Congressional Digest* 7 (February): 44–45.

Brostoff, Steven. 1996. Alternative disaster bill proposed. *National Underwriter: Property and Casualty/Risk and Benefits Management Edition,* 25 March, 3.

The budget of the United States government: Fiscal 1996. 1996. Washington, D.C.: U.S. Government Printing Office, June.

Camerer, Colin F., and Howard Kunreuther. 1989. Decision processes for low probability events: Policy implications. *Journal of Policy Analysis and Management* 8, no. 4 (Fall): 565–92.

Catalano, Peter. 1995. Hurricane alert! Expert predicts wave of killer hurricanes. *Popular Science* 247, no. 3 (September): 65–70.

Clinton pressed for additional flood aid. 1993. *Buffalo News,* 18 July, 1.

Commons, John R. 1919. Industrial relations. Address to the International Convention of Government Labor Officials, Madison, Wis., 3 June. In the microfilm ed. of the John R. Commons Papers, 1859–67, State Historical Society of Wisconsin, Division of Archives and Manuscripts, reel 17, frames 815–24.

Congressional Budget Office. 1996. Memorandum from Rachel Robertson, David Torregross, Kim Kowalewski, Perry Beider, Tim VandenBerg, and Pepper Santaluela (Congressional Budget Office) to Bill Hughes (House Committee on Transportation and Infrastructure). Washington, D.C., 2 February.

Cowen, Robert C. 1994. A sound method for forecasting hurricanes. *Christian Science Monitor,* 20 December, 13.

Critzer, Tess. 1995. U.S. insurers learn how to cope. *Insurance Industry International,* May, 11.

Dacy, Douglas, and Howard Kunreuther. 1969. *The economics of natural disasters: Implications for federal policy.* New York: Free Press.

Daniel, Pete. 1977. *Deep'n as it come: The 1927 Mississippi River Flood.* New York: Oxford University Press.

D'Arcy, Stephen P., and Virginia Grace France. 1992. Catastrophe futures: A better hedge for insurers. *Journal of Risk and Insurance* 59, no. 4 (December): 575–601.

Dewar, Helen. 1993. For Senate foes of spending, flood disaster spells relief. *Washington Post,* 5 August, A19.

Disastrous bonds. 1996. *Economist,* 31 August, 60.

Dreyfus, Jean-Marc. 1995. The C.C.R. (Caisse Centrale de Réassurance) and the reinsurance of natural disasters in France. Typescript. [In the possession of David A. Moss.]

Dunleavy, Jeanne H., Robin Edelman, Daniel J. Ryan, and C. Brett Lawless. 1996. *Catastrophes: A major paradigm shift for P/C insurers.* Oldwick, N.J.: A. M. Best, 25 March.

Durham, Wayne, Steve Johnson, and Julian Winston. 1995. Crisis in the wind—why action is needed now to prepare for tomorrow's "killer hurricanes." *CPCU Journal* 48, no. 1 (March): 17–34.

Emergency Supplemental Appropriations for Relief from the Major, Widespread Flooding in the Midwest Act of 1993. 1993. 103d Cong., 1st session. *U.S. Code Congressional and Administrative News* 3:1697.

Emerson, Bill, and Ted Stevens. 1995. Natural disasters: A budget time bomb. *Washington Post,* 31 October, A13.

Facts on File. 1993. *World News Digest,* 26 August, 624 E3.

Federal disaster assistance: Report of the Senate Task Force on Funding Disaster Relief. 1995. Washington, D.C.: U.S. Government Printing Office.

Federal Emergency Management Agency. 1993. *A citizen's guide to disaster assistance.* Washington, D.C.

Ferrara, Peter. 1995. Privatize federal disaster relief? *Washington Times,* 7 April, A18.

$5.7-billion disaster relief bill is approved, sent to Clinton. 1993. *St. Petersburg Times,* 7 August, 5A.

Freemantle, Tony. 1993. "Flood summit" centers on aid; Clinton asked for funds, not troops. *Houston Chronicle,* 18 July, A1.

Freivogel, William. 1993. Flood of money: Federal aid is sometimes uncoordinated and arbitrary. *St. Louis Post-Dispatch,* 26 September, 1B.

Galbraith, John Kenneth. [1958] 1984. *Affluent Society.* Boston: Houghton Mifflin.

Gastel, Ruth. 1996a. *Catastrophes: Insurance issues.* Insurance Information Institute Reports. New York, October.

———. 1996b. *Earthquakes: Risk and insurance issues.* Insurance Information Institute Reports. New York,.October.

Gettlin, Robert. 1996. Passage of disaster bill faces difficult future. *Best's Review: Property-Casualty Insurance Edition* 97, no. 2 (June): 8, 112.

Goodwin, Barry K., and Vincent H. Smith. 1995. *The economics of crop insurance and disaster aid.* Washington, D.C.: American Enterprise Institute Press.

Greene, Mark R. 1976. The government as an insurer. *Journal of Risk and Insurance* 43 (3 September): 393–407.

———. 1979. A review and evaluation of selected government programs to handle risk. *Annals of the American Academy of Political and Social Sciences* 443 (May): 129–44.

Grievous faults. 1995. *Economist,* 21 January, 79–80.

Hegger, Susan. 1993. Carnahan, Edgar, 4 other governors press Clinton for relief. *St. Louis Post-Dispatch,* 28 July, 9A.

Hoover, Herbert. 1952. *The Memoirs of Herbert Hoover: The cabinet and the presidency, 1920–1933.* New York: Macmillan.

Hoyt, William G., and Walter B. Langbein. 1955. *Floods.* Princeton, N.J.: Princeton University Press.

Hurd, Charles. 1959. *The compact history of the American Red Cross.* New York: Hawthorn.

Insurance Research Council. 1995. *Public attitude monitor, 1995.* Wheaton, Ill., November.

Jaffee, Dwight M., and Thomas Russell. 1997. Catastrophe insurance, capital markets, and uninsurable risks. *Journal of Risk and Insurance* 64, no. 2:205–30.

Keohe, Louise. 1995. California halts insurance "panic." *Financial Times,* 29 July, 3.

Kersnar, Scott. 1996. California earthquake insurance crisis boils over on FAIR plan. *National Mortgage News,* 10 June, 6.

Kielmas, Maria. 1996. French reinsurer Caisse Centrale de Réassurances accustomed to battling with forces of nature. *Business Insurance,* 7 October, G2.

Koenig, Robert L. 1993. Upper Mississippi lacks coordination of flood control. *St. Louis Post-Dispatch,* 29 August, 1A.

Koepp, Stephen. 1987. Rolling back regulation: A debate rages over how much freedom should be given to industry. *Time,* 6 July, 50–52.

Krauss, Clifford. 1993. The Midwest flooding; House approves flood relief after fight on deficit. *New York Times,* 28 July, A1.

Kunreuther, Howard. 1973. *Recovery from natural disasters: Insurance or federal aid.* Washington, D.C.: American Enterprise Institute.

———. 1993. Ambiguity and government risk-bearing for low probability events. In *Government risk-bearing: Proceedings of a conference held at the Federal Reserve Bank of Cleveland, May 1991,* ed. Mark S. Sniderman. Boston: Kluwer Academic.

Leggett, Jeremy. 1993. Who will underwrite the hurricane? *New Scientist* 139, no. 1885 (7 August): 28–33.

Lochhead, Carolyn. 1995. Talks begin on disaster insurance. *San Francisco Chronicle,* 19 October, A10.

Lohof, Bruce Alan. 1968. Hoover and the Mississippi Valley Flood: A case study of the political thought of Herbert Hoover. Ph.D. diss., Syracuse University.

Longman, Phillip. 1994. The politics of wind. *Florida Trends* 38, no. 4 (September): 30–40.

May, Peter J. 1985. *Recovering from catastrophes: Federal disaster relief policy and politics.* Westport, Conn.: Greenwood.

Message from the president relative to disaster assistance. 1970. 91st Congress, 2d sess., H. Doc. 91-323.

Mississippi River, hearings on H.R. 1749, a bill to prevent floods on the Mississippi River and improve navigation thereon. 1913. Washington, D.C.: U.S. Government Printing Office.

Monastersky, Richard. 1995. Los Angeles faces a dangerous quake debt. *Science News* 147, no. 3 (21 January): 37.

More aid arranged. 1993. *New York Times,* 24 September, A10.

Moss, David A. 1996. Government, markets, and uncertainty: An historical approach to public risk management in the United States. Working Paper no. 97-025. Harvard Business School, October.

———. 1998. Public risk management and the private sector: An exploratory essay. Working Paper no. 93-073. Harvard Business School, February.

Moss, David A., and Julie Rosenbaum. 1997. The Great Mississippi Flood of 1993. Case Study no. 797-097. Harvard Business School, 10 February.

Murphy, Susanne. 1995. Testimony on behalf of Bill Nelson, hearings on the Natural Disaster Protection Partnership Act of 1995 before the Subcommittee on Water Resources and Environment of the Committee on Transportation and Infrastructure. 104th Cong., 4th sess., 18 October.

National Oceanic and Atmospheric Administration. 1994. *The Great Flood of 1993: National disaster survey report.* Washington, D.C., February.

Navarro, Mireya. 1996. Florida facing crisis in insurance. *New York Times,* 25 April, A16.

Office of Emergency Preparedness. 1972. *Report to Congress: Disaster preparedness.* Washington, D.C.: U.S. Government Printing Office.

On the disaster dole. 1993. *Newsweek,* 2 August, 24.

Petch, Trevor. 1996. Developing options. *Financial Times,* 9 September, 7.

Phillips, Steven. 1994. *The Soil Conservation Service responds to the 1993 Midwest floods.* Washington, D.C.: U.S. Department of Agriculture, November.

Phinney, David. 1996. Congress considers dramatic changes in earthquake disaster assistance. Washington, D.C.: States News Service, 1 March.

Popkin, Roy S. 1990. The history and politics of disaster management in the United States. In *Nothing to fear: Risks and hazards in American society,* ed. Andrew Kirkby. Tucson: University of Arizona Press.

President Cleveland's veto statement. 16 February 1887. 49th Congress, 2d sess., Ex. Doc. 175.

Quackenbush, Chuck. 1996. On firmer ground. *San Diego Union-Tribune,* 6 October, G5.

Reeves, Richard. 1994. Californians: Let others pay. *Dallas Morning News,* 24 January, 15A.

Robin, Patricia McKinsey. 1984. The bit won't bite: The American Bilateral Investment Treaty Program. *American University Law Review* 33 (Summer): 931–58.

Scism, Leslie. 1996. California plan to sell quake policies is likely to reduce risks for insurers. *Wall Street Journal,* 4 September, A4.

Senate committee OKs aid bill. 1993. *Des Moines Register,* 31 July, 7.

Sharing the challenge: Floodplain management into the 21st century: Report of the Interagency Floodplain Management Review Committee. 1994. Washington, D.C.: U.S. Government Printing Office, June.

Sheets, Ken. 1993. After the flood. *Kiplinger's Personal Finance Magazine* 47, no. 10 (October): 67–71.

Small Business Administration Disaster Assistance Programs Hearings. 1994. Washington, D.C.: U.S. Government Printing Office.

Treaster, Joseph B. 1996. Insurer curbing sales of policies in storm areas. *New York Times,* 10 October, A1.

Unified National Program for Managing Flood Losses. 1966. 89th Cong., 2d sess., H. Doc. 465.

U.S. Army Corps of Engineers. 1993. *Annual flood damage report to Congress for fiscal year 1992.* Washington, D.C.

———. 1995. *Annual flood damage report to Congress for fiscal year 1994.* Washington, D.C.

U.S. Department of the Treasury. 1991. *Modernizing the financial system: Recommendations for safer, more competitive banks.* Washington, D.C., February.

Vega, Garcilaso de la. 1951. *The Florida of the Inca.* Translated by John Grier Varner and Jeannette Johnson Varner. Austin: University of Texas Press.

Wood, Daniel B. 1996. Lack of earthquake insurance rattles home-buyers. *Christian Science Monitor,* 3 June, 4.

Zolkos, Rodd. 1996. Reinsurance alternatives await in capital market. *Business Insurance,* 14 October, 1, 62–63.

Comment   Clement S. Dwyer Jr.

Florida is a microcosm of the problem that the insurance industry faces nationally.

There are four entities in Florida that deal with managing catastrophic risk in some fashion postevent: the Florida Hurricane Catastrophe Fund, the Florida Wind Pool, the Florida Residential Property and Casualty Joint Underwriting Association,[1] and the Guarantee Fund. In making sure that all these obligations are met, the first layer of defense is the ability of the securities to assess the industry on the basis of market share. The second is the ability to assess— particularly in the case of the Catastrophe Fund—all policies in force for a period of twenty years after the event. Florida has, therefore, in effect created an assessable mutual company. And I'm not talking only about homeowner's policies. I'm also talking about general liability policies, automobile policies, umbrella policies, whatever. The whole lot—except for workers' compensation—can be assessed to support catastrophe risk in the state. This is not what people think that they are getting when they contract for insurance coverage. Unfortunately, as Moss's paper makes clear, the market in this state is attempting to spread over a single state a risk of catastrophe exposure too great to be so diversified.

Florida presents us with a wonderful test case for the arguments surrounding the issues of affordability and availability of catastrophe insurance. In the wake

Clement S. Dwyer Jr. has been in the reinsurance industry for more than twenty-seven years as a broker, underwriter, and, most recently, an insurance-industry consultant in his firm, URSA Advisors, L.L.C. Mr. Dwyer is a director of several insurance and reinsurance companies and has acted as an adviser to the Florida Department of Insurance on various catastrophe-reinsurance issues.

1. This is the third largest homeowner's writer in the state of Florida. The last time I looked, it had about 925,000 policies in force, and, as the industry would complain, it is not the highest-cost provider. It bills itself as a residual market; however, it competes with the private sector.

of Hurricane Andrew, the Florida Commission on Hurricane Catastrophe Models was created (with the support of academics as well as industry practitioners and modeling companies). One of the early crises with which the commission was faced was whether the insurance commissioner would be forced to accept the rates for wind that the models produced. The rationale advanced in Tallahassee by Commissioner Nelson was that he was not going to give up control of the rate-setting process. What Florida presents us with, therefore, is an example of the political process standing in the way of market-clearing pricing.

I would also like to address the issue of cancellation and nonrenewal laws in the United States, which are poorly understood by many people. How long do you think that it would take, say, the Hartford Insurance Company to cancel all its business in New York's Nassau and Suffolk Counties? It would take fifty years (assuming that all policyholders pay their premiums) because an insurer can cancel only 2 percent of its policies per year in New York State. What has happened is that the state's insurance commissioner has expanded the FAIR Plan—and is, in fact, proposing to expand coverage further, to all downstate counties. Again, the market-clearing mechanisms of the private sector have been badly hindered by the regulatory process, and this problem is compounded as one moves across the country.

Another issue with which I have been struggling since coming to this conference is one involving the law of large numbers, where the loss of the few falls on the shoulders of the many. When does one cross from where the law of large numbers works to where it presents instead the problem of discrimination and cross-subsidization? Basic underwriting theory is a process of discriminating between good risks and bad. Unfortunately, that is not an easy thing to do. Moss raises the issue of cross-subsidization, and I myself believe that this is an issue that our society as a whole must address, but I am not sure of the proper forum in which to address it.

Specifically, the problem is whether the people of North Dakota should pay more for insurance so that the people of Palm Beach County can build expensive homes at the shore. I do not know how we can resolve this debate unless the country is prepared to accept coverage that is mandated at the point at which the mortgage originates. There is a clear conflict inherent in the operation of McCarran Ferguson, which delegates insurance regulation both to the states and to the federal government—the authority of the federal government extending only to those matters not explicitly delegated to the states. The insurance commissioners in North Dakota, Michigan, and Massachusetts therefore have a stake in the game in Florida. And the people clearly believe in them—not one elected insurance commissioner was not reelected in the most recent round of elections.

Moss's paper does a wonderful job of tracing the expansion of our society's expectations—pointing out that the nation as a whole is indeed prosperous enough to fulfill those expectations if it so desires. As far as the issue of federal involvement in the financing of catastrophe insurance is concerned, I believe that the proposed catastrophe bonds, Treasury catastrophe notes, and similar devices are excellent ideas because with them one develops a transparent price for the tail end of the distributions of losses. The reinsurance community does support such a development. We may, however, be expecting too much. This country works on a pay-as-you-go basis. And nothing will change unless a different political will is brought to the process than has been evinced heretofore.

In conclusion, I think that it will unfortunately take a major calamity to rationalize the system. Only then will the interested parties—the private sector, the consumer, the state regulator, and the federal regulator—recognize that they all must give up something. I don't say that this is a good way to solve the problem, but it may be the only way.

Comment   R. Glenn Hubbard

David Moss's illuminating paper considers the current state of federal disaster policy from a historical perspective. In a sweeping discussion of the evolution of federal disaster-relief policy since 1803 (when Congress assisted the victims of a fire in Portsmouth, N.H.), Moss highlights the rapid expansion of federal intervention after 1960. Arguing that this expansion is consistent with broader trends in government intervention in risk management, he suggests that expectations about intervention constrain the potential for rationalizing disaster policy. If unchecked, these expectations and constraints may lead to an exit of private insurers, further increasing disaster costs to taxpayers. Moss's paper closes by describing potential reforms and suggesting that the French policy of government reinsurance of natural catastrophe risks may serve as a good model for U.S. disaster policy in the future.

After describing the setting of the problems considered by Moss, I will organize my remarks in three areas: (1) lessons from political economy, (2) lessons from social insurance design, and (3) the role of private markets in disaster-risk management. While I will not discuss them in any detail, I recommend Moss's historical descriptions of disaster policy to anyone interested in the development of this increasingly costly area of federal intervention.

The Setting

Costs of property catastrophes in the United States have reached unprecedented levels in the 1990s. Total insured losses from natural disasters amounted to $75 billion between 1989 and 1995, where as they were only $51 billion for the whole of the period between 1950 and 1988 (see Borden and

R. Glenn Hubbard is the Russell L. Carson Professor of Economics and Finance at Columbia University and a research associate of the National Bureau of Economic Research.

Sarkar 1996). In addition, two developments suggest that high costs will remain for the foreseeable future. First, rising catastrophe-related costs offer some evidence that catastrophic risk has increased significantly in recent years. Second, rapid population growth in catastrophe-prone areas indicates a continuing trend toward increased costs of catastrophes. These developments do not bode well for private insurers. As a point of reference, U.S. primary-insurance-industry capital is about $20 billion (Canter, Cole, and Sandor, in press). This greater exposure raises the question of what role the federal government should play in disaster insurance or, more broadly, in disaster policy.

Federal intervention has grown in ad hoc phases and in systematic phases. Prior to the 1920s, federal responses were largely minor and coordinated with the Red Cross. Following the disastrous Mississippi Flood of 1927, the federal government increased spending on flood relief and effectively assumed responsibility for flood-control projects (see also the popular account in Barry 1997). The Federal Disaster Act of 1950 authorized a permanent relief fund with broad discretion (giving future officials the opportunity to feel their constituents' pain). This scope for intervention was expanded further by the 1970 disaster relief act. In tandem with relief polices, federal disaster insurance expanded in the 1960s and 1970s. The National Flood Insurance Act of 1968 and the Federal Crop Insurance Act of 1980 tried to substitute a federally backed insurance program for ad hoc disaster relief, but participation by propertyowners was poor. In 1978, the Federal Energy Management Agency (FEMA) was created to coordinate disaster programs distributed across several government agencies and to consolidate the management of escalating spending.

The Great Midwest Flood of 1993 was the proverbial watershed event in federal disaster relief, with FEMA overseeing the expenditure of more than $1 billion of disaster insurance (compared to the $10 million spent by the government in response to the 1927 flood). The Clinton administration requested additional payments to communities, small businesses, and farmers.

The problems emerge from this evolution of federal disaster relief and insurance policy. First, potential budget costs are significant, in the light of a federal commitment with no clearly articulated limits. Second, past government behavior makes statements that aid will not be forthcoming to individuals not meeting particular criteria or following prescribed rules not credible. Third, the combination of an expanding federal commitment and increased uncertainty about catastrophe risk may lead to widespread exit by private insurers putting further pressure on federal disaster intervention.

These concerns have led to proposals at the state and federal levels. Florida and California have established insurers or reinsurers of last resort, although states are poorly equipped to diversify catastrophe risks. At the federal level, 1994 legislation tightened enforcement of flood-insurance requirements in the National Flood Insurance Program, although credibility issues remain. The insurance industry has suggested the creation of the Natural Disaster Insurance

Corporation (NDIC), to be financed and administered collectively by private insurance; the NDIC would cap private insurers' disaster liability and would be authorized to borrow from the U.S. Treasury in the event of severe catastrophes. The Clinton administration proposed selling disaster-contingent claims on the open market, but the administration's proposal does little to encourage the development of private markets. The historical record suggests, however, that pressure for cross-subsidization across regions and credibility problems will limit the potential for success of the scheme.

Outside the United States, Moss identifies the French Caisse Centrale de Réassurance (CCR) as a possible model for reform. Mapping the scheme to the U.S. setting, a CCR-like approach would suggest the following. The federal government would require that specific coverage against natural catastrophes be included in every property-insurance policy. In addition, a premium surcharge would be mandated to pay for the additional coverage. Finally, such a plan would establish a federally guaranteed reinsurance program, allowing private insurers to cede most of risk (and premiums) to the government. I will return to this proposal in the context of social insurance below.

Lessons from Political Economy

As Moss's paper makes clear, economic analysis of government disaster policy must address "political economy" as well as "optimal policy" considerations. Historical developments in the U.S. banking industry offer some guidance for the present case. In the late nineteenth and early twentieth centuries, losses (generally by smaller, poorly diversified banks) in particular regions of a state generated political pressure for redistribution within a state—in the form of state deposit-insurance schemes (see, e.g., the discussion in Economides, Hubbard, and Palia 1996). The subsequent failure of state insurance schemes in the presence of larger banking crises ("catastrophes") led to political pressure for federal cross-subsidization (among banks and among regions of the country) of risk bearing through federal deposit insurance.

As is by now well known, the government assumption of bank deposit-risk management through deposit insurance failed key tests of insurance design. The presence of large amounts of insured or effectively insured deposits created the potential for moral hazard precisely when adverse shocks to industry capital appeared (as in the savings-and-loan industry in the early 1980s and the banking industry in the late 1980s). Moreover, it is difficult to motivate U.S.-styled deposit insurance as simply a response to a market failure.

Lessons from U.S. banking regulatory experience have shaped present banking-regulation proposals and offer guidance for casualty insurance. Chief among these are the importance of risk-based pricing and an expanded role for private markets in reinsurance of deposits to ensure market discipline. Economists generally argue that a public lender of last resort (such as the Federal Reserve in the United States) can be the final "catastrophic" reinsurer.

For disaster policy, experience of the political economy of banking regulation suggests the need to be wary of excessive cross-subsidization of risk and the need to encourage the develop of private reinsurance and market discipline.

Lessons from Social Insurance

Sidestepping the political economy of intervention, how might we set up a "social insurance" approach to disaster policy? The basic problem is that of systematic risk—in this case, the chance of a major catastrophe or series of major catastrophes that might bankrupt the private-insurance industry.

Social insurance principles suggest a way of organizing thoughts about deposit insurance. First, to mitigate the free-rider problem so endemic to disaster insurance, coverage for individuals and businesses must be (credibly) mandatory. Second, deductibles and coinsurance should align incentives for risk management by the insured. Third, private-sector reinsurance should be mobilized to pool risks across insurers in different regions with different exposures to catastrophic risks. Fourth, as in the banking analogy, the government's role would be limited to that of a lender of last resort. In the insurance context, this amounts to the combination of a catastrophic payment (mandatory insurance) with a deductible and coinsurance. The "lender-of-last-resort" role would replace ad hoc interventions.

To be successful, such a scheme based on social insurance principles must develop strong markets for private reinsurance. I say this for two reasons. First, private-reinsurance markets offer market discipline in the pricing and management of catastrophic disk. Second, absent well-functioning and deep private-reinsurance markets, the temptation for ad hoc government intervention in a disaster with large private losses becomes great, undermining the credibility of overall disaster policy.

Enhanced Role for Private Markets

The key to the improvement of private catastrophe insurance and reinsurance markets is the development and promotion of property-catastrophe-risk financial instruments ("securitization") of risk. In addition to the desirability of liquid financial markets for risk management, insurers have few additional avenues of assistance. Escalating prices for reinsurance combined with lower coverage amounts have made it more difficult for insurance companies to mitigate their risk through reinsurance. In addition, state regulatory restrictions limit (and in some cases prevent) companies from increasing premiums and reducing coverage in response to higher costs of reinsurance.

Since 1992, several financial instruments have emerged to securitize property-catastrophe risk. These instruments include exchange-traded options and futures, over-the-counter insurance products, and insurance swaps. As a consequence, individuals or businesses can take positions on the occurrence and cost of property catastrophes. Insurance companies can hedge their exposure by transferring property-catastrophe risk to a wide pool of willing investors.

While securitization represents an important and necessary development in enhancing the private sector's role in catastrophe management, instrument-design issues remain. Catastrophe-risk exposures can be specified by, for example, location, disaster type, and time of year. One must also sort out which participants bear which type of investment risk (i.e., among liquidity risk, basis risk, credit risk, adverse selection, or moral hazard). The most successful financial instruments will be those with low costs imposed by these investment risks.

For example, property-catastrophe options (traded on the Chicago Board of Trade [CBOT]) offer one approach. Most trades create "call spreads" comparable to purchasing a layer of insurance. The options offer minimal credit risk (given the role of the CBOT clearinghouse) and basis risk (unless for an insurance company because the payoff is based on aggregate industry claim payments). Adverse selection is minimized by the use of standardized instruments; moral hazard is mitigated by the use of an industry-based index. These advantages notwithstanding, liquidity risk remains a concern because of the low trading volume; many analysts believe that higher volume and lower liquidity risk are likely in the future (see Borden and Sarkar 1996).

Catastrophe bonds (or "act-of-God" bonds) are an example of an over-the-counter instrument. Such bonds create a link between the repayment and the catastrophe with variable coupon and principal repayments. As with the exchange-traded projects, liquidity risk remains a problem. Unlike the exchange-traded products, credit risk must be borne. While basis risk is nonexistent, the customized nature of the bonds could lead to adverse selection (if only the riskier insurance companies issue the bonds) and moral hazard (if the repayment is related to the issuer's individual catastrophe costs).

Finally, property-catastrophe swaps to be traded on the Catastrophic Risk Exchange (CATEX) are at an early stage of development. The swap is a bilateral agreement with reciprocal reinsurance between two insurers. Units of exchange are standardized by specifying "equivalent" risks and exposures. It is too early to assess the liquidity risk associated with these products. Counterparty credit risk must be borne. Basis risk, adverse selection, and moral hazard depend on the attributes of the individual swap design.

To summarize, recent market developments suggest that private markets can play a larger role in property-catastrophe risk management. Risks can be spread across a broader pool of individuals and business. These developments can reduce the effect of catastrophes on the insurance industry as a whole.

Conclusion

David Moss's interesting and readable paper highlights the need for economists, industry leaders, and policymakers to rethink federal disaster policy in the United States. The history of federal involvement in disaster insurance and relief—combined with experience with government intervention in risk management in other industries—leads one to be concerned about the need to maintain healthy private markets for managing risk. Lessons from both the political economy of regulation and social insurance design point out the need for well-functioning private-reinsurance mechanism. Recent developments of financial instruments for managing property-catastrophe risk offer an encouraging sign for private-insurance and -reinsurance markets in the future.

References

Barry, John M. 1997. *Rising tide: The Great Mississippi Flood of 1927 and how it changed America.* New York: Simon & Schuster.

Borden, Sara, and Asani Sarkar. 1996. Securitizing property catastrophe risk. *Current Issues in Economics and Finance* (Federal Reserve Bank of New York) 2 (August): 1–6.

Canter, Michael S., Joseph B. Cole, and Richard L. Sandor. In press. Catastrophe options on the Chicago Board of Trade: A new asset class for the capital markets and a new hedging tool for the insurance industry. *Financial Derivatives and Risk Management.*

Economides, Nicholas, R. Glenn Hubbard, and Darius Palia. 1996. The political economy of branching restrictions and deposit insurance: A model of monopolistic competition among small and large banks. *Journal of Law and Economics* 40 (October): 667–704.

9   The Moral Hazard of Insuring the Insurers

James G. Bohn and Brian J. Hall

9.1 Motivation

It has long been understood that insurance creates both benefits (risk reduction) and costs (moral hazard–induced distortions to incentives). The existence of so many insurance contracts in the market suggests that, in a wide variety of cases, the benefits exceed the costs of insurance coverage. But what happens if the company providing insurance fails and is unable to pay off policyholders? Presumably, there should be a market for insurance against insurance-company failure. But this just pushes the problem back a step. What if the insurer of the insurer fails? If consumers desire genuine protection against risk, the market, with or without the government's help, must figure out how to insure the insurers.

In the United States, the response to this problem has been the organization of quasi-governmental "guaranty funds" at the state level, each of which serves as the insurer of the insurance companies operating in that state. The state guaranty funds are implicitly backed by state governments, giving policyholders reasonable certainty that their claims will be paid even if their insurance company becomes insolvent.

But, just as insurance distorts incentives to individuals, the second-level insurance provided by the guaranty funds distorts the incentives of insurance companies. That is, guaranty-fund insurance creates incentives for insurance companies, especially those on the brink of failure, to engage in too much risk. But what form might this moral hazard take? Where might one look for evi-

James G. Bohn is an economist at the Board of Governors of the Federal Reserve System. Brian J. Hall is associate professor of business administration at the Harvard Business School and a faculty research fellow of the National Bureau of Economic Research.

The authors thank David Scharfstein, Christopher McGhee, Anne Gron, and Neil Doherty for helpful comments and Tom Gunderson for excellent research assistance.

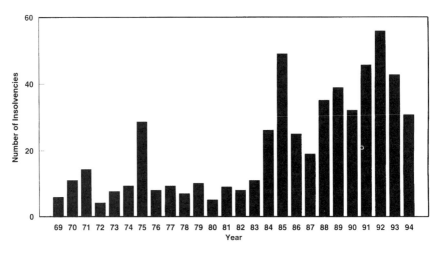

Fig. 9.1   Number of property-casualty insurer insolvencies

dence of excessive risk? Does such evidence exist? These questions are the subject of this paper.

A major motivation for this study was a finding in previous research (Bohn and Hall 1995; Hall 1996) that the costs of resolving property-casualty insurance-company failures are surprisingly large. The total cost of resolving a property-casualty insurer failure[1] is in the range of 100–120 percent of the company's preinsolvency assets. This number is three to four times larger than analogous cost estimates of resolving depository-institution failures.[2] Moreover, both the number of property-casualty insurer insolvencies and the total costs of these insolvencies have risen in the last decade (see figs. 9.1 and 9.2). These large resolution costs suggest that the perverse incentives created by the guaranty-fund system may be large. That is, moral hazard may be an explanation for these large costs.

The starting point for our analysis is the parallel between deposit insurance and the insurance provided by guaranty funds, both of which provide second-level insurance against insolvency.[3] The existence of (flat-rate) deposit insurance enables banks to engage in risky behavior without paying the appropriate

1. The total cost of resolving failures is equal to the costs of paying claims, plus the administrative costs of the liquidators and guaranty funds, minus recoveries from asset sales. Bohn and Hall (1995) found that the ratio of costs to preinsolvency assets was equal to one. Using an updated data set, Hall (1996) found this number to be about 1.2.

2. James (1991), Bovenzie and Murton (1988), and Barth, Bartholomew and Bradley (1991) all find that the net cost of resolving bank failures is about one-third of preinsolvency assets.

3. There are two main differences between the deposit-insurance and guaranty-fund systems. First, unlike the bank-insurance fund, the guaranty funds are not prefunded (assessments are levied after insolvencies occur since there is no "fund"). Second, the guaranty funds are operated at the state rather than the federal level. The guaranty-fund system is described in the next section.

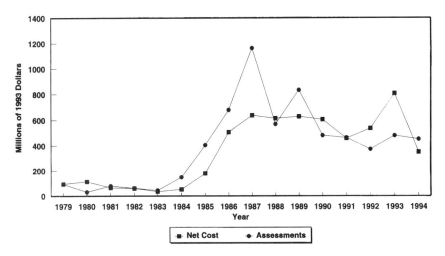

Fig. 9.2   Aggregate net cost of resolving property-casualty insurer insolvencies and total guaranty fund assessments

price for their risk taking.[4] Because depositors are insured against the risk of bank failure, they do not have incentives to monitor or discipline banks. Deposits represent a risk-free, and *adverse-selection-free,* form of borrowing for banks. This enables even the riskiest of banks to borrow in capital markets. Indeed, by raising deposit rates by small amounts, banks were able to attract large amounts of deposits (made easier by an active brokered deposit market), which they then invested in risky loans.[5] The existence of deposit insurance (albeit in combination with other factors) is widely believed to be the main cause of the savings-and-loan debacle, which in the end cost taxpayers approximately $150 billion.

Although it has been much less studied by academics, the insurance provided by guaranty funds creates similarly perverse incentives.[6] Although insurance companies do not accept deposits, they do receive premiums. Since there is a lag between the time that premiums are received and the time that losses are paid out, attracting premiums is a way to borrow from policyholders. The key similarity between the two systems is that guaranty-fund insurance diminishes the incentives of policyholders to monitor or discipline insurance companies, just as deposit insurance decreases the incentives for depositors to monitor banks. Thus, the guaranty-fund system creates a peculiar way for insurance companies to borrow with little discipline from capital markets—by writing

4. For an analytic proof, see Merton (1977).

5. For analysis of the savings-and-loan crisis and the perverse incentives created by deposit insurance, see Kane (1989).

6. Cummins (1988) analyzes how guaranty funds affect risk taking and how a risk-based premium structure can reduce the perverse incentives of guaranty funds.

premiums. Consistent with this possibility, we find evidence of excessive premium growth by property-casualty insurers in the years before insolvency. Moreover, this premium growth is more pronounced in long-tail lines, which have a long lag between premium payments and policyholder claims and therefore represent a more attractive way for insurance companies to borrow from policyholders.

This paper proceeds as follows. In the next section, we provide some background on the guaranty-fund system and describe the guaranty-fund rules. In the third section, we discuss the theory of how the guaranty funds create perverse incentives for insurance companies, especially those on the brink of failure. In the fourth section, we describe our data and present evidence on the degree of preinsolvency premium growth. In the fifth section, we disaggregate the premium growth into lines (e.g., personal property, corporate liability, etc.) and show that much of the fast growth in premiums is in long-tail lines. The sixth section contains some evidence on the relation between state regulatory resources and premium growth. The final section summarizes and contains additional discussion and interpretation of the results.

9.2 Guaranty Fund Background and Description of Rules

The guaranty-fund system was a response to a federal initiative in the late 1960s to establish a guaranty system for insurance companies similar to the FDIC.[7] Worried about a federal government "takeover" of insurance-company regulation, the National Association of Insurance Commissioners (NAIC) proposed model legislation for the establishment of guaranty funds at the state level. By the early 1970s, about three-fourths of the states had adopted guaranty-fund provisions that were closely based on the NAIC's model act. Most of the other states followed shortly thereafter.

Guaranty funds are generally nonprofit associations of all companies licensed to write insurance within a state in lines covered by the guaranty fund. Insurance companies are required to be a part of the guaranty-fund system in order to obtain a license. The board of each guaranty fund is composed of representatives from member firms and from the state insurance commissioner's office.

The state insurance departments, not the guaranty funds, are responsible for the regulation and oversight of insurance companies, which includes the prevention and detection of insurance-company insolvencies. Thus, involvement of the guaranty fund comes only after a company is declared to be insolvent, at which point the guaranty fund takes over the files of the failed insurer and pays the claims of policyholders.

In most cases, guaranty funds pay the full amount of policyholder claims in the same way that payment would be made by insurance companies. However,

---

7. Much of the material in this section is derived from Bohn and Hall (1995), Duncan (1987), and Epton and Bixby (1976).

there are some caps and deductibles. In most states, and in most lines, the caps on the funds' liability per claim are in the $300,000–$500,000 range. Thus, for the vast majority of claims, especially in personal lines, the caps are rarely binding. In addition, the deductibles are very small, ranging from $0.00 to $200 per claim, with most funds having a deductible of $100. Note also that, since guaranty funds pay only for the claims of the policyholders residing in their state, a failure of a multistate insurance company involves action on the part of multiple guaranty funds.

State insurance departments are responsible for the liquidation of the assets of the failed insurer. The proceeds of the liquidation are turned over to the guaranty funds to pay the claims of policyholders. Hall (1996) has shown, however, that, after paying all expenses related to the liquidation process, the state regulatory departments turn over an average of only thirty-seven cents for each dollar of preinsolvency assets. Thus, there is typically a large shortfall between the assets of the failed insurers and the obligations of the guaranty funds. The guaranty funds cover this shortfall by levying assessments against the solvent companies doing business in the state of the insolvent firms. The magnitude of assessments is directly proportional to a firm's share of direct premiums written within a state in lines covered by the fund.[8] Thus, the size of assessments is not related to any measure of a company's insolvency risk. Guaranty funds also make assessments to cover their administrative, legal, and other expenses.

Guaranty funds are not really funds since all but New York operate on a postassessment basis. That is, guaranty funds maintain no reserves and assess member insurance companies only after an insolvency occurs.[9] In most states, the assessment amount is capped at 2 percent of premiums written per year, although some states maintain lower caps. In addition, most state regulations contain provisions that enable companies to partially offset assessments. For example, most states include the cost of assessments as a factor in determining premiums. In addition, many states allow insurers to recover a portion of their assessment with credits against their premium taxes, which shifts a portion of the costs of the insolvency to other state taxpayers.

9.3   Theory: Guaranty-Fund Insurance and Moral Hazard

We begin by thinking about an insurance company that is insolvent or nearly insolvent but still operating because it has not yet been "caught" by the regulators. The company is having trouble meeting its expenses because of misman-

---

8. Guaranty funds are typically organized into separate accounts covering broad lines of insurance. The most common form of organization has three separate accounts—workers' compensation, automobile, and "all other" types of insurance. However, different states operate as few as one or as many as six accounts.

9. New York State adopted guaranty-fund legislation in 1947. Unlike other funds, New York's operates on a preassessment basis. The state maintains a fund of $150–$200 million for the resolution of insurance failures. Firms writing insurance in the state are assessed whenever the fund balance falls below the lower bound.

agement, higher than expected losses, or some other circumstance. The management of the firm would like the firm to continue operations. That is, the firm needs to find some cash in order to continue operating (and to pay its employees' and executives' salaries, among other things). There are three main options available to such a firm:

Option 1. The company could raise outside financing. However, if the market requires the company to pay something even close to the appropriate risk premium, such financing would be extremely costly. In addition, such a company may not be able to raise any outside financing at all because of credit rationing (see Stiglitz and Weiss 1981). Moreover, the current owners of such a firm are likely to have some knowledge of the firm's financial circumstances and are therefore reluctant to inject additional capital.

Option 2. The company could sell off some of its assets to raise cash.[10] However, such an action may be very transparent to regulators since assets are fairly easy to measure and value (at least relative to liabilities) and such firms do not want to become noticed by the regulators. These firms have an incentive to behave in ways that increase their riskiness, but they must balance the benefits of engaging in risky behavior against the costs of increasing the probability of getting caught.

Option 3. The company could attract more premiums, perhaps at prices below expected costs. The key insight is that selling premiums is similar to taking out a loan; premium payments represent an immediate inflow of cash and require (probabalistic) payments to be made at a later date. However, because the guaranty fund protects policyholders against insolvency risk, this type of "loan" (i.e., selling of premiums) is an *adverse-selection-free* form of finance. In order to borrow in this peculiar way, firms do not have to pay a large risk premium (because the guaranty funds protects the lenders, who in this case are the policyholders); nor do insurance companies need to worry about being credit rationed out of the market when they borrow in this way. Perhaps equally important, it seems likely that option 3 would be less transparent to regulators than option 2 (selling assets) since reserving (which involves the estimation of the liability created by a particular policy) is an inexact science. That is, if a company needs cash and wants to game the system, it is likely to be easier to write more premiums and reduce its reported liabilities (by underestimating its future losses) than to sell off its assets, which are more easily measured by regulators.

To see why writing premiums is essentially borrowing money from policyholders consider the following equation:

---

10. In related work, Hall (1996) presents evidence that the assets of many failed companies are of poor quality, which is consistent with this possibility.

$$(P_t - C_t)(1 + r_t) = E_t(L_{t+1}),$$

where P is premiums, C is costs, r is the interest rate, and L is losses. The left-hand side of the equation shows the revenues, net of the cost to operate the company, that a company generates during the year from writing premiums. Assuming for simplicity that all losses come in the subsequent period, the right-hand side shows the expectation of next-period losses at time $t + 1$. Competitive pressures, or, more precisely, a zero-profit condition, imply equality between the two in expectation. Note that, when a firm writes a policy, it essentially borrows premiums (net of costs), which it then pays back to policyholders with interest.

This equation can be rewritten as:

$$P_t - C_t = \frac{E_t(L_{t+1})}{(1 + r_t)}.$$

The left-hand side is equal to borrowing by the insurance company, and the right-hand side is equal to the net present value of (collective) repayment by policyholders. Without guaranty-fund insurance, an insolvent or nearly insolvent company's repayments would be heavily discounted by lenders (policyholders). In practice, this would mean that premium prices would have to be lowered substantially. However, the existence of guaranty-fund insurance removes the riskiness of "lending" to insurance companies, enabling them to borrow at something close to the risk-free rate. This implies that, because of guaranty-fund insurance, highly risky insurance companies should be able to increase their premiums (and, therefore, their cash flow) substantially with only small changes in premium prices.

As noted earlier, our story of how the guaranty-fund system affects the incentives of insurance companies is very similar to models in the banking literature about the moral hazard problems associated with deposit insurance. Deposit insurance enables banks, even risky ones, to borrow from depositors at the risk-free rate. The incentive to borrow at the risk-free rate and use the funds to make high-risk loans is especially attractive to poorly capitalized banks. Deposit insurance and limited liability combine to give the owners of the company what is essentially a put option. For banks "at the money" or "out of the money" (insolvent or nearly insolvent), increasing the volatility of their earnings increases the value of the bank.

That same principle applies to insurance companies. The incentive to borrow excessively from policyholders (attract premiums) and to use the money to make risky investments (perhaps by writing high-risk policies and/or under-reserving) is especially strong for insurance companies that are already insolvent. Like the banks, they face "heads-I-win-tails-somebody-else-loses" incentives. Indeed, Kane (1989) has argued that the combination of poorly capitalized banks, deposit insurance, and regulatory forbearance created what he termed savings-and-loan zombies, so-called because they sucked the life out of the healthy savings and loans by competing away their business with their aggressively risky behavior. This put the solvent savings and loans at risk, which in turn created more zombies. Although we do not test for this in our empirical section, our analysis of the incentives created by the guaranty funds suggests at least the possibility that the guaranty-fund system could create zombie insurance companies.

Finally, it should be noted that an extreme case of our story of how insurance companies can game the guaranty-fund system is through a Ponzi scheme. In our previous story, insurance companies were gaming the system by maximizing the expected value of the company, which involved high risks since the downside is essentially capped at zero. Under a Ponzi scheme, even a company that has no hope of ever becoming solvent can play. A company can increase premium growth while writing negative net present value (NPV) policies. When the losses occur, the company can pay these claims by writing even more negative NPV policies. A company can then live to another day, with all the benefits to management that are associated with continued operations. As is well known, however, all Ponzi schemes eventually fail. We come back to this issue in the final section, where the results are discussed and interpreted.

9.4   Preinsolvency Premium Growth

One way to examine the moral hazard effects of guaranty-fund insurance is to analyze how company financial condition correlates with risk-taking behavior. Ideally, one could analyze whether exogenously determined poor financial conditions were associated with excessive premium growth and other types of risk-taking behavior. However, in addition to the difficulty in finding a good instrument for financial condition, even using uninstrumented capital ratios as a measure of financial condition may be problematic. If our measure of capital is quite noisy (because companies that are gaming the system are also able to manipulate their book-value measure of capital), then a correlation between truly low capital rates and game playing may be hard to detect. Moreover, if, in addition to those companies gaming the system, there are many responsible companies—companies with negative shocks to their capital positions behave conservatively in the next period in order to regain their preshock financial status (a type of mean reversion)—then it will be difficult to find evidence of gaming the system even if such evidence exists. Thus, although this approach (analyzing all companies in poor financial condition) has considerable merit, it also has potentially serious problems. We thus decided to take a different approach.

Our approach is to examine the preinsolvency behavior of companies that become insolvent. While this approach does not represent a formal test proving causality between the guaranty fund and risk taking (measured by excessive premium growth in this case), it does have an obvious advantage: if game playing does exist and is serious enough to cause a significant number of insolvencies, then one should be able to detect a pattern of excessive premium growth prior to insolvency in a sample of failed companies.

9.4.1   Data Description

Our sample consists of property-casualty insurance firms that failed between 1987 and 1995. The initial set of failed firms was assembled from *Best's Insurance Reports* and the list of failures involving guaranty-fund activity provided by the National Conference of Insurance Guaranty Funds (see NCIGF 1991–93). For each failed firm, we searched Best's and Lexis/Nexis for the date on which the firm was declared insolvent.[11] All our analysis was conducted at the firm rather than the group level. We define year t as the year in which the firm was found to be insolvent. Years prior to the year of failure are henceforth referred to as $t - 1$, the calendar year prior to the year in which the firm was found insolvent, $t - 2$, $t - 3$, and so forth.

The set of firms was then merged with accounting information from the National Association of Insurance Commissioners's (NAIC) annual statement database. Firms that did not file annual statements in the three years prior to insolvency were omitted from the sample. Thus, we have information concerning the financial position and business mix of each active firm for the three-year period prior to assumption of management of the firm by regulators. There are 135 failed insurance companies in our sample.

9.4.2   Results

In this section, we look for evidence that insurance companies are gaming the system by examining the preinsolvency premium growth of firms that fail. Figure 9.3 plots the distribution of failed companies in terms of their premium growth in the two years prior to insolvency. This represents premium growth from year $t - 3$ to year $t - 1$ since t is defined to be the year of insolvency. Specifically, the figure plots the percentage of (failed) property-casualty insurance companies that had premium growth of 0–10 percent, 10–20 percent, and so on in the two-year period prior to insolvency.[12] The striking feature of the distribution is the extremely high number of companies in the "high-premium-growth" tail, both as a proportion of the total and relative to the proportion of companies in the center of the distribution.[13] For example, more than 35 percent of failed companies had total premium growth of more than 50 percent (in real terms) in the two years prior to failure.

---

11. The sequence of events involved in the takeover of a failed insurance company by the regulators is similar across states; however, terminology differs substantially. For our purposes, a court order declaring the insurer insolvent, the placement of the firm in rehabilitation, and the placement of the firm in conservation are equivalent since all three events entail the regulators assuming primary responsibility for the management of the firm.

12. A very similar pattern emerged when we looked at premium growth in the year prior to failure ($t - 2$ to $t - 1$), but we focus on growth rates in the two years prior to insolvency to decrease the possibility that idiosyncratic factors in one year generate noisy growth rates.

13. Note that, in its *Insolvency Report* (1991), A. M. Best also reports high premium growth for property-casualty insurance companies that subsequently failed.

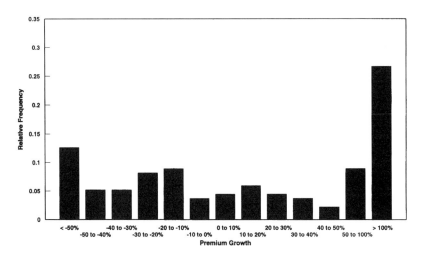

Fig. 9.3   Premium growth from year $t - 3$ to year $t - 1$, 135 failed firms

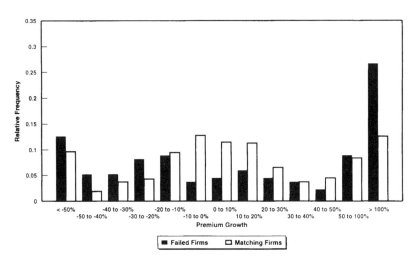

Fig. 9.4   Premium growth from year $t - 3$ to year $t - 1$, 135 failed and 540 solvent firms matched by size and year

In order to determine whether the large percentage of high-growth firms in the failed sample is unusual, we compared our sample with a matched sample—on the basis of asset size and year failed. In order to reduce noise, we picked four matches (the two nearest larger and the two nearest smaller) for each of our 135 failed firms. The two-year premium-growth rates are plotted in figure 9.4. While the matched sample also contains a reasonably large number of high-growth companies, presumably because these firms are relatively small by industry standards, the percentage of high-growth firms is less than half the percentage of high-growth companies in the failed sample. The evidence suggests that there is an unusually large percentage of firms that grew quickly prior to failure. This is consistent with the view that the incentives created by the guaranty funds are leading to moral-hazard-induced fast premium growth.

9.5   Premium Growth and Business Composition

In the previous section, we showed that a disproportionate number of failed insurance companies had unusually high premium growth prior to failure. In this section, we disaggregate the premiums into line composition to determine which lines were associated with this growth. The key question is, If insurance companies are gaming the system, which lines are they likely to increase the most?

9.5.1   Long-Tail Lines

There are several reasons to suspect that insurance companies that seek to game the system are likely to use premium growth in long-tail lines. First, it is harder to estimate the future losses in long-tail lines precisely. Liability claims are less predictable than, for example, physical damage from automobile accidents. While insurance companies normally find uncertainty about future losses an unattractive feature, it is a desirable characteristic for a company that wishes to game the system by underreserving. Second, the simple fact that long-tail lines create long-term borrowing opportunities for insurance-company gamers makes premium growth in these lines attractive. The one thing desired by insurance companies that want to game the system is more time. Increasing premium growth in long-tail lines enables companies to buy that time.

9.5.2   Results

In order to test this possibility, we divided our failed sample into fast-growth (real premium growth of over 50 percent between year $t - 3$ and year $t - 1$) companies and slow-growth companies. We then looked at how the fraction of premiums in long-tail lines changed for the fast-growth firms relative to the slow-growth firms in a variety of lines of business. (The precise definitions of how we categorized the lines of business appears in the appendix.) The results are presented in table 9.1. The first three columns show the results for the forty-seven fast-growth companies. The fraction of premiums written in the specific line is shown for $t - 3$, then $t - 1$, followed by the change between the two years. The results are then repeated for the eighty-seven slow-growth firms in the next three columns.

The results indicate that fast-growth companies increased their fraction of premiums in long-tail lines from an average of about 31 percent to almost 70

Table 9.1   **Failed Firms Partitioned by Growth Rates**[a]

Line of Business	Fast Mean $t-3$	Fast Mean $t-1$	Change in Fast	Slow Mean $t-3$	Slow Mean $t-1$	Change in Slow
% in long-tail lines	30.98	69.79	+38.81	62.56	59.84	−2.73
% in personal property	28.25	21.14	−7.10	18.69	16.78	−1.91
% in personal liability	14.53	40.00	+25.47	28.21	24.94	−3.27
% in corporate property	41.51	12.79	−28.71	22.78	29.53	6.74
% in corporate liability	15.70	26.05	+10.35	30.31	28.74	−1.56
% in workers' compensation	13.61	9.74	−3.88	13.44	12.85	−.59
% in automobile	38.31	58.43	+20.12	40.38	36.01	−4.36

	Statistical Tests of Changes			
	Change in Fast	Change in Slow	t-Test (p-value)	Wilcoxon (p-value)
% in long-tail lines	+38.81	−2.73	.0263	.0396
% in personal property	−7.10	−1.91	.5089	.6031
% in personal liability	+25.47	−3.27	.0111	.0041
% in corporate property	−28.71	6.74	.0370	.1691
% in corporate liability	+10.35	−1.56	.3962	.7364
% in worker's compensation	−3.88	−.59	.2404	.9762
% in automobile	+20.12	−4.36	.0069	.0193

[a]Includes forty-seven high-growth and eighty-seven low-growth failed firms.

percent. This represents a 39 percentage point increase in the share of business in long-tail lines. By contrast, the fraction of premiums in long-tail lines for the slow-growth firms was essentially unchanged, falling by about 3 percentage points. Moreover, both a t-test and a Wilcoxon rank sum test, which are shown in the bottom portion of table 9.1, confirm that the differential change in the share between fast-growth firms (38.8 percent) and slow-growth firms (−2.7 percent) is statistically significant. The strong relative movement into long-tail lines for the potential gamers (firms with fast premium growth) is therefore consistent with our theory that increasing long-tail lines is a desirable way to game the system.

In order to determine more precisely which lines fast-growth insurers are moving into, we adopt narrower definitions of the insurer's lines of business. The results are shown in the next six rows of table 9.1. First, the four combinations of personal/corporate and property/liability are considered. Then, workers' compensation and automobile are considered. Two results stand out. First, while there is some change in the lines of the fast-growth firms, none of the categories of lines change significantly for the slow-growth firms. Unlike the fast-growth companies, these slow-growth companies march forward toward insolvency with little aggregate change in the composition of their business.

Second, the primary reason for the increase in the fraction of premiums in long-tail lines for the fast-growth firms is the increase in personal, not corporate, liability lines, as indicated by the aggregate 25 percentage point increase in the share in personal liability lines. There is only a 10 percent increase in the share of corporate-liability lines, and this change is not statistically different from the near-zero (-1.6 percent) change in the corporate-liability share for the slow-growth firms.

There are at least two reasons why gaming firms may choose to increase growth in personal liability premiums rather than in corporate-liability premiums. First, losses in corporate-liability lines tend to be larger and are therefore more likely to exceed the guaranty-fund caps. Thus, corporate buyers of liability insurance may care about the solvency of insurers in a way that individual buyers do not. Second, corporate-insurance purchasers are likely to be better informed about the rules and the financial condition of the insurer than individual purchasers of liability insurance. That is, the relative inability of individuals who purchase liability insurance (which consists primarily of automobile-liability insurance) to learn about and understand the guaranty-fund rules may make growth in this category ideal for companies that want to game the guaranty-fund system. The large (20 percent) increase in the fraction of premiums in automobile for the fast-growth firms, shown in the last row, is consistent with this story.

In order to test the robustness of these basis results, we compared the fast-growth failed companies with a matched sample of fast-growth nonfailed (again, greater than 50 percent growth) companies. Each high-growth failed firm was matched by size and year with four high-growth healthy firms. The results, shown in table 9.2 and using the same procedure as in table 9.1, tell the same basic story. All the comparisons are basically the same, which is not surprising given that, like the slow-growth failed firms, the fast-growth non-failed firms show little change in any of the lines of business. The fact that potential gamers (fast-growth failed firms) increase their fraction of premiums in long-tail lines (especially personal liability) while a similar set of fast-growing nongaming firms does not strengthen the case that premium line changes of the gamers is unusual.[14]

As a final test, we compared the slow-growth failures with a matched set

---

14. If companies are gaming the system with fast premium growth, then, unless they are all Ponzi schemes, some companies should be expected to succeed (i.e., to gamble and remain solvent). Our ability to find a matched sample of fast-growing nonfailed firms is consistent with this story. That is, our sample of fast-growth nonfailures may include some "gamers" that succeed.

Table 9.2   High-Growth Firms Partitioned by Failure[a]

Line of Business	Failed Mean $t-3$	Failed Mean $t-1$	Change in Failed	Matched Mean $t-3$	Matched Mean $t-1$	Change in Matched
% in long-tail lines	30.98	69.79	+38.81	45.21	48.40	+3.19
% in personal property	28.25	21.14	−7.10	26.42	24.64	−1.79
% in personal liability	14.53	40.00	+25.47	17.86	19.21	+1.35
% in corporate property	41.51	12.79	−28.71	35.11	33.41	−1.71
% in corporate liability	15.70	26.05	+10.35	20.59	22.74	+2.15
% in workers' compensation	13.61	9.74	−3.88	4.21	6.14	+1.93
% in automobile	38.31	58.43	+20.12	34.69	33.15	+.46

	Statistical Tests of Changes			
	Change in Failed	Change in Matched	t-Test (p-value)	Wilcoxon (p-value)
% in long-tail lines	+38.81	+3.19	.0483	.0406
% in personal property	−7.10	−1.79	.4952	.2984
% in personal liability	+25.47	+1.35	.0160	.0002
% in corporate property	−28.71	−1.71	.0909	.1042
% in corporate liability	+10.35	+2.15	.5551	.0231
% in workers' compensation	−3.88	−1.93	.0338	.0514
% in automobile	+20.12	+.46	.0036	.0009

[a]Includes 47 high-growth failed firms and 187 high-growth solvent firms matched by the calendar year of the annual statement and assets in year $t-2$.

(again, matched by size and year) of slow-growth nonfailures. Results of the comparison appear in table 9.3. Neither group showed any significant change in its line of business,[15] so it is not surprising that the statistical tests show no statistical differences between (the changes in) the two groups. Both the failed slow-growth and the nonfailed slow-growth companies seem to be marching forward with little change in their mixes, the former into insolvency, the latter into relative prosperity.

Finally, we used regression analysis to determine whether the relative changes in business composition hold controlling for various factors. We combine the samples of failed and matched firms from tables 9.2 and 9.3 to determine whether the potential gamers (fast-growth failed firms) changed their business composition relative to nongamers. The change in the share of a firm's

15. It has already been established in table 9.1 above that the slow-growth failed companies did not change their line mix significantly.

Table 9.3   **Slow-Growth Firms Partitioned by Failure**[a]

Line of Business	Failed Mean $t-3$	Failed Mean $t-1$	Change in Failed	Matched Mean $t-3$	Matched Mean $t-1$	Change in Matched
% in long-tail lines	62.56	59.84	−2.73	44.15	44.90	+.75
% in personal property	18.69	16.78	−1.91	30.66	29.76	−.90
% in personal liability	28.21	24.94	−3.27	15.42	16.61	+1.19
% in corporate property	22.78	29.53	6.74	31.89	32.63	+.72
% in corporate liability	30.31	28.74	−1.56	22.03	20.98	−1.04
% in workers' compensation	13.44	12.85	−.59	6.00	6.06	+.06
% in automobile	40.38	36.01	−4.36	29.21	30.02	+.81

	Statistical Tests of Changes			
	Change in Failed	Change in Matched	t-Test (p-value)	Wilcoxon (p-value)
% in long-tail lines	−2.73	+.75	.4816	.8847
% in personal property	−1.91	−.90	.5533	.5380
% in personal liability	−3.27	+1.19	.4149	.5453
% in corporate property	+6.74	+.72	.3028	.8102
% in corporate liability	−1.56	−1.04	.8227	.1136
% in workers' compensation	−.59	+.06	.6106	.1098
% in automobile	−4.36	+.81	.4177	.2793

[a]Includes 87 slow-growth failed firms and 350 matching solvent firms matched by the calendar year of the annual statement and assets in year $t-2$.

line of business was regressed on a constant, FAST (equals one if a fast-growth firm), FAILED (equals one if failed), and FASTFAIL, the interaction of FAST and FAILED. FASTFAIL is the coefficient of interest since this coefficient indicates how gamers change their business composition relative to nongamers. We also included additional control variables, which are defined in the appendix. An indicator for MUTUAL was included. ASSETS was included as a proxy for size, and LEVER, the ratio of liabilities to assets, was included to capture the capital position of the firm.

The results, shown in tables 9.4 and 9.5, tell a similar story. In the specification with the change in the fraction of long-tail lines as the dependent variable, the coefficient on the interaction term FASTFAIL is positive and statistically significant, indicating a significant increase (about 39 percentage points) in the fraction of long-tail lines for potential gamers. Moreover, as before, this increase is in personal liability and automobile lines, as indicated by the positive and significant coefficients on FASTFAIL in those two specifications. Con-

Table 9.4   Change in Business Composition prior to Failure

Variable	Long-Tail Lines	Personal Property	Personal Liability
INTERCEPT	.0047	−.0194	.0362**
	(.0256)	(.0195)	(.0166)
FAST	.0282*	−.0073	−.0057
	(.0165)	(.0134)	(.0118)
FAILED	−.0313	−.0145	−.0039
	(.0473)	(.0190)	(.0511)
FASTFAIL	.3899**	−.0436	.2876***
	(.1801)	(.0781)	(.1094)
MUTUAL	.0123	−.0036	−.0030
	(.0153)	(.0142)	(.0104)
ASSETS	.0737*	−.0305	−.0257
	(.0439)	(.0279)	(.0318)
LEVER	−.0088	.0257	−.0438
	(.0503)	(.0440)	(.0303)
Adjusted R^2	.0542	−.001	.0497

Note: Dependent variable is the change in the share of a firm's business in each line between year $t - 3$ and year $t - 1$, where $t = 0$ is the year of insolvency. Sample contains 134 failed and 532 matched solvent firms. All independent variables are defined in the appendix. Heteroskedasticity-consistent standard errors are given in parentheses.

*Significant at the 10 percent level.
**Significant at the 5 percent level.
***Significant at the 1 percent level.

versely, when corporate liability is the dependent variable, the coefficient on FASTFAIL is positive, but the magnitude is small (0.08) and not close to being statistically significant. In sum, the results of tables 9.4 and 9.5 corroborate the findings of the earlier tables.

9.6   Regulatory Resources and Excessive Premium Growth

The final issue that we address is whether there is any evidence that a higher level of resource expenditures by state insurance regulators is effective in reducing the amount of excessive premium growth. To the extent that companies are gaming the system in the way we have described, one would expect that increased regulatory scrutiny, which is likely to be positively correlated with the state's regulatory resources, would reduce the degree of game playing.

In order to test this idea, we employ a logit model with high growth as the dependent variable and various measures of regulatory resources as the explanatory variables. As in the earlier sections, we define high-growth firms as those that increase premium growth by 50 percent or more between year $t - 3$ and year $t - 1$. We also include the same control variables as in tables 9.4 and 9.5.

The measures of regulatory resources include BUDCO1 and BUDCO2, the state regulatory budget divided by the number of insurance companies in the

Table 9.5   **Change in Business Composition prior to Failure**

Variable	Commercial Property	Commercial Liability	Workers' Compensation	Automobile
INTERCEPT	.0203	−.0372*	−.0010	.0370**
	(.0240)	(.0189)	(.0108)	(.0179)
FAST	−.0297*	.0428***	.0203*	−.0125
	(.0159)	(.0151)	(.0110)	(.0170)
FAILED	.0600	−.0068	−.0066	−.0450
	(.0555)	(.0230)	(.0136)	(.0596)
FASTFAIL	−.3280**	.0838	−.0515*	.2505***
	(.1648)	(.1379)	(.0289)	(.0895)
MUTUAL	−.0141	.0207*	−.0020	−.0046
	(.0149)	(.0121)	(.0042)	(.0177)
ASSETS	−.0142	.0706	.0539	−.0390
	(.0366)	(.1182)	(.0472)	(.0398)
LEVER	−.0162	.0342	.0011	−.0508
	(.0510)	(.0323)	(.0200)	(.0354)
Adjusted R^2	.0374	.0141	.0153	.0325

Note: Dependent variable is the change in the share of a firm's business in each line between year $t - 3$ and year $t - 1$, where $t = 0$ is the year of insolvency. Sample contains 134 failed and 532 matched solvent firms. All independent variables are defined in the appendix. Heteroskedasticity-consistent standard errors are given in parentheses.

*Significant at the 10 percent level.
**Significant at the 5 percent level.
***Significant at the 1 percent level.

state (determined two ways; for precise definitions, see the appendix), and EXAMCO1 and EXAMCO2, the number of examiners in the state's regulatory office divided by the number of companies (again, defined two ways). Greater regulatory resources may limit the ability of insurers to game the system. An increased number of examiners may make it more likely that regulators will be able to detect unusual activity by an insurer. Regulators can then either take action to curtail the activities of a firm or petition the court to declare the insurer insolvent and placed under state supervision. In most cases, the entity filing the petition of insolvency is the office of the insurance commissioner in an insurer's state of domicile. Thus, the resources available to the commissioner in the state of domicile should have some effect on the ability of an insurer to game the guaranty fund.

The problem, of course, is that none of the measures of regulatory resources are exogenous. In particular, one might expect that an increase in insurance-company risk taking might lead to a greater need for regulatory resources. This biases the results against finding that more regulatory resources lead to lower game playing. Nevertheless, we believe that this exercise is worth doing to see if there is evidence of a regulatory effect in spite of this bias.

The results with the failed sample are shown in table 9.6. In all four cases, the coefficient on regulatory resources is negative, indicating that more re-

Table 9.6   Logit Model of the Likelihood of Fast Premium Growth for Failed Property and Casualty Insurers

	Model 1	Model 2	Model 3	Model 4
INTERCEPT	1.0048	1.0262*	1.5290**	1.4910**
	(.5417)	(.5686)	(.6407)	(.7285)
MUTUAL	−1.2641	−1.2363	−1.1423	−1.2244
	(.8476)	(.8529)	(.8470)	(.8601)
ASSETS	−24.5389**	−23.8942**	−20.8848*	−19.0954*
	(11.9010)	(11.8983)	(11.4587)	(11.0735)
LEVER	−.9775	−1.0433	−1.0532	−1.1231
	(.8233)	(.8228)	(.8276)	(.8156)
BUDCO1	−5.7852**			
	(2.7468)			
BUDCO2		−2.9895*		
		(1.7026)		
EXAMCO1			−6.0972**	
			(2.7409)	
EXAMCO2				−2.5846
				(1.7036)
Pseudo R^2	.1169	.0951	.1288	.1050

Note: Fast premium growth is defined as a 50 percent or greater real increase in direct premium writings between $t − 3$ and $t − 1$, where $t = 0$ is the year of insolvency. Dependent variable = 1 if company exhibited high growth in direct premium writings, 0 otherwise. $N = 132$ with 47 high-growth firms and 85 low-growth firms in each model. Independent variables are defined in the appendix. Asymptotic standard errors are given in parentheses. Excludes firms domiciled in Puerto Rico and U.S. territories.

*Significant at the 10 percent level.

**Significant at the 5 percent level.

sources are associated with a decreased probability that the company is a high-growth gamer. Moreover, two of the coefficients are significant at the 5 percent confidence level, and one is significant at the 10 percent level. In terms of the implied magnitude of the effect, the coefficients imply that a 10 percent increase in the amount of budgetary resources is associated with approximately a 0.9 percent decrease in the probability that the firm is high growth (model 1). Using model 3, the results indicate that a 10 percent increase in the number of examiners is associated with a 2 percent decrease in the probability that the firm is high growth. Thus, the magnitudes of the coefficients imply a modest, but not insignificant, effect.

The same tests are then repeated for the nonfailed sample. These results are shown in table 9.7. The coefficients on the budgetary variables are again negative, but, as expected, the effects are smaller in magnitude.[16] Moreover, none

16. The effect of a change in regulatory resources on the likelihood of a solvent firm falling into the fast-growth category is about one-fifth as large as it is for the corresponding model using failed firms.

Table 9.7   **Logit Model of the Likelihood of Fast Premium Growth for the Matched Set of Solvent Property and Casualty Insurers**

	Model 1	Model 2	Model 3	Model 4
INTERCEPT	.5620***	.5270**	.5893***	.5513**
	(.2083)	(.2197)	(.2148)	(.2255)
MUTUAL	−1.3015***	−1.2939***	−1.2952***	−1.2956***
	(.2739)	(.2747)	(.2734)	(.2740)
ASSETS	−19.8502***	−19.7396***	−19.6684***	−19.7042***
	(5.4194)	(5.4325)	(5.4016)	(5.4087)
LEVER	−1.0957***	−1.1231***	1.1020***	−1.1245***
	(.3818)	(.3813)	(.3813)	(.3791)
BUDCO1	−1.2001			
	(1.5740)			
BUDCO2		−.2637		
		(.9450)		
EXAMCO1			−.5244	
			(.5619)	
EXAMCO2				−.1340
				(.2944)
Pseudo R^2	.1276	.1269	.1281	.1271

Note: Fast growth is defined as a 50 percent or greater real increase in direct premium writings between $t - 3$ and $t - 1$, where $t = 0$ is the year of insolvency. Dependent variable = 1 if company exhibited high growth in direct premium writings, 0 otherwise. $N = 526$ with 186 high-growth firms and 340 low-growth firms in each model. Independent variables are defined in the appendix. Asymptotic standard errors are given in parentheses. Excludes firms domiciled in Puerto Rico and U.S. territories.

**Significant at the 5 percent level.
***Significant at the 1 percent level.

are statistically significant. These results should be interpreted with the caveat that they are weak and are biased in the direction of not finding a relation between regulatory resources and game playing. Nevertheless, taken together, the results suggest that more regulatory resources may be effective in curbing excessive premium growth by firms attempting to game the guaranty-fund system.

9.7   Summary and Conclusion

The savings-and-loan and commercial banking crisis of the late 1980s and 1990s led to a large literature on the moral hazard effects of deposit insurance. Research on the moral hazard of the guaranty-fund system—the moral hazard of insuring the insurers—pales in comparison. This paper is an attempt to fill that gap.

We first explain the mechanism through which the guaranty-fund system may create moral hazard and then describe how this moral hazard might manifest itself in terms of insurance-company behavior. We start with a parallel between bank deposit insurance and guaranty-fund insurance, both of which provide second-level insurance against the failure of the relevant financial institution. Just as deposit insurance enables banks to borrow at the risk-free rate from insured depositors, guaranty-fund insurance enables insurance companies to borrow at (approximately) the risk-free rate from policyholders. The key insight is that premium payments are similar to borrowed funds since there is a lag, which is particularly long in long-tail lines, between premium payments and policyholder claims. Thus, we argue that one way that insurance companies can game the guaranty-fund system is through a peculiar type of borrowing—fast premium growth.

The patterns that emerge in the data are consistent with this story. More than one-third of insolvent property-casualty insurance companies had very high premium growth in the two years prior to failure. And, as might be expected if companies are gaming the system in the way we have described, this premium growth was more pronounced in long-tail than in short-tail lines. Moreover, the increase in long-tail lines was driven by personal liability lines—where the guaranty-fund caps are less likely to be binding—rather than corporate-liability lines. Finally, it was shown that excessive premium growth was less pronounced in states that had greater regulatory resources. Taken together, the results are strikingly consistent with the moral hazard story that we have described.

Despite this, it is possible that the risky insurance-company behavior that we have documented would have occurred even without the guaranty-fund system. For example, it may be the case that insurance companies take advantage of buyers who are relatively uninformed about the financial condition of the firm. Thus, insurance companies may be able to game the system by increasing premium growth to these "credit-insensitive" buyers. Indeed, this story is consistent with the evidence that premium growth was more pronounced in personal lines than in corporate lines; it seems likely that individuals are less informed than corporations about the financial condition of insurance companies.

Although our analysis reveals some striking patterns consistent with guaranty-fund-induced moral hazard, it is clear that additional research is needed to establish the extent to which the risky behavior documented in this paper is caused by the existence of the guaranty-fund system. One potential direction for future research is to make use of the state variation in guaranty-fund caps. Although this variation is not large, such an approach has the potential to provide a purer test of the proposition that guaranty-fund insurance creates moral hazard. In addition, if good insurance-company data can be found for the 1960s, another possibility is to compare insurance-company behavior before and after the introduction of the guaranty-fund system. Finally, as discussed in section 9.4, yet another approach is to start with the set of all insurance companies and then analyze how firm financial conditions influence firm risk taking.

Additional research is also needed to increase our understanding of the nature and degree of insurance-company risk taking. This study has considered only one type of moral hazard—excessive premium growth. Our understanding of the incentive effects of insurance-company regulation would be greatly increased by an investigation of other ways in which insurance companies engage in excessively risky behavior.

Appendix

Business Mix Definitions

Personal property	= Farmowner's and homeowner's multiple peril, automobile physical damage.
Personal liability	= Automobile liability.
Corporate property	= Commercial multiple peril, fire, allied lines, earthquake, aircraft, inland and ocean marine, financial guarantee lines.
Corporate liability	= Workers' compensation, medical malpractice, products and other liability, accident and health Lines.
Long-tail lines	= Personal and corporate-liability lines and financial guarantee lines.
Automobile	= Automobile liability and automobile physical damage.
Workers' compensation	= Workers' compensation.

Data Definitions

FAST   = FAST = 1 if the direct premiums written by the insurer increased by more than 50 percent in real terms in the two years prior to insolvency, that is, between year $t - 3$ and year $t - 1$.

FASTFAIL = FASTFAIL = 1 if FAST = 1 and the firm became insolvent in year t, 0 otherwise.

MUTUAL = MUTUAL = 1 if the firm has a mutual form of ownership, 0 otherwise.

ASSETS = The assets of the firm in billions of 1994 dollars on the annual statement filed on 31 December of year $t - 3$, where year t is the year of insolvency.

LEVER   = The ratio of liabilities to assets of the firm on 31 December of year $t - 3$, where t is the year the firm was found insolvent.

BUDCO1 = The budget of the insurance commission in the state of domicile divided by the number of firms domiciled in that state. Insurance commission budget is for the year 1990, and the number of firms domiciled in the state is taken from *Best's Solvency Study—Property/Casualty.*

EXAMCO1 = The number of examiners employed by the insurance commission in the state of domicile divided by the number of firms domiciled in that state. The number of examiners is for the year 1990, and the number of firms domiciled in the state is taken from *Best's Solvency Study—Property/Casualty.*

BUDCO2 = Same as BUDCO1 with the exception that the number of firms domiciled in the state was obtained from the 1990 demographics file of the NAIC annual statement database.

EXAMCO2 = Same as EXAMCO1 with the exception that the number of firms domiciled in the state was obtained from the 1990 demographics file of the NAIC annual statement database.

References

Barth, J., P. Bartholmew, and M. Bradley. 1991. Determinants of thrift resolution costs. *Journal of Finance* 45:731–54.

A. M. Best. Various years. *Best's solvency study—property/casualty.* Oldwick, N.J.

———. Various years. *Best's insurance reports.* Oldwick, N.J.

———. 1991. *Insolvency report.* Oldwick, N.J.

Bohn, James G., and Brian J. Hall. 1995. Property and casualty solvency funds as a tax and social insurance system. Working Paper no. 5206. Cambridge, Mass.: National Bureau of Economic Research, August.

Bovenzie, J., and A. Murton. 1988. Resolution costs and bank failures. *FDIC Banking Review* 1:1–13.

Cummins, J. David. 1988. Risk-based premiums for insurance guarantee funds. *Journal of Finance* 43:823–39.

Duncan, M. 1987. Property-liability post assessment guaranty funds. In *Issues in insurance* (4th ed.), ed. Everett D. Randall. Malvern, Pa.: American Institute for Property and Liability Underwriters.

Epton, B., and R. Bixby. 1976. Insurance guaranty funds: A reassessment. *DePaul Law Review* 25:227–63.

Hall, Brian J. 1996. Regulatory free cash flow and the high cost of insurance company failures. Discussion Paper no. 1782. Harvard Institute of Economic Research, September.

James, Christopher M. 1991. The losses realized in bank failures. *Journal of Finance* 46:1223–42.

Kane, Edward J. 1989. *The S&L insurance mess: How did it happen?* Washington, D.C.: Urban Institute Press.

Merton, Robert C. 1977. An analytic derivation of the cost of deposit insurance and loan guarantees: An application of modern option pricing theory. *Journal of Banking and Finance* 1:3–11.

National Conference of Insurance Guaranty Funds (NCIGF). 1991–93. *Assessment and financial information.* Indianapolis.

Stiglitz, Joseph, and Andrew Weiss. 1981. Credit rationing in markets with imperfect information. *American Economic Review* 71:393–410.

Comment   Christopher M. McGhee

The Bohn and Hall paper provides a clear exposition on an important aspect of the risk-management issues that one needs to try to understand when thinking about the insurance industry.

There are essentially two main parts of Hall and Bohn's thesis. First, when insurance companies are on the brink of insolvency, they raise cash the cheapest way they can. For insurance companies, this means that they write more premium and that this growth is concentrated in long-tail personal lines classes, especially personal automobile liability. Intuitively, this seems logical, and the data that Hall and Bohn present is reasonably convincing. A point that is not examined in the paper, but that also seems likely, is that, given that these companies operate in a competitive marketplace (a safe assumption in the United States), they can do this only by cutting prices. There is a reasonable, if not high, probability that they do this at prices that are too low. It would be helpful to attempt to ascertain if this speeds and/or deepens the insurance company's insolvency. It seems plausible that it would at least deepen the insolvency. If one were to discover that insurance companies, in fact, generate new business by cutting prices, then it would be interesting to try and see what effect insurance market cycles might have on the data. The point is simply that, if prices are high relative to risk at a given point in time, companies engaging in this "inappropriate" behavior might get away with it for a longer period of time than if the market were soft. Said another way, one might expect to see a lag in the insolvency rate relative to the period of rapid premium growth under these circumstances. It is also clear that, if the business is being "bought" by these companies by cutting prices, this complicates Hall's and Bohn's analysis significantly, as one needs to know whether consumers are credit insensitive or, conversely, whether they are willing to take the increased credit risk if they get enough price discount.

The second main part of the thesis posits how insurance companies can convince consumers to pay them premium, that is, effectively loan them the use of their premium dollars. The authors suggest that the presence of state guaranty funds makes these consumers less credit sensitive than they would otherwise be if no guaranty fund existed. The authors conclude that the rapid premium growth of many insurers, particularly in long-tail lines for private individuals, in the two years preceding their insolvency suggests that this is true. On this point, I am less convinced as there are other possibilities that could explain the data.

Let me pose an alternative explanation. One could categorize buyers of insurance in many different ways, but, here, I suggest that we categorize and rank them into four categories on the basis of their credit sensitivity (or rather lack of it), as follows.

Christopher M. McGhee is a managing director of Marsh and McLennan Securities Corporation, the investment banking subsidiary of Marsh and McLennan Companies.

The first group would be those individuals who are not credit sensitive with respect to the premiums that they pay for insurance. One can come up with at least three reasons why this might be true. First, the consumer thinks of insurance premiums as a tax (as might be the case for mandatory automobile insurance) and as such tries only to get the cheapest premium. Second, this group may perceive that the credit risk is so small that it essentially does not matter. After all, these consumers might say, "I really care a lot only if the insurance company won't pay when I have a loss, and the chances that I have a loss are so small that I don't really think I'm going to have one. Otherwise I lose only my premium." (But most consumers think that they "lose" their premium when they pay it anyway.) Consumers, one might guess, would think of this credit decision very differently than when they put their life savings in a bank. Cursory review of some of the data that Hall and others have provided suggests, in fact, that the expected value of the credit risk that consumers face when they lend to banks is an order of magnitude or two greater than when buying insurance policies. Finally, this group would include those who just do not know enough to think about credit risk—the truly credit-risk insensitive.

Our next three groups are all credit sensitive, but their judgments are influenced by different factors and information.

Our second group is credit sensitive, but these consumers' own credit-risk evaluation is unaffected by the presence of guaranty funds. This is because they may not know that they exist. Indeed, this is not implausible when one considers that, in about half the states, insurance agents operate under a "gag" rule that enjoins them from telling their customers that a guaranty fund even exists. This group may rely instead on ratings from the rating agencies, and rating agencies may be slow to catch "misbehaving" insurers until it is too late.

Our third group of insurance buyers is also credit sensitive, but these consumers are affected by the presence of guaranty funds. Bohn and Hall suggest that consumers fall into this category. It bears considering, however, that in this group one might also include those individuals who do not know of the existence of the guaranty funds explicitly but simply think that the government will pay if a failure occurs. It would be interesting to attempt to ascertain whether this perception varies depending on the cause of insolvency, that is, whether the insolvency is caused by a disaster (e.g., a hurricane or an earthquake) or by a "normal" insolvency. Note that there is a potentially important counterargument to critics of guaranty funds embedded here. That is, if people think that the government will step in to help them out in the event of a failure, and if they think this regardless of whether they know of the existence of guaranty funds, then it could be argued that having the guaranty funds is beneficial because at least it provides a well understood and reasonably orderly process for handling the claims of insolvent companies.

Our fourth group of insurance consumers is made up of the most sophisticated buyers of insurance. Here, again, the presence or absence of guaranty funds has little to do with their buying decisions. This group knows that guaranty funds exist. But they also know that limits apply on how much can be paid out from a guaranty fund. They are likely to be aware that, if they buy from an insurance company that then becomes insolvent and they then have to make a claim against the state guaranty fund, significant time delays in actually getting paid would almost certainly occur. Such time delays are not very palatable to customers who have just suffered a large financial loss. Furthermore, this group may know that the state guaranty funds are unfunded and may not have confidence that the funds could pay one hundred cents on the dollar if a really large insolvency, or a series of insolvencies, occurred. Those in this group are likely to rely on the credit assessment of rating agencies and their own intermediaries for credit information. It is worth noting that a large percentage of commercial insurance business is placed through insurance brokers. Brokers work for the insured and therefore may be more focused on protecting the interests of their clients than would insurance agents who are legal representatives of the insurance carrier.

These are our four groups. We might consider who falls into each of our four categories. Taking our fourth group first (our very sophisticated buyers), one might reasonably think that this includes many, if not most, buyers of commercial insurance.

The other three categories would presumably be composed predominately of private individuals buying personal lines coverages. I suspect that consumers who buy only automobile insurance are more likely to fall into category 1, our least-credit-sensitive group. I suspect this because one might guess that, if they have a mortgage, most home buyers are influenced by the lending institution to use "A"-rated security or better, at least for their home loan, and thus are educated to at least some modest extent to be credit sensitive.

An insurance company with declining credit worthiness trying to rapidly grow its premium writings would presumably go after the less-sophisticated buyers of insurance in categories 1, 2, and 3, with special emphasis on category 1, that is, our credit-insensitive group. The authors' data is consistent with this, as rapid premium growth was concentrated in the sale of personal automobile insurance.

Under my alternative explanation, only one of our four groups actually is sensitive to the presence of the guaranty funds, and it is possible that most of the rapid premium growth may not come from this group.

What matters, of course, is how much of the buying population falls into each of our categories. Bohn and Hall's analysis would be significantly extended by attempting to measure the credit sensitivity of the insurance-buying population. Note that the fact that guaranty funds were created strongly suggests that many believe that a significant portion of the population is credit insensitive. The authors have acknowledged that further research on this subject is needed. Nevertheless, the paper is an excellent start with regard to the public policy issues that the presence of guaranty funds create.

As a postscript, it may be instructive to note that the presence of moral hazard has been well understood in the reinsurance industry and that the reinsurers (the insurers of insurers) structure what they sell to respond to this risk. Without going into any detail, I would simply note that, traditionally, reinsurers have effectively been selling long-term contracts, but with an annual right to review their deals, change the terms, or exit completely. In this review process, information gathering much beyond what is publicly available is taken into account. This gives the reinsurer powerful protection from being gamed overtime by an insurer. Note that this "behavior-regulation" effect is largely absent in guaranty funds. One might try to examine, therefore, whether the presence or absence of reinsurance correlates with insolvency.

Comment   David Scharfstein

Insurance companies have long understood the concept of moral hazard—that insuring their clients against adverse events induces them to take less caution than they otherwise would. If James Bohn and Brian Hall are correct, as I think they are, insurance companies have learned a lesson from their clients. Insurance companies are themselves insured by state guaranty funds. The result of "insuring the insurers," according to Bohn and Hall, is that insurers become aggressive risk takers when they become financially distressed.

Bohn and Hall start by observing that insurers can increase revenues by offering insurance policies at more attractive premiums. Because they are insured by state guaranty funds, customers care little about whether the insurance company will have enough capital to pay any future claims. Thus, financially distressed insurers have an easy way of avoiding liquidation in the short run; they simply price low, increase premiums written, and use the income to pay off short-term loans. Of course, in the longer run, there will be claims against the insurers, and they will not have the capital to meet their obligations. Instead, the guaranty funds foot the bill. The story is not too different from the savings-and-loan failures of the 1980s and the subsequent bailouts.

The paper marshals three pieces of evidence that together suggest that the description given above is a valid one. First, Bohn and Hall find that many property-and-casualty insurers failed after very high premium growth. Second, much of the premium growth is in long-tail lines, where there is much greater uncertainty about future losses. The greater uncertainty means that the insurer could get lucky and have limited losses. And, third, this risk-taking behavior is less pronounced in states where regulatory oversight is greater.

The first two facts alone are not enough to tell a compelling story that failed insurers game the system by taking excessive risk when they get into financial

David Scharfstein is the Dai-Ichi Kangyo Bank Professor of Management at the Sloan School of Management, Massachusetts Institute of Technology.

trouble. The bankruptcy courts are littered with companies—financial and non-financial alike—that took risks and lost. For example, the airline People Express went bankrupt after a period of rapid growth. In the year that it went bankrupt alone, its revenue grew by nearly 25 percent. It gambled, and it lost. It is the third fact—in combination with the other two—that convinces me that failed insurers were taking excessive risk; they gambled less when there was more regulatory oversight. This tells us that many of the insurers consciously exacerbated the problem by using the state guaranty funds to subsidize their risk-taking behavior.

While Bohn and Hall have identified the moral hazard costs of the state guaranty fund, it is hard to go from their analysis to any claims about whether the system is worthwhile. Because the analysis looks only at the insurers that actually failed, we do not know anything about the insurers that were able to avoid distress owing to the guarantees of the fund. For example, absent a state guaranty fund, it would be difficult for an insurer with some unlucky large losses to get any new business or retain its old customers because of a fear that their claims would not be paid. The loss of these customers would exacerbate the problem and make it more likely that the insurer would not be able to pay. Default would be a self-fulfilling prophecy. This argument is similar to the rationale behind deposit insurance for banks.

To get some sense of the costs and benefits of state guaranty funds, it might be better to analyze the behavior of distressed or poorly performing insurers rather than just the failed insurers. The critical question is how these insurers respond to distress. Some will choose to take excessive risk and will fail; others will recover without taking excessive risk. Thus, one could estimate the fraction of insurers that accelerate premium growth (particularly in long-tail lines) after the onset of distress. And one could estimate the extent to which this is related to regulatory oversight and caps on guaranty funds. These estimates will give some sense of the extent to which state guaranty funds induce inefficiencies.

Finally, it is worth thinking about how one could improve the current system. Ideally, just as there is risk-based deposit insurance, one would like insurers to pay risk-based insurance premiums; that is, less well-capitalized insurers should pay more into the state guaranty funds. In this way, insurers internalize at least some of the costs of taking excessive risk. However, the current system is the exact opposite of what one would want. The more highly capitalized, less risky insurers end up paying more to the state guaranty funds because they are forced to bail out their bankrupt competitors. One would hope that, just as the bank defaults led to changes in the way banks are regulated, the defaults of property and casualty insurers would also lead to changes in the way insurers are regulated.

10   Index Hedge Performance: Insurer Market Penetration and Basis Risk

John A. Major

Index-based financial instruments bring transparency and efficiency to both sides of risk transfer, to investor and hedger alike. Unfortunately, to the extent that an index is anonymous and commoditized, it cannot correlate perfectly with a specific portfolio. Thus, hedging with index-based financial instruments brings with it basis risk. The result is "significant practical and philosophical barriers" to the financing of property/casualty catastrophe risks by means of catastrophe derivatives (Foppert 1993). This study explores the basis risk between catastrophe futures and portfolios of insured homeowners' building risks subject to the hurricane peril.[1]

A concrete example of the influence of market penetration on basis risk can be seen in figures 10.1–10.3. Figure 10.1 is a map of the Miami, Florida, vicin-

John A. Major is senior vice president at Guy Carpenter and Company, Inc. He is an Associate of the Society of Actuaries.

This research was financially supported by Guy Carpenter and Co. and by the NBER Project on the Financing of Property/Casualty Risks. The author would like to thank the following people for their comments, support, and assistance: Kenneth Froot, Richard Kane, Ben Lashkari, Susan Lesser, John Mahon, Diane Major, John Mangano, Chris McGhee, Jonathan Norton, Virginia O'Brien, André Perold, Jaime Rosario, Aaron Stern, Brandon Sweitzer, Bruce Thomas, and Janene Thomas.

This paper is in no way intended to be an endorsement of, or a solicitation to trade in, financial instruments or securities related to, or based on, the indices described herein. The paper is a highly technical, academic analysis and should not be viewed as an advertisement or sales literature relating to index-based financial instruments. The data referenced in the paper are historical in nature and should not be presumed to be indicative of future data. The estimates and methodology contained in the paper are based on information that is believed to be reliable; however, Guy Carpenter and Co., Inc., does not guarantee the reliability of such estimates and methodologies.

Prospective investors in index-based financial instruments should not rely on this paper in evaluating the merits of such an investment. As of this writing neither Guy Carpenter and Co. nor any of its employees are licensed to sell securities or advise others on the merits of investing in particular securities. The paper should not be construed, in any way, as an invitation or offer to invest or trade in securities.

1. Section 10.4 below comments on the all-lines, all-coverages, all-perils context.

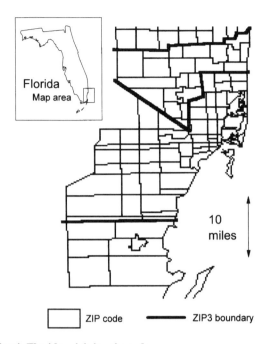

Fig. 10.1   Miami, Florida, vicinity zip codes

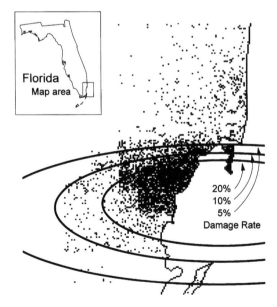

Fig. 10.2   Effect of Hurricane Andrew on the homeowner's-insurance industry
Note: Each dot represents $1 million of losses to the insurance industry.

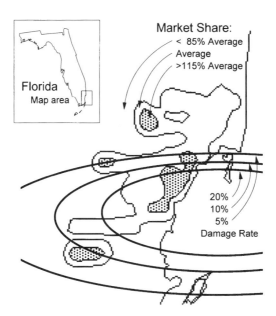

Fig. 10.3   Market penetration vs. damage rate

ity, from just south of Ft. Lauderdale to just north of Key Largo. The polygons depict zip codes, with the bolder lines marking the boundaries of zip sectional centers.[2] Figures 10.2 and 10.3 register to the same scale and placement as figure 10.1.

Figure 10.2 shows the effect of Hurricane Andrew on the homeowner's-insurance industry in Florida. Three levels of contours represent the damage rate (losses divided by exposed value) caused by the hurricane. Near the center of the contours, the damage rate approached 50 percent. Each dot represents $1 million of losses to the industry. The densest portion of losses is not centered in the damage-rate contours because of the population-density gradient. The highest concentration of exposed value, the center of the Hialeah–Miami–Miami Beach metropolitan area, is to the north of the 5 percent contour line. The population density decreases steadily as one moves south. Had the hurricane made landfall ten miles north or south of where it did, there could have been a factor-of-two change in the industry outcome.

Figure 10.3 shows the market penetration of a particular homeowner's in-surer at the time of the hurricane. Imagine that this company had held a com-moditized cat contract instead of reinsurance, a contract that would reimburse it a share of the industry losses from a natural disaster equal to its share of

2. A zip (zone improvement plan) code is a unit of geography defined by the U.S. Postal Service and designated by a five-digit number. On average, residential zip codes contain about two thousand households. Sectional centers are administrative units composed of all zips with the same first three digits.

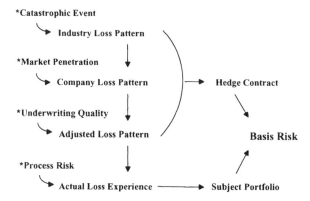

Fig. 10.4   Influences on hedge performance

exposures in southeastern Florida. Basis risk emerges in the mismatch between expectations and outcomes: its share of exposures is not uniform across the area. This company had the misfortune to have its peak market penetration almost coincide with the peak damage rates. Its actual damages were about 25 percent higher than its expected industry share, so the hedge would have underperformed, leaving the company with 20 percent of its losses not covered. On the other hand, if the hurricane had come in just ten miles south of where it did, the hedge would have netted the company a profit.

The influences on both the losses experienced by a portfolio of insured risks and the recoveries available from an index-based hedge, as illustrated in figure 10.4, can be classified as follows:

The catastrophic event itself. This is the industrywide pattern of losses arrayed in space.

The market penetration of the subject portfolio. Multiplying this pattern by industry losses produces an estimate of the subject company's losses.

Underwriting quality. This includes nonspatial characteristics of the subject portfolio, such as deductibles, policy forms, risk-selection standards, and claim-settlement practices. These characteristics contribute to loss variation, even after the event and market penetration have been taken into account. To the extent that they are understood, a hedge can be adjusted for them.

Process risk. This is the ultimately unpredictable component of loss variation.

Basis risk is the random variation of the difference between the hedge-contract payout and the actual loss experience of the subject portfolio. Two types of basis risk are considered. *Conditional basis risk* refers to the variation due to the influence of factors other than the events. It addresses such questions as, How would the hedge perform if an event like Andrew were to occur? Given an implicit class of events—"like Andrew"—the relation between the portfolio's loss and the contractual recovery has a random character. For some events in the class, the insurer is "lucky" in that, say, its penetration is low in the most heavily damaged areas. This variation is termed *conditional basis risk*. Considering all sources of variation, that is, allowing varying events to influence outcomes as well, yields the more familiar definition of basis risk. Here, the term *unconditional basis risk* is used to emphasize the distinction.

To operationalize the notion of conditional basis risk, this study uses an equivalence principle: the subject portfolio is a random draw from a class of portfolios sharing the same *market characteristics*. Conditional basis risk can then be treated as the sampling behavior of hedge outcomes in a specific event when portfolios are drawn from the market-characteristics equivalence class. The motivation for this definition is that, ex ante, the hedger posing the question about conditional performance has an event firmly in mind but does not know where it will strike the portfolio. Intuitively, the idea is to "shift the event" to different parts of the subject portfolio yet maintain all industry-specific attributes of the event. The equivalence principle does this by exchanging the portfolio for an equivalent version. Section 10.1 defines the market-characteristics equivalence class by showing how to characterize a portfolio in a small number of parameters, the *market-characteristics vector*. It also develops a model of the distribution of this vector as well as a model of process risk.

This study models catastrophe indices built up from the insurance industry's catastrophe losses from an event, along with corresponding exposures, by zip code. A hedging instrument is some linear combination of the zip-by-zip losses reported by the index. For a futures contract based on a single-valued statewide index (e.g., the Property Claim Services [PCS] cat index), that linear combination consists of a single constant applied to all zip codes in a state.

Section 10.2 shows the use of these models in a Monte Carlo simulation (Metropolis and Ulam 1949; Rubinstein 1981) of catastrophe-index hedging. It explores the influence of insurer market penetration on basis risk by contrasting the performance of statewide and zip-based contracts. Conditional and unconditional measures of basis risk, correlation coefficients, and optimal hedge ratios are presented.

This study assumes no underwriting-quality influence. The boundary between underwriting quality and process risk is indistinct; it is determined by the extent to which risk characteristics can be taken into account. If an insurer kept and made use of detailed records concerning the construction and materials of each house in its portfolio, these factors would be considered part of underwriting quality. If not, they would be considered part of process risk. To the extent that a hedger understands its own practices and portfolio characteristics vis-à-vis the industry and their implications for loss experience, it can adjust its use of index contracts accordingly.[3] In this sense, the study assumes perfect self-knowledge; hedge-performance estimates reported here should therefore be considered upper bounds.

Section 10.3 discusses related work. Section 10.4 makes concluding remarks. The appendix discusses the modeling of insurer market penetration in detail.

10.1   A Model of the Underlying

10.1.1   Introduction

Consider a state consisting of a set of zip codes symbolized by z. The companies doing business in the state are symbolized by c. Let $R_{z,c}$ denote the risk count (number of insured homes) that company c has in zip code z. Let R_z denote the sum across all companies, that is, the total market, in zip code z. Let R_c and R be the respective sums over all the zips in the state. $M_c = R_c/R$, the risk-count share of company c, is a key parameter throughout this study.[4] Let $v_{z,c,i}$ be the insured value of the ith risk and $\bar{v}_{z,c}$, $\bar{v}_z$, and $\bar{v}$ the average values for the respective groups.

The objective of sections 10.1.2–10.1.4 below is to characterize the pattern of penetration and values for company c in a small number of parameters, the *market-characteristics vector*. In section 10.1.5 below, a second level of modeling considers the distribution of the market-characteristics vector itself.

A catastrophic event is represented as a schedule of damage rate (expected loss–to–value ratio) by zip code. Section 10.1.6 below factors damage rate into its frequency and severity components. Loss can then be modeled as a compound Poisson process (Beard, Pentikäinen, and Pesonen 1984).

10.1.2   The Market Characteristics of One Company

The simplest model of risk count is to assume that $R_{z,c}$ follows a Poisson distribution.[5] Since zip codes vary in population, it makes sense to represent the Poisson mean as $\lambda_{z,c} = \pi_c \cdot R_z$. However, constant penetration π_c is implausible because realized penetration varies much more than Poisson. This leads to a two-stage hierarchical model $\lambda_{z,c} = \pi_{z,c} \cdot R_z$, where $\pi_{z,c}$ is itself a random variable. A logical choice would be lognormal, yielding $\lambda_{z,c} = \exp(\mu_c + \xi_{z,c}) \cdot R_z$, where μ_c is constant, and $\xi_{z,c} \sim \text{Normal}(0, \sigma_c^2)$. Even this is inadequate be-

---

3. Underwriting quality also influences the reported index values. If less than the full industry is incorporated into an index, there is sampling error. Careful index construction and the central limit theorem can assure that this error remains small relative to the hedger's variation.

4. While *market share* is usually defined as the share of premiums received by the company, it will be convenient to deal with shares of risk count and shares of total insured value.

5. Since market share rarely exceeds 20 percent, the Poisson process can be used rather than the more technically correct but cumbersome binomial process.

cause penetration is spatially autocorrelated.[6] A case study illustrating spatial autocorrelation is presented in the appendix.

There are two fundamental approaches to the analysis of spatial structure.[7] Metric methods (Whittle 1954) deal with distance relations between observations. Occurrence methods (Grieg-Smith 1964; Kershaw 1964) count observations in quadrats (random samples of areas). This study treats zip codes as quadrats at one level of scale and zip sectional centers (three-digit zip codes) as quadrats at a larger scale. This leads to a model of the form

$$\lambda_{z,c} = \exp(\mu_c + \xi_{z,c} + \zeta_{z3,c}) \cdot R_z,$$

$$R_{z,c} \sim \text{Poisson}(\lambda_{z,c}),$$

with μ_c constant, $\xi_{z,c} \sim \text{Normal}(0, \sigma_c^2)$, $z3$ symbolizing three-digit zips, and $\zeta_{z3,c} \sim \text{Normal}(0, \tau_c^2)$.

The selection of risks within a zip is not homogeneous either. Another two-level hierarchical component of the model accounts for differential selection of homes by value:

$$\bar{v}_{z,c} = \exp(\varepsilon_{z,c}) - \bar{v}^{(1-\beta_c)} \cdot \bar{v}_z^{\beta_c},$$

$$v_{z,c,i} = \bar{v}_{z,c} \cdot \exp(\phi_{z,c,i}),$$

where $\varepsilon_{z,c} \sim \text{Normal}(\alpha_c, \upsilon_c^2)$, and $\phi_{z,c,i} \sim \text{Normal}(-\frac{1}{2} \cdot \omega_c^2, \omega_c^2)$.[8]

The pattern of risk count and values for a particular company in a particular state is thus abstracted as being the result of a random process characterized by a *market-characteristics* vector of seven parameters, $\vartheta = \langle \mu, \sigma, \tau, \alpha, \beta, \upsilon, \omega \rangle$.

10.1.3 Market-Characteristics Data

As part of its risk-management consulting, Guy Carpenter has acquired portfolio descriptions of many property-casualty insurers. Ten companies were chosen at random from the database. Property-exposure data, dating from 1988 to 1995, were extracted for nine states to obtain a total of twenty-four company-state combinations. States were chosen by importance sampling (Kahn 1950), where the weighting was proportional to the PCS historical catastrophe loss totals, with some concession to the presence of data exhibited by the companies. A Latin Square protocol (Cochran and Cox 1957) was fol-

---

6. Zip codes near one another have more similar penetration rates than widely separated zip codes.

7. Typically, the first step in analyzing spatial autocorrelation is to consider exogenous characteristics of the geographic areas, themselves spatially autocorrelated, as potential regressors. For example, one might test whether penetration is a function of median housing value. Company-independent factors are unavailable for this purpose because the study adopts the stance that 100 percent of the market is penetrated by 100 percent of the companies.

8. The choice of $-\frac{1}{2} \cdot \omega_c^2$ for the mean of $\phi_{z,c,i}$ enforces $E[v_{z,c,i}] = \bar{v}_{z,c}$.

Table 10.1   **Penetration Study Data**

State	Zip Codes All	Zip Codes > 50 OOHU	A	B	C	D	E	F	G	H	I	J
FL	941	907	✓	✓	✓							
MA	564	545	✓			✓	✓					
MD	484	449			✓			✓	✓			
MN	946	895									✓	✓
MT	375	296							✓	✓		
NC	859	819			✓	✓				✓		
NJ	626	610				✓		✓	✓			
NY	1,890	1,750		✓	✓							
TX	1,968	1,804	✓				✓			✓		

Note: OOHU = owner-occupied housing units.

Table 10.2   **Distribution of Risk-Count Share** $M_c = R_c/R$

Size Class	Risk-Count Share (%)	Number of Company-States
1	.2–.5	5
2	.5–1.0	3
3	1.0–2.0	7
4	2.0–5.0	5
5	5.0–10.0	4
Total		24

lowed so that every state could be paired with at least two companies and every company with at least two states.[9] Zip codes where the 1990 Census of Population and Housing reported at least fifty owner-occupied housing units were kept.[10] This typically retained 99.9 percent of the housing units in the state. Tables 10.1 and 10.2 summarize.

10.1.4   Fitting the Market Characteristics

Maximum-likelihood estimation of hierarchical models is notoriously difficult, involving high-dimensional integration of analytically intractable integrands (Hill 1965; Tiao and Tan 1965). Modern methods to solve these problems include integral approximations (Tierney and Kadane 1986), the EM algorithm (Dempster, Laird, and Rubin 1977), and Gibbs sampling (Gelfand and Smith 1990). Computational efficiency is important in this study because of the number of observations (sometimes over fifteen hundred zip codes) and the need to make estimates for each of the twenty-four cases.[11]

9. There was a failure to meet the criterion; one company had usable data in only one state.
10. Zip-code tabulations of census data were obtained from Claritas, Inc.
11. In addition, ninety-six estimation cycles were executed in bootstrap replications.

Table 10.3   **Occurrence of Zero Risk Count among Zips**

Size Class	Risk-Count Share (%)	Frequency of $R_{z,c} = 0$ (%)
1	.2–.5	42.4
2	.5–1.0	44.0
3	1.0–2.0	12.6
4	2.0–5.0	8.0
5	5.0–10.0	6.6

Could one substitute observed risk count $R_{z,c}$ for the Poisson parameter $\lambda_{z,c}$ and estimate μ_c, σ_c, and τ_c by performing analysis of variance (ANOVA) (Fisher 1942) directly on $\ln(R_{z,c}/R_z)$? This has some justification; variation among the $R_{z,c}$ is much greater than Poisson. However, it fails because $R_{z,c}$ is very often zero. Table 10.3 summarizes, pooling cases in each size class.

Therefore, a more sophisticated approach to estimating the $\lambda_{z,c}$ is used: an empirical Bayes technique (Robbins 1951, 1955) treats the "true" unobservable penetration rates $\pi_{z,c}$ as parameters that underlie the observed Poisson risk counts. These parameters, as random variables in their own right, follow a prior distribution driven by hyperparameters estimated from the "crude" observed penetration rates. The estimated prior allows a Bayes posterior point estimate of the realized-penetration-rate parameters $\pi_{z,c}$. This procedure is detailed in the appendix.

The next step in the analysis is to conduct a random-effects ANOVA with the following model:

$$\ln(\pi_{z,c}) \;=\; \ln(\lambda_{z,c}/R_z) \;=\; \mu_c \;+\; \xi_{z,c} \;+\; \zeta_{z3,c},$$

where μ_c is constant, $\xi_{z,c} \sim \text{Normal}(0, \sigma_c^2)$, and $\zeta_{z3,c} \sim \text{Normal}(0, \tau_c^2)$.

Henderson's Method I (Henderson 1953) is used to estimate μ_c and the variance components σ_c^2 and τ_c^2. While not the most sophisticated approach, it has the advantage of being very fast computationally because it relies on sums-of-squares equations and uses no iteration.

The final step is to develop the distribution of insured property values. The model[12]

$$\ln(\bar{v}_{z,c}/\bar{v}) \;=\; \alpha_c \;+\; \beta_c \cdot \ln(\bar{v}_z/\bar{v}) \;+\; \varepsilon_{z,c},$$

where $\varepsilon_{z,c} \sim \text{Normal}(0, \upsilon_c^2)$, is fitted by weighted least squares, with weights proportional to $R_{z,c}$.

Unfortunately, the data consist of aggregates by zip code and so are insufficient to fit

$$\ln(v_{z,c,i}) \;=\; \ln(\bar{v}_{z,c}) \;+\; \phi_{z,c,i},$$

---

12. Median housing values in the census data were used in preference to means.

where $\phi_{z,c,i} \sim \text{Normal}(-\frac{1}{2} \cdot \omega_c^2, \omega_c^2)$. To estimate ω_c, detailed risk-by-risk data are needed. Fortunately, such detail was available from another study of one company in one state, and the estimated value there was $\omega_c = 0.51$.

By the above process, the twenty-four cases were abstracted to points ϑ_c in a seven-dimensional parameter space. Since there is only the single fixed value for ω, it is not useful to include it in the parameter space. It is, however, useful to augment the parameterization by the new variable $\kappa_c = \ln(M_c) = \ln(R_c/R)$, representing the observed risk-count share of the company. Given such a point $\vartheta_c = <\kappa, \mu, \sigma, \tau, \alpha, \beta, \upsilon>$, simulation can construct a pattern of risk count and aggregate value with the specified spatial characteristics according to the hierarchical model

$$\xi_z \sim \text{Normal}(0, \sigma^2),$$

$$\zeta_{z3} \sim \text{Normal}(0, \tau^2),$$

$$\lambda_z = \exp(\mu + \xi_z + \zeta_{z3}) \cdot R_z,$$

$$R_{z,c} \sim \text{Poisson}(\lambda_z),$$

$$\varepsilon_z \sim \text{Normal}(0, \upsilon^2),$$

$$\bar{v}_{z,c} = \exp(\alpha + \varepsilon_z) \cdot \bar{v}^{(1-\beta)} \cdot \bar{v}_z^\beta,$$

$$\omega = 0.51,$$

$$\phi_{z,i} \sim \text{Normal}\left(-\frac{1}{2} \cdot \omega^2, \omega^2\right),$$

$$v_{z,c,i} = \bar{v}_{z,c} \cdot \exp(\phi_{z,i}).$$

10.1.5   The Distribution of Market Characteristics

The next step is to investigate the multivariate distribution of ϑ. Table 10.4, above the diagonal, shows the correlations of the ϑ parameters. (The lower-left triangle is discussed below.) For $N = 24$ cases, the two–tail 5 percent critical value is $|\rho| > 0.4043$; six pairs show significant correlations. That κ and μ show a high correlation is not surprising: the expected value of M according to the model is $\exp[\mu + \frac{1}{2} \cdot (\sigma^2 + \tau^2)]$.

Other correlations suggest that companies of different overall penetration behave differently in the details of their penetration. For example, negative correlation of σ and τ with κ and μ suggests that higher penetrations are more uniformly achieved. Figure 10.5 shows this relation in more detail. There was no apparent distinction between agency companies and direct writers.

Following this lead, σ, τ, and α were regressed against κ. For σ and α, simple least squares was used. Because the standard errors of the τ estimates were relatively high, weighted least squares was used with weights proportional to the inverse of the standard errors for τ values fitted in section 10.1.4

Table 10.4   **Correlation Coefficients between Penetration Model Parameters**

	μ	σ	τ	α	β	υ	
κ	.94	−.32	−.59	−.38	−.24	.13	κ
		−.51	−.72	−.50	−.19	.12	μ
			.51	.31	−.14	−.09	σ
τ*		−.40		.34	.09	.15	τ
α*		.21	−.15		.21	.01	α
β		−.23	.00	.13		−.36	β
υ		−.06	−.24	.06			
		σ*	τ*	α*			

Note: See text for key.

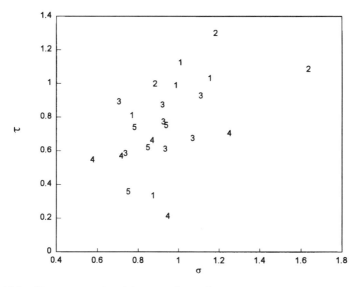

Fig. 10.5   Sigma vs. tau by risk-count share class

above. Table 10.4, below the diagonal, shows correlations where the (starred) κ-modeled parameters have been replaced by their residuals. No remaining correlation is significant.

The conditional distribution of ϑ on κ is therefore represented as

$$\mu = \kappa - \frac{1}{2} \cdot (\sigma^2 + \tau^2),$$

$$\sigma \sim \text{Normal}(m = 0.6674 - 0.0649 \cdot \kappa, \; s = 0.2146),$$

$$\tau \sim \text{Normal}(m = 0.2783 - 0.0913 \cdot \kappa, \; s = 0.2327),$$

$$\alpha \sim \text{Normal}(m = -0.2569 - 0.1387 \cdot \kappa, \; s = 0.3851),$$

$$\beta \sim \text{Normal}(m = 0.5497, \; s = 0.1514),$$

$$\upsilon \sim \text{Normal}(m = 0.4303, \; s = 0.0852).$$

10.1.6   Process Risk

The total insured value that company c has exposed to catastrophe risk in zip code z is given by $v_{z,c} = \sum_i v_{z,c,i} = R_{z,c} \cdot \overline{v}_{z,c}$. Given a particular catastrophic event in the state, let the random variable representing the loss incurred by the ith risk be $L_{z,c,i}$. The damage rate (loss-to-value ratio) is $d_{z,c,i} = L_{z,c,i}/v_{z,c,i}$. Let $d_{z,c}$, d_z, and d_c be damage rates for the aggregates. In particular, note that d_z represents the aggregate industry damage rate in zip code z.

Assume that $d_{z,c,i}$ are conditionally independent and identically distributed given z and c.[13] Let $f_{z,c}$ be the probability that the ith risk incurs a loss $L_{z,c,i} > 0$. This is the *damage-rate frequency*. Let $m_{z,c}$ and $s^2_{z,c}$ be the mean and variance of $d_{z,c,i} | (L_{z,c,i} > 0)$, the *damage-rate severity*. Because $L_{z,c,i} = d_{z,c,i} \cdot v_{z,c,i}$ and d and v are assumed independent, treat $L_{z,c}$ as a compound Poisson process with rate $\ell_{z,c} = R_{z,c} \cdot f_{z,c}$, expected severity $E[L_{z,c,i} | L_{z,c,i} > 0] = m_{z,c} \cdot v_{z,c}$, and variance of severity $\text{Var}[L_{z,c,i} | L_{z,c,i} > 0] = \overline{v}^2_{z,c} \cdot s^2_{z,c} + (m^2_{z,c} + s^2_{z,c}) \cdot \text{Var}[v_{z,c,i}]$.

Event descriptions specify values for d_z, but the equation $E[d_{z,c}] = f_{z,c} \cdot m_{z,c}$ needs to be factored, and $s^2_{z,c}$ needs to be estimated. First assume that process risk in zip code z operates on all companies homogeneously: drop the subscript c, and reduce the problems to factoring $E[d_{z,c}] = d_z = f_z \cdot m_z$ and estimating s^2_z. This assumes away company-specific differences in the expected damage rate in a given zip code, the "underwriting-quality effects" mentioned above.

Friedman (1984) offers a solution to the factoring and estimating problems. To separate frequency from severity, refer to his table 2. His columns 2, 3, and 4 correspond to this study's f_z, m_z, and d_z, respectively.[14] He shows an almost perfect loglinear relation between f_z and d_z, namely, $f = 2.155 \cdot (d)^{0.6132}$. Adopt that, cap f_z at one, and derive $m_z = d_z / f_z$.

For s^2_z, refer to Friedman's figure 14. This graph shows selected percentage points of the distribution of severity as a function of wind speed. Beta distributions with coefficients of variation of 1.0 fit this reasonably well; therefore, $s^2_z = m^2_z$ can be assumed.

In summary, given a zip code z with company exposure specified by $R_{z,c}$ and $\overline{v}_{z,c}$ and an event specified by a damage rate d_z, model the losses, $L_{z,c}$, as a compound Poisson process with Poisson rate $\ell_{z,c}$ and severity parameters $m_{z,c}$ (mean) and $\ell^2_{z,c}$ (variance), where

$$a = 2.155, \; b = 0.6132,$$

$$f_z = \min[1, \; a \cdot (d_z)^b],$$

$$m_z = d_z / f_z,$$

---

13. Studies at Guy Carpenter have found only a mild dependence of d on v.
14. Friedman uses counties, not zip codes, as the unit of geography.

$$\ell_{z,c} = R_{z,c} f_z,$$

$$n_{z,c} = m_z \bar{v}_{z,c},$$

$$\ell_{z,c}^2 = m_z^2 \cdot (\bar{v}_{z,c}^2 + 2 \cdot \text{Var}[v_{z,c,i}]).$$

In particular, this implies

$$E[L_{z,c}] = R_{z,c} \cdot d_z \cdot \bar{v}_{z,c},$$

$$\text{Var}[L_{z,c}] = 2 \cdot R_{z,c} \cdot d_z^2/f_z \cdot \bar{v}_{z,c}^2 \cdot \exp(\omega^2).$$

10.2   Simulating Hedge Performance

10.2.1   Introduction

This section uses the model of the underlying to analyze an insurer hedging its portfolio. Section 10.2.2 below describes three nested cycles of the simulation. The innermost cycle, starting with a specific event and company, simulates conditional basis risk. The intermediate cycle, starting with a specific company, iterates events through the innermost cycle to simulate unconditional basis risk. The outermost cycle samples market characteristics across a spectrum of companies. How events and companies are sampled is discussed in section 10.2.3 below.

There are several statistics of hedge performance available. The correlation coefficient $\rho(L, G)$ between the risk being hedged L and the hedge instrument G is most often quoted. The optimal hedge ratio, that is, the value of α minimizing the variance of outcomes $\text{Var}[L - \alpha \cdot G]$, is also frequently used.[15] The minimum variance is a true *measure* of performance.

Standard deviation, the square root of variance, is more easily intuited than variance because it is expressed in the same units as the hedge. This study therefore represents basis risk in terms of the *volatility* of the hedge, defined here as $\varsigma(\alpha, G) = (\text{Var}[L_c - \alpha \cdot G])^{1/2}/E[L]$. In particular, $\varsigma(0, G)$, the "unhedged volatility," is the coefficient of variation of L; $\varsigma(\alpha_{opt}, G)$, the "attained volatility," is the minimum standard deviation of the hedge, expressed relative to $E[L]$. Hedge-performance results are presented in sections 10.2.4–10.2.6 below.

10.2.2   Theory

Consider a group of reporting companies $g = 1, 2, \ldots, N$, and let $U_z = \Sigma_g v_{z,g}$ and $K_z = \Sigma_g L_{z,g}$ represent the group's total exposed values and losses incurred from the event in zip code z, respectively.

Consider two loss indices tailored to company c. First is the statewide version:

15. These are related by $\alpha_{opt} = \rho(L, G) \cdot (\text{Var}[L]/\text{Var}[G])^{1/2}$.

$$H_c = (\Sigma_z K_z) \cdot (\Sigma_z v_{z,c})/(\Sigma_z U_z).$$

This corresponds to a situation where only the statewide aggregate losses and values are reported. The company's hedge can only be a simple proportion of the reported losses.

Second is the ZIP-based index:

$$I_c = \Sigma_z I_{z,c} = \Sigma_z (K_z \cdot v_{z,c}/U_z).$$

This corresponds to a situation where individual zip-code losses and values are reported. The hedge reflects the company's specific pattern of zip-by-zip penetration.

Assume that the index reporting group consists of the entire industry, $U_z = v_z$. This permits the following simplifications: $d = (\Sigma_z d_z \cdot v_z)/(\Sigma_z v_z)$, $H_c = d \cdot \Sigma_z v_{z,c}$, and $I_c = \Sigma_z (d_z \cdot v_{z,c})$, where v_z is the aggregate industry value insured in zip code z.

Because of the way it was defined (see sec. 10.1.6 above), $E[L_{z,c}] = I_{z,c}$; therefore, a zip-based hedge, as modeled, is able to reflect the loss experience of the subject company, except for the effects of process risk. A hedge based on the statewide index, on the other hand, is also subject to market-penetration heterogeneity effects.

The objective is, then, to evaluate $\text{Var}[L_c - \alpha \cdot H_c]$ and $\text{Var}[L_c - \alpha \cdot I_c]$ for arbitrary hedge ratios α.[16] The accumulation of sufficient statistics proceeds via Monte Carlo simulation.

The inner loop of the simulation takes as input the specification of a company, ϑ_c, and the specification of an event $\eta = \{d_z\}$ as it affects a state $\{\bar{v}, \{<R_z, \bar{v}_z>\}\}$.[17] Fifty realizations of a pattern of market penetration $\{<R_{z,c}^{(s)}, \bar{v}_{z,c}^{(s)}>\}_{s=1,\ldots,50}$ corresponding to ϑ_c are drawn by simple random sampling according to the models of section 10.1.4 above. Hedge results $H_c^{(s)}$ and $I_c^{(s)}$ are computed according to the preceding discussion. Process risk in each zip code, $\text{Var}[L_c^{(s)}|\eta]$, is computed according to section 10.1.6 above and totaled across zips for $\text{Var}[L_c^{(s)}|\eta]$. Then the (event-conditional) expectations and variance-covariance matrix of L, H, and I, are tabulated. Since process risk is uncorrelated with anything else, the only moment affected by process risk is $\text{Var}[L_c | \eta] = \text{Var}_s[E[L_c^{(s)}|\eta]] + E_s[\text{Var}[L_c^{(s)}|\eta]] = \text{Var}_s[I_c^{(s)}|\eta] + E_s[\text{Var}[L_c^{(s)}|\eta]]$. Optimal hedge ratios, correlation coefficients, and conditional basis-risk measures are then computed. Note that the optimal hedge ratio for the zip-based index, conditional on event, is one.[18]

The intermediate loop of the simulation takes as input the specification of a

---

16. While it may be possible to improve the zip-based hedge by allowing α to vary between zip codes, this refinement will not be considered here.

17. For events that cross state lines, the state components are simulated individually, and the appropriate moments are summed together.

18. This is because the covariance between I and L is equal to the variance of I: $\text{Covar}[L_c, I_c|\eta] = \text{Covar}_s[E[L_c^{(s)}|\eta], I_c^{(s)}|\eta] + E_s[\text{Covar}[L_c^{(s)}, I_c^{(s)}|\eta]] = \text{Covar}_s[I_c^{(s)}, I_c^{(s)}|\eta] + 0 = \text{Var}_s[I_c^{(s)}|\eta]$.

company, ϑ_c, and produces as output the unconditional moments, hedge ratios, correlations, and basis-risk measures. This requires sampling events in a framework of possible hedge contracts.

Two common types of catastrophe reinsurance contracts are *annual aggregate* and *per occurrence* contracts. The former type responds to the total catastrophe losses experienced by an insured portfolio during a year. The latter, more common, type responds to the losses caused by a single event. Per occurrence contracts also usually have *reinstatement* provisions that allow the contract to be renewed (for a price) after a claim has been submitted.

In this study, index hedging emulates the per occurrence type of contract. An event is therefore defined as one of the following: (1) a hurricane with a minimum specified damage[19] to the industry or (2) an entire year without such a hurricane.

Conditional hedge statistics are combined across events, taking event probability into account, to obtain unconditional hedge statistics.[20] For example, the calculation of covariance between L and H proceeds as

$$\text{Cov}[L, H] = \Sigma_\eta P_\eta \cdot \text{Cov}[L, H|\eta] + \Sigma_\eta P_\eta$$
$$\cdot E[L|\eta] \cdot E[H|\eta] - (\Sigma_\eta P_\eta \cdot E[L|\eta]) \cdot (\Sigma_\eta P_\eta \cdot E[H|\eta]),$$

where P_η represents the sampling probability of event η. Note that the optimal *unconditional* hedge ratio for the zip-based index is also one.[21]

Analysis across the spectrum of insurers occurs in the outer layer of simulation, where a random sample of market-characteristics vectors, ϑ_c, is drawn according to section 10.1.5 above.

10.2.3   Sampling Issues

Historical damages[22] from catastrophes since 1949 were obtained from PCS and adjusted for socioeconomic growth by Guy Carpenter actuarial staff (Mahon 1995) to restate them as contemporaneous events. Hurricanes were isolated from other types of events. The threshold hurricane selected was Hurricane Allen, which struck Texas on 4 August 1980 and inflicted $58 million (1980 dollars) in insured damages. Since 1949, there were thirty-seven hurri-

---

19. The effect of a threshold level of damage is to approximate smaller events by zero.

20. It might be argued that the proper way to compute unconditional results is to compute variances conditional on particular realizations of market penetration $< R_{z,c}^{(s)}, \bar{v}_{z,c}^{(s)} >$ and then to take expectation with respect to all the realizations in a market-characteristics class ϑ_c. This approach makes it difficult to assess conditional hedge performance and raises issues of possible "overfitting" of hedge ratios to the limited number of events in the simulation. Numerical studies found that this alternative approach produced state-based hedge-volatility estimates approximately 10–12 percent lower than the estimates shown later in this paper.

21. Again, this is because the covariance between I and L is equal to the variance of I: $\text{Cov}[L, I] = \Sigma_\eta P_\eta \cdot \text{Cov}[L, I | \eta] + \Sigma_\eta P_\eta \cdot E[L | \eta] \cdot E[I | \eta] - (\Sigma_\eta P_\eta \cdot E[L | \eta]) \cdot (\Sigma_\eta P_\eta \cdot E[I | \eta]) = \Sigma_\eta P_\eta \cdot \text{Var}_s[I^{(s)} | \eta] + \Sigma_\eta P_\eta \cdot E_s[I^{(s)}|\eta]^2 - (\Sigma_\eta P_\eta \cdot E_s[I^{(s)}|\eta])^2 = E_\eta[\text{Var}[I|\eta]] + \text{Var}_\eta[E[I|\eta]] = \text{Var}[I]$.

22. Historical damages included all lines and coverages.

Table 10.5   **Simulated Hurricanes**

Hurricane	Date	States Used
Connie	11 August 1955	Virginia, North Carolina, Delaware, Maryland
Debra	24 July 1959	Texas
Donna	9 September 1960	Florida, Massachusetts, New York, Rhode Island
Carla	9 September 1961	Texas
Betsy	7 September 1965	Florida, Louisiana
Alicia	16 August 1983	Texas
Elena	30 August 1985	Florida, Alabama, Mississippi
Andrew	24 August 1992	Florida
Erin	1 August 1995	Florida

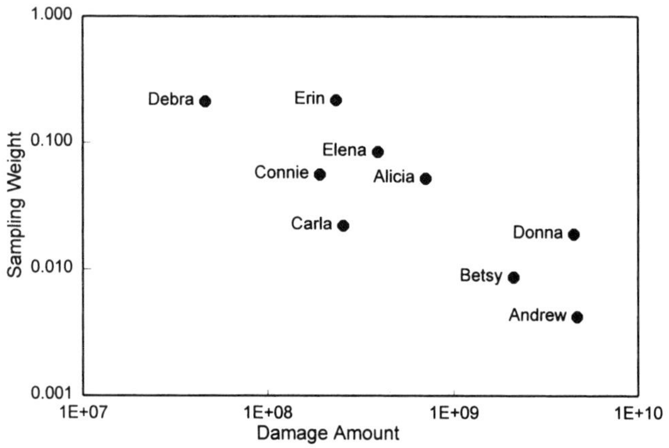

Fig. 10.6   Simulated hurricanes

canes causing at least as much (contemporary-equivalent) damage and eighteen years without such a hurricane.

Nine hurricanes were chosen as an importance sample of the thirty-seven candidates, where the importance weight was proportional to the adjusted damage estimate. They are listed in table 10.5. Their patterns,[23] that is, homeowner's-building-coverage damage rates $\{d_z\}$, were obtained from USWIND.[24] Figure 10.6 shows the hurricane simulated industry damage versus sampling weight P_η. The nonevent, a year with no hurricane, is not shown. It has a sampling weight of $18/55 = 0.327$.

For the outer simulation loop, six values of risk-count share (M or, equivalently, κ) were selected. For each value, Latin Hypercube stratified sampling (McKay, Conover, and Beckman 1979) was used to draw a sample of twenty

---

23. In cases where a hurricane caused damage to several states, not all states were used for detailed simulation. The worst-hit states were selected so as to account for at least 90 percent of all the simulated damages.

24. USWIND is a hurricane catastrophe model developed by EQECAT Inc.

Table 10.6   **Simulated Market-Share Classes (%)**

Risk-Count Share	Average TIV Share	Minimum TIV Share	Maximum TIV Share
.20	.43	.18	.85
.50	.95	.40	1.76
1.00	1.72	.78	3.21
2.00	3.20	1.24	7.52
5.00	6.88	2.56	13.80
10.00	12.51	5.85	23.30

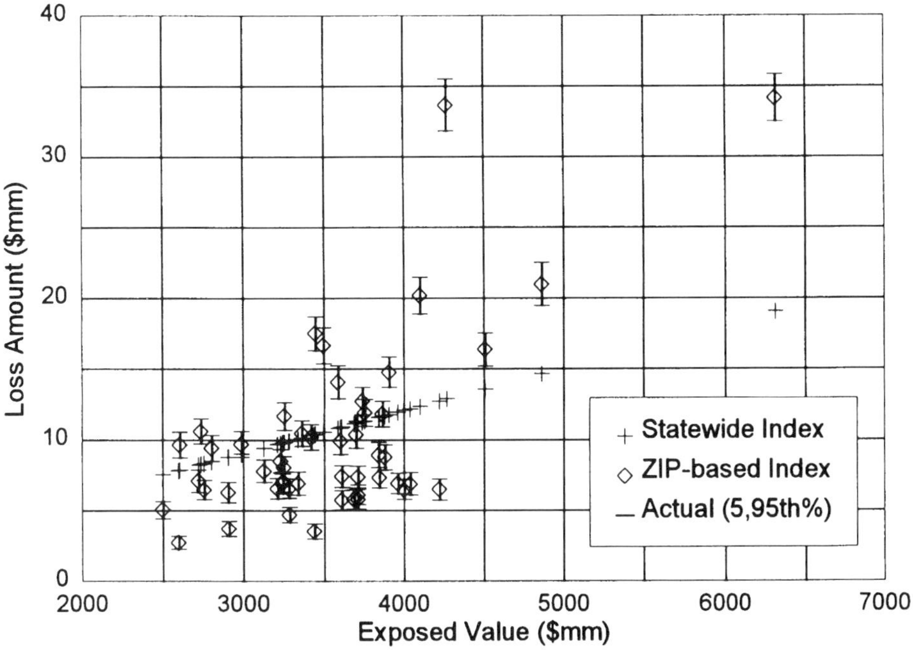

Fig. 10.7   Simulated loss and index outcomes, 1 percent company in Hurricane Alicia

values from the distribution of $\vartheta|\kappa$. The values are presented in table 10.6. Note that the share of total insured value (TIV) varies within risk-count share classes. This is visible in figure 10.12 below.

10.2.4   Example

Figure 10.7 shows the simulation of a 1 percent risk-count share company in Hurricane Alicia. The simulated outcomes occur in fifty sets of three vertically collinear symbols. The horizontal axis represents the total (statewide) exposed value. Vertically, the crosses represent the value of the statewide index; it is

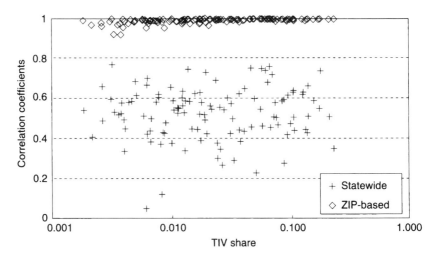

Fig. 10.8   Correlation coefficients between loss experience and indices, conditional on Hurricane Alicia

proportional to exposed value, at the 0.3 percent statewide damage rate. The diamonds represent the value of the zip-based index. The bars span the fifth to the ninety-fifth percentile values for the actual loss.[25]

The correlation between the statewide index and the losses is 0.661; between the zip-based index and the losses it is 0.996. The optimal hedge ratio for the statewide index is 2.17. These outcomes correspond to an unhedged volatility of 0.627, attained volatility of 0.471 for the statewide hedge, and attained volatility of 0.056 for the zip-based hedge.

10.2.5   Conditional Basis-Risk Results

Figure 10.8 shows the correlation coefficients, conditional on Hurricane Alicia, between loss experience and both the statewide index H and the zip-based index I for all simulated companies. Figure 10.9 shows the associated optimal hedge ratios for the statewide hedge.[26] Figures 10.10, 10.11, and 10.12 show basis risk as attained volatilities. Figure 10.12 repeats the information in figure 10.11 with the vertical axis rendered on a logarithmic scale. Table 10.7 summarizes for the six risk-count share classes. Conditionally, the statewide hedge reduces the volatility of results by a modest amount, whereas the zip-based hedge achieves a dramatic reduction.

Figure 10.13 shows attained volatility, relative to unhedged volatility, for all events. The vertical bars represent the mean, plus or minus one standard devia-

25. Recall that actual losses are not simulated in detail; rather, the expected value of losses and process risk variance are simulated. A normal distribution is assumed in locating the percentage points on this graph.
26. Recall that the optimal hedge ratio for the zip-based hedge, conditional on event, is always one.

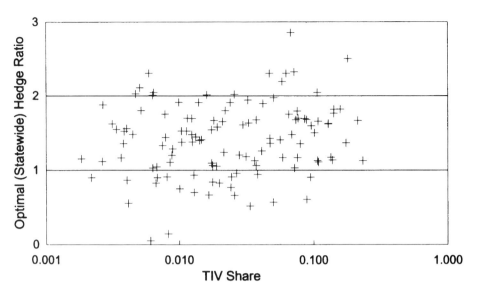

Fig. 10.9 Optimal conditional hedge ratios, statewide index, conditional on Hurricane Alicia

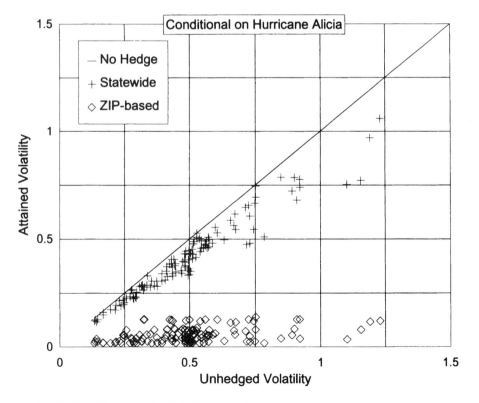

Fig. 10.10 Conditional volatility comparison

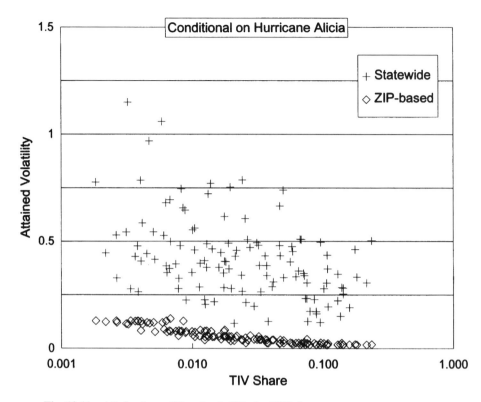

Fig. 10.11   Attained conditional volatility by TIV share

tion, of this ratio across all simulated companies. Hurricane Alicia is fairly typical of the simulated events. Only in Hurricane Donna does the statewide hedge achieve results consistently better than a 25 percent reduction in conditional volatility. The zip-based hedge typically achieves over a 70 percent reduction in volatility. Figure 10.14 shows the mean unhedged volatilities themselves. Again, Alicia is typical, and Donna exhibits an unusually low value.

10.2.6   Unconditional Basis-Risk Results

This section addresses unconditional hedge performance across all events, including the nonevent (a year without a severe hurricane).

Figure 10.15 shows the correlation coefficients between loss experience and both the statewide index H and the zip-based index I for all simulated companies. Figure 10.16 shows the associated optimal hedge ratios for the statewide hedge.[27] Figures 10.17 and 10.18 show basis risk as attained volatilities. The two figures differ in that, in figure 10.18, the vertical axis is logarithmic. Table

---

27. Recall that the optimal unconditional hedge ratio for the zip-based hedge is always one.

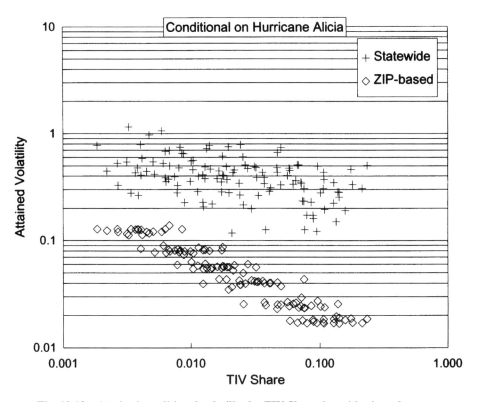

Fig. 10.12 **Attained conditional volatility by TIV Share, logarithmic scale**

Table 10.7   **Average Performance Statistics, Conditional on Hurricane Alicia**

	Optimal Hedge Ratio	Correlation Coefficient		Attained Volatility		
Risk-Count Share (%)	Statewide	Statewide	Zip Based	No Hedge	Statewide	Zip Based
.2	1.57	.530	.973	.711	.582	.124
.5	1.25	.500	.986	.555	.466	.081
1.0	1.44	.522	.991	.503	.426	.056
2.0	1.40	.496	.993	.483	.409	.040
5.0	1.53	.543	.996	.424	.339	.025
10.0	1.58	.545	.998	.371	.299	.018

10.8 summarizes for the six risk-count share classes. Figure 10.19 shows attained volatilities expressed as a fraction of unhedged volatility. Table 10.9 summarizes.

On an unconditional basis, both hedges achieve meaningful reductions in volatility. However, whereas the statewide index typically reduces volatility

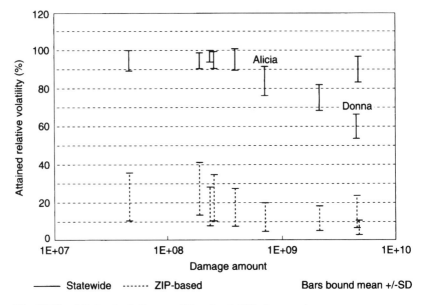

Fig. 10.13   Attained relative conditional volatility by event

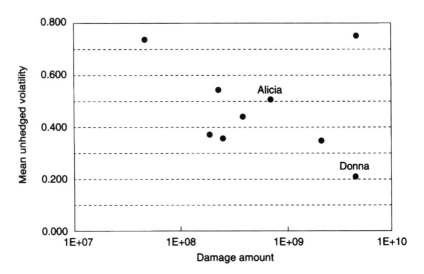

Fig. 10.14   Unhedged conditional volatility by event

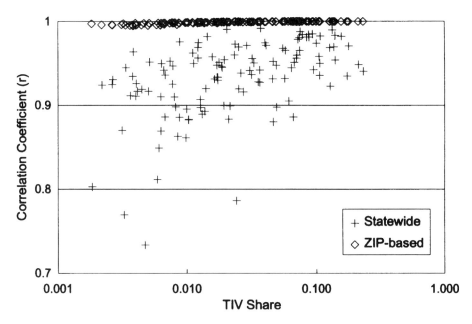

Fig. 10.15   Unconditional correlation coefficients between loss experience
and indices

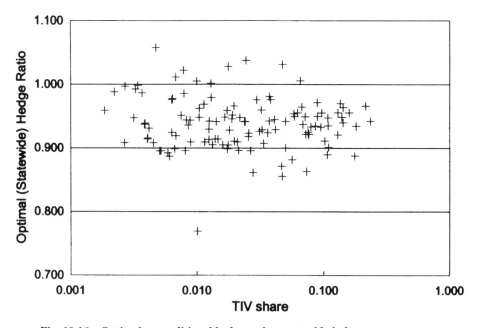

Fig. 10.16   Optimal unconditional hedge ratios, statewide index

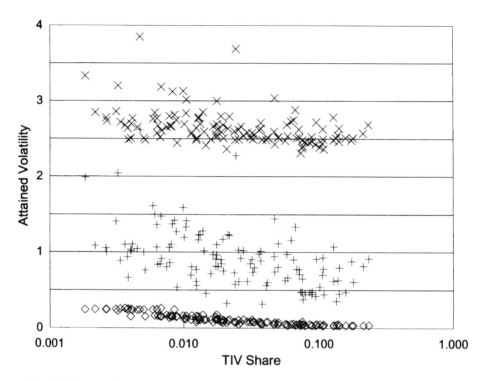

$\times$ No Hedge   + Statewide $\diamond$ ZIP-based

Fig. 10.17   Attained unconditional volatility by TIV share

50–75 percent, the zip-based hedge reduces it 90–99 percent. The reason for this is the conditional volatility, which is nearly unaffected by the statewide hedge but is reduced 70 percent or more by the zip-based hedge.

Differences in hedge performance among the simulated companies appear in both conditional and unconditional analyses. The attained volatility of the zip-based hedge shows clear "banding" by risk-count share, with no evidence of trending with TIV or even much variation within risk-count share class. The statewide hedge attained volatilities show a generally decreasing trend with TIV share and considerable variation, which can be interpreted as sensitivity to the details of the market-characteristics parameters. The unhedged volatility shows a less pronounced downward trend with increasing TIV share and perhaps a bit less sensitivity to market characteristics.

10.3   Related Work

The theory of hedging with financial futures and other derivatives is well established in the finance literature. More recent work in applying this theory

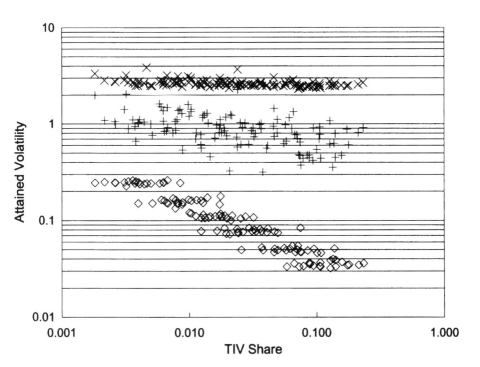

× No Hedge   + Statewide   ◇ ZIP-based

Fig. 10.18   Attained unconditional volatility by TIV share, logarithmic scale

Table 10.8   Average Performance Statistics, across All Events, for Hedges Based on a Hurricane Futures Index

Risk-Count Share (%)	Optimal Hedge Ratio Statewide	Correlation Coefficient		Attained Volatility		
		Statewide	Zip Based	No Hedge	Statewide	Zip Based
.2	.955	.886	.996	2.842	1.295	.245
.5	.938	.921	.998	2.722	1.045	.158
1.0	.927	.929	.999	2.626	.955	.112
2.0	.934	.942	1.000	2.612	.850	.078
5.0	.941	.954	1.000	2.568	.744	.050
10.0	.939	.960	1.000	2.540	.682	.035

to the case of property-casualty insurance exposures and catastrophe instruments includes Bühlmann (1996) and Meyers (1996). In both of these, the parameter of interest is the correlation coefficient between the experience of the subject portfolio and that of the catastrophe instrument being purchased.

For both the subject portfolio and the hedging instrument, Bühlmann as-

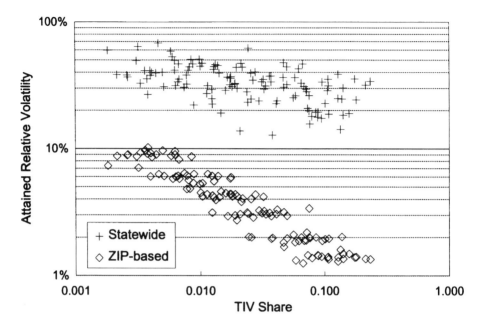

Fig. 10.19   Unconditional attained relative volatility

Table 10.9   **Mean Reduction in Volatility for Hedges Based on a Hurricane Futures Index (%)**

Risk-Count Share	Mean Attained Volatility/ Unhedged Volatility		Risk-Count Share	Mean Attained Volatility/ Unhedged Volatility	
	Statewide	Zip Based		Statewide	Zip Based
.2	44.6	8.7	2.0	31.7	3.0
.5	38.0	5.8	5.0	28.5	1.9
1.0	36.1	4.3	10.0	26.5	1.4

sumes a mixture of catastrophe and noncatastrophe risk. Meyers models a futures contract based on the (catastrophe-only) PCS index but, like Bühlmann, considers a mixed-subject portfolio. Generally, catastrophe experience is assumed independent of noncatastrophe experience, and all noncatastrophe experience is assumed mutually independent. Correlation coefficients between mixed portfolios can therefore be easily derived from those of the corresponding pure catastrophe components. In both papers, the authors use artificial examples to motivate the discussion.

There have been numerous empirical assessments of hedge performance. D'Arcy and France (1992) correlate underwriting profits with national PCS losses. Hoyt and Williams (1995) and Harrington, Mann, and Niehaus (1995) analyze loss ratios hedged against national or broad regional industry indices. Weber and Belonsky (1996) correlate company losses with national and regional PCS indices. Correlations between large company experience and regional indices in hurricane-prone areas were found to be typically in the 0.6–0.7 range. More recently, Harrington and Niehaus (1997) compare hedge performance of regional indices to tailored state-level indices. They find a state-based PCS hedge to attain correlations typically in the 0.75–0.8 range.

The use of empirical Bayes methods in the actuarial literature is not new. Lamm-Tennant, Starks, and Stokes (1992) use an empirical Bayes technique to assess the profitability of insurers. Major and Riedinger (1992, 1995) use empirical Bayes estimates in a computerized search for insurance-claim fraud. The implicit connections with Bayesian credibility theory (Herzog 1990; Klugman 1992) point to a large body of literature.

The use of simulation in the analysis of catastrophe risk is certainly not new. Friedman's pioneering work (Friedman 1969, 1972, 1975, 1979, 1984; Friedman and Mangano 1983) is the template from which subsequent analysts have started. Recently, Insurance Services Office (1996) made use of simulation to assess the volatility of catastrophe losses relative to surplus. In particular, they found coefficients of variation of 2.8 for earthquakes in the industry as a whole and 1.8–7.4 for all perils combined in selected insurer groups.

Analysis of the occurrence of hurricanes spans a considerable segment of the literature, including Friedman's work, Ho et al. (1987), Ho, Schwerdt, and Goodyear (1975), Schwerdt, Ho, and Watkins (1979), Georgiou, Davenport, and Vickery (1983), Twisdale, Vickery, and Hardy (1994), and Major and Mangano (1995).

10.4 Concluding Remarks

Within the context and limitations of the study, hedging with a statewide catastrophe index was shown to be afflicted by substantial basis risk caused by the variation in market penetration of insured portfolios. This analysis was limited in a number of dimensions, however. In particular, it explored only one type of peril (hurricane) and one type of insured risk (residential buildings). Drawing inferences to the general case of all lines requires projecting the behavior of the components of basis risk to other structures and coverages.

Drawing inferences to the general case of all perils requires dealing with other damage-generating mechanisms. Among 213 PCS-recorded events with contemporary severity to the industry at least as great as Hurricane Allen, only thirty-seven were hurricanes. Only three were earthquakes. While representing only 19 percent of the events, these two types accounted for roughly half the loss dollars. Nonhurricane wind events (tornadoes, thunderstorms, winter storms, tropical storms, etc.) accounted for most of the remaining events and

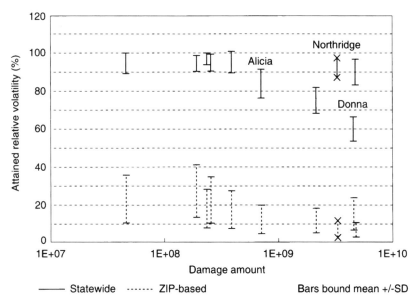

Fig. 10.20   Attained relative volatility by event, including Northridge

loss dollars.[28] The largest 14 of these 213 events, at least fifteen times as severe as Hurricane Allen,[29] accounted for half the losses. Of those, ten were hurricanes (65 percent of the losses), and one was an earthquake (12 percent of the losses).

The largest earthquake was that in Northridge on 17 January 1994, causing $12.5 billion in insured damages. Figures 10.20 and 10.21 reproduce the information in figures 10.13 and 10.14 above, with simulated Northridge results superimposed.[30]

Northridge does not appear strikingly different from the simulated hurricanes.[31] If Northridge is typical of large earthquakes in this regard, then the conclusions of the study would not change significantly by extending the scope of the perils because the dominant events are hurricanes and earthquakes. On the other hand, if earthquakes are subject to larger variation of market penetration and process risk, then hedge performance would be worse than reported here. However, the overall conclusion, that market-penetration variation causes substantial basis risk, seems irrefutable.

28. But most of the *total* damage to portfolios was located away from hurricane- and earthquake-prone areas.

29. This cutoff is roughly the median of the nine events simulated here.

30. A uniform earthquake-insurance coverage factor of approximately 20 percent was assumed, whereas 100 percent of homes were assumed covered for hurricane losses.

31. Of course, the simulation is based on the underlying model fitted to homeowner's penetration, not earthquake-insurance penetration. Nonetheless, the spatial scale of damages turns out to be typical of hurricanes.

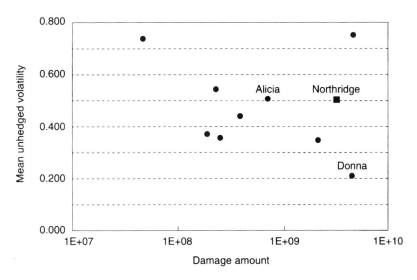

Fig. 10.21   **Unhedged conditional volatility by event, including Northridge**

Underwriting quality is also not dealt with in this study. No hedgers will have perfect knowledge of the effects of their portfolios' physical and financial characteristics or their own underwriting risk-selection standards and claim-settlement practices. Unhedged variation may be substantially understated in this study. The performance results shown here must be regarded as best case.

Appendix
An Empirical Bayes Approach to Imputing Penetration Rates

Methodology

Searle, Casella, and McCulloch (1992) define empirical Bayes estimation as "using a marginal distribution to estimate parameters in a hierarchical model, and substituting these estimates for their corresponding parameters in a formal Bayes estimator." This section describes such an approach to estimating $\pi_{z,c}$, the underlying (unobservable) risk-count penetration rate in zip code z for company c.

The estimate is based on the posterior modal value for $\psi_{z,c} = \ln(\pi_{z,c})$, given the observed risk count $R_{z,c}$ and total industry risk count R_z, that $R_{z,c}$ is Poisson distributed with expectation $\lambda_{z,c} = \exp(\psi_{z,c}) \cdot R_z$, and a normal prior distribution for $\psi_{z,c}$.

To obtain the prior, values of $\ln(R_{z,c}/R_z)$ are first examined across all zips where $R_{z,c} > 0$. This subset is treated as a left-censored sample from a normal distribution. The rate of censoring, along with the twenty-fifth and seventy-fifth percentiles of the sample, allows the estimation of the mean and standard deviation of the full, uncensored distribution.[32] The same procedure is applied to subsamples grouped by zip sectional center (zip3). The prior for $\psi_{z,c}$ is then taken to be a normal with standard deviation equal to that estimated from the statewide sample and mean equal to a weighted average of the statewide and zip3 estimates. The statewide weight is the observed rate of censoring in the zip3.

Given the prior mean μ and standard deviation σ from the previous calculation, the posterior modal $\psi_{z,c}$ is the solution to the equation

$$\partial[L(\psi, R_{z,c}|R_z)]/\partial\psi = 0,$$

where the joint likelihood of the data and the parameter is proportional to

$$L(\psi, R_{z,c}|R_z) = \exp\left\{-\frac{1}{2} \cdot [(\psi - \mu)/\sigma]^2\right\}$$
$$\cdot \exp[-\exp(\psi) \cdot R_z] \cdot [\exp(\psi) \cdot R_z]^{R_{z,c}}.$$

Since $\lambda = \exp(\psi) \cdot R_z$, solving for the zero derivative reduces to solving

$$\ln(\lambda) + \sigma^2 \cdot \lambda = \mu + \sigma^2 \cdot R_{z,c} + \ln(R_z).$$

As $R_{z,c}$ gets large, the estimated value for $\lambda_{z,c}$ converges to $R_{z,c}$. When $R_{z,c}$ is zero, the estimated penetration rate $\lambda_{z,c}/R_z$ decreases as R_z increases.

A Market-Penetration Case Study

Consider a case from the data presented in section 10.1.3 above. The subject company has a risk-count share of 1–2 percent in the state of Maryland, and 12.9 percent of the zips have a zero risk count. The observed penetration rates, $R_{z,c}/R_z$ are shown in figure 10A.1. Each symbol in the charts represents one zip code. The points were randomly perturbed horizontally for better visibility.

The presence of spatial autocorrelation can be seen by means of analysis of variance where zip sectional center (zip3) is taken as the treatment effect in table 10A.1.

The F-statistic has $p = 2.2 \cdot 10^{-14}$, which is highly significant. However, the significance test is predicated on normally distributed errors, which is clearly not the case.

The next step is to impute the underlying penetration rates, filtering out, as it were, the variation arising from Poisson sampling. Figures 10A.2 and 10A.3

---

32. Using the interquartile range improves robustness of the estimates. Also, the entire sample cannot be used because the censoring has an element of randomness to it.

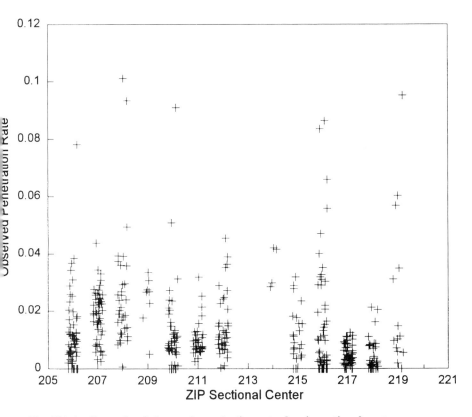

Fig. 10A.1   **Example of observed penetration rates by zip sectional center**

Table 10A.1   **Analysis of Variance of Penetration Rate**

Source of Variation	df	SS	MS	F
Zip3	12	.0192	.00160	8.42
Error	435	.0828	.00019	
Total	447	.1020		

Note: SS = sum of squares; MS = mean square.

show the results. Each symbol represents one zip code. Figure 10A.3 zooms in on those zips with an estimated penetration rate less than half a percent. No zip code is (ever) estimated to have a zero penetration rate.

Figure 10A.4 shows the resulting estimated penetration rates ($\pi_{z,c}$) by three-digit zip. The vertical axis is logarithmic. This figure makes spatial autocorrelation visually apparent. For example, penetration rates in zips 208xx (Bethesda)

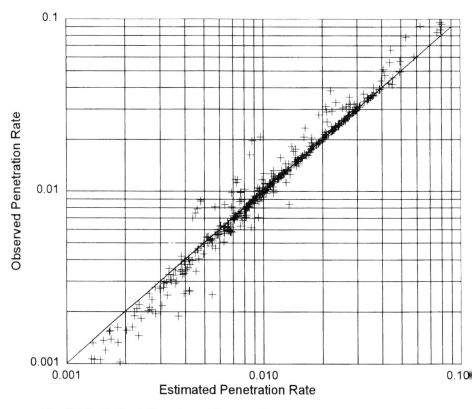

Fig. 10A.2   Estimated vs. observed penetration rates

tend to be above 1 percent, while those in zips 217xx (Frederick) are almost all below 1 percent.

Analysis of variance of the logs of $\pi_{z,c}$ results are given in table 10A.2.

This has $p = 7.7 \cdot 10^{-38}$. Figure 10A.4 suggests that normality assumptions are reasonable in the logarithmic domain. Therefore, zip3 has an effect; therefore, spatial autocorrelation is present. All twenty-four cases had zip3 effects significant at the 1 percent level or better.

For the risk-count penetration parameters of ϑ, the variance components are computed by

$$\text{zip (error) effect: } \sigma^2 = \text{SS(ERROR)}/\text{df(ERROR)} = 0.544,$$

$$\text{zip3 effect: } \tau^2 = [\text{SS(ZIP3)} - \text{df(ZIP3)} \cdot \sigma^2]/[N - (\Sigma N_i^2)/N] = 0.337,$$

which correspond to $\sigma_c = 0.74$ (.03) and $\tau_c = 0.58$ (.24), where standard errors (Searle 1956) are expressed as coefficients of variation.

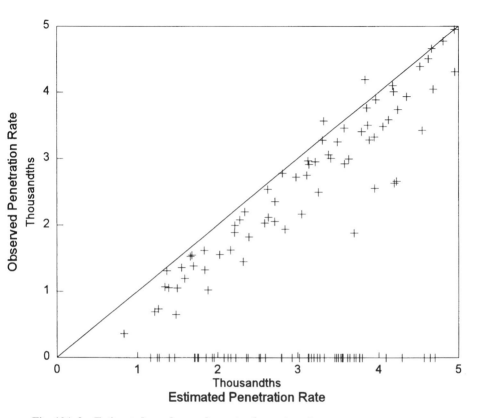

Fig. 10A.3   **Estimated vs. observed penetration rates, close up**

Table 10A.2   **Analysis of Variance of Log Imputed Penetration Rate**

Source of Variation	df	SS	MS	F
Zip3	12	142.93	11.9112	21.9
Error	435	236.56	.5443	
Total	447	379.49		

Note: SS = sum of squares; MS = mean square.

The Question of Bias

To assess the estimation procedure, twelve of the twenty-four cases were replicated eight times each by parametric bootstrap (Efron and Tibshirani 1993) and reestimated. The median bias among the cases was −2.75 percent for the zip effect and −8.0 percent for the zip3 effect. While the former was statistically significant, it was judged small enough to ignore. The latter was not statistically significant.

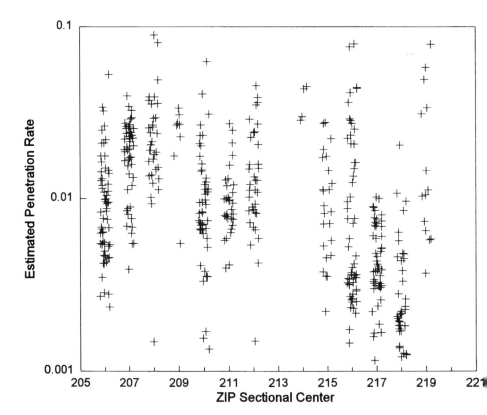

Fig. 10A.4   Example of estimated penetration rates by zip sectional center

References

Beard, R. E., T. Pentikäinen, and E. Pesonen. 1984. *Risk theory: The stochastic basis of insurance.* London: Chapman & Hall.

Bühlmann, H. 1996. Crosshedging of insurance portfolios. In *1995 Bowles Symposium: Securitization of insurance risk,* ed. H. Bühlmann. Monograph no. M-FI96-3. Schaumburg, Ill.: Society of Actuaries.

Cochran, W. G., and G. M. Cox. 1957. *Experimental design.* 2d ed. New York: Wiley.

D'Arcy, S. P., and V. G. France. 1992. Catastrophe futures: A better hedge for insurers. *Journal of Risk and Insurance* 59, no. 4:575–600.

Dempster, A. P., N. M. Laird, and D. B. Rubin. 1977. Maximum likelihood from incomplete data via the EM algorithm. *Journal of the Royal Statistical Society,* ser. B, 39:1–38.

Efron, B., and R. J. Tibshirani. 1993. *An introduction to the bootstrap.* New York: Chapman & Hall.

Fisher, R. A. 1942. *The design of experiments.* 3d ed. Edinburgh: Oliver & Boyd.

Foppert, D. 1993. Uncertain futures. *Best's Review, Property/Casualty Insurance Edition* 93, no. 11:20.

Friedman, D. G. 1969. Computer simulation of the earthquake hazard. In *Geologic hazards and public problems conference proceedings,* ed. R. A. Olson and M. Wallace, 153–81. Washington, D.C.: U.S. Government Printing Office/Office of Emergency Preparedness, Executive Office of the President.

———. 1972. Insurance and the natural hazards. *International Journal for Actuarial Studies in Non-Life Insurance and Risk Theory* (Amsterdam) 7, pt. 1:4–58.

———. 1975. *Computer simulation in natural hazard assessment.* Monograph no. NSF-RA-E-75-002. Boulder, Colo.: Institute of Behavioral Science, University of Colorado.

———. 1979. A possible national simulation model using geographic coordinates. In *Natural hazards data resources: Uses and needs* (Monograph no. 27), ed. S. K. Tubbesing. Boulder, Colo.: Program on Technology, Environment, and Man, Institute of Behavioral Science, University of Colorado.

———. 1984. Natural hazard risk assessment for an insurance program. *Geneva Papers on Risk and Insurance* 9, no. 30 (January): 57–128.

Friedman, D. G., and J. J. Mangano. 1983. Actuarial approach to the estimation of storm surge probabilities on an open beach in Lee County, Florida. In *Report of Committee on Coastal Flooding from Hurricanes.* Washington, D.C.: National Research Council, National Academy of Sciences.

Gelfand, A. E., and A. F. M. Smith. 1990. Sampling-based approaches to calculating marginal densities. *Journal of the American Statistical Association* 85:398–409.

Georgiou, P. N., A. G. Davenport, and B. J. Vickery. 1983. Design wind speeds in regions dominated by tropical cyclones. *Journal of Wind Engineering and Industrial Aerodynamics* 13:139–52.

Grieg-Smith, P. 1964. *Quantitative plant ecology.* London: Butterworth.

Harrington, S. E., S. V. Mann, and G. Niehaus. 1995. Insurer capital structure decisions and the viability of insurance derivatives. *Journal of Risk and Insurance* 62, no. 3:483–508.

Harrington, S. E., and G. Niehaus. 1997. Basis risk with catastrophe insurance derivative contracts. Paper presented at the Fifth International Conference on Insurance Solvency and Finance, London, 17 June.

Henderson, C. R. 1953. Estimation of variance and covariance components. *Biometrics* 9:226–52.

Herzog, T. N. 1990. Credibility: The Bayesian model versus Bühlmann's model. *Transactions of the Society of Actuaries* 41:43–81.

Hill, B. M. 1965. Inference about variance components in the one-way model. *Journal of the American Statistical Association* 60:806–25.

Ho, F. P., R. W. Schwerdt, and H. V. Goodyear. 1975. *Some climatological characteristics of hurricanes and tropical storms, Gulf and East Coasts of the United States.* National Oceanic and Atmospheric Administration Technical Report no. NWS 15. Washington, D.C.: U.S. Department of Commerce, National Oceanic and Atmospheric Administration, National Weather Service.

Ho, F. P., J. C. Su, K. L. Hanevich, R. J. Smith, and F. P. Richards. 1987. *Hurricane climatology for the Atlantic and Gulf Coasts of the United States.* National Oceanic and Atmospheric Administration Technical Report no. NWS 38. Washington, D.C.: U.S. Department of Commerce, National Oceanic and Atmospheric Administration, National Weather Service.

Hoyt, R. E., and R. D. Williams. 1995. The effectiveness of catastrophe futures as a hedging mechanism for insurers. *Journal of Insurance Regulation* 14:27–64.

Insurance Services Office. 1996. *Managing catastrophe risk.* New York.

Kahn, H. 1950. Modifications of the Monte Carlo method. *Proceedings, Seminar on Scientific Computations, November 16–18, 1949,* ed. C. C. Hurd. New York: IBM.

Kershaw, K. A. 1964. *Quantitative and dynamic ecology.* London: Edward Arnold.

Klugman, S. A. 1992. *Bayesian statistics in actuarial science with emphasis on credibility.* Boston: Kluwer Academic.

Lamm-Tennant, J., L. T. Starks, and L. Stokes. 1992. An empirical Bayes approach to estimating loss ratios. *Journal of Risk and Insurance* 59, no. 3:426–42.

Mahon, J. B. 1995. Forecast of US insured catastrophe losses. Internal memorandum. New York: Guy Carpenter & Co., 19 January.

Major, J. A., and J. J. Mangano. 1995. Selecting among rules induced from a hurricane database. *Journal of Intelligent Information Systems* 4:39–52.

Major, J. A., and D. R. Riedinger. 1992. EFD: A hybrid knowledge/statistical-based system for the detection of fraud. *International Journal of Intelligent Systems* 7, no. 7:687–703.

———. 1995. EFD: Heuristic statistics for insurance fraud detection. In *Intelligent systems for finance and business,* ed. S. Goonatilake and P. Treleaven. Chichester: Wiley.

McKay, M. D., W. J. Conover, and R. J. Beckman. 1979. A comparison of three methods for selecting values of input variables in the analysis of output from a computer code. *Technometrics* 21:239–45.

Metropolis, N., and S. Ulam. 1949. The Monte Carlo method. *Journal of the American Statistical Association* 44:335.

Meyers, G. G. 1996. A buyer's guide for options and futures on a catastrophe index. In *CAS 1996 Discussion Paper Program: Alternative markets/self-insurance.* Arlington, Va.: Casualty Actuarial Society.

Robbins, H. 1951. Asymptotically subminimax solutions of compound statistical decision problems. In *Proceedings of the Second Berkeley Symposium on Mathematics, Statistics, and Probability,* ed. Jerzy Neyman. Berkeley: University of California Press.

———. 1955. An empirical Bayes approach to statistics. In *Proceedings of the Third Berkeley Symposium on Mathematics, Statistics, and Probability,* vol. 1, ed. Jerzy Neyman. Berkeley: University of California Press.

Rubinstein, R. Y. 1981. *Simulation and the Monte Carlo method.* New York: Wiley.

Schwerdt, R. W., F. P. Ho, and R. R. Watkins. 1979. *Meteorological criteria for standard project hurricane and probable maximum hurricane wind fields, Gulf and East Coasts of the United States.* National Oceanic and Atmospheric Administration Technical Report no. NWS 23. Washington, D.C.: U.S. Department of Commerce, National Oceanic and Atmospheric Administration, National Weather Service.

Searle, S. R. 1956. Matrix methods in variance and covariance components analysis. *Annals of Mathematical Statistics* 27:737–48.

Searle, S. R., G. Casella, and C. E. McCulloch. 1992. *Variance components.* New York: Wiley.

Tiao, G. C., and W. Y. Tan. 1965. Bayesian analysis of random effects models in the analysis of variance I: Posterior distribution of the variance components. *Biometrika* 52:37–53.

Tierney, L., and J. B. Kadane. 1986. Accurate approximations for posterior moments and marginal densities. *Journal of the American Statistical Association* 81:82–86.

Twisdale, L. A., P. J. Vickery, and M. B. Hardy. 1994. Uncertainties in the prediction of hurricane windspeeds. In *Hurricanes of 1992: Lessons learned and implications for the future,* ed. R. A. Cook and M. Soltani. New York: American Society of Civil Engineers.

Weber, M., and G. Belonsky. 1996. Cat option critique. *Reinsurance* 27, no. 9:21–22.

Whittle, P. 1954. On stationary processes in the plane. *Biometrika* 41:434–49.

Comment   André F. Perold

Basis risk has been a central issue in many of the papers and discussions at this conference. For example, we have heard claims that basis risk is a main source of insurer profitability but that it is also the risk that limits capacity; that broad-market hedging instruments are too coarse to effectively reduce basis risk and that finer hedges such as ones based on zip-code-level indices are needed; that large insurers can manage basis risk through broader distribution but that small insurers will require intermediation of basis risk; that reinsurers will earn spreads by buying and packaging idiosyncratic risks and hedge themselves by selling standardized, broad-market risks; and that the creation of reinsurance contracts, written on standardized zip-code-level indices, is necessary for the development of a deep and liquid market for contracts written on marketwide indices.

John Major's paper seeks to inform this discussion by empirically estimating basis risk. The paper estimates insurer-specific deviations from statewide indices and then examines the hedging effectiveness of contracts based on zip-code-level indices. Being the first study of its kind, the paper makes an important contribution to our understanding of basis risk.

In Major's model, firms are homogeneous with respect to underwriting quality, and their exposures within a zip code are near homogeneous in that they exhibit only small deviations from the index ("process risk"). Except for process risk, a firm's exposure within a zip code is thus proportional to its penetration of that zip code, and its statewide exposure is determined by its vector of zip-code-level penetrations. For example, if firm A writes insurance only in zip code 1, and if firm B writes insurance only in zip code 2, firm A's exposure will differ from firm B's to the extent that the losses in zip codes 1 and 2 are unrelated. A statewide hedge based on the sum of losses in zip codes 1 and 2 might therefore be quite ineffective. On the other hand, hedging instruments based on zip-code-level indices will allow firms A and B to hedge all but process risk.

The paper provides conditional as well as unconditional estimates of basis risk. *Conditional* refers to losses in a specific hurricane, while *unconditional* refers to losses simulated over multiple hurricanes. The difficult part is to model the variation in loss exposures for a given event. That is, different hurricane paths may result in the same total statewide damage, and the distribution of damage across these paths must be estimated. The paper does so by assuming that this distribution is the same as the distribution of market penetration across firms. In the example given above, this corresponds to assuming that a hurricane would hit zip code 1 or zip code 2 but not both.

André F. Perold is the Sylvan C. Coleman Professor of Financial Management at Harvard Business School.

The author thanks John Major and Peter Tufano for helpful comments.

To clarify, let v_z be the industry coverage of zip code z, let d_z be the industrywide loss, and let p_z be the penetration of a given firm. Ignoring process risk, the firm's losses are given by $\Sigma_z v_z p_z d_z$, while the industry's losses are given by $\Sigma_z v_z d_z$. The firm's basis—if using a hedging instrument based on the statewide index—is given by

$$B = \Sigma_z v_z p_z d_z - h\Sigma_z v_z d_z (\Sigma_z v_z p_z / \Sigma_z v_z),$$

where h is the hedge ratio, and the term in parentheses is the ratio of the firm's statewide exposure to the industry's statewide exposure. The firm's unconditional basis risk is given by the variation in B as a function of the vector $\{d_z\}$. The firm's conditional basis risk is determined by the variation in B as a function of $\{d_z\}$, holding fixed industry statewide losses $\Sigma_z v_z d_z$.

The key to understanding the paper's results is to note that basis risk is a symmetrical function of the vector of losses $\{d_z\}$ and the vector of market penetrations $\{p_{cz}\}$; that is, interchanging $\{d_z\}$ and $\{p_z\}$ leaves B unaffected. Thus, the variation in basis across firms (i.e., across realizations of market penetration) will be the same as the variation in basis across hurricane paths if the market-penetration vector $\{p_z\}$ is sampled from the same distribution from which the loss vector $\{d_z\}$ is drawn.

For reasons presumably of data availability, the paper simulates variation in basis risk by sampling from the distribution of market penetrations across firms. While this is a clever idea, my intuition is that the approach *understates* true basis risk. I suspect that firms are relatively more homogeneous with respect to market penetration than are the hurricane paths that result in a given amount of statewide damage.

The basic results of the paper are that unhedged losses have an unconditional coefficient of variation in the range 2.5–2.8. With the use of statewide hedging instruments, unconditional coefficients of variation are in the range 0.7–1.3; and, with the use of zip-code-level hedging instruments, the range is only 0.04–0.2. That these last numbers are not zero reflects the fact that the only risk remaining—process risk—is modeled as being very small.

In Major's simulations, the correlation between individual firm exposures and the statewide index is very high, ranging from 89 to 96 percent, while the correlation between individual firm exposures and the zip-code-level indices is extremely high, in excess of 99.5 percent. The extremely high zip-code-level correlation simply reflects the low level of process risk, while the high correlation with the statewide index might be the result of relatively low variation among firm market penetrations, as discussed above.

A Simple Model of Insurance Origination and Hedging

The results of the paper raise the important question of how the correlation between the insurer's portfolio and the hedging instrument might affect the optimal hedge ratio. The paper presents minimum-variance hedge ratios, which are independent of the cost of hedging. Quite possibly, however, instruments based on zip-code-level indices might be considerably less liquid than instruments based on statewide-level indices. For example, adverse selection likely will become more significant for finer hedges—especially if these hedges are used by firms with significant market penetration—resulting in these instruments having greater bid-offer spreads.[1] Thus, even though zip-code-level instruments might be better hedges because of higher correlations, the demand for these instruments might be dampened by higher transaction costs. In what follows, I attempt to model the trade-off between higher hedging costs and higher correlations in a simple way.

Consider a one-period model in which the firm originates q units of coverage, with expected profits $P(q)$ before hedging costs and deadweight capital costs. The firm hedges a fraction h (or hq units) of the risks that it has insured with an instrument that has correlation R with these risks. The hedging instrument is denominated so that its per unit variance, σ^2, is the same as the per unit variance of the risk being hedged. Absent hedging costs, the minimum-variance hedge ratio is optimal and is equal to R.

The per unit cost of hedging is S, which includes normal transaction costs such as the bid-ask spread as well as any "abnormal premium" in the pricing of the instrument. The abnormal premium is the instrument's expected return in excess of the risk-free rate, before transaction costs. There should be no abnormal premium in an efficient capital market if catastrophe risk is uncorrelated with priced factors. However, as discussed in Froot and O'Connell (chap. 5 in this volume), the pricing of catastrophe hedging instruments may presently contain significant abnormal premiums. The cost S is assumed here to be invariant to the quantity hedged, h.

The firm's demand for hedging stems from the deadweight cost of risk capital that the firm bears because of agency and information costs (see Merton and Perold 1993; Merton 1993; and Froot and Stein 1998). Applying the model developed in Perold (1998), these deadweight costs are proportional to the total risk of the firm. The functional form is

$$\text{Deadweight cost of risk capital} = k\sigma_F,$$

where k is a constant, and σ_F is the standard deviation of the firm's end-of-period cash flows. σ_F is given by

$$\sigma_F^2 = \sigma^2 q^2 \{1 + h^2 - 2Rh\}.$$

The value of the firm[2] is $P(q) - hqS - k\sigma_F$, which can be expressed as

$$\text{Firm value} = P(q) - q\{hS + k\sigma(1 + h^2 - 2Rh)^{1/2}\}.$$

---

1. For a discussion of the analogous problem in the stock market, see Gammill and Perold (1989).

2. Here, *firm value* refers to expected excess profits after deadweight costs of hedging and of risk capital. It represents the premium over *book value*, or invested capital, of the firm.

Maximizing over h yields the optimal hedge ratio

$$h^* = R - S\{(1 - R^2)/(k^2\sigma^2 - S^2)\}^{1/2}.$$

At the optimal hedge ratio, the value of the firm is

$$\text{Firm value} = P(q) - q\{SR + [(1 - R^2)(k^2\sigma^2 - S^2)]^{1/2}\}.$$

These results relate the optimal hedge ratio and firm value to the correlation and cost of the hedging instrument as follows. First, the firm hedges less as the cost of hedging rises; that is, h^* is decreasing in S. In addition, no hedging occurs if the cost of hedging is large relative to the firm's deadweight cost of risk capital, that is, if $S > k\sigma R$. Full hedging occurs when $R = 1$ even if $S > 0$, provided that $S < k\sigma R$. Firm value is increasing in R and decreasing in S.

This model can now be tied to the empirical findings of the paper. If the results are correct that the statewide index and zip-code-level index correlations differ by only 4–11 percent, then it may easily be that the benefits of the finer zip-code-based hedges are offset by higher costs of hedging. A numerical example illustrates the trade-off.

Let $P(q) = \$100$, $q = 100$, and $k\sigma = \$1.00$. With these values, if $R = 0$ so that the firm does no hedging, its deadweight cost of risk capital evaluates to $qk\sigma = \$100$, with the result that the value of the firm is zero. At the other extreme, if $S = 0$ and $R = 1$, all risk can be fully and costlessly hedged, and the firm therefore bears no deadweight cost of risk capital. The value of the firm then is $\$100$.

Tables 10C.1 and 10C.2 calculate the optimal hedge ratio and firm value, respectively, for various values of S and R. The tables show that the hedging costs need to be significant if these costs are to negate the benefits of higher correlations. For example, suppose that a *costless* broad-market hedging instrument is available and that its correlation with the firm's risks is $R = 0.7$.

Table 10C.1   **Optimal Hedge Ratio**

	\multicolumn{5}{c}{Cost of Hedging (S)}				
R	0	.1	.3	.5	.7
1.0	1.00	1.00	1.00	1.00	1.00
.9	.90	.86	.76	.65	.47
.8	.80	.74	.61	.45	.21
.7	.70	.63	.48	.29	.00
.6	.60	.52	.35	.14	.00
.5	.50	.41	.23	.00	.00
.4	.40	.31	.11	.00	.00
.3	.30	.20	.00	.00	.00
.2	.20	.10	.00	.00	.00
.1	.10	.00	.00	.00	.00

Table 10C.2   **Firm Value with Optimal Hedging**

	Cost of Hedging (S) ($)				
R	0	.1	.3	.5	.7
1.0	100.0	90.0	70.0	50.0	30.0
.9	56.4	47.6	31.4	17.3	5.9
.8	40.0	32.3	18.8	8.0	1.2
.7	28.6	21.9	10.9	3.2	.0
.6	20.0	14.4	5.7	.7	.0
.5	13.4	8.8	2.4	.0	.0
.4	8.3	4.8	.6	.0	.0
.3	4.6	2.1	.0	.0	.0
.2	2.0	.5	.0	.0	.0
.1	.5	.0	.0	.0	.0

The optimal hedge ratio for this instrument is 0.7, and the value of the firm is $28.60. If a finer instrument is available with correlation $R = 0.9$ and the cost of hedging is $S = 0.3$, the optimal hedge ratio is 0.76. The firm hedges $qh = 76$ units and incurs a hedging-related cost of $qhS = \$22.80$. Moreover, hedging reduces the firm's deadweight cost of risk capital from $100 to $45.80, and the value of the firm is therefore $100 - \$45.80 - \$22.80 = \$31.40$. Thus, improving the correlation from 0.7 to 0.9 has economic significance even if the cost of hedging is large. At an even larger cost of hedging, say, $S = 0.5$, the hedge ratio is still high, at 0.65, but the value of the firm is much lower, at $17.30.

These results are obviously most sensitive to the magnitude of the deadweight capital costs—which drive the demand for hedging in the first place. For example, if $k\sigma$ is small (e.g., $k\sigma = 0.1$), then the cost of hedging must only exceed 0.1 for no hedging to occur.

Conclusion

John Major's paper estimates the potentially significant increase in correlation, and consequent reduction in basis risk, that might be achieved with the use of hedging instruments based on zip-code-level indices. The paper does so by devising a simulation technique based principally on variation in market penetration across firms and the assumption that this variation is a good proxy for the distribution of damage across hurricane paths. The implications of the results for the demand for hedging with zip-code-level instruments are not obvious, however. There almost certainly will be greater costs associated with the use of these instruments. Depending on the reasons that firms hedge in the first place, these greater costs may offset the superior covariance properties of zip-code-level instruments.

References

Froot, Kenneth A., and Jeremy C. Stein. 1998. Risk management, capital budgeting and capital structure policy for financial institutions: An integrated approach. *Journal of Financial Economics* 47, no. 1 (January): 55–82.

Gammill, James F., Jr., and André F. Perold. 1989. The changing character of stock market liquidity. *Journal of Portfolio Management* 15, no. 3 (Spring): 13–18.

Merton, Robert C. 1993. Operation and regulation in financial intermediation: A functional perspective. In *Operation and regulation of financial markets,* ed. P. Englund. Stockholm: Economic Council.

Merton, Robert C., and André F. Perold. 1993. Theory of risk capital in financial firms. *Journal of Applied Corporate Finance* 6, no. 3 (Fall): 16–32.

Perold, André F. 1998. Capital allocation in financial firms. Working Paper no. 98-072. Harvard Business School.

11   Panel Discussions

**Panel I: Barriers to and Opportunities for
Low-Cost Trading of Catastrophic Risk**

Robert Litzenberger

What do I think about the impact of securitization? The first thought that comes to mind is disintermediation, analogous to what happened when major corporations issued commercial paper, and thereafter no longer relied on commercial banks for loans.

Similarly, we can think of securitization of insurance resulting in disintermediation at various levels: (1) large nonfinancial companies going to primary insurers, (2) insurers having exposures going to reinsurers, and (3) the reinsurers going to retrocessional market. At each level there are administrative and brokerage costs involved.

Let me talk a bit about disintermediation at the first level. Companies have already learned to self-insure many small risks and need insurance for the very large risks. We can picture a major integrated oil company insuring its oil platforms directly through its securitization. This would require more standardization and considerably less reliance on the legal system for resolutions of claims, so it's not the same as a traditional insurance contract. It might not be the right contract for certain companies that want the traditional insurance coverage.

One major issue in a securitization or a reinsurance contract is maintaining the proper incentives for careful underwriting. Thus, indemnity-based securitizations have to be written so that the original insurers or reinsurers maintain a substantial participation in the risk. Also, most investors don't have the exper-

---

Robert Litzenberger is a managing director of Goldman Sachs and Co.

tise to sort out the different types of exposures. To avoid adverse selection, the secession rules for a reinsurance securitization have to be written in such a way that cherry picking isn't possible. Partly because of these complications, many securitized transactions will be based on indices that relate to industrywide exposure. If the company has no control over the index, the moral hazard and adverse selection issues don't arise. Of course the problem with an index is the company's basis risk. I think issuers are going to have to think about insurance the way we think about other securities. In order to reduce risk we don't need perfect hedges. Storage of oats creates price exposure that is frequently hedged with another feed grain, corn, because corn futures are more liquid. They don't hedge one to one but minimize the associated tracking error. In government bond markets, on-the-run securities are used to hedge off-the-run securities and there is basis risk. The reliance on indices works out very well with firms with diversified exposures. If you look at a very specialized insurance company, a small company, an index security may create too large a basis risk. There will always be a role for reinsurers but the role may change. The large primary companies that are already adequately diversified may issue index-type securities using the capital markets directly. The small companies probably would use reinsurance. Reinsurers would pool exposures and use their expertise in managing basis risk. For the same amount of capital they could write more reinsurance because they are only exposed to basis risk. They are able to take on more "exposure" because they're able to offset the systematic component within indices and an attempt to balance out their book accordingly.

When discussing the limited capacity of the reinsurance for coverage of major cats, the question often asked is, If returns are so great, why is there not more equity placed in reinsurance companies? The problem is the extreme tail events. For example, consider the losses that are estimated based on current exposures if the following, large historical event were to occur: San Francisco earthquake (1905), $45 billion; New Madrid earthquake (1811), $42 billion; Great New England hurricane (1938), $25 billion. Offering coverage for such super cat exposures requires very high credit quality. Weaker credit reinsurance companies that have major reinsurance exposure to super cat are unlikely to survive such an event. The problem is, a AAA rate reinsurance company would have to have a huge amount of capital to insure such extreme tails. It's just not efficient to put that much equity, for example, in a Bermuda reinsurance company to support this type of activity.

Stewart C. Myers

Our problem is to understand how to obtain efficient, low-cost trading of catastrophic risks ("cat" risks or "cats"). We might start by asking where these risks are traded now.

Stewart C. Myers is the Gordon Y Billard Professor of Finance at the Sloan School of Management, Massachusetts Institute of Technology, and a member of the board of CAT Ltd.

If you buy the stock of a property-casualty company, you are trading cata-strophic risk. The stock market is absorbing those risks. We like to think that the stock market is an efficient absorber of risk. Why aren't we done?

The reason is obvious: no property-casualty company can completely avoid or reinsure cat risks. With limited liability, a stockholder in a property-casualty corporation does not bear much of the worst tail of the probability distribution of catastrophes. In order to cover that bad tail, an insurance company would have to carry massive amounts of collateral. Ordinary property-casualty com-panies don't have enough assets to cover the worst losses.

This raises a tax problem, at least for U.S. insurance companies. The farther you go out in the tail of bad cat outcomes, the greater the ratio of incremental collateral to incremental premium must be to cover possible losses. The worst cats are low-probability events. Once in a blue moon the insurance company's collateral gets hit by an exceptionally bad cat event. But most of the time that collateral just sits there, as if it were in a mutual fund. While it sits there, it is taxed. There is double taxation. The insurance company must compete with mutual funds or other investment vehicles to hold this collateral. The other investment vehicles are not double taxed.

There is a case for tax reform here. Suppose that you could set aside some assets, somehow segregate them, and designate them as collateral for extreme catastrophic losses—losses that haven't occurred yet but are going to occur sooner or later. The income on these segregated assets should not be subject to corporate tax. It could accumulate just like the income inside a pension plan. That would remove the double taxation and therefore the tax disincentive for insurance companies to hold collateral. Last evening, Ross Davidson suggested tax-deductible reserves against cats. This is another way of removing the tax disincentive to hold collateral.

I am not claiming that this tax incentive is the only reason the primary insur-ers don't hold more collateral in order to self-insure against catastrophes, but I think that it's an important one.

The next step in bearing cat risks is reinsurance. If you buy stock in a cat reinsurance company, you are absorbing cat risks. Given that reinsurers are apparently healthy, why aren't we done? First, they, too, don't have the capacity for much of the worst tail of the probability distribution, that is, for the most extreme cat events. They handle the middle cats, so to speak. Second, they appear to price cat reinsurance policies at a substantial markup over actuarial value. Look at cat risks from the viewpoint of standard capital market theory. These are uncorrelated risks, which do not amount to a large fraction of the total wealth in the economy. Therefore, they ought to be priced out at close to the risk-free rate of interest, of course taking account of the probability of occurrence. But reinsurance premiums are apparently far above that actuarial value, at least for the worst, lowest-probability catastrophes.

Yesterday, these excess reinsurance costs were attributed either to risk aver-sion or to some kind of capital constraint. I don't find either reason plausible. Something else is going on. I'll tell you what it is. Suppose that you set up a reinsurance company. You've got to pull together people, systems, and information. There is a substantial setup cost in order to write policies and actually make money off them. These costs are not second order. Once the costs are incurred, the reinsurance company has an intangible asset. Part of the markup of reinsurance premiums above actuarial value is a return on and of this asset.

If the reinsurance company operates successfully, it acquires further intangible assets. For example, good reinsurers learn as much or more about the risks that they are taking on as do their customers, the primary insurance companies. As a consequence, they develop relationships with these companies, and that, too, has an intangible value that shows up in the prices charged for reinsurance policies.

Once intangible assets are acquired, reinsurers begin to act as if they were risk averse—not because their ultimate investors are risk averse, but because their intangible assets are long-lived and they're at risk. If a cat takes on too much catastrophic risk—too many policies that go too far out in the bad tail of cat outcomes—it runs the risk of going bust and losing, or at least damaging, its intangible assets. Notice that the intangible assets are worth most right after the worst catastrophes. This reinforces the apparent risk aversion.

Yesterday, we spent a lot of time talking about what to do and not much time on what was really going on. I do not claim that my story about intangible assets is a complete corporate finance theory of insurance, but at least it is an example of how to think it through. It does not help to build agency models that basically assume one individual buying insurance from another. Reinsurance companies are corporations, with going-concern values and intangible assets. They have access to international capital markets. Corporate finance, not utility or stylized agency theory, is the appropriate mode of analysis.

Now let's turn back and ask why the primary insurers are willing to pay so much above actuarial value for cat reinsurance contracts. It is partly just the value of information. But primary insurers also have intangible assets and therefore act as if they are risk averse. In addition, their managers accept various financial transactions just to get things done—just to get through the day, so to speak. A manager of a primary insurance company has countless things to worry about. If, at small absolute cost, he or she can forget about worrying about a particular cat outcome, a reinsurance contract may be worth signing even though the price is high relative to actuarial value.

I haven't touched on securitization. Bob Litzenberger is the expert on that. But I am convinced that information is the reason that the securitization of cat risks is difficult. As you go further out on the tail of bad cat outcomes, information problems become worse. The further you go out on the tail, the thinner the information becomes. Adverse-selection or moral hazard problems therefore become more serious. Adverse selection may not be costly in absolute dollars, but, relative to the actuarial value of a very low-probability event, it can be fatal to securitization.

Of course, you can try to solve the information problems by designing the contracts or securities to depend on an index or some other attribute that's outside the control of the insurer. However, that creates a basis risk for the insurer, whose own losses will not match the index or attribute. As Bob Litzenberger pointed out, basis risk is less of a problem for bigger and more diversified companies and much more of a problem for the smaller companies.

Panel II: Similarities and Differences between Catastrophic Risk and Other Markets

Roberto Mendoza

I'd like to make two preliminary comments. The first one is that in reading through the papers that were prepared for this conference, my colleagues and I learned a great deal. An issue often raised is the extent to which fundamental academic research informs, influences, and changes practitioner behavior. I can tell you that in the case of this body of work, the answer is very much so. The second point I'd like to make, not simply in order to be provocative, is the assertion that, in fact, we are done. I do not believe that there is a problem. I think that the market currently securitizes catastrophic risk in an efficient manner.

The topic before us is the similarities and differences between catastrophic risk and other markets, and the fundamental similarity is obvious. You pay some money on day 1 and are faced with a range of outcomes. That is the similarity between catastrophic risk and every other market, whether investment in debt or equity or any kind of investment. Given the particular attributes of catastrophic risk, the differences are also very significant and have the potential to create material inefficiencies. I will address three of them.

First, unlike many other markets, the identity of the purchaser of the instrument is important to the insured. When you have a catastrophe, it makes a big difference as to who is there to pay. As a result, just as we've been discussing, securitization is involved in most cases—some kind of special purpose vehicle and some kind of mechanism to ensure that collateral exists to meet the payment. The creation of that special-purpose vehicle—and what is done with the assets placed in it—creates, in my view, a lack of seamlessness or an inefficiency, and therefore an increased cost.

Second, I would draw a distinction between the outcomes of investment in a so-called cat bond and those of investment in various other forms of high-yield instruments. Often, discussions of payoffs in cat bonds compared to high-yield bonds don't pay sufficient attention to a key difference. With a cat bond, you lose your money or at least a portion of it, but it *is* a loss. In the case of a default with a high-yield bond, you still have a claim, and that claim has optionality embedded in it, which may or may not be fairly valued by the market

Roberto Mendoza is vice chairman of J. P. Morgan.

at the time the default occurs. So, looking at the price of a defaulted bond versus the amount lost on a cat bond and looking at the price at a certain moment in time may not be a fair comparison because of potential market inefficiency in pricing the optionality in the case of the high-yield instrument—an inefficiency which may stem from illiquidity or information asymmetries.

Third, the comparison of the pay-offs of a cat bond and a traditional reinsurance contract often ignores the optionality in the latter when a catastrophe occurs. Reinsurance contracts incorporate an implied, sometimes explicit, renewal option, often at a higher price. As a result, comparing the three instruments—the high-yield bond, which defaults but has embedded optionality; the cat bond, which causes a loss, and that's it; and the traditional reinsurance contract, which has an implicit renewal option—is a complex undertaking. Indeed, it is much more complex than just looking at the quoted price of defaulted high-yield bond versus the loss on a cat bond at a moment in time.

I would argue that the securitization of catastrophic risk may not be debt-like in its nature but equity-like, which has implications for the conclusion of these remarks. The point with respect to the differences between the instruments is that securitization in the form of a cat bond has massive amounts of inefficiency built into it which must be overcome if securitization—in the sense we've been discussing—is going to dominate the alternative to traditional reinsurance.

Why are we going to all this trouble to see if the securitization of catastrophic risk can be done? I tread carefully here, given the audience. As I understand the theory, if you have a portfolio investor to whom you can provide a fairly priced (in an actuarial sense) totally uncorrelated asset, the overall riskiness of the portfolio will be reduced, increasing its value. If you can create such an instrument, the power of diversification will create greater value and therefore attract more capital at a lower rate and create capacity at an efficient price. That's the argument. But the theory has a very high hurdle to overcome—the inefficiencies of the securitization structure.

Is there, in fact, a problem today? This is why I wanted to get back to the assertion that we are done. I'd argue there is no problem today, and this is the reasoning: the assertion that there is a problem somehow relates to a combination of capacity and price. That assertion generally comes from the primary insurers, who say, "I can't get reinsurance at an economic price" or "I can't get it in the $25–$50 billion layer." What they are really saying is that they can only get it at a market price which may not allow them to make a sufficient profit. The market has shown a remarkable ability to generate equity capital to write these risks. And it isn't at all clear that there is a structural market inefficiency which inhibits either capacity or reasonable pricing. It may be that the business of providing primary catastrophic risk insurance is not a good business. It isn't written anywhere that all businesses are good businesses and have high returns on equity. Providing catastrophic risk insurance may not be a good business, and therefore what the insurers are really saying is, "I'm not in a very good business, and in order to make it a good business, find me some cheap reinsurance somewhere."

I'd like to touch for a moment on the tax point brought up by Professor Myers. It is a real issue, and there is a real solution. You establish the reinsurer in a jurisdiction where there isn't a tax and to which the premium payments are tax deductible. There is such a jurisdiction. It's called *Bermuda.* It's the fastest growing insurance center in the world. That's the reason we don't need legislation—we have an answer.

To repeat the bottom line: The securitization of catastrophic risk is an equity-like risk, not a debt-like risk. I believe the markets have, in effect, securitized catastrophic risk in the most efficient manner possible. They have done so by setting up catastrophic-risk reinsurers in tax-advantaged, favorably regulated jurisdictions, and these catastrophic-risk reinsurers earn very high returns on equity. The answer to the question of why the pricing for reinsurance is substantially above its actuarial value, if that is in fact the case, is that this is exactly why these reinsurers earn very high returns on equity. Not only do they earn very high returns on equity, but almost without exception they are in the process of returning equity to their shareholders. The market is working very elegantly. I submit that, if the insurers who are protesting insufficient capacity or high prices were willing to pay a price attractive to the reinsurers, the capacity would be there.

So, in summary, in my opinion, the objective of creating greater efficiency through securitization is a natural attribute of capital markets, which has occurred already, and we are done. The portfolio manager who buys the theory that the acquisition of a fairly priced, uncorrelated asset increases the value of his portfolio should prefer the common stock of a cat reinsurer to a cat bond, simply because the cat reinsurance company represents a more efficient form of securitization.

Andrew Alper

My conclusion coming down last night was that we were the "gut course" here, so welcome to Reinsurance 101. I'm pleased to be here today to discuss the securitization of insurance risk and to try to draw some comparisons to other securities markets. The comparison is pretty easy because we have a lot of good analogies. As we think about this market, there are many examples of other markets that have developed in a similar fashion to what we expect here.

Let me start by talking about why we are optimistic about the development of this market for securitized insurance risk. We have heard the analogy to mortgages all morning. The market for insurance risk today is relatively illiquid, not unlike the mortgage market of fifteen years ago. Fifteen years ago, banks built lending capacity through the issuance of debt and equity at the bank-holding-company level, through retained earnings, and through deposit

Andrew Alper is a managing director of Goldman Sachs & Co.

liabilities. The assets were originated and held on balance sheets, and there was virtually no liquidity in the secondary market for mortgage assets. Today, the financial flows between the capital markets and the insurance markets are likewise quite constrained. In response to Roberto's point, I think that the reinsurance business is not a very good one today. It doesn't have to be that way, however. I believe that securitization can make reinsurance a very good business, one in which reinsurers get paid, not for their balance sheets, but for value-added services. Mortgage-backed securities enable the free flow of capital between mortgage assets and alternative investments—stocks, bonds, commodities, etc.

In the insurance industry today, the only way to raise the capital to fund insurance risk is through the issuance of debt and equity at the insurance-holding-company level and, of course, the taking in of premiums. So far the analogy is pretty good. This constrained flow of capital means that, first, the capital that is raised tends to be trapped within the industry, hence the cycle. Bermuda was a very efficient reaction to the cats in the late 1980s. But the problem is that now we have $4 billion of capital in Bermuda, and it's trapped there, and we had to go through some fairly inefficient mechanisms to get it out and to try to smooth out the pricing cycle.

Second, there is a fairly long lag time, at least by capital market standards. It took a couple of years to raise the capital in Bermuda, and that's why we saw rates on line shoot up in the reinsurance markets. Now, the rapidity in the development of the capacity of the capital markets to fund risk is evinced by the growth in the mortgage-backed market. A number of people have commented that the mortgage-backed market was really a beneficiary of government assistance of some form, and I think that that is very true. I think that that assistance was a catalyst, but there have been other asset-backed markets that have developed since then that are not beneficiaries of government largesse. Here you see that the mortgage market grew from virtually nothing in the early 1980s to a $100 billion per year market in the 1990s.

When you consider the case of asset-backed securities without government assistance, by and large you see a very similar pattern. There was no issuance in 1985 and $80 billion per year in 1995. That is a lot of capacity flowing back and forth in the capital markets.

An interesting aside here is that the securitization market for consumer receivables dramatically changed the credit-card industry. Ten years ago, the major issuers were basically money-center banks that used their rather large balance sheets to fund consumer receivables. The major credit-card issuers today were unheard of ten years ago—MBNA, ADVANTA, etc.—and they have relatively small balance sheets. These are balance-sheet warehouses, and then they use the capital markets to fund risk. This is the topic of a separate discussion, but it is an interesting question if the same thing happens in the insurance market. What does it mean for the reinsurers and insurers currently in the market? Which will survive? Which will prosper? Which will become dinosaurs?

Clearly, there is some potential for security market activity in the area of natural disasters. The magnitude of the exposures is enormous. A $22 billion Gulf Coast loss dwarfs the $4 billion Bermuda capital. A $70 billion Los Angeles earthquake, a $100 billion New Madrid earthquake, a $75 billion Florida windstorm—these are basically uninsurable events given the capacity in the insurance and reinsurance markets today. There's roughly $230 billion in surplus in the U.S. property-casualty market. The $75 billion of insured losses over this period is a large, large chunk of that. Relative to the U.S. securities markets, various numbers are thrown around, but let's call it $13 trillion. $75 billion is a very small slice of a $13 trillion capital market, so, clearly, the capital markets have the capacity to absorb this kind of cat risk. And, by the way, a 1 percent fluctuation in the U.S. capital markets is an everyday event, so every day roughly $130 billion bounces in and out of the capital markets. I recognize that there is a difference between realized losses and trading losses, but the volatility is something that the market can handle.

The idea of insurance and reinsurance as being fungible with bonds and stocks really isn't all that crazy, and increasingly the insurance world is thinking about it this way. Insurance is just an option on capital, and, depending on the structure of the instrument, it can be either equity, like an excess-of-loss cat instrument, or debt, like finite-risk reinsurance in many forms. When rates shot up in the cat market, Allstate made a conscious decision not to buy reinsurance but instead to issue more equity. That is a direct comparison, a direct trade-off—equity in the balance sheet versus buying cat reinsurance.

Let me give a trivial example of how you might package insurance options to create a principal protected security. Assume that you have a special purpose reinsurer and an insurer buying the reinsurance and that the latter is paying a 10 percent rate on line for coverage. If you issue a $200 million bond and $100 million goes into a ten-year U.S. Treasury investment that rises to par in ten years, that's the principal protection right there. That $100 million is unavailable for reinsurance protection. The other $100 million *is* available for reinsurance protection. Assume that there is a 10 percent rate on line and that it earns, say, 6 percent through short-term investments; that's a 16 percent yield in that portion of it. The investor put in $200 million, so it's an 8 percent current coupon. What happens is that, if a triggering event takes place, the special purpose reinsurer has its assets diminished, and the rate on line goes down, staying in for whatever is left in the trust. At the end of ten years, if no event happens, the investor gets the $100 million from the U.S. Treasuries plus whatever is left in the trust, which gives a fairly attractive yield to maturity.

What are the probabilities of loss? A Moody study of the junk bond market covering roughly fifteen years at default rates reveals about a 4 percent probability of loss. The market today is about four hundred basis points over the U.S. Treasuries, so the market is having a multiple of pure loss of one times. The reinsurance market, however, has a much higher multiple. For a single event with losses totaling $20 billion, I am told that it's about a 4 percent probability. And these estimates fluctuate anywhere from 12 to 28 percent rate on line. A particular pricing point a month or two ago was a 17 percent rate on line, or four times the pure risk. Now, that figure may be a bit higher today, but it leaves lots of room for the securities market to get interested.

Given the ability to repackage insurance risks and to provide an attractive price in the capital markets, the question is, Who are the buyers, and what are their issues? I won't dwell on the buyers. But here are the issues, and these are my final points. The first is that right now we are in a very soft reinsurance cycle, and, therefore, the reinsurance market is very aggressively trying to capture these opportunities. That will not always be the case. Second, at this point in time, even though in theory the capital markets should be price competitive (because of the uncorrelated nature of the risk) and should price through the reinsurance market, investors in fact are saying, "We're just dumb investors; why should we buy this risk at a price below the reinsurance market where the pros buy it?" Over time, however, the capital markets should come to provide lower-cost reinsurance.

Finally, from the investor's perspective, right now security structures look too complex. A few years from now, however, these will look like trivial exercises. In any new market, it takes a while for people to get used to new structures. Investors must be educated as to what the risk is, what the probabilities are, what the probabilities mean. This is a time-consuming process, and the most important part of it is the availability and credibility of information. People in the market must have confidence that they know what they are buying and that they know how to trade it. There has to be secondary market liquidity. There has to be an ability to build diversified portfolios. We've seen the exact same thing in the junk bond market. We saw it in the swaps market. We saw it in the asset-backed market. What happens is that you have a flurry of activity, a lot of frustration, a lot of wheel spinning. Then, all of a sudden, critical mass is reached, information is available, people are comfortable with the process, liquidity develops, and capital market capacity explodes. I expect to see the same pattern here in the reinsurance and insurance sector.

Martin Feldstein

Thank you very much. What I got from that was that, even if we haven't arrived yet, we are on our way and getting closer every day.

Andrew and Roberto both seem to be saying that there are high rates of return available. Why? Why isn't more money going into this to drive that return down? And Roberto said that the equity is going back out. Given that there is a high rate of return, that this is one of the good businesses, and that there are other businesses that are not so good, why aren't we seeing more capital coming in?

Martin Feldstein is the George F. Baker Professor of Economics at Harvard University and president of the National Bureau of Economic Research.

Roberto Mendoza

I think that the difference between Andrew and me would be that one must distinguish between the economic attractiveness of a reinsurance business and that of the cat business. The cat reinsurance market, I would submit, offers a very high return on equity—on the order of 18–20 percent. Because the insureds aren't willing to pay the price, these businesses don't have sufficient opportunity to deploy their accumulated capital in insuring catastrophic risk and are therefore returning that capital to their investors.

Martin Feldstein

They are willing to pay the price to generate an 18–20 percent return on equity. So the question is, Why isn't there a little more selling moving down that curve so that the return on equity is 17 or 16 percent if that's a much better return than equity can get in some other market?

Roberto Mendoza

My answer to that would be twofold. To take a step back, the first thing would be to ask why an investor would buy this at all. I understand that the argument holds that the efficient frontier in an uncorrelated risk is pushed out. The issue not addressed by the securitized structure is, instead of selling someone securitized catastrophe risk, why not sell him the equity of a cat reinsurer, thereby driving down the cost of the capital for the cat reinsurer and allowing him to price more efficiently to the primary insurer? To answer your point, some of that is going on. But my gut reaction would be that, for the cat reinsurers, there still isn't sufficient demand because, for various reasons, the primary insurers would rather have no reinsurance. They don't protect themselves. They would rather have no reinsurance than pay the price to generate a 15 percent return on equity for the reinsurer.

Andrew Alper

I might repeat two points. One is with regard to the catastrophe reinsurers. As Roberto properly points out, the return is declining for these companies. It has been declining for the last two years. Pricing is off for their core business, and they are therefore returning capital because they don't see the same returns that they thought they could achieve when they were created—for which I applaud them. I think that's the right discipline. What we have not found is an excess profit. I believe that there are other ways to apply capital more efficiently than through a corporate structure with a lot of equity sitting in it. We haven't found that yet, for a variety of reasons. So partly this all comes to the reinsurance market, and part of it is the complexity. Again we are back to the point at which a new market is opened up to a broad investor group: the product must be simple, must be similar to things to which the investors are accustomed, and must fit the rules. That's why equity in Bermuda was perfectly logical. My firm raised capital for companies in the Bermuda market. It was the right thing to do to fill a void quickly because it was efficient and it was liquid. The real trick—something on which we are all spending a lot of time— is whether there is a next, more efficient mechanism for doing that? Again, we find the complexity burdensome, and it is taking us all longer than we wanted it to take.

Roberto Mendoza

I do believe that a fundamental difference of opinion exists between us on the issue of whether it can be done better. And that difference of opinion re- volves around the question of whether an equity-like risk or a debt-like risk has been transferred. I believe that there are more efficient ways of providing contingent liquidity. I'd argue with respect to real risk transfer that the market works just fine right now. And it is an equity market. The securities are liquid, and returns are very high. But, because the primary insurance company has external limitations on fair pricing—legislative, governmental, even societal— the ability to offload the risk to the markets, whether through securitization or the reinsurer, is constrained. That's what makes the primary insurance markets inefficient and unable to price at a level that provides an adequate return. It's not an inefficiency in the markets. The markets *are* efficient. It would be dan- gerous for us to underestimate the efficiency, liquidity, and reactive capacity of the markets. The inefficiency lies instead in the regulation of the insurer.

Panel III: Evolving Institutions for Redistributing Catastrophic Risk

Richard Sandor

The study of inchoate markets is something that has challenged economists over time, whether it be the structural changes in the sixteenth century in the formation of the Dutch East India Company and the invention of the limited- liability corporation, the standardization in the mortgage market, the develop- ment of Ginnie Maes, collateralized mortgage obligations (CMOs), or the junk bond market in the 1980s and 1990s and what happened there. This is just another challenging paradigm of that, and the input that the academic world can have is phenomenal.

We've seen various tools emerge—from an organized futures market in Chi- cago (the Chicago Board of Trade vis-à-vis the PCS index) to separate efforts by such leading investment bankers as Goldman Sachs, Morgan Stanley, and Merrill Lynch and major intermediaries like Guy Carpenter, all of whom were involved in one way or another in pushing this. I would like to say that, on the one hand, on the Chicago side you now have a contract that seems to be strug-

Richard Sandor is chairman and chief executive officer of Environmental Financial Products, Ltd., and chairman of Hedge Financial Products.

gling by a lot of standards, but, if you look at the numbers, the open interest there is larger than pork bellies and Treasury bills were at a comparable point in time. On the other hand, we have three major investment banks working on bond deals. All these people will give you their opinions on the pros and cons of these new risk-management tools, and then I'll wrap it up.

Richard Kane

I'm delighted to be here and to have this opportunity to share with you some thoughts about the emerging methods and institutions for distributing cat risks. From the start my firm has actually been at the forefront of thinking about this, which I suspect explains the large alumni group that we have here at the conference. During my brief remarks, you will detect some natural bias toward the continuing prominence of the broker in the transactions that we are doing. You shouldn't be surprised at that.

I'd like to offer some thoughts about the changing nature of the business as we look forward. Both the insurance and the reinsurance markets have been historically reactive. Ace and Excel were formed in response to the crisis of the mid-1980s. And, of course, additional Bermuda capacity came together following Hurricane Andrew. Now, for the first time, you can make a case that we are actually thinking ahead as an industry in that we are in the fortunate position of not yet having seen the megaevent that we have all been talking about and some have forecast. So we have the opportunity to prepare ourselves, and that's most of what we're here to talk about.

Most of you are familiar with my firm's view of risk, which is, in fact, the same as Andy Alper's. What you will not find in it is a very big role for government. It seems to me that we ought to be able to figure out how to deal with this as an industry without much government involvement.

A couple of questions as we think about the future: Can the current institutions and distribution methods access this broader, deeper capital base that we think we need to get into, and what should the role of current players be in the new world? I think that the answer to the first question is a definite yes. But, in order to achieve the required level of efficiency, some changes are going to be necessary. The role of the traditional players will also no doubt be questioned and tested as we move forward. In the past, our world was two-dimensional, with a very linear approach to investors. Only recently have we realized that those illusive investors and suppliers of capital are the same as the consumers themselves. I believe that there will be changes in both capital providers and the dynamic nature of the risk-transfer process. As more investors express interest in this emerging asset class, there will be a greater need for professional management. We will find this in risk management, providing new and better techniques. We will see this in approaches to the analysis and

Richard Kane is president and chief executive officer of the global services division of Guy Carpenter & Company, Inc.

management of exposure. There will be a continuing need to get closer to the sources of the deal flow and, in a very large measure, to information. A lot of what we have been talking about here is the need to continue to build on the information that's available to investors about what we are doing. And, finally, there will be a continued need for portfolio diversification within classes of business.

Investors will come at this with different appetites and needs. Some of them will wish to manage their portfolios actively. Clearly, one example of that would be an investment in a cat bond. More likely, we see people managing their own portfolios through exchange trading. Although, as we discussed yesterday, the basis-risk problem must be solved, as those solutions come forward there will be a big opportunity for folks to use the exchanges to deal with these issues. Most investors will require professional management and deal flow. There are a couple of ways to think about that. One is an equity investment in a reinsurance company. You could do that today, and, as Bob Mendoza suggested, you can go in and out of that very easily. The opportunity exists to do that, and it certainly is a way for new capital to participate in this industry. The other way would be participation in a fund. I believe that funds will be developed with special purposes that provide opportunities for investors to come in.

Now, on the subject of information, there was a comment in the *Wall Street Journal* last summer from an investment manager who said that we would have to become experts in meteorology. It would require a considerable investment in time and energy to analyze the new risks involved. This gets back to a point that we were discussing a few minutes ago about some of the issues involved in drawing an analogy between CMOs and cat risk. Information is one of those issues. Virtually all of us believe that we understand what a mortgage is all about, and, even though as the CMOs developed we made that activity much more complex by carving up the investment opportunities into smaller and smaller pieces with different flavors, we felt that we understood the basic mechanisms. This is not necessarily true with cat risk, and as an industry we have a significant need to educate investors so that they really understand what they are investing in.

What does this say about the role of an intermediary in this business? It continues basically the way it has been going. Historically, the brokers have been a catalyst for developing solutions to satisfy client needs. Think, for example, of the development of Centre Re and Mid-Ocean as well as residual market facilities. We need, frankly, to do this for survival purposes but, importantly, also because, in bringing real value to the industry, we need to continue to facilitate efficient risk transfer and to develop alternative markets. What all that means to us is that the intermediaries have an important role in a very complex industry. Transformers, exchanges, and funds are new, and the capacity requirements are significantly larger and will be sourced differently. But the basic business of efficiently providing risk-transfer facilities to insurance is largely unchanged.

Frank Pierson

Historically what has happened is that the insurer has all the cat risk and several different ways of getting rid of that risk. One of them was simply to go to the capital market and raise capital. Alternatively, it could send the risk to its reinsurer, and the reinsurer would then go out and raise capital. I have simplified this, eliminating retrocessional markets, and, yes, brokers are in here somewhere—I don't mean to leave them out. But this is the basic flow. The problem is that this structure causes a dilemma—the capital markets themselves can't, by law, originate the risk directly. I think that, in the future, the capital markets won't be able to go to an individual insured and say, "I can offer you a solution," as they might do when offering other financial products. It's got to be an insurance product of some sort, and an insurer is going to stay in the picture. So we have the starting point in the origination of the risk that is going to stay in place. Now what we have to figure out is how to get from that source out to the capital markets. I think that it's generally believed that insurers for most noncat risk have way too much capital. But for cat risk they don't have enough, and, under the current rate regulation and pricing environment, insurers can't charge enough in cat risk in advance. And, if they could, they have no way to put that money aside for a rainy day because of accounting and tax rules.

So, in trying to get rid of this risk, the insurance industry faces these dilemmas, and something is stopping it from getting to securitization, which I think people think of as the solution. Insurance regulation causes problems. Unlike someone who originates mortgages, insurers can't take their insurance and sell it to someone else. They are always at risk, and they all have to deal with the credit risk. Even if they sell it off to the market, they have a credit risk. If whoever they've sold that risk to doesn't perform, they have to perform.

There is an apparent or perceived information asymmetry that makes the market feel uncomfortable analyzing catastrophe risk, and we've had many conversations about changing the structures and indices involved. A good comment made this morning was that we should have an index based on a model. The actual choice of model doesn't matter, just as long as there is a model on which to base the investment.

A big factor involved in the slow acceptance of new approaches is simple inertia. It just takes a lot of big insurance companies a long time to do something new. Imagine both an insurer wish list and a capital markets wish list. Many items appear on both. Both markets want a commodity product. Unfortunately, by *commodity product* each market means something different. A commodity product in the capital market is standardized; every clause is the same, and everyone knows what it is. The insurance market wants a commodity product that can be customized differently in different situations. Where the capital

Frank Pierson is a managing director of the Zurich Centre Group.

markets want to be able to get in and, more important, get out, want liquidity, want to be able to understand the risks, want something that can be priced, and want some common trigger, insurers want as little basis risk as possible, want a product that's accountant friendly and tax efficient, long term and stable. I think that what's going to happen is that the reinsurer, in whatever form, will bridge these two wish lists.

For new approaches such as securitization to work, certain assumptions must be made. One assumption is that all insurers need short-term capital. They need this transitory capital when they need it, and they don't need it the rest of the time. One assumes that they can and will pay their own losses over a long period of time and that they truly are profitable.

Where does this lead in terms of what I think a reinsurer will look like? As I said earlier, I think that the insurer will still be the originator of risk, and so somehow it has to get rid of the risk. And I think that the insurer will have direct access to capital markets. Insurers will go out and get capital; they'll try cat bonds, CBOT futures, whatever. However they do it, they'll get directly to the capital market. Insurers of all sizes are going to use a reinsurer as an intermediary between them and the capital markets. And they're going to do it in several different ways.

One way is the reinsurer selling perfect hedges to the insurers. The perfect instrument to do that exists today—the reinsurance contract. The reinsurer can approach the insurer about the losses it wants to cede and then offer a contract that does exactly that. It will then turn around and, on the basis of some kind of index, buy imperfect hedges from the capital market. It can keep the basis risk, and it can manage that basis risk because it can craft its portfolio to be as close to or as far away from the index as it wants it to be. It can therefore manage how much it retains and how much it cedes out will be dictated by its own management's view of risk versus reward.

I think that a second role for reinsurers will be the standard role that they have today. They're just going to take a cat risk. They're going to say that it's attractively priced, that it's going to come in to me, and that I'm just going to retain it against my capital.

Finally, I think that the reinsurer is going act as an investor but also in some ways, as people have said, as a value-added manager or provider of information. The reinsurer is going to package risk through contingent equity puts, contingent surplus notes, etc. It's going to be the knowledge provider to the capital market. It's going to go out there and figure out how to craft some deals, figure out what the pricing should be, probably take shares of these deals, perhaps act as an arranger for a fee, perhaps act as a general partner in a partnership, and basically send out and design the covers for the market. Some companies are already doing it. My firm, for example, has a company called Insurance Partners. We go out to a market and say that we're going to design these kind of investments and ask those involved to commit to following our investment every time we create one. What you get as a result is a pool of committed capital that will back what you as the manager of these funds decide are good investments.

In summary, I think that what will happen is that we are moving away from being a reinsurer (whatever that is today) that takes in cat risk and retains it to being an organization that's going to have at least three different roles: being a basis-risk taker, being the usual cat-risk taker, and being a value-added adviser to the capital markets.

Joseph H. Umansky

The previous panelists as well as those who presented and discussed the papers yesterday cited various statistics regarding the size of a potential catastrophe loss relative to the size of the financial markets. I will therefore forgo the pleasure of requesting statistics. Instead, let us simply presume that there is demand among insurers and other institutions like state governments for large amounts of catastrophe protection. Let us also presume that there are sufficient reasons of return and diversification to make investors interested in accepting and trading insurance risk.

I will first address some of the specific needs of issuers (broadly speaking, the parties wanting protection) and the particular requirements of investors. I will then show several mechanisms for matching those interests.

Issuers

Insurers have not been able to get as much protection from catastrophic losses as they desired. On the supply side, the constraints exist on reinsurance capacity. On the demand side, large insurance portfolios generate huge exposures to single events like earthquakes and hurricanes. However, it is important to note that today there are specific shortfalls for certain types of catastrophes but that, overall, there is excess capital in the industry.

The motivation for buying reinsurance is solvency. But even for the largest firms, like AIG, where solvency is not an issue, there are concerns like earnings volatility and stability of credit ratings that make it desirable to have reasonably priced and collectable catastrophe protection.

In addition, it is necessary to get the proper accounting benefit for both GAAP and statutory purposes, get the appropriate tax treatment, satisfy rating-agency requirements, and maintain the confidence of lenders and investors. In approaching these concerns, the insurers are looking for cost-effective solutions through access to new investors, and, if these solutions are to be effective, they need to get the leverage and hence the pricing right.

Joseph H. Umansky is vice president and deputy comptroller of American International Group, Inc.

Investor Requirements

What do investors want? Like all of us, investors want high returns and low risk. That said, I note that investors are responsive to the idea of risk and return taken together in context. In this case, *context* means portfolio diversification. Pure insurance risk is only remotely connected to world financial markets. It would take a huge disaster actually to move interest rates or affect the stock market.

What do investors look for? They look for spreads above the risk-free rate commensurate with the risk that they are taking. They want manageable credit-risk exposure. Liquidity and secondary markets should not be dismissed as unimportant. They need an understandable product structure and price validation through independent indices or participation by knowledgeable investors.

The question that we now face is how to bring the issues and needs of the insurers together with the requirements of investors. A number of efforts have taken place to date. There are those who say that the reinsurance market works and capital market solutions are not only not required but will not work. I believe that capital market solutions will work, but the most efficient structure is not yet in front of us.

Docking: First Efforts

The first-generation attempts are the Chicago Board of Trade products, the Catastrophe Exchange, act-of-God bonds, and contingent notes.

The CBOT products depend on a poor index; insurers have a significant amount of basis risk. Trading activity has been such that it can provide only relatively low limits of coverage to the insurer and an illiquid security to the investor.

The Catastrophe Exchange swaps risks directly between counterparties. High search costs render it impracticable, and, as much as individual insurers would like to diversify the risk, most believe that they do their job better than someone else with a different risk profile. Therefore, the equivalents are very difficult to work out.

Most of the act-of-God bonds depend on the CBOT index, which creates basis risk for the insurer. If the triggers are based on actual performance, the investor is faced with the moral hazards, thereby creating additional uncertainty on the part of the investors. And the insurer is faced with a claim validation process that is incremental and could be burdensome. Also, the investor may be faced with regulatory issues on actual performance triggers since state insurance commissioners may deem the investment to be participation in the insurance business.

Other issues related to act-of-God bonds are the following:

Liquidity is a concern to investors. There is currently no mechanism to hedge or trade the risks in the bonds.

Initial indications by some investment bankers that the cost to insurers would be lower than traditional insurance have not materialized. While investors in act-of-God bonds may be new, they are not innocent capacity; they demand rates at least equal to the traditional market. This, together with the initial frictional cost, makes the act-of-God bonds at least as expensive as traditional insurance.

There continue to be a number of unresolved issues regarding the accounting and tax implications of act-of-God bonds. While economically the result may be the same, the steps through which one must go in order to accomplish the same accounting benefits are burdensome, and I question whether they work.

In today's market, act-of-God bonds face an uphill battle. If insurers or reinsurers can get traditional coverage at the same price, why should they take basis risk, accept more restrictive terms, face accounting problems, and go through a prolonged documentation process? Despite the difficulties, conditions are ever changing, and the challenge facing promoters of this product is to make them more friendly.

Contingent notes are standby liquidity facilities in a somewhat innovative form. They do nothing to help earnings, providing only some level of solvency to an insurer. Even when they are structured as surplus notes, there are limitations on the capital benefits. They do not represent true insurance, and they are not even triggered on an insurance contingency. These are very interesting structures, but it's important to note that they provide limited benefit.

Another structure that has been evolving is contingent capital. Contingent capital encompasses various classes of preferred or common stock that are putable to an investor in the event of a catastrophe. These structures provide liquidity and surplus but do not provide earnings relief. They also satisfy the concerns of the rating agencies, who are taking a much harder look at catastrophe exposures.

Docking: A Better Way

Perhaps I've painted an overly bleak picture. It is important to temper this with an observation.

The first car was no real match for a horse. The first steps in a breakthrough are often taken backward. The same is true in the insurance sector. Let me share with you how we can make a better match between issuers and investors, today, and then close with a glimpse of the future.

Pricing validation. Better docking requires first and foremost an index with some key characteristics. These include disaggregation by zip code, credibility on a zip-code basis, elimination or mitigation of variances in underwriting performance, consistency of reporting, and historical replicability. Beyond a credible and independent index, investors will take comfort in the participation of knowledgeable experts and quality issuers.

Credit risk. Once price is settled, someone still has to hold the ante in this game. The solutions to date have relied heavily on one-off trust structures, very similar to those used in mortgage- and asset-backed securities. A better solution might be a formal exchange, one that not only satisfies the credit function but also maintains valuable trading information, market demand, and price histories.

Future. Where does that leave us? First, issuers and investors must become accustomed to trading in *physical* as distinguished from *financial* risks. By that I mean that a Los Angeles earthquake will have a price just like ten-year Treasuries. Over time, investors will take different flavors of risk, for a price. Initially, the risks may be added on to more traditional securities. Eventually, these risk elements will trade independently of the underlying securities.

Once we have a broad range of freely traded risks, there will be changes in the capitalization of insurance firms. It may become too expensive for insurers to hold and finance all the risks themselves. Rather, the underwriting skills of the best insurers may be deployed as asset managers for pools of specialized investor money. Banks and thrifts both found it better to package and sell risks rather than finance them on balance sheet.

Will this happen in the insurance industry? The competitive environment, conditions in the markets, and regulations will control the nature and timing of any evolution. But the insurance industry might do well to ponder these examples.

Richard Sandor

I'd like to make one or two summary comments. What I heard our panelists talking about is that these are new markets and that a lot of work has to be done. Frank's point I think is right, but it presents an opportunity, not a problem. There is a role for a Myron Scholes, and a Fischer Black, and Harvard and Yale and MIT, in developing these models. There is a Nobel Prize out there for whoever does that. Admittedly the markets are inefficient and illiquid. But some of us like that. In fact, if you look at the early work of Working at Stanford University, he wrote that what hedgers do is speculate on the basis. When gold futures were introduced in the United States, the idea was to buy cheap Peruvian gold that was being dumped, refine it into bars, and sell it on the New York market. When bond futures started, Salomon Brothers went to the New York State Teachers Retirement Fund and tried to find cheap bonds to trade against the Chicago market. When stock index futures started, anybody who could buy the 500 stocks underlying the index could sell the futures. It was a bad hedge, but it was a great arbitrage. So, recognizing inefficient markets, people like myself are in the crop-insurance business. I don't mind when crop-insurance rates stay high and everybody gets disturbed about mad cow disease and pummels the cattle market because one of the legs of my trade holds steady and the other gets killed. The fact that there are disconnected markets and illiquidities just provides arbitrage and basis trading opportunities.

We should also look at the role of the broker, the role of the new insurer, and the credit issue. Some of the difficulties that we are encountering actually provide opportunities, both for the academics and for the people who view liabilities as dynamic and will trade them on a regular basis. As pointed out, some people want a perfect basis product. Other people will want to take the basis risk because they want basis profits. There is also the International Swap Dealers Association (ISDA) market, the swap market, which we haven't talked about. This is a $50 trillion market—institutional investors alone are represented by thirty banks. So that's another opportunity.

Panel IV: Implications for U.S. Insurers

James M. Stone

As some of you know, I am a person who has worn different hats over the last twenty years. I was an academic, and then I was a regulator, and now I am a business executive. All the papers for this conference appealed to me wearing one hat or another of these three. Since this is largely an academic crowd and that is the hat I least get to wear these days, let me say first that what attracted me most from an academic point of view was Ken Froot's finding that the reinsurance industry was charging fourteen times expected costs. If I were going to make an academic presentation myself this morning, I'd want to look at why he got that result. And I would focus on three things. First, is the figure really fourteen times? I'd argue that it probably isn't, that you get fourteen times only if you assume that the expected future cost for catastrophes looks just like the recent past. Many experts are viewing the past few decades as aberrantly calm, so the overall past cost probably doesn't look like the recent past cost. At least the insurance industry believes that that won't be the case. Second, are prices going to stay that high, or is this price-to-cost ratio a temporary blip? And my bet is that, for various reasons, it's a temporary blip and the price-to-cost ratio won't stay that high. Third, what are the institutional or industry structure reasons that would lead Froot's estimate to be more than you'd expect it to be? I think that the answer has something to do with the nature of the reinsurance industry. In particular, I would look to a subject that was not much talked about today—the importance of relationships and what is not written in the contract. These features of reinsurance cause some strange things to occur in this industry. But I am not going to be an academic today, so I won't pursue this thought any further right now.

Now I'll tell you what I would have talked about if I'd talked about regulation. We have all heard a lot of talk about the role of government in dealing with catastrophe and cataclysm, and we have heard almost as much about securitization. If I were going to talk from a regulator's point of view, I would want to talk about that. I think that securitization is coming, and I think that that's a good thing. I think that securitization and government action together

James M. Stone is chairman of the Plymouth Rock Company.

could be even better. In the climate of the next few years, a rational government program is probably unlikely, so securitization will probably come without it. But, at some point in the more distant future, the government may play some explicit role. In the meantime, I want to emphasize that the government plays a huge implicit role in the homeowner's catastrophe market anyway. It does this through insolvency funds, which affect whether people are credit sensitive when they choose their insurers. It, therefore, affects the capital structure of insurance companies. Companies must decide how much capital they want to put at risk, knowing that the insolvency fund is going to pick up after they stop and that they don't need vast cushions of capital to get customers. And we all assume that, in a cataclysm or a large enough catastrophe, the government is going to play some other bailout role, even though we don't know exactly what that role will be, and that, too, becomes part of the decision-making process as one makes rational business decisions about capitalization and risk. So the government is already playing a major role in this industry. Securitization, so far, is not. In the very near future, securitization will likely be part of the equation as well.

Finally, putting on the hat I am supposed to wear today, that of an executive in private industry, the points that I want to make are few. First, there may be some misimpression about the sophistication of reinsurance pricing. Reinsurance pricing for individual large risks can get pretty sophisticated, but most treaty reinsurance in the property area is very primitively priced now. One of the most important things that's going to happen in the near future (and my company is insisting that its reinsurers begin now) is that pricing will become much more sophisticated. Instead of a reinsurer charging x percent of whatever premium a primary carrier charges your customers, we want reinsurance prices that explicitly reflect location, construction, and concentration, and that means property by property.

Each time we add a property, we should know what it's going to cost us in reinsurance. If we could have that, we would be better off as a company, and I believe that our reinsurers would be better off as well. We would be better off as a company because this knowledge would help us as we select our book of business. We would be underwriting as we went along, taking into account the market pricing of the reinsurance that we're going to have to buy. This, in turn, would help us with the regulators. People have asked me how companies are going to deal with regulators on coming price shocks in property pricing for cat-prone properties. It would help if reinsurance were priced rationally and thus if there were some demonstrable reason why our prices had to reflect that. If we didn't get a rational reaction from the regulators, then it would tell us where to choose our business. So we are strongly urging our reinsurers to give us a more sophisticated method of pricing. That probably couldn't have been done ten years ago. Today, it is quite straightforward and easy to do. More precisely, it's not easy institutionally, but it's easy mathematically.

Let me conclude by returning to the argument here at the panel table: Is there a big problem today in the catastrophe reinsurance markets? My answer is that that really depends on what you call a problem. Are these markets inefficient? I would say that these markets are quite inefficient. Are they inefficient in a way that causes tremendous harm to either the industry or the public? I doubt it. They're not that inefficient. Are they so inefficient that they should divert government attention? No. Are they inefficient enough to create marvelous business opportunities? Absolutely.

Robert P. Irvan

As you know, I work for an insurance company, and, when people in an insurance company speak to a group like this, it's customary to compare the real world with some other world that academics deal with. I thought that I might relay a few experiences that illustrate this difference. I once had an underwriter tell me that, on a block of business for which he was responsible, he'd averaged 3 percent profit for the last five years, which added up to a 15 percent return on equity! That person has now moved on to the reinsurance industry, which may explain some of the unusual price decreases that the academics here have not been able to understand. We also use a one-hundred-year return period when looking at our capacity and at the maximum amount of catastrophe exposure that we would like to accept. However, we happen to have more than we would like to write on Nantucket and Martha's Vineyard. Some of our underwriters object to our modeling, pointing out, quite logically in their opinion, that most of the homes that we insure there are well over a hundred years old. We point out, on the other hand, that a hundred years ago, those same homes may not have been beachfront properties. These anecdotes do make me wonder just who lives in the real world and who lives in some other world.

The subject today is implications for the insurance industry, and I must admit that I don't know what they are. I believe that that's almost the consensus of the whole group. I'd like to go back to an old economic phrase that can be summarized as, It all depends. And I think that there are a lot of things going on that will make us look back ten years from now and say, We should have seen this coming. But it's probably not predictable.

Very briefly, we are dealing with uncertainty. There are a number of ways to handle uncertainty. We have already talked about them, but the key point is that the competitor with the lowest price wins, time after time and in every field. For that reason, I would expect that companies will be forced to explore aggressively a number of different strategies.

Now, with that in mind, I want to talk about some assumptions that I use. I'm responsible, among other things, for the purchase of reinsurance. My firm spends about $350 million a year on reinsurance. (1) I assume that the frequency of large catastrophes will increase over the next few years, regardless

Robert P. Irvan is senior vice president and chief financial officer of Cigna P&C.

of what anyone thinks about global warming. (2) If nothing else, the values at risk are increasing. (3) Mitigation will not have a major effect within any reasonable time horizon. And I also anticipate that (4) sooner or later, and more likely sooner than later, we will experience a megacatastrophe, in Florida, on the New Madrid, or the like, that will change the entire landscape, both figuratively and literally.

(5) I believe that regulators will continue to behave like regulators, for the most part, reasonable, serving as a buffer between what the industry would like to do in response to events and what the public will accept. But they will also regulate market exit and entry. I have to think about that when I buy reinsurance. We have to think about it when we actually write insurance. Regulators are going to set terms that we would like to change at times. They will continue to be more concerned than we would like with affordability rather than solvency, although over time they do adjust to reality. And, following a major catastrophe, we will face major constraints that will temporarily worsen because the regulators are behaving like a buffer.

Rating agencies are very important to most insurance companies. I believe that they are going to shift their emphasis away from assets and earnings and toward catastrophes and that they will improve the amount of data that they get from companies. They will then increase the importance of a company's cat management on its rating.

I might point out that reinsurers' share of catastrophe losses over the last few years has dropped. Hugo, for example, had a 43 percent share paid by the reinsurers. By the time you get to Northridge, it was 21 percent. Reinsurers are accepting less and less risk, buying more finite reinsurance, transferring less true risk, and engaging in more temporal displacements. In short, regulators are not letting primary companies shift the risk to the insured as fast as the reinsurers are shifting the risk to the primary companies.

I do think that catastrophe modeling will improve and that this is going to make a major difference in the demand for capacity from the capital markets. Company data will become more accurate, companies will continue to find exposures that they did not know they had, underlying science will be updated, and every time we have a major cat, we're going to discover that in some fundamental way the model was wrong. And each time we'll say that, if we had known that, we would have been better off. But then the next cat will reveal another source of uncertainty. Having said that, uncertainty will be reduced. When I think of the way we have handled our risk as an industry over the last few years, I think of a big box of rocks. What the models do is allow us to shake that box a lot and let things settle and then fill up some of the cracks between the large rocks with some gravel and then some sand. As a result of all this, the demand for more capacity outside the industry will lessen. There is a lot of capacity that simply is not being used by insurance companies right now, if they could trade their exposure with other companies or with reinsurers more selectively. Partly because of that unused capacity, the return on equity on the cat portfolios will improve, and this will dampen the demand for reinsurance.

Capital markets have already found a way to fund catastrophe exposures. We've already mentioned in the last few days what's happened in Bermuda. I also agree that cats tend to be more of an equity issue than a debt issue and while we need a Black-Scholes theory for cats, we also need a Miller-Modigliani to help us decide what the right mix should be. Or maybe there is no right mix.

Reinsurance markets are reasonably effective at transferring risk. That's something that is often not taken into account by people advancing the need for capital market involvement. I think that, in the long run, capital markets will provide a commodity-type product and not the tailor-made product that most reinsurance companies provide and most insurance companies need.

Having said that, I thought about different scenarios. One involves how much more cat cost we're going to have in the future. Will it go up sharply? Or will it stay at about the same level? Will we get some major breakthrough in the capital market? Will we get more government involvement? Over time, the capital markets will probably make some improvements, but, because of inertia, there will be no fundamental change. On the other hand, if we get a lot more cats, and if the capital markets have not responded rapidly enough, then I would anticipate far more government involvement. And that is something that, as a member of the insurance industry and as someone who believes in the free market, I would really not like to see. It is, however, a highly likely occurrence if we get a devastating earthquake along the New Madrid. We will wind up funding a large portion of the losses, but we have very little effect on policy.

Even if the capital markets enter in a major way, if we have a megaloss or another large Andrew or two Andrews, we may still have trouble meeting society's capacity needs immediately afterward.

Having said all this, I believe that the capital markets should continue to try to sell their existing products, both to insurers and, more likely, to reinsurers. Driven by demand, they should innovate, innovate, innovate, while still emulating the coverages that reinsurance companies provide.

Another option, one that I both fear and wonder about, is having the capital markets entering the risk management field in some other way and protecting the balance sheet of a company just beyond cats. Cats would then become just a by-product.

What should insurance companies and reinsurers do? First, prepare for the worst. It's always a good idea. They should control their aggregates with a big margin for error. Do as much as you can on your own risk portfolio first, then seek as much outside help as you can get, including the capital markets, and don't be afraid of innovation because, in the long run, we're going to need it. And after all this you still have to worry a lot at night.

If I had to summarize, I would say that the future will bring us further consolidation in the reinsurance and primary markets, which may change the land-scape with regard to the purchase of reinsurance. I think that we will see a reduction in the risk charge as more knowledge is traded between insurance companies and reinsurance companies and as the models improve, we'll see cost shifting to exposures causing the cost. Over time, states like California and Florida will be forced to allow their insureds to pay more realistic rates, both on the coast and within the state. And interior states and interior areas will pay less. Insurer portfolios will have more geographic diversity, either by trading or by what they write.

I do anticipate a larger role for capital markets. What I do not know is whether I should put a *much* in front of the *larger.*

Dennis Chookaszian

What I'd like to do is just give you a few thoughts.

First, regarding the comment that Jim made earlier about Ken Froot's finding that the reinsurance industry was charging fourteen times expected costs, that's a very important point, not because the figure is fourteen, but because it's not one. Fourteen is a big number. That's the reason why about five years ago, when people were trying to put together this whole securitization idea, many insurers said, "Hey, we don't want this to happen." Why? Because insurers liked fourteen. Reinsurers were not exactly excited about the idea of having the number come down because of securitization. Even primary insurers were not sure that it was going to help that much. What's changed is that securitiza-tion is going to become a reality and that companies must choose sides. One must decide whether it makes sense. Getting in the middle doesn't make any sense at all. Five years ago securitization made no sense. It was contrary to the best interests of many companies. Now that it's going to happen, however, you see a number of insurers jumping in to participate. That's the big change.

My second point is insurers versus reinsurers. Each carries very different implications. My company is both an insurer and a reinsurer, a situation that reminds me of Harry Truman's remark about wanting to have only one-armed economists because the two-armed variety kept saying, "On the other hand . . . on the other hand. . . ." That's very much what happens in our industry. Securitization looks good from one vantage point and bad from another. What might be good for the insurer is not necessarily good for the reinsurer, and vice versa. So you are going to see differences in the industry.

Finally, I'd like to get into the whole question of where it is going to go. And I'll give you the old crystal ball forecast, being ever mindful of the old adage, He who lives by the crystal ball learns to eat cracked glass. But, having said that, let me give you a few thoughts on what's happening in the insurance industry. Over the last five years or so, there have been some major changes taking place in the industry. Andy Grove from Intel wrote a great book on

Dennis Chookaszian is chairman and chief executive officer of CNA.

change. He talks about 10× changes that are ten times more powerful than other changes. It's like the difference between a windstorm and a hurricane. He talks about how important such changes are and about how your objective as a business is to get ahead of such changes and capitalize on the opportunities they bring. I'll give you five changes that I think are 10× changes happening in the insurance industry today. One change is the inroads that banking is making into the insurance business. Another change is the whole employee leasing business and the way it's going to change the distribution of insurance. Another is the Internet and electronic commerce and what these are going to do to the distribution of the product. Another is the outsourcing of business processes by smaller insurers to large service providers. Finally, we have securitization.

These are five transformations that are going to change our industry. In the case of securitization, the effect is going to be set against a backdrop of profound restructuring. The insurance industry is restructuring on three levels. First is a consolidation restructuring. You are going to see more consolidations, similar to what you've seen on the casualty side with CNA's acquisition of Continental and the Travelers/Aetna merger. You're going to see more of that happening, but not that much more. The top twenty property-casualty companies write roughly half the premium volume. My guess is that there will be perhaps three consolidations over the next five years. On the reinsurance side, I think that you'll see a proportionately higher degree of consolidation. The barriers to consolidation are smaller in the reinsurance markets than they are in the primary markets.

The second level is financial restructuring. The industry is no longer supported by the traditional capital base. It is now supported on the mutual company side by the advent of things like surplus notes and greater availability of capital than in the past. And, on the stock company side, you have more investor capital coming in and more of a movement to look to short-term results. You hear more talk about quarterly earnings in the insurance business than I've heard in the last thirty years or so. And the best evidence of this short-term view is the use of the term *exit strategy*. Exit strategy was a leveraged buyout idea of twenty to thirty years ago, and now you hear insurance companies talking about exit strategy. That idea is totally inconsistent with the long-term view of what we're trying to do in insurance. Suppose that you are a customer buying an insurance product that will pay you over fifty years. Then you don't want to know that your insurance company is thinking about an exit strategy. So it isn't a very good thing from a long-term perspective, but it's a reality of life.

Finally, the third level is liability restructuring. It already has started in transactions such as Equitas, the CIGNA good bank/bad bank, and the Home/Zurich consolidation. These are all various forms of liability restructuring, and securitization is nothing more than another attempt to do that. So, in short, what I think you're going to see is a tremendous set of changes that will reshape the industry, changes driven by some of these ideas that I mentioned, and the whole securitization market is going to be a major part of that.

Contributors

Andrew Alper
Partner
Goldman Sachs & Co.
85 Broad St., 18th Floor
New York, NY 10004

James G. Bohn
Board of Governors of the Federal
   Reserve System
Mail Stop 93
20th & C Streets
Washington, DC 20551

David F. Bradford
Woodrow Wilson School
Princeton University
Princeton, NJ 08544

Dennis H. Chookaszian
Chairman and CEO
CNA Insurance Companies
CNA Plaza
Chicago, IL 60685

John H. Cochrane
Graduate School of Business
University of Chicago
1101 East 58th Street
Chicago, IL 60637

J. David Cummins
The Wharton School
3641 Locust Walk
Philadelphia, PA 19104

David M. Cutler
Department of Economics
Harvard University
Cambridge, MA 02138

Sanjiv Das
Graduate School of Business
Harvard University
361 Morgan Hall, Soldiers Field
Boston, MA 02163

Ross J. Davidson Jr.
Vice President
USAA
9800 Fredericksburg Rd.
C3W
San Antonio, TX 78288

Peter Diamond
Department of Economics
Massachusetts Institute of Technology
Room E52-344
50 Memorial Drive
Cambridge, MA 02139

Clement S. Dwyer Jr.
URSA Advisors, LLC
4 Indian Ln.
Califon, NJ 07830

Martin Feldstein
NBER
1050 Massachusetts Avenue
Cambridge, MA 02138

Kenneth A. Froot
Graduate School of Business
Harvard University
Soldiers Field Road
Boston, MA 02163

James R. Garven
Department of Finance
2158 CEBA
E. J. Ourso College of Business
    Administration
Louisiana State University
Baton Rouge, LA 70803

Steven F. Goldberg
USAA
P&C Underwriting and Pricing F03W
9800 Fredericksburg Rd.
San Antonio, TX 78288

Anne Gron
Graduate School of Management—M&S
Northwestern University
2001 Sheridan Rd.
Evanston, IL 60208

Brian J. Hall
Harvard Business School
284 Baker West
Boston, MA 02163

James R. Hines Jr.
University of Michigan Business School
701 Tappan St.
Ann Arbor, MI 48109

R. Glenn Hubbard
Graduate School of Business
Columbia University
609 Uris Hall
New York, NY 10027

Robert P. Irvan
Senior Vice President
Chief Financial Officer
CIGNA Property & Casualty
1601 Chestnut Street
TL56C
Philadelphia, PA 19192

Dwight Jaffee
Haas School of Business
University of California
Berkeley, CA 94720

Richard Kane
Guy Carpenter and Co.
2 World Trade Center
52nd Floor
New York, NY 10008

Paul R. Kleindorfer
Wharton School
University of Pennsylvania
Pennsylvania, PA 19104

Howard C. Kunreuther
Wharton School
University of Pennsylvania
Philadelphia, PA 19104

Christopher M. Lewis
Ernst and Young
1225 Connecticut Ave. NW
Washington, DC 20036

Robert H. Litzenberger
Goldman Sachs & Co.
32 Old Slip
17th Floor
New York, NY 10004

Kyle D. Logue
University of Michigan Law School
Hutchins Hall
Ann Arbor, MI 48109

John A. Major
Guy Carpenter and Co.
2 World Trade Center
52nd Floor
New York, NY 10048

Christopher M. McGhee
Marsh and McLennan Securities Corp.
2 World Trade Center, 52nd Floor
New York, NY 10048

Roberto Mendoza
Vice Chairman
JP Morgan & Co., Inc.
60 Wall Street
New York, NY 10260

David A. Moss
Morgan 261
Harvard Business School
Soldiers Field Road
Boston, MA 02163

Kevin C. Murdock
Graduate School of Business
518 Memorial Way
Stanford University
Stanford, CA 94305

Stewart C. Myers
Sloan School of Management
MIT, Room E52-451
50 Memorial Drive
Cambridge, MA 02139

Paul G. J. O'Connell
Emerging Markets Finance
5 Revere Street
Cambridge, MA 02138

Paolo M. Pellegrini
Global Risk Advisors LLC
845 Third Avenue
New York, NY 10022

André F. Perold
Sloan School of Business
Harvard University
Morgan Hall 367
Cambridge, MA 02139

Richard D. Phillips
Department of Risk Management
    and Insurance
Georgia State University
P.O. Box 4036
Atlanta, GA 30302

Frank Pierson
ZC Group
1 Chase Manhattan Plaza
35th Floor
New York, NY 10005

Raghuram Rajan
University of Chicago
Graduate School of Business
1101 E. 58th Street
Chicago, IL 60637

Richard Sandor
Environmental Financial Products
111 W. Jackson Boulevard
14th Floor
Chicago, IL 60604

David Scharfstein
Sloan School of Management
Massachusetts Institute of Technology
Room E52-433
50 Memorial Drive
Cambridge, MA 02139

Jeremy C. Stein
Sloan School of Management
Massachusetts Institute of Technology
E52-448
Cambridge, MA 02139

James M. Stone
President
Plymouth Rock
695 Atlantic Avenue
Boston, MA 02111

James A. Tilley
Managing Director
Morgan Stanley Dean Witter
750 Seventh Ave.
New York, NY 10010

Joseph H. Umansky
American International Group, Inc.
70 Pine Street
New York, NY 10270

Richard J. Zeckhauser
JFK School of Government
Harvard University
79 JFK Street
Cambridge, MA 02138

Author Index

Subject Index